VOICES OF HISTORY

1944–45

VOICES OF
HISTORY

1944-45

Speeches and Papers of
ROOSEVELT, CHURCHILL,
STALIN, CHIANG, HITLER
AND OTHER LEADERS

Delivered During 1944

NATHAN AUSUBEL, *Editor*

GRAMERCY PUBLISHING COMPANY
NEW YORK

COPYRIGHT 1945 BY GRAMERCY PUBLISHING COMPANY

PRINTED IN THE UNITED STATES OF AMERICA

EDITOR'S FOREWORD

The purpose of this annual is to bring into one convenient volume the significant state papers and the important speeches of the chief statesmen and officials of the world.

Every speech is reprinted exactly as given in the source. Where possible the source is official. Nothing has been added or taken away, and all are published without comment.

The arrangement is chronological because all documents are interrelated. In fact, many of the speeches take on the aspect of an international debate. This is especially true of the speeches of Churchill and Hitler.

Speeches and statements of the enemy are included because it is impossible to understand fully the year 1944 without knowing what Hitler and Tojo told both their people and the world.

In reprinting the speeches of Winston Churchill in the House of Commons, the interpolations of members are included so that the speaker's words may carry full meaning.

The speeches of the enemy leaders were monitored by the FCC. At times words were not distinct, but in all the speeches there is sufficient text for full meaning.

As suggested by Dr. Charles A. Beard in his introduction to the 1941 edition, speeches by leaders other than officials of state are outside the scope of this book. However, due to the great historical importance of the United States' second wartime Presidential election, and inasmuch as the role of opposition candidate may be considered quasi-official, the Democratic and Republican party platforms and most of the campaign speeches of President Roosevelt and Governor Thomas E. Dewey are included.

The chronology is intended to serve as a guide and background for the reader in placing events and to establish their historical interrelation. Likewise, maps are included to show the contemporary locations of the battle fronts.

ACKNOWLEDGMENTS

The publication of *Voices of History* would be impossible without the active cooperation of many people and organizations.

Acknowledgment is gratefully given to:

The *New York Times* for permission to reprint speeches, state papers and maps from their columns, and for granting us the use of C. B. Palmer's able summary of 1944.

The White House for supplying press releases of President Roosevelt's speeches, messages and statements.

The British Library of Information for helpful suggestion and the use of the *British Speeches of the Day* and the *Parliamentary Debates*.

The *United Nations Review* for texts of speeches by many foreign statesmen.

The *Information Bulletin* of the Embassy of the USSR in Washington.

The *Department of State Bulletin* for many U. S. speeches and papers.

The New York Office of the O. W. I. for making available the texts of speeches and documents from Axis sources as recorded by the Foreign Broadcast Intelligence Service of the Federal Communications Commission, without which this volume could not be complete.

We are grateful for other aid and cooperation impossible to list in detail.

Finally, the editor wants to thank the many people, organizations and institutions whose recognition of the value of the first three volumes in this series has led to its continuance.

CONTENTS

CONTENTS

CONTENTS

CONTENTS

A REVIEW OF THE YEAR 1944

By C. B. Palmer [1]

A year ago the Axis held more than 20,000,000 square miles of the earth's land and sea areas. Today the Axis holds 13,581,000 square miles.

These figures are in a way a measure of Allied victories in 1944. They are also a measure of the tasks remaining.

Allied hopes were that 1944 would be the year of decision in Europe. Then full attention could be turned to the Pacific and the defeat of Japan. The year fell short of expectations in the west, in fact it ended with the Allies beating back a Nazi waging counter-attack. Nevertheless, in both theatres of war the Allies could count unprecedented military triumphs.

Never in modern times had western Europe been invaded over water. Never before had an offensive been waged over such immense distances as in the Pacific. Never before had land, sea and air forces been welded into such a team for the defeat of such strongly emplaced foes.

Germany and Japan began the year fighting everywhere far from their own boundaries. As the year ended, Allied troops held more than 1,000 square miles of German soil, on both fronts. The islands of Japan were under air attack one to eight times a week; the Pacific front had moved 2,500 miles closer to Tokyo. In neither Europe nor the Far East had a decision been reached. Yet the decisive forces—encirclement, blockade, attrition, penetration—were at work.

Governments Return

Evidence of the progress of war was found in political problems that rose in its wake. Five exiled Governments returned to their homelands—French, Belgian, Luxembourg, Greek and Filipino. Three Axis countries—Bulgaria, Rumania and Finland—were knocked out of the war and a fourth—Hungary —was tottering. Liberation and conquest brought to the fore political stresses. These posed immediate tests for statesmen's skill. In the longer view there was the problem of securing the peace. In grand concert and between nation and nation there was a searching for formulas and philosophies.

These developments—military and diplomatic—had their impact on the home front. For a while the expectation of an early end to the war in Europe gave impetus to planning for demobilization and reconversion. It also brought into the spotlight America's role in the family of nations. It colored very strongly the 1944 elections. Choosing a President and a Congress, the people sought to determine their post-war road in both internal and foreign affairs.

As the year ended, however, the war itself once more dominated all thoughts. The battles were getting tougher, not easier.

[1] *New York Times.*

THE WAR IN EUROPE

A year ago Gen. Dwight D. Eisenhower was still in North Africa, newly named to command the proposed invasion of Europe from the west.

Today General Eisenhower's headquarters are in Paris; eight Allied armies stand in France, the Low Countries, Germany.

The greatest drama in military history was staged in Europe in 1944. As the year began, a Wehrmacht totaling 6,000,000 men stood astride the Continent from the English Channel to the Dnieper—1,800 miles—and from the North Cape to Crete—2,500 miles. It had great water barriers and mountain chains to bolster the power of its arms.

Grand Strategy

But in November, 1943, the decision had been made at Teheran by Prime Minister Churchill, Marshal Stalin and President Roosevelt. In 1944 a grand offensive from west, east and south would be launched against the Nazis. The problems were enormous. There was no land front in the west; the invasion base was Britain, 3,000 miles from the American arsenals and training camps. In the south the front was a hundred-mile line across lower Italy. In the east the bulk of the German armies was massed against the Russians, along a 2,000-mile front from the Arctic Ocean to the Black Sea.

The answer was planning and preparation. General Eisenhower, who had been Allied Commander in Chief in the Mediterranean, went to England (Jan. 16) to start work with his Anglo-American staff. The flood of troops to Britain swelled. The strategic bombing of Germany was methodically increased, its primary purposes to cripple the Luftwaffe against the time of invasion. In the south the Italian campaign, which had made slow progress through the mountains below Cassino, was stepped up with the leapfrog move to Anzio, thirty miles from Rome (Jan. 22).

All these were part of the preliminary strategy of keeping the Germans spread out, uncertain, wearing them down however they could be reached.

On D-day (June 6) the sky was alive with 11,000 Allied planes, the English Channel swarmed with 4,000 ships. Onto the beaches of Normandy poured 250,000 men in the first twenty-four hours. More than 118,000 tons of bombs in the preceding month had smashed the Germans' transportation network over a broad area.

The Break-Through

The great task for the Allies was to get their main strength onto the Continent, get room for maneuver, then slice up the enemy. The fall of Cherbourg (June 25), the break-out into Brittany (July 27) after seven weeks of harrowing hedgerow fighting, the race across France (Orléans fell on Aug. 17; Paris on Aug. 25) broke the Wehrmacht. The invasion of southern France (Aug. 15) sped the process.

Meanwhile the three-front strategy had come into play. Just as some Wehrmacht units reached France from the east, the Red Army struck (June 23). Then began a vast offensive which was to sweep the Germans out of White Russia and the eastern half of Poland, knock Rumania and Bulgaria out of the war and swing up the Danube to Budapest.

The summer's blows cost the Wehrmacht an estimated 3,000,000 men. They also produced a convulsion in the Reich. A "bomb plot"—real or fake— against Adolf Hitler (July 20) was a signal for a new purge, a shift of generals, a grant of higher power to Gestapo Chief Heinrich Himmler. Then came (July 24) the new decrees for "total mobilization."

There was another reaction in the enemy camp. Soon after invasion started, Hitler unveiled his "vengeance weapon"—V-1, the robot bomb sent blindly against London and southern England. V-1 and its larger companion V-2— a stratospheric rocket—took a toll of more than 5,000 lives in less than three months.

When the Allied winter offensive (Nov. 16) threatened the industrial Ruhr and Saar regions of the western Reich the Germans struck back (Dec. 16). Surprise and a massing of power on a single sector of the front carried them westward forty miles to the Meuse. Then the Allies rallied and hurled the Nazis back.

THE PACIFIC WAR

A year ago Truk seemed a formidable obstacle in the Pacific.
Today the Americans are 2,000 miles beyond Truk.

After two years of slow and arduous moves all around Japan's Pacific perimeter, the Army and Navy in 1944 began to strike daring blows in dazzling profusion.

The first of the great moves was the invasion of the Marshalls, which the Japanese had held for twenty years and which they had made an interlocking system of bases; they were invaded (Feb. 1). The technique was to strike not at the nearest point but in deep, by-passing the enemy's strongest points, smashing his airfields.

Then it was the turn of the southern flank to move ahead. General MacArthur struck blows in rapid succession, covering 2,500 miles in less than five months. Great pockets of Japanese were left behind in New Guinea.

Nimitz's Blow

The right flank, under Admiral Nimitz and powered by the gigantic Task Force 58, moved again. It was a strike of 1,200 miles from the Marshalls into part of Japan's main defenses, the ladder of islands reaching directly to Tokyo. The invasion of Saipan (June 14) called out the full savagery of Japanese resistance. Before it was conquered Americans suffered 15,000 casualties, 2,300 of them killed. The Japanese forces of 23,000 were wiped out.

In human as well as strategic terms the next major move was perhaps the greatest of the Pacific campaign. This was the invasion of the Philippines (Oct. 20). Again the reaction was savage. The Japanese fleet emerged—to suffer the worst naval defeat ever inflicted. Sixty-nine ships, including some of the most important of his fleet, were sunk (Oct. 23–25). Japan persisted in trying to reinforce the Leyte garrison and lost sixty-eight more ships and an estimated 112,000 lives. Before that battle was over General MacArthur had struck out again, to Mindoro in the western Philippines, at the edge of the South China Sea, only 150 miles from Manila and 750 miles from the China coast.

If these great advances were shaping the defeat of Japan there were other omens also. The year 1944 saw the emergence of a mighty new air weapon— the Superfortress. First from China (June 15), then from Saipan (Nov. 24), these giants began the strategic hammering of Japan's industries.

Japan was not wholly on the passive defense during the year. Twice she launched offensives. Both were aimed at knocking China out of the war. The first was the drive from Burma into India. This was intended to cut the new supply line—air and road—into China from the southwest. Japan's other offensive was staged in China. Fearing the encroachment from the south-west as well as from the Pacific, the Japanese set out to split China in two and cut her supply line from India. In part they succeeded. Drives from north and south established a land corridor from Tientsin all the way to Indo-China and on down the Malay Peninsula.

THE DIPLOMATIC FRONT

A year ago the great coalition was united on the single task of routing the Nazis on the battlefield.

Today the coalition faces the complex task of restoring freedom and stability to a war-torn world.

Out of the military successes of 1944 arose grave problems of peace. The most immediate of these was the conflict between the old order and the new, the old being the political and social regimes that obtained when war broke out, the new being revolutionary forces centering in the resistance groups that had fought fascism all through the war. The longer-range problem focused in the question of securing the peace: Was there to be an over-all security organization built on common action—like that envisioned at Dum-barton Oaks—or was there to be a revival of the network of alliances and treaties which preceded both world wars? As the year ended, the latter method was already being implemented. This raised the further question: Could the two concepts be reconciled, could broad cooperation be welded to bilateral agreements?

The immediate consequences of liberation were many and troublesome. The captive peoples had had no political expression for four years and more. Starvation and misery had made nerves taut. How much and what kind of assistance should the Allies give in setting up new regimes? With whom should they deal as representing the wishes of the liberated peoples? There were conflicting claims from rival political groups. The Allied decisions would indicate recognition; Allied arms would constitute authority.

Russia and Poland

In the east, Russia, invaded twice in a generation by the Germans, was concerned with safeguarding her boundaries. Moscow said the areas of old Poland occupied by the Red Army in 1939 were thenceforth part of Russia. Moscow also said that the Polish Government in Exile, in London, was tinged with fascism and was not representative of the people. When the London group refused to accede to a plan for compensating Poland with parts of Germany, the Russians sponsored a Polish Committee of Liberation (July 30) as the body it would deal with. In view of the deadlock, Prime Minister Churchill said (Dec. 15) the London Poles must reconcile themselves to Moscow's plan.

In the south, in both Italy and Greece, Britain's role came under scrutiny. The interim Italian Government, appointed by various political groups rather than elected by the people, underwent crisis after crisis. British opposition to Count Carlo Sforza led to a reshaping of the Cabinet (Dec. 9). In many quarters the cry arose that Britain was interfering to save the monarchy; American Secretary of State Stettinius issued a statement (Dec. 5) which was read as criticism of Britain. A similar but more violent situation arose in Greece. Civil strife followed the return of the Greek Government from

Cairo (Oct. 18). British troops battled with anti-monarchist resistance groups. A visit by Mr. Churchill (Dec. 25) and a proposal for a regency seemed to offer a temporary solution.

In this way the immediate effects of liberation were linked to the future. The old question of "spheres of influence"—Russia's among adjoining states, Britain's in the areas fringing her Mediterranean lifeline—was beclouding the prospects for amicable settlements of Europe's problems.

Return to Alliances

At the same time, moves which seemed to foreshadow regional groupings of nations by treaties—a western bloc sponsored by Britain, an eastern bloc sponsored by Russia—were under way. France and Russia signed an agreement (Dec. 10) whose principal effect would be to curb German aggression but which many felt might lead to a revival of complex alliances. At Dumbarton Oaks (Aug. 21–Oct. 7) spokesmen for the United Nations had envisioned a permanent, broad-scale organization of large and small powers which could deal with international disputes and act against aggression. There had not been full agreement on the structure but there were high hopes agreement could be reached.

THE HOME FRONT

A year ago American casualties in World War II stood at 140,000.

Today they stand at 628,000, not counting the toll of the German counteroffensive.

Never have the American people been more aware of the cost of war than they are as 1944 ends. One part of that cost is entered on the honor rolls of killed, wounded, missing and prisoners. Another part is told in the rising demands on civilians.

These factors have been reflected in the changing mood of the public as the year progressed. In the spring as events moved toward D-day there was tenseness, yet general confidence. Through the Normandy fighting there was anxiety. With the break-through and the race across France there was surging optimism. Then there was reaction. The slow progress in the autumn, the savage German resistance to the Allied offensive, finally the Nazi counterattack, brought the nation to a mood of grim reality as to what the home front faced after a year of unprecedented effort.

The American share in making possible the grand offensives of 1944 was enormous. As the year began the nation had already spent $153,000,000,000 on defense and armaments programs. The President estimated (Jan. 10) that $90,000,000,000 would be needed for the next fiscal year. About 40 per cent would come from taxation and the rest would have to be borrowed.

Demand for Men

More war goods than ever before were produced but at some points the factories lagged behind the rising schedules. The result was a straining for manpower. The total pool was ample, but there were shortages in certain lines and certain areas. To force men into key jobs Selective Service and employment regulations were tightened (March 1 and 14; Dec. 19–22). Another stringency developed when rationing regulations which had been eased (March 2 and May 4) were tightened again (Dec. 23).

In the forefront of people's minds through much of the year was the election. Its beginnings were clouded by uncertainty about the candidacies of certain leading figures. Wendell Willkie was an early contender but he withdrew after defeat in an initial test, the Wisconsin primaries (April 4). Gov. Thomas E. Dewey of New York and President Roosevelt were named to head their tickets, with Gov. John W. Bricker of Ohio and Senator Harry S. Truman of Missouri as running mates, at the Republican and Democratic conventions (June 30 and July 20). On election day (Nov. 7) 47,971,156 people voted (approximately 2,800,000 service men and women). They chose Roosevelt and Truman by 3,592,769, the smallest plurality since 1916 but a 432–99 sweep in the electoral vote. A more strongly Democratic Congress, 243 seats to the Republicans' 190, was returned.

JANUARY

January 1, 1944

The Red Army, in the greatest victory since Stalingrad, pursued the demoralized German troops to within twenty-seven miles of the Polish border, capturing 300 towns.

3

The Argentine Government recognized the new Bolivian Government which seized power by a military coup d'état.

4

The Red Army, continuing its offensive west of Kiev, smashed across the 1939 Russian-Polish border, capturing Novograd-Volynski and Olevsk.

5

The London Polish Government-in-Exile announced that it had instructed its underground adherents in Poland neither to hinder nor to assist the Red Army fighting against the Germans in their country.

6

In a speech to Spanish army officers General Franco warned all combatant countries to keep "hands off" Spain.

7

While not naming Argentina, Secretary of State Cordell Hull made clear that the Bolivian coup d'état was inspired and aided by pro-Axis forces outside the country.

8

The Second Ukrainian Army captured the railroad bastion of Kirovograd in the Dnieper Bend, having routed 100,000 Germans in a four-day offensive.

10

The Special Fascist Tribunal at Verona condemned to death former Italian Foreign Minister and son-in-law of Mussolini, Count Ciano. Also receiving the death sentence were seventeen members of the former Fascist Grand Council, including Marshal De Bono, the Italian commander of the disastrous campaigns in Eritrea and Libya.

12

Immediate punishment of all traitors to France and collaborationists with Germany was asked by the French Consultative Assembly.

13

The Soviet Government denounced the Franco dictatorship of Spain as an ally of the Axis.

THE RED ARMY'S ADVANCE RAISES POLITICAL ISSUES

Courtesy New York Times

January, 1944

14

The U. S. Selective Service System informed Congress that the Army and Navy required 700,000 additional men in the first six months of 1944.

The London Polish Government-in-Exile offered to discuss "all outstanding questions" with Soviet Russia provided the U. S. and Britain would sit in on the discussions.

15

The Peruvian Government charged that a number of native fascist conspirators, including Germans and Japanese, had plotted a New Year's coup.

16

The Red Army opened a new attack in the Nevel sector below Lake Ilmen, cutting the railroad from Novosokolniki to Leningrad.

Japanese opened Burma campaign.

General Dwight D. Eisenhower arrived in London to assume command of the invasion of western Europe.

Marshal Tito declared that his Partisan army had brought the German army in Yugoslavia to a halt and that his troops had seized the initiative in several sectors.

17

The Soviet Government rejected the offer by the London Polish Government-in-Exile to enter into negotiations on the Russian-Polish boundary question and refused to consider renewing ruptured diplomatic relations.

Secretary of State Cordell Hull announced that the United States Government had offered its good offices to the Russian Government in an effort to reconcile Soviet-Polish differences and to reëstablish diplomatic relations between them.

19

Foreign Secretary Anthony Eden announced in Commons: "I myself have informed the Spanish Government through the Spanish Ambassador to London of the most serious effect which this continuing unneutral assistance to our enemies in this struggle against our allies must have on Anglo-Spanish relations now and in the future."

20

Twenty-nine-month siege of Leningrad lifted.

21

Premier Hideki Tojo told the Japanese Diet that the outcome of the Pacific War, where there was "only a hair's breadth between final victory and defeat," would be determined by air power.

22

In a surprise attack British and American troops landed on the Italian shore a short distance south of Rome.

25

Allied troops pushed twelve miles inland below Rome to the Appian Way without meeting real German opposition.

Foreign Minister Alberto Gilbert announced that the Argentine Government would take severe measures against German espionage.

The House of Representatives voted $1,350,000,000 for United States participation in UNRRA.

The British Ministry of Economic Welfare made known that the so-called neutral countries of Spain, Switzerland, Sweden, Portugal and Turkey were supplying Germany with vital military supplies.

26

President Pedro Ramirez signed a decree declaring diplomatic relations between Argentina and Germany and Japan were at an end.

Secretary of State Hull announced that the Soviet Government had declined for the present the tender of good offices by the U. S. Government to restore relations between the U.S.S.R. and the London Polish Government-in-Exile.

President Roosevelt described the "States' rights" soldier-vote measure as "a fraud on the soldiers and sailors and marines."

27

A joint statement by the U. S. Army and Navy announced the torture and murder of 5,200 Americans and many times that number of Filipinos captured on Bataan and Corregidor by the Japanese.

Secretary of State Cordell Hull charged Japan with violation of the Geneva Prisoners-of-War Convention and with "inhuman cruelty or callous failure to provide the necessities of life" to American prisoners of war.

28

The British Government joined the U. S. in shutting off oil supplies to Franco Spain because of its continued support of Germany.

29

President Roosevelt hailed the action of President Pedro Ramirez in leading Argentina to her break of diplomatic relations with the Axis.

30

On the eleventh anniversary of the Nazi seizure of power in Germany, Adolf Hitler broadcast a warning to all the nations in Europe against the "Bolshevist menace."

31

The greatest naval force since the Battle of Jutland in World War I, supported by a gigantic air armada, attacked the Japanese on the Marshall Islands.

STATEMENT BY PRESIDENT ROOSEVELT ON THE ANNIVERSARY OF THE SIGNING OF THE DECLARATION BY THE UNITED NATIONS

January 1, 1944 [1]

Many of us in the United States are observing this first day of the New Year as a day of prayer and reflection and are considering the deeper issues which affect us as part of the family of nations at a crucial moment in history. It is fitting on this day that we direct our thoughts to the concept of the United Nations which came into being on another and infinitely bleaker New Year's Day two years ago.

[1] White House news release.

It was but three weeks after Pearl Harbor that the Declaration by United Nations was promulgated at Washington. Twenty-six nations subscribed immediately, eight more have adhered subsequently, all pledging themselves to stand together in the struggle against common enemies.

Two years ago the United Nations were on the defensive in every part of the world. Today we are on the offensive. The walls are closing in remorselessly on our enemies. Our armed forces are gathering for new and greater assaults which will bring about the downfall of the Axis aggressors.

The United Nations are giving attention also to the different kind of struggle which must follow the military phase, the struggle against disease, malnutrition, unemployment, and many other forms of economic and social distress.

To make all of us secure against future aggression and to open the way for enhanced well-being of nations and individuals everywhere, we must maintain in the peace to come the mutually beneficial cooperation we have achieved in war. On the threshold of the New Year, as we look toward the tremendous tasks ahead, let us pledge ourselves that this cooperation shall continue both for winning the final victory on the battlefield and for establishing an international organization of all peace-loving nations to maintain peace and security in generations to come.

NEW YEAR'S ADDRESS BY SOVIET PRESIDENT MIKHAIL KALININ

January 1, 1944 [1]

Dear Comrades! Citizens of the Soviet Union! Men and women workers! Men and women collective farmers! Soviet intellectuals! Red Army and Navy men, commanders and political workers! Men and women guerrillas! Residents of Soviet districts temporarily captured by the German-fascist occupationists!

I greet and congratulate you upon the coming New Year.

Comrades, this is the third time our country meets the New Year in the conditions of hard struggle against German fascism. All the interests and thoughts of our people are bound with the war, while the people's energy and aspirations are directed toward a single great patriotic aim—the earliest expulsion of the enemy from the Soviet Union, the victory over the German invaders.

It is quite natural that today, the day of the coming New Year, every Soviet citizen asks himself—what have we accomplished during the past year, and in the first place, on the front of struggle against the German invaders?

One must say bluntly—much has been accomplished. Certainly this falls short of our desire—to completely clear Soviet territory of the fascist brigands; but still our military achievements are enormous.

The past year was a year of radical turn in the course of the war. The beginning of 1943 was marked by the historic victory scored by our troops at Stalingrad, and the summer by another important victory at Kursk and Belgorod. As a result of the Red Army's offensive operations, two-thirds of the territory temporarily occupied by the Germans has been liberated from the enemy. The Red Army completely liberated from the Germans the

[1] Information Bulletin, Embassy of the U.S.S.R.

Krasnodar and Stavropol territories, the Kalmykia, Kabardino-Balkaria, Voronezh, Kursk, Rostov, Smolensk and Stalingrad Regions. The Ukraine east of the Dnieper has been delivered from German bondage with its large— in regard to population and industrial importance—Regions of Stalino, Voroshilovgrad, Kharkov, Poltava, Sumy and Chernigov. Large parts of the Dniepropetrovsk and Zaporozhye Regions, with the regional centers of Dniepropetrovsk and Zaporozhye, have been cleared of the Germans. Parts of the Kiev, Kirovograd, Zhitomir and Nikolayev Regions have also been liberated. More than thirty districts of the Gomel, Mogilev, Vitebsk and Polessye Regions of Byelorussia, and the regional center—the town of Gomel —have been cleared of the German invaders.

This is evidence of the grave defeat sustained by the German army on the Soviet front during 1943.

One of the most important successes scored by our Red Army during the past year was doubtless the forcing of the Dnieper—the liberation of the city of Kiev, the establishment and expansion of places d'armes in the Ukraine west of the Dnieper.

The Germans particularly clung to the Dnieper as to their most important defensive line, but the Red Army dislodged them from these positions and tirelessly drives them back westward toward the Soviet frontiers, driving deep wedges into the German defenses. The blows dealt by the Red Army to the fascist invaders are gradually sobering not only the German command but the entire leading gang of Hitlerites. The Urals, and the Baku oil have been forgotten, the desire to encircle Moscow has been lost, and, which is especially significant, the Germans have begun to regard "elastic retreat" and "shortening the front line" as their best strategy.

This explanation of the fate of German war plans is laughable; but evidently the German command has no better explanation. And, as the saying goes, nothing can be made out of nothing. As to the so-called German "elastic retreat," the Red Army knows well that the Germans do not abandon voluntarily a single yard of Soviet soil; they have to be knocked out of Soviet territory in the stiff fighting which our army carries on day in and day out. The true helpers of our Red Army are our valiant men and women guerrillas. They perform great deeds by ruthlessly annihilating the enemy.

For the sake of justice one must say that the Red Army's successes on the front are largely made possible by the self-sacrificing labor of Soviet men and women in factories and plants, in pits and mines, in transport and in agriculture. Workers, collective farmers, Soviet intellectuals, all the peoples of the Soviet Union, have worked this year with still greater success, supplying their army with everything.

And the best reward for the energy, enthusiasm and high sense of patriotic duty displayed by the Soviet people in their labor is the appraisal given to the work of the Soviet rear by the Supreme Commander-in-Chief, Marshal of the Soviet Union Stalin.

This year, parallel with the Red Army's blows, our Allies have also waged an incessant struggle against the German-fascist troops. Anglo-American troops ousted the Germans from Northern Africa, Sicily, Sardinia and Corsica. At present the scene of struggle has been shifted to Southern Italy, where the Allied troops are steadily forging ahead toward Rome—capital of Italy. The Anglo-American Air Force has acted effectively, destroying military industrial objectives of Germany. Germany's strongest ally in Europe—Italy— has surrendered, while the Italian people on a growing scale joins the struggle against the Germans.

The joint struggle against German fascism has brought about close political rapprochement between the Allies. The Moscow Conference held at the close of October of this year, with the participation of the Ministers of Foreign Affairs of the United States of America, Great Britain and the Soviet Union, insured the further business-like rapprochement between the Allies and paved the way for the meeting of the leaders of the Allied countries.

From November 28 to December 1 was held the Conference of leaders of the Three Allied Powers—Chairman of the Council of People's Commissars of the USSR Stalin, the President of the United States of America Roosevelt, and the Prime Minister of Great Britain Churchill—in Teheran. The Conference went down in history as the Teheran Conference of the three great Powers of the world.

Indeed, the Teheran Conference is the great event of our days, a historical milestone in the struggle against the German aggressor. All German efforts to cause disunity among the freedom-loving peoples were blasted. The leaders of the three great Powers arrived at full accord in matters of war and peace. They arrived at the very thing which is craved by the masses of the peoples in the occupied countries, worn out with suffering under the German jackboot.

A great contribution to the cause of struggle against German aggression is the recently concluded treaty of friendship, mutual assistance and postwar collaboration between the Soviet Union and the Czechoslovak Republic.

As you see, comrades, our successes in 1943 are enormous. However, for complete victory over the enemy all of us, at the front as well as in the rear, following the leader's call, must exert all our strength and will to achieve this aim.

Comrades, men and women citizens of the Soviet Union! Red Army men, commanders and political workers!

On behalf of the Soviet Government and the Central Committee of our Party, I congratulate you upon the New Year.

Long live our Red Army which, under the leadership of Marshal of the Soviet Union Comrade Stalin, in the New Year of 1944 will deal the final blow to the fascist invaders and will completely clear them from the territory of the Soviet Union.

A Happy New Year, Comrades!

PRESIDENT CHIANG KAI-SHEK'S NEW YEAR'S
MESSAGE TO THE CHINESE PEOPLE

January 1, 1944 [1]

Today is New Year's Day of 1944. It was exactly fifty years ago today that Dr. Sun Yat-sen started the revolutionary movement for the salvation of China by organizing the Hsing Chung Hui.

Through seven years of bitter resistance against Japan we have laid a solid foundation for victory. We and our Allies are now exchanging news of military success and preparing for an all-front offensive. This New Year's Day marks the dawn of a new era and its celebration, which the Army and people in our country share with comrades in arms of all other peace-loving and anti-aggression nations, should be of special significance.

The outstanding development in the global war during the past year was

[1] Chinese News Service.

that the cornerstone for the victory of the United Nations was solidly laid, while the Axis forces in North Africa suffered a smashing defeat and the whole of Libya was cleared of the Nazi horde. This was followed by the Allied occupation of Sicily and Italy's surrender. On the eastern European front, the Soviet forces scored repeated victories, completely dislodging the Germans from positions along the Dnieper.

Japan has also suffered reverses everywhere in the Pacific and China theaters. With the recent Allied landings on New Britain and other strategic points, Japan's second line of defense in the Pacific from the Solomons to the Bismarck Sea has been broken. In the China theater she has encountered unexpected heavy blows at the hands of our defenders in all her futile attacks in the provinces of Kwangtung, Chekiang, Kiangsi, Kiangsu, Shantung, Hopei, Anhwei, Shansi, and Suiyuan. In her third major campaign in Hunan and Hupeh, we were able to inflict upon her a most crushing defeat, and especially in the battle of Changteh she had a taste of the splendid fighting quality of our troops. In all her four attacks in western Yunnan she failed to dislodge our forces from their rock-like defenses along the Nu River. Throughout the past year the Japanese had nothing but defeats and failures in both offense and defense.

The fate of the Axis partners, Japan and Germany, can now be said to be sealed. The United Nations have become stronger, as more and more nations have joined their ranks, while non-belligerent countries have become more and more friendly and sympathetic to them. The past year therefore was a turning point in the titanic World War.

While the concerted efforts of the United Nations have been to a considerable extent accountable for this happy turn of events during the year, when the initiative passed into Allied hands, there is a more important factor to be considered. This lies in the traditional love for democracy and freedom of the American people, who treat all the peoples of the world as their equals. Their broadmindedness and farsightedness have led the American Government to adopt a just and enlightened world policy and to translate that policy into action with success. Thus America has played a significant role in turning the tide of the World War and in laying the foundation of victory for the United Nations. The Axis brigands have been subjected to a psychological disarmament under the censure of justice and righteousness. This point I wish to impress most emphatically on our Army and our people, a point which is also worthy of worldwide attention.

It should be emphasized that the foundation of victory is that our war is a war for the establishment of justice and the liberation of mankind. Only in this spirit, given full expression, may victory be won and permanent peace achieved.

During the past year our international relations were readjusted first by the relinquishment by the powers concerned of their extraterritorial and related rights in China and then by the passage of the American Congress of the bill for the repeal of the Chinese Exclusion Act. We have concluded new treaties on the basis of equality and entered into treaties of amity with friendly nations whereby our traditional relations of friendship with them have been enhanced. Thus our century-old aspirations for national independence and freedom may now be said to have been realized. In October last year we signed with America, Great Britain, and the Soviet Union at Moscow a joint declaration on collective security. This, together with a joint declaration signed by the United Nations at Washington on New Year's Day 1942 which it supplements, provides for the attainment of the common war aims and lays down the principle for the establishment of an international peace machinery. Later, at the Cairo and Teheran conferences agreements were reached on common war strategy in Europe and Asia and on the punishment of war criminals in the East and West.

In the light of the important events of the past year, the peoples of the world, amid the gunfire of a cataclysmic war, can already visualize the advent of peace and dawn of righteousness. Peoples who have been trampled down by the aggressors can now be sure of their future emancipation and rebirth.

Here I wish to report to the Army and people of our country the impressions I received during my participation in the Cairo Conference, which, I am sure, you will be glad to hear. In 1938 I pointed out that ever since the Meiji reform Japan had consistently followed a policy of continental aggression to satisfy her ambition for the enslavement of China and domination of East Asia as a first step toward world conquest. To crush such ambitious designs of Japan, we must strive to liberate the Korean people and regain Formosa as one of the aims of our resistance.

At the Cairo Conference, America, Great Britain, and China unanimously agreed to strip Japan of all the Pacific Islands she has seized or occupied since the first World War and to drive her out of all the territories which she has despoiled by force or out of greed. She has to restore to us the four Northeastern Provinces, Formosa, and the Pescadores. She has to permit Korea to be free and independent. Thus we have received absolute assurances of attaining the aims of our sacred war of resistance. This will not only cheer our fellow countrymen in Formosa, the Pescadores, and the Northeast, as well as the people of Korea, but all the oppressed and maltreated Asiatic people both in the Pacific and Asia mainland may look forward with hope for liberation.

In the intimate talks I had with President Roosevelt and Prime Minister Churchill at Cairo, we considered steps for mutual co-operation and agreed upon certain plans for the prosecution of the war. We also touched upon the question of the disposal of the enemy after the war.

One important problem in this connection concerns Japan's form of government. When President Roosevelt asked my views, I frankly replied: "It is my opinion that all the Japanese militarists must be wiped out and the Japanese political system must be purged of every vestige of aggressive elements. As to what form of government Japan should adopt, that question can better be left to the awakened and repentant Japanese people to decide for themselves."

I also said: "If the Japanese people should rise in a revolution to punish their war mongers and to overthrow their militarist government, we should respect their spontaneous will and allow them to choose their own form of government." President Roosevelt fully approved of my idea. This opinion of ours is entirely based on the spirit of the joint declaration of the United Nations in 1942.

Today I make public this conversation with President Roosevelt at Cairo in order to impress upon our Army and people that after victory we hope not only to set free all the peoples who have been oppressed and enslaved by the enemy, but also to give a helping hand to the innocent and harmless people in Japan.

I have returned from the Cairo Conference with renewed devotion to the ideals of justice and peace. I may tell you that the deepest impressions I have of President Roosevelt are of his unflinching faith, his firm determination to emancipate all the world's oppressed peoples, and his sincere desire to help China become a truly free and independent nation. His basic policy is the attainment of real peace in the world and genuine equality among men, and he thinks that in such a future world as he visualizes China must be one of the pillars. This spirit of his arises from his innate love of justice and right-eousness and his policy is based upon the peaceful relations of mutual trust between the American and Chinese peoples during the last 150 years.

I also had several intimate talks with Prime Minister Churchill. This reso-lute, farsighted, and deeply emotional statesman of Great Britain impressed me by his frankness and straightforwardness. Mr. Churchill has an inflexible determination to crush Japan with the concerted efforts of the United Nations and fully shares our faith in Sino-British co-operation in war and in peace. Our talks have contributed immensely toward a better understanding between our two countries.

I wish further to tell you, aside from America and Great Britain, the Soviet Union, which participated in the Teheran Conference, has also consistently hoped that China succeed in its national reconstruction program and enjoy independence and freedom.

I am deeply convinced that the United Nations, of one heart and of one purpose, are truly engaged in a war to end all wars and that it is for this lofty ideal that the Allies are fighting gallantly on every front. To live up to the expectations of our Allies, our Army and people should redouble their efforts to make their nation strong and independent in order to meet the respon-sibilities of the times.

Since the Cairo Conference the aims of the common war against Japan have been clarified. The decision that the three powers are to bring increasing pressure to bear upon Japan will soon be carried into action. Henceforth the burden of our Army and people will become increasingly heavy, as the im-portant task of encircling the Japanese on the Asiatic mainland will fall pri-marily upon our shoulders. We must realize that in her defensive war Japan will have to make the China theater her last line of defense, where she will take her last and most stubborn stand.

In the decisive battle on the China front all our soldiers and people must give all they have and all they are. They should be truly aware that it is no easy task to win victory.

This coming year will see the beginning of the decisive stage when the land, sea, and air forces of the United Nations will carry the war to Japan's home islands and to all the seas surrounding her. Judging from our present position as compared with that of the enemy, I believe that if we prosecute the war in strict accordance with the strategy we have agreed upon, we can certainly defeat Japan in the Pacific and Indian Oceans to such an extent that either she has to surrender unconditionally or none of her forces will be able to survive the impact of our pressure. In this offensive on an unprecedented scale we of China should collaborate with the Allied forces and exert our utmost efforts. We should not only do so in our theater, but should counter-attack the enemy in other sectors of the East Asia mainland, wherever an opportunity presents itself, with a view to smashing to its very roots Japan's so-called Greater East Asia fortress. We must realize that only when Japan is utterly crushed in the China theater and only when China attains an all-front victory can permanent world peace be established.

To sum up, it is beyond doubt that the enemy is bound to lose. This is the inevitable outcome of the war but the coming year will see our fighting expand in scope and increase in severity. We must see to it that every one of our soldiers and every one of our civilians shall solemnly discharge his God-given duty. We have to fight on the one hand and reconstruct on the other, and we should begrudge no sacrifices. I want all our Army and people, treasuring their past achievements and looking ahead to the glorious future, to fulfill their obligations and show greater strength and spirit of sacrifice in their struggle for the realization of the ideals of our national revolution. There are four guiding principles by which they must strictly abide. First, co-operation between the Army and people must be strengthened; second, every citizen must perform the duty he owes to the state and contribute everything to the nation's cause; third, through economy and thrift material resources must be saved as much as possible with a view to meeting the needs of replenishment at the front; and, fourth, everybody must live a life of self-respect and honor by observing the tenets of the New Life Movement.

All our officers and men in the various war areas should do their utmost to expedite military preparation so that when the forthcoming great offensive unfolds itself this year they will make a contribution to the state that will be remembered forever. Thus may we realize our seven-year-old motto: "Victory is certain in war; success is certain in reconstruction."

PREMIER HIDEKI TOJO'S NEW YEAR'S ADDRESS

January 4, 1944 [1]

Upon welcoming the new spring of the year 1944, I, together with you, humbly congratulate the long life of His Imperial Majesty and at the same time express our congratulation for the continuous prosperity of the Royal Houses. Taking this opportunity, I also express our heartfelt appreciation to your services through considerable hardships during the past year, as well as express our desire for your further good services during this year.

Today, on the first day when the Administration commences its activities in the third year of the G.E.A. War, as you know already, the wartime Government Civil Service Act has been decided upon and was publicly announced. Here I have been given this opportunity to express, with you who hold important positions in the Central Government, our determination in successful application of the regulations, and this is indeed very gratifying.

Now Imperial Japan faces a grave situation which determines the future of our Nation and which also determines the rise or fall of Asia. Under the august virtue of His Imperial Majesty, we must strive, with the complete cooperation of the entire Nation, with unwavering spirit, to break through difficulties and must make this third year of the G.E.A. War, the year during which we firmly establish our foundation for the decision of victory and for our certain victory.

At this moment, the duties of us, the Government officials, bear great importance. Now, whether the duties of the Government officials are being carried out successfully or not will be immediately reflected upon the fighting spirit of the people, and it also will influence the activities of the people, which in turn will greatly influence the effort for the prosecution of the war.

As you know already, as for the quality of the Government officials, not only . . . in 1887. . . . Thus, we, the Government officials, began to imprint (them) deeply into our hearts. The reason each Cabinet in the past has carried out reforms of Government officials was nothing more than an expression of effort to maintain the foregoing principle.

[1] Office of War Information.

However, today, when the responsibilities of the Government officials have increased in importance, and when the number of the Government officials have been increased greatly, the fact that we have been granted an Imperial Ordinance, which clearly shows in particular the main points therein, is indeed very gratifying, and I, together with you, express our heartfelt gratitude. I expect that all of us Government officials upon our return to our respective places will firmly fulfill our services under the wartime, so that there may not be any regret, by carefully studying the points which have been graciously indicated in this ordinance and by mutual assistance.

In the wartime Government Civil Service Act, first of all there is the following passage: "Anyone who is serving the Government must fulfill his true duties, based upon the true principle of our national polity, with sincere service throughout, in mutual cooperation, and with extraordinary determination. Under the present condition, the responsibilities of the Government officials have increased in importance. You must expect to do your part, by firmly observing the regulations and adopting each rule with great adaptability, so that you may not hinder the smooth prosecution of the sacred war."

As I think deep, having the Government officials participate in functions of administrative affairs by sacrificing themselves under one unified guidance for the interest of the prosecution of the war and in accordance with the profound national polity of our Nation is the most important requirement, and this spirit will be the foundation of all other affairs.

It is needless to mention this here, but the officials are delegates of His Imperial Majesty the Emperor. Therefore, the Government officials must bear in mind that it is the fundamental principle that they must serve His Majesty with the determination to sacrifice all they have so that each one of the people who are the (children) may enjoy equal (rights) with all others. I firmly believe that any person who serves as a Government official must render his service, based upon this principle, with his unwavering sincerity and supreme loyalty.

The next point of the ordinance is as follows: "The Government officials must particularly realize the importance of their responsibility under wartime, and must particularly fulfill their duties by combining every possible effort and improvement." As I reflect upon the past, most of all serving in the Government must realize the importance of their responsibility in time of war. They must constantly reflect upon their work in prosecuting their duties even if there is something lacking; and at the same time, of course, they must strive with the expectation that they will fulfill their duties with certainty by overcoming any hardship by effort and new improvements.

As is commonly believed, the success and failure of any work is dependent on the person who is responsible for it. The success in (administration) will be mainly determined by the strength or the weakness of the persons in responsible positions. The brave deeds and strong (word missing) in war are not determined by the strength of a person, but they are determined by the strength of the sense of responsibility of the person. Hence, in order to carry out any administrative work under a protracted war in the most effective and speedy manner, it is extremely important that the men in the responsible positions prosecute their duties with a further vigorous sense of responsibility.

From this sense of responsibility alone can extraordinary effort be obtained and can they be able to carry out our affairs in the most appropriate way. If they should face their duties with fear to hold responsibilities, or take minimum responsibilities in maintaining the principle of wishing that nothing would happen, such an attitude would be difficult to excuse.

Now, the current situation is not an easy one. The responsibilities must be fulfilled by a gallant effort with an ardent spirit which will enable us to hold an attitude that we will fulfill our duty with our lives. To hold a firm sense of responsibility and to take our responsibilities with our very lives, and to render service with our fullest effort—this determination is the fundamental spirit, I believe, through which we can give our service to our Nation.

In the Imperial Ordinance it is provided that—I quote: "Government officials must have foresight and good judgment and must constantly expend their thoughts to the fullest degree and must endeavor in harmony and cooperation to have all their administrative policies contribute toward the consummation of the sacred war." I feel that today all administrative duties must be concentrated on the one object of winning the G.E.A. War.

In this connection, it is especially necessary that you yourselves always take to your respective duties earnestly. If you perform your duties with politics in mind, you will never be able to carry on active and proper Government administration which will meet the exigencies of this great war. You must literally change your attitude to one on a wartime basis. This is an urgent demand of the decisive war situation. Of course, Government officials are divided into higher and lower classes. Among them there are outstanding officials who excel in the discharge of their duties, and also there are officials who are developing themselves into officials of that caliber.

With regard to the respective realms of your administrative duties, you must at least concentrate on means and ways which will be most fitting to the present decisive war situation, and which will achieve the highest results. In addition, you must most certainly pledge yourselves to exert your most strenuous efforts constantly to stimulate the increase of fighting power, a duty which is urgent during the present situation.

It is very essential that a decisive change be effected by those who are not in tune with the existing situation. What I should like to emphasize in particular with regard to this point is the element of time which is an absolutely necessary factor in the prosecution of a war.

We must most certainly devote ourselves to the (word missing) Imperial Ordinance and extend our fullest cooperation to conform to the war situation, striving toward the prosecution of administration in a most expedient manner. A difference of one second can become the deciding factor between victory and defeat. Administrative policies which ignore the element of time are of no value. If we Government officials should impose aimless restrictions on our time, wasting our breath because we have not carefully considered the element of time, such an action would be truly (regrettable).

In the Imperial Ordinance it is also provided that Government officials, in wartime especially, must issue orders of public service in all fields to subordinate officials, and with a spirit of self-sacrifice must strive toward discharging thoroughly these (word missing). I feel that all higher officials must always clearly designate public service to subordinate officials, and especially must issue appropriate (declarations). The subordinate officials must promptly and (faithfully) execute these instructions.

In order to do this, it is necessary for higher officials to bear in mind the need for clear-cut and detailed decisions. In short, those making these decisions occupy the position of (leaders), and must bear in mind their duty to the State with a strong and lofty sense of responsibility (while) exerting their efforts appropriately on special studies, thereby fully prosecuting the (two words missing). During wartime this is especially essential. It is the sense of responsibility held by the Commanding Officers of the Armed Forces that is responsible for immediately making use of their fighting strength.

However, even in the Government administrative world, just how great and good are the results which are being manifested in the administration by means of the sense of responsibility of such leaders has been very clearly shown by the facts in connection with the recent application of administration laws. Hence those occupying the position of leaders must truly exert their wholehearted efforts, and especially those connected with the increase of production must pay their fullest attention to this matter of sense of responsibility.

In the Imperial Ordinance it is next provided that—I quote—"Government officials, especially during wartime, must preserve the honor of their colleagues and, without losing any time, must strive toward the prosecution of Government administrative policies." I feel that in striving for the attainment of good results which will bring compensation, there will be an increasing number of new ideas and methods, but these are urgent matters, and it is only natural for them to arise. Furthermore, if you have any ideas or opinions, you should express them without hesitation.

However, once you have made a responsible decision on matters of public duty with regard to administration in general, you must without losing any time and with the fullest determination embark on your task. This attitude is especially necessary for Government officials in time of war. In carrying out war matters to cope with the war situation, care must be exercised that they are done on time and that (full) advantage of the opportunity is taken. Such things as losing time, or not being able to attain the ultimate objective even after a decision has been made on policy, or expressing complaints, criticism, or dissatisfaction, or fulfilling responsibility in order to (retrieve) time, must be immediately (done away with).

We must not forget that such a thing as criticism of munitions production, which is an especially urgent matter during the present situation, and of production in other fields will without question have a great effect on the attitude of the people. In the Imperial Ordinance it is next provided that—I quote—"Government officials, particularly in wartime, must exercise their fullest abilities and take to their tasks with a spirit of (love)."

I feel that each and every subject of the Nation is fighting this great war by offering fullest service. This fact must be borne deeply in mind by those who are Government officials. As the people's living conditions become more difficult during wartime, and as hardships and sufferings mount one upon another, I feel more than ever the need that Government officials contact the people with a spirit of self-sacrifice and diligence in the application of administrative policies, fully realizing the existing situation as regards the people's living conditions and the psychology of the people.

Particularly, in pushing forward with Government measures, Government officials must (bear in mind) that there are not a few (cases) in which a feeling of unhappiness and cheerlessness is rising among the people. During the present war situation, it is not permissible that these matters be ignored. The contact made by each and every Government official with the people, by showing their respect and loyalty to the country, will have a great effect on the emergency increase of fighting power and on domestic consolidations. For instance, even if you are a Government official of the lowest rank and are in contact with the people, you must clearly bear in mind that the spiritual ties between Government officials and people must not be impaired.

In the Imperial Ordinance it is next provided that—I quote—"Government officials, especially during wartime, must concentrate on ways and means of uniting the people, and with sincerity (several words missing), and thereby exert their efforts in the prosecution of administrative policies." It is needless for me to say that each Government official must obey orders, regardless of whether his duty is of a military or an ordinary nature.

As I have said previously, as the people's living conditions become more complex and more strained in the cause of the attainment of victory, and as the (word missing) become wider in scope in the (word missing) of the people's living conditions and the establishment of security in people's economy, Government officials are especially required of (several words missing).

I believe that at this juncture it is especially essential for Government officials to exert further efforts in the preparation of business affairs (of the Government), not merely (considering) themselves, and to dash into those duties which concern the changing of the people's way of life during wartime to a decisive wartime way of life, with the one object of establishing security of wartime (two words missing) economy, thereby discharging their duties as models to the Nation.

In the Imperial Ordinance it is next provided that—I quote—"Government officials, particularly in wartime, must exercise care in speech and must exercise circumspection in order to protect military secrets." I feel that it is a matter of course that silence of (word missing) speech is necessary. During the present situation in particular, care must be exercised day and night. Especially in order to deal with information concerning foreign countries, it is necessary for Government officials to exercise care in (word missing) of their speech.

In short, Government officials during wartime must exercise circumspection for the protection of military secrets, and must at least exert their fullest efforts so that fear will not be created among the people due to carelessness of speech.

Furthermore, simultaneously with the promulgation of the Wartime Civil Service Act, the Wartime Civil Service Disciplinary Act was also promulgated in addition to the previously effected Civil Service Disciplinary Act. This act clearly indicates that Civil Service officials must discipline themselves in the prosecution of their duties in time of war, and if any person among them should violate our national laws, particularly in time of war, in the least degree, fullest measures must be taken to cope with such cases.

Also, in addition to the punishment, namely, discharge from duty (word missing), demotion and reprimand, which are provided for in the present Civil Service Disciplinary Act, another punishment, domiciliary confinement, has been added. In this manner, the act provides that the most appropriate punishment may be given in accordance with each case.

In addition to this, with the gracious concern of His Imperial Majesty, an Imperial Ordinance was promulgated which provides ways to compensate Government officials and employees when they retire from office or when they are rehired. That is, for officials and employees in each Government office, including those who have been reinstated in Government service, who retire from office after having rendered meritorious service, and particularly should they become disabled or are forced to retire due to physical injuries received in the prosecution of their duties, the ordinance provides that special compensation may be given in reward for meritorious service rendered.

Furthermore, the Government is contemplating a measure to reward, by increase in salary or other means, those who have rendered meritorious service and who are still in office.

In short, when all Government officials in complete and harmonious cooperation strive with the expectation of making contributions toward the prosecution of the war by concentrating all measures toward this aim in the speediest manner, with the spirit of self-sacrifice and a strong sense of responsibility in the execution of their duties, great administrative efficiency will be attained for the first time, in the interest of the prosecution of the war.

Therefore, if Government officials should forget to keep up with the current situation, lose self-confidence or self-respect, or their attitude toward the people should be unkind and insincere, not only will the Government officials lose the confidence of the people but the effects of this will indeed be very great. This situation must absolutely be corrected.

I again call this to your attention. The mental attitude of the Government officials in time of war must be positive to the fullest degree in time of war. Of course, to fight well in the war is very important. But, in time of war, for each official to render concrete and voluntary contribution in his respective working place, and for each one to make a contribution even in a small way toward the successful prosecution of the war, is most important of all.

Officials should not abuse their official position, nor should they seek to avoid criticism by merely fulfilling their duties. They should voluntarily criticize themselves and, at the same time, it is very essential, more than anything else, that they have a spirit of voluntary willingness for advancement, which will enable them to strive for the attainment of ultimate victory by sacrificing themselves, no matter with what difficulty they may be confronted.

Today, at this very urgent moment of the current situation which will decide the rise or fall of Imperial Japan, and which also will determine the rise or fall of the G.E.A. Sphere, the fact that the Wartime Civil Service Disciplinary Act has been decided upon and was promulgated is indeed very gratifying, and we are filled with trepidation. Gentlemen, the determination of victory or defeat is, ultimately, entirely dependent on the success or failure of the 100,000,000 people to exert their efforts.

Furthermore, that which enables our people to exert their total strength is, therefore, entirely dependent on the (word missing) and effort of us, the Government officials. I, together with you, gentlemen, will lead others in putting these regulations into practice, and we pledge to exert every ounce of our strength in the execution of our duties.

POLISH GOVERNMENT-IN-EXILE'S STATEMENT ON RED ARMY'S DRIVE INTO POLAND

January 5, 1944 [1]

In their victorious struggle against the German invader, Soviet forces are reported to have crossed the frontier of Poland.

This fact is another proof of the breaking-down of German resistance and it foreshadows the inevitable military defeat of Germany. It fills the Polish nation with hope that the hour of liberation is drawing near. Poland was the first nation to take up the German challenge and it has been fighting against the invaders for more than four years, at a cost of tremendous sacrifices and

[1] Polish Information Center.

sufferings, without producing a single Quisling and rejecting every form of compromise or collaboration with the aggressor.'

The underground movement, among its many activities, concentrated upon attacking the Germans in their most sensitive spots, upon sabotage in every possible form and upon the carrying out of many death sentences on German officials whose conduct had been particularly outrageous.

Polish forces, twice reorganized outside their country, have been fighting ceaselessly in the air, at sea and on land, side by side with our Allies, and there is no front on which Polish blood has not been mingled with the blood of other defenders of freedom.

There is no country in the world where Poles have not contributed to furthering the common cause. The Polish nation, therefore, is entitled to expect full justice and redress as soon as it is set free from enemy occupation.

The first condition of such justice is the earliest re-establishment of Polish sovereign administration in the liberated territories of the Polish Republic, and the protection of the lives and property of Polish citizens.

The Polish Government, as the only legal steward and spokesman of the Polish nation, recognized by Poles at home and abroad as well as by the Allied and free governments, is conscious of the contribution of Poland to the war and is responsible for the fate of the nation. It affirms its indestructible right to independence, confirmed by the principles of the Atlantic Charter common to all the United Nations and by binding international treaties.

The provisions of those treaties, based on the free agreement of the parties, not on the enforcement of the will of one side to the detriment of the other, cannot be revised by accomplished facts. The conduct of the Polish nation in the course of the present war has proved that it has never recognized and will not recognize solutions imposed by force.

The Polish Government expects that the Soviet Union, sharing its view as to the importance of future friendly relations between the two countries, in the interests of peace and with the view of preventing German revenge, will not fail to respect the rights and interests of the Polish Republic and its citizens.

Acting in that belief, the Polish Government instructed the underground authorities in Poland on October 27, 1943, to continue and to intensify their resistance to the German invaders, to avoid all conflicts with Soviet armies entering Poland in their battle against the Germans and to enter into co-operation with Soviet commanders in the event of resumption of Polish-Soviet relations.

If a Polish-Soviet agreement, such as the Polish Government has declared itself willing to conclude, had preceded the crossing of the frontier of Poland by Soviet forces, such an agreement would have enabled the Polish underground army to co-ordinate its action against the Germans with Soviet military authorities.

The Polish Government still considers such an arrangement highly desirable. At this crucial moment, the importance of which in relation to the outcome of the war in Europe is evident to everyone, the Polish Government issues the above declaration, confident in final victory and in the triumph of the just principles for which the United Nations stand.

This declaration has been handed to all the United Nations with which the Polish Government has diplomatic relations.

RUSSIAN DECLARATION ON SOVIET-POLISH FRONTIER

January 5, 1944 [1]

On January 5, a declaration of the exiled Polish Government on the question of Soviet-Polish relations was published in London. It contained a number of erroneous affirmations, including an erroneous affirmation concerning the Soviet-Polish frontier.

As is known, the Soviet Constitution established a Soviet-Polish frontier corresponding with the desires of the population of the western Ukraine and western White Russia, expressed in a plebiscite carried out on broad democratic principles in the year 1939. The territories of the western Ukraine, populated in an overwhelming majority by Ukrainians, were incorporated into the Soviet Ukraine, while the territories of western White Russia, populated in an overwhelming majority by White Russians, were incorporated into Soviet White Russia.

The injustice caused by the Riga Treaty in the year 1921, which was forced on the Soviet Union with regard to Ukrainians inhabiting the western Ukraine and White Russians inhabiting western White Russia, was thus rectified. The entry of the western Ukraine and western White Russia into the Soviet Union not only did not interfere with the interests of Poland but, on the contrary, created a reliable basis for a firm and permanent friendship between the Polish people and the neighboring Ukrainian, White Russian and Russian peoples.

The Soviet Government has repeatedly declared that it stands for the re-establishment of a strong and independent Poland and for friendship between the Soviet Union and Poland. The Soviet Government declares that it is striving toward the establishment of friendship between the U.S.S.R. and Poland on the basis of firm good-neighborly relations and mutual respect, and, should the Polish people so desire, on the basis of an alliance of mutual assistance against the Germans as the principal enemies of the Soviet Union and Poland. Poland's adherence to the Soviet-Czechoslovak treaty of friendship, mutual assistance and postwar co-operation could assist in the realization of this task.

The successes of Soviet troops on the Soviet-German front speed day by day the liberation of the occupied territories of the Soviet Union from the German invaders. The selfless struggle of the Red Army and the fighting operations of our Allies that are unfolding bring the rout of the Hitlerite war machine nearer and bring liberation to Poland and other nations from the yoke of the German invaders.

In this war of liberation the Union of Polish Patriots in the U.S.S.R. and the Polish army corps created by it and operating on the front against the Germans hand in hand with the Red Army are already fulfilling their gallant tasks.

Now an opportunity for the restoration of Poland as a strong and independent State is opening. But Poland must be reborn, not by the occupation of Ukrainian and White Russian territories, but by the return of territories seized from Poland by the Germans. Only thus can confidence and friendship among the Polish, Ukrainian, White Russian and Russian peoples be estab-

[1] The United Nations Review.

lished. The eastern borders of Poland can be fixed by agreement with the Soviet Union.

The Soviet Government does not consider the frontiers of the year 1939 to be unchangeable. The borders can be corrected in favor of Poland on such lines that districts in which the Polish population predominates be handed over to Poland. In such case the Soviet-Polish border could approximately follow the so-called Curzon Line, which was adopted in the year 1919 by the Supreme Council of Allied Powers and which provided for the incorporation of the western Ukraine and western White Russia into the Soviet Union.

Poland's western borders must be extended through the joining to Poland of age-old Polish lands taken away from Poland by Germany, without which it is impossible to unite the whole of the Polish people in its own state, which thus will acquire a necessary outlet to the Baltic Sea.

The just striving of the Polish people for complete unity in a strong and independent state must receive recognition and support. The emigre Polish Government, cut off from its people, has proved incapable of establishing friendly relations with the Soviet Union. It has proved equally incapable of organizing an active struggle against the German invaders in Poland itself. Moreover, with its wrong policy, it frequently plays into the hands of the German invaders. At the same time, the interests of Poland and the Soviet Union lie in the establishment of firm and friendly relations between our two countries and in the unity of the Soviet and Polish peoples in the struggle against the common outside enemy, as the common cause of all the Allies requires.

PRIME MINISTER MIKOLAJCZYK'S BROADCAST TO POLAND

January 6, 1944 [1]

Poles! We are entering a turning point of history. According to dispatches from Moscow, the Soviet forces advancing in bitter victorious fighting against the Germans have crossed the Polish frontier. Defeat of our mortal enemies, the Germans, against whom we have been fighting without respite since the first of September, 1939, draws closer. It inspires us with hopes of prompt liberation and brings nearer the moment of our final reckoning with the Germans which will come irrespective of political situation!

We should have preferred to meet the Soviet troops not merely as Allies of our Allies, fighting against the same common enemy, but as our own Allies as well. You know that on October 27th our government ordered the underground authorities in Poland to extend the existing plan of general organized and unswerving resistance against the Germans, and to intensify the struggle against the enemy, to avoid all conflicts that might possibly arise in view of the absence of Polish-Soviet diplomatic relations, to establish co-operation with Soviet commanders if such relations should be resumed.

We know that the responsible leaders of the Directorate of Underground Resistance have received those orders. Only a few days ago we took further steps, aiming at further co-ordination of your struggle for the freedom and independence of our country with the common war effort of all United Nations. Our struggle started on the first of September, 1939, the day of the German invasion. We have been carrying it on ceaselessly and systematically,

[1] Polish Information Center.

without mercy, and we shall deal with the enemy within our means and possibilities, without respite until he is finally defeated.

Our strength is based on Poland's imperishable right to independence, and on the declarations and obligations of our Allies and of the United Nations. We demand respect for the rights and interests of the Polish Republic, its supreme authorities and its citizens in any war situation and at every stage of the development of the international political situation.

We are performing our duty and claim recognition and respect for our rights, that is all. Acting as we are, we are entitled to believe firmly that in the struggle in which we are facing hate, violence, murder and robbery, the eternal principles of morality, justice and law as well as those of the Atlantic Charter and Four Freedoms are on our side—Poland will win strength, freedom and independence.

I am convinced that in this moment of most severe trial and in the final round of the fight against the Germans, you will carry out the orders of the Polish Government and of the Directorate of Underground Resistance with calm, determination, discipline and solidarity.

The moment has come when I can reveal certain decisions taken by the Polish Government, in close consultation with the People in Poland, that had to remain secret until today. The whole world knows that Hitlerite rule in Poland is only surface deep. The Germans never managed to master your hearts, your thoughts or make you their servants.

In the Polish underground there exists a complete Polish state, fully organized in all phases of State administration, political, military, social and economic. The highest authorities of that State acting abroad on its behalf, reside in London. The Polish State never ceased to exist. All that happened was that under the pressure of events its organs had to become secret with the exception of those which had to remain in the open for the purpose of carrying out their duties outside the country.

Acting in consultation with our authorities in Poland, I submitted to the cabinet (I was then Minister of the Interior) a draft decree concerning the temporary organization of administration on the territories of the Polish Republic. This was duly signed on September 1st, 1942, by the President, Prime Minister Sikorski and all members of the Government.

Our purpose in making public the existence of such a decree is to make plain to the Polish citizens in the Motherland, the legal basis of the authority and competence of that member of the Polish Cabinet who, as Deputy Prime Minister, is a delegate of the Polish Government in Poland.

He has full authority to carry out all the functions of the Government concerning Home Administration. The delegate of the Government carries out his duties in accordance with orders and instructions of the Government of the Republic, with the assistance of his staff, its network of administrative offices acting in close co-operation with the Polish political representation and with the Commander of the Polish Underground Forces. Thus the onerous State duty of assuring continuity of the legal Government in Underground Poland is carried on.

The time may be close at hand for the Directorate of Underground Resistance to reveal itself. The Polish Government decided therefore by a special vote to make public the decree of the first of September, 1942. The delegate of the Government, a member of the Cabinet appointed by the President of the Polish Republic, will perform in Poland, until the return of the Prime Minister, the duties of Deputy Prime Minister just as the Deputy Prime Minister does in London, during the absence of the Prime Minister.

The delegate of the Government in Poland will reveal his name and official residence in due time. You are familiar with his declarations, and with instructions bearing the signature of the Government's delegate. I am convinced they will continue to be obeyed by you, as scrupulously as they have been hitherto, and that your sense of responsibility as citizens of the Polish Republic, which never failed in times of hardest trial, will not fail now.

Citizens of the Republic! Everyone of you, even in the most remote parts of our country, knows his rights and duties. Our instructions and orders reach you. By carrying them out strictly, with solidarity, determination and calm, in the days of final test that are at hand, you will fulfill your duties in the struggle for our rights: a strong, free and independent Poland, with free and happy citizens.

PRESIDENT ROOSEVELT'S ANNUAL MESSAGE TO CONGRESS

January 11, 1944 [1]

TO THE CONGRESS OF THE UNITED STATES:

This nation in the past two years has become an active partner in the world's greatest war against human slavery.

We have joined with likeminded people in order to defend ourselves in a world that has been gravely threatened with gangster rule.

But I do not think that any of us Americans can be content with mere survival. Sacrifices that we and our Allies are making impose upon us all a sacred obligation to see to it that out of this war we and our children will gain something better than survival.

We are united in determination that this war shall not be followed by another interim which leads to new disaster—that we shall not repeat the tragic errors of ostrich isolationism—that we shall not repeat the excesses of the wild Twenties when this nation went for a joy ride on a roller coaster which ended in a tragic crash.

When Mr. Hull went to Moscow in October, and when I went to Cairo and Teheran in November, we knew that we were in agreement with our Allies in our common determination to fight and win this war. But there were many vital questions concerning the future peace, and they were discussed in an atmosphere of complete candor and harmony.

In the last war such discussions, such meetings, did not even begin until the shooting had stopped and the delegates began to assemble at the peace table. There had been no previous opportunities for man to man discussions which lead to meetings of minds. The result was a peace which was not a peace.

That was a mistake which we are not repeating in this war.

And right here I want to address a word or two to some suspicious souls who are fearful that Mr. Hull or I have made "commitments" for the future which might pledge this nation to secret treaties, or to enacting the role of Santa Claus.

To such suspicious souls—using a polite terminology—I wish to say that Mr. Churchill and Marshal Stalin and Generalissimo Chiang Kai-shek are all

[1] *New York Times.*

thoroughly conversant with the provisions of our Constitution. And so is Mr. Hull. And so am I.

Of course, we made some commitments. We most certainly committed ourselves to very large and very specific military plans which require the use of all Allied forces to bring about the defeat of our enemies at the earliest possible time.

But there were no secret treaties or political or financial commitments.

The one supreme objective for the future, which we discussed for each nation individually, and for all the United Nations, can be summed up in one word: Security.

And that means not only physical security which provides safety from attacks by aggressors. It means also economic security, social security, moral security—in a family of nations.

In the plain down-to-earth talks that I had with the Generalissimo and Marshal Stalin and Prime Minister Churchill it was abundantly clear that they are all most deeply interested in the resumption of peaceful progress by their own peoples—progress toward a better life. All our Allies want freedom to develop their lands and resources, to build up industry, to increase education and individual opportunity and to raise standards of living.

All our Allies have learned by bitter experience that real development will not be possible if they are to be diverted from their purposes by repeated wars —or even threats of war.

China and Russia are truly united with Britain and America in recognition of this essential fact:

The best interests of each nation, large and small, demand that all freedom-loving nations shall join together in a just and durable system of peace. In the present world situation, evidenced by the actions of Germany, Italy and Japan, unquestioned military control over disturbers of the peace is as necessary among nations as it is among citizens in a community. And an equally basic essential to peace is a decent standard of living for all individual men and women and children in all nations. Freedom from fear is eternally linked with freedom from want.

There are people who burrow through our nation like unseeing moles, and attempt to spread the suspicion that if other nations are encouraged to raise their standards of living, our own American standard of living must of necessity be depressed.

The fact is the very contrary. It has been shown time and again that if the standard of living of any country goes up, so does its purchasing power—and that such a rise encourages a better standard of living in neighboring countries with whom it trades. That is just plain common sense—and it is the kind of plain common sense that provided the basis for our discussions at Moscow, Cairo and Teheran.

Returning from my journeyings, I must confess to a sense of "letdown" when I found many evidences of faulty perspective here in Washington. The faulty perspective consists in overemphasizing lesser problems and thereby underemphasizing the first and greatest problem.

The overwhelming majority of our people have met the demands of this war with magnificent courage and understanding. They have accepted inconveniences; they have accepted hardships; they have accepted tragic sacrifices. And they are ready and eager to make whatever further contributions are needed to win the war as quickly as possible—if only they are given the chance to know what is required of them.

However, while the majority goes on about its great work without complaint, a noisy minority maintains an uproar of demands for special favors for special groups. There are pests who swarm through the lobbies of the Congress and the cocktail bars of Washington, representing these special groups as opposed to the basic interests of the nation as a whole. They have come to look upon the war primarily as a chance to make profits for themselves at the expense of their neighbors—profits in money or in terms of political or social preferment.

Such selfish agitation can be highly dangerous in wartime. It creates confusion. It damages morale. It hampers our national effort. It muddies the waters, and therefore prolongs the war.

If we analyze American history impartially, we cannot escape the fact that in our past we have not always forgotten individual and selfish and partisan interests in time of war—we have not always been united in purpose and direction. We cannot overlook the serious dissensions and the lack of unity in our War of the Revolution, in our War of 1812, in our War Between the States, when the survival of the Union itself was at stake.

In the First World War we came closer to national unity than in any previous war. But that war lasted only a year and a half, and increasing signs of unity began to appear during the final months of the conflict.

In this war we have been compelled to learn how dependent upon each other are all groups and sections of the population of America.

Increased food costs, for example, will bring new demands for wage increases from all war workers, which will in turn raise all prices of all things, including those things which the farmers themselves have to buy. Increased wages or prices will each in turn produce the same results. They all have a particularly disastrous result on all fixed-income groups.

And I hope you will remember that all of us in this Government represent the fixed-income group just as much as we represent business owners, workers and farmers. This group of fixed-income people include: teachers, clergy, policemen, firemen, widows and minors on fixed incomes, wives and dependents of our soldiers and sailors, and old age pensioners. They and their families add up to one-quarter of our 130,000,000 people. They have few or no high-pressure representatives at the Capitol. In a period of gross inflation they would be the worst sufferers.

If ever there was a time to subordinate individual or group selfishness to the national good, that time is now. Disunity at home—bickerings, self-seeking partisanship, stoppages of work, inflation, business as usual, politics as usual, luxury as usual—these are the influences which can undermine the morale of the brave men ready to die at the front for us here.

Those who are doing most of the complaining are not deliberately striving to sabotage the national war effort. They are laboring under the delusion that the time is past when we must make prodigious sacrifices—that the war is already won and we can begin to slacken off. But the dangerous folly of that point of view can be measured by the distance that separates our troops from their ultimate objectives in Berlin and Tokyo—and by the sum of all the perils that lie along the way.

Overconfidence and complacency are among our deadliest enemies. Last spring—after notable victories at Stalingrad and in Tunisia and against U-boats on the high seas—overconfidence became so pronounced that war production fell off. In two months, June and July, 1943, more than a thousand airplanes that could have been made and should have been made were not made. Those who failed to make them were not on strike. They were merely saying, "The war's in the bag—so let's relax!"

That attitude on the part of anyone—Government or management or labor —can lengthen this war. It can kill American boys.

Let us remember the lessons of 1918. In the summer of that year the tide turned in favor of the Allies. But this Government did not relax. In fact, our national effort was stepped up. In August, 1918, the draft age limits were broadened from 21–31 to 18–45. The President called for "force to the utmost," and his call was heeded. And in November, only three months later, Germany surrendered.

That is the way to fight and win a war—all out—and not with half-an-eye on the battlefronts abroad and the other eye-and-a-half on personal, selfish, or political interests here at home.

Therefore, in order to concentrate all our energies and resources on winning the war, and to maintain a fair and stable economy at home, I recommend that the Congress adopt:

1. A realistic tax law—which will tax all unreasonable profits, both individual and corporate, and reduce the ultimate cost of the war to our sons and daughters. The tax bill now under consideration by the Congress does not begin to meet this test.

2. A continuation of the law for the renegotiation of war contracts—which will prevent exorbitant profits and assure fair prices to the Government. For two long years I have pleaded with the Congress to take undue profits out of the war.

3. A cost of food law—which will enable the Government (a) to place a reasonable floor under the prices the farmer may expect for his production, and (b) to place a ceiling on the prices a consumer will have to pay for the food he buys. This should apply to necessities only; and will require public funds to carry out. It will cost in appropriations about 1 per cent of the present annual cost of the war.

4. Early enactment of the stabilization statute of October, 1942. This expires June 30, 1944, and if it is not extended well in advance the country might just as well expect price chaos by summer. We cannot have stabilization by wishful thinking. We must take positive action to maintain the integrity of the American dollar.

5. A national service law—which, for the duration of the war, will prevent strikes, and, with certain appropriate exceptions, will make available for war production or for any other essential services every able-bodied adult in the nation.

These five measures together form a just and equitable whole. I would not recommend a national service law unless the other laws were passed to keep down the cost of living, to share equitably the burdens of taxation, to hold the stabilization line, and to prevent undue profits.

The Federal Government already has the basic power to draft capital and property of all kinds for war purposes on a basis of just compensation.

As you know, I have for three years hesitated to recommend a national service act. Today, however, I am convinced of its necessity. Although I believe that we and our Allies can win the war without such a measure, I am certain that nothing less than total mobilization of all our resources of manpower and capital will guarantee an earlier victory, and reduce the toll of suffering and sorrow and blood.

I have received a joint recommendation for this law from the heads of the War Department, the Navy Department, and the Maritime Commission. These are the men who bear responsibility for the procurement of the necessary arms and equipment, and for the successful prosecution of the war in the field. They say:

When the very life of the nation is in peril the responsibility for service is common to all men and women. In such a time there can be no discrimination between the men and women who are assigned by the Government to its defense at the battle front and the men and women assigned to produce the vital materials essential to successful military operations. A prompt enactment of a national service law would be merely an expression of the universality of this responsibility.

I believe the country will agree that those statements are the solemn truth.

National service is the most democratic way to wage a war. Like selective service for the armed forces, it rests on the obligation of each citizen to serve his nation to his utmost where he is best qualified.

It does not mean reduction in wages. It does not mean loss of retirement and seniority rights and benefits. It does not mean that any substantial numbers of war workers will be disturbed in their present jobs. Let these facts be wholly clear.

Experience in other democratic nations at war—Britain, Canada, Australia and New Zealand—has shown that the very existence of national service makes unnecessary the widespread use of compulsory power. National service has proved to be a unifying moral force—based on an equal and comprehensive legal obligation of all people in a nation at war.

There are millions of American men and women who are not in this war at all. It is not because they do not want to be in it. But they want to know where they can best do their share. National service provides that direction. It will be a means by which every man and woman can find that inner satisfaction which comes from making the fullest contribution to victory.

I know that all civilian workers will be glad to be able to say many years hence to their grandchildren: "Yes, I, too, was in service in the great war. I was on duty in an airplane factory, and I helped make hundreds of fighting planes. The Government told me that in doing that I was performing my most useful work in the service of my country."

It is argued that we have passed the stage in the war where national service is necessary. But our soldiers and sailors know that this is not true. We are going forward on a long, rough road—and, in all journeys, the last miles are the hardest. And it is for that final effort—for the total defeat of our enemies—that we must mobilize our total resources. The national war program calls for the employment of more people in 1944 than in 1943.

It is my conviction that the American people will welcome this win-the-war measure which is based on the eternally just principle of "Fair for one, fair for all."

It will give our people at home the assurance that they are standing four-square behind our soldiers and sailors. And it will give our enemies demoralizing assurance that we mean business—that we, 130,000,000 Americans, are on the march to Rome, Berlin and Tokyo.

I hope that the Congress will recognize that, although this is a political year, national service is an issue which transcends politics. Great power must be used for great purposes.

As to the machinery for this measure, the Congress itself should determine its nature—but it should be wholly non-partisan in its make-up.

Our armed forces are valiantly fulfilling their responsibilities to our country and our people. Now the Congress faces the responsibility for taking those measures which are essential to national security in this the most decisive phase of the nation's greatest war.

Several alleged reasons have prevented the enactment of legislation which would preserve for our soldiers and sailors and marines the fundamental prerogative of citizenship—the right to vote. No amount of legalistic argument can becloud this issue in the eyes of these 10,000,000 American citizens. Surely the signers of the Constitution did not intend a document which, even in wartime, would be construed to take away the franchise of any of those who are fighting to preserve the Constitution itself.

Our soldiers and sailors and marines know that the overwhelming majority of them will be deprived of the opportunity to vote if the voting machinery is left exclusively to the States under existing State laws—and that there is no likelihood of these laws being changed in time to enable them to vote at the next election. The Army and Navy have reported that it will be impossible effectively to administer forty-eight different soldier voting laws. It is the duty of the Congress to remove this unjustifiable discrimination against the men and women of our armed forces—and to do it as quickly as possible.

It is our duty now to begin to lay plans and determine the strategy for the winning of a lasting peace and the establishment of an American standard of living higher than ever before known. We cannot be content, no matter how high the general standard of living may be, if some fraction of our people—whether it be one-third or one-fifth or one-tenth—is ill-fed, ill-clothed, ill-housed, and insecure.

This Republic had its beginning, and grew to its present strength, under the protection of certain inalienable political rights—among them the right of free speech, free press, free worship, trial by jury, freedom from unreasonable searches and seizures. They were our rights to life and liberty.

As our nation has grown in size and stature, however—as our industrial economy expanded—these political rights proved inadequate to assure us equality in the pursuit of happiness.

We have come to a clear realization of the fact that true individual freedom cannot exist without economic security and independence. "Necessitous men are not free men." People who are hungry and out of a job are the stuff of which dictatorships are made.

In our day these economic truths have become accepted as self-evident. We have accepted, so to speak, a second Bill of Rights under which a new basis of security and prosperity can be established for all, regardless of station, race or creed.

Among these are:

The right to a useful and remunerative job in the industries or shops or farms or mines of the nation;

The right to earn enough to provide adequate food and clothing and recreation;

The right of every farmer to raise and sell his products at a return which will give him and his family a decent living;

The right of every business man, large and small, to trade in an atmosphere of freedom from unfair competition and domination by monopolies at home or abroad;

The right of every family to a decent home;

The right to adequate medical care and the opportunity to achieve and enjoy good health;

The right to adequate protection from the economic fears of old age, sickness, accident and unemployment;

The right to a good education.

All of these rights spell security. And after this war is won we must be prepared to move forward, in the implementation of these rights, to new goals of human happiness and well-being.

America's own rightful place in the world depends in large part upon how fully these and similar rights have been carried into practice for our citizens. For unless there is security here at home there cannot be lasting peace in the world.

One of the great American industrialists of our day—a man who has rendered yeoman service to his country in this crisis—recently emphasized the grave dangers of "rightist reaction" in this nation. All clear-thinking business men share his concern. Indeed, if such reaction should develop—if history were to repeat itself and we were to return to the so-called "normalcy" of the 1929's—then it is certain that even though we shall have conquered our enemies on the battlefields abroad, we shall have yielded to the spirit of fascism here at home.

I ask the Congress to explore the means for implementing this economic Bill of Rights, for it is definitely the responsibility of Congress so to do. Many of these problems are already before committees of the Congress in the form of proposed legislation. I shall from time to time communicate with the Congress with respect to these and further proposals. In the event that no adequate program of progress is evolved, I am certain that the nation will be conscious of the fact.

Our fighting men abroad, and their families at home, expect such a program and have the right to insist upon it. It is to their demands that this Government should pay heed, rather than to the whining demands of selfish pressure groups, who seek to feather their nests while young Americans are dying.

The foreign policy that we have been following—a policy that guided us to Moscow, Cairo and Teheran—is based on the common sense principle which was best expressed by Benjamin Franklin on July 4, 1776: "We must all hang together, or assuredly we shall all hang separately."

I have often said that there are no two fronts for America in this war. There is only one front. There is one line of duty, which extends from the hearts of the people at home to the men of our attacking forces in our farthest outposts. When we speak of our total effort we speak of the factory and the field and the mine as well as the battlefield—we speak of the soldier and the civilian, the citizen and his Government.

Each and every one of us has a solemn obligation under God to serve this nation in its most critical hour, to keep this nation great, to make this nation greater in a better world.

FRANKLIN D. ROOSEVELT

THE WHITE HOUSE,
January 11, 1944.

DECLARATION OF THE SOVIET GOVERNMENT ON SOVIET-POLISH RELATIONS

January 11, 1944 [1]

TASS is authorized by the Soviet Government to declare the following:
On January 5 in London was published a declaration of the emigre Polish

[1] Information Bulletin, Embassy of the U.S.S.R.

government on Soviet-Polish relations which contains a number of incorrect assertions, including an incorrect assertion about the Soviet-Polish frontier.

As is well-known, the Soviet Constitution established the Soviet-Polish frontier in conformity with the will of the population of Western Ukraine and Western Byelorussia, as expressed through a plebiscite conducted on a broad democratic basis in 1939. Then the territories of the Western Ukraine in which Ukrainians form the overwhelming majority of the population were incorporated with the Soviet Ukraine, and the territories of Western Byelorussia in which Byelorussians form an overwhelming majority of the population were incorporated with Soviet Byelorussia. The injustice committed by the Riga Treaty of 1921, which was imposed upon the Soviet Union, in regard of the Ukrainians inhabiting the Western Ukraine and the Byelorussians inhabiting Western Byelorussia, was thus rectified.

The incorporation of Western Ukraine and Western Byelorussia with the Soviet Union not only did not violate the interests of Poland, but on the contrary created a reliable foundation for stable and permanent friendship between the Polish people and its neighbors—the Ukrainian and Byelorussian and Russian peoples.

The Soviet Government has repeatedly stated that it stands for the re-establishment of a strong and independent Poland and for friendship between the Soviet Union and Poland. The Soviet Government declares again that it seeks to establish friendship between the USSR and Poland on the basis of stable, good-neighborly relations and mutual respect and, if the Polish people will so desire—on the basis of an alliance for mutual assistance against the Germans as the chief enemies of the Soviet Union and Poland.

Poland's joining of the Soviet-Czechoslovak treaty of friendship, mutual assistance and postwar collaboration could contribute to the accomplishment of this task.

The successes scored by Soviet troops on the Soviet-German front daily accelerate the liberation of the occupied territories of the Soviet Union from the German invaders. The self-sacrificing struggle of the Red Army and the developing war operations of our Allies bring nearer the utter defeat of the Hitlerite war machine and are bringing to Poland and other nations liberation from the yoke of the German occupationists.

The Union of Polish Patriots in the USSR and the Polish Army Corps formed by it, which acts on the front against the Germans hand-in-hand with the Red Army, are already fulfilling their glorious tasks in this struggle for liberation.

At present the possibility is opening for the rebirth of Poland as a strong and independent state. However, Poland must be reborn not through the seizure of Ukrainian and Byelorussian lands, but through the restoration to Poland of lands which belonged to Poland from time immemorial and were wrested by the Germans from her. Only in this way trust and friendship could be established between the Polish, Ukrainian, Byelorussian and Russian peoples.

The eastern frontiers of Poland can be established by agreement with the Soviet Union. The Soviet Government does not regard the frontiers of 1939 as unalterable. These frontiers can be modified in Poland's favor so that the areas in which the Polish population forms a majority be turned over to Poland. In this case the Soviet-Polish frontier could pass approximately along the so-called Curzon line, which was adopted in 1919 by the Supreme Council of the Allied Powers, and which provides for inclusion of the Western Ukraine and Western Byelorussia into the Soviet Union.

The western frontiers of Poland must be extended through incorporation with Poland of ancient Polish lands previously wrested by Germany, without which it is impossible to unite the whole Polish people in its state, which thereby will receive a needed outlet to the Baltic Sea.

The just aspiration of the Polish people for its full reunion in a strong and independent state must receive recognition and support.

The emigre Polish government, isolated from its people, proved incapable of establishment of friendly relations with the Soviet Union. It also proved incapable of organizing active struggle against the German invaders within Poland herself. Furthermore, by its incorrect policy it not infrequently plays into the hands of the German occupationists.

However, the interests of Poland and the Soviet Union consist in that stable, friendly relations be established between our countries and that the people of Poland and the Soviet Union unite in struggle against the common external enemy, as demanded by the common cause of all the Allies.

PRESIDENT ROOSEVELT'S BUDGET MESSAGE TO CONGRESS

January 13, 1944 [1]

TO THE CONGRESS OF THE UNITED STATES:

The budget transmitted herewith covers the period ending June 30, 1945. This is a period which I am certain will be crucial in the history of the United States and of mankind, a period which will see decisive action in this global war. While we move toward complete defeat of our enemies, we must lay the groundwork to return the nation to peaceful pursuits. This double task is the essence of the Government's program and must be reflected in the budget.

The budget for the fiscal year 1945 anticipates a total of Federal expenditures (in general and special accounts and net outlays of Government corporations, excluding debt retirement) of $100,000,000,000—slightly more than the revised estimates for the fiscal year now under way.

In substantial measure these expenditures will be made under appropriations already enacted. I am transmitting herewith specific recommendations for appropriations of $17,000,000,000, of which $7,000,000,000 are for war purposes. For most of the war appropriations I shall submit detailed recommendations in the spring. I estimate that these recommendations will amount to $53,000,000,000.

The estimated total of $70,000,000,000 of appropriations in the general and special accounts for the fiscal year 1945 compares with a total of $100,-000,000,000 of actual appropriations for the fiscal year 1944. Reappropriations, additional to the above totals for recommended new appropriations, are estimated to be $38,000,000,000 for the fiscal year 1945 and $15,000,000,000 for the fiscal year 1944.

Since there is always—and particularly for war procurement—a lag between appropriations and the related obligations and subsequent expenditures, a large part of the recommended appropriations will not be translated into expenditures until later fiscal periods. We shall continue to adjust our war program promptly to changing strategic necessities, and I shall use all the authority available to the executive branch to prevent needless expenditures.

[1] *New York Times.*

Four Phases in the War Program

As we win the battle of producing the instruments of modern war, we enter the period of decisive action on many battlefields throughout the world. We have attained superiority in war production. Production alone, however, does not assure victory. We must fight and fight hard.

In June, 1940, when France fell, we recognized that we were in mortal danger and that only by building our strength to the utmost would we have a chance to maintain peace or to attain victory if we were attacked. We then embarked on a program of preparedness, converting our factories and constructing a new munitions industry of gigantic size. At the time of Pearl Harbor, we were in the first stages of training the Army, strengthening the Navy, and developing a munitions industry.

In the period of defensive war, we had to be satisfied with fighting a delaying action and with delivering munitions to our Allies while we gained precious time.

The anxious year of defensive warfare came to an end with the attack on Guadalcanal and the invasion of Africa in late 1942. Thus began the period of aggressive deployment of our forces. During that time we had to build up and fill up the pipelines for military supplies of all kinds as well as establish material reserves for future aggressive operations. The munitions program was then limited only by our productive resources and shipping facilities.

With pride in the over-all achievements of American management and labor, I can say that we are now well equipped, with pride in the military leadership of the Allied forces, I can say that we are now in a strategic position to make full use of our equipment for decisive blows by land, by sea and by air.

The size and composition of our war expenditures reflect these various phases of the preparedness and war program, as the following table indicates:

WAR EXPENDITURES

(Including Net Outlays of Government Corporations)

Period	Average Annual Rate (in Billions)	Estimated P.C. of Total		
		Munitions, Including Ships	*Pay, Sub- sistence	War Con- struction
Preparedness:				
July, 1940–November, 1941	$9.8	50	30	20
Defensive war:				
December, 1941–October, 1942	45.7	56	22	22
Aggressive deployment:				
November, 1942–December, 1943	83.5	59	28	13
Offensive war:				
†January, 1944–June, 1944	97.0	64	30	6
July, 1944–June, 1945 (fiscal year 1945)	90.0	63	33	4

* Including also agricultural lend-lease and other civilian war activities.
† On basis of $92,000,000,000 for fiscal year 1944.

The rapid increase in war expenditures mirrors a gigantic effort. We have converted and diverted approximately half of our resources to war purposes. In the production of munitions we now almost equal the rest of the world combined. Expenditures for industrial facilities and other war construction, which reached their peak in the fall of 1942, have declined since then and will decline further.

The total $22,000,000,000 public and private expansion of industrial plant and equipment should suffice by and large for the foreseeable needs of the far-flung battlefronts, and in addition provide capacity for unexpected contingencies. Expenditures for pay and subsistence of the armed forces are still increasing because of the continuing growth of our military forces and increased allowances to the wives, children and other dependents of our fighting men. Expenditures for subsistence and other purposes would have to be higher were it not for the fact that our field forces stationed abroad are receiving considerable supplies and services from our Allies under reciprocal lend-lease arrangements.

THE MUNITIONS PROGRAM

At the present time it is extremely difficult to estimate necessary expenditures for munitions. In the past, such estimates were based on maximum output in the light of available facilities, raw materials and manpower. This maximum was always less than enough to fill the requirements established by our military leaders.

The situation is quite different now. We have excess supplies in some types of munitions, deficiencies in others. Whether at any time we have an excess or a deficiency depends on rapidly changing strategic conditions. Every effort is made to adapt production to these changing conditions as promptly as possible. A special committee under the Joint Chiefs of Staff is scrutinizing the military requirements item by item and cutting out or cutting back programs no longer justified in view of strategic developments. The lend-lease requirements of our Allies are subject to similar scrutiny by other agencies.

In most cases in which contracts have been canceled, the same contractor has received other more urgent orders; plants, raw materials and labor could not be released for production for civilian use in these cases. We have canceled, for instance, orders for many escort vessels in order to push construction of landing vessels.

In a number of cases, however, labor and material have been released for urgent domestic needs of indirect war importance. We shall release for civilian production any facilities, manpower or raw material that are no longer needed for war production, but only when we are sure that by doing so we will not impair the war effort. I know that none of us wants any cut in the production of munitions needed at the battlefronts simply to permit an increased production for civilian comforts.

RELIEF AND REHABILITATION IN LIBERATED AREAS

As we close in on the enemy we are confronted with the necessity of initiating the restoration of civilian life and productivity in the liberated areas. Both relief and the commencement of the process of rehabilitation will be necessary requirements of military occupation.

In liberated areas, relief must, of necessity, be a military problem at the outset. This job will be turned over to civilian administration as soon as feasible. For this reason the United Nations Relief and Rehabilitation Administration recently has been created. Appropriate committees of Congress are now considering enabling legislation that will permit the United States to make its proportionate contribution.

SUMMARY OF WAR PROGRAM

Estimates of Expenditures and Appropriations

It is now expected that war expenditures (including net outlays of Government corporations for war activities) for the current fiscal year will amount to $92,000,000,000, $8,000,000,000 below the $100,000,000,000 estimate submitted in my budget message of a year ago. In certain types of munitions we have fallen short of our objectives, but by and large the cut in the estimate of expenditures is due to changes in the war program.

For the fiscal year 1945—the year ending eighteen months hence—war expenditures are estimated at $90,000,000,000. I emphasize, however, that this estimate is tentative; it is based on the assumption that the war will continue throughout the fiscal year 1945. In our military planning, in our production planning, and in our financial planning we cannot rely with safety on hopes of earlier victory.

If the war should continue on all fronts throughout the fiscal year 1945 or longer, we shall be prepared. If an unfavorable turn in military events should result in an increased demand for munitions, we shall, with available facilities, pour out even more munitions than scheduled, and expenditures will be larger.

If, on the other hand, victory should be achieved on one of the major fronts earlier than assumed, I assure the Congress and the nation that war production will be promptly adjusted to the changed requirements, and war expenditures in the fiscal year 1945 may be less than estimated at the present time. Because of termination payments, mustering-out pay, and similar demobilization expenditures, however, the reduction in cash expenditures will of necessity lag considerably behind any curtailment of war production.

The total war program as measured by appropriations, contract authorizations, and Government corporation commitments from June, 1940, through December, 1943, totals $344,000,000,000. Of this amount, $264,000,000,000 have been obligated already, and it is estimated that $307,000,000,000 will have been obligated by the end of the current fiscal year. Unobligated balances total $80,000,000,000 now and will be reduced to about $38,000,000,000 by June 30, 1944, assuming that additional supplemental appropriations of $1,500,000,000 will be provided before the end of the current fiscal year.

Through December, 1943, we have spent $153,000,000,000 for war and it is estimated that $202,000,000,000 will have been spent by the end of the current fiscal year, leaving $105,000,000,000 in outstanding obligations to be liquidated in later fiscal years.

It will be necessary to request additional appropriations for obligations to be incurred in the fiscal year 1945. Detailed recommendations for most of the war appropriations will be made in the spring, as last year. The tentative estimate for the fiscal year 1945 is $60,000,000,000 of new war appropriations and $10,000,000,000 of new contract authorizations.

I also intend to recommend that an estimated $38,000,000,000 of unobligated appropriations be reappropriated for the coming fiscal year.

The new appropriations include $18,000,000,000 to liquidate prior contract authorizations. The additions to the war program therefore will amount to $42,000,000,000 new appropriations (excluding appropriations for the liquidation of prior contract authorizations), $10,000,000,000 new contract authorizations, and $1,500,000,000 estimated supplementals for this year. These additions will bring the total war program to $397,000,000,000 for the fiscal year 1945.

Enactment of these requests will permit the Government to incur new obligations totaling $90,000,000,000 in the fiscal year 1945. This, together with the unliquidated obligations on June 30, 1944, would permit the expenditure of $195,000,000,000 in the fiscal year 1945 and subsequent years, when appropriations have been made to liquidate contract authorizations.

As stated earlier, it is estimated that $90,000,000,000 will be spent for war purposes in the fiscal year 1945. Assuming that it will be necessary to obligate all appropriations and contract authorizations, we shall finish the fiscal year 1945 with about $105,000,000,000 of unliquidated obligations—the same amount as the unliquidated obligations existing at the beginning of the fiscal year.

I hope that this total war program will never be fully obligated and spent. Congressional approval of the estimated new appropriations and contract authorizations will be necessary, however, to permit our military leaders and our procurement agencies the flexibility they must have in planning and executing the job ahead.

WARTIME READJUSTMENTS AND PREPARATION FOR PEACE

Demobilization begins long before hostilities end. While we are still expanding war production, we have already terminated more than $12,000,000,-000 of war contracts; while we are still increasing the size of the armed forces, we have already discharged a million men and women. If hostilities end on one major front before they end on other fronts, large-scale demobilization adjustments will be possible and necessary while we are still fighting a major war.

The problems of adjustment cover a wide range-contract termination, reconversion of war plant, disposal of Government-owned property, shifting of men to peacetime employment, and many others. Our approach to these problems must be positive, not negative. Our objective must be a permanently high level of national income and a correspondingly high standard of living.

To achieve this end there must be concerted efforts by industry, labor and Government and a well-planned demobilization program. As men, materials and facilities are released from war service and production, such resources must be channeled into civilian production on a basis that will assure a high and stable level of production, consumption and employment. The soldier, the worker, the business man and the farmer must have assurance against economic chaos.

Just as economic mobilization for total war required many interrelated measures, so adequate reconversion to civilian production will require many interrelated adjustments of fiscal policy, production policy, price policy and labor policy. At this time I shall discuss, but briefly, certain aspects of a demobilization program.

CONTRACT TERMINATION, DISPOSAL OF SURPLUS PROPERTY AND INDUSTRIAL RECONVERSION

The problems pertaining to the termination of contracts, the disposal of war surpluses and the reconversion of industry, already before us, will take on increased significance during the war and after.

Contract termination will become a problem of large magnitude. A considerable number of contracts has already been terminated. Should victory be achieved on one front, the volume of contract termination and related settlement problems will increase markedly even during the war. Raw materials, goods in process and overhead costs incurred on the assumption that contracts will be completed, all involve settlement problems when contracts are terminated. The timing of future contract terminations is, of course, uncertain; but it is evident that the volume of such terminations and the amount of related claims and payments will be very large.

It will be necessary to dispose of a vast amount of Government property. Our war program has required the expenditure of approximately $15,000,-000,000 by the Government for new industrial plant and equipment and over $13,000,000,000 for non-industrial construction and land.

In addition, the Government owns scores of billions of dollars of raw materials, merchant ships, aircraft, munitions and a wide variety of other commodities. The value of Government property that will become surplus during and after the war is as uncertain as the vicissitudes of war. There can be no doubt, however, that a very large amount of public funds will be involved.

The policies followed in contract termination and the disposal of surplus property will have a major impact on the speed and effectiveness of the reconversion of industry and of the re-employment of those released from war service and war production. Such policies will also have a major bearing on the stability and pattern of the nation's economy for many years to come.

It is, therefore, imperative to develop a unified program to deal with the interrelated problems of contract termination, surplus property disposal and industrial reconversion. To facilitate the development of co-ordinated policies pertaining to these fields, a war and post-war adjustment unit has been established in the Office of War Mobilization. A joint contract termination board, including representatives of the several contracting agencies, has also been established in that office to develop recommendations for a unified program relating to the settlement of terminated war contracts. Recommendations pertaining to contract termination and disposition of surplus war properties are now in preparation.

The disposition of war surpluses should be closely co-ordinated with the permanent management of Government property. To provide a foundation for such co-ordination, I hope that machinery for the permanent management of Government property can be established in the very near future.

MANPOWER DEMOBILIZATION AND RE-EMPLOYMENT

Demobilization of war workers and members of the armed forces also starts long before the war ends. Since Jan. 1, 1942, we have discharged a million men and women from active military duty because of age, physical and mental disabilities and other reasons.

Both service men and war workers will need active help in finding their way back into gainful and productive peacetime employment. Many have gained exceptional skills and shown managerial ability in wartime; they should have an opportunity to contribute these skills and aptitudes to civilian activities.

Certain re-employment rights in private and Government employment have been assured to members of the armed forces and, in limited instances, to those who transferred to war jobs. Many of these will be able to resume their pre-war employment.

This war, however, is causing substantial changes in the geographic, technological and market structures of industry. Many employers will be recruiting employees in excess of their pre-war labor force. Many employees and ex-service men will be looking for new employment opportunities because they had no employment before the war or because their previous jobs no longer exist.

It is imperative that we be on guard against any weakening of the administrative agencies which have been established for the purpose of job placement, counseling and training. To master this great task of re-employment we must maintain and strengthen during the demobilization period a unified national employment and counseling service. Adequate provisions for job re-training, education and rehabilitation must supplement the placement service. Special measures are needed to increase the opportunities for the employment of ex-service men, particularly those disabled in war service.

PUBLIC WORKS PLANNING

Our reconversion policy should have as a major aim the stimulation of private investment and employment. There will, however, be an urgent need for certain public works in the post-war period. As a result of the war the normal construction work of Federal, State and local Governments has been curtailed. Many new facilities will be needed.

Careful advance planning and evaluation are essential to assure that priority will be given those projects that fill the greatest need relative to their cost, as well as to assure that their construction will be timed in accordance with employment requirements.

It is my hope that adequate machinery for the general planning and evaluation of public works in relation to broader economic activities can be established at all levels of Government and that there can be close co-ordination both in planning and in completing essential projects. Thus, public works activities of the various communities and areas would be effectively co-ordinated with broad national programs and interests.

I have directed the various Federal agencies to submit estimates of appropriations for making detailed plans for Federal public works and improvements. I have asked the Bureau of the Budget to assume a continuing responsibility for co-ordinating the advance preparation of Federal public works and improvement programs to be undertaken when the war is over.

VETERANS' LEGISLATION AND SOCIAL SECURITY

Last July I recommended to the Congress a minimum program to assist service men and service women in meeting some of the problems they will face when discharged. This included mustering-out pay for every member of the armed forces sufficient to provide for a reasonable period after discharge. I also urged an educational and training program to enable those demobilized from the armed forces to further their education and training and to prepare for peacetime employment. I am confident that the Congress will take early action along these lines.

The permanent program of social security initially adopted in 1935 provides a framework within which many of the problems of demobilization can be met. This framework of unemployment insurance and retirement benefits must be reinforced and extended so that we shall be better equipped for readjustment of the labor force and for the demobilization of the armed forces and civilian war workers.

Pressing economic need has forced many workers to continue in employment or seek work even when disability, old age, or care of young children would have made retirement from the labor force preferable. Extension at the present time of the coverage of the Federal Old-Age and Survivors Insurance system to many groups now denied protection, and expansion of the scope of the system to include disability benefits, would permit these workers to retire after the war. The old-age and survivors insurance system should also be amended to give those in the armed forces credit for the period of their military service.

The proposed changes in the social security law would provide the necessary minimum protection for nearly all individuals and their families, including veterans of the present war.

They would provide benefits additional to veterans' pensions, veterans' compensation, and national service life insurance in case of death or disability attributable to military service.

I repeat my recommendation that the present unemployment insurance system be strengthened so that we shall be able to provide the necessary protection to the millions of workers who may be affected by reconversion of industry.

I prefer an extension of coverage and liberalization of unemployment benefits to any special legislation, such as that providing for dismissal payments through war contractors. I also recommend the adoption of a program of Federal unemployment allowances for members of the armed forces.

Furthermore, I suggest Congress consider the establishment of unemployment insurance for maritime employees and a temporary system of unemployment allowances for those in Federal service who, because of their wartime employment, have been unable to build up rights under the existing system.

INTERNATIONAL PROBLEMS OF READJUSTMENT

In the international field, as in the domestic field, there is no sharp distinction between war and post-war policies. For example, the program under Lend-Lease and reciprocal lend-lease arrangements is designed to facilitate the effective prosecution of the war and at the same time to help lay the foundation for post-war settlement and international prosperity.

We are now engaged in discussion with other members of the United Nations to work out plans to expedite the international flow of capital into worth-while long-term investments, to remove obstacles to international trade, and to stabilize currencies. The United Nations are working toward a permanent international organization for food and agriculture. We are also considering co-operative arrangements to facilitate maritime and air transportation.

The success of these international policies depends to a considerable extent on the success of our domestic demobilization policy, and vice versa. The more prosperous the United States, the more it will demand the products of other countries, both in the form of raw materials for its industries and in the form of manufactured goods to meet consumers' demands. Our purchases will, in turn, provide other countries with the means to buy more of our exports, more and more, our prosperity and world prosperity become interdependent.

THE FARM AND FOOD PROGRAM

Farm output in 1943 has been the largest in our nation's history. This bountiful production has enabled us to maintain the best-fed army in the world, to send much needed food to our Allies, and to eat better ourselves than civilians in any other country. Although some of us at home did not have all the particular foods we wanted, more of us were nutritionally well fed than ever before. Our farmers have accomplished this through hard work and intelligent use of their resources.

The year 1944 will be more critical on the food front in view of increasing food requirements for our armed forces, our Allies and the starving populations in territories formerly occupied by the enemy. To meet these needs, farm production must be larger than in 1943. Barring unfavorable weather conditions, I believe this objective can and will be achieved through even better use of our farm labor, land, machinery and other resources.

Farmers, spurred on by their desire to make the utmost contribution to the war effort, will do their level best to get the job done. It is the Government's responsibility to facilitate their efforts. The major emphasis of our 1944 program will be to develop and encourage balanced production, efficient farming practices and the full use of all our agricultural resources.

Much of the Government's assistance to agriculture in the past ten years has been intended to re-establish farmers' purchasing power. This has been achieved—and more. Farm prices in 1943 were 115 per cent of parity, and farm income in 1943 is estimated at 150 per cent of parity.

On the price side, the problem of the Government is no longer to increase farm prices generally, but rather to adjust relationships among prices of the various farm products in harmony with relative production needs. To this end the War Food Administrator, in co-operation with the Price Administrator and with the approval of the Director of Economic Stabilization, has prepared a full schedule of support prices for war crops and other critical commodities with the objective of encouraging 1944 production of each crop in the quantity desired without increasing the general level of farm prices.

This schedule should be announced well in advance of planting time. The carrying out of these support prices, however, will depend upon Congressional action on the Commodity Credit Corporation Bill. The schedule of support prices must be implemented by appropriate measures such as loans, purchase and sale programs, ceilings and related production aids.

A stable farm price level is basic if we are to prevent inflation. I have often declared my belief that the judicious use of subsidies is necessary if consumer prices are to be kept from rising. I repeat it again. Only if we succeed in preventing an appreciable rise in the general level of both farm prices and wages, however, can we continue to hold the cost of living stable with a moderate use of subsidies. The cost-of-living index was 124.1 in November, 1943 —the same as in April.

In order that the Federal Government may fulfill its responsibility in the 1944 farm and food program, I am recommending appropriations of $659,-000,000 for the Department of Agriculture including the War Food Administration. This is approximately $314,000,000 less than the current appropriations for these agencies. The recommendation includes provision for conservation and use of agricultural land resources, the soil conservation service, the Farm Security Administration, the exportation and domestic consumption of agricultural commodities, the administration of the Sugar Act, and research and other long-established functions of the Department of Agriculture. It does not include provision for potential losses of the Commodity Credit Corporation.

The over-all decrease of $314,000,000 results largely from the omission of a recommendation for parity payments and a reduction in the recommended appropriation for conservation and use of agricultural land resources.

TOTAL FEDERAL EXPENDITURES

The estimates of Federal expenditures are intimately related to the stabilization program. If we permit general increases in wages in the war industries, in farm prices, or in profits on war contracts, Federal expenditures will increase correspondingly. The estimates presented in this budget are based on the assumption that the wage and price line will be held, and I am convinced that the line can be held.

Wages, farm prices, and profits havê reached levels which should be exceeded only in rare cases of special war requirements and not by attempts of pressure groups to promote their special interests. If we take the point of view that our efforts to secure stabilization can be relaxed just because production is nearing its peak, we shall be sacrificing one of the main objectives of the stabilization program—to reduce the dangers of economic disorganization in the demobilization period.

The following figures (with millions omitted) summarize Federal expenditures in recent years for the war program, for interest on the public debt and for all other activities.

Classification	*1945	*1944	†1943	†1942
War activities:				
General and special accounts	$88,200	$88,500	$72,109	$26,011
Government corporations (expenditures less receipts)	1,800	3,500	2,976	2,255
Total	$90,000	$92,000	$75,085	$28,266
Interest on public debt	3,750	2,650	1,808	1,260
Other activities:				
General and special accounts:				
Veterans' pensions and benefits	1,252	865	600	552
Refunds of taxes and customs, including excess-profits tax refund bonds	1,799	412	79	94
All other	2,953	3,524	3,583	4,479
Government corporations (expenditures less receipts)	15	—175	—1,476	—440
Total expenditures	$99,769	$99,276	$79,679	$34,211

* Estimated.   † Actual.

As I have pointed out repeatedly, there is not much realism in the customary distinction between war expenditures and other expenditures, often called "non-war" expenditures. Practically all Government activities under present conditions are related directly or indirectly to the war. War expenditures, as identified for budgetary purposes, include only those made under appropriations which the Congress has designated "Defense" or "War" or obviously enacted for war purposes.

Another group of expenditures is emerging as a result of the present war. Already large, this aftermath-of-war category will become a dominant factor in future budgets. For the fiscal year 1945 it includes, for example, about three-fourths of the interest on the public debt; more than half of the expenditures for insurance, pensions, and other benefits for veterans; and a large amount for refunds of war taxes. Expenditures for contract termination, now included in war procurement, also belong in this group.

Expenditures for veterans' pensions and benefits and for tax refunds are expected to rise sharply during the fiscal year 1945. Tax refunds include $1,000,000,000 for issuance of post-war bonds for the refundable portion of corporate excess-profits taxes. The issuance of refund bonds is, of course, not a cash expenditure.

Excluding expenditures for veterans and refunds, the total for "other" activities is expected to continue next year the steady decline which has been maintained since 1939. The estimate for the fiscal year 1945 is $2,953,000,-000—barely half the comparable total of $5,897,000,000 expended in 1939. It is $571,000,000 below the revised estimates for the current fiscal year.

This latter decrease will occur despite some increases in so-called "non-war" expenditures. Among the increases are $129,000,000 in some subdivisions of the Treasury, Justice, State and Agriculture Departments, the General Accounting Office, the National Advisory Committee for Aeronautics, and the Social Security program. For the most part, these increases reflect war-necessitated expansions of workloads under "non-war" appropriations.

Major reductions are expected in aids to agriculture, general public works, work relief, the Department of Commerce, War Department civil functions, and the Federal Works Agency. These items total $553,000,000 less than the corresponding items for the present fiscal year. The Post Office expects to have no deficit, but rather a surplus of $11,000,000.

For all purposes other than direct war activities, I am recommending appropriations, in general and special accounts, of $10,115,000,000, including $3,750,000,000 for interest on the public debt and $590,000,000 for statutory debt retirement under permanent appropriation. The total of $5,775,000,000 for other purposes is an increase of $1,321,000,000 over the amount enacted by the Congress for the current fiscal year including anticipated supplemental appropriations. This increase, like the expenditure estimates, reflects primarily the large volume of veterans' benefits and tax refunds occasioned by the present war, and if these items are excluded there is a decrease of $434,-000,000.

The estimated expenditures and recommended appropriations assume application of the Overtime Pay Act with present coverage throughout the fiscal year 1945. Current provisions for overtime pay for most Federal Government employees have been operative only since May 1, 1943; they will expire June 30, 1945, unless terminated earlier by the Congress.

The overtime pay law provides for quarterly determinations by the Director of the Bureau of the Budget of the number of employes required for the proper and efficient exercise of the functions of each department or agency. Although nearly half of the civilian personnel of the Government are not covered by the act, I believe the determinations have effectively supplemented other budgetary controls.

Other factors contributing to savings in Government use of manpower have been the legislation authorizing overtime work and pay, suggestions made by Congressional committees, general manpower controls, curtailment and consolidation of activities, and the unremitting efforts of the Civil Service Commission and the heads of operating agencies to use personnel more effectively.

More than a year ago I notified the heads of all departments and agencies that I expected them to eliminate every nonvital service, to seize every opportunity for improving the speed and efficiency of operations, and to conserve manpower, materials and money. Each of these officials is now being asked to take stock of what his agency has accomplished and to continue aggressive efforts for improvement in the management and economical functioning of his organization.

One result of all these efforts has been a material reduction in Government personnel. The latest reported total of paid civilian employees of the executive branch in continental United States was 2,798,000 in October, 1943; there were 154,500 additional in Alaska, the Panama Canal Zone and overseas. Nearly three-fourths were in the War and Navy Departments and other war agencies.

The total number employed in the continental United States in October was 205,000 below the peak of June, 1943. The bulk of the reduction was in the war agencies; they reduced personnel by 167,000 from June to October, while the so-called nonwar agencies reduced personnel by 38,000. The earlier rise was in the war agencies. Other agencies as a group have been reducing personnel steadily for eighteen months or more, although during all that time they have been devoting more and more of their efforts directly to war activities.

There has been during the past year, too much unfounded disparagement of Government employment. No one can estimate what this has cost in impaired morale, employee turn-over, recruitment difficulties, and retardation of essential war work. Thousands of Americans entered the Government service or have remained in it with single-hearted determination to contribute to victory. Yet Government employees frequently have had to bear an unjustified stigma, somehow associated with the mistaken assumption that nearly all of them occupy armchair jobs.

Of course, it is true that thousands of Government employees work at desks. In Government, as elsewhere, the manual workers are not the only producers. Modern armies cannot operate without quartermasters, paymasters, communication systems; ships and planes cannot be built without drafting, procurement, accounting; indeed, no organized activity in our complex society can succeed without writing and record-keeping.

Even so, the large majority of employees in the war agencies are engaged in mechanical operations. Among the so-called nonwar agencies the postal service alone accounts for more than two-fifths of all the personnel. These facts are too frequently disregarded by critics who fail to look behind personnel statistics to the work the employees do.

THE REVENUE AND BORROWING PROGRAM

Summary of Federal Finances

Net receipts under present legislation are estimated at a little more than $41,000,000,000 for the current fiscal year and at somewhat less than $41,-000,000,000 for the fiscal year 1945. Receipts in these years will be about $19,000,000,000 above those of the fiscal year 1943. This rise reflects increased tax rates in the Revenue Act of 1942, the current Tax Payment Act of 1943, and the higher level of incomes and profits.

Net receipts from all sources in the fiscal year 1945 are expected to be somewhat lower than in the current fiscal year, despite the fact that some items, notably corporation taxes, will increase further. Substantial collections in the present fiscal year, mainly in connection with transition to a current basis for individual income taxes, will not recur in 1945 and later years. Estimates of receipts in this budget are subject to modification if the pending revenue bill is enacted.

Total expenditures for the fiscal year 1945 are estimated to exceed net receipts by $59,000,000,000. Without further legislation the deficit will amount to 59 per cent of total expenditures, approximately the same as the comparable ratio for the current fiscal year.

SUMMARY OF FEDERAL FINANCES

(Excluding Debt Retirement and Trust Funds)

(In Millions)

Classification	*1945	*1944	†1943	†1942
Total expenditures	$99,769	$99,276	$79,679	$34,211
Total receipts	43,425	42,578	23,385	13,668
Deduct: Net appropriations for Federal old-age and survivors' insurance trust fund	2,656	1,392	1,103	869
Net receipts	40,769	41,186	22,282	12,799
Excess of expenditures over receipts	59,000	58,090	57,397	21,412

* Estimated.   † Actual.

In view of these prospective deficits, I recommend the earliest possible enactment of additional fiscal legislation.

The amount which the Federal trust funds, especially the Old-Age and Survivors' Insurance Fund, can invest in Treasury bonds has been estimated under the assumption that the increased Federal insurance contribution rates which were scheduled for Jan. 1, 1944, will become effective on March 1, 1944.

The Congress decided to postpone the effective date of the increase sixty days in order to gain time for further consideration of the increase on social security rates. I earnestly urge the Congress to retain at this time the scheduled increase in rates. High employment and low rates of retirement during the war have added to social insurance reserves. However, liabilities for future benefits based on the increased wartime employment and wages have risen concurrently.

The increase in contributions provided by existing law should now become effective so that the contributions will be more nearly in accord with the value of the insurance provided and so that reserves may be built up to aid in financing future benefit payments.

The Need for Additional Taxes

In my budget message last year I recommended legislation to collect $16,-000,000,000 in additional taxes, savings, or both. I also pointed out the importance of simplifying taxation and of putting taxes, as far as feasible, on a pay-as-you-go basis. I repeated previous recommendations for making our tax laws more fair and equitable.

Provision for collection of individual income taxes on a pay-as-you-go basis was made in 1943 by the passage of the current Tax Payment Act.

In October, 1943, the Administration's revenue program was presented, calling for additional wartime taxes in the amount of $10,500,000,000. Those recommendations are still under consideration by the Congress, and I wish at this time to stress the need for additional wartime taxes in at least the amount requested in October.

The developments of the past year have not lessened the needs for additional revenue and nothing has occurred to indicate that the Administration's tax program is more than a minimum. Indeed, the necessity for additional revenue becomes increasingly acute as the war continues. The debt has risen at a record rate, and the prospect is for a continued rise with little or no diminution in rate during the months to come.

Let us face the fact—the failure thus far to enact an adequate fiscal program has aggravated the difficulties of maintaining economic stabilization.

Increases in income should be limited to reasonable rewards for additional effort. A wartime tax policy directed to that objective is a necessary support to wage and price stabilization. It is, furthermore, an important wartime contribution to post-war fiscal planning.

The time to impose high taxes is now when incomes are high and goods are scarce. In this situation, if we do not now pay in taxes all that we can, we shall be treating unfairly those who must face the accumulated bill after the war. Individual incomes will be approximately 40 per cent higher in the calendar year 1944 than in 1941, after payment of all taxes, Federal, State, and local. Corporate profits after taxes are running at an all-time high.

The time to relax some wartime taxes will come when goods are again plentiful, after reconversion of industry to peacetime production.

In view of these facts, I must urge upon the Congress the need for additional revenue beyond that provided in the bill now pending before the Senate. I also recommend tax simplification to reduce the burdens of compliance of the many millions of taxpayers by elimination of returns where feasible and by other measures—provided such changes do not result in substantial impairment of receipts for the Treasury or of equity for taxpayers.

Renegotiation of War Contracts

The American people are united in their resolution to prevent war profiteering. Taxation alone is not enough. One of the most constructive attempts ever made to reduce profiteering at the expense of the Government in wartime was the Renegotiation Law, enacted by the Congress in April, 1942. That statute gives to the major procurement agencies the right and charges them with the duty to re-examine their war contracts and subcontracts and to recover excessive amounts paid under them, as well as to reduce inordinately high prices being charged for goods still to be delivered.

The record of performance under that statute has been good. The cost of our procurement program has already been reduced by over $5,000,000,000 by contractors' agreements to refund money already paid them by the Government for war matériel and by price reductions granted the Government on goods still to be delivered. A considerable part of this amount would have escaped even wartime taxes.

Many wartime profits are not subject to excess-profits taxation; moreover, even taxes paid may be refunded under various provisions of the present excess-profits tax law. The recapture of exorbitant war profits, in my judgment, should be definitely assured by renegotiation.

To measure the benefits of the renegotiation statute in terms of dollars recovered from war contractors is to understate its beneficial effect. The statute is enabling us to combine speed of procurement with fair prices for the goods the Government must buy. Without it the war procurement program would be handicapped.

Of late I have been disturbed by proposals, apparently being seriously considered in the Congress, which will, if adopted, greatly restrict the operation of the statute if not destroy its effectiveness. I believe adoption of such proposals would be a serious mistake. In spite of criticism leveled at the statute by highly articulate special pleaders, I think it can fairly be said that the statute has proved to be very helpful in preventing or reducing excessive profits, and that renegotiation has been carried out with fairness and equity.

The Public Debt

Wartime spending leaves its legacy of post-war debt. By June 30, 1944, the public debt is expected to reach $198,000,000,000, and a year later, $258,000,-000,000. Even higher totals will be reached if advance financing builds up cash balances. In any case it will soon be necessary to request legislation authorizing a further increase in the debt limit from the present level of $210,000,000,000. In view of these huge totals, administration of the public debt and of related fiscal policies must receive double care and scrutiny.

The primary achievement of our debt policy has been the maintenance of low and stable rates of interest. Average interest rates payable on the public debt now are less than 2 per cent. Interest received from all new issues is fully taxable. As a result, the net cost per dollar borrowed since Pearl Harbor has been about a third the cost of borrowing in the First World War.

A debt of $258,000,000,000 will require gross interest payments of $5,000,-000,000 annually at the present average rate. With a national income of $125,000,000,000 or more, these payments need not prove oppressive. I am confident that we can devise a tax structure and other appropriate economic policies which will permit both payment of interest, and gradual repayment of principal during years of prosperity, without impairing the stability and growth of the national income.

We have sought to secure the broadest possible distribution of our debt, not only to fight against inflation, but also to assure a wide distribution of income from the debt. For these two reasons it has been our deliberate policy to offer the highest rates of interest on those bonds which are sold to individual purchasers in limited amounts.

Over 50,000,000 subscribers to war bonds now own a direct financial stake in the United States. More than a third of all the resources of life insurance companies and mutual savings banks and half of all the assets of commercial banks consist of Government bonds. These individual investors, as well as bank depositors and insurance policy holders, can count upon the soundness of these assets.

Every dollar accumulated by individuals, corporations, or other non-financial institutions adds to rainy-day reserves of these bondholders. Businesses with heavy costs of reconversion will be able to defray such costs in part through liquidation of bonds. State and local governments will be able to finance some public works programs without levying additional taxes or borrowing additional funds. Individuals who are temporarily unemployed will be able to redeem war bonds, besides relying upon unemployment compensation and other provisions.

An increase in wartime debt is unavoidable. War expenditures must continue at high levels until our enemies are defeated; a bare minimum of regular Government activity must be preserved; interest must be paid regularly on the outstanding debt. The executive departments are using their best efforts to hold down all these outlays, wherever reductions are consistent with maximum war effort. The only effective way now to control the volume of the debt and to minimize post-war adjustments is to adopt a truly stiff fiscal program.

This war was inevitable because peaceful nations cannot live in the same world with nations that have become tools in the hands of irresponsible cliques bent on conquest. That obstacle to peace will be removed by destruction of the German and Japanese war machines and by establishing lasting co-operation among the nations united in the fight for freedom.

In this budget I have outlined the financial requirements for victory. I have also outlined some of the measures required to aid in the reconversion of our war economy and to help discharged soldiers and dismissed war workers find their way back into civilian life and peacetime employment.

Military victory is not enough. We shall not have completed the defense of our way of life until we also solve the second task, the reconstruction of an economy in which everyone willing to work can find for himself a place in productive employment. The enemy, though beaten on the battlefields, may still arise in our midst if we fail in the task of reconstruction.

Victory will be not only a cause for joy over an accomplishment but at the same time a challenge to another great undertaking. You and I have the responsibility to prepare for victory and for peace. Let us make sure that the budget, the Government's work plan, serves both ends.

FRANKLIN D. ROOSEVELT

Jan. 10, 1944.

POLISH GOVERNMENT-IN-EXILE'S DECLARATION ON SOVIET COMMUNIQUÉ

January 15, 1944 [1]

The Polish Government have taken cognizance of the declaration of the Soviet Government contained in the Tass communiqué of the 11th of January, which was issued as a reply to the declaration of the Polish Government of January 5th.

The Soviet communiqué contains a number of statements to which complete answer is afforded by the ceaseless struggle against the Germans waged at the heaviest cost by the Polish Nation under the direction of the Polish Government.

In their earnest anxiety to safeguard the complete solidarity of the United Nations, especially at this decisive stage of their struggle against the common enemy, the Polish Government consider it to be preferable now to refrain from further public discussions.

While the Polish Government cannot recognize unilateral decisions or accomplished facts which have taken place or might take place on the territory of the Polish Republic, they have repeatedly expressed their sincere desire for the Polish-Soviet agreement on terms which would be just and acceptable to both sides.

To this end the Polish Government are approaching the British and the USA Governments with the view of securing through their intermediary the discussion by the Polish and the Soviet Governments with participation of the British and American Governments of all outstanding questions, the settlement of which should lead to friendly and permanent co-operation between Poland and the Soviet Union.

The Polish Government believes this to be desirable in the interest of victory of the United Nations and harmonious relations in postwar Europe.

[1] Polish Information Center.

PREMIER HIDEKI TOJO'S ADDRESS AT OPENING OF 84TH DIET

January 21, 1944 [1]

Previously, on the opening ceremony of the Diet session, His Imperial Majesty, the Emperor, has granted an especially gracious Imperial Rescript, and we were deeply moved with trepidation. I, together with you, reverently acknowledge the will of His Imperial Majesty, the Emperor, and firmly pledge that we all will exert our fullest effort in the prosecution of our important duties under wartime conditions, so that we may speedily attain the objective of this sacred war and thereby put His Imperial Majesty, the Emperor, at ease.

As I reflect on the past, it is already two years and some months since the outbreak of the Greater East Asia War, and our officers and men are gallantly and dauntlessly fighting on the general war front under the august virtue of His Imperial Majesty. I, together with you, express our heartfelt appreciation to the gallant and valiant fighting of our officers and men of the Imperial forces and, at the same time, offer our deepest condolence and congratulation to the heroic souls of officers and men who died on the battlefield.

To the members of the bereaved families we express our sympathy from the bottom of our hearts, and at the same time we pray for the speedy recovery of our wounded and sick officers and men so that they may again serve on the battlefield. Furthermore, I, together with you, express our heartfelt respect to the people who are continuing to fight gallantly and valiantly.

Looking at the general scope of the G.E.A. War, the counteroffensives of the enemy are further growing in intensity and persistency. Despite the tremendous damage they have suffered, as you already know well, the enemies are simply extending their bases by depending on their numerical superiority. They are also attacking our sea lane, whose influences over our transportation efficiency cannot be overlooked.

In coping with such an acute and prevailing condition, our officers and men on the fighting front are inflicting disastrous damage on the enemy by gallantly and dauntlessly fighting on all fronts, and are advantageous, as well, in utilizing actively the strategic superiority we won at the beginning of the war. The great and brilliant war achievements of our forces recently attained —particularly in the Solomons and Gilbert areas, and on the China front— are indeed unprecedented in the history of the world. The only people who are ignorant of this fact are the people of the U. S. and Britain, whose eyes have been blinded by their leaders.

However, the greatness of the damage being inflicted on the personnel of the enemy during this period is especially noteworthy. The future of the U. S. and Britain, who daringly challenged us, confronted by the officers and men of the Imperial Forces, whose persistent spirit will never allow them to stop until they crush completely the superior enemy forces with a handful of men—is indeed very dark and tragic, and the only thing that awaits them in the future is ultimate defeat.

In response to the gallant and dauntless fighting of our officers and men on the battlefront, the 100,000,000 people have also arisen with greater determination. Now the students have been mobilized for the fighting front

[1] Office of War Information.

and a special military conscription ordinance has also been put into effect. These measures have long been in effect in the enemy nations. However, the fact that Imperial Japan has now determined to adopt these measures indicates that Japan, compared with the enemy nations of the U. S. and Britain, still has enough reserve manpower for mobilization. It also illustrates the unwavering determination of Imperial Japan to destroy these enemies.

Meanwhile, the increase of fighting strength, particularly in the air, is drastically and continuously following the line of upward progress by overcoming numerous hardships and difficulties in the various fields, and the prevailing production capacity is more than twice greater than that of last year.

As you know already, the Munitions Ministry was newly established in November of last year, and on Jan. 15 the transfer of all administrative affairs from the War and Navy Ministries, in regard to the production of airplanes, was completed. Thus the Munitions Ministry has completed its preparations, and is now able, fully and concretely, to exert its efforts for airplane production. In this manner we can now expect to see a drastic increase in plane production, an increase several times greater than the present production capacity, for the structure for airplane production has been fully solidified.

Of course, in regard to the increase and strengthening of fighting power, there are still many more points which need improvement and effort in response to the demands of this fierce and decisive war operation, and this we feel very keenly. If the superior technical ability of our 100,000,000 people, who have shown unsurpassable ability and efficiency by exceeding the world production standard within a short time in the field of war industries, should be turned to production of airplanes, and their skill expressed to a maximum degree, it is very certain that we may be able to effect a drastic increase in the production of planes.

The Government, with the cooperation of the people and with the confidence mentioned in the foregoing, will constantly strive for improvement and greater effort, and is firmly determined that a drastic increase in plane production will be materialized in response to demands from the fighting front.

Judging from their war strategy the enemies, constantly striking back in desperation, and regardless of the tremendous damage inflicted on them recently on the South Pacific front, particularly the U. S., are secretly contemplating a plot to end the war in a short period, although loudly mouthing protracted war, and it is very obvious.

This is chiefly due to the fact that the enemies in planning strategy face a disadvantageous war, for they must depend on a vast and long supply line to continue their war, as well as on an acutely unstable feeling, at home and overseas. In short, her war production on which America relies the most has already reached its peak. Also, in view of their material and manpower resources, the enemies' unstable feeling is growing constantly. In Britain, on the other hand, the national power has already been drained and the degree of wear on the Nation is constantly increasing.

The enemies fully appreciate the facts that, if (1) more time should be given to Imperial Japan, Japan's strategic strongholds will be solidified further; (2) that the munitions resources in the Southern Regions will further be converted into fighting power; and (3) that the Asiatics will be further solidified to strengthen their unity, thus making (the enemies) completely helpless to challenge the position that will be held by Imperial Japan, and they fear this the most.

The leaders of the U. S. and Britain, who are spreading useless principles, and are dragging the people into the sufferings of war, cannot help but dare to attempt useless and atrocious deeds in an effort to save their faces on being confronted with the people's dissatisfaction and weariness that grows greater as the war goes on.

It is also very natural for the Allied Nations, whose relationship contains a fundamental contradiction to their national interests, to strive aimlessly in an effort to patch up the situation before it becomes too late. Now the enemies are in a dilemma. Now is the best chance to crush the enemies thoroughly and drive them into unavoidable catastrophe, for the enemy is in a dilemma, and we should never let this opportunity escape us. This is the reason Imperial Japan is striving, maintaining herself very calmly and coolly, to strike harder blows on the enemy by grasping this good opportunity.

The hammering I spoke of in the foregoing is already being realized. To have been struck such a tremendous blow, such as we have witnessed in the six air battles off Bougainville Island, and the four air battles off the Gilbert Islands, must be fatal even to the U. S. who is relying on numerical superiority. This is not hard to imagine.

Especially when we think of the fact that several tens of thousands of officers and men of the enemy have been sent to the bottom of the Southern Sea within a short period, it is very easy for us to imagine the disastrous influences it has brought forth on the enemy. It is also very understandable that the enemy leaders are desperately attempting to conceal this undeniable truth.

And the thing that manifests further the greatness of the Imperial Forces' power and, at the same time, enables a shift to offensive operation without losing the opportunity, is the increase and strengthening of fighting power, particularly in the air, for which the 100,000,000 people are now striving with their fullest effort. It is needless for me to waste words here over the fact that we must constantly solidify our preparation, mentally and materially, for a protracted war. For what is called "preparations for protracted war" means nothing else than establishing a concrete offensive structure that will enable us to strike the enemy, particularly a structure that will enable us to inflict a fatal blow on the enemy as the situation arises. There is also no need for wasting words on this.

In short, the demand for prosecuting the war in the future is the need for a structure enabling us to crush the enemy's fighting power by grasping the opportunity for a general counteroffensive while the enemy is in a dilemma and, at the same time, for a structure also enabling us to expand drastically and strengthen our fighting strength, particularly our air strength. Such a structure will enable us to crush the enemy, while it solidifies preparations, both mental and material, to cope with a protracted war and to help us turn to an offensive and, finally, to bring the enemies to their knees.

In accordance with the demands for the prosecution of this decisive war, as I mentioned in the foregoing, the Government from last autumn adopted various measures for the conversion of domestic structures into the war with the intention of perfecting the decisive wartime structure of the nation. However, I wish to explain the policies on which the Government wishes to exert its fullest effort in the future.

Whether we are successful or not in supplying superior airplanes sufficiently and speedily to the fighting front now will determine the trend of the war and will also determine success or failure in this war. To produce a large number of planes speedily, quantity and time elements are absolutely essential in strengthening air fighting strength. Of course, this is not an easy task. However, for the sake of ultimate victory, we must fulfill this requirement no matter how we may do it.

As I have already mentioned in the foregoing, the Government, together with the people, expects to fulfill this objective with unwavering confidence. And, for the increase and strengthening of fighting power, particularly air fighting power, the increased production of essential raw war materials such as iron, light metals, coal, and other materials, as well as the strengthening of the National Labor Service Mobilization, and security and improvement of sea and land transportation power, are recognized as essential requirements.

In regard to the increased production of important war materials, the Government is exerting its fullest effort, under an epoch-making plan, for increase of production in response to the demands of the fighting front, so that nothing regrettable may be felt later. Parallel to this, in regard to the strengthening of the National Labor Service, the Government intends to adopt various measures to increase quantity, that is, to increase the number of men, and to improve the skill of the workers.

In regard to the strengthening of the people's mobilization, although it will considerably influence the livelihood of the people and increase the people's responsibility, the Government intends to exert its fullest effort in the application of this measure to cope with the future exigency of the war situation. Of course, I firmly believe without the slightest doubt that the people will gladly and voluntarily cooperate with the Government.

In regard to the matter of improvement in quality, the Government acknowledges the fact that there are many points which still need improvement and development. The Government will further concentrate its effort and the sense of responsibility of the proper authorities on these points, so that there may be nothing left to regret.

As for the security and improvement of sea and land transportation, the damages sustained by our sea transportation cannot be regarded lightly. At this point, the Government will strengthen the sea transportation power by comprehensively strengthening the land transportation and speeding up shipbuilding, by overcoming various difficulties, and by adopting various measures in regard to seamen used in transportation convoy (word missing) and longshoremen.

In cooperation with the various measures mentioned in the foregoing, security in foodstuffs also is an essential requirement for ultimate victory. Concerning the solidification of the self-sufficiency system in foodstuffs, the Government has endeavored to assure its security by adopting careful programs. Imperial Japan has now approached this condition by an epoch-making increase in production of potatoes and wheat, in addition to rice, due to the efforts of the people, as well as the extraordinary cooperation of Manchukuo, where there is nothing for us to worry about, no matter how long this war may continue.

The people in agricultural villages who are concentrating their full effort for the increase of foodstuffs production by breaking through all difficulties, through many ups and downs, and by young and old, men and women, aiding and depending on each other in accordance with the unsurpassable patriotism and endeavor which is the traditional spirit of the farmers of Imperial Japan, impress us deeply beyond expression.

The importance of security in foodstuffs during wartime, particularly when a war becomes a protracted one, is fully illustrated in the history of war, the

First European War. The Government will make further endeavors for the increase of foodstuffs production, as well as for smooth operation of rationing, and intends further to strengthen self-sufficiency in foodstuffs. In this respect the Government also wishes to receive the fullest cooperation of the people.

Along with the progress of the war, of course, the Government will strive to increase and strengthen taxes and people's savings, and the Government has provided the most appropriate measures for the most efficient utilization of funds for industries. The Government expects to perfect the security and strengthening of these measures by the cooperation of the people.

Parallel with the aforementioned measures, the conversion of the wartime structure into one for the decisive wartime is the fundamental premise for all other measures. In view of this unprecedentedly great war, efficiency in fulfillment of their duties by Government officials will immediately be reflected upon the people, and it will affect the fighting spirit of the people, and also will tremendously influence efficiency in the prosecution of the war.

At this crucial moment, the wartime Civil Service Administrative Act has been adopted and proclaimed, clarifying the duties of Government officials under wartime conditions. At this time we, the Government officials, are firmly resolved that we will, by self-criticism and by training and improving ourselves, thoroughly fulfill our services in wartime.

The important points of the Government's domestic measures are as I have mentioned in the foregoing, but at this point I wish to express my special desire, that is, confidence in ultimate victory which flows in our Nation through the hearts of the people; that is, a firm confidence that we are going to win the ultimate victory in the G.E.A. War.

It is needless to mention it here especially but, in the last analysis, a war is a battle between one man and another. Now all the leading nations in the world have already engaged in war several years by mobilizing their total national strength; therefore the victory falls into the hand of that people which firmly believes that the ultimate victory is in their hands. The decision of ultimate victory is made only by a split second.

In this war we must be fully prepared to be confronted with more acute and greater sufferings. However, when we are suffering from the increase of difficulties, of course the enemy is also suffering from a tremendous increase of difficulties and distress. In this, both sides will wear down in extreme weariness, and the side which loses its fighting spirit even a second earlier will be vanquished. Such a development in this war is inevitable, and it is easy to predict it.

In connection with this, the people of the nations who are challenging Imperial Japan, whose national policy is unsurpassable in the world, and whose war structure is indomitable, are indeed very unfortunate and should really be pitied.

The extreme patriotism of the Yamato race which, for ruler, has the Imperial Household, whose history is unbroken for 3,000 years and is following a steady upward progress, is the best in the world. And, in this G.E.A. War, in which our Nation had no choice but to rise for the sake of self-existence and self-prosperity, our Nation will continue its speedy forward advance with a passion which will burn everything which encounters it.

The more that the hardships press upon us and the more the difficulties which pile upon another in our sight, that much more will the spirit of us, the 100,000,000 people, become fierce and firm. Our gallant soldiers, only a handful in number, fought against enemy forces several times as large, nay, several tens of times larger than themselves, and gallantly died together previously on Attu Island and recently at Tarawa and Makin islands. These deeds constantly reveal to the enemy the true nature of us, the 100,000,000 people. That is the spirit of the Yamato race.

However, we should not forget that there are numerous unseen (efforts) by our gallant and dauntless officers and men, who also are willing to die gladly like the heroes on Attu, Tarawa, and Makin islands. Indeed, this great spiritual power which will even make devils cry is constantly flowing throughout the veins of us, the 100,000,000 people, and this is our underlying strength. Because we have this spiritual power, which is unsurpassed by any other Nation in the world, we always will win and will be able to win the ultimate victory in this war of justice.

What the enemies secretly fear in us is the very spiritual power of ours. With this spiritual power as our foundation, when an epoch-making increase in our fighting strength has been realized by effective application of the measures which I mentioned in the foregoing, only victory lies ahead of us.

Turning our eyes on the situation in the G.E.A. Sphere, we recall the G.E.A. Conference which was held during November, last year, as you already know. This conference was realized while our Nation prosecuted the G.E.A. War and carried on the establishment of the G.E.A. Sphere as Premiers and leaders of the various nations in the G.E.A. Sphere gathered in a hall in an intimate atmosphere.

These delegates earnestly participated in discussions concerning the future of the G.E.A. Sphere, and finally reached common agreements. That is, the announcement has been declared to the world that the G.E.A. War will be successfully consummated, based upon the five great principles, namely, common existence and common prosperity, independence and self-defense, enhancement of civilization, economic development, and contribution to the progress of mankind, thereby making contributions for the establishment of world peace.

Of course, the G.E.A. Joint Declaration indicates that the great ideal of our Imperial Japan completely coincides with the ideal of the G.E.A. Sphere, and this declaration also solemnly declared the common ideal of the G.E.A. Sphere to the entire world. The 1,000,000,000 people of the G.E.A. Sphere, with further closer collaboration among them and by repelling the (word missing) of the U. S. and Britain, are striving with the fullest effort for the establishment of the G.E.A. Sphere, based upon humanity and justice, so that they may make a contribution for world peace.

To the earnest cooperation of the people in the G.E.A. Sphere toward Japan, we have no words to express our appreciation. Taking this opportunity, I, together with you, express our heartfelt appreciation to the people of the G.E.A. Sphere.

The state of complete unity between Japan and Manchukuo now has been further solidified. Beginning with the signing of the basic treaty with China, the signing of the treaty between Japan and Thailand in regard to her new territories, and the independence of Burma and the Philippine Islands—all these have been materialized in succession. The grant of political participation of the local inhabitants in Malai (Malaya), Sumatra, Djawa (Java), Borneo and the Celebes also is being put into effect gradually, and the cooperation extended by the local inhabitants to the Imperial Government is indeed very impressive.

The leaders of various nations in the G.E.A. Sphere, despite atrocious exploitations and indiscriminate bombings, are gallantly fighting against the enemy, and by quickly and wisely understanding the situation they are voluntarily guiding their people, and the peoples are sturdily striving with fullest speed toward the ultimate victory with unwavering confidence.

Recently the U. S. and Britain are raiding nonmilitary facilities in various nations in the G.E.A. Sphere and subjecting innocent civilians to their bombings, wounding or killing them. To many persons in the G.E.A. Sphere who lost their lives or lost homes because of malicious deeds of the enemy, I hereby express our heartfelt sympathy.

The condemnable enemy's atrocity is something which neither God nor man can forgive. For this reason, Imperial Japan is firmly resolved to deal a blow (tetsuzui—sledge-hammer blow) of righteous vengeance and punishment. This resolute determination of Imperial Japan should be noted and imprinted well into the minds of the people of America and Britain.

Today the unity of the 1,000,000,000 people of G.E.A. is day by day strengthened and solidified, and the great enterprise to establish the G.E.A. Sphere and the liberation of G.E.A. is advancing with strong, gigantic strides.

The luring of the Chungking Regime to a discussion conference at Cairo at this time by the enemy, America and Britain, is nothing more than an exposure of the psychological break between Chungking and Anglo-America. And, confronted with a situation where Asia has returned to her original state, based upon the principle of neighborly relationship, independence, and self-government, Chungking already has lost its objective in fighting against Japan, and the people of Chungking are turning their eyes toward a new direction. As for the enemy, due to our encirclement operation, they are clinging fast to force of habit and are accepting (several words missing) being unable to do anything about it.

Furthermore, the people under the Chungking Regime have achieved only empty promises of aid and have been given a dream-talk. They have acquired useless prolongation (of the war) and an increase of suffering through the war.

The U. S. and Britain, who previously had boasted of a general counter-offensive in Burma, thereby to give aid to Chungking, have seen the passing of the monsoon period and greeted the cold season, which is past its middle period. In this way our enemy waits in vain for another season to roll by. Just how vain, unreliable, and faulty is the (word missing) humanitarianism which the U. S. and Britain profess to have is fully illustrated by the various races that live under the rule of the British, and by the Negroes who live in the U. S.

The desire of our country to share the happiness of co-prosperity among all nations, and to remove all racial discrimination, is a desire long cherished. It is our perpetual ideal. On the other hand, the U. S. and Britain and other anti-Axis nations (few words missing) aspire to send the gloriously prosperous and new G.E.A. Sphere back again to its former state and subject it to random exploitation. All the G.E.A. nations are working together to prevent such an occurrence, and we, the G.E.A. nations, cannot acknowledge such a situation.

The people of India, in particular, are gallantly withstanding extreme poverty and suffering due to the domination of the U. S. and Britain. For them our heart cries out with sympathy. The liberation of India is the ardent desire of the 1,000,000,000 people of Asia which they cannot suppress in spite of themselves. Numerous Indian patriots, led by Subhas Chandra Bose, have already risen for the independence of their country.

Leader Chandra Bose, who represented the Provisional Government of

Free India, was welcomed to the G.E.A. Conference held in Tokyo last year. As you are well informed, the Imperial Government announced during this conference that it has pledged itself to transfer the Andaman and Nicober Islands, which are under the control of the Imperial Forces, and thus took the first step to aid India in its movement toward attainment of freedom.

In an endeavor to acquire prestige and independence, through Leader Chandra Bose, the great undertaking of the liberation of India is steadily making progress. Today the 400,000,000 Indians who are revolting against the mentally malicious British and Americans are responding, and have begun to take action in this justified movement. And in keeping with the progress of the independence movement, a vigorous movement, the first of its kind since India was fettered, is about to overspread the whole of India.

Thus the hope that the day when the Provisional Government of Free India will take command over India is not very far away, and, in coping with this situation, the Imperial Government of Japan, together with the other nations of the G.E.A. Sphere, will extend actual power in the form of positive aid to India in order to bring about its liberation. I take this opportunity doubly to reaffirm this fact before the world.

Turning our eyes toward the European situation, our friendly Nation, Germany, is sturdily striving forward to destroy the enemy, the U. S. and Britain, by holding an unwavering structure in the midst of numerous ups and downs. There are considerable difficulties that Germany confronts at present, which we fully comprehend. However, the people of Germany are overcoming all difficulties and, with an ever-growing fighting spirit, are fighting gallantly and valiantly with firm confidence in their ultimate victory.

Germany, which has already gone through many tests and has completed preparations to cope with the pending great decisive war, will inflict fatal blows by taking advantage of their opportunities against the armies of the U. S. and Britain in land battles in which the Germans excel, and she is ready to deal blows so hard that the enemy, the U. S. and Britain, will never be able to rise again. This free and daring operation of the German Forces, which will come eventually, will indeed be worthy of our expectations.

Based upon the noble principle of humanity and justice, both the Nations of Japan and Germany are united firmly by the blood shed in a common war against the U. S. and Britain, and by the forever unchanging mutual understanding, in order that we may be able to make contributions toward the establishment of a New World Order. The collaboration of Japan and Germany, particularly in the spiritual ties, is growing more intimate as the war increases in intensity.

And, under the firm leadership of Premier Mussolini, Italy began a new life, and endeavors to restore itself to a normal state of affairs by steadily advancing her preparations.

I, together with you, express our heartfelt respect to the gallant and valiant fighting of the Axis Nations in Europe, centered around Germany. I firmly pledge that we further solidify our collaboration, from the East and the West, and achieve our common objective by crushing the U. S. and Britain.

In the foregoing, I have explained the policy of the Government in coping with this fierce, decisive war. I appeal to you to fully comprehend the intentions of the Government, and I sincerely hope that you will give speedy approval to those legislative bills which have been submitted to you by the Government.

VICE-PRESIDENT HENRY A. WALLACE'S
JACKSON DAY DINNER ADDRESS

January 24, 1944 [1]

Tonight we are all thinking about the young men of America, the best equipped men who ever went to war. We hope and pray that victory will soon be theirs and ours and that our sons will return home safely. All soldiers should be given a genuine and simple ballot that will be counted.

We as individuals are here tonight because the people, suffering from the Hoover-Mellon-Wall Street collapse, demanded a New Deal. The people believed in Roosevelt, the Democratic Party and the New Deal in 1932 because they felt that the New Deal stood for human rights first and property rights second. The people confirmed their faith in Roosevelt and the New Deal in 1936 and 1940.

The New Deal is not dead. If it were dead the Democratic Party would be dead, and well dead. But the Democratic Party is not dead and the New Deal has yet to attain its full strength. The New Deal is as old as the wants of man. The New Deal is Amos proclaiming the needs of the poor in the land of Israel. The New Deal is New England citizens dumping tea in the Boston Harbor. The New Deal is Andrew Jackson marching in the twentieth century. The New Deal is Abraham Lincoln preaching freedom for the oppressed. The New Deal is the new freedom of Woodrow Wilson fighting the cartels as they try to establish national and international fascism. The New Deal is Franklin D. Roosevelt.

In the peace to come the freedom of Jackson, Lincoln, Wilson and Roosevelt means the economic right of the people to the great abundance of the America of tomorrow. The freedom of Jackson, Lincoln, Wilson and Roosevelt in the peace to come also means that personal liberty must move hand in hand with that abundance. This freedom stands for justice and fair play for all the classes and all the regions in terms of the welfare of the plain folks.

The doorway to this freedom is blocked by the deliberate misrepresentation of the paid hirelings of the special interests. Because of these hirelings the worker on the farm and in the factory has often been condemned without a hearing as a saboteur of the war effort. These paid hirelings try to create dissension between the fighter on the farm, the fighter in the factory and the fighter at the front. They shall not succeed because all three fighting fronts have the same two objectives, quick victory in war, justice and jobs in peace. Justice and jobs for our workers and servicemen will give prosperity to our farmers and adequate profits for business.

The Democratic Party will always be first in the hearts of the people if it applies to the ever-changing problems of war and peace the resolute courage and patient humanity of the founding fathers of the New Deal, Jackson and Lincoln.

One man more than any other in all history has given dynamic power and economic expression to the ageless New Deal. That man is Roosevelt. Roosevelt has never denied the principles of the New Deal and he never will. They are a part of his very being. Roosevelt, God willing, will in the future give the New Deal a firmer foundation than it has ever had before. So on with

[1] Office of the Vice-President.

the New Deal, on with winning the war and forward march for peace, justice and jobs.

PRESIDENT ROOSEVELT'S MESSAGE TO CONGRESS ON THE SERVICEMEN'S VOTE

January 26, 1944 [1]

TO THE CONGRESS OF THE UNITED STATES:

The American people are very much concerned over the fact that the vast majority of the 11,000,000 members of the armed forces of the United States are going to be deprived of their right to vote in the important national election this fall, unless the Congress promptly enacts adequate legislation.

The men and women who are in the armed forces are rightfully indignant about it. They have left their homes and jobs and schools to meet and defeat the enemies who would destroy all our democratic institutions, including our right to vote. Our men cannot understand why the fact that they are fighting should disqualify them from voting.

It has been clear for some time that practical difficulties and the element of time make it virtually impossible for soldiers and sailors and marines spread all over the world to comply with the different voting laws of forty-eight States and that unless something is done about it, they will be denied the right to vote.

For example, the statutes of four of the States permit no absentee voting at all in general elections. Eleven other States require registration in person in order to be able to vote. Others permit absentee registration; but in some instances the procedure is so complicated and the time is so limited that soldiers and sailors in distant parts of the world cannot practically comply with the State requirements.

But even if the registration requirements were met, there are still innumerable difficulties involved. For example, Private John Smith in Australia, and his brother Joe who is on a destroyer off the coast of Italy, who think they are entitled to vote as well as to fight, find that they have to write in and ask the appropriate public official in their own State for absentee ballots.

In every State those ballots cannot even be printed until after the primary elections—and in fourteen States the primaries do not take place until September. In due time the ballots are printed—but they cannot always be sent out immediately, since in about half the States the absentee ballots cannot be mailed until thirty days or less before the election.

Weeks after they are mailed out, they reach John Smith in Australia and Joe aboard his destroyer. Even assuming that John and Joe, in the meantime, have not been transferred to another station or ship, or have not been wounded and sent to a hospital, it is doubtful whether the ballots will get back in time to be counted. If they have been moved, as is very likely, the ballots may not even reach them before election day.

In fourteen States the procedure is even more time-consuming and cumbersome—for instead of writing for an official ballot John and Joe must first obtain special application forms for official ballots, which must be received and filled out and returned before the ballots themselves are even mailed to them.

[1] *New York Times.*

The Congress in September, 1942, took cognizance of this intolerable situation facing millions of our citizens and passed a Federal absentee balloting statute (Public Law 712). That law did three things: It provided for a Federal ballot to be prepared by the States; it abrogated State requirements for registration and poll tax payments in so far as they apply to members of the armed forces, and it required the War and Navy Departments to distribute postal cards to members of the armed forces with which they might request Federal absentee ballots from their State election officials.

The Federal law was a slight improvement in that it provided absentee voting procedures in those cases where there had been no action by the States. It also eliminated some of the strict procedural requirements contained in many of the State laws. The great defect in that statute, however, was that it still involved a time lag, so that the voter might not receive his ballot in time to return to be counted.

This defect is inherent, and cannot be avoided, in any statute under which the forwarding of ballots for distribution must wait until the candidates have been selected in the primaries, or which requires correspondence between the local election officials and soldiers and sailors who may be transferred or moved at any minute.

If any proof were necessary to show how ineffective this Federal statute was—the fact is that out of 5,700,000 men in our armed forces at the time of the general elections of 1942, only 28,000 servicemen's votes were counted under the Federal statute.

The need for new legislation is evident if we are really sincere—and not merely rendering lip service to our soldiers and sailors.

By the 1944 elections there will be more than 5,000,000 Americans outside the limits of the United States in our armed forces and Merchant Marine. They, and the millions more who will be stationed within the United States waiting the day to join their comrades on the battlefronts, will all be subject to frequent, rapid, and unpredictable transfer to other points outside and inside the United States. This is particularly true in the case of the Navy and Merchant Marine, components of which are at sea for weeks at a time and are constantly changing their ports of entry and debarkation.

Some people—I am sure with their tongues in their cheeks—say that the solution to this problem is simply that the respective States improve their own absentee ballot machinery. In fact, there is now pending before the House of Representatives a meaningless bill, passed by the Senate Dec. 3, 1943, which presumes to meet this complicated and difficult situation by some futile language which "recommends to the several States the immediate enactment of appropriate legislation to enable each person absent from his place of residence and serving in the armed services of the United States * * * who is eligible to vote in any election district or precinct, to vote by absentee ballot in any general election held in his election district or precinct in time of war." This "recommendation" is itself proof of the unworkability of existing State laws.

I consider such proposed legislation a fraud on the soldiers and sailors and marines now training and fighting for us and for our sacred rights. It is a fraud upon the American people. It would not enable any soldier to vote with any greater facility than was provided by Public Law 712, under which only a negligible number of soldiers' votes were cast.

This "recommendation" contained in this piece of legislation may be heeded by a few States but will not—in fact, cannot—be carried out by all the States. Two States would require a constitutional amendment in order to adopt a practical method of absentee voting—which is obviously impossible to do before the November elections. Only a handful of the States—nine—will have Legislatures regularly in session this year; and, to date, only eight other States have called special sessions of their Legislatures for this purpose.

Besides, the Secretary of War, who will have the bulk of the administrative responsibility for distributing and collecting the ballots, has stated: "No procedure for offering the vote to servicemen can be effectively administered by the War and Navy Departments in time of war unless it is uniform and as simple as possible. Especially is this true with regard to the voting of persons outside the United States. * * * An army engaged in waging war cannot accommodate that primary function to multiple differences in the requirements of the forty-eight States as to voting procedure."

I am convinced that even if all the States tried to carry out the "recommendations" contained in this bill, the most that could be accomplished practically would be to authorize the Army and Navy to distribute and collect ballots prepared by the States in response to postcard requests from servicemen—the very procedure set forth in Public Law 712, which has been such a failure.

What is needed is a complete change of machinery for absentee balloting, which will give the members of our armed forces and merchant marine all over the world an opportunity to cast their ballots without time-consuming correspondence and without waiting for each separate State to hold its primary, print its ballots, and send them out for voting.

The recent bills proposed by Senators Green and Lucas and by Congressman Worley, S. 1612, H. R. 3982, seem to me to do this job. They set up proper and efficient machinery for absentee balloting. These bills propose that blank ballots on special paper suitable for air delivery be sent by the War and Navy Departments to all the fronts and camps and stations out in the field, well in advance of election day.

Immediately after primary elections are held, the names of the various candidates would be radioed or wired to the various military, naval and merchant marine units throughout the world—on the high seas, on every front and at every training station. The lists of candidates would then be made available to the voters, and the ballots would be distributed for marking in secrecy.

But even if the candidates' names had not been made available in an area in time to allow the ballots to be sent back to the United States, the voters could cast their votes by designating merely the name of the party of the candidates they desired to vote for. The voting date would be fixed in each area in sufficient time to get the ballots back home before election day, even if the actual names of the candidates had not been received in that particular area. The ballots would be collected and transmitted back to the United States by the quickest method of delivery for forwarding to the appropriate State election officials.

Each State, under these bills, would determine for itself whether or not the voter is qualified to vote under the laws of his State. Each State would count the ballots in the same way in which it counts the other ballots that are cast in the State. The sole exceptions would be those conditions of registration and payment of poll tax which could not be satisfied because of the absence of a voter from his State of residence by reason of the war. Those conditions were abrogated by the Congress when it passed the existing Federal absentee balloting law (Public Law 712).

There is nothing in such a proposed statute which violates the rights of the States. The Federal Government merely provides quick machinery for getting the ballots to the troops and back again. Certainly it does not violate States' rights any more than Public Law 712, which was passed by a substantial majority of the Congress in September, 1942, and which specifically provided that no member of the armed forces had to register or pay a poll tax in order to vote in a Federal election. It is no more violative of States' rights than the Soldiers and Sailors Civil Relief Act, which the Congress passed in October, 1940—more than a year before the war began.

It is true that these bills do not provide a simplified method of voting for State and local officials. The Congress has not the same authority to provide a simplified voting procedure for the thousands of State and local candidates that it has for Federal candidates. Nor would it be practicable to do so. The inclusion of all the State and local candidates would increase the size and weight of the ballot so as to make air delivery a physical impossibility.

Furthermore, the transmission and distribution of names of the many thousands of State and local candidates throughout the United States to each voter in every military and naval unit and merchant ship raise insuperable difficulties.

Since these bills provide that if any voter wishes he may use the procedure of his own State for absentee balloting, he is given, to the extent that there is any possibility of doing so, an opportunity to vote for State and local candidates. In fact, since they provide for a postcard system to implement the State laws, each voter is given at least as great an opportunity to vote for State and local candidates as he would have under any legislation.

The inclusion of other groups of voters who are engaged abroad in war work of various kinds would be desirable. But as to members of our armed forces and merchant marine, I deem the legislation imperative.

Our millions of fighting men do not have any lobby or pressure group on Capitol Hill to see that justice is done for them. They are not ordinarily permitted to write their Congressman on pending legislation; nor do they put "ads" in the papers or stimulate editorial writers or columnists to make special appeals for them. It certainly would appear unnecessary that our soldiers and sailors and merchant marine have to make a special effort to retain their right to vote.

As their Commander in Chief, I am sure that I can express their wishes in this matter and their resentment against the discrimination which is being practiced against them.

The American people cannot believe that the Congress will permit those who are fighting for political freedom to be deprived of a voice in choosing the personnel of their own Federal Government.

I have been informed that it would be possible, under the rules of the Congress, for a soldiers' vote bill to be rejected or passed without any roll-call, thus making it impossible for the voters of the country—military or civilian —to be able to determine just how their own Representative or Senator had voted on such a bill.

I have hesitated to say anything to the Congress on this matter for the simple reason that the making of these rules is solely within the discretion of the two houses of the legislative branch of the Government. I realize that the Executive as such has nothing to do with the making or the enforcement of these rules. Nevertheless, there are times, I think, when the President can speak as an interested citizen.

I think that there would be widespread resentment on the part of the people of the nation if they were unable to find out how their individual representatives had expressed themselves on this legislation—which goes to the root of the right of citizenship.

As I have said, this is solely a legislative matter, but I think most Americans will agree with me that every member of the two houses of Congress ought to be willing in justice "to stand up and be counted."

FRANKLIN D. ROOSEVELT

THE WHITE HOUSE,
    Jan. 26, 1944.

ARGENTINE GOVERNMENT DECREE BREAKING RELATIONS WITH THE AXIS

January 26, 1944 [1]

Decree Breaking Relations

In view of proofs obtained by the Federal police as to the existence of a vast espionage network damaging the close and traditional ties of friendship of the republic, threatening the national sovereignty, harming the foreign policy of this Government, and plotting against the security of the continent, and considering:

That this criminal activity is directly imputable to the Governments of the Axis because such acts were similar to those perpetrated earlier by other agents who now are in the hands of justice;

That the continuance of these illicit activities makes the residence in our republic of the German and Japanese diplomatic representatives incompatible with continental security, especially in view of the exceptional privileges given diplomatists;

That the gravity and persistence of the proved facts and the evident participation of foreign diplomatic representatives in the activities of espionage oblige the definition of Argentina's international policy in the light of new circumstances:

The President of the Argentine nation decrees:

Effective immediately, diplomatic relations are broken with the Governments of Germany and Japan. Passports are to be given the diplomatic representatives of both countries. The Ministry of Foreign Relations will take the necessary steps for the exchange of Argentine diplomatic and consular functionaries in those countries.

Government Statement

The Minister of Foreign Relations and Religion, Brig. Gen. Alberto Gilbert, declared in the late hours of the night that the Argentine Government has decided to proceed immediately with the rupture of diplomatic relations with Germany and Japan.

This attitude is based on the fact that investigations ordered by the National Government, referred to in a communiqué of the Foreign Ministry of Jan. 21, have permitted it to prove conclusively the existence in the country of a vast network of espionage. Statements made by detained persons demonstrate that the activity of espionage, which was the reason for criminal proceedings against a number of persons and for the retirement of the then

[1] *New York Times.*

German Naval Attaché, Capt. Dietrich Niebuhr, has continued to develop in prejudice to the interests of the country and in open violation of the policies of the Government and of duties imposed on the republic and its inhabitants by the Decree of Neutrality of Sept. 4, 1939, and the decrees of Dec. 9 and 18, 1941.

This attitude by a group of foreigners, who have forgotten their elemental obligations to the country under whose protection they were, not only involves the individuals directly responsible for this criminal activity, but also involves the personal responsibility of the diplomatic agents who gave aid and who sheltered them with the privileges and immunities conceived for the development of good and pacific relations of cordiality, but never for the protection and concealment of acts of aggression against the very country which accepts them.

The Government finds itself facing repeated acts that previously had been the object of condemnation by the Government and by public opinion.

Repetition of these activities by other persons, the organization into a band by such persons and their resources, the aid they found in the agents of the German Government, removes all possibility that this matter could be considered spontaneous acts of the spies themselves.

All of that plan evidently responds to a plan conceived by the Governments of the Axis to make the territory of the republic the center of their activities, with complete indifference to their duties to respect the Argentine Republic, and with indifference to the dangers that such activity could cause to our neutral nation.

That plan, then, consists of an unfriendly act executed in Argentina by hidden agents of the Axis countries; which obliges this nation to adopt elemental measures to secure its own defense.

That systematic espionage activity within the territory of this nation has convinced the Argentine Government that it is not possible to continue maintaining diplomatic relations with the Government of Germany.

This decision made, the maintenance of diplomatic relations with Japan resulted equally incompatible.

Faced with the disregard of their rights by representatives of the Governments of the Axis, who have attempted to execute acts of aggression against other American countries from Argentine territory, the Government of the nation, in defense of its own dignity and of its sovereignty, resolved to take such measures of security that the present situation warrants, beginning with the delivery of their passports to the representatives of Germany and Japan, and recalling the Argentine diplomatic agents accredited to those countries.

We also thus give expression to the concept of American solidarity which has been the fundamental basis of Argentine foreign policy from the first days of the revolution for emancipation.

Argentina has never been remiss in affirming that sentiment of fraternal union with its neighbors. It has been and continues to be disposed to demonstrate once again that it feels—as its own—the dangers and worries of the other American countries.

STATE DEPARTMENT REPRESENTATIONS TO JAPAN ON JAPANESE ATROCITIES

January 27, 1944 [1]

Below are the texts of two telegrams sent to the American Legation in Bern for communication to the Japanese Government through the Swiss Government representing the interests of the United States in Japan. In these communications the Government of the United States again made comprehensive representations to the Japanese Government concerning abuses and neglect to which American nationals in Japanese custody had been subjected and called for amelioration of the treatment accorded them.

JANUARY 27, 1944.

Please request Swiss Legation Toyko to deliver the following textually to the Japanese Government:

The Government of the United States refers to its communication delivered to the Japanese Government on December 23, 1942 by the Swiss Legation in Tokyo in charge of American interests in Japan and Japanese-occupied territory concerning reports that the Government of the United States had received of the mistreatment of American nationals in Japanese hands. The Swiss Legation in Tokyo on May 28, 1943 forwarded to the Government of the United States a preliminary reply from the Japanese Government to this communication in which that Government stated that it would communicate in due course the results of investigations concerning each instance referred to in the note of the Government of the United States. No reports of investigations regarding these instances have yet been received.

The Government of the United States has taken due note of the statements of the Japanese Government "concerning the special circumstances prevailing in areas which have until recently been fields of battle" and concerning "the manifold difficulties which exist in areas occupied by the Japanese forces or where military operations are still being carried on." The Government of the United States points out, however, that the regions in which Americans have been taken prisoner or interned have long ceased to be scenes of active military operations and that the Japanese holding authorities have therefore had ample opportunity to establish an orderly and humane internment program in accordance with their Government's undertakings. Despite this fact the Government of the United States continues to receive reports that the great proportion of American nationals are the victims either of inhuman cruelty or of callous failure to provide the necessities of life on the part of the Japanese holding authorities, in violation of the common laws of civilization and of the Japanese Government's undertaking to apply to American nationals the humane provisions of the Geneva Prisoners of War Convention.

There follows a statement of the principal categories of the deprivation of rights, cruelties, wanton neglect, mistreatment and hardships to which, according to information received by the Government of the United States from many sources, Americans in Japanese custody have been subjected.

I. Representatives of the Swiss Government entrusted with the protection of American interests in Japan and Japanese-occupied territory have not been permitted to go to every place without exception where prisoners of war and civilian internees are interned, have not been permitted to interview with-

[1] State Department Bulletin.

out witnesses the persons held, and have not had access to all places occupied by the prisoners (Article 86 of the Geneva Prisoners of War Convention).

II. Representatives of the International Red Cross Committee have been refused permission to visit most of the places where American nationals are held by the Japanese authorities (Articles 79 and 88).

III. American nationals have not been permitted to forward complaints to the Japanese holding authorities or to representatives of the protecting power (Article 42).

IV. The Japanese authorities have punished and have threatened to punish American nationals for complaining concerning the conditions of captivity (Article 42).

V. The Japanese Government has failed to furnish needed clothing to American nationals (Article 12).

VI. The Japanese authorities have confiscated personal effects from American civilian internees and prisoners of war (Article 6).

VII. American prisoners of war and civilian internees have been subjected to insults and public curiosity (Article 2).

VIII. Civilians and prisoners of war interned by Japan are suffering from malnutrition and deficiency diseases because of the failure and refusal of the detaining authorities to provide health sustaining food for their charges, or to permit the United States to make regular shipments on a continuing basis under appropriate neutral guarantees of supplemental food and medical supplies. (Article 11 and the specific reciprocal undertaking of Japan to take into account national differences in diet.)

IX. The Japanese authorities have devoted to improper and forbidden uses the profits of the sale of goods in camp canteens instead of devoting them to the welfare of the persons held in the camps (Article 12).

X. Contrary to the specific undertaking of the Japanese Government, the detaining authorities have compelled civilians to perform labor other than that connected with the administration, maintenance and management of internment camps. Officer prisoners of war have been forced to labor and non-commissioned officers to do other than supervisory labor (Article 27).

XI. Prisoners of war have been required to perform labor that has a direct relation with war operations (Article 31).

XII. Medical care has in many instances been denied to prisoners of war and civilian internees and when given has been generally so poor as to cause unnecessary suffering and unnecessary deaths (Article 14).

XIII. The Japanese Government has reported the names of only a part of the American prisoners of war and civilian internees in its hands (Article 77) and of American combatants found dead by Japanese forces (Article 4 of the Convention for the Amelioration of the Condition of the Sick and Wounded of Armies in the Field, to which Japan is a contracting party).

XIV. The Japanese Government has not permitted internees and prisoners of war freely to exercise their religion (Article 16).

XV. The Japanese Government has not posted the Convention in camps in English translation, thus depriving American prisoners of war and civilian internees of knowledge of their rights thereunder (Article 84).

XVI. The Japanese Government has failed to provide adequate equipment and accommodations in prisoner of war and civilian internment camps and transports, but on the contrary forced them to subsist in inhumane conditions (Article 10).

XVII. The Japanese Government has completely failed to apply the provisions of the Geneva Prisoners of War Convention (Title III, Section V,

Chapter 3) with regard to trial and punishment of prisoners of war despite the fact that violations of its undertaking in this respect have repeatedly been called to its attention, but on the contrary has imposed cruel and inhuman punishments without trial.

XVIII. The Japanese authorities have inflicted corporal punishment and torture upon American nationals (Article 46).

The Government of the United States emphasizes that it has based the foregoing charges only on information obtained from reliable sources. Many well-authenticated cases can be cited in support of each of the charges.

The Government of the United States also desires to state most emphatically that, as the Japanese Government can assure itself from an objective examination of the reports submitted to it by the Spanish, Swedish, and International Red Cross representatives who have repeatedly visited all places where Japanese are held by the United States, the United States has consistently and fully applied the provisions of the Geneva Prisoners of War Convention in the treatment of all Japanese nationals held by it as prisoners of war or (so far as they are adaptable) as civilian internees, detainees or evacuees in relocation centers. Japanese nationals have enjoyed high standards of housing, food, clothing, and medical care. The American authorities have furthermore freely and willingly accepted from the representatives of the protecting Powers and the International Red Cross Committee suggestions for the improvement of conditions under which Japanese nationals live in American camps and centers and have given effect to many of these suggestions, most of which, in view of the high standards normally maintained, are directed toward the obtaining of extraordinary benefits and privileges of a recreational, educational or spiritual nature.

The Government of the United States demands that the Japanese Government immediately take note of the charges made above and take immediate steps to raise the treatment accorded American nationals held by Japan to the standard provided by the Geneva Prisoners of War Convention, which the United States and the Japanese Governments have mutually undertaken to apply. The Government of the United States also expects the Japanese Government to take proper disciplinary or penal action with regard to those of its officials, employees, and agents who have violated its undertakings with respect to the Geneva Convention and the international Common Laws of decency.

The Government of the United States again directs the attention of the Japanese Government to the system of neutral supervision provided in Article 86 of the Geneva Convention. The Government of the United States again reminds the Japanese Government of the complete fulfillment of the provisions of this Article as respects the activities of the Government of Spain acting as protecting Power for Japanese interests in the continental United States and of the Government of Sweden as protecting Power for Japanese interests in Hawaii.

The Government of the United States therefore expects the Japanese Government, in accordance with recognized practice of civilized states, fully to implement the provisions of the Geneva Prisoners of War Convention. The United States Government demands that the Japanese Government will, among other things, promptly implement the provisions of Article 86 in respect to the activities of the Government of Switzerland as protecting Power for American interests in Japan and Japanese-controlled territory and will make it possible for the Government of Switzerland to give to the Government of the United States assurances to the effect that Swiss representatives have been able to convince themselves by the full exercise of the rights granted under Article 86 that the abuses set forth in the foregoing statement have been completely rectified or that steps have been taken in that direction that are considered by Switzerland to be adequate.

The United States Government until the present has refrained from publishing in this country the facts known to it regarding outrages perpetrated upon its nationals, both prisoners of war and civilian internees, by the Japanese. The United States Government hopes that as these facts are now again officially called to the Japanese Government's attention that Government will adopt a policy of according to United States nationals in its hands the treatment to which they are entitled, and will permit representatives of the protecting Power to make such investigations and inspections as are necessary in order to give assurances to this Government that improved treatment is in fact being accorded to American nationals. In such case this Government would be in a position to assure the American people that the treatment of American nationals by the Japanese authorities had been brought into conformity with the standards recognized by civilized nations.

HULL

JANUARY 27, 1944.

There are recited in the following numbered sections, the numbers of which correspond to the numbered charges in the Department's urgent telegram of even date, examples of some of the specific incidents upon which this Government bases the charges made by it against the Japanese Government in the telegram under reference. The specific incidents have been selected from the numerous ones that have been reported from many reliable sources to this Government. Ask the Swiss Government to forward this statement textually to its Minister in Tokyo with the request that he present it to the Japanese Government simultaneously with the telegram under reference and that he call upon the Japanese Government promptly to rectify all existing derelictions and take such further steps as will preclude their recurrence.

The Minister should further seek for himself or his representatives permission, in accordance with Article 86 of the Convention, to visit each place without exception where American nationals are detained and request of the Japanese Government the amelioration of any improper conditions that he may find to exist.

The Swiss Minister in Tokyo should be particularly asked to report promptly and fully all steps taken by the Japanese Government in conformity with the foregoing.

Charges I and II. Prisoner of war and civilian internment camps in the Philippines, French Indochina, Thailand, Manchuria, Burma, Malaya, and the Dutch East Indies, and prisoner of war camp No. 1 in Formosa have never been visited by Swiss representatives although they have repeatedly requested permission to make such visits. None of these camps except the one at Mukden are known to have been visited by International Red Cross representatives. In recent months visits have not been allowed to the prisoner of war camps near Tokyo and Yokohama, and the prisoner of war camps in and near Hong Kong, although the Swiss representatives have requested permission to make such visits.

The value of such few visits as have been permitted to some camps has been minimized by restrictions. Swiss representatives at Shanghai have been closely escorted by several representatives of the Japanese Consulate General at Shanghai during their visits to camps and have not been allowed to see all parts of camps or to have free discussion with the internees. Similar situations prevail with respect to the civilian internment camps and prisoner of war camps in metropolitan Japan and Formosa.

By contrast, all of the camps, stations, and centers where Japanese nationals are held by the United States have been repeatedly visited and fully inspected by representatives of Spain and Sweden who have spoken at length without witnesses with the inmates, and International Red Cross representatives have been and are being allowed freely to visit the camps in the United States and Hawaii where Japanese nationals are held.

Charge III. Communications addressed by the persons held to the protecting Power concerning conditions of captivity in several of the civilian camps near Shanghai, among them Ash Camp and Chapei, remain undelivered. The same situation exists with respect to the civilian internment camp in Baguio, and in most if not all of the camps where American prisoners of war are held. Persons held at Baguio, Chefoo, Saigon, and at times in the Philippine prisoner of war camps were denied permission to address the camp commander.

Charge IV. On one occasion during the summer of 1943 all of the persons held at the Columbia Country Club, Shanghai, were punished by cancellation of dental appointments because complaints were made to representatives of the Swiss Consulate General. During the same period, at Camp B, Yanchow, the entire camp was deprived of a meal by the Camp Commandant because complaints had been made concerning the delivery of spoiled food.

There are cited under Section XVIII below, cases of prisoners of war being struck because they asked for food or water.

Charge V. Civilian internees at Hong Kong have gone without footwear and civilian internees at Kobe have suffered from lack of warm clothing. In 1942 and 1943, American and Filipino prisoners of war in the Philippines and civilian internees at Baguio were forced to labor without shoes and clad only in loin cloths.

Charge VI. This is reported to have been the case at the following camps: prisoner of war camps in the Philippine Islands, prisoner of war enclosures at Mariveles Bay, Philippine Islands, civilian internment camps at Baguio, Canton, Chefoo, Peking, Manila, Tsingtao, Weihsien, and Yangchow, and at the Ash Camp, Chapei Camp, Lunghwa Camp, and Pootung Camp, in or near Shanghai. The articles most needed by the prisoners and internees have been taken. For example, Japanese soldiers took the shoes from an American officer prisoner of war who was forced to walk unshod from Bataan to San Fernando during the march which began about April 10, 1942. Although the prisoners constantly suffered from lack of drinking water canteens were taken from prisoners during this march; one of these victims was Lieutenant Colonel William E. Dyess.

At Corregidor a Japanese soldier was seen by Lieutenant Commander Melvyn H. McCoy with one arm covered from elbow to wrist and the other arm half covered with wrist watches taken from American and Filipino prisoners of war.

Charge VII. American prisoners of war in Manila were forced by Japanese soldiers to allow themselves to be photographed operating captured American military equipment in connection with the production of the Japanese propaganda film "Rip down the Stars and Stripes."

Prisoners of war from Corregidor being taken to Manila were not landed at the port of Manila but were unloaded outside the city and were forced to march through the entire city to Bilibid Prison about May 23, 1942.

Japanese school children, soldiers, and civilians have been admitted to internment camps and encouraged to satisfy curiosity regarding the persons held. Such tours were conducted at Baguio, Hong Kong, and Tsingtao.

Charge VIII. Deficiency diseases such as beriberi, pellagra, scurvy, sprue, et cetera, are common throughout Japanese internment camps. These diseases are least common in the civilian internment camps (called assembly centers) at Shanghai and in some other camps where the persons held have but recently been taken into custody or where trade by the internees themselves with outside private suppliers is allowed. It appears therefore that the great prevalence of deficiency diseases in prisoner of war camps where internees have been solely dependent upon the Japanese authorities for their food supply over an extended period is directly due to the callous failure of these authorities to utilize the possibilities of a health sustaining diet afforded by available local products. The responsibility for much of the suffering and many of the deaths from these diseases of American and Filipino prisoners of war rests directly upon the Japanese authorities. As a specific example, prisoners of war at Davao Penal Colony suffering from grave vitamin deficiencies could see from their camp trees bearing citrus fruit that they were not allowed to pluck. They were not even allowed to retrieve lemons seen floating by on a stream that runs through the camp.

Charge IX. For example, in the prisoner of war camps at Hong Kong, the profits of the canteens have not been used by the holding authorities for the benefit of the prisoners.

Charge X. At Baguio civilian internees have been forced to repair sawmill machinery without remuneration.

Officer prisoners of war have been compelled by Major Mida, the Camp Commandant at Davao Penal Colony, to perform all kinds of labor including menial tasks such as scrubbing floors, cleaning latrines used by Japanese troops and working in the kitchens of Japanese officers.

Charge XI. Ten American engineers were required to go to Corregidor in July 1942 to assist in rebuilding the military installations on that island, and prisoners of war have been worked in a machine tool shop in the arsenal at Mukden.

Charge XII. The condition of health of prisoners of war in the Philippine Islands is deplorable. At San Fernando in April 1942, American and Filipino prisoners were held in a barbed-wire enclosure so overcrowded that sleep and rest were impossible. So many of them were sick and so little care was given to the sick that human excrement covered the whole area. The enclosure at San Fernando was more than 100 kilometers from Bataan and the abominable treatment given to the prisoners there cannot be explained by battle conditions. The prisoners were forced to walk this distance in seven days under merciless driving. Many who were unable to keep up with the march were shot or bayoneted by the guards. During this journey, as well as at other times when prisoners of war were moved in the Philippine Islands, they were assembled in the open sun even when the detaining authorities could have allowed them to assemble in the shade. American and Filipino prisoners are known to have been buried alive along the roadside and persistent reports have been received of men who tried to rise from their graves but were beaten down with shovels and buried alive.

At Camp O'Donnell conditions were so bad that 2,200 Americans and more than 20,000 Filipinos are reliably reported to have died in the first few months of their detention. There is no doubt that a large number of these deaths could have been prevented had the Japanese authorities provided minimum medical care for the prisoners. The so-called hospital there was absolutely inadequate to meet the situation. Prisoners of war lay sick and naked on the floor, receiving no attention and too sick to move from their own excrement. The hospital was so overcrowded that Americans were laid on the ground outside in the heat of the blazing sun. The American doctors in the camp were given no medicine, and even had no water to wash the human waste from the bodies of the patients. Eventually, when quinine was issued, there was only enough properly to take care of ten cases of malaria, while thousands of prisoners were suffering from the disease. Over two hundred out of three hundred prisoners from Camp O'Donnell died while they were on a work detail in Batangas.

At Cabanatuan there was no medicine for the treatment of malaria until after the prisoners had been in the camp for five months. The first shipment of medicines from the Philippine Red Cross was held up by the camp authorities on the pretext that they must make an inventory of the shipment. This they were so dilatory in doing that many deaths occurred before the medicine was released. Because of lack of medicines and food, scurvy broke out in the camp in the Fall of 1942. Since the prisoners had been at the camp for some months before this disease became prevalent, the responsibility for it rests upon the detaining authorities.

It is reported that in the autumn of 1943 fifty percent of the American prisoners of war at Davao had a poor chance to live and that the detaining authorities had again cut the prisoners' food ration and had withdrawn all medical attention.

Though the medical care provided for civilian internees by the Japanese camp authorities appears to have been better than that provided for prisoners of war, it still does not meet the obligations placed on the holding authorities by their Government's own free undertaking and by the laws of humanity. At the civilian internment camp, Camp John Hay, childbirth took place on the floor of a small storeroom. At the same camp a female internee who was insane and whose presence was a danger to the other internees was not removed from the camp. A dentist who was interned at the camp was not permitted to bring in his own equipment. The Los Banos Camp was established at a recognized endemic center of malaria, yet quinine was not provided, and the internees were not allowed to go outside of the fence to take antimalarial measures.

The Japanese authorities have not provided sufficient medical care for the American civilians held in camps in and near Shanghai and the internees have themselves had to pay for hospitalization and medical treatment. Deaths directly traceable to inadequate care have occurred.

Even in metropolitan Japan, the Japanese authorities have failed to provide medical treatment for civilian internees, and it has been necessary for Americans held at Myoshi, Yamakita, and Sumire to pay for their own medical and dental care.

Charge XIV. For example, the internees at Camp John Hay were not allowed to hold religious services during the first several months of the camp's operation, and priests have not been allowed to minister to prisoners held by the Japanese in French Indochina.

Charge XV. No copy of an English translation of the text of the Geneva Prisoners of War Convention has been available to civilian internees or prisoners of war nor have the Japanese authorities taken other steps to inform the persons held of their rights under the terms of the Convention. Reports have been received of the Japanese authorities informing prisoners of war that they were captives, having no rights under international law or treaty.

Charge XVI. At Camp O'Donnell many of the men had to live without shelter during 1942. In one case twenty-three officers were assigned to a shack, fourteen by twenty feet in size. Drinking water was extremely scarce, it being necessary to stand in line six to ten hours to get a drink. Officers had no bath for the first thirty-five days in the camp and had but one gallon of water each in which to have their first baths after that delay. The kitchen equipment consisted of cauldrons and a fifty-five gallon drum. Camotes were cooked in the cauldrons, mashed with a piece of timber, and each man was served one spoonful as his ration.

In late October 1942, approximately 970 prisoners of war were transferred from the Manila area to the Davao Penal Colony on a transport vessel providing only twenty inches per man of sleeping space. Conditions on the vessel were so bad that two deaths occurred, and subsequently because of weakness some fifty percent of the prisoners fell by the roadside on the march from the water front at Lasang, Davao to the Penal Colony.

The places used by the Japanese authorities for the internment of American civilians in the Philippine Islands were inadequate for the number of persons interned. At the Brent School at Baguio, twenty to thirty civilians were assigned sleeping accommodations in a room which had been intended for the use of one person.

At the Columbia Country Club at Shanghai the internees were obliged to spend CRB $10,000 of their own funds to have a building deloused so that they might use it for a needed dormitory. At Weihsien no (repeat no) refrigeration equipment was furnished by the Japanese authorities and some of the few household refrigerators of the internees were taken from them and were used by the Japanese guards, with the result that food spoiled during the summer of 1943. The lack of sanitary facilities is reported from all of these camps.

Charge XVII. American personnel have suffered death and imprisonment for participation in military operations. Death and long-term imprisonment have been imposed for attempts to escape for which the maximum penalty under the Geneva Convention is thirty days arrest. Neither the American Government nor its protecting Power has been informed in the manner provided by the Convention of these cases or of many other instances when Americans were subjected to illegal punishment. Specific instances are cited under the next charge.

Charge XVIII. Prisoners of war who were marched from Bataan to San Fernando in April 1942 were brutally treated by Japanese guards. The guards clubbed prisoners who tried to get water, and one prisoner was hit on the head with a club for helping a fellow prisoner who had been knocked down by a Japanese army truck. A colonel who pointed to a can of salmon by the side of the road and asked for food for the prisoners was struck on the side of his head with the can by a Japanese officer. The colonel's face was cut open. Another colonel who had found a sympathetic Filipino with a cart was horsewhipped in the face for trying to give transportation to persons unable to walk. At Lubao a Filipino who had been run through and gutted by the Japanese was hung over a barbed-wire fence. An American Lieutenant Colonel was killed by a Japanese as he broke ranks to get a drink at a stream.

Japanese sentries used rifle butts and bayonets indiscriminately in forcing exhausted prisoners of war to keep moving on the march from the Cabanatuan railroad station to Camp No. 2 in late May 1942.

At Cabanatuan Lieutenant Colonels Lloyd Biggs and Howard Breitung and Lieutenant R. D. Gilbert, attempting to escape during September 1942, were severely beaten about the legs and feet and then taken out of the camp and tied to posts, were stripped and were kept tied up for two days. Their hands were tied behind their backs to the posts so that they could not sit down. Passing Filipinos were forced to beat them in the face with clubs. No food or water was given to them. After two days of torture they were taken away and, according to the statements of Japanese guards, they were killed, one of them by decapitation. Other Americans were similarly tortured and shot without trial at Cabanatuan in June or July 1942 because they endeavored to bring food into the camp. After being tied to a fence post inside the camp for two days they were shot.

At Cabanatuan during the summer of 1942 the following incidents occurred: A Japanese sentry beat a private so brutally with a shovel across the back and the thigh that it was necessary to send him to the hospital. Another American was crippled for months after his ankle was struck by a stone thrown by a Japanese. One Japanese sentry used the shaft of a golf club to beat American prisoners, and two Americans, caught while obtaining food from Filipinos, were beaten unmercifully on the face and body. An officer was struck behind the ear with a riding crop by a Japanese interpreter. The same officer was again beaten at Davao Penal Colony and is now suffering from partial paralysis of the left side as the result of these beatings. Enlisted men who attempted to escape were beaten and put to hard labor in chains.

At the Davao Penal Colony, about April 1, 1943, Sergeant McFee was shot and killed by a Japanese guard after catching a canteen full of water which had been thrown to him by another prisoner on the opposite side of the fence. The Japanese authorities attempted to explain this shooting as an effort to prevent escape. However, the guard shot the sergeant several times and, in addition, shot into the barrack on the opposite side of the fence toward the prisoner who had thrown the canteen. At about the same time and place an officer returning from a work detail tried to bring back some sugarcane for the men in the hospital. For this he was tied to a stake for twenty-four hours and severely beaten.

In the internment camp at Baguio a boy of sixteen was knocked down by a Japanese guard for talking to an internee girl, and an elderly internee was struck with a whip when he failed to rise rapidly from his chair at the approach of a Japanese officer. Mr. R. Gray died at Baguio on March 15, 1942 after being beaten and given the water cure by police authorities.

At Santo Tomas, Mr. Krogstadt died in a military prison after being corporally punished for his attempted escape.

HULL

PRESIDENT ROOSEVELT'S ADDRESS OPENING FIFTH WAR LOAN DRIVE

January 29, 1944 [1]

LADIES AND GENTLEMEN:

All our fighting men overseas today have their appointed stations on the far-flung battlefronts of the world. We at home have ours, too. We need, we are proud of, our fighting men—most decidedly. But, during the anxious times ahead, let us not forget that they need us, too.

[1] *New York Times.*

It goes almost without saying that we must continue to forge the weapons of victory—the hundreds of thousands of items, large and small, essential to the waging of the war. This has been the major task from the very start. And it is still a major task. This is the very worst time for any war worker to think of leaving his machine or to look for a peacetime job.

And it goes almost without saying, too, that we must continue to provide our Government with the funds necessary for waging war not only by the payment of taxes—which, after all, is an obligation of American citizenship —but also by the purchase of war bonds—an act of free choice which every citizen has to make for himself under the guidance of his own conscience.

Something All Should Do

Whatever else any of us may be doing, the purchase of war bonds and stamps is something all of us can do and should do to help win the war.

I am happy to report tonight that it is something which nearly everyone seems to be doing. Although there are now approximately 67,000,000 persons who have or earn some form of income (including the armed forces) 81,000,-000 persons or their children have already bought war bonds. They have bought more than 600,000,000 individual bonds; their purchases have totaled more than $32,000,000,000. These are the purchases of individual men and women and children.

Any one who would have said this was possible a few years ago would have been put down as a starry-eyed visionary. But of such visions is the stuff of America. Of course, there are always pessimists with us, everywhere, a few here and a few there. I am reminded of the fact that after the fall of France in 1940 I asked the Congress for money for the production by the United States of 50,000 airplanes per year.

Well, I was called crazy—it was said that the figure was fantastic; that it could not be done, and yet today we are building airplanes at the rate of 100,000 a year.

Link Between Bonds, War

There is a direct connection between the bonds you have bought and the stream of men and equipment now rushing over the English Channel for the liberation of Europe. There is a direct connection between your war bonds and every part of this global war today.

Tonight, therefore, on the opening of this Fifth War Loan drive, it is appropriate for us to take a broad look at this panorama of world war, for the success or failure of the drive is going to have so much to do with the speed with which we can accomplish victory and then peace.

While I know that the chief interest tonight is centered on the English Channel and on the beaches and the farms and the cities of Normandy, we should not lose sight of the fact that our armed forces are engaged on other battle fronts all over the world, and that no one front can be considered alone without its proper relation to all.

It is worth while, therefore, to make over-all comparisons with the past. Let us compare today with just two years ago—June, 1942. At that time Germany was in control of practically all of Europe, and was steadily driving the Russians back toward the Ural Mountains. Germany was practically in control of North Africa and the Mediterranean and was beating at the gates of the Suez Canal, and the route to India. Italy was still an important military and supply factor—as subsequent, long campaigns have proved.

Situation in the Pacific

Japan was in control of the western Aleutian Islands; and in the South Pacific was knocking at the gates of Australia and New Zealand—and also was threatening India. Japan had seized control of most of the Central Pacific.

American armed forces on land and sea and in the air were still very definitely on the defensive, and in the building-up stage. Our Allies were bearing the heat and the brunt of the attack.

In 1942 Washington heaved a sigh of relief that the first war bond issue had been cheerfully oversubscribed by the American people. Way back in those days, two years ago, America was still hearing from many "amateur strategists" and political critics, some of whom were doing more good for Hitler than for the United States.

Two years ago, but we are on the offensive all over the world—bringing the attack to our enemies.

In the Pacific, by relentless submarine and naval attacks, amphibious thrusts, and ever-mounting air attacks, we have deprived the Japs of the power to check the momentum of our ever-growing and ever-advancing military forces. We have reduced the Jap shipping by more than three million tons. We have overcome their original advantages in the air. We have cut off from that return to the homeland tens of thousands of beleaguered Japanese troops who now face starvation or ultimate surrender. And we have cut down their naval strength, so that for many months they have avoided all risk of encounter with our naval forces.

Long Way to Tokyo

True, we still have a long way to go to Tokyo. But, carrying out our original strategy of eliminating our European enemy first and then turning all our strength to the Pacific, we can force the Japanese to unconditional surrender or to national suicide much more rapidly than has been thought possible.

Turning now to our enemy who is first on the list for destruction—Germany has her back against the wall—in fact three walls at once.

On the south—We have broken the German hold on central Italy. On June 4 the city of Rome fell to the Allied armies. And allowing the enemy no respite, the Allies are now pressing hard on the heels of the Germans as they retreat northward in ever-growing confusion.

On the East—Our gallant Soviet Allies have driven the enemy back from the lands which were invaded three years ago. And the great Soviet armies are now initiating crushing blows.

Results of Air Blows

Overhead—Vast Allied air fleets of bombers and fighters have been waging a bitter air war over Germany and western Europe. They have had two major objectives: to destroy German war industries which maintain the German armies and air forces; and to shoot the German Luftwaffe out of the air. As a result German production has been whittled down continuously, and the German fighter forces now have only a fraction of their former power.

This great air campaign, strategic and tactical, is going to continue—with increasing power.

And on the West—The hammer blow which struck the coast of France last Tuesday morning, less than a week ago, was the culmination of many months of careful planning and strenuous preparation.

Millions of tons of weapons and supplies, hundreds of thousands of men assembled in England are now being poured into the great battle in Europe.

I think that from the standpoint of our enemy we have achieved the impossible. We have broken through their supposedly impregnable wall in northern France. But the assault has been costly in men and costly in materials. Some of our landings were desperate adventures; but from advices received so far, the losses were lower than our commanders had estimated would occur. We have established a firm foothold; we are now prepared to meet the inevitable counter-attacks of the Germans—with power and with confidence. We all pray that we will have far more soon than a firm foothold.

Americans have all worked together to make this day possible.

The liberation forces now streaming across the Channel and up the beaches and through the fields and the forests of France are using thousands and thousands of planes and ships and tanks and heavy guns. They are carrying with them many thousands of items needed for their dangerous, stupendous undertaking. There is a shortage of nothing—nothing! And this must continue.

What has been done in the United States since those days of 1940—when France fell—in raising and equipping and transporting our fighting forces, and in producing weapons and supplies for war, has been nothing short of a miracle.

It was largely due to American teamwork—teamwork among capital and labor and agriculture, between the armed forces and the civilian economy—indeed among all of them.

And everyone, every man or woman or child, who bought a war bond helped—and helped mightily!

There are still many people in the United States who have not bought war bonds, or who have not bought as many as they can afford. Everyone knows for himself whether he falls into that category or not. In some cases his neighbors know, too. To the consciences of those people, this appeal by the President of the United States is very much in order.

So all of the things which we use in this war, everything we send to our fighting Allies, costs money—a lot of money. One sure way every man, woman and child can keep faith with those who have given, and are giving, their lives is to provide the money which is needed to win the final victory.

I urge all Americans to buy war bonds without stint. Swell the mighty chorus to bring us nearer to victory!

GENERAL CHARLES DE GAULLE'S SPEECH AT THE BRAZZAVILLE CONFERENCE

January 30, 1944 [1]

LADIES AND GENTLEMEN:

If what we are actually undertaking were to be judged by mistakes in the past, we could wonder that the French government has decided to call a Congress at Brazzaville at this moment. Yesterday's false prudence would no

[1] French News and Information Service.

doubt advise us to wait since the war is not yet ended. But we cannot tell what tomorrow's peace will be like. Also, the most urgent question for France is the future of her overseas territories.

Gentlemen, the government believes that nothing could be less justified than this self-effacement, nor rasher than this prudence, because present conditions, although they are painful and complicated, force us to act energetically rather than to wait. Perhaps there is no cause to exaggerate the reasons which press us to examine the whole of French African problems, but nevertheless we believe that the great events which are disrupting the world should cause us to lose no time. We believe also that the horrible trial which France is enduring under the German occupation does not lessen any of France's duties or rights and that this gathering of representative people from all the French territories in Africa, which is now an accomplished fact, provides us with an excellent opportunity through the initiative and under the direction of the Commission of Colonies to compare the experiences and ideas of the men who have the honor and responsibility of governing our African territories in the name of France.

Where else but in Brazzaville should this conference have taken place? Brazzaville which for many cruel years was literally the refuge of our honor and independence and which will remain as an example of the most praise-worthy French effort of the last half century. Frenchmen have responded to the call of a civilizing vocation many centuries old and under the stimulus of Republic governments and the leadership of such colonists as Gallieni, Jadot, Savorgnan de Brazza, Binger, Marchand, Foureau, Lamy, Borguis, Desbordes, Lyautey, Gouraud and Mangin, have made their way through this continent, pacified and opened up to the world a large portion of Darkest Africa whose poverty-stricken and varied tribes had until then been kept in a state of misery and inaccessibility because of the vastness, the formidable natural barriers and the exceedingly hard climate of their land.

To realize what we have done toward developing Africa's natural resources and for the welfare of the men who live there, one only needs to travel across our territories and to admit this fact one needs only to be greathearted.

Just as a stone gains impetus as it rolls down hill so the work we have begun here brings us constantly new and increasingly hard tasks. Even when the present World War began it was necessary to establish conditions on new bases in order that the men who live in Africa should progress and that French sovereignty should be exercised. Is it necessary to say that the war has actually precipitated this development? First, because this has been up to now mainly an African war and the relative and absolute importance of Africa's territories, communications, resources and military effectives has been shown in the bright light of theaters of war. Finally and chiefly because one of the stakes in this war is the condition of mankind and during the action of physical forces such as this war has everywhere set in motion there is not a man in the entire world who has not raised his head to look beyond the years and ponder on the destiny of his people. Among the imperial powers none feels this appeal more than France does. None feels more deeply than France the need to learn from past events in order to set the 60,000,000 men whose fate is linked with our 42,000,000 inhabitants on the way to the world of the future. First because France is a nation whose genius is destined to raise mankind step by step to the heights of dignity and brotherhood where all men may one day be united; secondly because when France at the time of her temporary defeat was driven back into the metropole and was in dire extremity, she found in her overseas territories a refuge, resources and now a springboard for her liberation and this has created a permanent bond between France and her Empire. And finally, it is for this reason that the new France, profiting by her tragic experience, has determined that in all matters concerning those who depend upon her she will nobly and generously choose new pathways as well as new methods for realizing their destiny. Does this mean that France wishes to continue its mission overseas by enclosing these territories within barriers which would isolate them from the world and particularly from other African countries? Indeed not: And to prove it we need only remember how French Equatorial Africa and the French Cameroons as soon as they were liberated, entered into relations with neighboring countries such as the Belgian Congo, British Nigeria and the Anglo-Egyptian Sudan. I take the Governor-General as my witness. We have only to recall that the whole Empire, with the temporary exception of Indo-China, is largely contributing by its strategic positions, its production, its communications as well as by providing military forces and air bases to the Allies' common war effort.

We believe that in the world of tomorrow an autocracy will be neither desirable nor possible for anyone. We believe that from the point of view of the development of the riches and great systems of communication of Africa this continent for the most part constitutes one whole.

But we are positive that there would be no progress, that progress would be impossible if the men who are living in their native land under the French flag could not benefit by it morally and materially; if this development did not lead them up to a higher level so that someday they could take part in the management of their own affairs. This is the mission of France in Africa. This must be our aim.

We have no illusions about the length of time needed for these stages. Governors-General, Governors, you know Africa well enough to judge what can gradually be done and what it is practical to attempt. And for our part, we know very well that it will be the responsibility of the French nation itself to change the structure of the Empire at the right moment or to undertake any other reforms she may have decided upon during her sovereignty.

Gentlemen, you will examine social, political, economic and other programs which will be submitted to the government in order to be progressively carried out. You must act so that each one of our territories through its development and the human progress of its populations, will become an integral part of the French community with its own character, interests, inspirations and future.

Gentlemen, the French African Conference of Brazzaville is open.

CHANCELLOR ADOLF HITLER'S ADDRESS ON 11TH ANNIVERSARY OF NATIONAL SOCIALIST RÉGIME

January 30, 1944 [1]

In the fifth year of this the greatest of wars, the causes and the sense and purpose of this world struggle cannot any longer be unclear to anyone. For the time in which it could still seem that this struggle was one of European conflicts, instigated again and again by Britain to render the Continent power-

[1] *New York Times.*

less and to maintain the balance of power in favor of the British Empire, is long past.

Those who since 1936 in London dealt in systematic war mongering have now become not the leaders but those who are led. The spirits they hoped to use, according to the old British custom, have once more become the masters themselves and are too powerful for them. No matter how this struggle may end, Britain, finally and irrevocably, has lost her role in the Continent.

The eyes of the world will be opened about the importance of the Jewish question quite independently of the result of this struggle. Millions of war prisoners will become propagandists about this. The question no longer is whether it is possible to say who will have hegemony at the end of this struggle, either the European family of nations represented by the strongest state among it or the Bolshevist Colossus. Either Germany will be victorious on behalf of the whole of Europe or Soviet Russia will be the victor.

Statements spread abroad by some British newspapers to the effect that Russia, after beating Germany eventually, would no longer have any reason to penetrate farther into Europe and would be satisfied with education—that is to say, extermination—of the German people, are nothing but Jewish falsehoods. The same applies to insinuations that Britain would then immediately take the lead in a new fight against Soviet Russia.

The victor in this struggle certainly will not let British newspaper writers determine his aims in this war. Secondly, in the event bolshevism is finally victorious, the sorry remains of Europe will hardly be ready to continue the struggle against the European-Asiatic Soviet colossus under England's leadership. Even less so, as England's military chances in such a struggle must be considered hopeless.

Furthermore, every European knows that at best this small surviving remnant of Europe would receive only the honor—like the Canadian, Australian and South African troops—to carry on their own bloody burden in the struggle for the maintenance of British domination and to save British manpower and lives.

One thing, therefore, is quite certain: in this struggle there can be only one victor, and that will be either Germany or Soviet Russia. German victory means the preservation of Europe and a victory by Soviet Russia means its destruction. That is so clear that even every Englishman who is not completely pig-headed should know it.

If with real British hypocrisy they pretend the outcome might after all be different, that is only because of the fact that the guilty war criminals in London no longer see the possibility of disentangling themselves from the entanglements of their own creation.

The way back is already blocked to them by their Jewish wire-pullers and instigators in respect to their internal policy, too. For Britain, as well as the United States, the question no longer exists as to whether after this war they want to fight bolshevism. But the question is only whether after this war they will be able to resist bolshevism at home.

What in the practical sense Europe may expect of British war promises is most clearly shown by the British and American attitude toward the fate of the Poles, Finns, Baltic States and the whole of southeast Europe.

By the unscrupulous promises of guarantees to help Poland, that State was driven into war against Germany. By the blatant lie that other States must be saved from Germany, they were compelled to accept treaties of assistance, and with the same lying phrases one after the other of these countries has been dropped. They had to be sacrificed, not because the individual Englishman wanted it, but because England in case of a bolshevist victory would be unable to prevent this outcome.

Not only are they—in view of their own position, which is entirely contaminated by bolshevism—unable to conduct successfully any other policy, but also every state that, like England, has sold its soul to Judaism will sooner or later succumb to this pest, unless at the last minute it pulls itself together to expel these bacteria by force from its body.

The opinion that it would be possible to live together peaceably and even to live in harmony with these ferments of decomposition is nothing but the belief that the body in time will reach a state in which it will assimiliate cholera bacillus.

The question of the salvation of Europe and the European states is one, therefore, that cannot be solved exclusively by the National Socialist German people and its army. If, however, the Reich is crushed, no other state in Europe could put up resistance to this new invasion of Huns. They know this quite well in the Kremlin.

Therefore, out of sheer precaution for the future, the Kremlin would in case of victory decide on the complete extermination of the German people. This aim is also the openly admitted intention of international Jewry. It is quite irrelevant in this connection whether Jewish advocates of this aim are in England or in America or elsewhere in the various countries of Europe, or whether they are directing from their central office in Moscow.

It is also quite irrelevant whether European or non-European statesmen are ready to admit this fact or not, or whether in one country or another people believe it is possible to decontaminate themselves from the bacteria they had grown themselves by their servile attitude.

Unless Germany is victorious, the fate of these States in northern, southern and central Europe will be determined within a few months. Ten years later the oldest cultural Continent would have lost its essential traits of individuality. Gone would be the picture so beloved by all of us, of the cultural and material development existing for more than 2,500 years.

The bearers of this culture, the leaders of nations, would perish somewhere in the woods and swamps of Siberia, if they were not finished off before by being shot in the neck.

Jewry could then celebrate the destruction of Europe by a second triumphant Purim festival. [The Purim festival marks the deliverance of the Jews from Haman.] That German people today are capable of conducting this decisive life and death struggle for their own preservation and for the preservation of the European Continent is due to the grace of God, who, after its long struggle for power—now eleven years old—has let National Socialism victoriously achieve its aim.

Without Jan. 30, 1933, and without the National Socialist revolution, without its gigantic internal work of purification and construction, there would be no power in Europe today capable of opposing the bolshevist colossus. The Germany of that time was so weakened by the growing Jewish infection that it could hardly think of mastering the bolshevist danger in the interior. Even less could it oppose it abroad.

As in other countries, economic ruin was brought about by Jewry, rendering unemployed several million Germans. The destruction of the peasantry, trade and industry was planned in preparation for an interior collapse. This was furthered by the maintenance of a senseless class society that helped turn into hate the reason of the masses in order to convert them into a willing instrument of bolshevism.

By mobilizing these proletarian slaves it was hoped that after the annihilation of their national intelligence they could be still more degraded into complete coolies. But even if this process of bolshevist revolt did not reach full success inside Germany, the German state with its Weimar constitution would, in the face of the great tasks of modern world policy, only have been a ridiculous and helpless body.

To be prepared for this conflict, not only problems of power but mostly problems of a social and economic character had to be solved.

When National Socialism eleven years ago without delay started realizing its program, it succeeded just in the nick of time in setting up a state that had enough strength in its external relations to fulfill that European mission which in ancient times Greece had against the Persians, Rome against the Carthaginians, and, in later centuries, the Western World against Eastern tribes.

In addition to many others, four great tasks therefore confronted us in 1933. On their solution depended not only the future of the Reich but also the salvation of Europe, perhaps even that of all human civilization.

First: By solving its inner social problems Germany had to find again the social peace it had lost at home. This meant that the elements that split up the nation into classes, the bourgeoisie and the proletariat, had to be abolished in their many forms and replaced by a national community. Appeal to reason had to be supplemented by ruthless elimination of those elements in all camps which offered vicious resistance.

Second: Unification of the nation in the field of social policy had to be supplemented by that in the field of national policy. That means that the Reich, which was disunited and divided not only into many political parties but also into many small states, had to be replaced by a unified National Socialist state, conceived and led so as to be able to stand up effectively even to the strongest tests of the future.

[There was no explanation of the absence of the third and fourth tasks.]

Only the solution of all these tasks could have as its result a state capable at home and abroad of waging a struggle for its own defense and for the defense of the European family of nations.

When, eleven years ago, the Nazi movement had obtained power in this state after a long struggle within legal limits, the true foundations for the successful solution of these tasks had already been created. The German national community had found its embodiment in the Nazi movement itself.

Therefore, it was not the state that in the course of the years had shaped the Nazi movement, but the movement that shaped the state. Whatever great things have been accomplished since then, the first achievements of the Nazi revolution are undoubtedly due to the building up of the German national community, its transformation carried out by cautious steps but persistently and firmly, of the old state, made up of various opposing classes of society, into the new socialist organism, the state of the nation and the people.

Thus alone Germany has become immune from all attempts to infect her with the bolshevik virus. The fact that in the Reich today any young German, without regard to his birth, his origin, his wealth, his education or the position of his parents, can attain any position on his personal merits is one of the most decisive feats of the Nazi revolution.

How rapidly this socialist revolution of the structure of our nation is taking place is proved most convincingly by the present war, for the armed forces, too, have now been included in the sphere of this development. More than sixty per cent of our young officers now come from the ranks. Thus they form a bridge with hundreds of thousands of workers and peasants, of members of the lower and middle classes.

This unified state, based on a solid national and political organization, had to create forthwith armed forces which in their intellectual disposition, in their mental attitude, in their numerical strength and material equipment would be an adequate instrument to carry out the task of self defense.

After the rest of the world had refused all German offers to limit armaments the Reich had to shape its own armaments accordingly.

In order to be able to preserve Germany's existence in Europe with some chance of success it was necessary to unite into one all those countries which were either inhabited by Germans or had belonged for more than 1,000 years to the German Reich, thus constituting areas that from a national and economic viewpoint were indispensable for the preservation of the Reich, that is, for its political and military defense.

One day history will note it as one of the greatest achievements that in our great state we have succeeded in starting and carrying through a socialist revolution that, without destroying any national property and without in any way restricting the creative powers of the old classes of society, brought about the complete equality of all citizens. This development will be further continued by National Socialism with imperturbable and determined consistency. Thereby, nazism will deprive international Jewry of all opportunities of undermining from within the structure of our nation.

The National Socialist community can already be regarded as the unassailable core of all European self-defense. For only a state that in its own interior is completely free from anti-social centers of infection is able to oppose bolshevism with full assurance in its external relations.

The Jews, themselves, have lost all power in our great Reich. By perpetrating this war against Nazi Germany they will have helped to spread the ideas of the National Socialist revolution and to bring within the reach of other nations the elements of scientific study and the actual solution of this question.

The World War of 1939 will be known in history as a repetition on a gigantic scale of the trial against our party in 1924 [the Munich trial]. Just as then the attack, which had been meant to destroy our movement, spread our ideas with the force and rapidity of an explosion over the rest of Germany.

In similar fashion this present struggle will within a few years open the eyes of the people about the Jewish question and vindicate the Nazi answer to it and the measure taken to get rid of it as obvious and well worthy of imitation.

The greatness of this historic conflict will open the eyes and minds of nations and train them to think and act in these gigantic historical dimensions. Millions of soldiers and war prisoners will turn into millions of propagandists for this knowledge.

This gigantic struggle, which has now been raging for five years, proves better than anything else that the Nazi revolution has provided the German people with arms to maintain itself by means of internal organization, economically as well as with regard to power. This struggle can take no other course than any other great war on this earth. The ups and downs of events can, therefore, depress only him who has not learned to see or think historically.

The path from the vision of the half-blind soldier of 1918 to the reality of the Nazi state of 1944 was more tremendous and certainly more difficult than the path of the Reich of today to final victory.

That at the end of this struggle there will be victory for Germany, and consequently for Europe, against the criminal attackers in the east and west is not only an expression of the belief of every National Socialist, but an inner certainty. The guarantors of this victory today are not only the soldiers at the front but the fighting homeland also.

As the first World War gave birth to nazism, the second will confirm and strengthen it. However difficult it may be, the homeland will never be spared the end. It is conscious of its fate, and as its sons are fighting at the front, so is it working and fighting valiantly for its fate at home.

The enemy's attempts to bring the German Reich to collapse by high explosives and incendiary bombs will only strengthen the German people's determination and create that hardened and firm state that will shape European history in centuries to come.

But that this gigantic world-shattering process of formation is accompanied by suffering and pain confirms the eternal law of development, which not only applies to all great struggles but also reveals the fate of the world to any simple man on earth. As a natural consequence, this reorganization of our people imposes the greatest demands on the fighting front and the home front also.

However much the storm may rage around our fortress, the day will come when, like every tempest, it will abate and from behind the dark clouds the sun will shine and smile on those who steadfastly and unshakingly remained faithful to their belief and who did their duty.

The bigger today's worries, the higher one day the Almighty will regard, judge and recompense the achievements of those who, against a world of foes, held their flag in loyal hands and carried it forward undaunted. Therefore this struggle will result—despite all the deviltries of our enemies—in the greatest victory of the German Reich.

FEBRUARY

February 1, 1944

The Supreme Soviet of the U.S.S.R. approved Foreign Commissar Vyacheslaff M. Molotov's proposal to change the Russian constitutional system to allow the sixteen constituent republics to have their own armies and diplomatic corps.

American marines and soldiers landed on Japanese territory for the first time and established beachheads near Roi and Kwajalein Islands in the Marshalls.

2

Allied troops by-passed Cassino and broke through the German Gustav Line on a front of several miles.

U. S. Marines captured Roi Island in the Marshalls, the first pre-war Japanese territory to fall to American forces.

3

The House of Representatives defied President Roosevelt and defeated the Administration-sponsored Worley bill which would have provided a Federal ballot for the armed forces in the November elections.

The Spanish Cabinet announced that "the Government has discussed all precautionary measures that may be necessary to see that Spanish neutrality is respected."

4

The Argentine Government published a decree severing diplomatic relations with Bulgaria, Vichy France, Hungary and Rumania.

5

Secretary of the Interior Ickes, in his capacity as President of the Petroleum Reserves Corporation, announced that the U. S. Government would lay a 1,200-mile oil pipeline across Saudi Arabia, from the Persian Gulf refineries to the Mediterranean, as a war measure.

6

All of Kwajalein Atoll came into American hands.

Wendell L. Willkie started his "all-out" drive for the Republican presidential nomination by entering the Nebraska preferential primary.

8

Secretary of State Cordell Hull confirmed that he had renewed his warning to Finland that if she continued in the war she must be prepared to take the consequences.

9

The U. S. Senate voted down the Administration's $1,500,000,000 plan for food subsidies, 49 to 26.

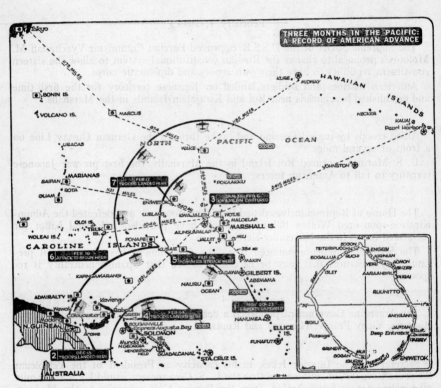

Courtesy New York Times

February, 1944

11

President Roosevelt met with the American Chiefs of Staff to confer on the crisis in the Italian campaign.

12

Prime Minister Winston Churchill stated that there was no justification for pessimism about the long stalemated battle on the Anzio beachhead.

14

Field Marshal Gen. von Rundstedt pledged a German fight to the finish against the expected Allied invasion of France.

15

A military coup d'état of pro-Nazi army officers forced a crisis in Argentina when it became known that the Government was about to declare war on the Axis. Foreign Minister Alberto Gilbert was forcibly ousted.

17

The great naval and air battle against Truk was begun by powerful units of the Pacific Fleet.

The British Government issued a White Paper proposing a free health service for all.

18

The Red Army captured Staraya Russa, below Leningrad.

U. S. naval, air and sea forces scored a big victory over the Japanese at Truk.

19

Premier Hideki Tojo carried out a Japanese Cabinet shakeup "to cope with the important phases of both politics and war."

Americans captured the Japanese air base on Engebi Island of Eniwetok Atoll.

21

Officially admitting heavy losses in the American attack on Truk, the Japanese High Command replaced Field Marshal Gen. Sugiyama with General Hideki Tojo, and Admiral of the Fleet Osami Nagano with Admiral Shigetaro Shimada, the Navy Minister.

The U. S. Government decided to continue its oil embargo against Spain during March to show its impatience with that country's friendly relations with Germany.

22

Soviet troops captured the great iron mining center of Krivoi Rog in the Dnieper Bend after four months of furious fighting.

U. S. carrier planes struck at the important Japanese naval and air base of Saipan in the Marianas, only 1,300 miles from Tokyo.

23

Foreign Secretary Anthony Eden declared in Commons: "We are absolutely free to interest ourselves in the affairs of Europe and the nations of Europe and no spheres of influence have been agreed to by anybody."

24

Senator Alben W. Barkley tendered his resignation as Senate Majority Leader to a conference of Democratic leaders in protest of President Roosevelt's tax bill veto message, but was immediately re-elected. The House overrode President Roosevelt's tax veto by 299–95.

Chile crushed a vast Nazi spy ring, arresting 100 agents and seizing a clandestine short wave radio.

28

As a result of destroying a Japanese force of 8,000 in the Ngakyedauk Pass, the Allied armies in Burma prevented an invasion of India.

29

The *Times* of London, in a special editorial, called for an economically and politically strong Germany after the war. It also opposed its dismemberment in any way.

FOREIGN COMMISSAR MOLOTOV'S REPORT TO THE SUPREME SOVIET OF THE U.S.S.R.

February 1, 1944 [1]

COMRADES DEPUTIES:

The question of the transformation of two People's Commissariats—the People's Commissariat of Defense and the People's Commissariat of Foreign Affairs—from Union into Union-Republican People's Commissariats has been posed before the Supreme Soviet.

The Council of People's Commissars believes that this question is quite ripe. This is not a matter of the ordinary reorganization of two People's Commissariats. This is primarily a matter of placing new and most responsible tasks before the Union Republics. The question has been posed of new tasks and rights of Union Republics, firstly in the matter of the defense of our country, and secondly in the sphere of external relations with foreign states, and in this connection, of important transformations in our Union State.

Heretofore the Union Republics took part in the common work of creation of the organization and equipment of the Red Army. Our Army was created as an All-Union Army, and there existed no separate army formations of the Republics. Now it is proposed to institute army formations of Republics, which should form component parts of the Red Army. In this connection there arises the need for the creation of People's Commissariats of Defense in the Union Republics, as well as the necessity of the transformation of the Union People's Commissariat of Defense into a Union-Republican People's Commissariat.

After the foundation of the Union of Soviet Republics in 1922, foreign political relations were wholly concentrated in the Union People's Commissariat of Foreign Affairs, to which individual Republics delegated their powers in foreign relations. Now the Government of the Union proposes that Union Republics be granted powers to enter into direct relations with foreign states and conclude agreements with them. Naturally, the granting of powers to the Republics in the sphere of foreign relations renders it necessary to create People's Commissariats of Foreign Affairs in the Union Republics and to transform the Union People's Commissariat of Foreign Affairs into a Union-Republican People's Commissariat.

The meaning of the proposed transformation is perfectly clear. This transformation signifies the great expansion of activities of the Union Republics which has become possible as a result of their political, economic and cultural growth, or, in other words, as a result of their national development. One

[1] Information Bulletin, Embassy of the U.S.S.R.

cannot fail to see in this a new, important step in the practical solution of the national problem in the multi-national Soviet State; one cannot fail to see in this a new victory for our Lenin-Stalin national policy.

This transformation, however, has become possible not merely as a result of the strengthening of our Republics. It has become possible as a result of the achieved strengthening of our Union State as a whole. The strengthening of the Soviet Union that has taken place is most convincingly proved by the manner in which our Red Army, which bears the whole brunt of the struggle with the main forces of the most dangerous enemy, is beating the German-fascist army and successfully brings nearer the time of the complete expulsion of the enemy from Soviet territory and his utter defeat.

Now it is more than obvious how scandalously the enemy's calculations on the Red Army's defeat fell through and how nearsighted were the Hitlerites' calculations on causing disunity among the peoples of the Soviet Union. Our Army, which was joined by millions of people from all the nations in the Soviet Union and which receives such invaluable help from our guerrillas in the enemy's rear, proves more and more successfully with every day how strong our country has become, how powerful the Soviet system is, how great the friendship of the Soviet peoples is.

The present proposal on the transformations in the organization of defense and in foreign relations, providing for a great expansion of the functions of the Union Republics, should serve as a new confirmation of our confidence in the strength and growth of the forces of the Soviet Union. This confidence is demonstrated all the more forcefully that we propose to effect these transformations at the height of a Patriotic War, when the forces of our peoples are strained so greatly and when not every state would venture to undertake such important transformations.

I. *Transformation of the People's Commissariat of Defense*

I proceed to the question of the transformation of the People's Commissariat of Defense. It is proposed by the draft of the law to establish that the Union Republics organize army formations of the Republics, and that the People's Commissariat of Defense is transformed from a Union into a Union-Republican People's Commissariat. It is proposed accordingly to make the necessary addenda to the All-Union Constitution.

Now, too, we have national army formations in the Red Army. Our Army has Lithuanian, Latvian, Estonian, Georgian, Azerbaijanian, Armenian, Kazakh and certain other army formations. Some of these army units were created during the Patriotic War. Now that all the peoples of the Soviet Union strive to take their place in the ranks of the Red Army, creation of army formations of the Republics is of great importance to us. As is well known, in Tsarist Russia certain nationalities and peoples were not conscripted for military service. For instance, the Uzbeks, Kazakhs, Tajiks, Turkmenians, Kirghizians, and most of the peoples of the Northern Caucasus, also peoples of the North, were not subject to conscription. Tsarism, naturally, did not trust peoples which it kept in a colonial or semi-colonial status. The Tsarist power even did not do anything to prepare these peoples for gradual induction into the army.

In the Soviet time, the situation has changed radically. The legislation naturally contains no legal restrictions for some or other nationalities as regards conscription. But a certain time had to pass in order to render possible actual realization of conscriptions to the Red Army in all parts of the Soviet Union. Partial conscriptions to the Red Army were carried out in past years even in those districts of the USSR where no conscriptions took place in old times. National army units were formed in the Red Army as well, but up to recent time these formations could not really develop. Now the situation has changed for the better. Adequate possibilities have been created for army formations in the Union Republics. All the Republics have not only cadres of rank and file fighters, but also certain cadres of commanding personnel capable of directing respective army units. Thus at present the creation of army formations in the Union Republics can be placed on a firm foundation.

But to realize this task it is necessary to have Republican People's Commissariats of Defense, and consequently there arises the necessity of the transformation of the Union People's Commissariat of Defense into a Union-Republican People's Commissariat. It is to be expected that this will also increase the attention paid by the Republics to the organization of military training in schools and institutions of higher education, of which we stand in need. Under such conditions, the creation of army formations in the Republics as component parts of the Red Army will play a not insignificant, positive part.

How will this affect our Red Army? Will this contribute to its strengthening, to the growth of its might? Yes, this is beyond any doubt. Our Army has always been close to and cherished by the peoples of the Soviet Union. In the course of the Patriotic War, still stronger became the love of the peoples of the USSR for their Army, still stronger and more universal became the pride of the Soviet people in the successes and heroism of the Red Army. Indeed, who fails to see what a glorious struggle is waged by our Army for the liberation of the Ukraine, for the liberation of Byelorussia? Who fails to appreciate whole-heartedly what the Red Army does to prepare the imminent liberation of Lithuania, Latvia, Estonia, Moldavia and the Karelo-Finnish Republic? Who fails to remember that Soviet troops saved Azerbaijan, Georgia and Armenia from the invasion of German fascism? Who of our Soviet people does not glorify our Army for having defended our Capital —Moscow, for having routed the Germans at Stalingrad and launched an offensive along the whole front, for having defended Leningrad and fully lifted the blockade from it, and for now chasing the enemy hordes from the native soil without giving him any respite? Who, save those plagued by fascism, fails to understand now that the Red Army fulfills a mission of liberation not only with regard to its own motherland, but also with regard to all democratic countries which fight for their honor, freedom and independence against the mortal danger presented by fascism?

Who further does not know that the men and women workers of our mills and factories, that the men and women peasants on the collective farms, that our intelligentsia, that all the Soviet people, are ready to give all their strength to enhance the might of the Red Army, that by their self-sacrificing labor they discharge by actual deeds their duty to the motherland, to the heroic Red Army?

The formation of army units of the Republic should serve to strengthen further our Army as the defender of our country, as the reliable bulwark of the Soviet Union. The enemies of the Soviet Union need not doubt that as a result of these new army formations the forces of our State will grow still stronger. This will make them more cautious in the future.

This new embodiment of the growing friendship of the peoples of the Soviet Union will contribute to the further growth of the prestige of our country with the nations of the East and West.

II. *Transformation of People's Commissariat of Foreign Affairs*

Of no lesser significance is the transformation of the All-Union People's Commissariat of Foreign Affairs into a Union-Republican People's Commissariat. Before the foundation of the Soviet Union, along with the People's Commissariat of Foreign Affairs of the Russian Soviet Federative Socialist Republic there existed People's Commissariats of Foreign Affairs in the Ukraine, Byelorussia, Georgia, Armenia and Azerbaijan, which on certain occasions maintained foreign relations with other states. During the early period when our State was not yet gathered into one Union State, but consisted of separate parts, a number of treaties and agreements were concluded between individual Soviet Republics and foreign states. On some occasions representatives of the Russian SFSR were specially authorized by other Soviet Republics to participate in international conferences and to conclude treaties with other states on behalf of all or several Soviet Republics.

Comrade Stalin said at the first All-Union Congress of Soviets that "at that time the Soviet Republics, although they acted together, marched separately, occupied primarily by the problem of their existence." That was inevitable at the initial stage. When the USSR was founded in accordance with the common will of the Union Republics, it was decided to unify relations with foreign states in one center. Then was created the All-Union People's Commissariat of Foreign Affairs, in which were vested the powers of the People's Commissariats of Foreign Affairs of the separate Soviet Republics. Since then, up to our days, the Soviet State was represented abroad through All-Union diplomatic representatives. Treaties and agreements with foreign states were also concluded only on behalf of the Union. This was necessary at a certain stage of the development of our State and yielded its positive results by having strengthened the State and highly enhanced its part in international affairs. But even then, as far back as at the Party Congress in 1923, Comrade Stalin said: "We shall still take up the national question more than once, since national and international conditions are subject to changes and may still change. I do not preclude the possibility that subsequently we may have to separate certain commissariats which we are now merging in the Union of Republics . . ."

Being the best authority on the national question, not only in our Party and not only in our country, Comrade Stalin, who together with the great Lenin laid the foundation of the Soviet Union, pointed out even then that changes in the international situation and the national development would more than once call forth organizational changes in the machine of the Soviet State. No other state of affairs can be imagined, especially in such a young and rapidly gaining strength organism as the Soviet Union is.

Now the question of the foreign relations of the Union Republics stands differently from the way it stood two decades ago when the Soviet Union was being founded. It grew out of the vital needs of the Republics and its solution is dictated by the interests of the Union as a whole. The time is long past when certain foreign states tried not to notice the existence of the Soviet Republic born in the October Revolution. Now, on the contrary, among foreign states there is a growing desire to establish and develop diplomatic relations with our State.

Certainly under conditions of World War this meets with peculiar, not insignificant difficulties, but still even in the years of war the international connections of the USSR have been steadily extending. One may even say that it was just in the years of the war that the international connections of the Soviet Union have risen to a new and higher level. The facts are universally known. For the first time during the existence of Soviet power, we have established not only friendly but even allied relations with Great Britain. Similar good relations have been formed between us and the United States of America. A powerful anti-Hitler coalition has been formed, headed by the Soviet Union, Great Britain and the United States of America, a coalition whose military and political importance for the whole range of democratic states can hardly be overestimated. The recently concluded Soviet-Czechoslovak Treaty may serve as an example of the strengthening of friendly relations of the Soviet Union with European states. The foundations have been laid for the cooperation of large and small democratic countries, not only in time of war against a common enemy, but also in the postwar period for the sake of safeguarding peace against new encroachments on the part of aggressive powers.

As is well known, the Moscow and Teheran Conferences played a most eminent part in the development and strengthening of the anti-Hitler coalition. Now as never before, great is the confidence of the peoples of the anti-Hitler camp in near and complete victory, in joint crushing blows of the Allies at the common enemy, which are already not distant, as well as confidence that the alliance and friendship of the anti-fascist countries will be steeled in this common struggle.

And still it cannot be said that this general positive course of development of the international connections of the Soviet Union could fully cover not only the requirements of the whole Union but also the multifarious and growing requirements of the Union Republics in foreign affairs. Thus the Union Republics have quite a few specific economic and cultural requirements which cannot be covered in full measure by All-Union representation abroad and also by treaties and agreements of the Union with other states. These national requirements of the Republics can be met better by means of direct relations of the Republics with the corresponding states. Naturally, questions of this kind require special concrete elaboration in Union and Republican organs. It cannot be denied either that a certain time will be required to organize these external activities of the Republics. Such questions are not solved after a cut and dried pattern. It is indisputable, however, that the problem of emerging into the arena of external activities has already acquired vital importance for a number of Republics.

Lastly, it should be acknowledged that this is in the interests not only of this or that individual Union Republic, but also in the interests of the entire cause of the expansion of international connections and the strengthening of the cooperation of the USSR with other states, which is of such importance in time of war and which will yield fruit also in the postwar period.

Such are the grounds on which the necessity of the transformation of the People's Commissariat of Foreign Affairs from a Union into a Union-Republican People's Commissariat should be recognized. Whereas in the initial period there existed only Republican People's Commissariats of Foreign Affairs, and in the second period only a Union Commissariat of Foreign Affairs, now the People's Commissariat of Foreign Affairs should be transformed into a more complex and ramified organization—into a Union-Republican People's Commissariat.

It remains for me to add a few words on our diplomatic practice. It is necessary to note that the absence of special provisions in the Soviet Constitution as regards the rights of Union Republics to exchange of representations with other states and to the maintenance of foreign relations, is sometimes interpreted to the direct detriment of the interests of the Soviet Republics and of the Soviet Union as a whole. The proposed addition will serve to eliminate facts of this kind.

III. *New Forward Stride in Solution of National Problem*

The proposed transformation of the People's Commissariat of Foreign Affairs and the People's Commissariat of Defense is a new forward stride in the solution of the national problem in the Soviet Union. This transformation is in direct accord with the principles of our Lenin-Stalin national policy. The realization of measures of this kind at the present time means that the Soviet State has reached a new level in its development, turning into a more complex and virile organism. In this one cannot fail to see fresh evidence of the great significance of the socialist principles of the organization of the Soviet Union.

In his report to the Congress of Soviets which adopted the Constitution of the USSR in 1936, Comrade Stalin thus characterized the victory of the national policy of the Soviet power which insured the success of the formation of a multi-national state on the basis of socialism:

"The absence of exploiting classes which are the principal organizers of strife between nations; the absence of exploitation which cultivates mutual distrust and kindles nationalist passions; the fact that power is in the hands of the working class which is the foe of all enslavement and the true vehicle of the ideas of internationalism; the actual practice of mutual aid among the peoples in all spheres of economic and social life; and finally, the flourishing national culture of the peoples of the USSR, a culture which is national in form and socialist in content—all these and similar factors have brought about a radical change in the aspect of the peoples of the USSR; their feeling of mutual distrust has disappeared, a feeling of mutual friendship has developed among them, and thus real fraternal cooperation among the peoples has been established within the system of a single Union State. As a result, we now have a fully-formed multi-national socialist State which has stood all tests and whose stability might well be envied by any national state in any part of the world."

Seven years—and what years!—have passed since then. Soon it will be three years that we have been waging the great Patriotic War against German fascism and its allies, which use the material and manpower resources of nearly the whole of Europe in their struggle against the Soviet Union. This has been a new—and the most serious at that—test for our multi-national State. But the Soviet Union has passed this test, too, with flying colors.

On the 26th anniversary of the October Revolution, Comrade Stalin thus summed up the latest period:

"All the peoples of the Soviet Union have risen as one to defend their motherland, rightly considering the present Patriotic War the common cause of all working people, irrespective of nationality or religion. By now the Hitlerite politicians have themselves seen how hopelessly stupid were their hopes of discord and strife among the peoples of the Soviet Union. The friendship of the peoples of our country has withstood all hardships and trials of war and has become tempered still further in the common struggle of all Soviet people against the fascist invaders."

This—in Comrade Stalin's words—is one of the decisive sources of the strength of the Soviet Union.

Let us sum up. Carrying out under the present conditions important State transformations, we must of course pose the question of how this will affect the Red Army and its deep rear in the country. In other words, are we making a step toward the strengthening or toward the weakening of the USSR?

Everything said above permits to give a definite answer to this question. The transformation of the People's Commissariat of Foreign Affairs and the People's Commissariat of Defense which follows from the expansion of the tasks and functions of the Union Republics within the country and beyond its confines, far from running counter to the interests of the strengthening of our Union, on the contrary is being effected in the name of and for the purpose of the further strengthening of our great State.

Since the time when the Soviet Union was founded, the Constitution has insured to the Union Republics such a supreme expression of their sovereign rights as the right of free secession from the USSR. But as time passes the stronger becomes the desire of the peoples of the Soviet Union to live in close friendship among themselves, to help one another and to march together through all trials under the guidance of Soviet power.

The recognition by the Union of the increased requirements of the Republics in their state activities, including foreign activities, and legislative provision for these needs of the Republics, only serves to strengthen the fraternal relations among the peoples of our country and reveals still more fully the historic meaning of the existence of the Soviet Union to the peoples of the East and West.

It should be recognized further that the new forward stride in the solution of the national problem in the USSR is of great importance from the viewpoint of all progressive humanity. At a time when German fascism—this worst product of imperialism!—has reared its head and unleashed a World War to strangle its neighbors, to destroy free states and impose its bandit imperialist policy upon other peoples of Europe, and after that upon the peoples of the whole world—the new success in the realization of the Lenin-Stalin national policy in the Soviet State will have especially great international significance. This step of the Soviet power will constitute a new moral-political blow at fascism and its man-hating policy, hostile to its core to the interest of the free national development of peoples.

The Soviet Union and its Allies are already successfully beating fascism, which imposed this war, hastening the time of its utter military defeat. But we know that matters should not be restricted to the military defeat of the fascist forces. It is necessary to bring to completion the moral-political defeat of fascism as well. To this, we are certain, will successfully contribute those State transformations in the Soviet Union which are now submitted for your approval.

I express assurance that the Supreme Soviet will demonstrate the unanimity of the Soviet people in the solution of the question of the proposed State transformations.

TEXTS OF THE SOVIET AUTONOMY DECREES

February 1, 1944 [1]

With the aim of widening international connections and strengthening the collaboration of the U.S.S.R. with other States and taking into consideration the growing need of the Union Republics in the establishment of direct

[1] The United Nations Review.

relations with foreign States, the Supreme Soviet of the U.S.S.R. decrees:

1. A Union Republic may enter into direct relations with foreign States and conclude agreements with them.

2. To introduce into the Constitution of the U.S.S.R. the following additions:

A. To add to Article XIV point (A) of the Constitution after the words: "representation of the Union in international relations, conclusion and ratification of treaties with foreign States" the words: "the establishment of the general character of the relations between the Union Republic and foreign States." This point thus reads as follows:

(A) Representation of the Union in international relations, conclusion and ratification of treaties with other States and the establishment of the general character of the relations of the Union Republic and foreign States.

B. To add to the Constitution of the U.S.S.R. Article XVIII (A) to read thus: "Each Union Republic has the right to enter into direct relation with foreign States, to conclude agreements with them and exchange diplomatic and consular representatives with them."

C. To supplement Article LX of the Constitution of the U.S.S.R. with point (E) reading: "Establishment of the representation of the Union Republic in international relations."

3. To transform the People's Commissariat for Foreign Affairs from an All-Union into a Union-Republican People's Commissariat.

KALININ,
Chairman of the Presidium of the Supreme Soviet of the U.S.S.R.
GORKIN,
Secretary.

The Supreme Soviet of the U.S.S.R., with the aim of strengthening the defensive power of the U.S.S.R., decrees:

1. To establish that the Union Republics shall organize military formations of the Republics.

2. To add to the Constitution of the U.S.S.R. the following additions:

A. To supplement Article XIV, point (H) of the Constitution after the words "organizing the defense of the U.S.S.R. and directing all armed forces of the U.S.S.R.," the words: "the establishing of the directing principles of the organization of military formations of the Union Republics."

This point thus reads:

"(H) Organizing the defense of the U.S.S.R., directing all armed forces of the U.S.S.R., the establishment of the directing principles of the organization of military formations of the Union Republics."

B. To supplement the Constitution of the U.S.S.R. with Article XVIII-B, as follows:

"Each Union Republic has its republican military formation."

C. To supplement Article LX of the Constitution of the U.S.S.R. with point (E) as follows:

"Establishes the method of the creation of military formations of the Union Republic."

3. To transform the People's Commissariat for Defense from an All-Union into a Union-Republican People's Commissariat.

KALININ,
Chairman of the Presidium of the Supreme Soviet of the U.S.S.R.
GORKIN,
Secretary of the Supreme Soviet of the U.S.S.R.

LINCOLN'S DAY ADDRESS BY VICE-PRESIDENT HENRY A. WALLACE

February 12, 1944 [1]

Until the end of time men will come here to pay tribute to the memory of Abraham Lincoln. He who speaks here should speak from the heart, and briefly.

Every schoolboy, every American and all lovers of freedom everywhere know the Lincoln story. He was born poor, he united a nation torn asunder and he freed men. Lincoln was a man of faith who looked beyond private sorrow and public woe. His name and his deeds will live forever.

Within a few months after Abraham Lincoln became President we were engaged in a terrible war which was not won until a few days before his tragic death. It was not an easy war to win. The opposing armies in the field were strong. Those who gave lip service to the United States but who found fault with everything Lincoln said and did were powerful. Influential newspapers continually and severely criticized him. At one time, only a few months before he was renominated for President, he had only one supporter in Congress. This great man who spoke truly when he said, "I have never willingly planted a thorn in any man's bosom," was misrepresented and maligned by swarms of little men. Lincoln, nevertheless, bent his great energies to winning the war and planning for the peace. He was struck down while the people of the United States, North and South, were celebrating the return of peace.

We meet tonight in the midst of another great war. Ten million American fighting men are engaged in work as important as any which has ever been done on this earth. As soon as this war has been won the soldiers and the workers in war plants will be ready to make peacetime goods. There must be jobs for all willing workers. We have come out of the dark cellars of unemployment and doles, and we must never go back. The people have a right to ask, "Why can we not work and get enough to eat and wear in peace as we have in war?" The answer is, "We can and we must!!" With full employment the people of the United States can have the things they have always wanted, better homes, better schools, better household furnishings and more time to spend with their children.

Those who are blinded by fear say that we must go back to the old days—the days of hunger and despair. We must not heed them. They are not of the stature to which Lincoln grew.

The future calls for faith and work—faith and intelligent planning. Peace, goodwill, jobs, health and family security are possible and obtainable, and should become the tools of man's march toward the fuller and richer life. If Lincoln were here today he would concern himself with striving for a better tomorrow.

Short-sighted, fearful people in Lincoln's day said that we could never recover from the wreckage of the Civil War. Lincoln himself looked ahead with hope and confidence. He planned for New Frontiers—for the West that was to be. The American enterprise and the American Government of 1864 knew that the men who returned to civilian life needed work to do. The

[1] Office of the Vice-President.

jobs that were provided by the building of the West saved us from chaos after the Civil War.

This experience of our grandfathers is a lamp for our feet.

Who does not wish to see swamps drained, harbors deepened, dams built, soil saved, inventions encouraged and new and better goods for use and comfort provided for men everywhere? The man who cannot see, the man who fears and waits is not of the stuff of which Lincoln was made. Rather he is like the Copperheads whom Lincoln fought—those who wanted peace at the price of a divided nation. Those who seek a people's peace have the right to see through Lincoln's eyes, and our duty is continually to work with vigilance always against the national and international carpetbaggers who would starve and enslave the world.

Lincoln said, "Trust the common people." He believed in their common sense and in their ultimate unselfishness. Today, while democracy is menaced abroad and while American Fascists are trying to enslave us here, the words and deeds and inspiration of Lincoln give strength to those who battle in the people's cause.

So long as there is human need in the United States it is criminal for men to be idle, whether they be the idle poor or the idle rich. It is bad business and bad morals to allow believers in scarcity to hold down production while people need goods and men are out of work. The people of America are our most precious possession. The poorest people of America are our most valuable, untapped market. Men are more important than dollars. Abraham Lincoln believed this. Shortly before he became President he said that he was both for the man and for the dollar, but in case of conflict he was for the man before the dollar. He believed and died believing that the rights of man were more precious than the rights of private property.

Those who fight for us in this war belong to many parties, many creeds and many races. This is a people's war. The peace must be a people's peace. Lincoln would have it so. We will fight unceasingly against anyone who puts the dollar above the man. We will win the people's peace.

SPEECH BY SEÑOR DR. DON ADRIÁN C. ESCOBAR UPON PRESENTATION OF LETTERS OF CREDENCE AS AMBASSADOR OF ARGENTINA TO THE UNITED STATES

February 15, 1944 [1]

MR. PRESIDENT:

I have the honor to deliver to you the letters of credence with which my Government accredits me as Ambassador Extraordinary and Plenipotentiary and the letters of recall of my distinguished predecessor; and in this circumstance it is a pleasure for me to transmit to you the sentiments of admiration and fraternal friendship which the Government and people of Argentina cherish toward the great Republic of the North, with which we have always been joined by spiritual, material, and moral bonds which time has consolidated to the point of their becoming indestructible.

[1] State Department Bulletin.

The Argentine people has just been stirred to its innermost depths by two very grave occurrences: one of these, the tragic catastrophe of San Juan which cost many lives and enormous material destruction. That disaster furnished occasion for putting to the test once again the solidarity of feeling among the American nations, and I am pleased to repeat to Your Excellency the gratitude of my country for the part which your country had in that sincere and spontaneous gesture. The other is the categorical determination which my Government has taken, interpreting the desire of our people, to break off relations with Germany and Japan, in view of the seriousness of activities which wounded its most noble sentiments. The Argentine Government could not permit countries to which we are closely bound by traditional ties of friendship to be injured, since those activities not only infringed on the national sovereignty but compromised its foreign policy and attacked the security of the continent.

Argentina knows and feels that the destiny of America is her own destiny. This thought, Mr. President, which is a double imperative, historical and geographical, contains a high significance for the relations among the sovereign countries of America which act with rectitude—relations which cannot be altered in spite of the differences which may arise in the evaluation of some essential questions.' They must be clarified and settled in a friendly and cordial atmosphere, since today, as yesterday and as tomorrow, the common objective cannot be other than the most complete reciprocal understanding. Thus ideas will be discussed, certain interests will for the moment be divergent, but over and above the occasional and ephemeral clash of ideas and interests is placed respect for the immutable principles of morality and justice.

My country does not, in any manner, practice isolation. It has maintained and will always maintain the necessity for the closest union among the peoples of America. Its history proclaims this. It does not seek benefits, nor shares, nor advantages. It recognizes fully the rights of others and firmly maintains its own. It has an honorable and untarnished tradition: it loves peace and never soiled its name by any aggression; it submitted its fundamental questions to arbitration, it set up principles and doctrines universally recognized, and at congresses and conferences defined its policy with generous and broad concepts, which have been incorporated as juridical standards in the common patrimony of the nations of America.

We desire, Mr. President, that the legal gains achieved at the Pan American congresses be consolidated; that the solidarity sealed at Lima be a living reality. To this end we have proposed to the limitrophe countries, without the most remote political aim, the study and formation of customs unions for the better economic development of the countries, members of such unions, and the attainment of a higher standard of living for the populations concerned. And it is our keenest desire to leave the doors wide open to the whole continent to adhere to this regime, thereby converting to a harmonious reality the dreams of Washington, of Bolivar, of San Martín and so many great men of America.

The good-neighbor policy, which you initiated, Mr. President, found in my country a sympathetic echo and instantaneous welcome and, as you have said in speeches which are famous, it must be understood that this new policy of the United States has a permanent character. For our part, I need not assure you that we shall tend toward the permanence of this reciprocal goodneighborhood. We must all be good neighbors and, morever, good and sincere friends.

From its first days as an independent nation Argentina practiced good-neighborliness and made of fraternity an article of faith: she made an offering of the blood of her sons and her well-being for other American peoples fighting on the fields of battle for most noble ideals and contributing to the freedom of half a continent.

When the peoples of America suffered misfortunes Argentina hastened to their aid with solicitude. But she did not limit her efforts to them but also offered her aid to distant and dissimilar countries when they were passing through a difficult situation. Thus, Argentina will now be present to aid the countries which are suffering the horrors of war, carrying out her mission with Christian generosity and diligent zeal.

The Government of my country will contribute, within its means, to the great work of aid, reconstruction, and rehabilitation to take care of the disasters and calamities which are scourging the world.

I hope that you, Excellency, who know my country, which had the gratification of receiving you with cordial rejoicing, will offer me the necessary opportunities to the end that I may discharge my mission which is, without reservation, that of a true rapprochement with the United States, of increasing cooperation, of sincere understanding and loyal friendship.

Mr. President, in the name of the Argentine people and Government I formulate good wishes for the prosperity of the United States, and express their warm desire for your personal happiness.

PRESIDENT ROOSEVELT'S REPLY TO AMBASSADOR ESCOBAR

February 17, 1944 [1]

MR. AMBASSADOR:

I am indeed happy to greet you and to receive the letters accrediting you as Ambassador Extraordinary and Plenipotentiary of the Argentine Government near the Government of the United States of America. I accept at the same time the letters of recall of your distinguished predecessor, Dr. Felipe Espil, who will be remembered by his many friends in this country with deep affection and high esteem. Dr. Espil during his many years of service in the United States labored devotedly and unceasingly to bring about a deeper understanding between our two Governments and peoples.

I thank you for your expression of the sentiments of admiration and friendship cherished by the Government and people of Argentina for the United States. Similar sentiments have traditionally characterized the attitude of the Government and people of this country for the Argentine Republic. The two events referred to by you—namely, the disastrous earthquake at San Juan and the recent action of your Government in severing diplomatic relations with the Axis powers—have given rise to renewed demonstrations of that attitude.

The tragic loss of life which occurred at San Juan aroused feelings of deep sympathy here as well as a desire to be of assistance to the afflicted people of that region.

The action of the Argentine Government in severing relations with Germany and Japan and Axis satellites has been received with satisfaction by

[1] Dept. of State Bulletin.

free people everywhere. The importance of this and other related matters connected with the eradication of subversive activities in the promotion of the security of the Western Hemisphere against the continuing aggressions of the enemies of our civilization is manifest.

These aggressions have taken manifold forms.

They have included espionage conducted under the auspices of the diplomatic missions of the Axis nations.

Industries producing for United Nations war purposes have been sabotaged by agents of the Axis powers.

All manner of subversive activities have been engaged in not only for the purpose of impeding the war effort of the United Nations but even in some cases with the object of overthrowing by violent means governments friendly to our common cause.

All of these activities would have involved the most serious peril to our common interests if they had not been combated by the energetic and united action of the American republics. With the decision of your Government to cooperate fully in promoting the security of the continent, the Axis is severely handicapped in its conduct of operations in this hemisphere.

I am pleased to express my whole-hearted agreement with your observations concerning the policy of the good neighbor. That policy not only has long-term implications of incalculable importance; it has also enabled the American republics in a time of serious peril and grave threat to their independence to concert measures and take steps in unison for their common defense. I am confident that the people of the United States have adopted this policy as a part of their permanent political philosophy.

I am very happy to extend to you, Mr. Ambassador, a most cordial welcome and to assure you of my own desire and of the desire of the officials of this Government to render you every possible assistance in the fulfillment of your mission. I am pleased also to have this opportunity of extending through you my best wishes for the happiness and welfare of the people of Argentina.

ADDRESS BY LORD WAVELL, VICEROY OF INDIA, AT JOINT SESSION OF LEGISLATIVE ASSEMBLY AND COUNCIL OF STATE OF INDIA

February 17, 1944 [1]

It has been the practice of Viceroys to address the Legislature at the first opportunity after taking office. Hitherto it has happened that the earliest opportunity has been about six months after the Viceroy's arrival. For myself, as you know, the first opportunity occurred within so short a time that I felt obliged to postpone the occasion. I have now spent some four very busy months in my post and I am prepared to offer you such views and guidance as I can at this momentous stage of India's history. You need not regard them as final views. I always look forward to making fresh contacts, and gaining fresh knowledge. But they indicate certain principles on which action for the progress of India must, I consider, be based.

The last address to you by the Viceroy was at the end of the longest term of office in the history of the appointment. It was not only the longest term, but the most exciting. Lord Linlithgow's patience, strength and administrative

[1] British Speeches of the Day.

skill were shown to the full in those difficult years. The war inevitably interrupted or hampered much of the work which was nearest to his heart, to
further the material prosperity and constitutional progress of India. As time
goes by the greatness of the service which he rendered to India in those critical
years will become even more apparent.

Though not entirely a stranger to this Legislature, I have till lately served
India as a soldier. As a soldier in the positions which I have held during
this war I know better, perhaps, than anyone what the United Nations owe
to India for our success in the struggle against Nazism and Fascism, and the
barbarous ambitions of Japan. I shall do my best to see that the debt is
acknowledged and paid, not only with tributes of words, but with practical
aid. I shall also try to pay my personal debt to the Indian soldier for his
gallant and enduring service by doing my best to further the welfare of the
Indian peoples, of whom the Indian soldier is a fitting representative. Though
the soldier stands in the limelight, it is not only to the soldier that the United
Nations owe gratitude; the Indian worker, also, and many others in India
have made a very great and vital contribution to the war effort.

My first task here is to assist the South East Asia Command to drive the
enemy from the gates of India. There can be no peace or prosperity for
India or anyone else until Japanese ambitions are utterly destroyed.

"You May Be Proud of Your Contribution"

I need say little to you on the general course of the war. You have seen for
yourselves how the United Nations took and withstood the dangerous shocks
of three years of war—a war for which their enemies had planned and prepared while they had planned for peace and how they rallied from those shocks
in irresistible strength. You have seen how the spirit of the British people
flashed like a sword from its sheath at the challenge of the disasters in
France; how they faced a triumphant Germany for one year almost alone
and unequipped, but undaunted; how they won the Battle of Britain against
the mighty German Air Force, and the Battle of the Atlantic against Germany's many U-boats, and—with the aid of the Dominions and India, and the
United States—the Battle of the Mediterranean and Africa against the combined strength of the German and Italian sea, land and air forces. You have
seen how Russia met the mightiest, most formidably equipped, most mobile,
most highly trained, most arrogantly confident, force of fighting men ever
launched by land; and has hurled them back in defeat and ruin, as she did
another would-be world conqueror 130 years ago. As one who has seen much
of the Russian soldier, both in peace and war, I have watched with special
interest the prowess of the army and the people, whom I have always liked
and admired. You have seen, too, how the United States of America
recovered from the treacherous surprises of Pearl Harbor and Manila, and
how powerful a fighting machine she has organized to carry her counter-
offensive to Japan. You have seen China indomitable for over six years,
though almost unarmed. You are joined with four of the toughest nations
of the world in spirit and action. The end is certain and you may be proud
of your contribution to it.

When the end will come it is difficult yet to say. Germany is reeling under
a series of shocks, physical and moral, which may well put her out of the
ring at an early date, though we must not count on it. We shall then be
able to intensify the war against Japan. You realize the physical difficulties
of the reconquest of Burma and of other territory seized by the Japs early

in the war. It will be accomplished, but it needs careful training and preparation.

Food Problems

India, as one of the principal bases of the war against Japan must be stable and organized. To maintain stability we must solve our economic problems. Food, which is the most important of them, was so fully debated in both Houses at the last session of the Legislature that I need say little here about it. It is an All-India problem which my Government is trying to organize on an All-India basis. The key points in our plan are strict supervision of dealers under the Food Grains Control Order, avoidance of competitive buying in the procurement of Government requirements, statutory price control, control over movements and rationing in the larger towns. We rely for success on the administrative energy of the Provincial Governments—and on parallel action in the Indian States—and I am glad to say that during the past four months we have made progress. We are not out of the wood yet, but, backed by substantial imports, I believe we can improve our food position greatly in 1944. Our aim is not to favor the townsman at the expense of the cultivator but to see that staple food grains are available to all at prices at once fair to the cultivator and within the means of the poorer members of our population. The Grow More Food campaign has already produced valuable additions to our supplies and will, I am sure, produce more. There is likely to be a world shortage for some years after the war during the period of recovery and India must be prepared to stand by herself as far as possible. A bold agricultural policy will be necessary.

The situation in Bengal is special and has caused my Government grave anxiety. But there, too, conditions have improved and I trust will continue to improve. We must run no risk of last year's disaster being repeated.

The food problem is closely linked with the inflationary threat which we are determined to avert. The Finance Member will deal fully with this in introducing the Budget and I do not intend to speak now of the remedies he will propose. I need only say there has been a distinct improvement in the rate of savings and that we have made some progress in increasing the supply and bringing down the price, of consumers' goods manufactured in India, as well as of those imported from abroad. The new Department of Industries and Civil Supplies has formidable tasks ahead of it, but it has made a good start with standard cloth, i.e., release of woolen goods to the general public and control of prices of imported drugs.

The transportation system has been subjected to great strains which it has supported creditably, thanks to the fine work of our railwaymen, to whose steadiness and regularity we owe a great deal. I know that conditions of travel are not easy for the general public; I am afraid that is inevitable.

A good harvest, the presence of easier and better paid work than in the coalfields, difficulties about the supply of food and the epidemic of malaria combined to draw labor away from the mines and make their return slow. Labor conditions are beginning to return to normal, but there is much to be done to improve the raising and distribution of coal and conditions in the coalfields. My Government has appointed a Coal Commissioner to study all the factors bearing on production and movement and to see that the policy of the departments concerned is effectively carried out. We shall, I hope, effect considerable improvement, though it may take time.

Preparation for the Future

Unless and until some other form of Government can be established with general consent the present Government of India—mainly an Indian Government—will continue to carry out to the best of its ability—and I am satisfied it is very good ability—two primary purposes of any Government: the maintenance of law and order, the duties of internal administration and the preparation for the work ahead at the end of the war. The winning of this war is our first task, but it must not exclude preparation for the future.

We are approaching the end of the greatest of all wars. On the whole, in view of the scale of the dangers and disasters to the world as a whole India has come through it with less hurt than any other nation in the front line. And the war has, in many directions enhanced her opportunities and prospects. It has hastened her industrial development, it will increase food production, and it has strengthened her financial position. That it has not brought, as in certain other countries, increased unity of spirit and purpose is an unhappy circumstance which we all deplore. There is, however, nothing more unprofitable than to indulge in recriminations about the past. We must look forward and not back.

India's Economic Assets

The postwar world will be for India a world of great opportunities and great dangers, wherein she has an outstanding role to play. It is our present business to prepare her materially and morally for these testing years. Let us count our blessings. First, India's great undeveloped resources in agriculture and industry. Her soil is not yet cultivated to its full fruitfulness. With improvement in methods, in irrigation and fertilization, we can increase our food supply greatly, both in quality and quantity. We can much improve the breed of cattle. There is wide scope for development in India's main industry, agriculture.

There are also great commercial possibilities in India. There are mineral resources still undeveloped; there is abundant labor, a portion whereof has now attained a considerable degree of technical skill. India has many experienced and able men of business. Her financial position at the end of this war should be a good one. There are almost unlimited markets, internal and external, for her produce.

Such are her main economic assets. She has, however, also many economic difficulties and disabilities. The pressure of an increasing population, the small percentage of educated persons, the low standard of health services, the poor conditions wherein the greater part of both the agricultural and laboring populations live, the flagrant contrast between wealth and poverty, the inadequacy of communications all make the immensity of the problem which confronts India in raising her standard of living. Our task is to use, rightly and to the best advantage, her great economic assets; not to increase the wealth of a few, but to raise the many from poverty to a decent standard of comfort. A hard task indeed, but a noble task which calls from all for the spirit of co-operation, the spirit of hope and the spirit of sacrifice.

The present Government means to prepare the way for India's postwar development with all the earnestness of spirit and with all the resources, official and non-official, which it can enlist.

We have to consider first of all the "Winding Up" process that follows all wars—demobilization and resettlement of soldiers; the termination of wartime contracts with industry, and the orderly return of industrial labor to peace-time tasks; the dispersal of property and stocks of goods acquired for war purposes.

Plans for India's Economic Development

Our great aim must be to plan for economic and social development so as to raise our standards of living and general welfare. We must lift the poor man of India from poverty to security, from ill-health to vigor, from ignorance to understanding, and our rate of progress must no longer be at the bullock-cart standard, but at least at the pace of the handy and serviceable jeep.

As you know the development of India is being dealt with by a committee of my Executive Council, which is assisted by a number of other committees with a strong non-official element. I am considering means to strengthen our planning organization and to accelerate our progress. Much useful prelimi-nary work has been done and we have now reached the stage whereat, for certain subjects at least, as for example the demobilization and resettlement of soldiers, definite planning can begin in some detail. Over the greater part of the field our actual conduct after the war will depend to some extent, often to a great extent, on international factors—such as tariff policy and interna-tional currency—whereof we can at present know little. But we need not wait on these; on big questions of policy we have to make certain broad assump-tions and we are now deciding what our assumptions should be. Concurrently we are appointing individual development officers—not committees—to draw up outline plans for subjects such as electrification, industries, road develop-ment, irrigation and agriculture. We are also arranging to give opportunities for bodies of Indians connected with industry, the health services and other branches of development to visit the United Kingdom and, if required, the United States of America, to study for the benefit of India the latest develop-ments in their line of work. For the main social services we already have the Educational Adviser's memorandum and shall later have a report of the Bhore Committee on Medicine and Public Health. I believe that during 1944 our plans will take shape; they must cover the whole of India and other Provinces and the States will, I am sure, co-operate with the Center in pro-ducing the best and most comprehensive possible statement of our needs. I and my Government are in earnest in doing all we can to further India's progress after the war.

We welcome constructive suggestions; and my Government are examining with interest the plan recently propounded by seven prominent business men. The views of the authors of this plan on the objects to be achieved are in principle the same as those of my Government—we must work for a sub-stantial increase in the standards of living and social welfare. We may, on examination, differ on the methods to be employed, their relative importance to the plan as a whole, the part to be played by the State and by private enterprise, and the financial practicability of development on the scale con-templated within the time suggested by the authors; but our aim is similar and we welcome any sincere contribution to the problem that sets people thinking, and makes them realize both the possibilities and the pitfalls ahead of us.

As I said at Calcutta, it may in the initial stages be necessary for the Government of India and the Provincial Governments to devote a larger proportion of the resources available for economic development to agricultural and industrial development so as to increase the wealth of the country. But you may rest well assured that the vital matters of health and education will not be allowed to stand still, and that the recommendations of the Educational Adviser and the Bhore Committee will receive most earnest consideration.

India's Political Future

So much for India's economic future. It should be possible, if all goes well, to make good progress, and to lay plans well ahead. It is more difficult at present to plan India's political future in any detail. I can state to you what I know is the point of view of practically the whole of the British people and of His Majesty's present Government, and, I am confident, of any future Government of the United Kingdom. It is their genuine desire to see India a prosperous country, a united country, enjoying complete and unqualified self-government as a willing partner of the British Commonwealth. That last desire is not prompted by any sense of imperialism, or wish for domination, but by the real belief that in such an association India can best find security and help in the testing years ahead, and that peace in the East can so be best assured.

I am absolutely convinced, not only that the above represents the genuine desire of the British people, but that they wish to see an early realization of it. It is qualified only at present by the absolute determination to let nothing stand in the way of the earliest possible defeat of Germany and Japan; and by the resolve to see that in the solution of the constitutional problem full account is taken of the interests of those who have loyally supported us in this war, and at all other times—the soldiers who have served the common cause, people who have worked with us, the rulers and populations of States to whom we are pledged, and minorities who have trusted us to see that they get a fair deal. We are bound in justice, and in honor, in the interests of progress, to hand over India to an Indian rule which can maintain the peace and order and progress which we have endeavored to establish. I believe that we should take some risk to further this, but until the two main Indian Parties, at least, can come to terms, I do not see any immediate hope of progress.

The Cripps Offer Repeated

The Cripps offer was a bold and generous offer, and gave India a great opportunity to progress towards the solution of her problems. Be well assured that it was not made in any panic. I can say that with certainty, because I was Commander-in-Chief at the time, and in that position I know there was no panic in the Councils of those in authority, either in India or in the United Kingdom. We are not a people who panic easily in the face of danger. The offer was made in the hope that when the war had come so close to India, and threatened its national life, that it might arouse, as in other countries, a spirit of unity and co-operation that would have overridden political differences in the hour of danger. That hope was not fulfilled. There is no profit in recriminations about the reasons for the reaction to the Cripps offer. But since that offer has been stated more than once by His Majesty's Government to be still open, it may be as well to restate it here. Nearly two years have passed since the Cripps draft declaration was made public, but it stands forth today as a solemn pledge of His Majesty's Government that India shall have full control of her own destiny among the nations of the Commonwealth and the world. It declared in unmistakable terms that India should have the same status as the Dominions or the United Kingdom itself, under a Constitution of her own devising. It also embodied a constructive suggestion by His Majesty's Government to aid India in the attainment of that status. The proposals made provision for the setting up of a Constitution-making body, representative both of British India and the Indian States, and His Majesty's Government undertook to accept and implement the Constitution framed by this body, subject to two conditions. First, the Declaration recognized the right of any province not to accede to the Indian Union. Such provinces could either retain their present constitutional position; or, if they so desired, His Majesty's Government would agree with them upon a new Constitution giving them the same status as the new Indian Union itself. Second, the Declaration made provision for the signing of a treaty between His Majesty's Government and the Constitution-making body to provide for matters arising out of the transfer of power, including the protection of racial and religious minorities. It was made clear beyond all doubt that this treaty would not impose any restrictions upon the power of the Indian Union to decide its future relationship with the other States of the British Commonwealth of Nations.

The Cripps offer was an offer to India of full self-government, of the right to frame her own Constitution, and even the right, if she so desired, to sever her partnership with the British Commonwealth. Because of the military situation—which still obtains—it was provided that, pending the framing of a future Constitution, the direction of defense should remain the responsibility of His Majesty's Government, but it was contemplated that the Indian leaders should be associated not only with the Government of their country—under the exisiting Constitution, necessarily, till a new Constitution was framed and accepted—but with the councils of the Commonwealth and the United Nations.

The offer of co-operation in the Government on this basis by the leaders of Indian opinion is still open to those who have a genuine desire to further the prosecution of the war and the welfare of India. But the demand for the release of those leaders who are in detention is utterly barren until there is some sign on their part of willingness to co-operate. It needs no consultation with any one or anything but his own conscience for any one of those under detention to decide whether he will withdraw from the "Quit India" resolution and the policy which had such tragic consequences, and will co-operate in the great tasks ahead.

Political Unity and Geographic Unity

Not least of those tasks is a preliminary examination of the Constitutional problems of India by an authoritative body of Indians. We should be ready to give this body every assistance which it might desire in carrying out its task. For the present the country's Government must continue to be a joint British and Indian affair—with the ultimate responsibility still remaining with the British Parliament, though it is exercised through a predominantly Indian Executive—until it can be transferred to the fresh Constitution. But framing that future Constitution is essentially and properly an Indian responsibility. Until they can agree on its form, the transfer of power cannot be made. We offered a suggestion in the Cripps proposals which may or may not have been suitable. If Indians can devise a method which will produce agreement more readily, so much the better. If I may offer a personal opinion born of some experience, the smaller the body which discusses a difficult and controversial problem, the more likely it is that a profitable solution will emerge. On the main problem of Indian unity, the differences between Hindu and Muslim, I can only say this—you cannot alter geography. From a point of view of Defense, of relations with the outside world and of many internal and external economic problems, India is a natural unit. What arrangements you decide to make for the two great communities and certain other important minorities, as well as the Indian States, to live within that unit and make the best use of its wealth and opportunities is for Indians to decide. That two communities and even two nations can make arrangements to live together in spite of differing cultures or religions, history provides many examples. Solutions of the problem have varied. England and Scotland after centuries of strife arrived at absolute union; in Canada, British and French elements reached federal agreement which operates satisfactorily; French, Italian and German elements in Switzerland agreed on a different form of federation. In all the above there were religious as well as racial differences. In the United States many elements, racial and religious, have fused into one great nation with a federal structure after the bitter experience of a disastrous civil war. In Ireland conflicting elements have so far failed to unite and Ireland has a sort of Pakistan, though the analogy of course is only relative. The Soviet Union in Russia seems to have devised a new modification of its already flexible system, which will also no doubt repay careful study. These examples are before India for her constitutionalists to study. It is for her to say which will most nearly fulfill her own needs. But no man can alter geography.

I have spoken to you frankly and bluntly as I have been taught to speak as a soldier. Let me restate the main principles which guide me in my heavy task and responsibility. Our primary object, overriding all others, must be not merely to make certain of winning the war—the United Nations have already done that by endurance through adversities, by sacrifice of comforts, by unity of spirit and by unremitting hard work—but to win it as speedily as possible and with the least drain on future prosperity. That is the great administrative task. The second task is to prepare for the future, and politically we cannot settle the future of this country without the full co-operation of the British and Indian peoples, and the co-operation within India of Hindus, Muslims and other minority groups and of the Indian States.

I am conscious of the co-operation of many elements in this country— eminent and patriotic Indians of my Executive Council and of Provincial Governments; the Fighting Forces of India—the largest forces ever raised in history by voluntary enlistment; leaders and workers of industry who have made such a contribution to the war; Rulers of the Indian States. All these place India first in their thoughts and aims, but they have a practical view of the necessity for co-operation to realize progress. There is an important element which stands aloof. I recognize how much ability and high-mindedness it contains; but I deplore its present policy and methods as barren and unpractical. I should like to have the co-operation of this element in solving the present and future problems of India. If its leaders feel that they cannot consent to take part in the present Government of India, they may still be able to assist in considering the future problems. But I see no reason to release those responsible for the declaration of August 8, 1942, until I am convinced that their policy of non-co-operation and even of obstruction has been withdrawn, not in sackcloth and ashes—that helps no one—but in recognition of their mistaken and unprofitable policy.

Fine Administrative Services

During the last three months I have visited seven out of eleven of the main provinces of British India and two Indian States. I am setting out tomorrow to visit two more provinces. I have seen something of rural life as well as of towns. I wonder whether in considering India's economic and political problems we always remember how much of India is countryside and how little urban, how many live in villages, and how few, comparatively, in towns. I am impressed everywhere by the work which is being done for the betterment of India both by officials and non-officials. India has a very small official administration for its size, but it has very fine Services; the way in which they have stood up to the additional strain of work thrown on them by the war has been admirable. There are also very large numbers of non-official bodies and persons who are doing great work for India. There is much good will and wisdom in India if we can harness it to the common purpose.

I have no desire to make insidious comparisons, but I do feel it worth while to point out that a coalition government by Indians for Indians is not an impossible ideal. It is being carried out at the Centre without friction; it has been carried on for nearly seven years with conspicuous success in the Punjab. Thanks to the leadership of men of good sense, good will and good courage the affairs of that province have prospered with a minimum of communal friction; they have administered their province in the interests of the province, but also with regard to the interests of India and the war effort of the United Nations to which the Punjab has made so striking a contribution. I will make bold enough to say that had all the provinces worked the 1935 Act in the same spirit and with the same efficiency India would now be very close to complete self-government.

"We Have Come a Long Way Together"

We have come a long way together up a steep and difficult mountain at the summit of which lies complete Indian self-government. We are almost within sight of the top, but as with most mountain climbs that are worth doing, the final cliffs are the steepest and most baffling of all. At such a time it is doubly necessary to test each handhold and foothold and to cut adequate steps in the slippery ice so that the whole party roped together may not fall back in ruin. It is not the moment that prudent mountaineers choose to unrope, to dismiss their guides and, after a violent dispute, to take separate routes towards different peaks. We must go on together. We cannot halt too long at the heights which we have reached and we cannot with honor or safety turn back. We may have to pause to reconnoiter or cut steps but we must endeavor to go on climbing even though the rate may seem slow to impatient watchers or to the climbers themselves.

Finally, we must keep in mind the splendor of the view that lies before us when the summit is reached—the prospect of India at peace within herself, a partner in our great Commonwealth of Nations, mother of great people, the shield for peace in the East, busy and prosperous yet with leisure to develop the thought and poetry and art which are the real salt of life and of which India has already contributed much to the world. It is not an immediate vision, but I do not think it unattainable if we work together with patience, good sense and good will.

I believe firmly in the future of India. I am a sincere friend of India and should like to help her to political advance, but my military training has made me quite certain that no objective is ever gained without the fullest measure of co-operation from all concerned.

PRESIDENT ROOSEVELT'S EXECUTIVE ORDER ESTABLISHING THE SURPLUS WAR PROPERTY ADMINISTRATION

February 21, 1944 [1]

By virtue of the authority vested in me by the Constitution and Statutes of the United States, particularly the First War Powers Act, 1941, as President of the United States, and as Commander-in-Chief of the Army and Navy, it is hereby ordered as follows:

(1) There is hereby established in the Office of War Mobilization, the Surplus War Property Administration (hereinafter referred to as the "Administration"), the powers and functions of which, subject to the general supervision of the Director of War Mobilization, shall be exercised by a Surplus War Property Administrator (hereinafter referred to as the "Administrator"), to be appointed by the Director of War Mobilization.

(2) With the assistance of a Surplus War Property Policy Board, composed of a representative from each of the following: State Department, Treasury Department, War Department, Navy Department, Justice Department, Reconstruction Finance Corporation, Smaller War Plants Corporation, United States Maritime Commission, War Production Board, Bureau of the Budget, War Food Administration, Federal Works Agency, Civil Aeronautics Board, and the Foreign Economic Administration, it shall be the function of the Administration, to the full extent that such matters are provided for or permitted by law:

Scope of the Agency

(a) To have general supervision and direction of the handling and disposition of surplus war property.

(b) To have general supervision and direction of the transfer of any surplus war property in the possession of any Government agency to any other Government agency whenever in the judgment of the Administration such transfer is appropriate.

(c) Unless otherwise directed by the Director of War Mobilization, to assign, so far as it is deemed feasible by the Administration, surplus war property for disposition, as follows: Consumer goods to the procurement division of the Department of the Treasury; capital and producers' goods, including plants, equipment, materials, scrap and other industrial property, to a subsidiary of the Reconstruction Finance Corporation, created pursuant to Section 5D (3) of the Reconstruction Finance Act, as amended; ships and maritime property to the United States Maritime Commission; and food to the War Food Administration; provided that surplus war property to be disposed of outside the United States, unless otherwise directed by the Director of War Mobilization, shall be assigned, so far as it is deemed feasible by the Administration, to the Foreign Economic Administration.

[1] *New York Times.*

Broad Functions Conferred

(3) All functions, powers, and duties relating to the transfer or disposition of surplus war property, heretofore conferred by law on any Government agency may, to the extent necessary to carry out the provisions of this order, be exercised also by the Administration.

(4) The Administrator may prescribe regulations and issue directions necessary to effectuate the purposes of this order; and no Government agency shall transfer or dispose of surplus war property in contravention thereof. Each Government agency shall submit such information and reports with respect to surplus war property and in such form and at such times as the Administrator shall direct. When requested by the Administration, a Government agency shall execute such documents for the transfer of title or for any other purpose or take such steps as the Administration shall determine to be necessary or proper to transfer or dispose of surplus war property or otherwise to carry out the provisions of this order.

(5) The Administrator may perform the functions and exercise the powers, authority, and discretion conferred on the Administration by this order by such officials and such agencies and in such manner as the Administrator, subject to the provisions of this order, may determine. In carrying out the purposes of this order, the Administration may utilize the services of any other Government agency. The Administration, within the limit of funds which may be made available, may employ necessary personnel and make provision for supplies, facilities, and services necessary to discharge the responsibilities of the Administration.

(6) As used in this order:

(a) "Government agency" means any executive department, independent establishment, agency, commission, board, bureau, division, administration, office, service, independent regulatory commission or board, and any Government-owned or Government-controlled corporation.

(b) "Surplus war property" means any property, real or personal, including but not limited to plants, facilities, equipment, machines, accessories, parts, assemblies, products, commodities, materials, and supplies in the possession of or controlled by any Government agency whether new or used, in use or in storage, which are in excess of the needs of such agency or are not required for the performance of the duties and functions of such agency and which are determined, subject to the authority of the Office of War Mobilization, to be surplus by such agency.

All prior executive orders, in so far as they are in conflict herewith, are amended accordingly.

U. S. NOTE TO IRELAND ON IRISH NEUTRALITY

February 21, 1944 [1]

United States Request for the Removal of Axis Diplomatic and Consular Representatives from Ireland

The Secretary of State announced on March 10, 1944 that the American Government on February 21 had made a request to the Irish Government

[1] State Department Bulletin.

for the removal of Axis consular and diplomatic representatives whose presence in Ireland must be regarded as constituting a danger to the lives of American soldiers and to the success of the Allied military operations. The Irish Government has now replied that it is impossible for it to comply with this request. The text of the note delivered to Prime Minister de Valera on February 21, 1944 by the American Minister in Dublin, on instructions from the Department, reads as follows:

"Your Excellency will recall that in your speech at Cork delivered on the fourteenth of December, 1941 you expressed sentiments of special friendship for the American people on the occasion of their entry into the present war and closed by saying, 'The policy of the state remains unchanged. We can only be a friendly neutral.' As you will also recall, extracts of this speech were transmitted to the President by your Minister in Washington. The President, while conveying his appreciation for this expression of friendship, stated his confidence that the Irish Government and the Irish people, whose freedom is at stake no less than ours, would know how to meet their responsibilities in this situation.

"It has become increasingly apparent that despite the declared desire of the Irish Government that its neutrality should not operate in favor of either of the belligerents, it has in fact operated and continues to operate in favor of the Axis powers and against the United Nations on whom your security and the maintenance of your national economy depend. One of the gravest and most inequitable results of this situation is the opportunity for highly organized espionage which the geographical position of Ireland affords the Axis and denies the United Nations. Situated as you are in close proximity to Britain, divided only by an intangible boundary from Northern Ireland, where are situated important American bases, with continuous traffic to and from both countries, Axis agents enjoy almost unrestricted opportunity for bringing military information of vital importance from Great Britain and Northern Ireland into Ireland and from there transmitting it by various routes and methods to Germany. No opportunity corresponding to this is open to the United Nations, for the Axis has no military dispositions which may be observed from Ireland.

"We do not question the good faith of the Irish Government in its efforts to suppress Axis espionage. Whether or to what extent it has succeeded in preventing acts of espionage against American shipping and American forces in Great Britain and Northern Ireland is, of course, impossible to determine with certainty. Nevertheless it is a fact that German and Japanese diplomatic and consular representatives still continue to reside in Dublin and enjoy the special privileges and immunities customarily accorded to such officials. That Axis representatives in neutral countries use these special privileges and immunities as a cloak for espionage activities against the United Nations has been demonstrated over and over again. It would be naïve to assume that Axis agencies have not exploited conditions to the full in Ireland as they have in other countries. It is our understanding that the German Legation in Dublin, until recently at least, has had in its possession a radio sending set. This is evidence of the intention of the German Government to use this means of communication. Supporting evidence is furnished by the two parachutists equipped wih radio sending sets recently dropped on your territory by German planes.

"As you know from common report, United Nations' military operations are in preparation in both Britain and Northern Ireland. It is vital that information from which may be deduced their nature and direction should not reach the enemy. Not only the success of the operations but the lives of thousands of United Nations' soldiers are at stake.

"We request therefore, that the Irish Government take appropriate steps for the recall of German and Japanese representatives in Ireland. We should be lacking in candor if we did not state our hope that this action will take the form of severance of all diplomatic relations between Ireland and these two countries. You will, of course, readily understand the compelling reasons why we ask as an absolute minimum the removal of these Axis representatives whose presence in Ireland must inevitably be regarded as constituting a danger to the lives of American soldiers and to the success of Allied military operations.

"It is hardly necessary to point out that time is of extreme importance and that we trust Your Excellency will favor us with your reply at your early convenience."

PRESIDENT ROOSEVELT'S MESSAGE TO CONGRESS VETOING THE TAX BILL

February 22, 1944 [1]

I return herewith, without my approval, H. R. 3687, entitled "An Act to Provide Revenue, and for Other Purposes."

I regret that I found it necessary in the midst of this great war to be compelled to do this in what I regard as the public interest.

Many months ago, after careful examination of the finances of the nation, I asked the Congress for legislation to raise $10,500,000,000 over and above the existing revenue system. Since then persons prominent in our national life have stated in no uncertain terms that my figure was too low.

The measure before me purports to increase the national revenue by a little over $2,000,000,000. Actually, however, the bill in its net results will enrich the Treasury by less than $1,000,000,000.

As a tax bill, therefore, I am compelled to decide that it is wholly ineffective toward that end.

More specifically the bill purports to provide $2,100,000,000 in new revenues. At the same time it cancels out automatic increases in the social security tax which would yield $1,100,000,000. In addition it grants relief from existing taxes which would cost the Treasury at least $150,000,000 and possibly much more.

In this respect it is not a tax bill, but a tax relief bill providing relief not for the needy but for the greedy.

The elimination of automatic increases provided in the Social Security Law comes at a time when industry and labor are best able to adjust themselves to such increases. These automatic increases are required to meet the claims that are being built up against the social security fund. Such a postponement does not seem wise.

The clause relating to renegotiating of war contracts terminates the present renegotiation authority on Dec. 31 of this year. This seems unwise at this time because no person can at present determine what a renegotiation time limit should be. More experience is needed. The formal right of appeal to the tax court that is granted by this bill is an inept provision. The present tax

[1] *New York Times.*

court exists for a wholly different purpose and does not have the personnel or the time to assume this heavy load.

The bill is replete with provisions which not only afford indefensible special privileges to favored groups but set dangerous precedents for the future. This tendency toward the embodiment of special privileges in our legislation is in itself sufficiently dangerous to counterbalance the loss of a very inadequate sum in additional revenues.

Among these special privileges are:

(a) Permission for corporations reorganized in bankruptcy to retain the high excess profits credit and depreciation basis attributable to the contributions of stockholders who are usually eliminated in the reorganization. This privilege inures to the benefit of bondholders who, in many cases, have purchased their bonds in the speculative market for far less than their face value. It may open the door to further windfall profits in this market because of the undeserved benefit received by reorganized corporations.

(b) Percentage depletion allowances, questionable in any case, are now extended to such minerals as vermiculite, potash, feldspar, mica, talc, lepidolite, barite and spodumene. In the case of some of these minerals the War Production Board refused to certify that current output was inadequate for war needs.

(c) The lumber industry is permitted to treat income from the cutting of timber, including selective logging, as a capital gain rather than annual income. As a grower and seller of timber, I think that timber should be treated as a crop and therefore as income when it is sold. This would encourage reforestation.

(d) Natural gas pipe lines are exempted from the excess profits tax without justification and in a manner which might well lead oil companies to request similar treatment for their pipe lines.

(e) Commercial airlines are granted an unjustifiable extension of the tax subsidy on their airmail contracts.

It has been suggested by some that I should give my approval to this bill on the ground that having asked the Congress for a loaf of bread to take care of this war for the sake of this and succeeding generations, I should be content with a small piece of crust. I might have done so if I had not noted that the small piece of crust contained so many extraneous and inedible materials.

In regard to that part of the bill which relates to wholly unobjectionable tax increases, may I respectfully suggest to the Congress that the excise taxes can easily and quickly be levied. This can be accomplished by the passage of a simple joint resolution enacting those provisions of the bill which increase the excise taxes. I should be glad to approve such a measure. This would preserve the principal revenue provisions of the bill without the objectionable features I have criticized.

In another most important respect this bill would disappoint and fail the American taxpayers. Every one of them, including ourselves, is disappointed, confused and bewildered over the practical results of last year's tax bill. The Ruml plan was not the product of this Administration. It resulted from a widespread campaign based on the attractive slogan of "pay-as-you-go." But, as was said many years ago in the State of New York in regard to that same slogan, "You don't pay and you don't go."

The nation will readily understand that it is not the fault of the Treasury Department that the income taxpayers are flooded with forms to fill out which are so complex that even certified public accountants cannot interpret them. No, it is squarely the fault of the Congress of the United States in using language in drafting the law which not even a dictionary or a thesaurus can make clear.

The American taxpayer has been promised of late that tax laws and returns will be drastically simplified. This bill does not make good that promise. It ignores the most obvious step toward simplifying taxes by failing to eliminate the clumsy Victory tax. For fear of dropping from the tax rolls those taxpayers who are at the bottom of the income scale, the bill retains the Victory tax—while at the same time it grants extensive concessions to many special interest groups.

The suggestion of withholding at graduated rates, which would relieve millions of people of the task of filing declarations of estimated income, was not adopted.

I trust, therefore, that the Congress, after all these delays, will act as quickly as possible for simplification of the tax laws, which will make possible the simplification of the forms and computations now demanded of the individual taxpayers. These taxpayers, now engaged in an effort to win the greatest war this nation has ever faced, are not in a mood to study higher mathematics.

The responsibility of the Congress of the United States is to supply the Government of the United States as a whole with adequate revenue for wartime needs, to provide fiscal support for the stabilization program, to hold firm against the tide of special privileges, and to achieve real simplicity for millions of small income taxpayers.

In the interest of strengthening the home front, in the interest of speeding the day of victory, I urge the earliest possible action.

PRIME MINISTER CHURCHILL'S SPEECH IN COMMONS ON THE MILITARY AND POLITICAL SCENE

February 22, 1944 [1]

This is no time for sorrow or rejoicing. This is a time for preparation, effort, and resolve. The war is still going on. I have never taken the view that the end of the war in Europe is at hand or that Hitler is about to collapse, and I have certainly given no guarantee, or even held out any expectation, that the year 1944 would see the end of the European war. Nor have I given any guarantee the other way.

On the whole my information—and I have a good deal—goes to show that Hitler and his police are still in full control and that the Nazi party and the generals have decided to hang together. The strength of the German Army is about 300 divisions, though many of these are substantially reduced in numbers. The fighting quality of the troops is high. The German General Staff system, which we failed to liquidate after the last war, represents an order comprising many thousands of highly trained officers and a school of doctrine of long unbroken continuity. It possesses great skill both in handling troops in action and in their rapid movement from place to place. The recent fighting in Italy should leave no possible doubt on these points.

It is true that the results of our bombing have had a noteworthy effect

[1] British Speeches of the Day.

on German munitions production. In the people they have produced a dull apathy, which also affects munitions production and all A.R.P. services. The splendid victories of our Soviet Allies on the Eastern front are inflicting immense losses upon the enemy. The fact that so many of the enemy's divisions have been drawn into Italy and into Yugoslavia, while other large bodies of his troops are held in France and the Low Countries by the fear of invasion, has been a help to these victories.

Moreover, the Anglo-American bombing of Germany, absorbing as it does about 3,000,000 Germans, has drawn, together with other British and American activities, four-fifths of the German fighter force to the British and American front—four-fifths of the fighter force and, I believe, a majority probably even of the bombers are against us and our American Allies. This also has been of assistance to the Soviet Union, and I think these statements should be made in justice to the Western Allies. They in no way detract from the glory of the Russian arms.

It must also be borne in mind, in surveying the general foundations of the scene as we see it today, that as the German troops retreat westwards they will find many opportunities of narrowing their front, and that if they choose to cut their losses in the Balkans or in the Italian peninsula at any time, a considerable number of divisions can be made available for the purpose of strengthening their central reserve. It is far from my wish to make any boastful statements about the part which this island is playing in the war. It has, however, been borne in on me that the interests of the alliance as a whole may be prejudiced if its other members are left in ignorance of the British share in the great events which are unfolding. The Dominions also have the right to know that the Mother Country is playing its part.

I think it is therefore my duty to state a few facts which are not perhaps generally realized. For instance, since January 1, 1943, up to the present time—the middle of February—ships of the Royal Navy and aircraft of the Royal Air Force—that is to say, the forces of the Mother Country only— have sunk more than half the U-boats of which we have certain proof in the shape of living prisoners, and they have also destroyed forty per cent of the very large number of other U-boats, of which either corpses or fragments provide definite evidence of destruction. Again on the naval side, apart from enemy U-boats, we have sunk by British action alone since January 1, 1943, nineteen enemy warships and also a large number of E-boats, escort vessels, minesweepers, and other auxiliaries. British action has been predominantly responsible for sinking during this period 316 merchant ships, aggregating 835,000 tons.

In that same period 7,677 officers and men of the Royal Navy and about 4,200 merchant navy officers and men have lost their lives in British ships. This last, however, does not at all represent the total war sacrifice to date of our merchant seamen, because matters have improved very much lately. Since the beginning of the war the proportion of merchant seamen hailing from these islands alone who have been lost at sea on their vital duty has been about one-fifth of the average number engaged in this service.

The total of personnel, officers and men of the Royal Navy lost since the war started is just over thirty per cent of its pre-war strength, the figures being 41,000 killed out of 133,000, which was its total strength at the outbreak of war. Since January 1, 1943, ships of the Royal Navy have bombarded the enemy's coasts on 716 occasions. In the same period we have lost in action or had disabled for more than a year—serious disablement—ninety-five ships of war.

Turning to the air, the honor of bombing Berlin has fallen almost entirely to us. Up to the present we have delivered the main attack upon Germany. Excluding Dominion and Allied squadrons working with the Royal Air Force, the British islanders have lost 38,300 pilots and air crews killed and 10,400 missing, and over 10,000 aircraft—that is, since the beginning of the war—and they have made nearly 900,000 sorties into the North European theater.

As for the Army, the British Army was little more than a police force in 1939, yet they have fought in every part of the world—in Norway, France, Holland, Belgium, Egypt, Eritrea, Abyssinia, Somaliland, Madagascar, Syria, North Africa, Persia, Sicily, Italy, Greece, Crete, Burma, Malaya, and Hong Kong. I cannot in this speech attempt to describe these many campaigns, so infinitely varied in their characteristics, but history will record how much the contribution of our soldiers has been beyond all proportion to the available manpower of these islands.

The Anglo-American air attack upon Germany must be regarded as our chief offensive effort up to the present time. Till the middle of 1943 we had by far the largest forces in action. As the result of the enormous transportations across the Atlantic which have been made during 1943, the United States bomber force in this island now begins to surpass our own and will soon be substantially greater still, I rejoice to say. The efforts of the two forces fit well together, and, according to all past standards, our effort is in itself prodigious.

Take the latest example. During the forty-eight hours beginning at 3 a.m. on February 20, four great raids were made upon Germany. The first was against Leipzig on the night of 19–20 by the Royal Air Force, when nearly 1,000 machines were dispatched, of which seventy-nine were lost. On Sunday morning a tremendous American raid, nearly 1,000 strong, escorted by an even greater number of fighters, American and British, but mostly American, set out for German towns, including Leipzig, in broad daylight. The losses in this raid were greatly reduced by the fact that the enemy fighters had been scattered beforehand by the British operations of the night before. The fighters descend at bases other than their own and cannot be so readily handled on a second rapidly ensuing occasion, and the full effect of the American precision bombing was therefore realized.

Following hard upon this, on the night of 20–21 another British raid was delivered, this time on Stuttgart, in very great strength—600 or 700. The effect of the preceding twenty-four hours' bombing relieved this third raid to a very large extent. Finally, the American force went out on Monday, again in full scale, and drove home in the most effective manner our joint air superiority over the enemy. Taking them together, these four raids, in which over 9,000 tons of bombs were dropped by the two Allied and complementary air forces, constitute the most violent attacks which have yet been made on Germany, and they also prove the value of saturation in every aspect of the air war. That aspect will steadily increase as our forces develop and as the American forces come into their full scope and scale.

The spring and summer will see a vast increase in the force of the attacks directed upon all military targets in Germany and in German-occupied countries. Long-range bombing from Italy will penetrate effectively the southern parts of Germany. We look for very great restriction and dislocation of the entire German munitions supply, no matter how far the factories have been withdrawn. In addition, the precision of the American daylight attacks produces exceptional results upon particular points, not only in clear daylight, but now, thanks to the development of navigational aids, through cloud.

The whole of this air offensive constitutes the foundation upon which our plans for oversea invasion stand. Scales and degrees of attack will be reached far beyond the dimensions of anything which has yet been employed or indeed imagined. The idea that we should better or further restrict the use of this prime instrument for shortening the war will not be accepted by the Governments of the Allies. The proper course for German civilians and non-combatants is to quit the centers of munition production and take refuge in the countryside. We intend to make war production in its widest sense impossible in all German cities, towns, and factory centers.

Retaliation by the enemy has so far been modest, but we must expect it to increase. Hitler has great need to exaggerate his counter-attacks in order to placate his formerly deluded population, but besides these air attacks there is no doubt that the Germans are preparing on the French shore new means of attack on this country, either by pilotless aircraft or possibly rockets, or both, on a considerable scale. We have long been watching this with the utmost vigilance. We are striking at all evidences of these preparations on occasions when the weather is suitable for such action, and to the maximum extent possible without detracting from the strategic offensive against Germany. An elaborate scheme of bombing priorities, upon which a large band of highly skilled American and British officers are constantly at work in accordance with the directions given by the combined Chiefs of Staff in Washington, has governed our action for some time past, and is continually kept up to date and in relation to our strategic needs and aims. I do not believe that a better machinery could be devised.

It is always flexible enough to allow us to turn aside for some particularly tempting objective, as, for instance, Sofia, the capital of caitiff Bulgaria. The weather, of course, remains the final factor in the decision where our day or night activities shall be employed. That leaves very great responsibility in the hands of the officers who actually handle these great masses, enormous masses, of aircraft.

The use of our air power also affects the general war situation by the toll which it takes of the enemy's fighter aircraft both by day and night, but especially by the Americans by day, because they have very great actions with their formations of Flying Fortresses with enemy fighter aircraft. Already we have seen the German air program concentrated mainly on fighters, thus indicating how much they have been thrown onto the defensive in the air.

Now this new German fighter strength is being remorselessly worn down both in the air and in the factories, which are the objectives of the continuous attack. Every opportunity is and will be sought by us to force the enemy to expend and exhaust his fighter aircraft strength. Our production of aircraft —fighters and bombers—judged by every possible test, already far exceeds the Germans'. The Russian production is about equal to ours. The American production is double or treble the German production.

When I speak of production I mean not only that of aircraft, not only that of the machines, but of all that vast organization of training schools and ancillary services which minister to air power, and without whose efficiency air power could not manifest itself. What the experiences of Germany will be when her fighter defense has been almost completely eliminated and aircraft can go all over the country, by day or night, with nothing to fear, but the *Flak* —the anti-aircraft—has yet to be seen.

The same is true of the air power of Japan. That also is now being overmatched and worn down, and the production is incomparably small compared with that of the great Powers whom Japan has assailed. Whereas on former occasions when I have addressed the House and tried to give a general picture of the war in its scale and proportion, its structure and proportion, I have always set the war against the U-boat menace in the forefront, I deliberately, on this occasion, gave the primacy to the great developments in air power which have been achieved and are to be expected. This air power was the weapon which both the marauding States selected as their main tool of conquest. This was the sphere in which they were to triumph. This was the method by which the nations were to be subjugated to their rule. I shall not moralize further than to say that there is a strange, stern justice in the long swing of events.

Our other great joint Anglo-American offensive is in Italy. Many people have been disappointed with the progress there since the capture of Naples in October. This has been due to the extremely bad weather which marks the winter in these supposedly sunshine lands and which this year has been worse than usual. Secondly, and far more, it is because the Germans bit by bit have been drawn down into Italy and have decided to make extreme exertions for the retention of the city of Rome. In October, they began to move a number of divisions southwards from the valley of the Po and to construct a winter line south of Rome in order to confront and delay the advance of the Fifth and Eighth Armies under General Alexander.

We were, therefore, committed to a frontal advance in extremely mountainous country which gave every advantage to the defense. All rivers flow at right angles to our march, and the violent rains, this year above the normal, often turned these rivers into raging torrents, sweeping away all military bridges which had been thrown across them and sometimes leaving part of the assaulting force already committed to the attack, on the far side and beyond the reach of immediate reinforcements or support.

In addition to the difficulties I have mentioned, there has been the need to build up a very large supply of stores and vehicles of all kinds in Italy, and also the strategic air force which is being developed for the attack on southern Germany has made extremely large priority inroads upon our transportation, and especially upon those forms of transportation which are most in demand. An immense amount of work has, however, been done, and the results will become apparent later on.

Among the Allies we have, of course, much the larger army in Italy. The American Air Force in the Mediterranean, on the other hand, is larger than the British, and the two together possess an enormous superiority, quantitative and also, we believe, qualitative, over the enemy. We have, also, of course, the complete command of the seas where an American squadron is actively working with the British Fleet. Such being the position, many people wondered why it was not possible to make a large, amphibious turning movement either on the eastern or western side of Italy to facilitate the forward advance of the army.

The need for this was, of course, obvious to all the commanders, British and American, but the practicability of carrying it into effect depended upon this effort being properly fitted in with the general Allied program for the year. This program comprises larger issues and forces than those with which we are concerned in Italy. The difficulties which had hitherto obstructed action were, I am glad to say, removed at the conferences which were held at Carthage at Christmas and at Marrakesh in January. The conclusions were approved step by step by the President of the United States and the combined Chiefs of Staff.

All that the Supreme War direction could do was done by the first week in

January. Preparations had already been begun in anticipation of the final surmounting of difficulties and January 22 was fixed as the zero day by General Alexander, on whom rests the responsibility for fighting the battle. It was certainly no light matter to launch this considerable army—40,000 or 50,000 men in the first instance, with all the uncertainty of winter weather and all the unknowable strength of enemy fortifications—to launch it out upon the seas.

The operation itself was a model of combined work. The landing was virtually unopposed. Subsequent events did not, however, take the course which had been hoped or planned. In the upshot we got a great army ashore equipped with masses of artillery, tanks, and very many thousands of vehicles, and our troops moving inland came into contact with the enemy.

The German reactions to this descent have been remarkable. Hitler has apparently resolved to defend Rome with the same obstinacy which he showed in Stalingrad, in Tunisia, and, recently, in the Dnieper Bend. No fewer than seven extra German divisions were brought rapidly down from France, Northern Italy, and Yugoslavia, and a determined attempt has been made to destroy the bridgehead and drive us into the sea. Battles of prolonged and intense fierceness and fury have been fought. At the same time the American and British Fifth Army to the southward is pressing forward with all its strength. Another battle is raging there.

On both fronts there has been in the last week a most severe and continuous engagement, very full accounts of which have been given every day in the Press and in the official *communiqués*. Up to the present moment the enemy has sustained very heavy losses, but has not shaken the resistance of the bridgehead army. The forces are well matched, though we are definitely the stronger in artillery and armor, and, of course, when the weather is favorable, our air power plays an immense part. General Alexander has probably seen more fighting against the Germans than any living British commander and there is General Freyberg, who is also in the fray. But General Alexander says that the bitterness and fierceness of the fighting going on both at the bridgehead and at the Cassino front surpasses all his previous experience. He even used in one message to me the word "terrific." On the southern front, the Cassino front, British, American, Dominion, Indian, French, and Polish troops are fighting side by side in a noble comradeship. Their leaders are confident of final success. I can say no more than what I have said for I would not attempt to venture on a more confident prediction, but their leaders are confident and the troops are in the highest spirit of offensive vigor.

On broad grounds of strategy, Hitler's decision to send into the south of Italy as many as eighteen divisions, involving with their maintenance troops probably something like half a million men—half a million Germans—and his decision there in Italy to make a large secondary front is not unwelcome to the Allies. We must fight the Germans somewhere unless we are to stand still and watch the Russians. This wearing battle in Italy occupies troops which could not be occupied in other greater operations and it is an effective prelude to them. We have sufficient forces at our disposal in Africa to nourish the struggle as fast as they can be transported across the Mediterranean. The weather is likely to improve as the spring approaches, and as the skies clear the Allied air power will reach its fullest manifestations.

This time last year, February 22 to a day, when I remember I was ill in bed, I was deeply anxious about the situation in Tunisia, where we had just sustained an unpleasant check at the Kasserine Pass, but I placed my confidence then in General Alexander and in the British, American, and French troops who were engaged in the battle. I placed my confidence then in that leader and those troops and that is how I feel about it now.

In the discussions at Cairo and during my enforced stay amid the ruins of Carthage I was able by correspondence to settle with the President and with the War Cabinet here the remodelling of the commands for our joint operations in the Mediterranean and elsewhere. The principle which should obviously be followed between two allies working together as closely as we and the United States is that the nationality of the commander should generally follow the majority of the troops in any theater. In General Maitland Wilson and General Alexander we have at once the supreme commander in the Mediterranean and the fighting head of the Army in Italy. We and our American Ally have full confidence in these officers under whom the United States General Devers and General Clark, the most daring and gallant leader of the Fifth Army, are the corresponding American chiefs.

In Great Britain, on the other hand, where forces are being assembled for future operations of the greatest magnitude, General Eisenhower, with whom we have worked for so long, so happily, and so successfully, has been placed at the summit of the war direction, with Air Chief Marshal Tedder as his deputy and with his brilliant United States Chief of Staffs, the trusty General Bedell Smith—these are the central figures of this command under whom many distinguished commanders, British and American, are serving, including General Montgomery, and these officers will, when the time comes, and in accordance with the arrangements which have been made, lead our armies to the liberation of Europe.

As certain statements have been made in America—unofficial statements —about the relative strengths of the armies to be employed from here, I think, it is necessary to state that the British and American Armies at the outset of the struggle will be approximately equal, but that if its duration is prolonged the continuous flow of the American build-up at an enormous rate will naturally give them that superiority of numbers which would be expected from the great numbers which they dispose and which they desire above all things to bring into contact as speedily as possible with the enemy. Hence it is right that the Supreme Command should go to the commanders of the United States.

I would turn aside for one moment just to emphasize how perfect is the cooperation between the commanders of the British and the American Armies. Nothing like it has ever been seen before in allies. No doubt language is a great help, but there is more in it than that. In all previous alliances the staffs have worked with opposite numbers to each department and liaison officers, but in Africa General Eisenhower built up a uniform staff in which every place was filled with whoever was thought to be the best man and they all ordered each other about according to their rank without the slightest regard to what country they belonged. The same unity and brotherhood is being instituted here throughout the forces which are gathering in this country, and I cannot doubt that it will be found most serviceable and unique also in all the history of alliances.

I must now turn from actual military operations to the European political scene which influences all military affairs so vehemently. In this present war of so many nations against the Nazi tyranny there has at least been a common principle at work throughout Europe, and among conquered peoples there is a unity of hatred and a desire to revolt against the Germans such as has never been known against any race before. The penalties of national defeat are frightful. After the blinding flash of catastrophe, the stunning blow, the gaping wounds, there comes the onset of the diseases of defeat. The central principle of the nation's life is broken and all healthy normal control vanishes.

There are few societies that can withstand the conditions of subjugation. Indomitable patriots take different paths, quislings and collaborationists of all kinds abound, guerrilla leaders, each with their personal followers, quarrel and fight. There are already in Greece and Yugoslavia factions engaged in civil war one with another and animated by hatreds more fierce than those which should be reserved for the common foe. Among all these varied forces, the German oppressor develops his intrigues with cynical ruthlessness and merciless cruelty.

It is hard enough to understand the politics of one's own country; it is almost impossible to understand those of foreign countries. The sanest and the safest course for us to follow is to judge all parties and factions dispassionately by the test of their readiness and ability to fight the Germans, and thus lighten the burden of the Allied troops. It is no time for ideological prejudices for one side or the other, and certainly we, His Majesty's Government, have not indulged ourselves in this way at all. Thus in Italy we are working for the present through the Government of the King and Badoglio, in Yugoslavia we give our aid to Marshal Tito, in Greece, in spite of the fact that a British officer was murdered by the guerrilla organization called Elas, we are doing our best to bring about a reconciliation or at least a working agreement between the opposing forces.

I will say a word if the House will permit me about each of these unhappy countries; the principle which should govern us and which we are certainly following. We signed the Italian armistice on the basis of unconditional surrender with King Victor Emmanuel and Marshal Badoglio, who were, and up to the present are, the legitimate Government of Italy. On their authority the Italian Navy not without risk and loss surrendered to us, and practically all Italian troops and airmen who were not dominated by the Germans also obeyed the orders they received from the Crown. Since then these Italian forces have cooperated with us to the best of their ability and nearly 100 Italian ships of war are discharging valuable services in the Mediterranean and the Atlantic.

Italian troops have entered the front line in Italy, and although on one occasion they suffered severe casualties they continue to fight alongside our men. Very much larger numbers are engaged in indispensable services to the Allied Armies behind the front. Italian airmen are also fighting at our side. The battle in Italy, for reasons which I have already explained, will be hard and long. I am not yet convinced that any other Government can be formed at the present time in Italy which would command the same obedience from the Italian armed forces.

Should we succeed in the present battle and enter Rome, as I trust and believe we shall, we shall be free to review the whole Italian political situation and we shall do so with many advantages that we do not possess at the present time. But it is from Rome that a more broadly based Italian Government can be formed. Whether a Government thus formed will be so helpful to the Allies as the present dispensation I cannot tell. It might, of course, be a Government which would try to make its position good with the Italian people by resisting so much as it dared the demands made on them in the interests of the Allied Armies.

I should be sorry, however, to see an unsettling change made at a time when the battle is at its climax, swaying to and fro. When you have to hold a hot coffeepot it is better not to break the handle off until you are sure that you will get another convenient and serviceable handle or at any rate until there is a dish cloth handy. The representatives of the various Italian parties who assembled a fortnight ago at Bari are of course eager to become the Government of Italy. They will certainly have no elective authority and certainly no constitutional authority until the present King abdicates or he or his successor invites them to take office. It is by no means certain that they would have any effective authority over the Italian armed forces now fighting with us. Italy lies prostrate under its miseries and disasters. Food is scarce, shipping to bring it is voraciously absorbed by our ever-expanding military operations. I think we have gained 12,000,000 tons this year, yet the shortage continues because our great operations absorb every great ship as it comes and the movement of food is difficult.

It would be a mistake to suppose that the kind of political conditions or affairs exist in Italy as work so healthfully in unbeaten lands or countries which have not been shattered by war or stifled by a long period of Fascist rule. We shall see much more clearly how to proceed and have much more varied resources at our disposal if and when we are in possession of the capital city. The policy therefore which His Majesty's Government have agreed provisionally with the Government of the United States is to win the battle for Rome and take a new view when we are there.

On the other side of the Adriatic in the vast mountain regions of Yugoslavia, Albania, and Greece, an area of perhaps 800 miles from north to south and 300 to 400 miles from east to west, the magnificent resistance to the German invaders is in full and violent progress. With the surrender of Italy, with which I think Great Britain had something to do, having fought the Italians since the summer of 1940, sixty-two Italian divisions ceased to be a hostile fighting factor. Forty-three were disbanded and enslaved, apparently without any of the safeguards which attach to prisoners of war, by the Germans. Ten were disbanded by the guerrillas in the Balkans, and nine, which were stationed in the south of Italy, or in Corsica and Sardinia, came over to the Allies. Confronted with this situation, Hitler decided to reinforce the Balkan peninsula heavily, and at the present time no fewer than twenty German divisions are engaged in the Balkans. That is to say, there are twenty-five Germans divisions in Italy, of which eighteen are in the present battle south of Rome, and another twenty are spread over the vast area of the Balkans. Well, they might be worse employed.

In Yugoslavia, in spite of the most ferocious and murderous cruelties and reprisals perpetrated by the Germans not only against hostages but against the village populations, including women and children, the partisan forces have the upper hand. The Germans hold the principal towns and try to keep the railways working. They can march their columns of troops hither and thither about the country. They own the ground they stand on but nothing else. All the rest belongs to the valiant partisans. The German losses have been very heavy, and so far as actual fighting is concerned, greatly exceed the losses of the partisans, but the killing of hostages and civilians in cold blood adds to the German score, and adds to our score against the Germans.

In Yugoslavia two main forces are engaged in the field. First, there are the guerrilla bands under General Mihailovitch. These were the first to take the field, and represent to a certain extent the forces of old Serbia.

For some time after the defeat of the Yugoslav Army, these forces maintained guerrilla warfare. We were not able to send them any aid or supplies, except a few droppings from aeroplanes. The Germans retaliated for any guerrilla activities by shooting batches of 400 to 500 people together in

Belgrade. General Mihailovitch, I much regret to say, drifted gradually into the position where some of his commanders made accommodation with the Italian and German troops, which resulted in their being left alone in certain mountain areas and in return doing very little or nothing against the enemy.

However, a new and far more formidable champion appeared on the scene. In the autumn of 1941 Marshal Tito's partisans began a wild and furious war for existence against the Germans. They wrested weapons from the Germans' hands; they grew in numbers rapidly; no reprisals, however bloody, whether upon hostages or the villages, deterred them. For them, it was death or freedom. Soon they began to inflict heavy injury upon the Germans and became masters of wide regions. Led with great skill, organized on the guerrilla principle, they were at once elusive and deadly. They were here, there, and everywhere. Large-scale offensives have been launched against them by the Germans, but in every case the partisans, even when surrounded, have escaped, after inflicting great losses and toll upon the enemy.

The partisan movement soon outstripped in numbers the forces of General Mihailovitch. Not only Croats and Slovenes, but large numbers of Serbians joined with Marshal Tito, and he has at this moment more than a quarter of a million men with him and large quantities of arms taken from the enemy or from the Italians. And these men are organized, without losing their guerrilla qualities, into a considerable number of divisions and corps. The whole movement has taken shape and form without losing, as I say, the guerrilla quality without which it could not possibly succeed. These forces are, at this moment, holding in check no fewer than fourteen out of twenty German divisions in the Balkan peninsula. Around and within these heroic forces, a national and unifying movement has developed. The Communist element had the honour of being the beginners, but as the movement increased in strength and numbers, a modifying and unifying process has taken place, and national conceptions have supervened. In Marshal Tito, the partisans have found an outstanding leader, glorious in the fight for freedom.

Unhappily, perhaps inevitably, these new forces came into collision with those under General Mihailovitch, and their activities upset his commanders' accommodation with the enemy. He endeavored to repress them, and many tragic fights took place and bitter feuds sprang up between men of the same race and country, whose misfortunes were due only to the common foe. At the present time the followers of Marshal Tito outnumber manifold those of General Mihailovitch, who acts in the name of the royal Yugoslav Government. Of course the partisans of Marshal Tito are the only people who are doing any effective fighting against the Germans now.

For a long time past I have taken a particular interest in Marshal Tito's movement, and have tried, and am trying, by every available means to bring him help. A young friend of mine, an Oxford don, Captain Deakin, now Lieutenant-Colonel Deakin, D.S.O., entered Yugoslavia by parachute nearly a year ago, and was for eight months at Marshal Tito's headquarters. On one occasion both were wounded by the same bomb and they became friends. Certainly, it is a bond between people, but a bond which, I trust, we shall not have to institute in our own personal relationships. From Colonel Deakin's report we derived a lively picture of the whole struggle and its personalities.

Last autumn we sent a larger mission, under Brigadier Maclean, the hon. and gallant member for Lancaster. Having joined the Foreign Secretary and myself at Cairo to report, he has now re-entered Yugoslavia by parachute. I can assure the House that every effort in our power will be made to aid and sustain Marshal Tito and his gallant band. The Marshal sent me a message during my illness, and I have since been in constant and agreeable correspondence with him. We intend to back him with all the strength we can draw, having regard to our other main obligations.

What then, is the position of King Peter and the royal Yugoslav Government in Cairo? King Peter, as a boy of seventeen, escaped from the clutches of the Regent, and with the new royal Yugoslav Government found shelter in this country. We cannot dissociate ourselves in any way from him. He has undoubtedly suffered in the eyes of the partisans by the association of his Government with General Mihailovitch and his subordinate commanders. Here, in these islands, we are attached to the monarchical principle, and we have experienced the many blessings of constitutional monarchy—but we have no intention of obtruding our ideas upon the people of any country. Greeks, Yugoslavs, Italians, all will be perfectly free to settle what form their government shall take so far as we are concerned, when the will of the people can be obtained under conditions of comparative tranquillity.

In the meantime the position is a somewhat complicated one, and I hope to have the confidence of the House in working with my right hon. friend the Foreign Secretary to unravel it, as far as possible, in concert with our Russian and United States Allies, who both, I am glad to say, are now sending missions to Marshal Tito. Our feelings here, and everywhere else, I should like the House to see, follow the principle of keeping good faith with those who have kept good faith with us, and striving without prejudice or regard for political affections, to aid those who strike for freedom against the Nazi rule, and thus inflict the greatest injury upon the enemy.

I have now given the House the fullest account in my power of this difficult, and in some ways delicate, situation in Yugoslavia, and I do not desire to add to it in any way at the present time. I have to pick my words with care because the situation is complicated. The saddest case of all of what I may call the diseases of defeat is Greece. Every one can recall the sentiments of admiration which the heroic defense of Greece, first against the Italians and then against the German invader, aroused throughout the civilized world. It is, indeed, painful to see the confusion and the internecine strife which has broken out in Greece; attended as it is by so many instances of treachery and violence, all of which has been to the advantage of the German invader, who watched with contemptuous complacency Greeks killing Greeks with ammunition sent to them to kill Germans.

There is also present the idea that powerful elements among the guerrillas are thinking much less of driving out the foreign enemy than of seizing the title deeds of their country and establishing themselves as the dominant party, irrespective of the views of the masses of the nation after the war is over. Here the situation, like that in Yugoslavia, is also much obscure and changing. But it can be said beyond all doubt that the great mass of the Greek people wait with fortitude and longing the hour of their liberation from the cruel servitude and bondage into which they have been thrown, and so far as we are concerned they shall not wait in vain.

A very full account was given to the House in December by my right hon. friend the Foreign Secretary of the meeting of the heads of Governments in Cairo and Teheran, and also of the meetings of the Foreign Secretaries which he had previously attended in Moscow. Things move so fast nowadays that this already seems ancient history, and I have little to add to what he said or to what has since been published.

It was a great advantage and pleasure to me to meet for the first time Generalissimo Chiang Kai-shek and his wife. The Generalissimo is a world figure and the main hope and champion of China. Madame Chiang Kai-shek is also a most remarkable and fascinating personality. Her perfect command of English and complete comprehension of the world struggle as a whole enable her to be the best of all interpreters in matters in which she herself played a notable part.

Most of our time in Cairo, before we visited Teheran, was taken up in discussing the strategy and policy to be pursued against Japan, and the best means of pressing forward the war in the Indian and Pacific theaters with the utmost energy, and of course the fitting of these plans into the requirements of the Atlantic and Mediterranean theaters. At Teheran the long desired triple meeting between President Roosevelt, Marshal Stalin, and myself was at length achieved. The personal contacts which we established were, and will, I am convinced, prove to be, helpful to the common cause. There would be very few differences between the three great Powers if their chief representatives could meet once a month. At such meetings, both formal and informal, all difficulties can be brought out freely and frankly, and the most delicate matters can be approached without the risk of jars or misunderstandings, such as too often arise when written communications are the only channel. But geography imposes its baffling obstacles, and though I trust it may be possible to hold further meetings as the war proceeds, I have no definite suggestions to make to the House at the moment.

The question is asked, I have heard, "Have the good relations established at Moscow and Teheran proved durable, or have they faded during the weeks that have passed?" "Does the *Pravda* statement," for instance, it is asked, "or do the articles which have appeared in various organs of the Soviet Government, imply a cooling off in Anglo-Russian or American-Russian friendship and a rebirth of suspicion of the Western Allies on the part of Russia?"

I feel fully entitled to reassure the House on that all-important point. None of the ground made good at Moscow and Teheran has been lost. The three great Allies are absolutely united in their action against the common foe. They are equally resolved to pursue the war, at whatever cost, to a victorious conclusion, and they believe that a wide field of friendly cooperation lies before them after the destruction of Hitlerite Germany. It is upon such a prolonged, intimate, and honorable association that the future of the world depends.

I took occasion to raise personally with Marshal Stalin the question of the future of Poland. I pointed out that it was in fulfillment of our guarantee to Poland that Great Britain declared war upon Nazi Germany, that we had never weakened in our resolve, even during the period when we were all alone, and that the fate of the Polish nation holds a prime place in the thoughts and policy of His Majesty's Government and of the British Parliament. It was with great pleasure that I heard from Marshal Stalin that he, too, was resolved upon the creation and maintenance of a strong, integral, independent Poland as one of the leading Powers in Europe. He has several times repeated these declarations in public, and I am convinced that they represent the settled policy of the Soviet Union.

Here I may remind the House that we ourselves have never in the past guaranteed, on behalf of His Majesty's Government, any particular frontier line to Poland. We did not approve of the Polish occupation of Vilna in 1920. The British view in 1919 stands expressed in the so-called Curzon Line, which attempted to deal, at any rate partially, with the problem. I have always held the opinion that all questions of territorial settlement and readjustment should stand over until the end of the war, and that the victorious Powers should then arrive at formal and final agreement governing the articulation of Europe as a whole.

That is still the wish of His Majesty's Government. However, the advance of the Russian armies into Polish regions in which the Polish underground army is active makes it indispensable that some kind of friendly working agreement should be arrived at to govern the wartime conditions and enable all anti-Hitlerite forces to work together with the greatest advantage against the common foe. During the last few weeks the Foreign Secretary and I together have labored with the Polish Government in London with the object of establishing a working arrangement upon which the fighting forces can act, and upon which, I trust, an increasing structure of good will and comradeship may be built between Russia and Poland.

I have an intense sympathy with the Poles—that heroic race whose national spirit centuries of misfortune cannot quench, but I also have sympathy with the Russian standpoint. Twice in our lifetime Russia has been violently assaulted by Germany. Many millions of Russians have been slain and vast tracts of Russian soil devastated as a result of repeated German aggression. Russia has the right to reassurance against future attacks from the West, and we are going all the way with her to see that she gets it, not only by the might of her arms but by the approval and assent of the United Nations.

The liberation of Poland may presently be achieved by the Russian armies, after these armies have suffered millions of casualties in breaking the German military machine. I cannot feel that the Russian demand for reassurance about her western frontiers goes beyond the limits of what is reasonable or just. Marshal Stalin and I also spoke and agreed upon the need for Poland to obtain compensation at the expense of Germany, both in the north and in the west.

Here I may point out that the term "unconditional surrender" does not mean that the German people will be enslaved or destroyed. It means, however, that the Allies will not be bound to them at the moment of surrender by any pact or obligation. There will be, for instance, no question of the Atlantic Charter applying to Germany as a matter of right and barring territorial transferences or adjustments in enemy countries. No such arguments will be admitted by us as were used by Germany after the last war, saying that they surrendered in consequence of President Wilson's Fourteen Points. Unconditional surrender means that the victors have a free hand. It does not mean that they are entitled to behave in a barbarous manner, nor that they wish to blot out Germany from among the nations of Europe. If we are bound, we are bound by our own consciences to civilization. We are not to be bound to the Germans as the result of a bargain struck. That is the meaning of "unconditional surrender." It may be that I shall have a further statement to make to Parliament about Poland later on. For the present, what I have said, however incomplete, is all that His Majesty's Government are able to say upon the subject, and I hope that we shall not be pressed further in the debate, because matters are still under discussion.

I thank the House very much for giving me their attention and so much consideration. There are many dangers and difficulties in making speeches at this moment. First, it is a time for deeds and not words; secondly, I must find the narrow line between reproof and complacency at home and encouragement of the enemy abroad. One has to confront the country with the grave times through which we are still passing without depressing the soldiers who will have to fight and win the battles of 1944.

Moreover, this should be remembered. There was a time when we were all alone in this war and when we could speak for ourselves; but now that we are in the closest relation on either side with our great Allies, every word spoken has to be considered in relation to them. We have lived through periods of mortal danger, and I cannot say that the dangers are mortal now. They are, none the less, very serious, and we need all the support and good will that have attended us at the time when everyone felt that national existence was at stake.

There is, I gather, in some quarters, the feeling that the way to win the war is to knock the Government about, keep them up to the collar, and harry them from every side, and I find that hard to bear with Christian patience. Looking far abroad, it is also election year in the United States, and that is the time when naturally a lot of rough things have to be said about Great Britain, and when popularity is to be gained in that vast community in demonstrating Americanism in its highest form. We are ourselves well accustomed to the processes of elections, and I think we should not allow ourselves to be unduly concerned with anything that may be said or written there in the course of a great constitutional process which is taking place.

All this, however, accords none too well—this atmosphere and mood at home—with the responsibilities and burdens which weigh upon His Majesty's Ministers and which are very real and heavy. We are in the advent of the greatest joint operation between two Allies that has ever been planned in history. There is a desire in this country in many quarters to raise the old controversies between the different parties. There is also a mood in the Anglo-American alliance to awaken slumbering prejudices and let them have their run.

Yet Liberals, Labour men, and Tories are at this moment fighting and dying together at the front, and working together in a thousand ways at home; and Britons and Americans are linked together in the noblest comradeship of war under the fire and flail of the enemy. My hope is that the generous instincts of unity will not depart from us in these times of tremendous exertion and grievous sacrifices, and that we shall not fall apart abroad or at home so as to become the prey of little folk, who exist in every country, and who follow alongside the juggernaut car of the god of war to see what fun or notoriety they can extract from the proceedings.

There is one thing that we agreed at Teheran above all others, to which we are all bound in solemn compact, and that is to fall upon and smite the Hun by land, sea, and air with all the strength that is in us during the coming spring and summer. It is to this task that we must vow ourselves every day anew. It is to this ordeal that we must address our minds with all the moral fortitude we possess. The task is heavy, the toil is long, and the trial will be severe. Let us all try our best to do our duty. Victory may not be so far away, and will certainly not be denied us in the end.

DECLARATION BY SECRETARY OF THE TREASURY MORGENTHAU ON AXIS LOOTING

February 22, 1944 [1]

On January 5, 1943, the United States and certain others of the United Nations issued a warning to all concerned, and in particular to persons in

[1] Treasury Department.

neutral countries, that they intend to do their utmost to defeat the methods of dispossession practiced by the governments with which they are at war against the countries and peoples who have been so wantonly assaulted and despoiled. Furthermore, it has been announced many times that one of the purposes of the financial and property controls of the United States Government is to prevent the liquidation in the United States of assets looted by the Axis through duress and conquest.

One of the particular methods of dispossession practiced by the Axis powers has been the illegal seizure of large amounts of gold belongings to the nations they have occupied and plundered. The Axis powers have purported to sell such looted gold to various countries which continue to maintain diplomatic and commercial relations with the Axis, such gold thereby providing an important source of foreign exchange to the Axis and enabling the Axis to obtain much-needed imports from these countries.

The United States Treasury has already taken measures designed to protect the assets of the invaded countries and to prevent the Axis from disposing of looted currencies, securities, and other looted assets on the world market. Similarly, the United States Government cannot in any way condone the policy of systematic plundering adopted by the Axis or participate in any way directly or indirectly in the unlawful disposition of looted gold.

In view of the foregoing facts and considerations, the United States Government formally declares that it does not and will not recognize the transference of title to the looted gold which the Axis at any time holds or has disposed of in world markets. It further declares that it will be the policy of the United States Treasury not to buy any gold presently located outside of the territorial limits of the United States from any country which has not broken relations with the Axis, or from any country which after the date of this announcement acquires gold from any country which has not broken relations with the Axis, unless and until the United States Treasury is fully satisfied that such gold is not gold which was acquired directly or indirectly from the Axis powers or is not gold which any such country has been or is enabled to release as a result of the acquisition of gold directly or indirectly from the Axis powers.

It is understood that a similar Declaration is being issued simultaneously by the United Kingdom Treasury, and by the Union of Soviet Socialist Republics.

MARSHAL STALIN'S ORDER OF THE DAY ON 26TH ANNIVERSARY OF THE RED ARMY

February 23, 1944 [1]

ORDER OF THE DAY OF THE SUPREME COMMANDER-IN-CHIEF:

Comrades Red Army men and Red Navy men, sergeants, officers and generals, men and women guerrillas!

The peoples of our country meet the 26th Anniversary of the Red Army in the midst of the historical victories of Soviet troops over the German-fascist

[1] Information Bulletin, Embassy of the U.S.S.R.

troops. For over a year the Red Army has been conducting a victorious offensive, battering the armies of the Hitlerite invaders and sweeping them off Soviet soil. During this period the Red Army successfully carried out the winter campaign of 1942–43, won the summer battles of 1943 and developed the victorious winter offensive of 1943–44.

In these campaigns without parallel in the history of wars, the Red Army made a fighting advance to the west of up to 1,700 kilometers at places and cleared the enemy from nearly three-fourths of the Soviet territory he had captured.

In the course of the present winter campaign the Red Army liquidated the powerful defense of the Germans all along the Dnieper, from Zhlobin to Kherson, and thereby upset the Germans' calculations on the successful conduct of protracted defensive war on the Soviet-German front.

Within the three months of the winter campaign our gallant troops have won most important victories on the territories of the Ukraine west of the Dnieper; completed the liberation of the Kiev, Dniepropetrovsk and Zaporozhye Regions; liberated the entire Zhitomir Region and almost the whole of the Rovno and Kirovograd Regions, as well as a number of districts of the Vinnitsa, Nikolayev, Kamenetz-Podolsk and Volynia Regions. By resolute actions the Red Army liquidated the attempts of a German counter-offensive in the Zhitomir, Krivoi Rog and Uman areas. Soviet troops arranged a new Stalingrad for the Germans west of the Dnieper by surrounding and wiping out ten German divisions and one brigade in the Korsun-Shevchenkovsky area.

A great victory has been won by Soviet troops at Leningrad. Our troops broke the powerful system of permanent, deeply-echeloned fortifications of the enemy, routed a strong grouping of German troops and completely freed Leningrad from enemy blockade and barbarous shellings. Soviet soldiers are completing the clearing of the Leningrad and Kalinin Regions of the fascist fiends and have set foot on the soil of Soviet Estonia. The mass expulsion of the occupationists from Soviet Byelorussia is under way: the Gomel and Polessye Regions have been nearly wholly liberated, as well as a number of districts of the Mogilev and Vitebsk Regions.

Under the unfavorable conditions of the present winter, having overcome the powerful defensive zones of the enemy, our troops within the three months of the winter campaign cleared of the invaders about 200,000 square kilometers of Soviet soil. The Red Army recaptured from the enemy over 13,000 inhabited localities, including eighty-two towns and 320 railway stations. New millions of Soviet citizens have been delivered from fascist captivity. Important agricultural and industrial areas with the richest resources of iron ore and manganese have been restored to our motherland. The Germans have lost these economically important areas to which they clung so desperately.

Now it is probably already obvious to everyone that Hitlerite Germany is irresistibly heading for catastrophe. True, the conditions for the prosecution of war in the present war are more favorable for Germany than during the last World War, when from the very beginning to the end of the war she waged a struggle on two fronts. However, a great drawback for Germany is the fact that in this war the Soviet Union proved to be much stronger than old Tsarist Russia was in the last war.

In the First World War six great powers—France, Russia, Great Britain, the United States of America, Japan and Italy—fought on two fronts against the German bloc. In the present war Italy and Japan went over to Germany's side, Finland joined the fascist bloc, Rumania who in the last war fought against Germany passed over, and up to the present Germany's main forces are still engaged on one front against the Soviet Union.

It is known from history that Germany always won a war when she fought on one front and, on the contrary, lost a war when she was forced to fight on two fronts. In the present war Germany, though fighting with her main forces on one front against the USSR, nevertheless not only proved unable to score a victory but has been placed on the verge of disaster by the powerful blows of the armed forces of the Soviet Union. If the Soviet Union fighting single-handed not only withstood the onslaught of the German war machine, but also inflicted decisive defeats upon the German-fascist troops, all the more hopeless will be the situation of Hitlerite Germany when the main forces of our Allies join in action and the powerful and growing offensive of the armies of all the Allied States develops against Hitlerite Germany.

The German-fascist brigands are now tossing about in search of ways to save themselves from disaster. Again they jumped at "total" mobilization in the rear, although Germany's manpower resources are depleted. The fascist ringleaders make desperate attempts to provoke discord in the camp of the anti-Hitler coalition and thereby to drag out the war. Hitlerite diplomats rush from one neutral country to another, strive to establish contacts with pro-Hitler elements, hinting at the possibility of a separate peace now with our State, now with our Allies.

All these subterfuges of the Hitlerites are doomed to failure, as the anti-Hitler coalition is founded on the vital interests of the Allies, who have set themselves the task of smashing Hitlerite Germany and her associates in Europe. It is this very community of basic interests that results in the consolidation of the fighting alliance of the USSR, Great Britain and the United States in the progress of the war. The hour is nearing of final reckoning for all the crimes committed by the Hitlerites on Soviet soil and in the occupied countries of Europe.

The victorious offensive of the Red Army became possible thanks to the new labor exploits of the Soviet people in all branches of our national economy. The working people of the Soviet Union buttressed the summer victories of the Red Army on the fronts with new production victories in the rear. Workers of our industry fulfill before the scheduled time and exceed programs fixed by the State; put into commission new factories, blast-furnaces and power stations; restore in the liberated districts at unparalleled speed the industry demolished by the occupationists.

The heroic efforts of the working class further strengthen the military material base of the Red Army and thus hasten the hour of our final victory. Soviet peasantry supplies the State with food for the Army and cities, with raw materials for industry and renders self-denying support to the Red Army. Soviet intelligentsia renders direct leading aid to the workers and peasants in developing production and meeting the requirements of the Red Army. The working people of the liberated districts daily extend their assistance to the Red Army—their liberator—and add the production of factories and agriculture undergoing restoration to the general stream of front-bound supplies. There is no doubt but that in the future, too, by its heroic labor and by the exertion of all its efforts, the Soviet people will insure the continuous growth of the productive forces of the country for the earliest and final defeat of the German-fascist invaders.

The creation of new army formations in the Union Republics, which has been prepared by the fighting companionship of the peoples of the USSR in the Patriot War and by the entire history of our State, will further strengthen the Red Army and will add new fighting forces to its ranks.

Comrades Red Army men, Red Navy men, sergeants, officers and generals, comrades men and women guerrillas!

In the great war of liberation for the freedom and independence of our motherland you have displayed miracles of heroism. The Red Army has achieved a resolute turn in the course of the war in our favor and now marches confidently toward final victory over the enemy. The enemy suffers one defeat after another.

However, he has not yet been smashed. Seeing approaching doom and the inevitability of retribution for all the monstrous crimes they committed on our soil, the Hitlerite bandits resist with the fury of doomed men. They hurl into battle their last forces and reserves, cling to every meter of Soviet ground, to every advantageous line. For this very reason, no matter how great our successes, we must, just as before, soberly appraise the enemy's strength, be vigilant not to permit self-conceit, complacency and heedlessness in our ranks. There has been no instance as yet in the history of wars of the enemy jumping into the abyss of himself. To win a war one must lead the enemy to the abyss and push him into it. Only shattering blows steadily growing in their power can crush the resistance of the enemy and bring us to final victory.

With this end in view it is necessary to continue to perfect the combat training of the men and the military art of the comanders of our Army. It is the duty of the Red Army to daily raise its military art to a higher level, incessantly and thoroughly to study the enemy's tactics, skillfully and in time to unriddle his insidious tricks, and oppose our own more perfect tactics to the enemy tactics. It is necessary that the combat experience and achievements of the foremost units and formations of the Red Army become the possession of all our troops, that the entire Red Army, all its men and officers, learn to batter the enemy in accordance with all the rules of modern military science.

Comrades Red Army men and Red Navy men, sergeants, officers and generals, men and women guerrillas! Greeting and congratulating you upon the 26th Anniversary of the Red Army, I order:

1. All rank and file and sergeants' personnel—infantrymen, mortar gunners, artillerymen, fliers, tankmen, sappers, signalmen, cavalrymen—to continue indefatigably to perfect their combat skill, to make full use of our splendid fighting equipment, to batter the enemy in the way he is battered by our glorious Guardsmen, to carry out precisely the orders of commanders, to strengthen discipline and order, to enhance organization.

2. Officers and generals of all arms—to perfect the art of direction of troops, the tactics of maneuvering, the interaction of all arms in the course of battle, to apply more boldly and widely the experience of the advanced units and formations of Guards in combat practice, to raise to a higher level the quality of the staff work and the work of the army rear establishments, to improve and develop our reconnaissance by every means.

3. The entire Red Army—by a skillful combination of fire and maneuver to break up the enemy's defense in its entire depth, to give the enemy no respite, to suppress in time enemy attempts to stem our offensive by counter-attacks, skillfully to organize the pursuit of the enemy, not to allow him to carry away his equipment, by bold maneuver to envelop the flanks of the enemy's troops, to break through to the enemy rear, to surround the enemy's troops, to split and wipe them out if they refuse to down arms.

4. Men and women guerrillas—to increase assistance to the Red Army,

to raid the enemy's headquarters and garrisons, to batter his rear establishments, to disrupt his communications and signal service, to deprive him of the possibility of bringing up his reserves.

5. To mark the great victories won by the armed forces of the Soviet State in the course of the past year, today, February 23, on the day of the 26th Anniversary of the Red Army, at 6 P.M., the valiant troops of the Red Army shall be saluted in Moscow, Leningrad, Kiev, Dniepropetrovsk, Gomel and Rostov with twenty-gun salvos.

Glory to our victorious Red Army!

Glory to Soviet arms!

Glory to our gallant men and women guerrillas!

Long live our great Soviet motherland!

Long live our Communist Party of the Soviet Union—inspirer and organizer of the great victories of the Red Army!

Death to the German invaders!

(Signed) Supreme Commander-in-Chief,
Marshal of the Soviet Union,
JOSEPH STALIN

PRESIDENT ROOSEVELT'S MESSAGE TO DE VALERA ON AMERICAN TROOPS IN THE BRITISH ISLES

February 26, 1944 [1]

I have received, through Mr. Brennan, Irish Minister in Washington, the text of your statement on January 27, last, following the arrival of American troops in the British Isles.

The decision to dispatch troops to the British Isles was reached in close consultation with the British Government as part of our strategic plan to defeat the Axis aggressors. There was not, and is not now, the slightest thought or intention of invading Irish territory or threatening Irish security. Far from constituting a threat to Ireland, the presence of these troops in neighboring territory can only contribute to the security of Ireland and of the whole British Isles, as well as furthering our total war effort.

I have noted in your previous statements expressions of gratitude for the long interest of the United States in Irish freedom. The special ties of blood and friendship between our two countries are recognized here no less than in Ireland and have never left us unconcerned with the problems and fate of Ireland.

At some future date when Axis aggression has been crushed by the military might of free peoples, the nations of the earth must gather about a peace table to plan the future world on foundations of liberty and justice everywhere. I think it only right that I make plain at this time that when that time comes the Irish Government in its own best interest should not stand alone but should be associated with its traditional friends, and, among them, the United States of America.

[1] Dept. of State Bulletin.

MARCH

March 1, 1944

An abortive revolt against the fascist Government of Argentina in behalf of the deposed Gen. Pedro Ramirez took place in Buenos Aires.

2

In their disappointment with Turkey's failure to help drive the Germans out of the Balkans, England and the U. S. ordered the halt of military supplies to that country under the Anglo-Turkish agreement.

Gen. Edelmiro Farrell, Acting President of Argentina by virtue of a military putsch, declared that the foreign policy of Argentina would continue unchanged.

3

The Government of Chile announced its determination to continue its recognition of Gen. Farrell's régime in Argentina.

President Roosevelt disclosed that the Italian Fleet would be distributed equally among the United States, Britain and Russia for purposes of prosecuting the war. Russia would get one-third of the Italian Fleet or the equivalent in American and British ships.

Acting Secretary of State Stettinius revealed that the United States Government had never entered into official relations with the Argentine régime headed by General Farrell.

4

U. S. Army Air Forces bombed Berlin for the first time.

The Japanese Government issued a series of unprecedented emergency defense measures ranging from the mobilization of high school students to the suppression of all evening newspapers.

Gen. George C. Marshall, Army Chief of Staff, asked the Senate Foreign Relations Committee to postpone action for military reasons on the resolution introduced by Senators Robert F. Wagner and Robert A. Taft putting the Senate on record as favoring continued Jewish immigration into Palestine.

6

Eight hundred Flying Fortresses and Liberators, escorted by hundreds of fighter planes, made the first round-the-clock bombing of Berlin and the rest of Germany.

8

Paraguay declared its intention of maintaining full relations with Gen. Farrell's military régime, observing that relations between the two countries "at no time have been interrupted."

9

Secretary of the Navy Frank Knox told the House Foreign Affairs Committee that the proposed 150-million Arabian oil pipeline project was a "military necessity."

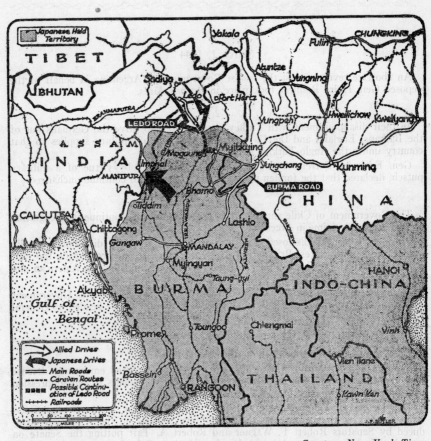

Courtesy New York Times

The Burma Front
March, 1944

In a joint statement President Roosevelt and Prime Minister Churchill declared that Allied ship losses in February were the lowest since U. S. entry into the war.

10

Upon the forced resignation of General Pedro Pablo Ramirez as President of Argentina, General Edelmiro Farrell assumed his office.

Prime Minister Eamon de Valera of Eire categorically rejected the U. S. Government's request that he close the German and Japanese Ministries in Dublin.

13

Marshal Badoglio announced that Russia and Italy had agreed to exchange ambassadors.

14

The Red Army swept across the lower Dnieper River and captured the Black Sea port of Kherson.

Prime Minister Churchill informed Commons that travel between Ireland and the rest of Britain would be halted on account of the presence of Axis agents in Eire.

U. S. Army bombers attacked the Japanese stronghold of Truk in the Caroline Islands . . . U. S. troops invaded Manus, the main island in the Admiralty group.

16

President Roosevelt called on the Finns to withdraw from their "hateful partnership" with Germany.

17

The expanding offensive of the Mediterranean Air Force against Festung Europa reached Vienna for the first time.

19

The Japanese launched an attack on the area of Imphal, capital of India's Manipur State.

20

Pierre Pucheu, former Vichy Minister of the Interior, who was found guilty of treason by a French military court, was executed in Algiers.

21

Wendell L. Willkie warned in Wisconsin that if the Republican Party campaigned on an isolationist plank President Roosevelt would be certain of reëlection.

Finland rejected the Russian armistice terms; Moscow placed full responsibility for the consequences on the Finnish Government.

22

The Germans announced their occupation of Hungary and their establishment of a new puppet government under Field Marshal Doeme Sztojay.

23

Secretary of State Cordell Hull approved the Soviet Union's qualified recognition of the Badoglio Government in Italy. He interpreted it as only a direct link with rather than diplomatic recognition of that Government.

27

The U. S. Supreme Court affirmed in two cases the authority of the Office of Price Administration to fix ceilings on the price of meat and rents.

29

Strong Pacific Fleet forces initiated heavy attacks on the Japanese-held Palau Islands.

Prime Minister Winston Churchill called for a vote of confidence in his coalition Government from the House of Commons.

30

The House of Commons handed Prime Minister Churchill the vote of confidence he sought.

31

Moscow announced that it had concluded an agreement with the Japanese to liquidate immediately all oil and coal concessions held by Japan on Sakhalin Island, twenty-six years before their legal deadline.

STATEMENT BY ACTING SECRETARY OF STATE
E. R. STETTINIUS, JR. ON U. S. RELATIONS
WITH ARGENTINA

March 4, 1944 [1]

The foreign policy of the United States since the beginning of the war has been governed primarily by considerations of support to the prosecution of the war. That applies to our relations with any country. That is the single uppermost point in our policy and must remain so.

Prior to February 25, the Argentine Government had been headed by General Ramírez. On January 26, 1944 his Government broke relations with the Axis and indicated that it proposed to go further in cooperating in the defense of the Western Hemisphere and the preservation of hemispheric security.

Suddenly, on February 25, under well-known circumstances, General Ramírez abandoned the active conduct of affairs. This Government has reason to believe that groups not in sympathy with the declared Argentine policy of joining the defense of the hemisphere were active in this turn of affairs.

The Department of State thereupon instructed Ambassador Armour to refrain from entering official relations with the new regime pending developments. This is the present status of our relations with the existing Argentine regime.

In all matters relating to the security and defense of the hemisphere, we must look to the substance rather than the form. We are in a bitter war with a ruthless enemy whose plan has included conquest of the Western Hemisphere. To deal with such grave issues on a purely technical basis would be to close our eyes to the realities of the situation.

The support, by important elements inimical to the United Nations war effort, of movements designed to limit action already taken could only be a matter of grave anxiety.

The United States has at all times had close ties with Argentina and the Argentine people. It has consistently hoped, and continues to hope, that Argentina will take the steps necessary to bring her fully and completely into the realm of hemispheric solidarity, so that Argentina will play a part worthy

[1] State Department Bulletin.

of her great traditions in the world-wide struggle on which the lives of all of the American countries, including Argentina, now depend. The policies and types of action, present and future, which would effectuate this full co-operation are fully known in Argentina, as in the rest of the hemisphere.

PRIME MINISTER EAMON DE VALERA'S REPLY TO U. S. STATE DEPARTMENT'S NOTE

March 10, 1944 [1]

The note of the American Government was handed to me by the American Minister on Feb. 21. I informed him at once that the request it contained was one with which it was impossible for the Irish Government to comply. The Irish Government have since given the matter careful consideration and I now confirm the reply which I then gave verbally.

The Irish Government have also received the assurance of the American Government, conveyed to the Irish Minister at Washington and later confirmed by the American Minister here in an interview with me on Feb. 29, to the effect that the American Government did not contemplate proceeding to military or other measures because of the reply which had been given.

The American Minister quoted in particular the President's personal message to me of Feb. 26, 1942, that "there is not now nor was there then the slightest thought or intention of invading the territory of Ireland or of threatening the security of the Irish" and added that this attitude was unchanged.

The Irish Government wish to express their appreciation of this assurance. They were indeed surprised that so grave a note as that of Feb. 21 should have been addressed to them. The terms of the note seemed to them altogether out of harmony with the facts and with the traditional relations of friendship between the Irish and American peoples.

They doubted that such a note could have been presented had the American Government been fully aware of the uniform friendly character of Irish neutrality in relation to the United States and of the measures which had been taken by the Irish Government, within the limits of their power, to safeguard American interests.

They felt, moreover, that the American Government should have realized that the removal of representatives of a foreign State on the demand of the Government to which they are accredited is universally recognized as the first step toward war, and that the Irish Government could not entertain the American proposal without a complete betrayal of their democratic trust. Irish neutrality represents the united will of the people and Parliament. It is the logical consequence of Irish history and of the forced partition of national territory.

Already before American entry into the war, the policy of the Irish Government toward Britain, America's ally, had been directed toward carrying out the intentions indicated in a statement of policy made by me in the *Dail Eireann* on May 29, 1935, namely that "our territory would never be permitted to be used as a base for attack upon Britain."

That policy has during the war been faithfully pursued. From the beginning, by the establishment of strong observation and defense forces, by a wide

[1] *New York Times.*

and rigorous censorship of press and communications, by an extensive anti-espionage organization and by every other means within our power, we have endeavored to prevent the leakage through Ireland of any information which might in any way endanger British lives or the safety of Great Britain.

Since the United States entered the war the same spirit of scrupulous regard for American interests has been shown. American officials have had an opportunity of seeing the measures which have been taken—they have indeed made favorable comments on their effectiveness—and it is satisfactory to observe that in the note itself not a single instance of neglect is alleged and no proof of injury to American interests is adduced. Should American lives be lost it will not be through any indifference or neglect of its duty on the part of this State.

As was known to the American officials, it is true that the German Minister had a wireless transmitter, but he had been for a long time debarred from using it and it has been in the custody of the Irish Government for some months. As regards the two parachutists dropped in Ireland last December, they were apprehended within a few hours. Two other agents dropped here since the war began met with a similar fate. The fifth, who arrived during the first year of the war, remained at large until Dec. 3, 1941, but the police were aware of his presence here almost from the first moment of landing, and successful activities on his part were rendered impossible.

The total number of persons, inclusive of these parachutists, suspected of intentions to engage in espionage, and now held in Irish prisons, is ten foreign and two Irish nationals. These are the facts, and it is doubtful if any other country can show such a record of care and successful vigilance.

The British Government have informed the Irish Government that they welcome the initiative of the American Government in sending the note and that they attached the utmost importance to it. The Irish Government do not wish to comment on this, except to remark that it is perhaps not known to the American Government that the feelings of the Irish people toward Britain have, during the war undergone a considerable change, precisely because Britain has not attempted to violate our neutrality.

The Irish Government feels sure that the American Government would agree that it would be regrettable if any incident now should alter that happy result.

The Irish Government are therefore safeguarding, and will continue to safeguard, the interests of the United States, but they must in all circumstances protect the neutrality of the Irish State and the democratic way of life of the Irish people. Their attitude will continue to be determined not by fear of any measures which could be employed against them, but by goodwill and the fundamental friendship existing between the two peoples.

POPE PIUS XII'S PLEA FOR ROME

March 12, 1944 [1]

In the tribulations that have deprived you of your family life you have been forced by the present calamity to be dispersed, to be without homes, perhaps separated from your beloved ones, often wandering about and without sufficient news of those with whom the ties of love and relationship connect

[1] *New York Times.*

you. Preoccupied with their fate as much as they are trembling for yours, resolve yourselves to have faith in your Heavenly Father, who in His love has promised to turn everything to the best—even the most serious and most bitter things.

As Vicar of Christ, I have come to give you words of blessing and comfort. You have crowded around us not to learn the anguish of our heart, but to hear from our lips and to read on our face that all your sufferings are ours and that we feel with you from the depth of our heart.

Be assured that there is not a single one of your sorrows and anxieties or physical and spiritual sufferings that does not pierce our soul more deeply and more painfully than any personal sufferings of our own.

From the day when our endeavors to avoid the scourge of war—the disastrous and fearsome consequences of which we foresaw—were unheard, our spiritual fatherhood, which already was in anxious solicitude in behalf of you in your innumerable multitudes, has been wholly bent toward alleviating your needs and your sufferings and to give the help of our unfortunately limited material resources in bread and clothing to those who had nothing left and needed everything, and to gather together those separated by fighting and invasions.

We spared no effort and we neglected nothing to prevent the sick and the people from experiencing the horrors of deportation and exile.

When harsh reality came to disillusion our most legitimate beliefs, we did all in our power to alleviate suffering but were conscious that all it was possible in our power to do was insufficient.

We cried out for help as would a father in his sorrow for his unfortunate sons, hoping to be heard far and near in those bosoms with a generous heart. And they have answered our appeal. Our deep gratitude remembers their names and offers them to God that He may enter them in the book of eternal reward.

But in this especially grave hour for the so-much-martyred city of Rome—torn in her living flesh, her inhabitants mutilated and wounded in horrible fashion, where sufferings have been most sharp and daily needs most pressing—we pray anew, we beg, we implore all those who have the means to help, either with material contributions or with the help of active work, not to deny their efficacious support and assistance.

Thus with towns stricken on nearly every continent by aerial war that knows no law nor restraint—in itself a terrible accusation against the cruelty of such fighting methods—how could we believe that anyone should ever dare to turn Rome, this noble city which belongs to all times and all places, on which the whole civilized world fixes its eyes in trepidation, to turn her into a field of battle and a theatre of war, thereby perpetrating an act as inglorious militarily as it is abominable in the eyes of God and humanity conscious of the highest spiritual and moral values.

We therefore once more appeal to the clear-sightedness and wisdom of responsible men on both belligerent sides who would not associate themselves with an act that no motive can ever justify in the eyes of history, but would rather turn their thoughts, their endeavors, desires and efforts toward a firm and lasting liberating peace.

[This paragraph as given to The Associated Press by the National Catholic Welfare Council in Washington read:

[We must therefore appeal once again to the clear-sighted vision and wisdom of responsible men in both belligerent camps; we feel certain that they will not wish to have their names associated with a deed which no motive could ever justify before history and that they would rather turn their thoughts, their intentions, their desires and labors toward the securing of a peace which will free mankind from all internal and external violence, so that their name may remain in benediction and not as a curse through the centuries on the face of the earth.]

Beloved Roman people, in the midst of a whirlwind of so many sufferings and trials, we recognize with bitterness of mind that any human help is unequal or inadequate to the extent of your sufferings, to alleviate which even the most generous helping hand of man cannot suffice.

Therefore, beloved sons and daughters, lift up your eyes to Him who will give you strength to carry your cross with warm faith and Christian fortitude —Jesus Christ, our Lord and Savior. To Him we wish to lead you. He, Himself invites you and tells you "come unto Me all ye that labor and are heavy laden and I will give you rest." He chose to undergo miseries of this earthly life, sufferings and afflictions, obstacles and most terrible tortures that can be inflicted by man. He precedes you with His cross: Follow Him.

He—the most innocent—bears His cross. Bear yours in penitence and expiation of our own sins and those others that provoke God's just punishments. He bears His cross for the salvation of the world. Bear yours with Him so faith and fear of God, Christian life and Christian love may come alive again in every heart, in every family, in social life and among all peoples. He bears His cross for the peace of the world; bear yours with Him to procure for yourselves and for the whole of mankind peace with God and peace among all nations.

Almighty God, who deigned in human shape to become our brother and the consolation of the afflicted, look down with grace and mercy upon this multitude of our sons and daughters whom war has deprived of their beloved homes; who look to their uncertain and dark future with sad anguish and the faith in Thee to which they clung in the serene and prosperous years, and which now that unspeakable sufferings have befallen them, has become more than ever their supreme support, their hope, their comfort on the hard and sorrowful path along which they have been led by events of war.

Oh Son of the Heavenly Father through the course of centuries and the succession of peoples, Thou shalt be at every moment our support, our consolation, our grace, our virtue, our justification, our mercy. Thou, who when still a child in the arms of Thy tender and beloved Mother Mary, and under the care of Thine earthly father, Joseph, had to abandon Thy home, grant those who today are wandering homeless the same obedience to the will of God which sanctified the sufferer.

Thou Master of the World who said of Thyself, "Foxes have their holes and birds of the air their nests, but the son of man has nowhere to lay his head," grant that these, our beloved children, anguished and tried by their privations, may draw from the example of Thy voluntary poverty that living faith, that divine strength, that Christian courage that will enable them to bear with true dignity and patience the bitterness of their unfortunate lives.

Eternal and Supreme Priest who, following the dictates of Divine Providence to gather all peoples in one single creed and under one shepherd, placed beauty and grace over Rome, before which the faithful of the entire universe bow with reverence and gratitude, take this town in this hour of increasing danger under the great wings of Thine omnipotence and protection; give counsel to those who live in it to look upon these days of fear and anguish as a time of spiritual meditation, of determination and a sincere return toward Thee and Thy law—so often neglected and violated.

Lord, in behalf of millions of people whom tremendous conflict has thrown into sorrow, misery and tears, we beseech Thee with the prayer of the holy liturgy: "Clement Lord, show us Thine ineffable mercy which may purify us of all those sins and save us from the penalties which we deserve for them. Grant to all those who trust Thee the possibility of seeing a day dawning in which shepherd and sheep, glorifying Thee and Thine infinite bounty, may acclaim with joy and gratitude 'we are saved through the mercy of the Lord.'"

Yes, today down here and for ever and ever. Amen.

SECRETARY OF STATE CORDELL HULL'S STATEMENT ON U. S. FOREIGN POLICY

March 21, 1944 [1]

BASES OF THE FOREIGN POLICY OF THE UNITED STATES

Our Fundamental National Interests—In determining our foreign policy we must first see clearly what our true national interests are. At the present time, the paramount aim of our foreign policy is to defeat our enemies as quickly as possible. Beyond final victory, our fundamental national interests are the assuring of our national security and the fostering of the economic and social well-being of our people.

International Cooperation—Cooperation between nations in the spirit of good neighbors, founded on the principles of liberty, equality, justice, morality, and law, is the most effective method of safeguarding and promoting the political, the economic, the social, and the cultural well-being of our nation and of all nations.

International Organization Backed by Force—Some international agency must be created which can—by force, if necessary—keep the peace among nations in the future. A system of organized international cooperation for the maintenance of peace must be based upon the willingness of the cooperating nations to use force, if necessary, to keep the peace. There must be certainty that adequate and appropriate means are available and will be used for this purpose.

Political Differences—Political differences which present a threat to the peace of the world should be submitted to agencies which would use the remedies of discussion, negotiation, conciliation, and good offices.

International Court of Justice—Disputes of a legal character which present a threat to the peace of the world should be adjudicated by an international court of justice whose decisions would be based upon application of principles of law.

Reduction of Arms—International cooperative action must include eventual adjustment of national armaments in such a manner that the rule of law cannot be successfully challenged that the burden of armaments may be reduced to a minimum.

Moscow Four-Nation Declaration—Through this declaration, the Soviet Union, Great Britain, the United States, and China have laid the foundation for cooperative effort in the post-war world toward enabling all peace-loving nations, large and small, to live in peace and security, to preserve

[1] *New York Times.*

the liberties and rights of civilized existence, and to enjoy expanded opportunities and facilities for economic, social, and spiritual progress.

Spheres of Influence and Alliances—As the provisions of the four-nation declaration are carried into effect, there will no longer be need for spheres of influence, for alliances, for balance of power, or any other of the special arrangements through which, in the unhappy past, the nations strove to safeguard their security or to promote their interests.

Surveillance Over Aggressor Nations—In the process of re-establishing international order, the United Nations must exercise surveillance over aggressor nations until such time as the latter demonstrate their willingness and ability to live at peace with other nations. How long such surveillance will need to continue must depend upon the rapidity with which the peoples of Germany, Japan, Italy and their satellites give convincing proof that they have repudiated and abandoned the monstrous philosophy of superior race and conquest by force and have embraced loyally the basic principles of peaceful processes.

International Trade Barriers—Excessive trade barriers of the many different kinds must be reduced, and practices which impose injuries on others and divert trade from its natural economic course must be avoided.

International Finance—Equally plain is the need for making national currencies once more freely exchangeable for each other at stable rates of exchange; for a system of financial relations so devised that materials can be produced and ways may be found of moving them where there are markets created by human need; for machinery through which capital may—for the development of the world's resources and for the stabilization of economic activity—move on equitable terms from financially stronger to financially weaker countries.

Atlantic Charter: Reciprocal Obligations—The pledge of the Atlantic Charter is of a system which will give every nation, large or small, a greater assurance of stable peace, greater opportunity for the realization of its aspirations to freedom, and greater facilities for material advancement. But that pledge implies an obligation for each nation to demonstrate its capacity for stable and progressive government, to fulfill scrupulously its established duties to other nations, to settle its international differences and disputes by none but peaceful methods, and to make its full contribution to the maintenance of enduring peace.

Sovereign Equality of Nations—Each sovereign nation, large or small, is in law and under law the equal of every other nation. The principle of sovereign equality of all peace-loving States, irrespective of size and strength, as partners in a future system of general security will be the foundation stone upon which the future international organization will be constructed.

Form of Government—Each nation should be free to decide for itself the forms and details of its governmental organization so long as it conducts its affairs in such a way as not to menace the peace and security of other nations.

Non-Intervention—All nations, large and small, which respect the right of others are entitled to freedom from outside interference in their internal affairs.

Liberty—There is no surer way for men and for nations to show themselves worthy of liberty than to fight for its preservation, in any way that is open to them, against those who would destroy it for all. Never did a plainer duty to fight against its foes devolve upon all peoples who prize liberty and all who aspire to it. All peoples who, with "a decent respect to the opinions of mankind," have qualified themselves to assume and to discharge the responsibilities of liberty are entitled to its enjoyment.

Dependent Peoples—There rests upon the independent nations a responsibility in relation to dependent peoples who aspire to liberty. It should be the duty of nations having political ties with such peoples to develop materially and educationally, to prepare themselves for the duties and responsibilities of self-government, and to attain liberty. An excellent example of what can be achieved is afforded in the record of our relationship with the Philippines.

PRESIDENT ROOSEVELT'S STATEMENT ON WAR REFUGEES

March 24, 1944 [1]

The United Nations are fighting to make a world in which tyranny and aggression cannot exist; a world based upon freedom, equality, and justice; a world in which all persons regardless of race, color, or creed may live in peace, honor, and dignity.

In the meantime in most of Europe and in parts of Asia the systematic torture and murder of civilians—men, women, and children—by the Nazis and the Japanese continue unabated. In areas subjugated by the aggressors innocent Poles, Czechs, Norwegians, Dutch, Danes, French, Greeks, Russians, Chinese, Filipinos—and many others—are being starved or frozen to death or murdered in cold blood in a campaign of savagery.

The slaughters of Warsaw, Lidice, Kharkov, and Nanking—the brutal torture and murder by the Japanese, not only of civilians but of our own gallant American soldiers and fliers—these are startling examples of what goes on day by day, year in and year out, wherever the Nazis and the Japs are in military control, free to follow their barbaric purpose.

In one of the blackest crimes of all history—begun by the Nazis in the day of peace and multiplied by them a hundred times in time of war—the wholesale systematic murder of the Jews of Europe goes on unabated every hour. As a result of the events of the last few days, hundreds of thousands of Jews, who while living under persecution have at least found a haven from death in Hungary and the Balkans, are now threatened with annihilation as Hitler's forces descend more heavily upon these lands. That these innocent people, who have already survived a decade of Hitler's fury, should perish on the very eve of triumph over the barbarism which their persecution symbolizes, would be a major tragedy.

It is therefore fitting that we should again proclaim our determination that none who participate in these acts of savagery shall go unpunished. The United Nations have made it clear that they will pursue the guilty and deliver them up in order that Justice be done. That warning applies not only to the leaders but also to their functionaries and subordinates in Germany and in the satellite countries. All who knowingly take part in the deportation of Jews to their death in Poland, or Norwegians and French to their death in Germany, are equally guilty with the executioner. All who share the guilt shall share the punishment.

Hitler is committing these crimes against humanity in the name of the

[1] White House news release.

German people. I ask every German and every man everywhere under Nazi domination to show the world by his action that in his heart he does not share these insane criminal desires. Let him hide these pursued victims, help them to get over their borders, and do what he can to save them from the Nazi hangman. I ask him also to keep watch and to record the evidence that will one day be used to convict the guilty.

In the meantime, and until the victory that is now assured is won, the United States will persevere in its efforts to rescue the victims of brutality of the Nazis and the Japs. In so far as the necessity of military operations permits, this Government will use all means at its command to aid the escape of all intended victims of the Nazi and Jap executioner—regardless of race or religion or color. We call upon the free peoples of Europe and Asia temporarily to open their frontiers to all victims of oppression. We shall find havens of refuge for them, and we shall find the means for their maintenance and support until the tyrant is driven from their homelands and they may return.

In the name of justice and humanity let all freedom-loving people rally to this righteous undertaking.

PREMIER HIDEKI TOJO'S SPEECH AT CLOSING OF 84TH DIET

March 25, 1944 [1]

The present Diet session was convoked at the most grave hour of the war situation, and the Government presented budget drafts and legislative bills which were necessary to meet this situation. Both the House of Peers and the House of Representatives have complied well with the demands of the times, and have fulfilled their urgent business matters with seriousness and celerity, attaining their mission with praise, for which I offer my hearty congratulations.

Supporting Germany which is about to make a complete change in the strength of the war by beginning an offensive again, the Imperial Nation of Japan is heartily looking forward to inflicting a firm and great attack from both east and west, against the officers and men of the U. S. and Britain who are rushing about madly with preparations for counterattacks.

The Government will readily put into practice the budget and legislative bills which have been approved at this time, and at the same time, without a moment's loss, will effectively and firmly put into operation the various measures, thereby maintaining increase of fighting strength and security of the people's livelihood with the intention to overcome this grave, decisive, wartime phase toward the attainment of the ultimate victory.

At this time, it is indeed noble and very reassuring that our 100,000,000 brothers have come to know the present conditions, accepting the difficulties which accumulate, making the increase of fighting strength in each and everyone's proper place their treasured resolve, and (accepting appointments) by laying down everything as a manifestation of the true aspect of our Imperial land. The situation is such that a still greater quantity and fast supply of reinforcements of fighting strength are absolutely necessary in order to annihilate the enemy who has relied on material strength from the

[1] Office of War Information.

very beginning. Here the 100,000,000 people firmly look forward to give our still greater exertions in the all-out rise to action, diligently and arduously, filling the demands of the operations of war so as to have the officers and men at the front manifest their true might freely.

PRIME MINISTER WINSTON CHURCHILL'S BROADCAST ON THE WAR OVERSEAS AND RECONSTRUCTION AT HOME

March 26, 1944 [1]

I hope you will not imagine that I am going to try to make you some extraordinary pronouncement tonight and tell you exactly how all the problems of mankind in war and peace are going to be solved. I only thought you would like me to have a short talk with you about how we are getting on, and to thank you for all the kindness with which you have treated me in spite of my many shortcomings.

It is a year almost to a day since I spoke to you on the broadcast here at home. This has been a time of disappointments as well as successes, but there is no doubt that the good news has far outweighed the bad, and that the progress of the United Nations towards their goal has been solid, continual and growing quicker. The long and terrible march which the rescuing powers are making is being accomplished stage by stage, and we can now say not only with hope, but with reason, that we shall reach the end of our journey in good order, and that the tragedy which threatened the whole world and might have put out all its lights and left our children and descendants in darkness and bondage, perhaps for centuries—that tragedy will not come to pass. He is a rash man who tries to prophesy when, how or under what conditions victory will come; but come it will. That, at least, is sure. It is also certain that unity of aims and action and singleness of purpose among us all— Britons at home, Allies abroad—will make it come the sooner.

A year ago the Eighth Army, which had marched 1,500 miles across the desert from Alamein, was in battle for the Mareth Line, and the First British Army and the American Army were beating their way forward through Tunisia. We were all confident of victory, but we did not know that in less than two months the enemy would be driven with heavy slaughter from the African continent leaving at one stroke 335,000 prisoners and dead in our hands. Since then the successful campaign in Sicily brought about the fall of Mussolini and the heartfelt repudiation by the Italian people of the Fascist creed.

Mussolini, indeed, escaped to eat the bread of affliction at Hitler's table, to shoot his son-in-law, and to help the Germans wreak vengeance upon the Italian masses whom he had professed to love, and over whom he had ruled for more than twenty years. This fate and judgment more terrible than death has overtaken the vainglorious dictator who stabbed France in the back and thought that his crime had gained him the empire of the Mediterranean.

The conquest of Sicily and Naples brought in their train the surrender of Sardinia and the liberation of Corsica—islands which had been expected to require for themselves a serious expedition and a hard campaign.

We now hold one-third of the mainland of Italy. Our progress has not been

[1] British Speeches of the Day.

as rapid or decisive as we had hoped, but I do not doubt that we shall be victors, both at the Anzio bridgehead and on the main front to the southward, and that Rome will be rescued.

Meanwhile, we have swept out of the struggle sixty-six Italian divisions, and we are holding in Italy, for the most part in close action, nearly twenty-five divisions and a noteworthy part of the German Air Force, all of whom can bleed and burn in the land of their former ally while other even more important events which might require their presence are impending elsewhere.

We have been disappointed in the Aegean Sea and its many islands which we have not yet succeeded in dominating. But these setbacks in the eastern Mediterranean are offset, and more than offset, by the panic and frenzy which prevail in Hungary, Rumania and Bulgaria, by the continued activities of the Greek guerrillas and, above all, by the heroic struggles of the Partisans of Yugoslavia under the leadership of Marshal Tito.

In the Near and Middle East we have certainly traveled a long way forward from those autumn days of 1940 when we stood all alone; when Mussolini was invading Egypt; when we were driven out of British Somaliland; when all Ethiopia was in Italian chains; and when we wondered whether we could defend the Suez Canal, the Nile valley, the Sudan and British East Africa. There is much still to be done in the Balkans and the eastern Mediterranean, but here again I do not doubt that the task will be finished in a workmanlike manner.

We who dwell in the British Isles must celebrate with joy and thankfulness our deliverance from the mortal U-boat peril—which deliverance lighted the year which has ended.

When I look back upon the fifty-five months of this hard and obstinate war, which makes ever more exacting demands upon our life-springs of energy and contrivance, I still rate highest among the dangers we have overcome the U-boat attack upon our shipping, without which we cannot live, or even receive the help which our Dominions and our grand, generous American Ally have sent us.

But there are other deliverances which we should never forget. There was the sea-mining peril which loomed so large in 1939 and which has been mastered by superior science and ingenuity, and by the often forgotten but almost unsurpassed devotion to duty of our minesweeper crews and the thousand ships they work and man that we may eat and live and thus fight for the good cause.

We have been delivered from the horrors of an invasion at a time when we were almost unarmed. We have endured without swerving or failing the utmost fury which Hitler could cast upon us from the air, and now the tables are turned and those who sought to destroy their enemies by the most fearful form of warfare are themselves reeling and writhing under the prodigious blows of British and American air power.

We had ourselves a large air force in this island this time last year; we have a larger one today. But besides all that, our American Allies have now definitely overtaken and outnumbered us in the mighty air force they have established here. The combination in true brotherhood of these two air forces, either of which is nearly as large in numbers and in power much greater than the whole air force of Germany, aided as it will be by another Allied air force in Italy, almost as large, which is now established there—these together will produce results in these coming months which I shall not attempt to measure in advance, but which will certainly be of enormous advantage to the cause of the Allies.

Not only have the British and Americans this great preponderance in numbers, which enables them to send out a thousand bombers as often as the enemy is able to send out a hundred against us, but also, by sharing all our secrets with one another, we have won the leadership in the marvels of Radar, both for attack and defense.

Surveying these famous and massive events—by land, sea and air—in the war waged by the two western Allies—Britain and the United States—against Hitlerism, we are entitled, nay bound, to be encouraged, to be thankful, and to resolve to do better than we have ever done before. It would be quite natural if our Soviet friends and Allies did not appreciate the complications and difficulties which attend all sea crossings—"amphibious" is the word—operations on a large scale. They are the people of the great land spaces, and when foes threaten the sacred soil of Russia, it is by land they march out to meet and attack them. Now our tasks are different. But the British and American people are filled with genuine admiration for the military triumphs of the Russian Army. I have paid repeated tributes to their splendid deeds, and now I must tell you that the advance of their armies from Stalingrad to the Dniester River, with vanguards reaching out towards the Prut—a distance of 900 miles accomplished in a single year—constitutes the greatest cause of Hitler's undoing.

Since I spoke to you last not only have the Hun invaders been driven from the land they had ravaged, but the guts of the German Army have been largely torn out by Russian valor and generalship. The peoples of all the Russias have been fortunate in finding in their supreme ordeal of agony a warrior leader, Marshal Stalin, whose authority enables him to combine and control the movements of armies numbered by many millions upon a front of nearly 2,000 miles, and to impart a unity and a concept to the war direction in the east which has been very good for Soviet Russia, and very good for all her Allies.

When a moment ago I spoke of the improvements for the Allied cause which are taking place in Hungary, and in the satellites in the Balkans, I was reserving the acknowledgment that the victorious advance of the Soviet Army had been the main cause of Hitler's approaching downfall in those regions. I have now dealt with the progress of the war against Hitlerite Germany, but I must also speak of the other gigantic war which is proceeding against the equally barbarous and brutal Japanese.

This war is waged in vast preponderance by the fleets, air forces and armies of the United States. We have accepted their leadership in the Pacific Ocean just as they have accepted our leadership in the Indian theater. We are proud of the contribution made by Australia and New Zealand against Japan. The debt which the British Empire and Commonwealth of Nations owes to the United States for the fact that their operations against the Japanese shielded Australia and New Zealand from Japanese aggression and from mortal peril during a period when the mother country was at full stretch in the struggle against Germany and Italy, that debt is one that will never be forgotten in any land where the Union Jack is flown.

Remarkable success has attended the work of the American Navy and of the American, Australian and New Zealand troops. The progress in New Guinea is constant. The American victories in the Pacific, and in particular their latest conquest and liberation of the Marshall Islands, constitute superb examples of the combination of naval, air and military force. It is possible that the war in the Pacific may progress more rapidly than was formerly thought possible. The Japanese are showing signs of growing weakness. The attrition of their shipping—especially their oil tankers—and of their air forces, on all of which President Roosevelt dwelt with sure foresight a year ago, has become not merely evident but obvious.

The Japanese have not felt strong enough to risk their fleet in a general engagement for the sake of their outer defense line. In this they have been prudent, considering the immense expansion of the United States naval power since the Japanese treacherous assault on Pearl Harbor. What fools the Japanese ruling caste were to bring against themselves the mighty latent war energies of the great Republic, all for the sake of carrying out a base and squalid ambuscade.

The British Empire and Commonwealth of Nations have pledged themselves to fight side by side with the United States against Japan no matter what it costs or how long it lasts. Actually, we have suffered from the Japanese injuries even greater than those which have roused the armed wrath of the American Union. In our theater of war, in Burma and the Bay of Bengal, we shall strive our utmost to aid the Americans in their contacts with China, and to add to our own. The more we can fight and engage the Japanese, and especially wear down their air power, the greater a diversion we make for the Pacific theater and the more help we give the operations of the United States.

In Burma those plans which were prepared last August at Quebec, are now being put into practice. Young men are at the helm. Admiral Mountbatten has infused a spirit of energy and confidence into the heavy forces gathered to recover Burma, and by that means to defend the frontiers of India and reopen the road to China. Our airborne operations enable us to attack the Japanese in the rear. They, for their part, have also got behind our front by infiltration at various places, and fierce fighting is going on at many points. It is too soon to proclaim results in this vast area of mountain and jungle, but in nearly every combat we are able to count three or four times more Japanese dead—and that is what matters—than we have ourselves suffered in killed, wounded and missing.

Individual fighting superiority in the jungle has definitely passed to the British and Indian soldiers as compared with the Japanese. Farther to the north, an American column of experienced jungle fighters and a considerable Chinese Army under General Stilwell of the United States Service, are progressing with equal mastery.

Later on I shall make to you or to Parliament a further report on all this hard fighting which, mind you, is not by any means decided yet. Meanwhile, we have placed a powerful battle fleet under Admiral Somerville in Indian waters in order to face the main part of the Japanese Fleet, should it turn westward after having declined battle against the Americans.

When I spoke a year ago, I drew attention to the possibility that there would be a long interval between the collapse of Hitler and the downfall of Japan. I still think there will be an interval, but I do not consider it will necessarily be as long an interval as I thought a year ago. But be it long or be it short, we shall go through with our American brothers with our utmost strength to the very end.

I have now tried to carry you—as if in a Mosquito aircraft on reconnoitering duty—over the world-wide expanse of this fell and ferocious war, and I trust you have gained not only some glimpse of particular scenes but also have a feeling of the relative size and urgency of the various things that are going on.

There are, as you see, quite a lot of things going on. Still, I remember that when I spoke to you on March 21 of last year I gave up the main part of what I said to what we are planning to do to make our island a better place for all its people after the war was over, whenever that should be. I told you there would have to be a general election and a new House of Commons, and that if I were still thought fit to be any further use I should put to the country a Four Years' Plan to cover the transition period between war and peace, and to bring the soldiers and sailors and airmen back to a land where there would be food and work and homes for all. I dwelt on how wrong it would be to make promises which could not be fulfilled, and for one set of politicians to try to outbid another in visionary scheming and dreaming. But I mentioned five or six large fields in which practical action would have to be taken. Let me remind you of them: reform on a great scale of the education of the people; a nation-wide uplifting of their physical health.

I spoke of the encouragement of agriculture and food production and the vigorous revival of healthy village life. I dwelt upon the importance of a national compulsory insurance scheme for all classes, for all purposes, from the cradle to the grave, and of a sound scheme of demobilization which would not delay the rebuilding of industry, and not seem unfair to the fighting men.

I spoke about the maintenance of full employment, and about the rebuilding of our cities and the housing of the people, and I made a few tentative suggestions about economic and financial policy—and what one may well call the importance of making both ends meet.

All this was to happen after the war was over. No promises were to be made beforehand; but every preparation that was possible without impeding the war effort, including legislative preparation, was to be set on foot.

Now, my friends, as your unfailing kindness encourages me to call you— I am a man who has no unsatisfied ambitions—except to beat the enemy and help you in any way I think right—and therefore I hope you will not suppose that in what I am going to say to you I am looking for votes or trying to glorify this party or that. But I do feel I may draw your attention to the fact that several of these large measures, which a year ago I told you might be accomplished after the war was over, have already been shaped and framed and presented to Parliament and the public.

For instance, you have the greatest scheme of improved education that has ever been attempted by a responsible government. This will soon be on the Statute Book. It involves a heavy cost upon the State, but I do not think we can maintain our position in the post-war world unless we are an exceptionally well-educated people and unless we can handle easily and with comprehension the problems and inventions of the new scientific age.

Then there is the very far-reaching policy of a National Health Service, which has already been laid before Parliament in outline, and has received a considerable measure of acceptance. Before this session is out we shall lay before you our proposals about the extensions of national insurance, upon which a vast amount of patient work has been done.

So here you have—or will have very shortly—three of the important measures which I thought would be put off till after the war, already fashioned and proclaimed at a time when no one can tell when the war will end. And all this has been done without relaxing the war effort or causing any party strife to mar the national unity.

But there are several other large problems upon which Ministers and their assistants have toiled and wrought, which are far advanced. And, indeed, if this process continues, and the war goes on long enough, the greater part of my Four Years' Plan of a year ago may well be perfected and largely in operation before we reach the General Election, and give the people the chance to say what they think about it.

Now I must say that one might have expected that His Majesty's Government would receive many compliments upon the remarkable progress we have made, not only with the war, but with the preparations for social and domestic welfare at the armistice or peace. Last October I thought the time had come to ask the King to appoint Lord Woolton to be Minister of Reconstruction with a seat in the War Cabinet. His was a record which rightly commanded respect. However, there is a large number of respectable and even eminent people who are not at all burdened with responsibility, who have a lot of leisure on their hands, and who feel most sincerely that the best work they can do at this present time of hard effort and anxiety is to belabor the Government with criticism, and condemn them as unprofitable servants because they are not, in the midst of this deadly struggle, ready at any moment to produce foolproof solutions for the whole future of the world, as between nation and nation, as between victors and vanquished, as between man and man, as between capital and labor, as between the State and the individual—and so forth and so on.

The harshest language is used, and this National Government which has led the Nation and the Empire, and, as I hold, a large part of the world, out of mortal danger, through the dark valleys into which they had wandered, largely through their own folly, back onto the broad uplands where the stars of peace and freedom shine, is reviled as a set of dawdlers and muddlers, unable to frame a policy, take a decision, or make a plan and act upon it. I know you around your firesides will not forget that this administration, formed in the hour of disaster by the leaders of the Conservative, Labor and Liberal parties banded together in good faith and good will, have brought the British Isles and the British Commonwealth and Empire out of the jaws of death, back from the mouth of hell, while all the world wondered. I know you will not forget that.

There are two subjects of domestic policy mentioned last year on which we have not yet produced an account of our course of action. The first is housing. We set before ourselves as a prime responsibility the provision of homes for all who need them, with priority for our Servicemen as and when they come home from the war. Let me first of all lay down this absolute rule: nothing can or must be done in housing or rehousing which, by weakening or clogging the war effort, prolongs the war. Neither labor nor material can be diverted in any way which hampers the vast operations which are in progress or impending. Subject to that, there are three ways in which the business of housing and rehousing the people should be attacked. Let me tell you about them.

Now, I do not take the view myself that we were a nation of slum dwellers before the war. Nearly 5,000,000 new approved houses or dwellings were built out of about 11,000,000 in this small island between the two wars, and the British people as a whole were better housed than almost any people on the Continent of Europe, or, I would add, in many parts of the United States of America.

But now about 1,000,000 homes have been destroyed or grievously damaged by the fire of the enemy. This offers a magnificent opportunity for rebuilding and replanning, and while we are at it we had better make a clean sweep of all those areas of which our civilization should be ashamed.

However, I have given my word that, so far as it may lie in my power, the soldiers, when they return from the war, and those who have been bombed out and made to double up with other families, shall be restored to homes of their own at the earliest possible moment. The first attack must evidently be made upon houses which are damaged, but which can be re-conditioned into proper dwellings. This must go forward during the war, and we hope to have broken the back of it during this year. It is a war measure, for our Allies are here among us in vast numbers and we must do our best for them.

The second attack on the housing problem will be made by what I call the prefabricated or emergency housing. On this the Minister of Works, Lord Portal, is working wonders. I hope we may make up to half a million of these, and for this purpose not only plans but actual preparations are being made during the war on a nation-wide scale. Factories are being assigned, the necessary set-up is being made ready, materials are being ear-marked as far as possible, the most convenient sites will be chosen—the whole business is to be treated as a military evolution, handled by the Government with private industry harnessed to its service. And I have every hope and a firm resolve that several hundred thousand of our young men will be able to marry several hundred thousand of our young women and make their own four years' plan.

Now what about these emergency houses? I've seen the full-sized model myself; and steps are being taken to make sure that a good number of housewives have a chance of expressing their views about it. These houses will make a heavy demand upon the steel industry, and will absorb in a great measure its overflow and expansion for war purposes. They are, in my opinion, far superior to the ordinary cottage as it exists today. Not only have they excellent baths, gas or electric kitchenettes, and refrigerators, but their walls carry fitted furniture—chests of drawers, hanging cupboards and tables, which today it would cost eighty pounds [about $320] to buy. Moreover, for the rest of the furniture, standard articles will be provided and mass produced, so that no heavy capital charge will fall upon the young couples, or others who may become tenants of the houses. Owing to the methods of mass production which will be used, I am assured that these houses, including the eighty pounds worth of fitted furniture, will be available at a very moderate rent.

All these emergency houses will be publicly owned, and it will not rest with any individual tenant to keep them in being after they have served their purpose of tiding over the return of the fighting men, and after permanent dwellings are available.

As much thought has been and will be put into this plan as was put into the invasion of Africa, though I readily admit that it does not bear comparison in scale with the kind of things we are working at now. The swift production of these temporary houses is the only way in which the immediate needs of our people can be met in the four and five years that follow the war.

In addition to this, and to the re-conditioning of the damaged dwellings, we have the program of permanent rebuilding which the Minister of Health, Mr. Willink, has recently outlined, and by which we shall have 200,000 or 300,000 permanent houses built or building by the end of the first two years after the defeat of Germany. For these, 200,000 sites are already owned by the local authorities.

Side by side with this comes the question of employment of the building trade. We do not want a frantic splurge of building, to be followed by a sharp contraction of the trade. I have a sympathy with the building trade and with the bricklayers. They are apt to be the first to be taken for the wars, and in time of peace they all know as they work at their job that when it is finished they may have to look for another. If we are to secure the best results, it will be necessary that our twelve years' plan for the building trade, on which Mr.

Bevin and Lord Portal have spent so much time, is a plan which will guarantee steady employment for long periods, and increased reward for increased efforts or superior skill; it will be necessary to see that that plan is carried out.

Then we are told by the busy wiseacres: "How can you build houses without the land to put them on? When are you going to tell us your plans for this?" But we have already declared in 1941 that all land needed for public purposes shall be taken at prices based on the standards of values of March 31, 1939. This was a formidable decision of State policy which selected property and land for a special restrictive imposition. Whereas stocks and shares and many classes of real property have gone up in value during the war, and when agricultural land, on account of the new proposals and new prospects open to farmers, has also risen in value, the State has the power, which it will on no account surrender, to claim all land needed bona fide for war industry or for public purposes at values fixed before wartime conditions supervened.

There are certain hard cases which will best be adjusted by parliamentary debate, but in the main you may be sure that ample land will be forthcoming, when and where it is needed, for all the houses, temporary or permanent, required to house our people far better than they have ever been housed before. Nobody need be deterred from planning for the future, by the fear that they may not be able to obtain the necessary land.

Legislation to enable the local authorities to secure any land required for the reconstruction of our towns has been promised, and will be presented to Parliament this session.

There are some comfortable people, of course, who want to put off everything until they have planned and got agreed to in every feature, a White Paper or a blueprint, for the regeneration of the world, before, of course, asking the electors how they feel about it. These people would rather postpone building homes for the returning troops until we had planned out every acre in the country to make sure the landscape is not spoiled. In time of war we have to face immediate needs and stern realities, and it surely is better to do that than to do nothing whilst preparing to do everything. Here is my difficulty; I put it frankly before you. I cannot take anything that will hinder the war, and no one—except the very clever ones—can tell when the war will end, or whether it will end suddenly or peter out. Therefore there must be an emergency plan, and that is what the Ministers concerned have been working at for sometime past. But in spite of this, and of all I've said, I cannot guarantee that everything will be perfect, or that if the end of the war came suddenly, as it might do, there will not be an interval when things will be pretty rough; but it will not be a long interval, and it will be child's play compared to what we have already gone through. Nor need we be frightened about the scale of this task. It looks to me a small one—this housing—compared to some of those we have handled, and are handling now. The value of the land involved is between one-twentieth and one-thirtieth of the cost of the houses to be built upon it. And our population itself is unhappily about to enter upon a period of decline—numerical decline—which can only be checked by the most robust treatment of housing and of all its ancillaries.

There is one other question on which I should like to dwell tonight, but for a reason which I shall mention later, I only intend to utter a passing reassurance. I mean demobilization. Now I know as much about this as most people, because I was Secretary of State for War and Air at the time of the great demobilization after the last war, when in about six months we brought home from abroad, released from military service and restored to their families, nearly 3,000,000 men. Great plans had been prepared before the Armistice by the planners to bring home all the key men first, and any soldier who could get a telegram from someone at home saying that he was wanted for a key job had priority over the man who had borne the burden and heat of the war. The troops did not think this was fair, and by the time I went to the War Office a convulsion of indiscipline shook the whole of our splendid army which had endured unmoved all danger, slaughter and privation. I persuaded the Cabinet to reverse this foolish and inequitable plan and to substitute the simple rule, *first out, first home,* with the result that discipline was immediately restored, and the process of demobilization went forward in a smooth and orderly fashion.

Now my friend, Mr. Bevin, the Minister of Labour, for whose deep sagacity and knowledge of the wage-earning masses I have high admiration—Mr. Bevin has devised a very much less crude, but equally fair and healthy scheme, in which I have the greatest confidence—in which all concerned may have the greatest confidence. Why am I not going to tell you all about it tonight? Or why will Mr. Bevin not tell you about it in the near future? Here is the reason. This is no time to talk about demobilization.

The hour of our greatest effort and action is approaching. We march with valiant allies who count on us as we count on them. The flashing eyes of all our soldiers, sailors and airmen must be fixed upon the enemy on their front. The only homeward road for all of us lies through the arch of victory. The magnificent armies of the United States are here, or are pouring in. Our own troops, the best trained and best equipped we have ever had, stand at their side in equal numbers and in true comradeship. Leaders are appointed in whom we all have faith. We shall require from our own people here, from Parliament, from the Press, from all classes, the same cool, strong nerves, the same toughness of fiber, which stood us in good stead in those days when we were all alone under the German blitz. And here I must warn you that in order to deceive and baffle the enemy as well as to exercise the Forces, there will be many false alarms, many feints and many dress rehearsals. We may also ourselves be the object of new forms of attack from the enemy. Britain can take it. She has never flinched or failed, and when the signal is given the whole circle of avenging nations will hurl themselves upon the foe, and batter out the life of the cruelest tyranny which has ever sought to bar the progress of mankind.

FOREIGN SECRETARY ANTHONY EDEN'S SPEECH ON POWER AND RESPONSIBILITY

March 28, 1944 [1]

For four years the greater part of Europe has lain under German rule. Nations have suffered, have writhed, have rebelled and been repressed with Nazi tyranny and ferocity.

Small powers whose territories gave valuable strategic or industrial prizes were the earliest victims. Austria and Czechoslovakia were among these. Pretexts were found or invented and the German armies marched in.

Poland by her refusal to yield first challenged this paralyzing process. But we and France could not bring her effective help and the German armies marched on.

[1] British Speeches of the Day.

France herself fell and still the dirty brown patch of Nazi tyranny spread wider until from Norway to Greece, from Brittany to the shores of the Black Sea, no land save only little Switzerland was free.

But in these last weeks there has been a new development. The process is being carried still further. Germany's satellites have now suffered with her other victims. Hitherto these wretched countries have been called upon to make a heavy contribution in life on every German front, but they have been left at least the semblance of control of their own affairs. And now all this, too, has been swept away. No shred of self-respect is left to these miserable henchmen of Nazi power.

And so all occupied Europe is today in torment and in ferment under the thinning crust of German domination. Many of these invaded countries have suffered to an extent and with an intensity of pain it is difficult for us to picture. These tragedies will leave their mark, scars cannot be healed all at once even when the day of liberation dawns.

The problems that beset South-Eastern Europe today are a forewarning of those that will confront us in many forms in many lands.

After the last war the problems of European reconstruction were immensely formidable. But this time the suffering has struck much deeper, the confusion is more widespread, and so the work of healing will require more time and patience.

There will be many mistakes; all cannot run smooth. Courage, perseverance, infinite patience will be needed. Above all an understanding that we cannot, at all times and in all places, wholly impose our judgment upon others.

None the less it must be our task to do everything in our power to help the countries of Europe who have endured so much for liberty and independence, to help them by encouragement and example and by every means in our power to build for themselves a new life from the wreckage of the old.

We must be clear about one factor. We must not expect the clock to start to strike again at the hour at which it left off when German invasion fell upon Europe. Many of these countries have been in the grip of the enemy for three years or more. They will not revert to the old life, we must help them to find the new.

In such conditions it is right that we should consider from time to time our own underlying purpose as a nation and how we propose to give it effect. It is certainly true that unless we set certain moral principles for our guide we shall be lost.

One can only navigate a ship by some fixed guide, a compass or, more roughly, the Pole Star. But the very act of navigation, down to the hands of the man at the wheel, is a constant correction of drift.

A ship, at any given moment, is hardly ever dead on her course; it is only by a multitude of approximations that she makes her landfall and is saved from disaster. But these approximations would only make confusion worse confounded unless they were designed to hold and keep one right line.

To apply this conception to the present situation I would say that the British people are convinced that they are fighting not only for their own liberties and the freedom of their own land but for the defeat of tyranny and for the good of the world as a whole. This is their landfall, and they are as determined to make it today as they were in the darkest hours of 1940.

It is very easy, I know, to be cynical about the moral principles which the greater part of our countrymen regard as being involved in the present struggle. It may be argued by some that they do not enter into it at all and that we are simply engaged in a struggle for existence and nothing else. It is indeed a struggle for existence in which we are engaged. If Hitler had overwhelmed this island our national life and all those liberties which our ancestors have won over the centuries would have been utterly destroyed.

But we should not have been the only ones to suffer. The victory which preserves our own independence will do the same for that of many other nations. It is not a reproach to us that we are fighting this tyranny on our own behalf when we are playing our part in saving others from it.

The philosophy of the naked struggle for existence—*der Kampf ums Dasein* —is the declared philosophy of Hitler. In *Mein Kampf* he has made it clear that as between nation and nation there are no obligations and that the law of the jungle is the only one that can prevail. This is also the view of Spengler, who went so far as to declare that "Man is a beast of prey."

Here is a conception which I feel that everyone in this island would instantly repudiate, but it is nevertheless a conception which has had a profound influence on German philosophy and on the German way of life. It is a conception which must be utterly rooted out if the world is to enjoy peace.

But if we say that we reject such a philosophy what is our positive creed which in international affairs shall guide us in the maze of day-to-day affairs? I suggest that it can only be the total antithesis to the Hitler philosophy; a conviction that nations are interdependent and that there will only be enduring peace if they strive to keep faith with one another.

This means, then, that our policies must be sustained by a moral purpose. I agree with the words of Quincy Adams, one of the most sagacious of American statesmen: "The more of pure moral principle that is carried into the policy of a Government, the wiser and more profound will that policy be." That, I feel sure, is also your conviction.

There, also you, the Churches, have your indispensable part to play, to marshal those moral and spiritual resources of which Christian humanity has accumulated through the centuries a store, now maybe hidden, but certainly not buried, beneath the weight of war and the suffering it brings.

Just as this moral principle lies at the root of the social structure within any nation, so must it lie at the root of any workable and endurable international system.

It is quite true that in the past efforts to apply it have only been temporarily successful, though they have occasionally succeeded for quite long periods.

But this does not mean that such attempts will always fail, and even if they did fail it would still be necessary to pursue the ideal of interdependence, for only thus can we escape from perpetual war and from one nation preying as a wolf upon another.

We tried to set out this conception in the documents which we agreed at the Moscow Conference and in the communique issued after the conference at Teheran. These statements recognize that after this war nations great and small will continue to exist and lead their individual lives. In other words, they accept that the world community will be composed of a number of independent States.

They do not contemplate that there will be any kind of super-State.

But we must realize that in the world in which we live, the independence of States can only be secured through international co-operation; that the independence of States means, in effect, the interdependence of States.

We shall see in the future, as the Moscow Declaration forecasts, a large number of States enjoying "Sovereign equality" varying from huge entities such as the Soviet Union, the United States, and the British Commonwealth of Nations to very small communities such as Luxemburg.

This being so we have to find a way by which all these separate units each with its own history and aspirations can work together for purposes so indispensable to them all.

These purposes may be described as peace, freedom and welfare.

I put peace first because we know only too well that we cannot have the other two without it. But peace itself would be a sterile thing if it were not accompanied by the right of free expression and development, and for that purpose we need an increase in human welfare so that men may have the time and opportunity for something else than the mere struggle for existence.

How should we do it?

Not, as I have said, by imposing the will of one nation or group of nations on all the rest but by those processes of ordered discussion inside the framework of freely accepted institutions by which alone permanent advance can be won.

This is the work upon which we are now engaged.

All peace-loving States have both the right and the duty to share in it and we must find a place for them all, great and small, in whatever institutions we set up.

Every State must have the right to make its voice heard in the discussion of the means by which we arrive at our common ends, if only because each has also a duty to contribute so far as its power extends towards the ends which we all seek.

When we speak of "peace-loving" States in Article 4 of the Moscow Declaration we do not mean by this definition merely to refrain from using physical force against others. We mean something more positive than that. We mean a readiness to contribute something towards the security and welfare of other States even at the cost of some sacrifice of immediate national interest.

But let us admit that though all States are equal in status they are not equal in power and consequently their duties must vary.

The responsibility for the preservation of peace must fall in the first instance on the Four Powers who signed the Moscow Declaration and I hope also on France when, as we all trust, without long delay she resumes her place among the Great Powers.

They must be able to confer together regularly on the major problems of the world and to give a decisive lead when action is necessary. They must, of course, associate other Powers with them in their task.

But we must recognize that those who bear the greatest responsibility, those on whose shoulders the burden will fall, must have the greater voice in deciding on any action to be taken in the general interest. All independent States must be free to declare their opinions and their grievances.

And all may profit by that.

But when it comes to deciding on action which only certain States, by their military power, are in a position effectively to take, we cannot simply count heads. The Great Powers have, and must have, special responsibilities in the field of security.

This does not mean that there will be a dictatorship of the Great Powers. Every free nation will have its own responsibility for peace, and its own contribution to make to it. But agreement among the Great Powers must be the foundation; for we have seen what happens when the Great Powers fall out among themselves.

The immediate result is that the smaller States are overwhelmed. The first problem, therefore, is to secure and maintain the co-operation of the Great Powers. This can only be done if we have some common purpose, some common set of principles.

It was these that we sought to set out in our conference at Moscow. But even when principles are agreed the task is far from complete. Their application presents continuing problems. Consultation between the three Great Powers is therefore continuous today over the whole field of our relations.

But for dealing with certain problems it is useful to have special machinery to help us in our task. This is taking shape, progress is being made.

For the first time here in London in the European Advisory Commission representatives of the three Great Powers, the United States of America, the Union of Soviet Socialist Republics, and ourselves have started work upon the solution of some of the more immediate problems we shall have to confront together. Useful and indeed essential work is being done on these, the fruits of which will become apparent in due course.

I have been speaking to you of peace as a matter of political and military security. But peace is something more than that.

Peace is a matter, too, of economic and social well-being. And here, too, the United Nations are working out a practical policy.

The success of the Food Conference at Hot Springs, the signing of U.N.R.R.A. Agreement, and the many Resolutions passed by the Atlantic City Relief Conference show not only that the Great Powers are prepared to give a lead, but also that all Powers, great and small, are willing and anxious to play their part in a world system.

It is difficult enough for a few Powers to reach agreement. How much greater is the difficulty in achieving positive results when forty or more United Nations meet round the table. That they have achieved such results is the remarkable feature of these economic conferences.

Moreover, the organizations which they have brought into being show that there is room for every State to find its proper place as a part of the international machine and so contribute to its effective running.

These achievements form only the beginning of what we hope to do by the same methods, but they give good ground for hope in the future.

Certain it is that if the world is to undertake successfully the great task of ensuring an expanding economy there must be much more co-operation in economic questions than there has been in the past.

But institutions alone, however cleverly constructed, cannot ensure success and so I return to the thought with which I began, that this great effort to obtain a more ordered and prosperous world community cannot succeed unless it is sustained by a moral purpose.

Here I am sure that the deep ambition of the mass of humanity is on our side and that you here in this Conference will help us. We need your prayers, your aid, your understanding. The task is arduous, the end is not in sight, but with faith we can win through.

PRESIDENT ROOSEVELT'S MESSAGE TO CONGRESS ON THE SERVICEMEN'S VOTE BILL

March 31, 1944 [1]

TO THE CONGRESS OF THE UNITED STATES:

I am permitting S. 1285, entitled "An Act to Facilitate Voting, in Time of War, by members of the land and naval forces, members of the Merchant Marine, and others, absent from the place of their residence, and to amend the act of Sept. 16, 1942, and for other purposes," to become law without my signature.

The bill is, in my judgment, wholly inadequate to assure to service men and women as far as is practically feasible the same opportunity which they would have to vote if they were at home.

Because of the confusing provisions of the bill and because of the difficulty of knowing just what will be the practical effect of the bill in operation, it is impossible for me to determine whether in fact more service men and women will be able to vote under the new measure than under existing law.

That determination will largely depend upon the extent to which the States cooperate to make the measure as effective as its provisions permit. In view of this situation, I have resolved the doubt, in favor of the action taken by the Congress, and am permitting the bill to become law without my approval.

In other words, this bill might fairly be called a standing invitation to the several States to make it practicable for their citizens to vote: in this sense the Congress is placing a certain responsibility on each State for action. But it will, of course, be understood by those in the armed services, who want to vote but cannot, that the Congress itself shares the responsibility through the complexities of this bill.

The issue regarding soldiers' voting has been confused. The issue is not whether soldiers should be allowed to vote a full ballot, including State and local offices, or a short ballot confined to Federal offices. I am, and always have been, anxious to have the Federal Government do everything within its power compatible with military operations to get the full State ballots to the men and women in the service.

I always have been, and I am now, anxious to have the States do everything within their power to get the full State ballots to the men and women in the service.

The real issue is whether after the States have done all that they are willing to do to get the full State ballots to the men and women in the service, and after the Federal Government has done everything within its power to get the full State ballots delivered to the men and women in the service, those who have not received their full State ballots should be given the right to cast a short, uniform Federal ballot which can readily be made available to them. This right, which should be assured to all men and women in the service, is largely nullified by the conditions which the provisions of this bill attach to its exercise.

In my judgment, the right of a soldier to vote the Federal ballot if he does not receive in time his State ballot should not be conditioned, as it is by this

[1] New York Times.

bill, upon his having made a prior application for a State ballot, or upon the prior certification by the Governor of the State that the Federal ballot is acceptable under State law. This bill provides a Federal ballot, but, because of these conditions, it does not provide the right to vote.

The Federal Government will and should do everything it can to get the State ballots to our men and women in the service. But it is not in my judgment true, as some have contended, that the Federal Government can assure the use of State ballots as readily as the use of Federal ballots. No matter what effort the Federal Government makes, in many cases it will not be possible to ensure the delivery in time of State ballots to designated individuals all over the world or their return in time to the respective States.

Some of the service men and women, not knowing where they will be a month hence or whether they will be alive, will not apply for their ballots. Others will not receive their State ballots in time or be able to get their ballots back to their States in time. Remember that a number of States will require a special form of application and that the postal-card application forms supplied by the Federal Government are only treated as an application for an application for a State ballot.

The Federal Government can ensure, and in my judgment it is the duty of the Federal Government to ensure, that every service man and woman who does not get his State ballot in time shall have the right to use a short and uniform Federal ballot.

It is in my judgment within the authority of the Congress to use its war powers to protect the political rights of our service men and women to vote for Federal offices as well as their civil rights with respect to their jobs and their homes. If Congress did not hesitate to protect their property rights by legislation which affected State law, there is no reason why Congress should hesitate to protect their political rights.

In 1942 Congress did exercise the war powers to provide Federal war ballots and they were counted in almost every State. What was constitutional in 1942, certainly is not unconstitutional in 1944.

In allowing the bill to become law, I wish to appeal to the States, upon whom the Congress has placed the primary responsibility for enabling our service people to vote, to cooperate to make the bill as fully effective as its defective provisions will allow.

The response of the Governors to my questions, and reports made to me by the War Department, indicate that many States have not yet taken action to make the bill as fully effective as it could be and that a considerable number of States do not presently contemplate taking such action.

I wish also to appeal to the Congress to take more adequate action to protect the political rights of our men and women in the service.

It is right and necessary that the States do all in their power to see that the State ballots reach the men and women in the service from their States. In particular, I appeal to them to see that their State laws allow sufficient time between the time that their absentee ballots are available for distribution and the time that they must be returned to be counted.

I also appeal to the States to see that the postal-card application forms for State ballots distributed by the Federal Government to the troops are treated as a sufficient application for their State ballot and not merely as a request for a formal application for a State ballot.

I also appeal to the States to authorize the use of the Federal ballots by all service people from their States who have not received their State ballots before an appropriate date, whether or not they have formally applied for them. No State or Federal red tape should take from our young folk in the service their right to vote.

I further appeal to the Congress to amend the present bill, S. 1285, so as to authorize all service men and women who have not received their State ballots by an appropriate date, whether or not they have formally applied for them, to use the Federal ballot without prior express authorization by the States. If the States do not accept the Federal ballot, that will be their responsibility. Under this bill, that responsibility is shared by the Congress.

Our boys on the battlefronts must not be denied an opportunitiy to vote simply because they are away from home. They are at the front fighting with their lives to defend our rights and our freedoms. We must assure them their rights and freedoms at home so that they will have a fair share in determining the kind of life to which they will return.

FRANKLIN D. ROOSEVELT

THE WHITE HOUSE,
March 31, 1944.

TEXT OF SOVIET-JAPANESE PROTOCOL ON LIQUIDATION OF JAPANESE OIL AND COAL CONCESSIONS IN NORTHERN SAKHALIN ISLAND

March 30, 1944 [1]

The Government of Japan and the Government of the U.S.S.R., as a result of negotiations conducted with the view to putting into force the understanding regarding annulment of Japanese oil and coal concessions in northern Sakhalin which was reached between the two Governments in connection with the pact of neutrality of April 13, 1941, have agreed upon the following articles:

ARTICLE I

The Government of Japan shall transfer all rights concerning Japanese oil and coal concessions in northern Sakhalin in accordance with stipulations of the present protocol and the terms for application of the protocol attached thereto.

Concession contracts concluded on Dec. 14, 1925, and additional contracts and agreements subsequently concluded between Japanese concessionaires on the one hand and the Government of the U.S.S.R. on the other hand shall be abrogated by virtue of the present protocol.

ARTICLE II

All property—installations, equipment, materials, spare stocks, provisions, etc.—possessed by the Japanese concessionaires in northern Sakhalin shall be transferred in their actual state, unless otherwise provided for in the present protocol and the terms for application of the protocol attached thereto, to the possession of the Government of the U.S.S.R.

[1] *New York Times.*

ARTICLE III

In connection with the preceding two articles the Government of the U.S.S.R. agrees to pay to the Government of Japan the sum of 5,000,000 rubles in accordance with stipulations of the terms for application of the protocol attached to the present protocol.

The Government of the U.S.S.R. will undertake to deliver each year to the Government of Japan 50,000 metric tons of oil produced in the Okha oil fields in northern Sakhalin on ordinary commercial terms for a period of five consecutive years after cessation of the present war.

ARTICLE IV

The Government of the U.S.S.R. guarantees removal from the concession territory, without hindrance and without taxation, of oil and coal stored and possessed by the Japanese concessionaires in accordance with stipulations of the terms for application of present protocol.

ARTICLE V

The present protocol shall come into force on the date of its signature.

The present protocol is done in the Japanese and Russian languages, both texts having equal force. In witness whereof the undersigned, duly authorized by their Governments, have signed the present protocol and have affixed their seals to it.

Done in duplicate in the city of Moscow on the 30th day of the third month of the 19th year of Showa, corresponding to March 30, 1944.

(This text, as transmitted by Domei, carried no signatures, but Japanese and Russian accounts of the agreements said the documents were signed by S. A. Lozovsky, Soviet Vice Commissar for Foreign Affairs, and Naotaka Sato, Japanese Ambassador in Moscow.)

SOVIET STATEMENT ON SOVIET-JAPANESE PROTOCOL

March 30, 1944 [1]

As the result of negotiations during the last few months between the Deputy People's Commissar for Foreign Affairs of the Union of Soviet Socialist Republics [Solomon A.] Lozovsky, and the Ambassador Extraordinary and Plenipotentiary of Japan to the U.S.S.R., Mr. Sato, a "protocol on the transfer to the Soviet Union of Japanese oil and coal concessions in northern Sakhalin," published in today's papers, was signed in Moscow March 30, 1944.

The agreement is also published below as to the order in which the property of Japanese oil and coal concessions in northern Sakhalin is to be handed over to the Soviet Government, signed by representatives of both powers March 10. Besides the aforementioned protocol, "the conditions of the carrying out of the protocol" were also signed March 30. In this document are set out details connected with the fulfillment of the stipulations of the protocol regarding

[1] *New York Times.*

the transfer to the Soviet Government of the rights and property of Japanese concessions in northern Sakhalin, terms of the evacuation to Japan of workers and employes, Japanese subjects engaged in oil and coal concessional enterprises, etc.

In 1925 the Soviet Government granted Japan oil and coal concessions in northern Sakhalin. Soviet-Japanese agreements on these concessions were concluded for a term of forty-five years, the agreement expiring in the year 1970. In the spring of 1941, in the course of negotiations for the concluding of the Soviet-Japanese neutrality pact, the Soviet Government put before the Japanese Government the question of the liquidation of the aforementioned Japanese concessions. Simultaneously with the signing on April 13, 1941, of the neutrality pact, the then Japanese Minister for Foreign Affairs, Mr. [Yosuke] Matsuoka handed the Soviet Government a written undertaking containing a commitment to solve in a few months the question of the liquidation of the concessions in northern Sakhalin. This undertaking was confirmed by Mr. Matsuoka May 31, 1941, by a new declaration handed the Soviet Government through the Japanese Ambassador in Moscow, Mr. [Yoshitsugu] Tatekawa.

At the same time the Japanese undertook to solve the question of the liquidation of the concessions not later than within six months from the day of the signing of the neutrality pact. This commitment was not carried out by the Japanese. Only as the result of negotiations concluded March 30 were the Soviet-Japanese agreements signed on the liquidation of Japanese concessions in northern Sakhalin and on the transfer to the Soviet Union of the whole property of the concessions on the conditions stipulated in the agreement. Thus, as the result of the present agreement, Japanese concessions in northern Sakhalin are being liquidated twenty-six years before the expiration of the term of the concession agreements.

Simultaneously, the Soviet-Japanese protocol established amendments in the conditions of Japanese fishing in Far Eastern waters of the U.S.S.R. The new Soviet-Japanese agreement on the fishing convention stipulates the following:

1. The exclusion of twenty-four fishing areas leased to Japanese fishing concerns and not put into exploitation for two consecutive years.
2. The right of Soviet organizations to acquire yearly 10 per cent of the Japanese fishing areas put up for sale.
3. Increase in the lease and other payments in gold paid by Japanese fishing concerns by 6 per cent as compared with 1943.

Amending the fishing convention of 1928, according to which fishing activities of Soviet organizations and Soviet citizens were subject to a number of essential limitations, the Soviet-Japanese agreement of March 30 stipulates that all these limitations are to be abolished. This agreement exempts from the fishing convention all questions relating to the fishing activities of Soviet organizations and Soviet citizens as being subject to the exclusive jurisdiction of organs of the Soviet state.

The present Soviet-Japanese agreement also provides that until the end of this war Japanese subjects and other foreigners are prohibited from fishing in certain fishing areas in the Far East established by the Soviet Government in July, 1941.

Furthermore, in accordance with the wishes of the Government of the U.S.S.R., the Japanese Government assumed an undertaking to guarantee that all fishing areas leased by Japanese subjects situated on the eastern coast of Kamchatka and in the Olutorski district are not to be exploited by Japanese lessees until the end of the war in the Pacific. On March 30 the Japanese Government informed the Government of the U.S.S.R. of its decision to close the Japanese consulate general in the town of Alexandrovsk and the Japanese vice consulate in the town of Okha in northern Sakhalin.

The same day the Soviet Government informed the Japanese Government of its decision to close the Soviet consulates in the Japanese towns of Hakodate and Tsuruga.

APRIL

April 2, 1944

The Red Army crossed into Axis territory for the first time when Russian troops fought their way across the Bessarabian frontier into Rumania.

3

Prime Minister Tsouderas of Greece resigned.

The German battleship Tirpitz was crippled by British carrier-based airplanes off North Cape in Norway.

The U. S. Supreme Court ruled by an eight to one decision that Negroes could not be barred legally from voting in the Texas Democratic primaries because such exclusion violated the 15th Amendment of the Constitution.

4

Gen. Charles de Gaulle enlarged the French Committee of National Liberation by appointing to it two Communist leaders.

5

Wendell L. Willkie, as a result of his overwhelming defeat in the Wisconsin Republican primary, announced his withdrawal as a candidate for the Republican nomination for President.

In preparation for the impending Allied invasion of Western Europe, Great Britain cut off telephone service to all parts of Ireland.

6

Gen. Henri Giraud offered his resignation to Gen. de Gaulle as Commander-in-Chief of the French Army.

7

President Roosevelt declared the Government's stabilization program a success on the eve of the first anniversary of his "hold-the-line" order.

8

Induction of all men over twenty-six was ordered halted by Maj. Gen. Lewis B. Hershey, Director of Selective Service.

9

Gen. de Gaulle dismissed Gen. Henri Giraud as Commander-in-Chief of the French armed forces. Gen. Giraud refused to give up his post, declaring Gen. de Gaulle's action illegal.

Secretary of State Cordell Hull, in defending his foreign policy, pledged the U. S. Government to the complete uprooting of fascism in all countries.

10

The Red Army recaptured the big Black Sea port and industrial city of Odessa.

President Avila Camacho of Mexico escaped an assassin's bullets.

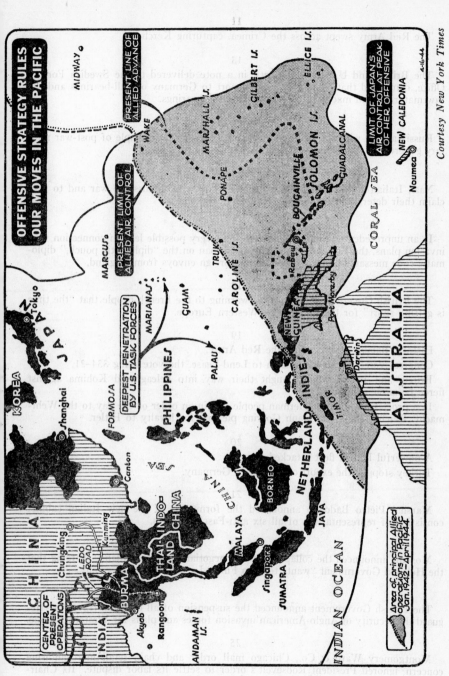

OFFENSIVE STRATEGY RULES OUR MOVES IN THE PACIFIC

PRESENT LINE OF ALLIED ADVANCE

PRESENT LIMIT OF ALLIED AIR CONTROL

LIMIT OF JAPAN'S AIR CONTROL AT PEAK OF HER OFFENSIVE

DEEPEST PENETRATION BY U.S. TASK FORCES

CENTER OF PRESENT OPERATIONS

Area of principal Allied operations in Pacific Jan. 1942–April 1944

April, 1944

11

The Red Army swept across the Crimea, capturing Kerch.

13

The British and U. S. governments, in a note delivered to the Swedish Foreign Office, demanded that Sweden halt her export to Germany of ball-bearings and the raw materials and machines used in making the bearings.

14

Russia agreed with the U. S. and Great Britain on the principle of post-war military government for Germany and her satellites.

15

Nazi, Italian and Japanese leaders met in Tokyo to discuss the war and to proclaim their determination to fight together to the end.

17

In an unprecedented move designed to seal every possible leak in connection with invasion plans, the British Government put a ban on the "diplomatic pouch," diplomatic code messages and the departure of foreign envoys from England.

18

The British Government broadcast a warning to the French people that "the time is getting short" for the invasion of Western Europe.

19

Historic Balaklava fell before the Red Army.

Congress voted a year's extension to Lend-Lease, the vote being 334–21.

British and Indian troops fought their way into beleaguered Kohima against fierce Japanese resistance.

In a proclamation to the German people and in an order of the day to the Wehrmacht, Reichsmarshal Hermann Goering pleaded for loyalty to Hitler.

20

A powerful British fleet attacked Sumatra.

Turkey stopped the export of chrome to Germany.

21

Marshal Pietro Badoglio announced the formation of the new Italian cabinet consisting of representatives of all six anti-Fascist parties.

23

Moscow announced the collapse of peace negotiations with Finland, charging that the Helsinki Government "wants to keep Finland as a vassal of Germany."

24

The British Government announced the suspension of all overseas travel to safeguard the security of Anglo-American invasion forces and plans for Western Europe.

25

Montgomery Ward & Co., Chicago mail order and chain retail merchandising concern, ignored President Roosevelt's order to settle its labor dispute. Its Chairman, Sewell Avery, challenged the President's authority to take over its properties.

Secretary of State Cordell Hull conferred with a bi-partisan group of Senators on the State Department's plan for post-war collaboration.

26

U. S. troops seized Montgomery Ward & Co. properties in Chicago after Sewell L. Avery, company chairman, had defied the Government.

27

Federal District Court Judge William H. Holley granted a temporary injunction to the Government, restraining officials of Montgomery Ward & Co. from interfering with the Government's operation of the plant. Sewell L. Avery, Company Board Chairman, was forcibly evicted by soldiers after he refused to yield control of the properties to Government officials.

28

The Bolivian Government announced that it had crushed the revolt against it. Secretary of the Navy Frank Knox died.

Premier Stalin and the American priest, the Rev. Stanislaus Orlemanski of Springfield, Mass., met to discuss the Polish situation.

30

General Douglas MacArthur stated that he would not accept the Republican nomination for the Presidency.

SECRETARY OF STATE CORDELL HULL'S BROADCAST ON U. S. FOREIGN POLICY

April 9, 1944 [1]

I want to talk with you this evening about the foreign policy of the United States. This is not, as some writers assume, a mysterious game carried on by diplomats with other diplomats in foreign offices all over the world. It is for us the task of focusing and giving effect in the world outside our borders to the will of 135 million people through the constitutional processes which govern our democracy. For this reason our foreign policy must be simple and direct and founded upon the interests and purposes of the American people. It has continuity of basic objectives because it is rooted in the traditions and aspirations of our people. It must, of course, be applied in the light of experience and the lessons of the past.

In talking about foreign policy it is well to remember, as Justice Holmes said, that a page of history is worth a volume of logic. There are three outstanding lessons in our recent history to which I particularly wish to draw your attention. In the first place, since the outbreak of the present war in Europe, we and those nations who are now our Allies have moved from relative weakness to strength. In the second place, during that same period we in this country have moved from a deep-seated tendency toward separate action to the knowledge and conviction that only through unity of action can there be achieved in this world the results which are essential for the continuance of free peoples. And, thirdly, we have moved from a careless tolerance of evil institutions to the conviction that free governments and Nazi and Fascist governments cannot exist together in this world because the very

[1] State Department Bulletin.

nature of the latter requires them to be aggressors and the very nature of free governments too often lays them open to treacherous and well-laid plans of attack.

An understanding of these points will help to clarify the policy which this Government has been and is following.

In 1940, with the fall of France, the peoples of the free world awoke with horror to find themselves on the very brink of defeat. Only Britain in the west and China in the east stood between them and disaster, and the space on which they stood was narrow and precarious. At that moment the free nations were militarily weak, and their enemies and potential enemies were strong and well prepared. Even before that this country had begun its preparations for self-defense. Soon thereafter we started upon the long hard road of mobilizing our great natural resources, our vast productive potentialities, and our reserves of manpower to defend ourselves and to strengthen those who were resisting the aggressors.

This was a major decision of foreign policy. Since that decision was made we have moved far from the former position. We and our Allies are attaining a strength which can leave no doubt as to the outcome. That outcome is far from achieved. There are desperate periods still before us, but we have built the strength which we sought and we need only to maintain the will to use it.

This decision which we have made and carried out was not a decision to make a mere sporadic effort. An episode is not a policy. The American people are determined to press forward with our Allies to the defeat of our enemies and destruction of the Nazi and Fascist systems which plunged us into the war. And they are also determined to go on, after the victory, with our Allies and all other nations which desire peace and freedom to establish and maintain in full strength the institutions without which peace and freedom cannot be an enduring reality. We cannot move in and out of international cooperation and in and out of participation in the responsibilities of a member of the family of nations. The political, material, and spiritual strength of the free and democratic nations not only is greatly dependent upon the strength which our full participation brings to the common effort but, as we now know, is a vital factor in our own strength. As it is with the keystone of an arch, neither the keystone nor the arch can stand alone.

This growth of our strength entails consequences in our foreign policy. Let us look first at our relations with the neutral nations.

In the two years following Pearl Harbor, while we were mustering our strength and helping to restore that of our Allies, our relations with these neutral nations and their attitude toward our enemies were conditioned by the position in which we found ourselves. We have constantly sought to keep before them what they, of course, know—that upon our victory hangs their very existence and freedom as independent nations. We have sought in every way to reduce the aid which their trade with the enemy gives him and to increase the strength which we might draw from them. But our power was limited. They and we have continually been forced to accept compromises which we certainly would not have chosen.

That period, I believe, is rapidly drawing to a close. It is clear to all that our strength and that of our Allies now makes only one outcome of this war possible. That strength now makes it clear that we are not asking these neutral nations to expose themselves to certain destruction when we ask them not to prolong the war, with its consequences of suffering and death, by sending aid to the enemy.

We can no longer acquiesce in these nations' drawing upon the resources of the Allied world when they at the same time contribute to the death of troops whose sacrifice contributes to their salvation as well as ours. We have scrupulously respected the sovereignty of these nations; and we have not coerced, nor shall we coerce, any nation to join us in the fight. We have said to these countries that it is no longer necessary for them to purchase protection against aggression by furnishing aid to our enemy—whether it be by permitting official German agents to carry on their activities of espionage against the Allies within neutral borders, or by sending to Germany the essential ingredients of the steel which kills our soldiers, or by permitting highly skilled workers and factories to supply products which can no longer issue from the smoking ruins of German factories. We ask them only, but with insistence, to cease aiding our enemy.

The Allied strength has now grown to the point where we are on the verge of great events. Of military events I cannot speak. It is enough that they are in the hands of men who have the complete trust of the American people. We await their development with absolute confidence. But I can and should discuss with you what may happen close upon the heels of military action.

As I look at the map of Europe, certain things seem clear to me. As the Nazis go down to defeat they will inevitably leave behind them in Germany and the satellite states of southeastern Europe a legacy of confusion. It is essential that we and our Allies establish the controls necessary to bring order out of this chaos as rapidly as possible and do everything possible to prevent its spread to the German-occupied countries of eastern and western Europe while they are in the throes of reestablishing government and repairing the most brutal ravages of the war. If confusion should spread throughout Europe it is difficult to over-emphasize the seriousness of the disaster that may follow. Therefore, for us, for the world, and for the countries concerned, a stable Europe should be an immediate objective of Allied policy.

Stability and order do not and cannot mean reaction. Order there must be to avoid chaos. But it must be achieved in a manner which will give full scope to men and women who look forward, men and women who will end Fascism and all its works and create the institutions of a free and democratic way of life.

We look with hope and with deep faith to a period of great democratic accomplishment in Europe. Liberation from the German yoke will give the peoples of Europe a new and magnificent opportunity to fulfill their democratic aspirations, both in building democratic political institutions of their own choice and in achieving the social and economic democracy on which political democracy must rest. It is important to our national interest to encourage the establishment in Europe of strong and progressive popular governments, dedicated like our own to improving the social welfare of the people as a whole—governments which will join the common effort of nations in creating the conditions of lasting peace and in promoting the expansion of production, employment, and the exchange and consumption of goods, which are the material foundations of the liberty and welfare of all peoples.

It is hard to imagine a stable Europe if there is instability in its component parts, of which France is one of the most important. What, then, is our policy toward France? Our first concern is to defeat the enemy, drive him from French territory and the territory of all the adjacent countries which he has overrun. To do this the supreme military commander must have unfettered authority. But we have no purpose or wish to govern France or to administer any affairs save those which are necessary for military operations against the enemy. It is of the utmost importance that civil authority in France should be exercised by Frenchmen, should be swiftly established, and should operate in accordance with advanced planning as fully as military operations will permit. It is essential that the material foundations of the life of the French people be at once restored or resumed. Only in this way can stability be achieved.

It has always been our thought in planning for this end that we should look to Frenchmen to undertake civil administration and assist them in that task without compromising in any way the right of the French people to choose the ultimate form and personnel of the government which they may wish to establish. That must be left to the free and untrammeled choice of the French people.

The President and I are clear, therefore, as to the need, from the outset, of French civil administration—and democratic French administration—in France. We are disposed to see the French Committee of National Liberation exercise leadership to establish law and order under the supervision of the Allied commander-in-chief. The Committee has given public assurance that it does not propose to perpetuate its authority. On the contrary, it has given assurance that it wishes at the earliest possible date to have the French people exercise their own sovereign will in accordance with French constitutional processes. The Committee is, of course, not the government of France, and we cannot recognize it as such. In accordance with this understanding of mutual purposes the Committee will have every opportunity to undertake civil administration and our cooperation and help in every practicable way in making it successful. It has been a symbol of the spirit of France and of French resistance. We have fully cooperated with it in all the military phases of the war effort, including the furnishing of arms and equipment to the French armed forces. Our central and abiding purpose is to aid the French people, our oldest friends, in providing a democratic, competent, and French administration of liberated French territory.

In Italy our interests are likewise in assisting in the development at the earliest moment of a free and democratic Italian government. As I said some moments ago, we have learned that there cannot be any compromise with Fascism—whether in Italy or in any other country. It must always be the enemy, and it must be our determined policy to do all in our power to end it. Here again, within these limits, it is not our purpose or policy to impose the ultimate form or personnel of government. Here again we wish to give every opportunity for a free expression of a free Italy. We had hoped that before this enough of Italy would have been freed so that we might have had at least a preliminary expression of that will. Events have not progressed according to our hopes.

The present situation, then, is this: In October, 1943 the President, Mr. Churchill, and Marshal Stalin accepted the active cooperation of the Italian Government and its armed forces as a co-belligerent in the war against Germany under the supervision of an Allied Control Commission. The declaration regarding Italy made at Moscow by the British, Soviet, and American Governments confirmed the policy initiated by the British and American Governments that the Italian Government shall be made more democratic by the introduction of representatives of those sections of the Italian people who have always opposed Fascism; that all institutions and organizations created by the Fascist regime shall be suppressed; that all Fascists or pro-Fascist elements shall be removed from the administration and from the institutions and organizations of a public character; and that democratic organs of local governments shall be created. Finally, it recites that nothing in the declaration should operate against the right of the Italian people "ultimately to choose their own form of government."

This policy has been and is being carried out. Only that part which calls for the introduction into the central government of more democratic elements has not yet been put into effect. This does not signify any change in the clear and announced policy. Thus far it has been thought by those chiefly responsible for the military situation that it would be prejudiced by an imposed reconstruction of the government, and a reconstruction by agreement has not yet been possible. But there is already promise of success in the activities of the political parties which are currently holding conferences with a view to drawing up a program for the political reconstruction of their country along democratic lines. The Permanent Executive Junta is seeking a solution which will provide for the cooperation of the liberal political groups within the government. Thus, after twenty-one years, we see a rebirth of political consciousness and activity in Italy, which points the way to the ultimate free expression of the Italian people in the choice of their government.

What I have said related to some of the most immediate of our problems and the effect of our policy toward them as we and our Allies have moved from a position of weakness to one of strength. There remain the more far-reaching relations between us and our Allies in dealing with our enemies and in providing for future peace, freedom from aggression, and opportunity for expanding material well-being. Here I would only mislead you if I spoke of definitive solutions. These require the slow, hard process, essential to enduring and accepted solutions among free peoples, of full discussion with our Allies and among our own people. But such discussion is now in progress. After two years of intensive study, the basis upon which our policy must be founded is soundly established; the direction is clear; and the general methods of accomplishment are emerging.

This basis of policy and these methods rest upon the second of the lessons which I said at the outset of my remarks was found in the pages of our recent history. It is that action upon these matters cannot be separate but must be agreed and united action. This is fundamental. It must underlie the entire range of our policy. The free nations have been brought to the very brink of destruction by allowing themselves to be separated and divided. If any lesson has ever been hammered home with blood and suffering, that one has been. And the lesson is not yet ended.

However difficult the road may be, there is no hope of turning victory into enduring peace unless the real interests of this country, the British Commonwealth, the Soviet Union, and China are harmonized and unless they agree and act together. This is the solid framework upon which all future policy and international organization must be built. It offers the fullest opportunity for the development of institutions in which all free nations may participate democratically, through which a reign of law and morality may arise, and through which the material interests of all may be advanced. But without an enduring understanding between these four nations upon their fundamental purposes, interests, and obligations to one another, all organizations to preserve peace are creations on paper and the path is wide open again for the rise of a new aggressor.

This essential understanding and unity of action among the four nations is not in substitution or derogation of unity among the United Nations. But it is basic to all organized international action because upon its reality depends the possibility of enduring peace and free institutions rather than new coalitions and a new pre-war period. Nor do I suggest that any conclusions of these four nations can or should be without the participation of the other United Nations. I am stating what I believe the common sense of my fellow countrymen and all men will recognize—that for these powers to become divided in their aims and fail to recognize and harmonize their basic interests can produce only disaster and that no machinery, as such, can produce this essential harmony and unity.

The road to agreement is a difficult one, as any man knows who has ever tried to get two other men, or a city council, or a trade gathering, or a legislative body, to agree upon anything. Agreement can be achieved only by trying to understand the other fellow's point of view and by going as far as possible to meet it.

Although the road to unity of purpose and action is long and difficult we have taken long strides upon our way. The Atlantic Charter was proclaimed by the President and the Prime Minister of Great Britain in August, 1941. Then, by the Declaration of the United Nations of January 1, 1942, these nations adopted the principles of the Atlantic Charter, agreed to devote all their resources to the winning of the war, and pledged themselves not to conclude a separate armistice or peace with their common enemies.

After that came the declaration signed at Moscow on October 30, 1943. Here the four nations who are carrying and must carry the chief burden of defeating their enemies renewed their determination by joint action to achieve this end. But they went further than this and pledged cooperation with one another to establish at the earliest practicable date, with other peace-loving states, an effective international organization to maintain peace and security, which in principle met with overwhelming non-partisan approval by the Congress in the Connally and Fulbright resolutions.

Further steps along the road of united allied action were taken at the conference at Cairo, where the President and Mr. Churchill met with Generalissimo Chiang Kai-shek, and at the conference at Teheran, where they met with Marshal Stalin. At Teheran the three Allies fighting in Europe reached complete agreement on military plans for winning the war and made plain their determination to achieve harmonious action in the period of peace. That concert among the Allies rests on broad foundations of common interests and common aspirations, and it will endure. The Teheran declaration made it clear also that in the tasks of peace we shall welcome the cooperation and active participation of all nations, large and small, which wish to enter into the world family of democratic nations.

The Cairo declaration as to the Pacific assured the liquidation of Japan's occupations and thefts of territory to deprive her of the power to attack her neighbors again, to restore Chinese territories to China, and freedom to the people of Korea.

No one knows better than we and our Allies who have signed these documents that they did not and do not settle all questions or provide a formula for the settlement of all questions or lay down a detailed blueprint for the future. Any man of experience knows that an attempt to do this would have been as futile as it would have been foolish.

There has been discussion recently of the Atlantic Charter and of its application to various situations. The Charter is an expression of fundamental objectives toward which we and our Allies are directing our policies. It states that the nations accepting it are not fighting for the sake of aggrandizement, territorial or otherwise. It lays down the common principles upon which rest the hope of liberty, economic opportunity, peace, and security through international cooperation. It is not a code of law from which detailed answers to every question can be distilled by painstaking analysis of its words and phrases. It points the direction in which solutions are to be sought; it does not give solutions. It charts the course upon which we are embarked and shall continue. That course includes the prevention of aggression and the establishment of world security. The Charter certainly does not prevent any steps, including those relating to enemy states, necessary to achieve these objectives. What is fundamental are the objectives of the Charter and the determination to achieve them.

It is hardly to be supposed that all the more than thirty boundary questions in Europe can be settled while the fighting is still in progress. This does not mean that certain questions may not and should not in the meantime be settled by friendly conference and agreement. We are at all times ready to further an understanding and settlement of questions which may arise between our Allies, as is exemplified by our offer to be of such service to Poland and the Soviet Union. Our offer is still open. Our policy upon these matters, as upon all others, is the fundamental necessity for agreed action and the prevention of disunity among us.

So it is with the basic conviction that we must have agreed action and unity of action that we have gone to work upon the form and substance of an international organization to maintain peace and prevent aggression and upon the economic and other cooperative arrangements which are necessary in order that we maintain our position as a working partner with other free nations. All of these matters are in different stages of development.

It is obvious, of course, that no matter how brilliant and desirable any course may seem it is wholly impracticable and impossible unless it is a course which finds basic acceptance, not only by our Allies but by the people of this country and by the legislative branch of this Government, which, under our Constitution, shares with the Executive power and responsibility for final action.

A proposal is worse than useless if it is not acceptable to those nations who must share with us the responsibility for its execution. It is dangerous for us and misleading to them if in the final outcome it does not have the necessary support in this country. It is, therefore, necessary both abroad and at home not to proceed by presenting elaborate proposals, which only produce divergence of opinion upon details, many of which may be immaterial. The only practicable course is to begin by obtaining agreement, first, upon broad principles, setting forth direction and general policy. We must then go on to explore alternative methods and finally settle upon a proposal which embodies the principal elements of agreement and leaves to future experience and discussion those matters of comparative detail which at present remain in the realm of speculation.

It is a difficult procedure and a slow procedure, as the time which has been required to work out the arrangements for such a universally accepted objective as international relief makes evident. It is a procedure in which misunderstanding, the premature hardening of positions, and uninformed criticism frequently cause months of delay and endless confusion, sometimes utter frustration. It is a procedure in which the people, who are sovereign, must not only educate their servants but must be willing to be educated by them.

In this way we are proceeding with the matter of an international organization to maintain peace and prevent aggression. Such an organization must be based upon firm and binding obligations that the member nations will not use force against each other and against any other nation except in accordance with the arrangements made. It must provide for the maintenance of adequate forces to preserve peace and it must provide the institutions and procedures for calling this force into action to preserve peace. But it must provide more than this. It must provide for an international court for the development and application of law to the settlement of international controversies which fall within the realm of law, for the development of machinery for adjusting controversies to which the field of law has not yet been extended, and for other institutions for the development of new rules to keep abreast of a changing world with new problems and new interests.

We are at a stage where much of the work of formulating plans for the organization to maintain peace has been accomplished. It is right and necessary that we should have the advice and help of an increasing number of members of the Congress. Accordingly, I have requested the Chairman of the Senate Committee on Foreign Relations to designate a representative, bipartisan group for this purpose. Following these and similar discussions with members of the House of Representatives, we shall be in a position to go forward again with other nations and, upon learning their views, be able to submit to the democratic processes of discussion a more concrete proposal.

With the same determination to achieve agreement and unity we talked with our Allies at Teheran regarding the treatment of Nazi Germany and with our Allies at Cairo regarding the treatment which should be accorded Japan. In the formulation of our policy toward our enemies we are moved both by the two lessons from our history of which I have spoken and by the third. This is that there can be no compromise with Fascism and Nazism. It must go everywhere. Its leaders, its institutions, the power which supports it must go. They can expect no negotiated peace, no compromise, no opportunity to return. Upon that this people and this Government are determined and our Allies are equally determined. We have found no difference of opinion among our Allies that the organization and purposes of the Nazi state and its Japanese counterpart, and the military system in all of its ramifications upon which they rest, are, and by their very nature must be, directed toward conquest. There was no disagreement that even after the defeat of the enemy there will be no security unless and until our victory is used to destroy these systems to their very foundation. The action which must be taken to achieve these ends must be, as I have said, agreed action. We are working with our Allies now upon these courses.

The conference at Moscow, as you will recall, established the European Advisory Commission, which is now at work in London upon the treatment of Germany. Out of these discussions will come back to the governments for their consideration proposals for concrete action.

Along with arrangements by which nations may be secure and free must go arrangements by which men and women who compose those nations may live and have the opportunity through their efforts to improve their material condition. As I said earlier, we will fail indeed if we win a victory only to let the free peoples of this world, through any absence of action on our part, sink into weakness and despair.

The heart of the matter lies in action which will stimulate and expand production in industry and agriculture and free international commerce from excessive and unreasonable restrictions. These are the essential prerequisites to maintaining and improving the standard of living in our own and in all countries. Production cannot go forward without arrangements to provide investment capital. Trade cannot be conducted without stable currencies in which payments can be promised and made. Trade cannot develop unless excessive barriers in the form of tariffs, preferences, quotas, exchange controls, monopolies, and subsidies, and others are reduced or eliminated. It needs also agreed arrangements under which communication systems between nations and transport by air and sea can develop. And much of all this will miss its mark of satisfying human needs unless we take agreed action for the improvement of labor standards and standards of health and nutrition.

I shall not on this occasion be able to explain the work which has been done—and it is extensive—in these fields. In many of them proposals are far advanced toward the stage of discussion with members of the Congress prior to formulation for public discussion.

I hope, however, that I have been able in some measure to bring before you the immensity of the task which lies before us all, the nature of the difficulties which are involved, and the conviction and purpose with which we are attacking them. Our foreign policy is comprehensive, is stable, and is known to all men. As the President has said, neither he nor I have made or will make any secret agreement or commitment, political or financial. The officials of the Government have not been unmindful of the responsibility resting upon them, nor have they spared either energy or such abilities as they possess in discharging that responsibility.

May I close with a word as to the responsibility which rests upon us. The United Nations will determine by action or lack of action whether this world will be visited by another war within the next twenty or twenty-five years, or whether policies of organized peace shall guide the course of the world. We are moving closer and closer to the hour of decision. Only the fullest measure of wisdom, unity, and alertness can enable us to meet that unprecedented responsibility.

All of these questions of foreign policy which, as I said earlier, is the matter of focusing and expressing your will in the world outside our borders, are difficult and often involve matters of controversy. Under our constitutional system the will of the American people in this field is not effective unless it is united will. If we are divided we are ineffective. We are in a year of a national election in which it is easy to arouse controversy on almost any subject, whether or not the subject is an issue in the campaign. You, therefore, as well as we who are in public office, bear a great responsibility. It is the responsibility of avoiding needless controversy in the formulation of your judgments. It is the responsibility for sober and considered thought and expression. It is the responsibility for patience both with our Allies and with those who must speak for you with them. Once before in our lifetime we fell into disunity and became ineffective in world affairs by reason of it. Should this happen again it will be a tragedy to you and to your children and to the world for generations.

SECRETARY OF STATE CORDELL HULL'S ADDRESS BEFORE THE PAN AMERICAN UNION

April 14, 1944 [1]

Pan American Day is an important anniversary to the nations of the Americas. We meet today to honor those whose vision and energy established

[1] State Department Bulletin.

and for more than fifty years have carried forward the Pan American Union and all that it signifies. It is well to ask ourselves why it is that we can meet in the midst of the greatest war of history and why it is that we have so great an achievement to commemorate. For in doing so we may more clearly see the guideposts which point the true direction in which we may go forward to new cooperation among ourselves and new cooperation with other nations of the earth.

Inter-American unity was not brought about by force and is not based upon the conception of a master race whose mission is to rule. It was not produced by nations with a homogeneous racial origin. It does not depend upon the bonds of a common language or a culture based on a common literature or common customs and habits.

Were these the only sources of international unity and common action, the future for the world would be dark indeed. But inter-American unity proves that there are other sources more subtle and even stronger—sources which offer hope to a world which can find no hope in the factors which I have mentioned. Our unity comes from a passionate devotion to human liberty and national independence which is so strong that it does not stop with the effort of each people to secure liberty for itself but goes on to respect as no less valid the desire of other peoples to achieve the same liberty in accordance with their own traditions and historic institutions. Although the language of Bolívar and San Martín was different from that of Washington and Jefferson, they were expressing the same purposes and principles, and they led their countrymen along the same paths. These are the paths along which inter-American unity has developed, growing ever stronger as the American nations have come to understand one another and to have trust and confidence in one another's purposes and to work together for purposes so identic that they produced, not division and jealousy, but unity of thought and action.

As the years have gone on, the true principles underlying inter-American unity have been made more specific as one inter-American conference has followed another. In the years between the world wars the trust and confidence between the American nations grew ever stronger while elsewhere the growth of ambitions of conquest by force brought division and fear. It is the common pride of the American republics and the good fortune of all mankind that the torch of international cooperation has burned at its brightest in the affairs of this hemisphere precisely at a time when it was being blacked out elsewhere. It is natural that the history of an international association which has endured longer than any other should provide encouraging guidance for the future.

At the Montevideo Conference in 1933 the American republics affirmed their belief in certain essential principles upon which cooperation between nations and international order must be based. Among them was the principle that every nation, large and small, was equal before the law of nations. Another was the right of every nation to develop its own institutions, free from intervention by others. We already see the beginning of a wider application of these basic principles. They were stated in the Atlantic Charter, the United Nations Declaration, and the declarations made at Moscow. Specifically, it was agreed at Moscow that membership in the world security organization must be upon the basis of the sovereign equality of all nations, weak as well as strong, and the right of every nation to a government of its own choice.

The American nations spoke with a united voice at Buenos Aires as early as 1936 and Lima in 1938 of the dangers to world peace which impended, and took united action to defend the hemisphere against them. When the attack came many of the American republics immediately sprang to the defense of the hemisphere. Shortly after the conference at Rio de Janeiro others took the same course. This chapter in our American history will ever be a gallant and glorious one. It teaches that unity of purpose, a common and passionate devotion to the maintenance of freedom, and mutual trust and confidence are the essential elements without which no amount of international organization and machinery can succeed. But it also teaches us and other nations that international organization and machinery are necessary. Successful as our common action has been, it has not been complete. And it took time, which may not always be available. Therefore, we learn that an international organization, whether in the field of inter-American cooperation or in the broader field of world peace, must have two main supports. It must gather its greatest strength from the rightness and justness of the principles upon which it is founded and the mutual trust of its members. It must also have such an essential framework and machinery and such an acceptance of their obligations on the part of its members as will enable it to act promptly and effectively in times of crisis.

Another guidepost for the future which our common experience before and during this war has raised is in the economic field. With the outbreak of the war the continent mobilized economically. The extent to which the products of the hemisphere have contributed to the growing success of the war against Germany and Japan cannot be overestimated. Millions of men and women throughout the hemisphere are devoting themselves unsparingly to the production of essential materials and to the forging of the weapons of our common victory. All this has been done under the great handicaps of the dislocations produced by the war.

At the end of the war all of our countries will be faced by problems of immense gravity. Out of the experience of our association in peace and in war we have learned that the expansion of material well-being can only come with an expansion of production and trade and hence an increase in consumption. We have learned too that no one nation can solve its problems by itself. An increase in production requires financing, a wise selection of the goods to be produced, and wise and fair commercial policies to enable goods to flow to their markets and necessary purchases to be made in return. All of this requires cooperative effort and the creation of international arrangements through which that effort may have concrete expression. But it requires something more than this. It requires the respect by each nation for each other nation, of which I have spoken, in the field of political relations. International cooperation in the economic field is the opposite of economic imperialism, by which one country seeks to exploit another. It is also the opposite of economic nationalism, by which each nation seeks to live unto itself.

We citizens of this hemisphere have great opportunities before us. The community of action among the American nations, already highly developed, will at the end of the war be indispensable in the advancement of our economic well-being and in the establishment of an international organization to prevent the recurrence of world wars. Together, as I have said, we foresaw, pointed out, and prepared against the dangers of war. Together we must foresee and prepare for the ever-greater common task of the peace. I believe that as in future years men of the Americas meet to commemorate this day they will see unfolded before their eyes ever-increasing evidence that the path along which inter-American cooperation has led is the path to human liberty and human welfare.

JOINT STATEMENT BY SECRETARIES STIMSON AND KNOX AND ADMIRAL LAND ON MANPOWER NEEDS IN THE ARMED SERVICES AND INDUSTRY

April 20, 1944 [1]

The joint statement on manpower needs in the armed services and industry issued by Secretaries Stimson and Knox and Admiral Land reads as follows:

The Secretary of War, the Secretary of the Navy and the chairman of the Maritime Commission announce that they have met today with representatives of the United States Chamber of Commerce, the National Association of Manufacturers and the Association of American Railroads to discuss the necessity for national war service legislation. Also present and joining in the discussion were Gen. George C. Marshall, Army Chief of Staff; Admiral Ernest J. King, Commander in Chief, United States Fleet, and Chief of Naval Operations; Lieut. Gen. Brehon H. Somervell; Assistant Secretary of the Navy Ralph A. Bard, Senator Warren R. Austin of Vermont and Representative James W. Wadsworth of New York.

Conferences had previously been had with national labor leaders.

Following today's meeting Secretary Stimson, Secretary Knox and Admiral Land issued a joint statement describing the need for legislation to provide adequate manpower for essential industries which must increase production despite transfer of some 1,400,000 of their employes to military service.

The statement:

After meeting with national leaders of organized labor we invited representatives of the United States Chamber of Commerce, the National Association of Manufacturers and the Association of American Railroads to meet with us for a discussion of the critical industrial manpower problem, and to solicit their support for war service legislation.

Before the end of the year we estimate that the armed services will require an additional 1,400,000 men. The uncertainties of the invasion may largely increase this total. Most of them—almost all—will be obtained through the democratic processes of the Selective Service System.

Most of them, too, will be drawn from vital industries which must not only obtain replacements for their employes called to the armed services but which must in many instances increase their working forces.

The nation has summoned 11,000,000 men to the colors. It is the essence of democracy that there should be equality of obligation as well as equality of privilege. If it is logical to require some to fight, then it is equally logical to require others to supply them the weapons. Only war service legislation can insure fair distribution of the burden we must all bear to win the victory in which we all will share.

Such legislation is necessary, in our opinion, to insure the success of essential war programs. Legislation of universal application is not, in our opinion, necessary. What is needed is a law so designed as to meet the actual conditions which confront the nation and its men on the fighting fronts. What those conditions are shall be stated.

[1] *New York Times.*

It is imperative that the country realize that the present methods of industrial service cannot do the whole job; that the American people must adopt some system of national industrial service which will provide workers for essential war industries, wherever shortages in manpower appear.

It is our thought that the War Work Service Act should first provide for the recruiting of voluntary industrial workers before the selective service principle is invoked. When a given war industry, in a given locality, is found suffering from a labor shortage, that fact should be proclaimed in a call for volunteers to fill the shortage. Emphatically, the law must prevent depletion in the ranks of other essential industries to man the one in distress, because one of the greatest of present difficulties is the excessive turnover in employment. The volunteers must come from labors not necessary to the nation's war needs.

In case sufficient volunteers do not appear in answer to the call, then the national selective service principle must be invoked to supply the essential need. That is our judgment. It is based on facts such as these:

Before the end of 1944 the Navy, Coast Guard and Marine Corps will require 635,000 men, of whom 230,000 will be needed as replacements.

In the same time the Army, which has reached its complement, will need 750,000 additional men as replacements;

That is a total of 1,390,000 men, a minimum total which may have to be greatly increased before 1945;

The greatest part of this number will be drawn from the shops and farms and mines, the factories and the railroads; most will have to be replaced because essential industries must keep on supplying our fighting forces with the materials and instruments of war;

The aircraft plants and the shipyards must not only be provided replacements for men called into the armed forces, but they must be given 200,000 additional workers to supply the demand for planes and ships;

Navy yards will need 5,000 additional workers just for the construction of submarines, alone;

In the shipyards building landing craft and all the amphibious warfare vessels, 18,000 workers above all replacements must be found before September. If we do not have the landing craft, we cannot take or hold the beaches!

In two East Coast yards alone, 11,000 men are immediately needed to build tankers to fuel our fleets.

These are but examples. Plants making synthetic rubber, tire fabrics and heavy-duty tires must have 19,000 more workers before September. Radio and radar factories are in urgent need now for 30,000 workers, more than 4,000 additional workers are needed in the manufacture of aviation gasoline. And all these are in addition to industrial replacements.

This nation sacrificed sixty bombers and 600 men to cripple the German ball-bearing industry in Schweinfurt, but it cannot obtain the workers here at home to fill the production lines of our own bearing and foundry industries upon which the armament program depends!

The railroads, upon which the nation depends for moving troops and the products of our factories and farms, assert that they are jeopardized by a shortage today of 100,000 men. The coal mines, source of the power that drives the wheels of industry and transportation, will send 45,000 workers into the armed forces this year from an already insufficient crew of miners. The lumber industry calls for 40,000 men at once.

Someone must step up to the bench, the lathe and desk of every war worker who leaves to fight for his country. More than that, the nation's working forces must be made flexible enough to fill the needs of high-priority military production. Disorderly migration of labor must be arrested. The turnover rate in war industries is alarming. We, as a people, are not meeting many of the labor shortages in critical programs, in the midst of a war for survival.

From March, 1943, to March, 1944, the civilian labor force declined by 1,500,000—equal to the number of men who will be drafted into the armed forces this year. In consequence the nation suffers with sixty-seven labor-shortage areas. Nearly every industrial center in the country needs workers. There are enough persons in most of these areas who are idle or employed in unessential work to make up these deficiencies.

Out of every 1,000 workers employed on Feb. 1, 1944, sixty-five quit. Only fifty-three workers are recruited to take their places. That means that last February the nation lost a net of twelve men out of every 1,000. Where 1,000 were turning out the munitions of war on Feb. 1 only 988 were working on Feb. 29.

Labor turnover has reached a rate of more than six per cent per month, three times the peacetime average.

In short, in order to keep a constant force of 100 men working an employer had to hire seventy-two new hands in the course of the year.

Why are they quitting? One reason is that successes in battle result in adverse trends in employment and production. Every victory seems to inspire in thousands the belief that the war is won. False public interpretation of what are only local victories on the perimeter of the enemies' strongholds may indeed imperil victory when we thrust at the foes' heart.

We have yet to meet the major forces of Germany, and of a Japan commanding a large share of the natural wealth and human resources of eastern Asia. We are still 2,000 miles from Tokyo, with all the enemy land and sea and air forces between us and that goal. For our fighting men the war is just entering its critical stage. For our civilian labor forces there must be no relaxation of effort.

We are poised for our greatest undertaking as a nation since we achieved our national independence and unity. We dare not falter at the front—or at home. Present methods have not and are not solving our critical manpower problems. There is little evidence to believe that they will provide for the greater problems of the future. The very real possibility that we may suddenly be forced to shift thousands of workers into the production of some entirely new weapon, which experience in combat or the secret inventions of our enemies demand, is a contingency which we cannot ignore.

In practice a National War Service Law would probably affect only a small proportion of the nation's employables, for most of the shortages are specific rather than general and the aggregate numbers needed to meet them are but a fraction of our potential working force. From the experience of our Allies it can be predicted that once the obligation to serve is made a duty by law the volunteers will come forward. Be that as it may, the need for a law to mobilize and maneuver the industrial manpower of the nation cannot, in our judgment, be denied or evaded.

Experience has taught us that we must use selective processes to man our fighting forces; experience is now teaching us that we must invoke the same national power to provide them the weapons.

PRIME MINISTER WINSTON CHURCHILL'S SPEECH IN COMMONS ON COMMONWEALTH AND EMPIRE UNITY

April 21, 1944 [1]

When we planned this Debate together through the usual channels, it was well understood that its main purpose was to enable the House to express its opinion, and that the Government would have no far-reaching declaration of policy to make. Indeed, it has been everywhere recognized that for us to commit ourselves to hard-and-fast lines of policy, or even to the advocacy of particular suggestions or proposals, would not be appropriate on the eve of the first meeting we have been able to arrange—after many attempts—of all the Dominion Prime Ministers since the war began. Thus viewed, I think it will be almost universally admitted that the Debate has been a great success, and has been of far-reaching usefulness; that the Motion * on which the Debate is founded is acceptable to all; that there is, as the Noble Lord has said, an all-party agreement on most fundamentals; and that the level of the discussion has been worthy of the breadth of the subject, and has been distinguished by speeches of a statesmanlike character, for I can use no other word for speeches such as I heard yesterday. . . . I much regret that I could not hear all the speeches which have been made, but I sat up till half past two this morning reading the full report of every speech, and I crave the indulgence of the House for not having been constantly on the Bench during this Debate, on account of some other things which, hon. Members may know, it is my duty to look after.

What has struck me most about the speeches to which I have listened or have read or upon which I have been kept well-informed, has been the great number of enormous topics, some of which have formerly been matters of heated controversy, and may be again, which Members have found it necessary, indeed have found it inevitable, to take for an airing. A great number of these questions concern our future, and they have been raised directly or indirectly. What changes are to be made in the political, economic, and defense structure of the British Commonwealth and Empire? In what way will an ever more closely knitted British Commonwealth and Empire become also, at the same time, more closely associated with the United States? How will this vast bloc of States and Nations, which will walk along together, speaking, to a large extent, the same language, reposing on the same body of common law, be merged in the supreme council for the maintenance of world peace? Should we draw closer to Europe—there is another question—and aim at creating, under the Supreme World Council, a living union, an entity in Europe, a United States of Europe? Or, again, should we concentrate upon our own Imperial and Commonwealth organization, or upon our fraternal association with the United States, and put our trust in the English Channel, in air power, and in sea power?

Other more familiar topics than these—because it is easy to see, from the recurrence of these topics in so many speeches, the way in which the modern

[1] British Speeches of the Day.

* "That the United Kingdom should do its utmost by close co-operation and regard for the different points of view of the nations of the Commonwealth to preserve in time of peace the unity of purpose and sentiment which has held them together in time of war."

mind of the House is moving—have been raised, like Free Trade versus Protection, Imperial Preference versus greater development of international trade, and international currency in relation to the policy of the United States and the existence of a vast sterling area. One even sees the gold standard peering around the corner, and, of course, British agriculture close at hand. My hon. Friend the Member for Eye said yesterday that the sole, or the main, lesson of the war was that the world was one and indivisible. I should myself have thought that the main obvious fact before our eyes is that the world is very seriously divided, and is conducting its controversies in a highly acrimonious manner. Certainly it seems sufficiently divided to give the peacemakers quite a considerable task to weld it into one common mutually-loving whole at the peace table. I cannot pretend to have provided myself with the answers to all these questions, with answers which would give satisfaction to all parties here at home, and cause no complications in our relations with foreign States, but I bid the House to take comfort from the fact that, great as our responsibilities are, no reasonable person could expect us to solve all the problems of the world while we are fighting for our lives. We must be generous, we must be fair to the future, we must leave something to be done by our descendants, if any.

My hon. Friend the Member for West Renfrew (Mr. Wedderburn), whose laudable desire to probe into the distant past is not always accompanied by historical precision, quoted—and I make no complaint of it—a speech which I made forty years ago against Mr. Joseph Chamberlain's policy of Protection and Imperial Preference which certainly does not, whatever else may be thought about it, reveal me as a very ardent supporter of those policies, and certainly makes it very odd that I should have, for the time being, the honor of leading the Conservative Party. I have no intention of passing my remaining years in explaining or withdrawing anything I have said in the past, still less in apologizing for it; but what I am concerned to do is to show to the House, and also to Members of my own Party, how strictly I have, during my stewardship, safeguarded the structure of Imperial Preference, which has arisen out of the controversies and achievements of the last forty years, against any danger of being swept away in the tumult of this war. At my first meeting with the President of the United States, at Argenta in Newfoundland, at the time of the so-called Atlantic Charter, and before the United States had entered the war—a meeting of very anxious and critical importance—I asked for the insertion of the following words which can be read in that document:

"With due respect for their existing obligations."

Those are the limiting words, and they were inserted for the express purpose of retaining in the House of Commons, and the Dominion Parliaments, the fullest possible rights and liberties over the question of Imperial Preference. Again, in February, 1942, when the United States was our closest Ally, I did not agree to Article 7 of the Mutual Aid Agreement, without having previously obtained from the President a definite assurance that we were no more committed to the abolition of Imperial Preference than the American Government were committed to the abolition of their high protective tariffs. The discussions as to how a greater volume of trade and a more harmonious flow of trade can be created in the immediate post-war years in agreement, leaves us, in every respect, so far as action is concerned, perfectly free. How could it otherwise be, when Parliament itself would not only have to debate the matters, but would have to legislate upon them, when they were brought before it? I am convinced myself that there should be a careful, searching, far-ranging discussion on the economics of the post-war world, and a sincere attempt made to reconcile conflicting interests wherever possible. There must be a wholehearted endeavor, begun in good time, to promote the greatest interchange of goods and services between the various communities of the world, and to strive for that process of betterment of standards of life in every country without which . . . expanding markets are impossible, and without which world prosperity is a dream which might easily turn into a nightmare.

My right hon. Friend the Member for Devonport (Mr. Hore-Belisha) made a remark which I particularly liked, when he said that the Empire is not a sick body. I cordially agree. But even I can look back to the days when it was considered to be moribund. There were, when I was young, some statesmen whose names are honored, who spoke of the Colonies as burdens, and of the Dominions as fruit which would fall from the tree when ripe. I did not live myself in the days when those speeches were made, but I remember well times of great anxiety about the Empire, at the end of the last century. I remember the South African war, and how shocked the War Office was, when Australia and New Zealand actually wanted to send contingents to fight, and how they eventually overcame their reluctance by adopting the immortal compromise "unmounted men preferred." My right hon. Friend, who is not here, has made great improvements since then. I have never thought myself that the Empire needed tying together with bits of string. I agree with my right hon. Friend the Member for Devonport that natural development, natural forces, mysterious natural forces, will carry everything before them, especially when those forces are fanned forward, as they will be, by the wings of victory in a righteous cause.

Then came another phase. Looking at the British Empire, say, thirty years ago, in 1914, on the eve of the first Great War, all foreign opinion, especially German opinion, was convinced that this vast structure of Empire, created and coming into full life in Victorian times, had reached a condition of ricketiness and looseness when a single violent shock would bring it clattering down and lay it low forever. Then came upon the world a most frightful war, incomparably greater than anything we had ever known, with slaughter far greater than any, thank God, we have suffered in this struggle. I remember coming out of the Cabinet meeting on an August afternoon in 1914, when war was certain, and the Fleet was already mobilized, with this feeling: "How are we to explain it all to Canada, Australia, South Africa and New Zealand; nay, how are we to explain it all to our own people in the short time left?" But, when we left the fierce controversy of the Cabinet room, and came out into the open air, the whole of the peoples of the British Empire, of every race and every clime, had already sprung to arms. Our old enemies, recent enemies, Generals Botha and Smuts, were already saddling their horses to rally their commandos to the attack on Germany; and Irishmen, whose names I always bear in my memory with regard, John Redmond and his brother, and others of the old Irish Parliamentary Party, which fought us for so many years in this House in pleading the cause of Ireland with great eloquence and Parliamentary renown—there they were, making these speeches of absolute support and unity with this country until everybody said everywhere, "The brightest spot in the world is Ireland." It may be that a grand opportunity was lost then. We must keep our eyes open. I always keep mine open on the Irish question.

We had a pretty dreary time between these two wars. But we have great responsibilities for the part we played—so we have, all of us—and so have the Americans in not making the League of Nations a reality and in not backing its principles with effective armed forces, and letting this deadly and vengeful foe arm at his leisure. But, underneath, the whole Empire and ourselves in these islands grew stronger and our resources multiplied. Little was said about our growth. Little was visible of our closer union, while the forces which had sent the Anzac Corps to the Dardanelles, and afterwards to the Hindenburg Line, and carried the Canadians to Vimy Ridge, were all growing, unseen, unnoticed, immeasurable, far below the surface of public life and political conflict. These are the natural processes to which my right hon. Friend so aptly referred. Then, this war broke out. The Mother Country —I must still ask leave to use this name; anyhow, I think it is rather dangerous to plunge into new nomenclature, and I am not sure that anything like "The Elder Sister Country" would be a very great success. There was that old song which I remember in my youth, "A Boy's Best Friend Is His Mother," and which seems to me to be sometimes worth humming again. The Mother Country I say was geographically involved, once again, in the struggles of Europe, and found it right and necessary to declare war upon Germany because Germany had violated Poland and we had guaranteed to defend Poland. Instantly, from all parts of the British Empire, with one lamentable exception, about which we must all search our hearts, came the same response. None of the disillusionments that had followed "the war to end wars," "the homes for heroes" and so forth—all good slogans in their day—none of the disillusionments which we had gone through, with the ups and downs of unemployment and great privations, none of these had affected in any way the living, growing, intensifying inner life of the British Commonwealth and Empire. When the signal came, from the poorest Colony to the most powerful Dominion, the great maxim held, "When the King declares war, the Empire is at war." The darkest moment came. Did anyone flinch? Was there one cry of pain or doubt or terror? No, Sir, darkness was turned into light and into a light which will never fade away.

What is this miracle? I think the word was used by some hon. Gentlemen yesterday. What is this miracle, for it is nothing less, that called men from the uttermost ends of the earth, some riding twenty days before they could reach their recruiting centers, some armies having to be sent 14,000 miles across the seas before they reached the battlefield? What is this force, this miracle which makes governments, as proud and sovereign as any that have ever existed, immediately cast aside all their fears, and immediately set themselves to aid a good cause and beat the common foe? You must look very deep into the heart of man, and then you will not find the answer unless you look with the eye of the spirit. Then it is that you learn that human beings are not dominated by material things but by ideas for which they are willing to give their lives or their life's work. Among the various forces that hold the British Empire together is, and I certainly do not object to the expression which my hon. Friend the Member for Seaham used, "enlightened self-interest"; that has a valued and important part to play, but I am sure he would make no mistake in placing that in front of those deeper and more mysterious influences which cause human beings to do most incalculable, improvident, and, from the narrow point of view, profitless things. It is our union in freedom and for the sake of our way of living which is the great fact, reinforced by tradition and sentiment, and it does not depend upon anything that could ever be written down in any account kept in some large volume.

We have had the Statute of Westminster, which some thought would involve the breaking of ties. There was a lot to be said about that on either

side. It has not impeded in the slightest degree the onward march of the
Commonwealth and Empire. It has not prevented the centripetal forces of our
vast organization from exerting their full strength. Here, after our failures—
we are not the only nation which had failures between the two wars—here,
after the Statute of Westminster, here after getting into this war, and dragging
in the Empire so unprepared—and they themselves no better prepared either
in arms or opinion—here amid the wreck of empires, states, nations, and
institutions of every kind, we find the British Commonwealth and Empire
more strongly united than ever before. In a world of confusion and ruin,
the old flag flies. We have not got to consider how to bind ourselves more
closely. It would pass the wit of man to do so. It is extraordinary what a poor
business it has become to sneer at the British Empire. Those who have tried
it in the United States have been discredited. Those who have tried it in the
Dominions have found no public backing, although there is free speech for
all opinions. Those who decry our Commonwealth of Nations and deride the
Mother Country have very little support.

The question before us is, How can we make things better? How can we
gain greater results from our already close ties? I do not think we should
embark upon that task with a sort of feeling that, if we do not do something,
everything is going to crash. I do not understand that. I do not feel like
that. The forces underlying our unity are superior to any temporary shortcomings for which any of us may become responsible. We have to consider
practical steps and to consider these coolly and sagely. The world is in
crisis. The British Commonwealth and Empire within itself was never more
united. Rudyard Kipling, that refreshing fountain of British Imperial ideas,
wrote of the Dominions:

"Daughter am I in my mother's house,
But Mistress in my own."

We have to take a step beyond that now. There is a family council.
Methods must be devised, without haste and without rest, to bring the nations
of the British Empire into intimate and secret counsel upon the march of
world events not only during this war—because that is done with great labor
and efficiency—but after the war, so that they know fully our position and
we theirs in regard to the march of events and the action which may have
to come from them. My right hon. Friend the Member for Devonport spoke
wisely and suggestively of "functional unity" within the Empire and also of
another applicable to the world at large. The question had been raised:
Should we have a permanent machinery like the Committee of Imperial
Defense, only on a larger scale, a kind of lively extension of the principle
which is embodied in the name of the Chief of the Imperial General Staff,
which Lord Haldane created by a farseeing decision, a sort of continuance, in
an Imperial form, of the machinery which I, at present, direct as Minister of
National Defense, should we set up something like this to be a standing and
perpetual committee of the British Empire? This is no more than an expansion on a much greater scale and in much more precise detail of the work
hitherto done by the Committee of Imperial Defense, which my right hon.
Friend mentioned. But should it extend into the sphere of maritime affairs,
of economic affairs and of financial affairs, and how far?

These are obviously matters which we must begin to explore together
when we meet informally our colleagues from the great Dominions. There are
some who would clothe the machinery of union with Ministerial authority,
there are others who would have it extended to both economic and military
affairs. I must say, speaking for myself, I see very little difficulty about the

first, about international bodies being developed with more vigor. We have, of course, representatives of the Dominions on the bodies which function under the Minister of Defense now. I see very little difficulty about the first; I see very great advantage about the second, namely, Ministerial contact. There must be frequent meetings of the Prime Ministers, and they must be attended by those they choose to bring with them, to discuss all aspects of Imperial policy and Imperial safety. Here as in so many cases time marches forward with a friendly step. The vast developments of air transport make a new bond of union—I think attention was drawn to it by my right hon. Friend opposite—and there are new facilities for meeting, which will make the councils of the British Commonwealth of Nations a unity much greater than ever was possible before, when the war is over and when the genius of the air is turned from the most horrible forms of destruction to the glories of peace.

It will be quite easy to have meetings of Prime Ministers or Imperial conferences, whatever you like to call them, every year or more often, on every serious occasion when we get to the times of peace, and we shall encourage them at any time in the period of war. It is not necessary that these meetings should always take place in London. They may take place in other great centers of our United Empire. Although I am still old-fashioned enough to consider Cockney London as the heart of the Empire, I am quite ready that we should take wing in the future. In this war we have already held, quite apart from the conferences with the President of the United States, a conference in Quebec where I sat for several days with the Dominion Cabinet, and we were all the guests of Canada, which I may say is a very agreeable thing to be. It is very likely, as the somber marches of the war succeed one another, when Hitler and Hitlerism are finished and blasted from the face of the earth, we shall have conferences of the British Empire and the United States in Australia about all these matters—and there are certainly some in which we find cause of complaint against the Japanese. When peace returns, and we should pray to God it soon may, the conferences of the Prime Ministers of the Dominions, among whom we trust India will be reckoned and with whom the Colonies will be associated, will, we hope, become frequent and regular facts and festivities of our annual life.

One last word before I sit down. Some assume that there must be an inherent antagonism between a world order to keep peace and vast national or federal organization which will evidently be in existence. I do not believe this is true. Both the world order and this great organization may be so fashioned as to be two parts of one tremendous whole. I have never conceived that a fraternal association with the United States would militate in any way against the unity of the British Commonwealth and Empire, or breed ill-feeling with our great Russian Ally, to whom we are bound by the twenty years treaty. I do not think we need choose this or that. With wisdom, and patience, and vigor, and courage, we may get the best of both. We have often said of our own British Empire:

"In My Father's house there are many mansions."

So in this far greater world structure, which we shall surely raise out of the ruins of desolating war, there will be room for all generous, free associations of a special character, so long as they are not disloyal to the world cause nor seek to bar the forward march of mankind.

JOINT STATEMENT BY MONETARY EXPERTS MEETING IN WASHINGTON TO DISCUSS ESTABLISHMENT OF A PROPOSED INTERNATIONAL STABILIZATION FUND

April 21, 1944 [1]

Sufficient discussion of the problems of international monetary cooperation has taken place at the technical level to justify a statement of principles. It is the consensus of opinion of the experts of the United and Associated Nations who have participated in these discussions that the most practical method of assuring international monetary cooperation is through the establishment of an international monetary fund. The principles set forth below are designed to constitute the basis for this fund.

Governments are not asked to give final approval to these principles until they have been embodied in the form of definite proposals by the delegates of the United and Associated Nations meeting in a formal conference.

I. *Purposes and Policies of the International Monetary Fund*

The fund will be guided in all its decisions by the purposes and policies set forth below:

1. To promote international monetary cooperation through a permanent institution which provides the machinery for consultation on international monetary problems.

2. To facilitate the expansion and balanced growth of international trade and to contribute in this way to the maintenance of a high level of employment and real income, which must be a primary objective of economic policy.

3. To give confidence to member countries by making the fund's resources available to them under adequate safeguards, thus giving members time to correct maladjustments in their balance of payments without resorting to measures destructive of national or international prosperity.

4. To promote exchange stability, to maintain orderly exchange arrangements among member countries and to avoid competitive exchange depreciation.

5. To assist in the establishment of multilateral payments facilities on current transactions among member countries and in the elimination of foreign exchange restrictions which hamper the growth of world trade.

6. To shorten the periods and lessen the degree of disequilibrium in the international balance of payments of member countries.

II. *Subscription to the Fund*

1. Member countries shall subscribe in gold and in their local funds amounts (quotas) to be agreed, which will amount altogether to about $8,000,000,000 if all the United and Associated Nations subscribe to the fund (corresponding to about $10,000,000,000 for the world as a whole).

2. The quotas may be revised from time to time, but changes shall require a four-fifths vote and no member's quota may be changed without its assent.

3. The obligatory gold subscription of a member country shall be fixed at 25 per cent of its subscription (quota) or 10 per cent of its holdings of gold and gold-convertible exchange, whichever is the smaller.

[1] *New York Times.*

III. *Transactions with the Fund*

1. Member countries shall deal with the fund only through their Treasury, central bank, stabilization fund or other fiscal agencies. The fund's account in a member's currency shall be kept at the central bank of the member country.

2. A member shall be entitled to buy another member's currency from the fund in exchange for its own currency on the following conditions:

(a) The member represents that the currency demanded is presently needed for making payments in that currency which are consistent with the purposes of the fund.

(b) The fund has not given notice that its holdings of the currency demanded have become scarce, in which case the provisions of VI, below, come into force.

(c) The fund's total holdings of the currency offered (after having been restored, if below that figure, to 75 per cent of the member's quota) have not been increased by more than 25 per cent of the member's quota during the previous twelve months and do not exceed 200 per cent of the quota.

(d) The fund has not previously given appropriate notice that the member is suspended from making further use of the fund's resources on the ground that it is using them in a manner contrary to the purposes and policies of the fund; but the fund shall not give such notice until it has presented to the member concerned a report setting forth its views and has allowed a suitable time for reply.

The fund may in its discretion and on terms which safeguard its interests waive any of the conditions above.

3. The operations on the fund's account will be limited to transactions for the purpose of supplying a member country on the member's initiative with another member's currency in exchange for its own currency or for gold. Transactions provided for under 4 and 7, below, are not subject to this limitation.

4. The fund will be entitled at its option, with a view to preventing a particular member's currency from becoming scarce:

(a) To borrow its currency from a member country;

(b) To offer gold to a member country in exchange for its currency.

5. So long as a member country is entitled to buy another member's currency from the fund in exchange for its own currency, it shall be prepared to buy its own currency from that member with that member's currency or with gold. This shall not apply to currency subject to restrictions in conformity with IX, 3, below, or to holdings of currency or with gold. This shall not apply to currency subject to restrictions in conformity with IX, 3, below, or to holdings of currency which have accumulated as a result of transactions of a current account nature effected before the removal by the member country of restrictions on multilateral clearing maintained or imposed under X, 2, below.

6. A member country desiring to obtain, directly or indirectly, the currency of another member country for gold is expected, provided that it can do so with equal advantage, to acquire the currency by the sale of gold to the fund. This shall not preclude the sale of newly mined gold by a gold-producing country on any market.

7. The fund may also acquire gold from member countries in accordance with the following provisions:

(a) A member country may repurchase from the fund for gold any part of the latter's holdings of its currency.

(b) So long as a member's holdings of gold and gold-convertible exchange exceed its quota, the fund in selling foreign exchange to that country shall require that one-half of the net sales of such exchange during the fund's financial year be paid for with gold.

(c) If at the end of the fund's financial year a member's holdings of gold and gold-convertible exchange have increased, the fund may require up to one-half of the increase to be used to repurchase part of the fund's holdings of its currency so long as this does not reduce the fund's holdings of a country's currency below 75 per cent of its quota or the member's holdings of gold and gold-convertible exchange below its quota.

IV. *Par Values of Member Currencies*

1. The par value of a member's currency shall be agreed with the fund when it is admitted to membership, and shall be expressed in terms of gold. All transactions between the fund and members shall be at par, subject to a fixed charge payable by the member making application to the fund, and all transactions in member currencies shall be at rates within an agreed percentage of parity.

2. Subject to 5, below, no change in the par value of a member's currency shall be made by the fund without the country's approval. Member countries agree not to propose a change in the parity of their currency unless they consider it appropriate to the correction of a fundamental disequilibrium. Changes shall be made only with the approval of the fund, subject to the provisions below.

3. The fund shall approve a requested change in the par value of a member's currency, if it is essential to the correction of a fundamental disequilibrium. In particular, the fund shall not reject a requested change, necessary to restore equilibrium, because of the domestic social or political policies of the country applying for a change. In considering a requested change, the fund shall take into consideration the extreme uncertainties prevailing at the time the parities of the currencies of the member countries were initially agreed upon.

4. After consulting the fund, a member country may change the established parity of its currency, provided the proposed change, inclusive of any previous change since the establishment of the fund, does not exceed 10 per cent. In the case of application for a further change, not covered by the above and not exceeding 10 per cent, the fund shall give its decision within two days of receiving the application, if the applicant so requests.

5. An agreed uniform change may be made in the gold value of member currencies, provided every member country having 10 per cent or more of the aggregate quotas approves.

V. *Capital Transactions*

1. A member country may not use the fund's resources to meet a large or sustained outflow of capital, and the fund may require a member country to exercise controls to prevent such use of the resources of the fund. This provision is not intended to prevent the use of the fund's resources for capital transactions of reasonable amount required for the expansion of exports or in the ordinary course of trade, banking or other businesses. Nor is it intended to prevent capital movements which are met out of a member country's own

resources of gold and foreign exchange, provided such capital movements are in accordance with the purposes of the fund.

2. Subject to VI, below, a member country may not use its control of capital movements to restrict payments for current transactions or to delay unduly the transfers of funds in settlement of commitments.

VI. *Apportionment of Scarce Currencies*

1. When it becomes evident to the fund that the demand for a member country's currency may soon exhaust the fund's holdings of that currency, the fund shall so inform member countries and propose an equitable method of apportioning the scarce currency. When a currency is thus declared scarce, the fund shall issue a report embodying the causes of the scarcity and containing recommendations designed to bring it to an end.

2. A decision by the fund to apportion a scarce currency shall operate as an authorization to a member country, after consultation with the fund, temporarily to restrict the freedom of exchange operations in the affected currency, and in determining the manner of restricting the demand and rationing the limited supply among its nationals the member country shall have complete jurisdiction.

VII. *Management*

1. The fund shall be governed by a board on which each member will be represented and by an executive committee. The executive committee shall consist of at least nine members including the representatives of the five countries with the largest quotas.

2. The distribution of voting power on the board and the executive committee shall be closely related to the quotas.

3. Subject to II, 2, and IV, 5, all matters shall be settled by a majority of the votes.

4. The fund shall publish at short intervals a statement of its position showing the extent of its holdings of member currencies and of gold and its transactions in gold.

VIII. *Withdrawal*

1. A member country may withdraw from the fund by giving notice in writing.

2. The reciprocal obligations of the fund and the country are to be liquidated within a reasonable time.

3. After a member country has given notice in writing of its withdrawal from the fund the fund may not dispose of its holdings of the country's currency except in accordance with the arrangements made under 2 above. After a country has given notice of withdrawal its use of the resources of the fund is subject to the approval of the fund.

IX. *The Obligations of Member Countries*

1. Not to buy gold at a price which exceeds the agreed parity of its currency by more than a prescribed margin and not to sell gold at a price which falls below the agreed parity by more than a prescribed margin.

2. Not to allow exchange transactions in its market in currencies of other members at rates outside a prescribed range based on the agreed parities.

3. Not to impose restrictions on payments for current international trans-

actions with other member countries (other than those involving transactions with other member countries; other than those involving capital transfers or in accordance with VI, above) or to engage in any discriminatory currency arrangements or multiple currency practices without the approval of the fund.

X. *Transitional Arrangements*

1. Since the fund is not intended to provide facilities for relief or reconstruction or to deal with international indebtedness arising out of the war, the agreement of a member country to Provisions III, 5, and IX, 3, above, shall not become operative until it is satisfied as to the arrangements at its disposal to facilitate the settlement of the balance of payments differences during the early post-war transition period by means which will not unduly encumber its facilities with the fund.

2. During the transition period member countries may maintain and adapt to changing circumstances exchange regulations of the character which have been in operation during the war, but they shall undertake to withdraw as soon as possible by progressive stages any restrictions which impede multilateral clearing on current account. In their exchange policy they shall pay continuous regard to the principles and objectives of the fund; and they shall take all possible measures to develop commercial and financial relations with other member countries which will facilitate international payments and the maintenance of exchange stability.

3. The fund may make representations to any member that conditions are favorable to withdrawal of particular restrictions or for the general abandonment of the restrictions inconsistent with IX, 3, above. Not later than three years after coming into force of the fund any member still retaining any restrictions inconsistent with IX, 3, shall consult with the fund as to their further retention.

4. In its relations with member countries the fund shall recognize that the transition period is one of change and adjustment, and in deciding on its attitude to any proposals presented by members it shall give the member country the benefit of any reasonable doubt.

STATEMENT OF ANDREI Y. VYSHINSKY, DEPUTY PEOPLE'S COMMISSAR OF FOREIGN AFFAIRS OF THE U.S.S.R., ON NEGOTIATIONS WITH FINLAND FOR AN ARMISTICE

April 22, 1944 [1]

As is already known from previously published reports of the Information Bureau of the People's Commissariat of Foreign Affairs of the USSR, in mid-February of this year the Finnish Government addressed the Soviet Government with a proposal to commence negotiations on the termination of war operations by Finland and on Finland's withdrawal from the war.

To this proposal the Soviet Government replied that it had no grounds to feel particular confidence in the present Finnish government, but if the Finns had no other possibility, the Soviet Government in the interests of peace agreed to negotiate with the present Finnish government on the cessation of

[1] Information Bulletin, Embassy of the U.S.S.R.

hostilities. The Soviet terms of armistice, formulated in the well-known six clauses, were published on March 1.

When the Soviet terms were being presented to the Finnish government, the latter was informed that if the Finnish government agreed to accept these terms the Soviet Government was prepared to receive Finland's representatives in Moscow to negotiate the conclusion of a concrete agreement. In its reply concerning the Soviet terms of armistice presented to the Soviet Legation in Stockholm on March 8, the Finnish government stated:

"The Finnish Government, which seriously strives to reestablish within the shortest time peaceful relations between Finland and the USSR, has closely studied the terms of armistice presented by the Soviet Union to Finland. The Finnish Government realizes that for Finland to be able to remain neutral after the conclusion of the armistice it is necessary that no foreign troops belonging to the belligerent country be stationed on her territory. However, this problem is so complicated that it requires more detailed discussion. Therefore the Finnish Government wishes to propose the commencement of negotiations, so that the Finns might explain their viewpoint on this and on other problems in connection with the terms of armistice proposed by the Soviet Government."

The Soviet Government found this reply unsatisfactory. This was communicated to the Finnish government and the latter's attention was drawn to the fact that the Soviet terms of armistice in the shape of the six clauses presented to Paasikivi were minimal and elementary and that only in the event of acceptance of these terms by the Finnish government, Soviet-Finnish negotiations on the cessation of hostilities were possible.

Informing the Finnish government of this, the Soviet Government declared that it would await a positive reply during one week, after which the Soviet Government would consider that the Finns had intentionally protracted the negotiations for some incomprehensible purposes and that they rejected the Soviet terms. On March 17, the Finnish government presented to the Soviet Government its reply, which said:

"Finland's Government, which, as previously, seriously strives for the reestablishment of peaceful relations and wishes to commence negotiations, cannot, however, declare beforehand acceptance of the terms in question, which affect the existence of the entire nation, without even being firmly certain of the interpretation of these terms and of their meaning."

Despite the fact that in essence this Finnish reply was negative, the Soviet Government deemed it possible to communicate to the Finnish government the following:

1. The Soviet Government does not object to the Finnish government sending one or several of its representatives to receive from the Soviet Government an interpretation of the Soviet terms of armistice.

2. The Soviet Government considers that Moscow would be the most appropriate place for representatives of the Finnish government to obtain the most exhaustive interpretation.

On March 26, a delegation of the Finnish government consisting of Paasikivi and Enkel arrived in Moscow. On March 27 and 29 the Finnish delegation met representatives of the Soviet Government Molotov and Dekanozov. As a result of the exchange of opinions between Soviet and Finnish representatives, the following Soviet proposals concerning peace with Finland were presented to the Finnish delegation:

1. Severance of relations with Germany and the internment of German troops and ships in Finland, or else the severance of relations with Germany

and the expulsion of German troops and ships from Finland not later than the close of the month of April. In either case the Soviet Government can render Finland aid with its armed forces.

2. Restitution of the Soviet-Finnish treaty of 1940 and the withdrawal of Finnish troops to the frontier of 1940 to be carried out in stages during the month of April.

3. Immediate repatriation of Soviet and Allied war prisoners, also Soviet and Allied civilians kept in concentration camps or used by the Finns for work; while should the USSR and Finland sign a peace treaty and not an armistice, the repatriation of war prisoners should be reciprocal.

4. Demobilization of fifty per cent of the Finnish army to be carried out during the month of May, and the transfer of the entire Finnish army to a peace footing to be carried out during June and July (this clause should form a part of the treaty or should be given the shape of a separate Soviet-Finnish agreement to be signed simultaneously with the peace or armistice treaty).

5. Compensation for damages caused by Finland to the Soviet Union by the hostilities and the occupation of Soviet territory, in the sum of 600 million American dollars, paid in the course of five years in goods (paper, cellulose, sea and river ships and various machinery).

6. Restoration to the Soviet Union of Petsamo and the Petsamo region, which the Soviet Union voluntarily ceded to Finland under the peace treaties of 1920 and 1940.

7. In the event of the acceptance by the Finnish party of the above six conditions, the Soviet Government deems it possible to renounce in favor of Finland its right to the lease of Hangoe and the area of Hangoe without any compensation.

As seen from the above text, these proposals gave concrete formulation of the clauses of the Soviet terms on the demobilization of the Finnish army, on compensation for damages which Finland caused the Soviet Union by hostilities and the occupation of Soviet territory, and also on Petsamo.

In addition, a new clause was introduced on the cessation of Hangoe and the area of Hangoe in favor of Finland.

As to the Finnish delegation, it did not propose any corrections of the Soviet armistice terms or present any proposals of its own concerning armistice terms.

On April 19, i.e., three weeks after the above Soviet armistice terms were presented to the Finns, the Finnish government communicated its reply to these terms through the medium of the Swedish Ministry of Foreign Affairs. This reply said:

"The Finnish Government received the proposals of the Government of the USSR concerning peace with Finland, which were presented on March 29 in more precise formulation to representatives of the Finnish Government Paasikivi and Enkel. These proposals were examined and studied by the Finnish Government and were submitted to the Diet for discussion.

"In the course of this it was considered that the acceptance of these proposals, which are partly impossible of realization even for technical reasons, would to a considerable extent weaken and violate the conditions under which Finland can continue to exist as an independent state, and would impose on the Finnish people burdens which, according to unanimous and competent testimony considerably exceed its strength.

"In view of this the Finnish Government, which seriously strives for the reestablishment of good and stable peaceful relations with its great neighbor in the East, regrets that the proposals which it recently received and carefully studied offer no possibility for the realization of this striving."

To this declaration of the Finnish government the Soviet Government sent the following reply on April 22:

"On April 19, the Soviet Government received the reply of the government of Finland to Soviet armistice terms presented in Moscow to the Finnish delegation composed of Paasikivi and Enkel.

"The Soviet Government notes that in its reply Finland's government declined the Soviet armistice terms as a basis for negotiations and discontinued negotiations on armistice."

The statement of the Finnish government that the Soviet proposals are allegedly partly impossible of realization for technical reasons is absolutely inconsistent. The Finnish delegation did not even raise any such question in Moscow. The Finnish government's attempt to evade responsibility as regards compensation for damages which Finland caused to the Soviet Union by hostilities and the occupation of Soviet territory cannot be justified by anything. As a result of the attack on the Soviet Union and occupation of its territory, Finland caused our country enormous losses and damages which she is obliged to compensate, in accordance with all the rules of justice. To write off this debt from Finland would mean to give a premium to the aggressor for acts of aggression, plunder and destruction.

The Finnish government's statement that the Soviet proposals would impose on the Finnish people a burden beyond its strength is groundless, since this question has not yet come under discussion and the Finnish delegation in Moscow did not state that it considered the problem of compensation for damages as the principal problem in the reestablishment of peace.

The negotiations with the Finnish delegation in Moscow made it clear that the main question for the Finnish government is the demand of the Soviet Government concerning the internment or expulsion of German troops stationed in Finland. The Finnish government asserts that acceptance of the Soviet proposals allegedly endangers the further existence of Finland as an independent state. This is certainly not true. Present-day Finland possesses no state independence. She lost it at the moment when she admitted German troops to her territory.

The point in question now is the restoration of Finland's lost independence by means of the expulsion of German troops from Finland and the cessation of hostilities. It is known that as a result of the fact that the Finnish government admitted German troops to its territory for a joint attack on the Soviet Union, the entire northern half of Finland fell into the hands of the Germans, who are the true masters there and who have converted Finland into a semi-occupied country.

But in the southern part of Finland the Finnish government does not possess full power either. In essence, after the Finnish government voluntarily yielded power in northern Finland to the Germans, it ceased to be master of its own home. In its relations with the German fascists, the Finnish government went to such lengths that already it cannot, and as a matter of fact, does not, wish to break with them. It placed its country at the service of the interests of Hitlerite Germany. Precisely for this reason the most difficult problem for the Finnish government was the demand for the internment or expulsion of German troops from Finland and for the severance of relations with Germany.

The present Finnish government does not wish to expel the German troops from Finland. It does not wish to reestablish peaceful relations. It prefers to leave its country in vassal subjection to Hitlerite Germany.

LORD HALIFAX'S SPEECH AT ANNUAL DINNER
OF AMERICAN SOCIETY OF
INTERNATIONAL LAW

April 29, 1944 [1]

You will, I am sure, feel it is only fitting that before I go on to speak of other things, I should say a word about a great American who must be much in our thoughts tonight. Others have more right than I have to speak of all that Frank Knox achieved for the service he loved so well; of that mighty battle fleet he did so much to build; of the robust judgment, the courage and fighting spirit he brought to the councils of the nation.

For my part I cannot forget that for three years I was honored by his friendship; that I learned, more and more, his value to our common cause and that, by word and example, he did as much as any man could do to foster a real comradeship in arms between your Navy and ours, and between your people and mine.

I am very glad to be here tonight to pay the tribute of a layman to the work which members of this association are doing in the field of international law. Particular significance attaches in these days to all that study, concerned as it is with so much that is directly at issue in this war. And, therefore, all thinking persons will have welcomed the statement, to which many members of this society have contributed, defining the action that seems requisite to lay "the basis of a just and enduring world peace, securing order under law to all nations."

There can be no field of inquiry closer to what I judge to be the public preoccupation at the present time. For I cannot doubt that the masses of the Allied peoples everywhere have two dominant thoughts, which can be truly said to include most of the things that matter to the world. The first is that they are determined to fight this war through and to finish it as quickly as they can; and the second is the question of how they can prevent there ever being another.

As to the first, we must all have a feeling of waiting on great events; waiting above all for the time when, now that the Allies have a preponderance of ships, planes, fighting material and men, we may strike decisive blows that will drive Germany and Japan out of the war. Meanwhile, our course is plain: It is to take no chance, to relax no effort, to hold back nothing that will hasten the day of victory.

The second thought is a question upon the answer to which depends the future of the human race. The best minds everywhere are working on it from every angle, for we realize how complex is the problem and how closely all parts of it are tied up together. Can we insure that the world will bind itself, both in written undertaking and in concrete act, to live in future, in the words of the preamble to the covenant of the League of Nations, "by the firm establishment of the understandings of international law as the actual rule of conduct among governments"? Or are the forces that would support and establish such a law once again to be swallowed by the jungle, of which the only maxim is:

"The good old rule, the simple plan,
That they should take who have the power

[1] *New York Times.*

And they should keep who can"?

Nations, like individuals, have great opportunities. They can convert them to large achievement or they can let them go. The nations have let go many opportunities; and, as we reflect upon the rate of growth in the destructive capacity of a scientific age, we should be the more grateful if we are allowed another chance. For if we do not take advantage of it the human race may come perilously near self-extermination.

Can we do better this time? The answer will depend upon whether or not we can be clear-sighted enough to recognize and face the real elements in the problem, pleasing or ugly as these may be.

Time was when there was real substance in the idea of the community of nations. The Roman Empire included within its borders the whole of the western civilized world, and in the shadow of its might peoples dwelt for generations in security. It vanished as a fact before the barbarian invasions and the division of the empire between Byzantium and Rome; but it survived as an idea in the concept of the unity of Christendom and in the shadowy supremacy of the Holy Roman Empire, which with the passage of years became, in the words of Voltaire, "neither holy nor Roman nor an empire." Such fragments of unity as remained at the close of the Middle Ages were further broken by the Reformation and the rise of strong national states. War followed war, with hardly a breathing space, while a few men patiently, but in vain, labored to rediscover the lost art of peace.

From their efforts we had the beginnings of a law of nations, with the publication in 1625 of Grotius' great work, "De Jure Belli et Pacis." Many different suggestions were made to restore the broken unity of Europe: the "Grand Design" associated with Sully, Minister of Henry IV of France; William Penn's "Essay Toward the Present and Future Peace of Europe"; the "Fundamental Treaty" of the Abbé Saint-Pierre; Kant's "Treatise on Perpetual Peace"; the Holy Alliance—to name the more famous only of these projects.

We had the great European Congresses—Westphalia, Utrecht, Vienna, Berlin. But these, for all their importance, were hardly more than glimmers in the surrounding gloom. In the seventeenth and eighteenth centuries every decade had its war; and even after 1815, when the British Navy sailed the seas without serious challenge, wars, though localized, continued; and in this uneasy fashion we reached the twentieth century, the first World War, and the great, but for the time at least unsuccessful, experiment of a League of Nations.

It is a long story. Why has humanity been so frustrated? Causes of failure to prevent war, like the actual causes of war, have varied at different times. In the Middle Ages and, indeed, later, religious and dynastic influences were far stronger breeders of wars than they are today; though these wars often left little mark upon the life of the ordinary population. It is also true that economic maladjustments, as we know them in the light of what we have learned in a century of mechanical invention, were less tormenting to our forefathers than they are to us. These maladjustments, with the economic disorders they produced, by pre-disposing people to accept bad advice, gave the gangster dictators exactly the opportunity they needed.

So one could go on, comparing and contrasting. But through all the variations we can plainly discover certain elements, forces, facts that in different circumstances remain fairly constant, and that go some way to explain the difficulties which have thwarted realization of the idea of international solidarity.

The first is, of course, that which we call nationalism, the sense which makes men, organized in a nation, conscious of their distinction from other national groups and leads them to prefer their own group to any other. Here, plainly, there is something which goes very deep both in history and human nature and has been a powerful force for both good and evil. But whatever its merits or demerits, it is in the world to stay, and no plan for more stable international order has a hope of succeeding that does not take it into full account.

The second fact is that wars induce in nations a desire for unity which peace often dissolves. Emotion is a stronger spur than reason, and when the storm clouds of war are emptying themselves upon the earth nations may register many good resolutions which are apt to fade when the skies clear.

"The devil was ill, the devil a monk would be;
The devil was well, the devil a monk was he."

The third thing, that we are very apt to forget, is how slow and difficult has been human progress and how very gradually we can expect to make large changes in human motive. The time has gone by when we might have been tempted to think of progress as something quasi-automatic, given enough mechanical aids to simplify, support and embellish daily life. We have seen too clearly how thin is the crust that separates man from animal and how easily something which we had thought firm and permanent can be thrown back into barbarism.

What, then, are we to think? For if we no longer can go to sleep with the thought of progress being easy and assured, we certainly cannot any longer take refuge in any kind of escapist philosophy. Neither as individuals nor as nations is it likely to be possible for us to stand on one side and keep out of the way of the traffic or to suppose that in a world that gets smaller every day political or economic conditions will allow any nation for long to enjoy the delusion of self-sufficiency.

Fortunately we can learn from our latest and greatest failure. It would not be hard to compile a list of the mistakes that the democracies made after 1918, but it all largely comes back to some very simple and very broad miscalculations.

You in the United States and we in the United Kingdom thought that what was so abundantly clear to us—namely, that for victors and vanquished alike war was a disastrous interlude—must be equally clear to everybody else. But it was not. And this instinctive misjudgment was responsible for giving many people a wholly exaggerated view of the strength of the League of Nations and of leading them to place quite undue faith in the mere signature of pacts and treaties.

This again led to our tragic mistake of putting the cart before the horse in the whole business of disarmament. Trusting to our own good intentions, believing that what was clear to us about war being a bad solution must also be clear to others, we pushed on with disarming ourselves and disarming by agreement our late Allies, while failing effectively to control the rearmament of those who had lately been our enemies.

I have called this putting the cart before the horse, because we did it all before we had established any firm system of security that would be called into operation if anything went wrong with our arrangements. And if there is one thing I would suppose was quite certain about our post-war actions this time, it is that neither you nor we shall be so mad as to disarm our nations except on a proved and established basis of security.

What does that mean? It means in the first place the refusal, by whatever action may seem the most sure, to the late aggressors of any opportunity to begin again. It means, secondly, the maintenance of these controls or prohibitions until we are satisfied that there is a real and a permanent change of heart. It means, finally, the refusal to permit any one-sided infraction of any terms that are imposed or accepted.

This last must be one of the fundamental principles of international action after the war. If law is to be effective, it must be applied always, everywhere and to all. We do not acquit a man of murder because he is a wealthy citizen, or because his victim was an old man who had not long to live. We do not acquit a man of theft because the amount he stole was not very large. Let the criminal get away with one crime and he is already half-way to the commission of another. And with Hitler, as with Japan, nothing succeeded so fatally as success.

I am not concerned to argue at what particular point they could have been halted in their depredations. No one knows better than I do how tragically our diplomacy, and I daresay yours, was hampered by the fact of which I spoke a moment ago—namely, that we had thrown away our strength. But that should not blind us to the truth that with each successful infraction, international law was weakened and the next crime came more easily.

Every part of this program makes two demands upon us. It demands the existence of force in some form which can, if necessary, be invoked as the law-abiding citizen invokes the policeman to keep order. It also demands the continued readiness of public opinion in all the peace-loving nations to remain resolute in this business of enforcement. Certainly our leaders must lead; but if they have insufficient regard for the thought of those who follow, they may not impossibly find themselves in the position that led the British statesman Disraeli on a historic occasion to describe the Prime Minister, Sir Robert Peel, as being "an emperor without his army."

Three weeks ago Mr. Hull addressed a serious and timely warning on this very point. "A proposal," he said, "is worse than useless if it is not acceptable to those nations who must share with us the responsibility for its execution. It is dangerous for us and misleading for them if in the final outcome it does not have the necessary support in this country." And what is true of the United States is true, with due allowance for variations of constitutional machinery, of other countries, too.

Can we, then, reasonably look forward to public opinion here and in the British Commonwealth being willing for the requisite period of time to accept the great responsibility that must go with power and that must surely accompany a victory, in the approach to which, through many almost miraculous deliveries, we can hardly fail to see the overruling hand of God?

The great powers cannot abdicate or delegate the responsibilities which their greatness has thrust upon them. They cannot take shelter behind a rampart of small states or suppose that a collective pronouncement of high intention can by itself and on all occasions take the place of action.

Nothing is more easy than to be gloomy about the future. It is easy to recall that in 1918 we had the same good intentions and made the same good resolutions. It is also true that at the end of this war the problems of peace are going to be much more difficult than they were at the end of the last war. Yet mankind never crosses the same river twice and it is perhaps reasonable to hope that the world will not twice make the same mistakes. Macaulay used to say that "no man who is correctly informed as to the past will be disposed to take a morose or disappointing view of the present."

And with all the disappointment and anxiety which we must feel, there is something to set upon the other side. During the last 150 years the world has made real progress toward recovery of the idea of a working society of nations. That progress is plainly, if unostentatiously, marked by a number of conventions and agreements, all of which, whatever may have been their intrinsic importance, plainly acknowledge that there is such a thing as an international community.

There were the numerous congresses and conferences of the nineteenth century, held either to liquidate or avert a war and important as registering the conviction that war is not merely the affair of the actual or potential combatants. And in 1918 we saw the culminating experiment of the League of Nations which, apart from its subsidiary, the International Labor Office, and its fruitful activities in the field of humanitarian and scientific endeavor, did realize, in a form however incomplete, the idea of an international society.

With all this slow but recognizable progress, large changes were bound to occur in the old conception of neutrality. So long as a war could be regarded as a private quarrel between two countries, other countries not directly concerned might hope to remain outside it. But one effect of the influence exerted upon world thought by the League of Nations has been to make war less the exclusive concern of combatants and more an offense against international law and order. In this war, more plainly even than in the last, we have found that no neutrality will avail by itself to protect the interests of a neutral or even to secure its national existence.

Furthermore, today the whole character of war has altered. Certainly this war is about something much more profound than frontiers or interests, as we used to understand them. And if the world should ever fail to keep the peace in the future, it is probably safe to assume that this would be because of a clash of fundamental ideas affecting all society.

The cumulative effect of these converging forces is to make it probable that the process of revising the old conception of neutrality will continue and that there will be a proportionate development in the idea that the protection of peace and world order are of common concern to all.

With all this, we must never lose sight of the momentum to war given by the economic and social disorders of our time. No political action by itself can be relied upon to keep war from the world unless we all realize how closely these problems belong to our peace and are prepared with resolution to meet and master them together. I do not say that we shall ever find their solution easy; but I am pretty sure that we shall never solve them separately.

The nations were far from accepting these truths twenty-five years ago, but they are a good deal nearer to them today. And as between the United States and the British Commonwealth, there is the further undoubted fact that the present war has brought us to a better knowledge of each other. It is leading both our peoples to realize that in discharging whatever responsibilities the needs of world security may place upon us, we are not and shall not be acting in any spirit of good fairy generosity to the world, but in the strictest temper of self-interest.

It is one of the crowning mercies of our times that there is no part of the earth's surface where American and British interests are in clash, or where, on the other hand, it is not to the highest advantage of both that they should stand together.

But there is perhaps something deeper than any of this, if we can truly make the thought real and our own. Our nations are now partners in this struggle. Many thousands from each nation are fighting side by side with the other in a comradeship of arms, and on a scale the like of which the world has seldom seen. Each day their unity is being welded and consecrated anew through sacrifice. They are our representatives, in that they are where they are because their respective nations have chosen them for that work. Most of us perhaps feel that they are more than our representatives, as with deep humility we read fractions of the single story of courage and devotion that filter back from them to us on our home fronts.

Must we not rightly feel, as they are part of us and we of them, that the best way to prove ourselves not unworthy of their company is to build that same fellowship between our peoples of which they, our noblest and our best, have shown the pattern? To do less would surely be to fail and to betray them by leaving their work half done. Nor are we likely to find any cause of greater inspiration in the days of peace than that to which those whom I have called our representatives have so freely surrendered themselves in war.

MAY

May 2, 1944

Under Allied pressure Spain agreed to cut its ore exports to Germany.

4

Dr. Joseph Goebbels informed the German people of "trump cards up our sleeves" when the invasion strikes. "There exist innumerable defense measures and weapons so far unknown."

5

Mohandas K. Gandhi, interned since August, 1942 by the British Government, was released from his confinement because of the critical condition of his health.

British troops launched a general counter-offensive on the Kohima front in India.

6

A Russian naval force and air units sank nineteen German transports and auxiliary vessels off Sevastopol.

7

General Charles de Gaulle called for a permanent alliance of France with the Soviet Union and cooperation with the Allies.

8

The Japanese launched a general offensive in eastern India, but were thrown back with heavy losses by British Indian troops.

9

The U. S. Government returned to its owners the Chicago plants of Montgomery Ward & Co.

10

President Roosevelt appointed Acting Secretary James V. Forrestal to succeed the late Frank Knox as Secretary of the Navy.

Premier Joseph Stalin announced the capture of Sevastopol, the Crimean Black Sea naval base, whose 250-day defense by the Russians in 1941–42 was one of the epic incidents of World War II.

Prime Minister Eamon de Valera's Government was beaten by the opposition, farmers and labor; a general election in Ireland was ordered.

11

In its campaign to drive the Japanese from north Burma, Chinese troops crossed the Salween River on a hundred-mile front.

The Allies opened their spring offensive in Italy against the lower Gustav Line.

Courtesy New York Times

The Allies Push Toward Rome
May, 1944

Lieut. Gen. Joseph W. Stilwell launched a new Chinese offensive against the north Burma Japanese bases at Kamaing, Mogaung and Myitkyina.

Selective Service Director Maj. Gen. Lewis B. Hershey issued orders staying the induction of most men of twenty-six through twenty-nine years for at least six months.

12

The Japanese Army invading Honan Province won control of the entire length of the vital Peiping-Hankow Railway, thus trapping several large Chinese forces.

A joint U. S.-British and Soviet declaration warned the Axis satellites for the last time to get out of the war.

16

Supported by the 14th U. S. Air Force, Chinese troops scored big advances in their Western Yunnan Province offensive.

Agreements were signed between Britain and the U. S. and the exiled governments of Norway, the Netherlands and Belgium providing for the control of civil affairs in those countries upon liberation.

17

Merrill's Marauders seized the Myitkyina airfield.

The Spanish Government under British pressure ordered German and Japanese agents out of Tangier across the strait from Gibraltar.

18

Allied Headquarters announced: "The Gustav Line has ceased to exist."

19

Two-thirds of the Hitler Line in Italy crumbled before American and French attacks.

King Peter of Yugoslavia dismissed his Yugoslav Government-in-Exile and invited Dr. Ivan Subasitch to form a pro-Tito Cabinet.

20

Vice-President Wallace left on a trip to Siberia and China for a first-hand study of conditions in those areas.

King Peter relieved pro-Nazi General Draja Mihailovitch of his post as Minister of War in the Yugoslav Government-in-Exile.

French forces turned the Adolf Hitler Line in Italy.

21

Professor Oscar Lange of the University of Chicago announced in Moscow that Marshal Stalin had given him the personal assurance—"It is in the interests of the Soviet Union that Poland be strong."

23

The Allied armies opened their drive on the Anzio beachhead.

24

American troops cut the Appian Way.

25

The Fifth Army's beachhead at Anzio established contact with the main front in Italy.

27

Dr. Joseph Goebbels invited the lynching of captured Allied fliers, saying: ". . . it is far too much to ask of us that we call on German soldiers and German police to intervene to protect these murderers from the fate they deserve."

American troops invaded Biak Island, 900 miles from the Philippines.

29

Secretary of State Cordell Hull announced his readiness to participate in a four-power discussion.

30

President Roosevelt announced the intention of the U. S. Government to offer its three major Allies a suggested program for international post-war security.

MARSHAL JOSEPH V. STALIN'S
ORDER OF THE DAY

May 1, 1944 [1]

ORDER OF THE DAY OF THE SUPREME COMMANDER-IN-CHIEF:

Comrades Red Army and Red Navy men, sergeants, officers and generals, men and women guerrillas! Working people of the Soviet Union! Brothers and sisters who have temporarily fallen under the yoke of the German oppressors and have been forcibly driven to fascist penal servitude in Germany!

On behalf of the Soviet Government and of our Bolshevik Party, I greet and congratulate you upon May Day!

The peoples of our country meet the day of May First in the midst of outstanding successes of the Red Army. Since the defeat of the German divisions at Stalingrad the Red Army has been conducting a practically incessant offensive. During this time the Red Army has made a fighting advance from the Volga to the Seret, from the foothills of the Caucasus to the Carpathians, exterminating the enemy vermin and sweeping it out of the Soviet land.

In the course of the winter campaign of 1943–44 the Red Army won the historic battle for the Dnieper and for the territories of the Ukraine west of the Dnieper, crushed the powerful German fortified defenses at Leningrad and in the Crimea, by skilful and vigorous actions overwhelmed the German defense on the water barriers of the Yuzhny Bug, the Dniester, the Prut and the Seret. Nearly the entire Ukraine, Moldavia, the Crimea, the Leningrad and Kalinin Regions, and a considerable part of Byelorussia, have been cleared of the German invaders.

The metallurgy of the south, the ore of Krivoi Rog, Kerch and Nikopol, the fertile lands between the Dnieper and the Prut, have been restored to the motherland. Tens of millions of Soviet people have been liberated from fascist slavery.

Acting in the great cause of the liberation of the native land from the fascist invaders, the Red Army emerged on our State frontiers with Rumania

[1] Information Bulletin, Embassy of the U.S.S.R.

and Czechoslovakia and now continues battering the enemy troops on the territory of Rumania.

The successes of the Red Army became possible due to the correct strategy and tactics of the Soviet Command, due to the high morale and offensive ardor of our men and commanders, due to our troops being well supplied with first-rate Soviet war equipment, due to the improved skill and training of our artillerymen, mortar gunners, tankmen, fliers, signalmen, sappers, infantrymen, cavalrymen and scouts.

A considerable contribution to these successes has been made by our great Allies, the United States of America and Great Britain, which hold a front in Italy against the Germans and divert a considerable part of the German troops from us, supply us with very valuable strategical raw materials and armaments, subject to systematic bombardments military objectives in Germany, and thus undermine the latter's military might.

The successes of the Red Army could, however, have proved unstable and could be reduced to nought after the very first serious counter-blow on the part of the enemy were not the Red Army backed from the rear by our entire Soviet people, by our entire country. In the battles for the motherland the Red Army has displayed unexampled heroism. But the Soviet people has not remained in debt to the Red Army.

Under difficult wartime conditions the Soviet people attained decisive successes in the mass production of armaments, ammunition, clothing and provisions and in their daily delivery to the fronts of the Red Army. During the past year the power of Soviet industry has substantially risen. Hundreds of new factories and mines, and dozens of power-stations, railway lines and bridges have been commissioned.

Fresh millions of Soviet people took their places at machines, mastered the most complex professions, became experts in their jobs. Our collective farms and State farms have stood the trials of war with credit. Under difficult wartime conditions, Soviet peasants work in the fields without folding their hands, supplying our Army and population with food and our industry with raw materials.

And our intelligentsia has enriched Soviet science and technology, culture and art, with new outstanding achievements and discoveries. Invaluable services in the cause of the defense of the motherland have been rendered by Soviet women, who work self-sacrificingly in the interests of the front, courageously bear all wartime hardships and inspire to fighting exploits the soldiers of the Red Army—the liberators of our motherland.

The Patriotic War has shown that the Soviet people is capable of performing miracles and emerging victorious from the hardest trials. Workers, collective farmers, intelligentsia, the whole Soviet people, are filled with determination to hasten the defeat of the enemy, to restore completely the economy ruined by the fascists, to make our country still stronger and more prosperous.

Under the blows of the Red Army the bloc of fascist states is cracking and falling to pieces. Fear and confusion now reign among Hitler's Rumanian, Hungarian, Finnish and Bulgarian "allies." At present these Hitler underlings, whose countries have been occupied or are being occupied by the Germans, cannot fail to see that Germany has lost the war. Rumania, Hungary, Finland and Bulgaria have only one possibility for escaping disaster: to break with the Germans and to withdraw from the war.

However, it is difficult to expect that the present governments of these countries will prove capable of breaking with the Germans. One should think that the peoples of these countries will have to take the cause of their liberation from the German yoke into their own hands. And the sooner the peoples of these countries realize to what an impasse the Hitlerites have brought them, the sooner they withdraw all support from their German enslavers and their underlings, the quislings in their own countries, the smaller will be the amount of sacrifices and destruction caused to these countries by the war, the more they can count upon understanding on the part of the democratic countries.

As a result of the successful offensive, the Red Army has emerged on our State frontiers on a stretch of over 400 kilometers and liberated more than three-quarters of occupied Soviet land from the German-fascist yoke. The object now is to clear the whole of our land of the fascist invaders and to reestablish the State frontiers of the Soviet Union along the entire line from the Black Sea to the Barents Sea.

But our tasks cannot be confined to the expulsion of enemy troops from our motherland. The German troops now resemble a wounded beast which is compelled to crawl back to the frontiers of its lair—Germany—in order to heal its wounds. But a wounded beast which has retired to its lair does not cease to be a dangerous beast. To rid our country and the countries allied with us from the danger of enslavement, the wounded beast must be pursued close on its heels and finished off in its own lair. And while pursuing the enemy we must deliver from German bondage our brothers, the Poles and Czechoslovaks, and others allied with us, the peoples of Western Europe, which are under the heel of Hitlerite Germany.

Obviously this task is more difficult than the expulsion of German troops from the Soviet Union. It can be accomplished only on the basis of the joint efforts of the Soviet Union, Great Britain and the United States of North America, by joint blows from the east dealt by our troops and from the west dealt by the troops of our Allies. There can be no doubt that only such a combined blow can crush completely Hitlerite Germany.

Comrades Red Army men and Red Navy men, sergeants, officers and generals, men and women guerrillas! Working people of the Soviet Union! Brothers and sisters who have temporarily fallen under the yoke of the German oppressors and have been forcibly driven to fascist penal servitude in Germany!

I greet and congratulate you upon the festival of May First!

I order: In honor of the historic victories of the Red Army on the front and to mark the great achievements of the workers, collective farmers and intelligentsia of the Soviet Union in the rear, today, on the day of the world festival of working people, at 8:00 P.M., a salute of twenty gun salvos shall be fired in Moscow, Leningrad, Gomel, Kiev, Kharkov, Rostov, Tbilisi, Simferopol and Odessa.

Long live our Soviet motherland!

Long live our Red Army and Navy!

Long live the great Soviet people!

Long live the friendship of the peoples of the Soviet Union!

Long live the Soviet men and women guerrillas!

Eternal glory to the heroes who fell in the battles for the freedom and independence of our motherland!

Death to the German invaders!

(Signed) Supreme Commander-in-Chief,
Marshal of the Soviet Union,
JOSEPH STALIN

MESSAGE FROM PRIME MINISTER WINSTON CHURCHILL TO PRIME MINISTER PAPANDREOU OF GREECE

May 1, 1944 [1]

I am very glad you have shown the firmness of character required to act as Prime Minister of Greece during this period when her light among the nations has been dimmed. His Majesty's Government will give you all support in your supreme task and duty of directing all Greek forces against the common foe who may, at any time, begin to reel or retreat. We have made our position as the ally of Greece and one of her oldest friends abundantly clear. The Nazi tyrant must be destroyed or expelled from the country.

After this has been done and reasonable tranquillity restored at the earliest moment the Greek nation, free from foreign interference of all kinds, will choose the form of democratic government under which they wish to live, whether it be a monarchy or a republic. The King is the servant of his people. I am sure he has no wish to force himself upon the Greek nation. Having begun the war against Italy in a victorious manner, he is now bound in honor to fight it through to the end against the Germans. No one has a constitutional right to stand between him and his duty.

We are responsible during the war for maintaining good relations with the Egyptian sovereign power whom we have protected against all German and Italian assaults. In the advent of solemn events in the military field we cannot allow sporadic disorders to break out among the Greek forces in Egypt who have been constitutionally placed under the supreme allied commander in the Mediterranean. We shall not hesitate to take any measures necessary for the performance of our duty. It is the Greek nation, not small bodies of soldiers, sailors, and politicians resting under our shield, who will decide the future. A free, independent, prosperous, and happy Greece would be dear to the British heart. We judge every Greek of every class and party according as they help to rescue the soil of Greece from the Hitlerite foe.

You have set yourself to face the perils and the toils of heading as Prime Minister a renewed attack by Greece on Germany whereby those ancient glories which were revived so recently in 1941 shall not cease to shine. In this task you will have our persevering and powerful support. Your watchwords should be "The union of all against the common foe," "The cleansing of the land from foreign butchers," "Free choice by the Greeks themselves of the government under which they wish to live."

ADDRESS BY GENERAL CHARLES DE GAULLE IN TUNIS ON THE ANNIVERSARY OF THE LIBERATION OF TUNISIA

May 7, 1944 [2]

Today, on the road that leads to victory, we are celebrating the first anniversary of the liberation of Tunisia. Not indeed with the intention of linger-

[1] British Information Services.
[2] French Press and Information Service.

ing, even for a moment, over this memory; for this war for life and for greatness can permit no halting. Nor to glorify ourselves with past success, for success will have meaning and value only when our principal aim is achieved. But just as a traveler climbing a hill seeks encouragement by looking at the road he has come along, so we, who have arrived at the supreme eve of battle, take comfort in turning back our thoughts to the ground already successfully covered. It is here that for the first time since the glorious days of 1914–1918 the American, British and French Armies found themselves reunited on the same battlefield. It is here that after long and stubborn combat more than 300,000 Germans and Italians laid down their arms before the Allies. It is here that the blows struck at the enemy by the Western Powers fighting for liberty began to be correlated with the gigantic offensive of the forces of the Soviet Union. It is here that soldiers belonging to the two groups into which treachery would have liked to divide the French Army, joined together and recognized each other for what they were. I mean, for good and brave men of the French soil. It is here that Hitler's attempts to break up our Empire ended in total failure and with them went Mussolini's absurd claims on Tunisia, united with us for ever.

It is here that reward, in the form of the enemy's rout and the traitor's confusion crowned the effort spent and the suffering endured by those exemplary Frenchmen of all political origins who had never surrendered and who thereby became the spark of the Resurrection.

Certainly, among the nations who are bearing the physical and moral hardships of the war, many could believe that the Tunisian victory would soon be followed by rapid and decisive successes. Particularly the French people, who —with their backs to the wall of their prison cell, with chains on their feet and handcuffs on their wrists, put up a fierce and exhausting struggle against the invaders—were inclined to hope that the speed of operations would permit them to escape sooner from their misery by contributing faster to their own liberation. It was naturally the same for the other European countries which are occupied—that is to say, tortured—by the enemy. For one of the primary effects of the common suffering is the appearance of a common psychology among the outraged national masses, from one end of our old continent to the other. History will judge at a later date the psychological and material reasons that have not yet made it possible to throw into battle in the West all the forces of the coalition. Everything indicates, however, that this is very near. Is it necessary to recall that France burns with impatient fury to take her place and play her part in this Allied action with everything that she is able to put into the battle either in front of the enemy or in his rear? For however burdensome this delay in which we see France's life-substance disappear, we have not submitted to it while doing nothing. What has been accomplished in the past year on metropolitan territory—in such terrible isolation and at such a price—to weaken the German war machine will one day, perhaps, make some impression on those who doubted France. What our Army has accomplished in twelve months, as much on the battlefields of Italy, around Aqua Fondata, from Croce to Belvedere, as on Corsican soil by completing the liberation of the island, begun by our forces of the interior, has continued to show after Bir Hakeim, Fezzan and Tunisia, that we are in full military rebirth. What has been achieved during the last year with respect to the war effort of all the Empire's territories, in spite of the difficulties of transportation by sea, by air and by land, and in spite of the loss of manpower caused by the mobilization of some and the physical exhaustion of others, might seem astonishing to the people who would like to ignore where French authority lies and to what degree France inspires confidence and devotion to the populations attached to her destiny. How could I fail to stress here the progress made in the last year with respect both to the mutual comprehension between Frenchmen and Tunisians, and the hope that the Tunisian people justly nourish for their own development under the protection and with the help of France. If we look at what has been accomplished in 341 days with respect to the rallying of the great mass of Frenchmen around their government, and for the war effort, we find enough to reassure certain anxious friends who seem afraid when liberation comes, to find a still feudal France ready for division under different authorities.

As a matter of fact we Frenchmen have neither these doubts nor these fears. For we know what France is. We know she is the people, the people who are openly and secretly aroused against the invader, the people in the Army, Navy and Air Force, eager to strike at the enemy, and entirely loyal to the national government, in a traditional diversity of feelings and tendencies, merged into one unprecedented unity, which progressively sweeps away all intrigues and diversions. To those who might not have the same certainty, let us suggest that they see and hear the people of Tunis, gathered together today as were yesterday Ajaccio, Alger, Oran, Constantine, Casablanca, Dakar and Brazzaville.

We suggest in all friendliness that they come tomorrow with us to the meeting places of the French people, on the Cannebière in Marseille, on the Place Bellecour in Lyon, on the Grenoble Place of Lille, on the Place Broglie in Strasbourg, or in any one of our liberated villages, or somewhere between the Arc de Triomphe de l'Etoile, and Notre Dame de Paris.

But at the moment when the armies of liberty are getting ready to bring to our soil the vicissitudes and the destructions of battle, at the moment when there is being planted in the minds of all the ideas and feelings from which will come the future orders of the world, at the moment when our people are stoically enduring the aerial bombings which prepare for the debarkation, we ardently hope that French realities will be definitely recognized. They alone, to begin with, can serve as a basis for the practical arrangements which would enable the Allied armies and their High Command—once they have set foot on metropolitan soil—to work together at their task which is and must remain exclusively strategic. We regret all the more, that the present interruption of communications between the French Government and its diplomatic and military representatives in London, creates a situation which makes it obviously impossible to settle anything concerning this matter. But in spite of this obstacle, as in spite of all others, we are perfectly confident about the issue of the great battle which will put to rout the hated enemy. We are perfectly assured that France alone will take care of what is France. We have the firm hope that the approaching victory will leave in nations that were invaded and in those that were not, the same spirit of reciprocal friendship which is necessary for their mutual co-operation, and their common well-being in the future.

Yes, I spoke of the future. Indeed, the men and women who are toiling, struggling and suffering cannot tear their thoughts away from what will follow their hardships, their struggle and their toil. At the very moment when the war is demanding of all men and women their greatest possible effort, it is only sound and human that they should look to the light that is shining behind the victory. They are measuring the gigantic task, that will be the reconstruction and rebirth of the country. But they are now sure of becoming again what they want to be—that is, free, strong and great—because they know where they have resolved to go.

Yes, they are resolved to take their place, that is to say the position to which they are called by their history, the genius of their race, and the role they have always played among the great peoples of the world. They know that they will arrive there only through their own effort, throughout the war and throughout the peace. They know that no matter how precious may be the friendship of others, it is from themselves alone, that will spring their new greatness. They have made out once and for all the balance sheet of their possibilities and also of their mistakes. Inside France they want to be hard-working, orderly and numerous in a democracy that is enlightened, healthy and strong. They want to be understanding, active and generous toward the territories and populations they are entrusted with leading toward a better future. This is so first of all with respect to the noble country of Tunisia. As to Europe to which the French people are linked by a bond so close that what hurts France hurts Europe which in turn would be doomed to chaos without the men and women of France—Europe that is still the great source of men's activities and even of wealth—Frenchmen wish, once the enemy has been routed, to become in the West the center of direct and practical co-operation, and in relation to the East, that is to say, first in relation with dear and powerful Russia, they wish to become permanent Allies. In the world where always and everywhere, can be found their friends, their influence and their interests, Frenchmen want to be the model artisans of that international and brotherly organization about which all men in the world are dreaming amidst hardships and divisions. France, suffering France, glorious France, new France, great France, forward.

BROADCAST TO BRITAIN BY PRIME MINISTER JOHN CURTIN OF AUSTRALIA

May 7, 1944 [1]

I speak to the people of Britain on behalf of 7,000,000 Australians.

Australia is the greatest land mass south of the Equator held by the British race. Along with 2,000,000 white people in South Africa and 1,500,000 in New Zealand we are the bastion of British institutions, the British way of life and the system of democratic government in the Southern World.

I suppose that the average citizen of the British Isles has some conception of Australia and Australians, whether it be because of the A.I.F. in the First World War, or Don Bradman's performances at Lord's, or the kangaroo and the Koala bear. Many, no doubt, have relatives who made their home in Australia. But that conception must have been enlarged enormously when Japan came into the war and Australia was faced with extinction as a free nation.

Then you must have realized that if Japan's onward march south engulfed Australia and New Zealand then all vestige of British freedom and liberty would have disappeared from the South Pacific. The Australian people stood firmly in the path of the aggressor because they knew that their most precious possession—their liberty—was the stake in the struggle. But they also stood

[1] British Speeches of the Day.

as the trustees for you, the people of Britain, for everything for which British people everywhere stand. Today, I can say with just pride, that that trusteeship has been carried out honorably and successfully.

What we did, we did to preserve our British way of life. We did it, too, for the United Nations. We did it for civilization itself against a barbaric, ruthless and fanatical enemy.

Let me tell you *how* we did it—how Australians undertook to marshal the maximum strength of which they were capable so as to meet an entirely transformed position in the Pacific. That was a task suddenly thrust on Australia after she had sent three A.I.F. divisions to the Middle East, another division to Malaya, maintained the flow of Australian air crews for the Battle of Britain and garrisoned numerous islands around Australia.

No country—not even this gallant little island—faced a greater danger with less resources than did Australia and the threat of invasion became such a grave possibility that the absolute priority of the fighting forces and their requirements became paramount over every other consideration.

That threat has now been removed because of four main factors. These are the gallantry of our own and the American forces; the skill of the commanders; the aid given by the United States and the splendid effort of the Australian people themselves. While Britain's resources have been committed in other theaters, we are grateful for the assistance you have extended to Australia. I can tell you that when the fact that British Spitfires had been in action against the Japanese was made known a great thrill ran through the Australian people.

Australia is now grappling with a task of no less magnitude. That is to maintain Australian combat forces, to feed and service Australian and Allied forces, to feed and maintain the Australian civil population and to produce vital food for Britain. All that imposes a terrific strain on Australia's manpower pool. Of the total male labor force, 40 per cent are serving in the forces or are engaged in direct war work while 60 per cent are engaged in providing food, clothing and other services for the Allied forces, in maintaining the civil population and in providing food for Britain.

Seventy-two per cent of Australian manpower is engaged in the fighting forces, in munitions-making and other essential industry. The corresponding figure for Britain is 75 per cent.

As I have said, that has imposed a strain. It has meant, too, that Australians have learned something of the rigors imposed on the British civil population. Food and clothes rationing, pegging of wages, curtailment of amenities and a general "do without" have combined to bring war very realistically to Australians. Australians suffer shortages which do not occur even in Britain.

Since Pearl Harbor, Australia has been almost completely pre-occupied with the war against Japan. But our airmen and our sailors have continued their fight, side by side with you, against the European enemy. Australian fighting men have given a new birth to the Anzac tradition established in the First World War. They have pushed the Japanese back from the very coast of Australia until the Allied retreat of 1942 has been turned into an Allied reconquest of 1944. Our men have fought under conditions worse than any army in any war anywhere in the world has suffered since the beginning of human combat.

I make it clear that Australia's pre-occupation with the war against Japan involves more than Australia. The interests at stake concern the whole British Commonwealth, the whole of the democratic nations throughout the world.

The issue in the Pacific, as in Europe, is between slavery and freedom. We, like you, have stood and fought for freedom. We, like you, do not mean to see the freedom we have helped to win for all people, everywhere in the world, diminished when peace comes.

The British Commonwealth, therefore, must recognize that the interests of all its members are involved in the ability of Australia to maintain and expand British institutions in the Pacific.

In particular, Australia wants her partners in the Commonwealth to understand the vital position Australia occupies in British Commonwealth affairs. That understanding has been amicably and fully reached with New Zealand and the Australia-New Zealand Agreement gives fullest recognition to and provides efficient machinery for that understanding.

Australia lays stress on the importance of the combined Allied military effort against Japan, and, while recognizing and accepting the strategy of "beat Hitler first," points out that because that will mean a prolonged war in the Pacific it is essential that a certain minimum effort must be maintained in the Pacific so that prolongation will not become stalemate.

I am happy to say that this point of view has been completely accepted by the Prime Ministers' Conference. The Commander-in-Chief of the Australian Military Forces (General Sir Thomas Blamey) who is in London with me, together with Australian naval and air force representatives in Britain, will discuss with the British Chiefs of Staff, the technical aspects of the case submitted by Australia. These discussions will aim at devising a satisfactory procedure for further consideration by the British and Australian Governments.

There is one thing more for me to say to the people of Britain. I have left it until the last, not in any sense of secondary or tertiary importance, but so that, I hope, my final words will remain with you.

I echo the thoughts of every Australian when I say: We Australians are proud to be of the stock which populates the British Isles. Our forebears were your forebears. Our sons and daughters are as your sons and daughters.

What has been done in the past four years in this fighting fortress of Britain will ring through the halls of fame forever. For ourselves, we say that when Britain alone stood against Hitler we are proud that we had the honor to be with you.

What has to be done in the future is in the hands of the peoples of the British Commonwealth and of men and women of goodwill elsewhere who subscribe to very much the same ideas and ideals. Our generation will have left its mark. Before we hand on the torch to our sons and daughters our remaining task is to think and plan so that their world may, in truth, be a new world.

There can be no going back to the "good old days." They were not good days and they have truly become old. We have to point the way to better days.

The responsibility is a grave one. In one of the Allied nations the other day it was said that the "British Commonwealth may well be studied as an object lesson in free association." The important word in that comment was "association." The partners in that association have a primary responsibility to each other, jointly and individually. By their behavior in the future, they may very well present to the world the blueprint for future happiness for all mankind. If they fail to do that, then they fail not only themselves but they may precipitate more misery, unhappiness and degradation into this suffering world.

So I say to the people of Britain, as I say to the people of my own country, we inherited something priceless, we have enhanced that heritage, let us be sure it is handed on untarnished.

Goodnight and may God bless you all.

ADDRESS BY PRIME MINISTER W. L. MACKENZIE KING OF CANADA TO BOTH HOUSES OF PARLIAMENT, AT WESTMINSTER, ON CANADA'S WAR EFFORT AND THE COMMONWEALTH

May 11, 1944 [1]

Prime Minister, Lord Chancellor, Mr. Speaker, My Lords and members of the House of Commons:

When I received from you, Prime Minister, the invitation to address members of both Houses of the Parliament of the United Kingdom, I found myself at a loss for words in which to acknowledge so high an honor. Your kindness in presiding on this occasion, your words of introduction, the traditions and associations of Westminster, and the presence in such numbers of members of the Lords and Commons add greatly to my sense of obligation.

I am only too well aware of all that it means to be the guest of the people of Britain, and to be speaking to them, and to others, from the heart of the British Commonwealth and Empire, at this moment of supreme crisis in human affairs. Your friendship and mine over many years of peace, and our close companionship throughout the years of war, afford me a support I greatly welcome in addressing this distinguished assembly.

Four years have now passed since you accepted the leadership of the people of Britain, and the leadership of the cause of human freedom. You and your colleagues have led this country, and the cause for which it stands, from the dark days of extreme peril, to this hour when at last the light is beginning to break. It is a source of confidence throughout the free world that you, Prime Minister, are continuing your leadership with a vision and a courage which have already become a legend.

I recognize that, for me, this occasion is designed as a welcome to Canada's representative at the meeting of Prime Ministers of the British Commonwealth. For the high compliment to Canada, and to other nations of the Commonwealth, I should like to express my gratitude and pride.

I know that the welcome you accord to me is equally heartfelt and generous towards the representatives of Australia, New Zealand and South Africa. I should like to say to Mr. Curtin, Mr. Fraser and Field Marshal Smuts how great is the admiration of the people of Canada of their leadership and of the heroic part which their countries have taken in this war. I should also like to say to them how glad I am that our presence in London at this time affords us not only exceptional opportunities of conferences but of making clear to the world the oneness of nations of the Commonwealth in the winning of the war, and in seeking international cooperation after the war.

Perhaps I may be allowed to convey a special message from the people of Canada.

No memory of happiness in the past is more cherished than the recollection

[1] Canadian Wartime Information Board.

of the visit of Their Majesties the King and Queen. In Canada, as in Britain, the years of war have heightened the admiration and increased the affection felt by men and women everywhere for our King and Queen. We have been inspired by their courage and devotion in sharing the dangers and sorrows of the people. In all the nations of the Commonwealth, their example has deepened the meaning and significance of our common allegiance to the Crown. The heroic endurance of the people of Britain is ever present in our minds. We shall never forget your resolution in the darkest days of the war. Nor shall we ever cease to remember the determination with which, amid destruction of your homes and in peril of your lives, you, the men, women and children of Britain, have continued to carry on your work, and to maintain your confidence in the future. Clearly the maintenance of human freedom has depended upon the preservation of the freedom of Britain. It is our greatest pride, as it is the greatest pride of other nations of the Commonwealth, that when, for so long a time, you alone bore the brunt of the attack, we stood with you in arms against the might of Nazi Germany. The free nations of the world can never forget that it was the indomitable resistance of the people of Britain that bought the precious time for the mobilization of the forces of freedom around the globe.

Britain has been an example to the world of the organization of a free people for a common task. You have astonished the world by the marvels of your industrial production, and by the skill and efficiency of your workers. You have never lost your faith. A new energy, a new confidence have been generated in your people. These will endure. And your faith, tested and tried in the fires of affliction, will be firmer and stronger than it has ever been.

When victory is won, you will still possess the same initiative, vigor and endurance; the same skills of hand and brain; the same qualities of mind and spirit. These have enabled the people of Britain to make a contribution to the winning of the war, which, man for man, no other nation has surpassed. In peace as in war, these qualities will remain. In the building of a better world after the war, Britain will be able, by the force of her example, to give the same leadership that she has given in the waging of war.

It is, however, not of Britain but of Canada that I am expected to speak on this occasion. I should like, therefore, if I may, to speak to you particularly of the spirit of Canada, as exemplified in Canada's war effort. I do this with less embarrassment, as a like spirit, I know, animates the war efforts of all the nations united in a common allegiance to the Crown.

I should like to speak, as well, of what that spirit signifies for the future of the British Commonwealth, and of the relations of the nations of the Commonwealth with other nations in the building of a new world order.

In speaking of Canada's war effort, it is not my intention to describe our contribution to the present world conflict primarily in terms of men and materials. What I should like to refer to are certain aspects which, viewed collectively, reveal the spirit of the Canadian people.

I place first the aspect I regard as most significant. Canada's war effort is a voluntary effort. It is the free expression of a free people. Like the other nations of the Commonwealth at war today, we entered the war of our own free will; and not as the result of any formal obligation. Ours was not primarily a response to a call of blood or race. It was the outcome of our deepest political instinct—a love of freedom and a sense of justice. As our decision was a voluntary decision, so the effort of our people in carrying on the war has been a voluntary effort. In Canada, as in other countries, controls and restrictions have been imposed in order to prosecute the war with vigor and efficiency. But at every stage these measures have received the overwhelming support of the Canadian people.

Canada's population numbers eleven and a half millions. Three quarters of a million of our finest young men are serving in the armed forces. This military demand on our manpower resources has not prevented our country from doubling its pre-war production. Thanks to the skill and devotion of our men and women, Canada is a granary, an arsenal, an airdrome, and a shipyard of freedom. Our country has become increasingly proud of the fact that every fighting man from Canada serving across the seas, on the seas, and in the air is a volunteer. We can say, in very truth, that Canada's effort in this war is a voluntary effort.

Canada's decision to enter the war was an immediate decision. When, in 1939, the last hopes of peace were fading from the world, I announced that, if Britain took up arms in the defense of freedom, our Government would ask Parliament to place Canada at Britain's side. When war came, there was no hesitation. As soon as Parliament could act, Canada was at war.

In those days, few if any of our people believed our country stood in immediate danger of attack. What we sensed immediately was the issue. We saw that a bitter struggle had begun between freedom and domination, and that the conflict would certainly spread. For the second time in a generation, Canada went to war to help prevent tyranny in Germany from extending its domination to other parts of the globe.

When the last war ended, the people of Canada, like other freedom-loving peoples, hoped and believed that peace and freedom had been assured to mankind for generations. In our National War Memorial, that hope and that faith were symbolized in the inseparably joined figures of peace and freedom. But all our history, all our political experience told us that freedom in Canada could not survive in a world that was no longer free.

From the beginning, our war effort was so planned and organized that we might reach, as rapidly as possible, the maximum effort our people could sustain during a long war. We expanded our navy as fast as we could build, or acquire the ships and train the men. We expanded our army to the highest strength we believed we could maintain in a long war. We expanded our air force to the limit of our capacity to secure the needed equipment, and to train personnel. The British Commonwealth Air Training Plan was expedited and expanded beyond all anticipations. The one hundred thousandth fighting airman has just completed his training. The co-operative training in Canada has vastly increased the joint strength in the air of the United Nations. We have expanded our war industries far beyond the needs of our own armed forces. Despite the withdrawal of hundreds of thousands of men from the farms, the fisheries, the mines and the forests, we have greatly enlarged our production of foodstuffs and raw materials. We are devoting about half our total production directly to the waging of war. We are paying about half of the financial cost of our war effort out of current revenue from taxation. Through victory loans and war savings, nearly every family is helping to finance the war.

In fighting men, in weapons and munitions, in food and in finance, we are seeking as a people to make our utmost contribution to the fight for world freedom. Our objective has been a total effort for total war, and we believe that objective is being attained.

Of the nations of the Western Hemisphere, Canada was the first to defend in arms the frontiers of the freedom of the new world. For more than two years, our country, alone in the Americas, was at war. In more ways than one our effort has been a pioneering effort.

Canada's contribution to the present war has been the greater because we live side by side with the United States. Without the harmony and reciprocity which exist between our two countries, neither could have achieved so much in the common cause. The ability of both Canada and the United States to defend the North American continent, and to fight abroad, has been greatly increased by our arrangements for joint defense, and by the pooling of resources. We have sought to make Canada's war effort, wherever possible, a co-operative effort. The extensive miltary works undertaken in Canada in conjunction with the United States have provided a remarkable instance of close and friendly co-operation. Ours is surely the supreme example of a smaller nation living in the fullest security and harmony side by side with a very powerful one.

As a part of our war policy, Canada is sharing, with other of the United Nations, ships, machines, weapons and other supplies which we are producing far in excess of the needs of our own armed forces. Since the war began, we have supplied to Britain, and to Britain's armed forces, war materials and other supplies worth nearly nine hundred million pounds ($4,000,000,000). Almost half of these supplies represent an outright contribution. Under our system of mutual aid, war materials have, for the past year, been supplied without payment to the United Nations, in accordance with strategic need. Canada is now supplying mutual aid to Britain, Australia, the Soviet Union, China and the French Committee of National Liberation.

As the war has progressed, our effort has become more and more a world-wide effort. Canadian-made machines and munitions of war have been used on all the fighting fronts. Canadian sailors and merchant seamen have served on all oceans. Our airmen have fought in the battle of the skies around the globe. From the early days of the war, our soldiers have helped to guard this Island. They have seen active service in the Pacific area, as well as at Dieppe, and in the Italian campaign. Today our army awaits the word of command to join with their comrades in the liberation of Europe. The morrow will witness Canadian forces taking part in a final assault upon Japan. Canada's effort has truly become a world-wide effort.

I need scarcely say that we are in this war to the end. Canada's fight for freedom will be a fight to the finish. It is clear to our people that this war is all one war; a monstrous conspiracy of the Fascist Powers to dominate and enslave the world. Having taken up arms of their own free will, the Canadian people will not relax until freedom is secure. Canada's effort will be an enduring effort.

We have also sought to look beyond the war; to make our effort a long-range effort. The Canadian people, no less than the people of Britain, whose sacrifices have been so great, need the promise of a brighter future. To sustain us in our endeavors, we all need the vision of a new world order. By co-ordinated action, by mutual aid, by continuous co-operation, the United Nations are achieving military victory. The widest measure of co-operation will be no less needed in the making and keeping of peace. While our primary aim, like yours, is military victory; our ultimate aim, like yours, is a better future for mankind.

Above all, our war effort must be viewed as a national effort. Our decision in 1939 was more than the free choice of a free Parliament. It was the most solemn act of a free nation. Our war effort appeals to our national pride. We have sought to make it worthy of Canada.

I have spoken of the war effort of Canada. May I hasten to say again that a like spirit has animated the war efforts of each of the other nations of the Commonwealth. With due allowance for varying conditions, the several aspects of Canada's war effort have been paralleled in Australia, New Zealand and South Africa. When war came, four nations, all of them thousands of miles from the scene of the conflict, ranged themselves at the side of Britain. To each, the issue was plain; from each the response was immediate. Each is seeking to put forth the utmost effort. The contributions of all bear the imprint of the initiative and self-reliance of the pioneer. Co-operation has marked their course throughout. Each is making a long-range effort which will prove to be an enduring effort. It is the pride of each that its war effort has been a national effort.

Nor have we far to seek to discover the cause of this identity of effort on the part of the nations of the Commonwealth. The spirit of a nation is not readily defined. It is known only as it is revealed. It resembles the flow of waters hidden beneath the earth's surface. From time to time, and from place to place, the waters having their origin in some secret source, reveal themselves as springs, or streams, or rivers. So also, from time to time, a nation's spirit wells up from its source and manifests itself in the collective acts of a people. Such collective action is quickened and heightened at a time of war. The war efforts of the nations of the Commonwealth owe their inspiration to a common source. That source is the love of freedom and the sense of justice which, through generations have been nurtured and cherished in Britain, as nowhere else in the world. The terrible events of 1940 revealed how great was the menace to freedom, and how suddenly freedom might be lost. So long as freedom endures, free men everywhere will owe to the people of Britain, a debt they can never repay. So long as Britain continues to maintain the spirit of freedom, and to defend the freedom of other nations, she need never doubt her own pre-eminence throughout the world. So long as Britain continues to share that spirit with the other nations of the Commonwealth, she need never fear for the strength or unity of the Commonwealth. The voluntary decisions by Britain, by Canada, by Australia, by New Zealand, and by South Africa are a supreme evidence of the unifying force of freedom.

This common effort springing from a common source has given a new strength and unity, a new meaning and significance to the British Commonwealth.

Without attempting to distinguish between the terms "British Empire" and "British Commonwealth," but looking rather to the evolution of this association of free nations, may I give to you what I believe to be the secret of its strength and of its unity, and the vision which I cherish of its future. "We, who look forward to larger brotherhoods and more exact standards of social justice, value and cherish the British Empire because it represents more than any other similar organization has ever represented, the peaceful co-operation of all sorts of men in all sorts of countries, and because we think it is, in that respect at least, a model of what we hope the whole world will some day become." This vision, I need scarcely say, is not mine alone; indeed, the words in which I have sought to portray it are not even my own. They were spoken thirty-seven years ago by one whose fame today is not surpassed in any part of the world, if, indeed, it has been equalled at any time in the world's history. They are the words of the present Prime Minister of Britain, uttered by Mr. Churchill in 1907. As they continue to reverberate down the years, they bring fresh inspiration to all who owe allegiance to the Crown, and increasing hope to mankind. Visions of youth, sometimes, "die away, and fade into the light of common day." They fade not because the vision is ever wholly lost, but because resolution wavers, because determination fails, because of seemingly insuperable obstacles. It has not been so with Mr. Churchill. He has not to ask

"Whither is fled the visionary gleam? Where is it now, the glory and the dream?"

The glory and the dream: are not they being realized at this very hour, in the strength and unity of the nations of the Commonwealth.

From time to time, it is suggested that we should seek new methods of communication and consultation.

It is true we have not, sitting in London continuously, a visible Imperial War Cabinet or Council. But we have, what is much more important, though invisible, a continuing conference of the Cabinets of the Commonwealth. It is a conference of Cabinets which deals, from day to day, and, not infrequently, from hour to hour, with policies of common concern. When decisions are taken, they are not the decisions of Prime Ministers, or other individual Ministers, meeting apart from their own colleagues, and away from their own countries, they are decisions reached after mature consideration by all members of the Cabinet of each country, with a full consciousness of their immediate responsibility to their respective Parliaments. I believe very strongly in close consultation, close co-operation, and effective co-ordination of policies. What more effective means of co-operation could have been found than those which, despite all the handicaps of war, have worked with such complete success; let us, by all means, seek to improve where we can. But in considering new methods of organization we cannot be too careful to see that, to our own peoples, the new methods will not appear as an attempt to limit their freedom of decision or, to peoples outside the Commonwealth, as an attempt to establish a separate bloc. Let us beware lest in changing the form, we lose the substance; or, for appearance's sake, sacrifice reality. I am told that, somewhere, over the grave of one who did not know when he was well off, there is the following epitaph: "I was well; I wanted to be better; and here I am."

In the passage I quoted from Mr. Churchill a moment ago, I gave only a part of what he said. He set forth as well the means of realizing his vision of peaceful co-operation. "Let us," he said, "seek to impress, year after year, upon the British Empire, an *inclusive* and not an *exclusive* character."

Like the nations of which it is composed, the British Commonwealth has within itself a spirit which is not exclusive, but the opposite of exclusive. Therein lies its strength. That spirit expressed itself in co-operation. Therein lies the secret of its unity. Co-operation is capable of indefinite expansion. Therein lies the hope of the future.

It is of the utmost importance to the Commonwealth that there should continue to be the greatest possible co-operation among its members. In like manner, it is, I believe, of the utmost importance to the future of mankind that, after the war, there should be the greatest possible co-operation among the nations of the world.

The war-time co-operation of the Commonwealth is not the product of formal institutional unity; it is the result of agreement upon policies of benefit to all. Moreover, they are policies that make an appeal "to all sorts of men in all sorts of countries," provided only they are men of goodwill.

If, at the close of hostilities, the strength and unity of the Commonwealth are to be maintained, those ends will be achieved not by policies which are exclusive, but by policies which can be shared with other nations. I am firmly convinced that the way to maintain the unity of the Commonwealth is to base that unity upon principles which can be extended to all nations. I am equally sure that the only way to maintain world unity is to base it upon principles that can be universally applied. The war has surely convinced all nations, from the smallest to the greatest, that there is no national security to be found in the isolation of any nation or group of nations. The future security of peace-loving nations will depend upon the extent and effectiveness of international co-operation. It is no less true that it is not the Great Powers only that are needed to defend, to preserve, and to extend freedom. We should be false to the freedom for which we are fighting if, at any time, we failed to remember that no nation liveth unto itself; and that nations, great and small, are members one of another.

But it is not merely the security of nations that is indivisible. Their prosperity also is indivisible. Few would wish to return to the years before the war, when almost every nation sought economic security in economic isolation from its neighbors. What happened was that the economic security of all nations was destroyed. Now is surely the time for the whole world to realize that. Just as no nation of itself can ensure its own safety so no nation or group of nations can in isolation ensure its own prosperity. For my part, I profoundly believe that both the security and the welfare of the nations of the British Commonwealth and, in large measure, the security and welfare of all peace-loving nations will depend on the capacity of the nations of the Commonwealth to give leadership in the pursuit of policies which, in character, are not exclusive, but inclusive. How far such policies can be successfully pursued will, of course, depend on the extent to which other nations are prepared to pursue similar policies. But let us, at least, wherever that is possible, give the lead that is in the interests of the world as a whole.

Over many years, Canada's relations have been especially friendly with the United States. Throughout the war, we have followed the path of co-operation. We like, also, to think that our country has had some part in bringing about a harmony of sentiment between the United States and the whole British Commonwealth. That harmony is the foundation of the close military collaboration which is proving so fruitful in this war.

It will ever be a prime object of Canadian policy to work for the maintenance of a fraternal association of the British and American peoples. When peace comes, it is our highest hope that the peoples of the British Commonwealth and the United States will continue to march at each other's side, united more closely than ever. But we equally hope that they will march in a larger company, in which all the nations united today in defense of freedom will remain united in the service of mankind.

We are approaching, in the European theatre, the supreme crisis of this long and terrible struggle. In this fateful hour, it is imperative that everything be done to maintain single-minded concentration on the achievement of victory. That is our first obligation. It is our duty to the humble people in all the Allied countries whose patient endurance, unremitting toil and ready acceptance of the burdens of war have made possible the immense strength in war materials and supplies of the United Nations. It is our duty, above all, to the millions of fighting men who, to defend our freedom and the freedom of mankind, are facing death at sea, on land and in the air.

The assurance of the unfailing support of our sailors, soldiers and airmen, is the supreme objective of the meetings of the Prime Ministers of the nations of the Commonwealth. We have met here, first and foremost, in order to do everything possible, by co-operation and by united action, to assure that support in largest possible measure on all the fighting fronts.

The present war is different from any war in the past. It is different in scale. In any accurate geographical sense, it is the first world war in history. It is a war that is being fought not only on land and at sea but, also in the clouds, miles above the surface of the earth. It is, moreover, a war that is not confined to the material realm. It is a struggle for the control of men's minds and men's souls. Its outcome will shape the moral destiny of the world. The support of our fighting men, and our debt to all who are near and dear to them must extend beyond the theatres of war. It must look beyond the end of hostilities. We owe it to all who bear the heat of the strife; we owe it to those who are crippled and maimed; we owe it to the many homes that are bereaved; we owe it to the memory of those who give their loves, to do all in our power to ensure that their service and their sacrifice shall not have been in vain.

In the past, the sacrifice of human life in war has been commemorated in monuments of stone or bronze. After this war, we must create something more fitting as a memorial. That, I believe, will be found only in securing for others the opportunities of a more abundant life. Already we, of the British Commonwealth and Empire, are a community of many nations, of many races and of many tongues. Already we have advanced far in the art of responsible government, in the practice of international co-operation, and in the application of the principle of mutual aid. Surely it is ours to help fashion a new world order in which social security and human welfare will become a part of the inheritance of mankind.

The war has been none of our making. We sought, above all else, the promotion of peace, of understanding and of goodwill. We deplored the extension of war to all parts of the world. Yet in the perspective of time, this world encircling danger may prove to have been a blessing in disguise. Only in this way, perhaps, could other nations, as well as our own, have come to see that the interests of mankind are one, and that the claims of humanity are supreme.

Our first duty is to win the war. But to win the war, we must keep the vision of a better future. We must never cease to strive for its fulfilment. No lesser vision will suffice to gain the victory over those who seek world domination and human enslavement. No lesser vision will enable us fittingly to honor the memory of the men and women who are giving their all for freedom and justice.

In the realization of this vision, the governments and peoples who owe a common allegiance to the Crown may well find the new meaning and significance of the British Commonwealth and Empire. It is for us to make of our association of free British nations, a model of what we hope the whole world will some day become.

DECLARATION BY AMERICAN, BRITISH AND SOVIET GOVERNMENTS REGARDING AXIS SATELLITES— HUNGARY, RUMANIA, BULGARIA AND FINLAND

May 12, 1944 [1]

Through the fateful policy of their leaders, the people of Hungary are suffering the humiliation of German occupation. Rumania is still bound to the Nazis in a war now bringing devastation to its own people. The Governments of Bulgaria and Finland have placed their countries in the service of Germany and remain in the war at Germany's side.

The Governments of Great Britain, the Soviet Union and the United States think it right that these peoples should realize the following facts:

1. The Axis satellites, Hungary, Rumania, Bulgaria and Finland, despite their realization of the inevitability of a crushing Nazi defeat and their desire to get out of the war are by their present policies and attitude contributing materially to the strength of the German war machine.

2. These nations still have it within their power, by withdrawing from the war and ceasing their collaboration with Germany and by resisting the forces of Nazism by every possible means, to shorten the European struggle, diminish their own ultimate sacrifices and contribute to the Allied victory.

3. While these nations cannot escape their responsibility for having participated in the war at the side of Nazi Germany, the longer they continue at war in collaboration with Germany the more disastrous will be the consequences to them and the more rigorous will be the terms which will be imposed upon them.

4. These nations must therefore decide now whether they intend to persist in their present hopeless and calamitous policy of opposing the inevitable Allied victory, while there is yet time for them to contribute to that victory.

PREMIER HIDEKI TOJO'S REPORT ON WAR PROGRESS AND PLANS

May 13–14, 1944 [2]

The agonies suffered by the enemy, America and Britain, are at last making themselves apparent on the surface. It is hard for them to conceal the restlessness in their impatience to end the war in a short time. (Word missing), and the resistance is intensely fierce; that is, the opposition is made on a large scale. More than that, boldly enough, the tempo of their advance has risen acutely.

However, the Imperial Army and Navy forces in this theater of war are dauntlessly giving them stiff battle and are inflicting severe blows on the enemy. Meanwhile, in the Burma theater, the Imperial forces crushed enemy (counteroffensives) in the making and, shoulder to shoulder with the Indians,

[1] State Department Bulletin.
[2] Office of War Information.

have already advanced into eastern India, and are now engaged in the reduction of the stronghold of Imphal.

At this point the surging movement for the acquisition of independence among the Indian people is being spurred sharply. It is nearing the dawn of the day of freedom and independence for India which has suffered under its bonds. The British Government, suddenly at this time, took steps to release Gandhi from prison. Such steps are substantially the usual British tricks which cunningly try to deceive the Indians. However, the Indian people, within whom the desire for freedom is already awakened, could not be deceived by this. In short, Gandhi's release does no more than expose Britain's weakness.

On the China continent, the unified advance of Japan and China, based on true and natural relationship between the two countries, is being cemented further day by day. At the same time, we are constantly dropping the iron hammer of punishment on the Chungking regime, which has not as yet become free of its illusions, and recently the Imperial forces with positiveness have been dealing crushing blows upon them.

Turning elsewhere and to our allied nations, Germany—in parallel with the Imperial forces waging brave battle on all fronts in G.E.A.—has reorganized its (resilient) structure and is already showing its (word missing). However, with the composure and self-assurance of one who can wait, Germany is awaiting the moment of decisive battle with America and England. A comprehensive view of the world situation as shown above tells us that the present time is the most decisive of all decisive periods.

The present is truly momentous. The Imperial troops, at all times and all places, have met this crucial situation. (Words missing). Needless to say, this G.E.A. War is the greatest war since the creation of this world. America and Britain who boast of having the greatest wealth and power (fukyo) in this world are throwing in their all for the overthrow of the Empire. Against this, Imperial Japan intends to fight to the bitter end and crush this inordinate ambition.

When Imperial Japan has fought this great war to a successful conclusion, then for the first time will a G.E.A. based on justice and morality truly be established, and a new world born. The responsibility resting on us, the 100,000,000 people, who are following the call of this holy war is truly great. The result of the deeply moving efforts of all of you, the people, since the outbreak of war till today, is astonishing and clearly shows the inexhaustible strength of Japan.

The Empire, at present, is supplying every type of munitions material by its productive power, with the raw materials of the Southern Regions added to that of Japan, Manchukuo, and China, and more than that, with two or more years of actual time, as the result of the (word missing) brilliant victories. In other words, while fighting an extremely fierce battle, the Empire is restoring production to one on a large scale.

The 100,000,000 people are forebearing all types of hardships, not to speak of inconveniences, in means of livelihood, and are manifesting impressive might. For example, the efforts of the people in the production of planes and construction of ships have resulted in production practically undreamed of before the outbreak of war. Moreover, materials essential to decisive victory such as oil, iron, and aluminum (words missing). Production of materials for war is increasing monthly, nay, daily.

As to food, Japan is now confident that it can maintain its position of self-sufficiency for the future on the basis of the Japan-Manchukuo self-sufficiency plan by means of the efforts of the people of Japan and the impressive cooperation of Manchukuo.

Turning to the subject of manpower, which is basic in the prosecution of war, the enemy America, particularly among the nations participating in the war, has reached the peak of mobilization of people; and, as it is extending its battle lines on a global scale, it is finding it difficult to replenish its military manpower, and is suffering more and more from manpower shortage in the field of industry.

Needless to say, this war of Greater East Asia is the greatest of wars which the world has ever witnessed. America and Britain, proud of their riches, are throwing every bit of their energy into the task of overthrowing Japan. However, victory or defeat in a war cannot be determined by money or materials alone. The fate of victory or defeat truly lies in the indomitable spiritual power of the people.

DECLARATION BY DOMINION PRIME MINISTERS AT CLOSE OF COMMONWEALTH CONFERENCE IN LONDON

May 18, 1944 [1]

We, the King's Prime Ministers of the United Kingdom, Canada, Australia, New Zealand and South Africa, have now, for the first time since the outbreak of the war, been able to meet together to discuss common problems and future plans. The representative of India at the War Cabinet and the Prime Minister of Southern Rhodesia have joined in our deliberations and are united with us.

At this memorable meeting in the fifth year of the war we give thanks for deliverance from the worst perils which have menaced us in the course of this long and terrible struggle against tyranny.

Though hard and bitter battles lie ahead, we now see before us, in the ever-growing might of the forces of the United Nations and in the defeats already inflicted upon the foe by land, by sea and in the air, the sure presage of our future victory.

To all our armed forces, who in many lands are preserving our liberty with their lives, and to peoples of all our countries whose efforts, fortitude and conviction have sustained the struggle, we express our admiration and gratitude.

We honor the famous deeds of the forces of the United States and of Soviet Russia and pay our tribute to the fighting tenacity of the many states and nations joined with us.

We remember, indeed, the prolonged stubborn resistance of China, the first to be attacked by the author of world-aggression, and we rejoice in the unquenchable spirit of our comrades in every country still in the grip of the enemy. We shall not turn from the conflict till they are restored to freedom. Not one who marches with us shall be abandoned.

We have examined the part which the British Empire and Commonwealth of Nations should bear against Germany and Japan, in harmony with our Allies. We are in cordial agreement with the general plans which have been laid before us. As in the days when we stood all alone against Germany, we

[1] British Speeches of the Day.

affirm our inflexible and unwavering resolve to continue in the general war with the utmost of our strength until the defeat and downfall of our cruel and barbarous foe has been accomplished. We shall hold back nothing to reach the goal and bring to the speediest end the agony of mankind.

We have also examined together the principles which determine our foreign policies, and their application to current problems. Here, too, we are in complete agreement. We are unitedly resolved to continue, shoulder to shoulder with our Allies, all needful exertion which will aid our fleets, armies and air forces during the war, and therefore to make sure of an enduring peace. We trust and pray that victory, which will certainly be won, will carry with it a sense of hope and freedom for all the world.

It is our aim that, when the storm and passion of war have passed away, all countries now overrun by the enemy shall be free to decide for themselves their future form of democratic government.

Mutual respect and honest conduct between nations is our chief desire. We are determined to work with all peace-loving peoples in order that tyranny and aggression shall be removed or, if need be, struck down wherever it raises its head. The people of the British Empire and Commonwealth of Nations willingly make their sacrifices to the common cause. We seek no advantages for ourselves at the cost of others. We desire the welfare and social advancement of all nations and that they may help each other to better and broader days.

We affirm that after the war a world organization to maintain peace and security should be set up and endowed with the necessary power and authority to prevent aggression and violence.

In a world torn by strife we have met here in unity. That unity finds its strength not in any formal bond but in the hidden spring from which human action flows. We rejoice in our inheritance, loyalties and ideals, and proclaim our sense of kinship to one another. Our system of free association has enabled us, each and all, to claim a full share of the common burden.

Although spread across the globe, we have stood together through the stress of two world wars, and have been welded the stronger thereby. We believe that when the war is won and peace returns, this same free association, this inherent unity of purpose, will make us able to do further service to mankind.

WINSTON S. CHURCHILL,
Prime Minister of the United Kingdom of Great
Britain and Northern Ireland.

W. L. MACKENZIE KING,
Prime Minister of Canada.

JOHN CURTIN,
Prime Minister of the Commonwealth of Australia.

PETER FRASER,
Prime Minister of New Zealand.

J. C. SMUTS,
Prime Minister of the Union of South Africa.

GENERAL DWIGHT D. EISENHOWER'S INSTRUCTIONS TO THE UNDERGROUND RESISTANCE MOVEMENTS OF EUROPE

May 20, 1944 [1]

When the Allies come to liberate you, they will rely on your help in many ways. In no more valuable way can this be given than by information about the enemy.

Start, therefore, today to observe him more and more closely. Observe the numbers of men and of vehicles by type. Note when they come and how, and the direction in which they are going.

Note the markings on their vehicles and try to find out the regiment, formations or groups to which they belong. Note their arms and their arrangements for supply of food and petrol. Note especially any large movement and the exact date.

Observe the faces and appearances of officers, especially senior officers, and of leaders among civilians. Endeavor to find out their names; note when they come and go and where they go to; learn the badges of their rank.

Try to discover the location of petrol, ammunition and supply depot and stores. Locations of headquarters and signal stations are especially important.

Note the times and routes of dispatch riders and whether they go singly or escorted.

Keep a watch on all bridges and note the water and lighting key points, which, if damaged, would destroy water and lighting systems.

Keep a look-out for the laying of mines or preparations for demolitions. Note especially any suspicious preparations that might be the laying of booby traps.

Let nothing escape you. Pool your knowledge. Take utmost care to give information to none but known patriots.

Be patient, above all, and hide your actions until the word is given.

PRIME MINISTER WINSTON CHURCHILL'S SPEECH IN COMMONS ON FOREIGN AFFAIRS

May 24, 1944 [2]

The meeting of Dominion Prime Ministers, which covered the best part of three weeks, has now concluded, and very full statements to Parliament and the public have been made, individually by the Prime Ministers themselves, and collectively by the declaration to which we have all subscribed. I could not pretend that we have arrived at hard and fast conclusions, or precise decisions upon all the questions which torment this afflicted globe, but it can fairly be said that, having discussed a great many of them, there was revealed a core of agreement which will enable the British Empire and Commonwealth to meet in discussion with other great organisms in the world in a firmly-

[1] *New York Times.*
[2] British Speeches of the Day.

knit array. We have advanced from vague generalities to more precise points of agreement, and we are in a position to carry on discussions with other countries, within the limits which we have imposed upon ourselves.

But this is a Debate upon Foreign Affairs, and nothing was more remarkable than the cordial agreement which was expressed by every one of the Dominion Prime Ministers on the general conduct of our Foreign Affairs and on the principles which govern that conduct, nor, I should add, on the skill and consistency with which they have been treated by my right hon. Friend the Foreign Secretary. The utmost confidence was expressed in him and in his handling of all those very difficult affairs, in spite of the complications by which they are surrounded, and, in spite of the need for prompt action which so often arises—for prompt action by the Mother Country before there is time to have full consultation. In spite of all these difficulties, the fullest confidence and pleasure was expressed in the work which my right hon. Friend has done. We therefore embark upon the present Debate with the backing of their goodwill from all these representatives of the Commonwealth and Empire—the word "Empire" is permitted to be used, which may be a great shock to certain strains of intellectual opinion. And we embark upon the present Debate not only with this backing of hearty goodwill, but with the feeling that this meeting of Prime Ministers from all over the Empire and the representatives of India in the midst of a second deadly war is in fact the highest pinnacle to which our world-wide family association has yet reached. At this time, in policy and in war, our objective is the same, namely, to beat the enemy as soon as possible; and I am not aware of any action or of any studied inaction for which His Majesty's Government are responsible that has not been directly related to that single and dominant purpose.

The duty of all persons responsible for the conduct of Foreign Affairs in a world war of this deadly character and of all who, in different ways, exercise influence is to help the fighting men to perform the heavy tasks entrusted to them and to ensure them all possible ease in execution and advantage in victory. Everyone in a position to guide public opinion, like Members of this House or of another place, or newspaper editors, broadcasters, calumnists —or columnists—I remember a tendency to throw the accent forward—and others—all of these should keep this very clear duty before their eyes. They should always think of the soldier in the battle and ask themselves whether what they say or write will make his task easier or harder. We long for the day to come when this slaughter will be over and then this additional restraint which imposes itself on every conscientious man in wartime can be relaxed or will vanish away entirely.

I must make my acknowledgments, first of all, to the very great degree with which these precepts are followed among those who accept the task of guiding public opinion, and especially in the House of Commons, which is always so careful of the public interest and which in other ways has shown itself to be possessed of those steadfast and unyielding qualities in the face of danger and fatigue for which it has always been renowned, but never more renowned than now. I shall try to practise what I have been preaching in the remarks I have to make, and I am sure the Committee will remember how many different audiences I have to address at the same moment, not only here but out of doors and not only in this Island, but throughout the Empire, not only among our Allies, great and small, west or east, but finally, among our enemies, besides, of course, satellites and neutrals of various hues. I must, therefore, pick my way among heated ploughshares, and in this ordeal the only guides are singleness and simplicity of purpose and a good or, at any rate, a well trained conscience.

Since I last spoke here on Foreign Affairs, just about three months ago, almost all the purposes which I mentioned to you have prospered, severally and collectively. First of all, let us survey the Mediterranean and the Balkan spheres. The great disappointment which I had last October, when I was not able to procure the necessary forces for gaining the command of the Aegean Sea following upon the collapse of Italy and gaining possession of the principal Italian islands, has, of course, been accompanied by an exaggerated attitude of caution on the part of Turkey. The hopes we cherished of Turkey boldly entering the war in February or March, or at least according us the necessary bases for air action—those hopes faded. After giving £20,000,000 worth of British and American arms to Turkey in 1943 alone, we have suspended the process and ceased to exhort Turkey to range herself with the victorious United Powers, with whom she has frequently declared that her sympathies lie, and with whom, I think, there is no doubt that her sympathies do lie. The Turks at the end of last year and the beginning of this year, magnified their dangers. Their military men took the gloomiest view of Russian prospects in South Russia and in the Crimea.

They never dreamed that by the early Summer the Red Army would be on the slopes of the Carpathians, drawn up along the Pruth and Serret Rivers, or that Odessa and Sevastopol would have been liberated and regained by the extraordinary valor, might and energy of the Soviet onslaught. Consequently the Turks did not measure with sufficient accuracy what might have occurred, or would occur, in Rumania and Bulgaria or, I may add, Hungary, what would be the result on all those countries of these tremendous Russian hammer blows struck, even in months which are particularly unsuitable for operations in these regions and which normally would be devoted to the process of replenishing the advancing front for future action. Having overrated their dangers, our Turkish friends increased their demands for supplies to such a point that, having regard to the means of communication and transport alone, the war would probably be over before these supplies could reach them.

We have, therefore, with great regret, discontinued the process of arming Turkey because it looks probable that, in spite of our disappointment in the Aegean, the great Allies will be able to win the war in the Balkans and generally throughout Southeastern Europe without Turkey being involved now at all, though, of course, the aid of Turkey would be a great help and acceleration of that process. This, of course, is a decision for Turkey to take. We have put no pressure upon them, other than the pressure of argument and of not giving the supplies we need for ourselves and other nations that are fighting. But the course which is being taken, and has been taken so far, by Turkey will not, in my view, procure for the Turks the strong position at the peace which would attend their joining the Allies.

I must, however, note the good service and significant gesture rendered to us by the Turkish Government quite recently, and it is said that it has been rendered to us on the personal initiative of Turkey's honored President, General Inonu, namely the complete cessation of all chrome exports to Germany. It is not too much to expect that the assistance given us in respect of chrome will also shortly be extended to cover other commodities, the export of which, even if of less importance than chrome, is of material assistance to the enemy. If so, we shall endeavor to compensate the Turkish people for the sacrifice which their co-operative action might entail by other means of importation.

I thought it right to speak bluntly. Turkey and Britain have a long history. They entered into relations with us before the war when things looked very black. They did their best through difficult times. I have thought it better to put things bluntly today, but I cannot conclude, notwithstanding anything I have said in criticism, without saying that we hope with increasing confidence that a still better day will dawn for the relations of Turkey with Britain and, indeed, with all the great Allies. Always in recent decades there has been in the Mediterranean a certain tension between Turkey and Italy on account of Italian ambitions in the Greek Islands and, also, possibly in the Adana Province of Turkey. The Turks could never be sure which way the Italian dictator would turn his would-be conquering sword. On that score Turkish anxiety has certainly been largely removed.

The fate of Italy is indeed terrible, and I personally find it very difficult to nourish animosity against the Italian people. The overwhelming mass of the nation rejoiced in the idea of being delivered from the subtle tyranny of the Fascists, and they wished, when Mussolini was overthrown, to take their place as speedily as possible by the side of the British and American armies who, it was expected, would quickly rid the country of the Germans. However, this did not happen. All the Italian forces which could have defended Italy had either been squandered by Mussolini in the African desert or by Hitler amid the Russian snows, or they were widely dispersed combatting, in a halfhearted way, the patriots of Yugoslavia. Hitler decided to make great exertions to retain Italy, just as he has decided to make great exertions to gain the mighty battle which is at the moment at its climax to the south of Rome. It may be that after the fall of Mussolini our action might have been more swift and audacious. As I have said before, it is no part of my submission to the House that no mistakes are made by us or by the common action of our Allies; but, anyhow, here is this beautiful country suffering the worst horrors of war, with the larger part still in the cruel and vengeful grip of the Nazis, and with a hideous prospect of the red-hot rake of the battle-line being drawn from sea to sea right up the whole length of the peninsula.

It is clear that the Germans will be driven out of Italy by the Allies, but what will happen on the moving battle fronts and what the Germans will do on their way out in the way of destruction to a people they hate and despise, and who, they allege, have betrayed them, cannot be imagined or forecast. All I can say is that we shall do our utmost to make the ordeal as short and as little destructive as possible. We have great hopes that the city of Rome may be preserved from the area of struggle of our armies. The House will recall that when I last spoke on foreign matters I expressed the view that it would be best that King Victor Emmanuel, and above all Marshal Badoglio, should remain at the head of the Executive of the Italian nation and Armed Forces until we reached Rome, when it was agreed by all that a general review of the position must be made.

Such a policy naturally entailed differences of opinion which were reflected not only among the Allied Governments but inside every Allied country. However, I am happy to say that after various unexpected happenings and many twists and turns the situation is now exactly what I ventured to suggest and as I described it to the House three months ago. In addition, far beyond my hopes, an Italian Government has been formed, of a broadly based character, around the King and Badoglio, and the King himself has decided that on the capture of Rome he will retire into private life forever and transfer his constitutional functions to his eldest son, the Prince of Piedmont, with the title of Lieutenant of the Realm.

I have good confidence in this new Italian Government which has been formed. It will require further strengthening and broadening, especially as we come more closely into touch with the populous industrial areas of the North—that is essential—but, at any rate, it is facing its responsibilities manfully and doing all in its power to aid the Allies in their advance. Here I may say we are doing our best to equip the Italian forces, who are eager to fight with us and not in the power of the Germans. They have played their part in the line on more than one occasion. Their fleet is discharging a most useful and important service for us not only in the Mediterranean but in the Atlantic; and the loyal Italian Air Force has also fought so well that I am making special efforts to supply them with improved aircraft of British manufacture. We are also doing our best to assist the Italian Government to grapple with the difficult financial and economic conditions which they inherited from Fascism and the war and which, though improving, are still severe behind the line of the Army. It is understood throughout Italy, and it is the firm intention of the United Nations, that Italy, like all other countries which are now associated with us, shall have a fair and free opportunity, as soon as the Germans are driven out and tranquility is restored, of deciding whatever form of democratic Government, whether monarchical or republican, they desire. They can choose freely for themselves. I emphasize, however, the word "democratic," because it is quite clear that we should not allow any form of Fascism to be restored or set up in any country with whom we have been at war.

From Italy one turns naturally to Spain, once the most famous Empire in the world and down to this day a strong community in a wide land, with a marked personality and distinguished culture among the nations of Europe. Some people think that our foreign policy towards Spain is best expressed by drawing comical or even rude caricatures of General Franco; but I think there is more to it than that. When our present Ambassador to Spain, the right hon. Gentleman the Member for Chelsea (Sir S. Hoare), went to Madrid almost exactly four years ago to a month, we arranged to keep his airplane waiting on the airfield, as it seemed almost certain that Spain, whose dominant party were under the influence of Germany because Germany had helped them so vigorously in the recently-ended civil war, would follow the example of Italy and join the victorious Germans in the war against Great Britain. Indeed, at this time the Germans proposed to the Spanish Government that triumphal marches of German troops should be held in the principal Spanish cities, and I have no doubt that they suggested to them that the Germans would undertake, in return for the virtual occupation of their country, the seizure of Gibraltar, which would then be handed back to a Germanized Spain. This last feature would have been easier said than done.

There is no doubt that if Spain had yielded to German blandishments and pressure at that juncture our burden would have been much heavier. The Straits of Gibraltar would have been closed and all access to Malta would have been cut off from the west. All the Spanish coast would have become the nesting place of German U-boats. I certainly did not feel at the time that I should like to see any of those things happen and none of them did happen. Our Ambassador deserves credit for the influence he rapidly acquired and which continually grew. In his work he was assisted by a gifted man, Mr.

Yencken, whose sudden death by airplane accident is a loss which I am sure has been noted by the House. But the main credit is undoubtedly due to the Spanish resolve to keep out of the war. They had had enough of war and they wished to keep out of it. [An Hon. Member: That is a matter of opinion.] Yes, I think so, and that is why my main principle of beating the enemy as soon as possible should be steadily followed. But they had had enough, and I think some of the sentiment may have been due to the fact that, looking back, the Spanish people, who are a people who do look back, could remember that Britain had helped Spain to free herself from the Napoleonic tyranny of 130 years ago. At any rate the critical moment passed; the Battle of Britain was won; the Island power which was expected to be ruined and subjugated in a few months was seen that very winter not only intact and far stronger in the homeland but also advancing by giant strides, under Wavell's guidance, along the African shore, taking perhaps a quarter of a million Italian prisoners on the way.

But another very serious crisis occurred in our relations with Spain before the operation designated "Torch," that is to say the descent of the United States and British forces upon North-West Africa, was begun. Before that operation was begun Spain's power to injure us was at its very highest. For a long time before this we had been steadily extending our airfield at Gibraltar and building it out into the sea, and for a month before zero hour, on 7th November, 1942, we had sometimes 600 airplanes crowded on this airfield in full range and in full view of the Spanish batteries. It was very difficult for the Spaniards to believe that these airplanes were intended to reinforce Malta, and I can assure the House that the passage of those critical days was very anxious indeed. However, the Spaniards continued absolutely friendly and tranquil. They asked no questions, they raised no inconveniences.

If, in some directions, they have taken an indulgent view of German U-boats in distress, or continued active exportations to Germany, they made amends on this occasion, in my view, so far as our advantage was concerned, for these irregularities by completely ignoring the situation at Gibraltar, where, apart from aircraft, enormous numbers of ships were anchored far outside the neutral waters inside the Bay of Algeciras, always under the command of Spanish shore guns. We should have suffered the greatest inconvenience if we had been ordered to move those ships. Indeed, I do not know how the vast convoys would have been marshaled and assembled. I must say that I shall always consider a service was rendered at this time by Spain, not only to the United Kingdom and to the British Empire and Commonwealth, but to the cause of the United Nations. I have, therefore, no sympathy with those who think it clever, and even funny, to insult and abuse the Government of Spain whenever occasion serves.

I have had the responsibility of guiding the Government while we have passed through mortal perils, and, therefore, I think I have some means of forming a correct judgment about the values of events at critical moments as they occur. I am very glad now that, after prolonged negotiations, a still better arrangement has been made with Spain, which deals in a satisfactory manner with the Italian ships which have taken refuge in Spanish harbors, and has led to the hauling down of the German flag in Tangier and the breaking of the shield over the Consulate, and which will, in a few days, be followed by the complete departure of the German representatives from Tangier, although they apparently still remain in Dublin. Finally, it has led to the agreement about Spanish wolfram, which has been reached without any affront to Spanish dignity, and has reduced the export of wolfram from Spain to Germany during the coming critical months to a few lorry-loads a month.

It is true that this agreement has been helped by the continuous victories of the Allies in many parts of the world, and especially in North Africa and Italy, and also by the immense threat by which the Germans conceive themselves to be menaced, by all this talk of an invasion from across the Channel. This, for what it is worth, has made it quite impossible for Hitler to consider reprisals on Spain. All his troops have had to be moved away from the frontier, and he has no inclination to face bitter guerrilla warfare, because he has got quite enough to satisfy himself in so many other countries which he is holding down by brute force.

As I am here today speaking kindly words about Spain, let me add that I hope she will be a strong influence for the peace of the Mediterranean after the war. Internal political problems in Spain are a matter for the Spaniards themselves. It is not for us—that is the Government—to meddle in such affairs—

[MR. SHINWELL (Seaham): Why then in Italy? My right hon. Friend did remark, as regards the restoration of the Government in Italy, that it could not be Fascist. That was his declaration. Why not in Spain?]

The reason is that Italy attacked us. We were at war with Italy. We struck Italy down. My hon. Friend, I am sure, will see that a very clear line of distinction can be drawn between nations we go to war with, and nations who leave us alone.

[DR. HADEN GUEST (Islington, North): Is not a Fascist Government anywhere, a preparation for an attack?]

I presume we do not include in our program of world renovation any forcible action against any Government whose internal form of administration does not come up to our own ideas, and any remarks I have made on that subject referred only to enemy Powers and their satellites who will have been struck down by force of arms. They are the ones who have ventured into the open and they are the ones whom we shall not allow to become, again, the expression of those peculiar doctrines associated with Fascism and Nazism, which have, undoubtedly, brought about the terrible struggle in which we are engaged. Surely, anyone could see the difference between the one and the other. There is all the difference in the world between a man who knocks you down and a man who leaves you alone. You may, conceivably, take an active interest in what happens to the former in case his inclination should recur, but we pass many people in the ordinary daily round of life about whose internal affairs and private quarrels we do not feel ourselves called upon to make continued inquiry.

Well, I say we speak the same words to the Spaniards in the hour of our strength as we did in the hour of our weakness. I look forward to increasingly good relations with Spain and to an extremely fertile trade between Spain and this country which will, I trust, grow even during the war and will expand after the peace. The iron from Bilbao and the North of Spain is of great value to this country both in war and peace. Our Ambassador now goes back to Spain for further important duties, and I have no doubt he goes with the good wishes of the large majority of the House and of all thoughtful and unprejudiced persons. I am sure that no one more than my hon. Friend opposite would wish that he should be successful in any work for the common cause. My hon. Friend has been often a vigilant and severe critic of His Majesty's Government, but as a real Opposition figure he has failed, because he never can conceal his satisfaction when we win—and we sometimes do.

I am happy to announce a hopeful turn in Greek affairs. When I spoke last on this I described them as the saddest case of all. We have passed through a crisis of a serious character since then. A Greek brigade and a large proportion of the Greek Navy mutinied, declaring themselves, in one way or other, on the side of the organization called E.A.M., the Greek freedom movement, and, of course, against the King and his Government. The King of Greece, who was in London, was advised by nearly everyone concerned in Cairo not to go back and warned that his life would be in danger. He returned the next day. The situation was then most serious. The Greek brigade was encircled by British forces some thirty miles away from Alexandria, and the Greek ships which had mutinied in Alexandria harbor were lying under the guns both of the shore batteries and of our superior naval forces which had rapidly gathered. This tension lasted for nearly three weeks. In due course the mutinies in the Fleet were suppressed. The disorderly ships were boarded by Greeks, under the orders of the Greek Government, and, with about fifty killed and wounded, the mutineers were collected and sent ashore. The mutinous brigade in the desert was assaulted by superior British forces, which captured the eminences commanding the camp, and the 4,000 men there surrendered. There were no casualties among the Greeks, but one British officer was killed in the attack upon the eminences. This is a matter which cannot be overlooked. The greatest patience and tact were shown by the British military and naval authorities involved, and, for some weeks past, order has been firmly established and the Greek forces who were misled into evil deeds by subversive movements have been interned for the time being.

The then Prime Minister, M. Tsouderos, had already tried, before these things happened, to arrange a meeting of all representatives of Greek opinion and to construct his administration so as to include them. He acquitted himself with dignity and was helped by M. Venizelos, the son of the great Venizelos whom we all esteemed so highly in the first world war. At this moment there emerged upon the scene M. Papandreou, a man greatly respected, who had lived throughout the war in Athens and was known as a man of remarkable character and one who would not be swayed by party interests, his own party being a very small one. M. Papandreou became the King's new Prime Minister, but before forming his Government he called a conference which met last week in the Lebanon. Every party in Greek life was represented there, including E.A.M., the Communists and others—a dozen parties or more. The fullest debate took place and all expressed their feelings freely.

This disclosed an appalling situation in Greece. The excesses of E.L.A.S., which is the military body operating under E.A.M., had so alienated the population in many parts that the Germans had been able to form security battalions of Greeks to fight the E.A.M. These security battalions were made up of men, in many cases, who would far rather have been out in the hills maintaining the guerrilla warfare. They had been completely alienated. At the same time, the state of hostility and suspicion which led last autumn to an actual civil war, existed between E.A.M. and the other resistance organizations, especially the E.D.E.S. under Colonel Zervas, a leader who commands the undivided support of the civilian population in his area and has always shown the strictest compliance with the orders sent him from G.H.Q., Middle East, under whom all his forces have been placed. Thus it seemed to be a question of all against all, and no one but the Germans rejoicing.

After prolonged discussion complete unity was reached at the Lebanon

Conference and all parties will be represented in the new Government which will devote itself to what is after all the only purpose worthy of consideration, namely the forming of a national army in which all the guerrilla bands will be incorporated and the driving, with this army, of the enemy from the country or, better still, destroying the enemy where he stands.

On Monday there was published in the newspapers the very agreeble letter which I received from the leaders of the Communists—that is more than I have ever received from the hon. Member for West Fife (Mr. Gallacher); perhaps he might write me one, to tell me that he confirms it—and the extreme Left wing party. There is published today in the papers the letter I have received from M. Papandreou, and another one to my right hon. Friend expressing the hopes which he has for the future of his Government, and thanks for the assistance we have given in getting round these troubles—what I call the diseases of defeat which Greece has now a chance of shaking off. I believe that the present situation—I hope and pray that it may be so—indicates that a new and fair start will come to Greece in her struggle to cleanse her native soil from the foreign invader. I have, therefore, to report to the House that a very marked and beneficial change has occurred in the situation in Greece, which is more than I could say when I last spoke upon this subject. There was trouble with the destroyer we were giving the Greeks here, and while matters remained so uncertain, we were not able to hand her over, but I have been in correspondence with the Admiralty, and I hope that as a result of this reconstructed government, and the new start that has been made, this ship will soon be manned and go to strengthen the Greek Navy as it returns to discipline and duty.

I gave some lengthy account last time of the position in Yugoslavia and of our relations with the different jurisdictions there. The difficulty and magnitude of this business are very great, and it must be remembered that not only three strongly marked races—the Serbs, Croats and Slovenes—are involved but, further south, the Albanians are also making a bold bid for freedom from German rule. But they, too, at the present time are split into several competing and even antagonistic groups. Nothing is easier than to espouse any one of the various causes in these different countries, with all their claims and counter-claims, and one can find complete satisfaction in telling the tale from that particular standpoint. The best and easiest kind of speech to make is to take a particular cause and run it home on a single-track mind without any consideration of anything else, but we have to think of policy as well as oratory, and we have to think of the problem as a whole, and also to relate our action to the main purpose which I proclaimed at the beginning of my speech, namely, beating the enemy as soon as possible and to gather all forces for that purpose in priority to any other purpose.

I can only tell the Committee today the further positions which have been reached in Yugoslavia as the result of the unremitting exertions of our foreign policy. They are, in my opinion, far more satisfactory than they were. I have received a message from King Peter that he has accepted the resignation of Mr. Puric and his Cabinet and is in process of forming a new and smaller Cabinet with the purpose of assisting active resistance in Yugoslavia and of uniting as far as possible all fighting elements in the country. I understand that this process of forming the new Government, involves the severance from the Royal Yugoslav Government of General Mihailovitch in his capacity as Minister of War. I understand also that the Ban of Croatia is an important factor in the new political arrangements, around whom, or beside whom certain other elements may group themselves for the purpose of beating the enemy and uniting Yugoslavia. This, of course, has the support of His Majesty's Government. We do not know what will happen in the Serbian part of Yugoslavia.

The reason why we have ceased to supply Mihailovitch with arms and support is a simple one. He has not been fighting the enemy and, moreover, some of his subordinates have made accommodations with the enemy from which have arisen armed conflicts with the forces of Marshal Tito, accompanied by many charges and counter-charges, and the loss of patriot lives to the German advantage. Mihailovitch certainly holds a powerful position locally as Commander-in-Chief and it does not mean that his ceasing to be Minister of War will rob him of his local influence. We cannot predict what he will do or what will happen. We have proclaimed ourselves the strong supporters of Marshal Tito because of his heroic and massive struggle against the German armies. We are sending, and planning to send, the largest possible supplies of weapons to him and to make the closest contacts with him. I had the advantage on Monday of a long conversation with General Velebit who has been over here on a military mission from Marshal Tito, and it has been arranged among other things that Marshal Tito shall send here a personal military representative in order that we may be kept in the closest touch with all that is being done and with the effect of it in Yugoslavia. This is, of course, additional to the contacts established with Marshal Tito at General Wilson's headquarters in Algiers and will, of course, be co-ordinated therewith.

It must be remembered, however, that this question does not turn on Mihailovitch alone; there is also a very large body, amounting to perhaps 200,000, of Serbian peasant proprietors who are anti-German but strongly Serbian and who naturally hold the views of a peasant ownership community in regard to property, less enthusiastic in regard to communism than some of those in Croatia or Slovenia. Marshal Tito has largely sunk his communist aspect in his character as a Yugoslav patriot leader. He repeatedly proclaims he has no intention of reversing the property and social systems which prevail in Serbia, but these facts are not accepted yet by the other side. The Serbians are a race with an historic past; it was from Serbia came the spark which fired the explosion of the first world war. We remember their historic retreat over the mountains. A very large number of Serbians are fighting with Marshal Tito's forces. Our object is that all forces in Yugoslavia, and the whole united strength of Serbia, may be made to work together under the military direction of Marshal Tito for a united, independent Yugoslavia which will expel from native soil the Hitlerite murderers and invaders, and destroy them until not one remains. The cruelties and atrocities of the Germans in Greece and in Yugoslavia exceed anything that we have heard, and we have heard terrible things, but the resistance of these historic mountaineers has been one of the most splendid features of the war. It will long be honored in history, and I am sure that children will read the romance of this struggle and will have imprinted on their minds that love of freedom, that readiness to give away life and comfort, and all there is around one, in order to gain the right to live unmolested on your native heath.

All I can say is that we must be given a little reasonable latitude to work together for this union. It would be quite easy, as I said just now, to take wholeheartedly one side or the other. I have made it very plain where my sympathies lie, but nothing would give greater pleasure to the Germans than to see all these hearty mountaineers engaged in intestine strife against one another. We cannot afford at this crisis to neglect anything which may obstruct a real unity throughout wide regions in which at present upwards of twelve German divisions are gripped in Yugoslavia alone and twenty in all —that is another eight in the Balkans and the Aegean Islands. All eyes must be turned upon the common foe. Perhaps we have had some success in this direction in Greece. At any rate it sums up our policy towards Yugoslavia, and the House will note that all questions of monarchy or republic or Leftism or Rightism are strictly subordinate to the main purpose which we have in mind. In one place we support a king, in another a Communist—there is no attempt by us to enforce particular ideologies. We only want to beat the enemy and then, with a happy and serene peace, let the best expression be given to the will of the people in every way.

For a long time past the Foreign Secretary and I have labored with all our strength to try to bring about a resumption of relations between the Soviet Government and the Polish Government which we recognize. Which we have always recognized since the days of General Sikorski. We were conscious of the difficulty of our task and some may say we should have been wiser not to attempt it. Well, we cannot accept that view. We are the Ally of both countries. We went to war because Germany made an unprovoked attack upon our Ally, Poland. We have signed a twenty years' Treaty with our Ally, the Soviet Union, and this Treaty is the foundation of our policy. Polish forces are fighting with our armies and have recently distinguished themselves remarkably well. Polish forces under Russian guidance are also fighting with the Soviet army against the common enemy.

Our effort to bring about a renewal of relations between the Polish Government and Russia in London has not succeeded. We deeply regret that fact, and we must take care to say nothing that would make agreement more difficult in the future. I must repeat that the essential part of any arrangement is regulation of the Polish eastern frontier, and that, in return for any withdrawal made by Poland in that quarter, she should receive other territories at the expense of Germany, which will give her an ample seaboard and a good, adequate and reasonable homeland in which the Polish nation may safely dwell. We must trust that, when we all engage in the struggle with the common foe, when nothing can surpass the bravery of our Polish Allies in Italy and daily on the sea, and in the air, and in the heroic resistance of the underground movement to the Germans. I have seen here men who came a few days ago out of Poland, who told me about it, and who are in relation with, and under the orders of, the present Polish Government in London. They are most anxious that this underground movement should not clash with the advancing Russian Army, but should help it, and orders have been sent by the Polish Government in London that the underground movement is to help the Russian Armies in as many ways as possible. There are many ways possible in which guerrillas can be successful, and we must trust that statesmanship will yet find some way through.

I have the impression—and it is no more than an impression—that things are not so bad as they may appear on the surface between Russia and Poland. I need not say that we—and I think I may certainly add, the United States —would welcome any arrangement between Russia and Poland, however it was brought about, whether directly between the Powers concerned, or with the help of His Majesty's Government, or any other Government. There is no question of pride on our part, only of sincere goodwill to both, and earnest and anxious aspirations to a solution of problems fraught with grave consequences to Europe and the harmony of the Grand Alliance. In the meantime, our relations, both with the Polish and the Soviet Governments, remain regulated by the public statements which have been made and repeated from time to time from this bench during the present war. There I leave this question, and I trust that if it is dealt with in Debate those who deal with it will always consider what we want, namely, the united action of all Poles, with all Russians, against all Germans.

We have to rejoice at the brilliant and skilful fighting of the French Moroccan and Algerian Divisions, and the brilliant leading they have had by their officers in the heart-shaking battle to which I have referred, and which is now at its climax. The French Committee of National Liberation, in Algiers, has the credit of having prepared these troops, which were armed and equipped by the United States under President Roosevelt's personal decision. The French Committee also places at the full service of the Allies, a powerful Navy including, in the *Richelieu,* one of the finest battleships in the world. They guide and govern a vast Empire, all of whose strategic points are freely placed at the disposal of the United Nations. They have a numerous and powerful underground army in France, sometimes called the Maquis, and sometimes the French Army of the Interior, which may be called upon to play an important part before the end of the war.

There is no doubt that this political entity, the French Committee of National Liberation, presides over, and directs, forces at the present time which, in the struggle against Hitler in Europe, give it the fourth place in the Grand Alliance. The reason why the United States and Great Britain has not been able to recognize it yet as the Government of France, or even as the Provisional Government of France, is because we are not sure that it represents the French nation in the same way as the Governments of Britain, the United States and Soviet Russia represent the whole body of their people. The Committee will, of course, exercise the leadership to establish law and order in the liberated areas of France under the supervision, while the military exigency lasts, of the supreme Allied Commander, but we do not wish to commit ourselves at this stage to imposing the Government of the French Committee upon all of France which might fall under our control without more knowledge than we now possess of the situation in the interior of France. At the same time I must make it clear that we shall have no dealings with the Vichy Government, or any one tainted with that association because they have decided to follow the path of collaboration with our enemies. Many of them have definitely desired, and worked for, a German victory.

In Norway and the Low Countries it is different. If we go there we shall find that continuity of lawful government is maintained by the Governments which we recognize, and with which we are in intimate relations. The Governments of King Haakon and Queen Wilhelmina are the lawfully founded Governments of those States, with perfect and unbroken continuity, and should our liberating Armies enter those countries we feel we should deal with them and also, as far as possible, with the Belgian and Danish Governments, although their Sovereigns are prisoners, but with whose countries we have the closest ties. On the other hand, we are not able to take a decision at this time to treat the French Committee of National Liberation, or the French Provisional Government, as it has been called, as the full, final, and lawful embodiment of the French Republic. It may be that the Committee itself may be able to aid us in the solution of these riddles and I must say that I think their decree governing their future action constitutes a most forceful and helpful step in that direction. With the full approval of the President of the United States I have invited General de Gaulle to pay us a visit over here in the near future and my right hon. Friend the Foreign Secretary has just showed me a telegram from Mr. Duff-Cooper, in Algiers, saying that he will be very glad to come. There is nothing like talking things over, and seeing where we can get to. I hope he will bring some members of his Government with him so that the whole matter can be reviewed.

As this war has progressed, it has become less ideological in its character, in my opinion. The Fascist power in Italy has been overthrown and will, in a reasonable period of time, be completely expunged, mainly by the Italian democracy themselves. If there is anything left over for the future we will look after it. Profound changes have taken place in Soviet Russia, the Trotskyite form of Communism has been completely wiped out. The victories of the Russian Armies have been attended by a great rise in the strength of the Russian State, and a remarkable broadening of its views. The religious side of Russian life has had a wonderful rebirth. The discipline and military etiquette of the Russian Armies are unsurpassed. . . . There is a new National Anthem, the music of which Premier Stalin sent me, which I asked the B.B.C. to play on the frequent occasions when there are great Russian victories to celebrate. The terms offered by Russia to Rumania make no suggestion of altering the standards of society in that country and were in many respects, if not in all, remarkably generous. Russia has been very patient with Finland. The Comintern has been abolished, which is sometimes forgotten. Quite recently, some of our representatives from the Ministry of Information were allowed to make a considerable tour in Russia, and found opportunities of seeing for themselves what they liked. They found an atmosphere of candid friendliness and a keen desire to see British films, and hear about our country and what it was doing in the war. The children in the schools were being informed about the war on the seas, and of its difficulties and its perils, and how the Northern convoys got through to Russia. There seemed a great desire among the people that Britain and Russia should be friends. These are very marked departures from the conceptions which were held some years ago, for reasons which we can all understand. . . .

We have no need to look back into the past and add up the tale and tally of recrimination. Many terrible things have happened. But we began thirty years ago to march forward with the Russians in the battle against the German tyranny of the Kaiser and we are now marching with them, and I trust we shall until all forms of German tyranny have been extirpated. As to Nazism, the other ideology, we intend to wipe that out utterly, however drastic may be the methods required. We are all agreed on that in this House, whatever our political views and doctrines may be. Throughout the whole of the British Dominions and the United States, and all the United Nations, there is only one opinion about that and for the rest, whatever may be said as to former differences, there is nothing that has occurred which should in any way make us regret the twenty years' Treaty which we have signed with the Russians, and which will be the dominating factor in the relations which we shall have with them.

I see that in some quarters I am expected today to lay out, quite plainly and decisively, the future plan of world organization, and also to set the Atlantic Charter in its exact and true relation to subsequent declarations and current events. It is easier to ask such questions than to answer them. We are working with thirty-three United Nations and, in particular, with two great Allies who, in some forms of power, far exceed the British Empire. Taking everything into consideration, including men and money, war effort, expanse of territory, we can claim to be an equal to those great Powers, but not, in my view, a superior. It would be a great mistake for me, as head of the

British Government, or, I may add—speaking to this Committee as a most respected institution—the Grand Alliance, or for the House, to take it upon ourselves, to lay down the law to all those different countries, including the two great Powers with which we have to work, if the world is to be brought back into a good condition.

This small Island and this marvellous structure of States and dependencies which have gathered round it, will, if we all hold together, occupy a worthy place in the vanguard of the nations. It is idle to suppose that we are the only people who are to prescribe what all other countries, for their own good, are to do. Many other ideas and forces come into play and nothing could be more unwise than for the meeting of Prime Ministers, for instance, to attempt to prescribe for all countries the way they should go. Consultations are always proceeding between the three great Powers and others, and every effort is being made to explore the future, to resolve difficulties and to obtain the greatest measure of common agreement on levels below the Ministerial level in a way which does not commit the Government.

A few things have already become quite clear and very prominent at the Conference which has just concluded. The first is that we will fight on all together until Germany is forced to capitulate and until Nazism is extirpated and the Nazi party are stripped of all continuing power of doing evil. The next is that the Atlantic Charter remains a guiding signpost, expressing a vast body of opinion amongst all the Powers now fighting together against tyranny. The third point is that the Atlantic Charter in no way binds us about the future of Germany, nor is it a bargain or contract with our enemies. It has no quality of an offer to our enemy. It was no offer to the Germans to surrender. If it had been an offer, that offer was rejected. But the principle of unconditional surrender, which has also been promulgated, will be adhered to as far as Nazi Germany and Japan are concerned, and that principle itself wipes away the danger of anything like Mr. Wilson's Fourteen Points being brought up by the Germans after their defeat, claiming that they surrendered in consideration of them.

I have repeatedly said that unconditional surrender gives the enemy no rights but relieves us from no duties. Justice will have to be done and retribution will fall upon the wicked and the cruel. The miscreants who set out to subjugate first Europe and then the world must be punished, and so must their agents who, in so many countries, have perpetrated horrible crimes and who must be brought back to face the judgment of the population, very likely in the very scenes of their atrocities. There is no question of Germany enjoying any guarantee that she will not undergo territorial changes if it should seem that the making of such changes renders more secure and more lasting the peace of Europe.

Scarred and armed with experience we intend to take better measures this time than could ever previously have been conceived in order to prevent a renewal, in the lifetime of our children or our grandchildren at least, of the horrible destruction of human values which has marked the last and the present world wars. We intend to set up a world order and organization, equipped with all the necessary attributes of power, in order to prevent the breaking out of future wars, or the long planning of them in advance, by restless and ambitious nations. For this purpose there must be a World Council, a controlling council, comprising the greatest States which emerge victorious from this war, who will be obligated to keep in being a certain minimum standard of armaments for the purpose of preserving peace. There must also be a world assembly of all Powers, whose relation to the world

Executive, or controlling power, for the purpose of maintaining peace I am in no position to define. I cannot say. If I did, I should only be stepping outside the bounds which are proper to us.

The shape of these bodies, and their relations to each other can only be settled after the formidable foes we are now facing have been beaten down and reduced to complete submission. It would be presumption for any one Power to prescribe in detail exactly what solution will be found. Anyone can see how many different alternatives there are. A mere attempt on our part to do so, or to put forward what is a majority view on this or that, might prejudice us in gaining consideration for our arguments when the time comes.

I shall not even attempt to parade the many questions of difficulty which will arise and which are present in our minds. Anyone can write down on paper at least a dozen large questions of this kind—should there be united forces of nations, or should there be a world police, and so on. There are other matters of a highly interesting character which should be discussed. But it would be stepping out of our place in the forward march for us to go beyond the gradual formulation of opinion, and ideas which are constantly going on inside the British Commonwealth and in contact with our principal Allies. It must not be supposed, however, that these questions cannot be answered and the difficulties cannot be overcome and that a complete victory will not be a powerful aid to the solution of all problems, and that the good will and practical common sense which exist in the majority of men and in the majority of nations will not find its full expression in the new structure which must regulate the affairs of every people in so far as they may clash with another people's. The future towards which we are marching, across bloody fields and frightful manifestations of destruction, must surely be based upon the broad and simple virtues and upon the nobility of mankind. It must be based upon a reign of law which upholds the principles of justice and fair play and which protects the weak against the strong if the weak have justice on their side. There must be an end to predatory exploitation and nationalistic ambitions.

This does not mean that nations should not be entitled to rejoice in their traditions and achievements, but they will not be allowed, by armed force, to gratify appetites of aggrandizement at the expense of other countries merely because they are smaller or weaker or less well prepared, and measures will be taken to have ample Armies, Fleets and Air Forces available to prevent anything like that coming about. We must undoubtedly in our world structure embody a great part of all that was gained to the world by the structure and formation of the League of Nations. But we must arm our world organization and make sure that, within the limits assigned to it, it has overwhelming military power. We must remember that we shall be hard put to it to gain our living, to repair the devastation that has been wrought and to give back that wider and more comfortable life which is so deeply desired. We must strive to preserve the reasonable rights and liberties of the individual. We must respect the rights and opinions of others, while holding firmly to our own faith and convictions.

There must be room in this new great structure of the world for the happiness and prosperity of all and in the end it must be capable of bringing happiness and prosperity even to the guilty and vanquished nations. There must be room within the great world organization for organisms like the British Empire and Commonwealth, as we now call it, and I trust that there will be room also for the fraternal association of the British Commonwealth and the

United States. We are bound by our twenty years' Treaty with Russia, and besides this—

I, for my part, hope to deserve to be called a good European—to try to raise the glorious continent of Europe, the parent of so many powerful States, from its present miserable condition as a kind of volcano of strife and tumult to its old glory of a family of nations and a vital expression of Christendom. I am sure these great entities which I have mentioned—the British Empire, the conception of a Europe truly united, the fraternal associations with the United States—will in no way disturb the general purposes of the world organization. In fact, they may help powerfully to make it run. I hope and pray that all this may be established and that we may be led to exert ourselves to secure these permanent and glorious achievements which alone can make amends to mankind for all the miseries and toil which have been their lot and for all the heroism and sacrifice which have been their glory.

FOREIGN MINISTER ANTHONY EDEN'S SPEECH IN COMMONS ON FOREIGN AFFAIRS

May 25, 1944 [1]

As I listened to this two-day debate I had the impression that there was a growing note of confidence about ourselves in the speeches. No doubt there are reasons for that outside these walls. Military events at the moment and good news from our armies would account for it. But I thought there was more to it than that. I think there was also the increased sense of unity which the meeting of the Prime Ministers of the Empire has given us. I felt an echo when the hon. Gentleman the Member for Seaham (Mr. Shinwell) said that international unity was difficult to achieve. I could not agree with him more wholeheartedly. I happened to be reading in a history the other day about one of my illustrious predecessors who had one period of office of about eighteen months. History just noted the term of office of Lord—by saying "No event of any international significance occurred." I thought that that was a time when I would have liked to be Secretary of State for Foreign Affairs. We live in very different times.

I would like at the beginning of my remarks to say something about the meeting of the Empire Prime Ministers. Many comments have been made in this Debate about that meeting, and I think it is right to say that it was probably at once the most successful and the most significant meeting of that kind which has ever been held. Both the men and the moment served to bring that about. Here were gathered together five statesmen of widely different character and experience but all united with the one purpose of trying to maintain and strengthen this Empire and Commonwealth and to ensure that the world should have the benefit of the service we could render it together. Of course that is the note as I conceive it, the only purpose of the British Commonwealth and Empire. We are not an exclusive organization, but we do think—and I make no apology for saying this—that we are the one really successful experiment in international co-operation that there has ever been. Out of that, we may suggest with becoming modesty to others, there may be something to be learned.

As I attended these proceedings I detected more than once what a strange,

[1] British Speeches of the Day.

indefinable and, if you like, what an illogical thing this British Empire is. Sometimes, the links that hold it together seem so frail as to be almost non-existent, or so frail that they would snap at the first pressure. That is the mistake which foreigners often make. It is the mistake that Ribbentrop made, though God knows I and others tried hard enough to make him believe it was wrong. This demonstration of reality of the strength of that relationship comes at a moment when it may be of real service to the world. Anyhow, it has so happened that in two world struggles in one generation, the British Commonwealth has shown itself to have a unity which nothing can break. In the second of these struggles it stood alone for a year or more.

How difficult it is to try to explain what brings these men together from these many corners of the world and leads them to feel such deep loyalty towards the British Empire. I cannot pretend to describe it, but perhaps like all really deep forces that move mankind, there is an element of mystery in it that cannot be put into words. I believe that to be true. Of this meeting, I must say that it owed its special character more than anything else to the leadership given it by our own Prime Minister. Sometimes here, within this Island with our vast controversies and frequent debates, it is difficult to stand back and view matters as they are seen in perspective by other lands and other peoples. Certain it is that the immense advantage of my right hon. Friend's position in the world was of quite invaluable aid in leadership in those discussions. There is another advantage. In the stress of war—and there is still a stress of war—nothing is more difficult than to avoid becoming immersed in the daily details of one's particular task, be it on foreign affairs, economic affairs, the Treasury, or whatever it is, and the burden is such that when you have a moment in which you are not occupied with your own affairs the Cabinet is discussing somebody else's affairs that are just a degree more tiresome than your own. When one is living like that, it is invaluable to be able to look at the problems which we have to face in company with a man like the Prime Minister. It is then that his experience is more valuable still. I can only say for myself that that experience was one that gave the greatest encouragement.

There was, it occurred to me, a feature in our meetings this time which I had not perceived before. I was privileged to attend the Imperial Conference in 1937. Since then we have developed to a very large extent the practice of sending the greatest possible amount of information to the Governments of all the Dominions so that today it is not merely a question of consulting them from time to time and asking their advice on some particular problem that arises, but it is the practice to give them fully all information that we have on day-to-day developments of foreign policy. The growth of that practice was immeasurably helpful at these meetings because the whole background of knowledge was present to an equal extent in the minds of all the men round the table. It may be there is more we can do in that regard. If there is we will gladly do it, for I am confident that this exchange of information is an indispensable element in true co-operation between the Dominions and ourselves. If as a result of that we get from time to time, when we give information about foreign affairs or whatever it may be, replies, questions, even criticism, we welcome them because they are all elements of strength to the British Commonwealth.

Having made those remarks on that aspect of our work, I want to plunge into the details of some matters which were discussed. More than one hon. Member in the Debate, talking about foreign affairs, has said that in wartime, of course, foreign policy must take second place to immediate military needs, and that is true. In wartime the Foreign Office has two duties: to help the Military arm, and as part of that help, to maintain, as far as lies in our power, unity among those who are fighting the common enemy. Also, so far as we can during wartime, it is to lay the foundations for co-operation afterwards. Those are the tasks on which we are engaged now. In wartime it sometimes happens that military needs may even conflict with political needs. I will put it another way—you may have to take decisions for short-term advantage which in the light of long-term policy you would prefer not to take —that sometimes does happen; but there is one aspect of the work we have done to which I would draw the attention of the Committee.

Despite all those difficulties, and I may say temptations, in this respect in wartime, we have not on any occasion in these four years of conflict entered into any secret engagement of any kind with anybody. I want the Committee to understand the importance of that; hon. Members like the hon. Member for West Leicester (Mr. H. Nicolson) who were present when the Treaty of Versailles was negotiated will remember what embarrassment was caused when secret treaties were pulled out of pockets, and engagements—often conflicting engagements—were all put on the table together. There is nothing of that kind on our part this time. To that extent we shall have an advantage.

I have said that one of our tasks is to try to help the Armed Forces. I will give briefly some examples of what I mean by that; for example, the negotiations with Portugal about the Azores, the negotiations with Spain over wolfram, the handling of our affairs with Turkey which led to the stoppage of chrome. I had, as one or two hon. Members have remarked in this Debate, the task of lending help to our Allies, among others, in trying to smooth out differences which arise even between Allies. Those are our tasks.

Here let me say one word about the neutral powers. My hon. Friend, the Member for West Leicester, was, I think, rather hard on us about the neutrals. He was inclined to criticize us for our treatment of them. I know they may sometimes regard our methods as harsh and arbitrary, and think that we take too little account of the rights of small nations. If they do, I can say truly we regret it.

I can also say we have asked no nation to take any step which violates its neutrality and we have asked no neutral who is also an Ally—of whom there are some—to take any step beyond that which is specifically within our rights according to the terms of our alliance, and we must insist to the limit on what are our rights. It is our duty to do everything in our power to shorten this struggle. And therefore, to the neutrals themselves I say, if sometimes we have seemed outspoken and urgent in our demands I regret it, but it is a fact that such action as we ask them to take is in their own interests, as anyone in this hour can see, if only it shortens the conflict which they as much as we wish to see brought to an end.

I must say that my sympathies and thoughts are more at the present time with occupied countries. I felt that the members of the Committee were many times right when they recalled the staunch Allies whom we have in Europe today. I think that at a time like this the Committee would like to send a message to those occupied countries—the smaller occupied countries of Europe—a message of encouragement and hope that their liberation may not be long delayed. I would like to speak of one or two of these countries. We had a remarkable speech just now—there were not quite so many Members present—from my hon. and gallant Friend, the Member for Blackpool (Wing Commander Robinson), just back from firsthand experience in the Balkans and Mediterranean. He told us of his experiences in a Greek ship, and how its sailors had twenty-four to twenty-five times taken that ship back into the Anzio Beachhead. We are greatly encouraged at the political unity which the Greek nation has at last achieved. We can neither forget the past of that country nor its own amazing achievements in this conflict at an earlier stage. After all, the Greeks were the first to debunk Mussolini. It was not we who did that. They defeated him and repelled him from their land. And we of this Committee would like to tell the Greek people we hope they are now united and that they will be able to work together and re-establish their reputation in the world. . . .

I wish to mention one or two others of these countries—Yugoslavia, Poland and Czechoslovakia. The suffering of all these countries has been great and the prayer for liberation is there. In particular I want to say a word about the northwestern countries, if I may so call them, which have been referred to in one or two speeches—Belgium, Norway and the Netherlands. Within the last few days we have signed agreements with the Governments of all three of them. The hon. Member for Kidderminster (Sir John Wardlaw Milne), asked whether we could perhaps make them public. We considered that in conjunction with our Allies who have signed similar agreements and we have found a difficulty in it because these agreements are not only political; they also contain military clauses affecting the action which must be taken if and when these countries are liberated. . . . It is quite proper. A secret agreement disposing of somebody else's belongings would be most improper, but if it is a secret agreement arranging how by military means you are going to free a country, I think that it is not very shocking. That is what they are. I can tell the hon. Member to relieve him from any strain of anxiety that so far as the political clauses are concerned, what they are designed to do is to give the Governments of those countries the full control of their own affairs at the earliest possible moment.

Now I come to a country which has been mentioned several times in this discussion—France. There is no part of our policy to which we attach more importance than the restoration of the independence and greatness of France. France is our nearest neighbor; for more than one thousand years our histories have been interlocked, sometimes in conflict. Sometimes the French got help from our northern neighbors, if I may speak as an Englishman for just one moment. But I think that as inhabitants of this Island we would acknowledge that no country has contributed more to the civilization of Europe, in the best sense of that term. For the future, we know that the French people will have their part to play in Europe, and we shall need them as they will need us if confidence and security are to live again in Europe. In the meanwhile, I would like, on behalf of the Government, and I hope of the Committee, to pay tribute to the spirit of resistance which the French people are showing, all the more despite the necessary bombardments which we are unhappily compelled to inflict upon them. I agree with what was said by the hon. Member for Bridgewater (Mr. Bartlett) yesterday. He said we must hand over the full responsibility for the Government of France to the French people as soon as is possible. I agree; there is no difference about that. There is not the least intention in our minds to inflict an AMGOT, as it is called, upon France or indeed upon any Allied country whatever, though, incidentally it is not in the least the kind of machine which the hon. Baronet, the Member for Barnstaple (Sir Richard Asland), so eloquently imagined yesterday. But be AMGOT good or ill, it has no connection with France or any Allied country when they are liberated.

In the light of these observations, I come to the special problem of recognition. I would like to try to put it in its true perspective. I regret that there is some misunderstanding as to the extent of recognition already accorded to the French Committee of National Liberation. For instance the hon. Gentleman the Member for Maldon asked why we did not recognize the Committee, as though there was no recognition at all. Of course that is not the position at present. We welcomed the unity of the Committee last year at Algiers. We were happy to recognize them last August as the body qualified to conduct the French effort in the war. We have gone much further than that since. We have dealt with the Committee as if they were the legitimate Government of all the French overseas territories. We have made agreements with them—financial agreements, economic agreements—on that basis. Our representative in Algiers has been given the rank of Ambassador and the French representative here, Monsieur Vienot, who is doing such good work, has been given a similar rank. More than that, we have dealt with the French Committee not only as if they were the Government in the territory where their writ runs already, but we are also dealing with them in matters which concern the metropolitan territory of France and as the French authority which will exercise leadership in France as her liberation proceeds.

Now I come to where I think the difficulty lies. In connection with these discussions, certain conversations have been necessary and these conversations and the progress of them have unhappily been interfered with by the restrictions which we felt compelled to institute over a wide area as a security measure on account of forthcoming operations. I say frankly that those restrictions are extremely troublesome to the conduct of foreign affairs, not in respect of one country alone. I would like to say at this box how grateful the Government are for the spirit in which the Diplomatic Corps as a whole have taken these quite unprecedented measures. But the House will understand, as I am sure our French friends will understand, that vexatious as these restrictions are, the needs of absolute military security must come first. That being so, we think that the best way to deal with the question of civil administration in France is to have direct conversations. It is for this purpose that the Prime Minister has invited General de Gaulle to come here. General de Gaulle has accepted. He will receive, I know, a warm welcome from all of us here. I feel confident nothing but good will come out of that meeting, and that when the whole situation can be surveyed we shall be able to clear away all misunderstandings, however formidable they may seem now. At least that is what we wish to do.

I will turn for a moment to another matter, to which I want to refer because of one or two speeches which were made about our attitude to Europe. I do not know whether hon. Members happened to see the two-column article which appeared in the *Times* on the 13th May containing an analysis of German propaganda. If not, I commend it as quite good reading. That analysis showed German propaganda had just two themes. One was that the Empire was breaking up. That is not working awfully well just now. The other was that we were disinteresting ourselves in certain parts of Europe: in other words, that a some place or other never specified—it may be Moscow, it may be Teheran—we had done a deal, it may be with Soviet Government or it may be with somebody else, by which we would cease to interest ourselves in certain parts of Europe. That is absolutely and categorically untrue. I would like to go further. In the first place, no arrangement of such a kind has been come to. In the second place, no arrangement of such a kind was suggested to us. In the third place, if anybody had suggested such an arrangement to us we would not have agreed to it. Otherwise, the report is approximately accurate.

It is, of course, true that there are certain parts of Europe—Western Europe and the Mediterranean—where our interests are more directly concerned than others. But as the right hon. Gentleman, the Member for Devonport (Mr. Hore-Belisha) emphasized in his speech we are above all Europeans, and our interest in Europe is not limited to any single part of Europe. What we seek is the security of the Continent which has suffered so much but which has given so much light and leading to the world in the past and could do it again if only it could recover its unity and prosperity. I am confident that the Governments of the Dominions perfectly well understand our position in this respect and that they endorse it. No great country should attempt to do more in its foreign policy than its strength will allow. But having said that, I think I can add, that as a result of this meeting and as a result of events in the war, the British Commonwealth's authority and influence in the world is at least as high as it has ever been; and that influence we should use, can use, and will use to promote the prosperity and the unity of Europe.

What do we want to achieve in our foreign policy? I would put it like this. We want in our relations with other countries to try to maintain a standard of honesty, of fair dealing and of international good faith. Foreign affairs are really not so very different in those respects from domestic affairs. Human intercourse is based on good faith, on the keeping of promises, on honoring the pledged word between man and man. I agree so much with what my noble Friend the Member for Lanark (Lord Dunglass) said yesterday—we are very glad, all of us, to welcome him back—about the consequences of the lowering of international standards. I remember myself venturing to make, some years ago, a speech in this House in which I said that I thought we were in the presence of the progressive deterioration of international standards. I say frankly that I think that process was one of the main contributory causes of the outbreak of this war. Why did the war become inevitable? It was because Hitler and Mussolini refused to observe the ordinary standards of international conduct in the day-to-day conduct of international affairs. It was more than that, because they used the desire of other nations to maintain those standards to obtain concessions, to profit by those concessions, and then to proceed to their next demand. They were encouraged by the desire of the peace-loving countries to avoid war if ever they could.

I remember an occasion in a conversation with Hitler—I think it was in 1933 or thereabouts—when he spoke to me of the Versailles Treaty, and he explained how the Treaty had been imposed on Germany, and how, therefore, he could never accept it. I said "What about the Treaty of Locarno?" He said "That is another thing. That was a freely negotiated Treaty. Germany signed that of her own free will. By that I stand"—or words to that effect. He said it with a fervor and an eloquence, which I confess entirely convinced me. I came back thinking "that is not such an unreasonable attitude" and so forth. Eighteen months after that, Locarno had gone the same way as the Treaty of Versailles. That was the method, that was the technique of those men. If those methods and those techniques are practised, whoever practises them, there cannot be enduring peace. So I say to the Committee: We cannot say to the world "You have got to do this; you have got to do that." That is beyond the power of forty-five million. But what we can do is in our own conduct and by our own leadership to try to establish and maintain those standards of international conduct without which there cannot be peace. That I conceive to be the duty of British foreign policy.

May I for a moment or two look a little into the future? When victory is won, the first task will be close collaboration between the British Commonwealth, the United States, the Soviet Union and China—but in the main, as far as Europe is concerned, between the first three—to ensure that Germany cannot start this business again. I want to speak for a moment about cooperation between these three in particular—ourselves, the United States and the Soviet Union. If I emphasize it, it is because I am convinced that if we can establish real understanding all else, though difficult, will be possible. But if we cannot establish that understanding, then the future is very dark indeed. Having said that I am not suggesting these three Powers should seek to impose some three-Power dictatorship on the world. That would be bad, very bad. But what they should do is serve the world in assuring at least for the outset that these two particular aggressors with whom we are now dealing are not in a military position to repeat in a few years' time what they did before. I hope I shall carry the Committee with me in that. There is nothing exclusive in our desire to work together. It is indispensable that we should so work together. May I mention the suggestion about co-operation in Western Europe? I think it may be desirable that we should have close, intimate and friendly relations with other countries in Western Europe, but neither my hon. Friend nor anybody else would suggest that on such a foundation alone such lasting security could be founded. We have to stretch wider than that.

I would like to say a word about our relations with these two Powers. My right hon. and gallant Friend the Member for Kelvingrove (Lieut.-Colonel Elliot) spoke about our relative size—our forty-five millions, and these two countries, one with one hundred forty millions and the other with two hundred millions. That is true, but on the other hand, I must tell the Committee that though I have been in many negotiations with these two Powers alone I have never felt any sense of inferiority, and I honestly don't believe that they felt any particular sense of superiority. I don't mean individually toward me, but toward this country. The reason is, of course, that though we are only forty-five millions, we have in this Island, a unique geographical position and a rather remarkable experience, because we are the center of a great Empire. I would suggest we need not overstress the size of our partners or underestimate our own significance. At any rate, of all our international troubles, that is the one that worries me least.

About the United States I think I can say that at this time our relations are as close and cordial as they have ever been. We had the other day the experience of a visit from Mr. Stettinius, the Undersecretary of State, who I think spoke to the hon. Members upstairs. That visit was remarkable, not only because of his own personality but because he brought with him a large number of representatives of the State Department, and they worked together with our own representatives in the Foreign Office with the result that apart from understanding at a higher level, there is now interlocked at every stage understanding by each of the other's policy. That is something quite new in our experience with the United States, or indeed with any country, and I think it will be of great service because although decisions must be taken by Ministers, it is good that all those down the hierarchy should understand each other's point of view. Recently we have had both from the President and Mr.

Hull statements that show American leaders are thinking on broad courageous and good neighborly lines.

Now I turn to our relations with the other great Power—our Ally Russia. There is in our minds no reservation when we say that we wish to work with the Soviet Union in the fullest and closest collaboration, but it is also in the interests of our two countries that we should accept the fact that there are certain difficulties in this task, and I agree with the right hon. Gentleman, the Member for Wakefield (Mr. A. Greenwood) that we do not gain much by ignoring them. There is first the legacy of suspicion difficult to describe and quite impossible to exaggerate. It is a suspicion which is not as many think, of modern growth, but which dates back to, and existed in the days of Tsarist Russia and will be found many times in the records of the Congress of Vienna and so forth. Unhappily, it has always played its part in Anglo-Russian relations and it has a habit of accumulating suspicions on their side which produce counter-suspicions on ours, and before we know where we are a mountain of suspicion is the result. For that there is only one cure—that bit by bit our peoples get to know each other better. We are ready, I say to our Soviet friends, to do anything in our power at any time to further that result.

There are other things—differences in form of government, differences in attitude to the individual, to the press, and so on. These are all pretty wide divergencies, and I repeat, that we do better to face them frankly. But on the other side there is something else to put in the scale. There is the fact that in three great world convulsions, in the Napoleonic war, in the last great war, and in this war, we have found ourselves allied and fighting together for the same purpose—to stop one man or one power dominating the whole of Europe. On each of the last occasions when we fought together we fell aside quickly soon after, but this time we have got to do better. We have an absolute conviction here in this country that the Soviet Union means to see this struggle through to the end. We have the same intention. I have been asked about the extent of our collaboration now. For instance, are we consulted on such matters as Soviet peace terms to Rumania, and the negotiations with Finland? The answer is we were consulted on both questions. In respect to Rumania we thought Mr. Molotov's speech, and the offer made, fair and just to Rumania. In respect to Finland, we deplored the fact that the Finnish Government had turned down the peace terms. On both these matters we were consulted. I do not want to belittle the extent of the effort which has got to be made in both these countries to make of this Twenty-Year Treaty a lasting reality of value to our two countries and to the world, but surely the Committee will feel that the stakes for the future in this matter are so huge that both of us must make every effort that we may succeed. Personally I believe we shall succeed.

I have been asked several questions about the situation in the Far East, particularly by the hon. Member for Kidderminster, the hon. and gallant Member for Renfrew (Major Lloyd) and many others. I think we are all conscious of the heavy burdens that China carries just now. We in this country are in our fifth year of war and, looking back on it, it seems a pretty long period. China is, however you reckon it, at least in her eighth year of war. Her people have suffered greatly, and many of her cities have been destroyed. We have been unable to carry to her all the help we would like to carry, and it is only by the remarkable efforts of the Air Force—quite unique efforts—in crossing the Himalayas that any assistance has reached her at all. Her ordeals have been long and stern. We pledge ourselves anew that we will not rest until Japan is defeated and China has restored to her all those territories wrongly seized from her. An hon. Member has asked me about supplies. In the main, of course, the supplies have to be for the United States Air Force which has been built up in China and for the needs of the Chinese armies under General Stilwell's leadership, but whatever space is left over, it is for the Chinese Government to say what priority they want for the goods that are sent to them. We all wish we could send more, but we are sending already to the limit of our capacity.

While speaking of the Far East I would like to make a statement upon the position of our prisoners in the hands of the Japanese. What I am now going to tell the Committee arose from a suggestion made, I think, by the hon. Member for Seaham on the 28th of January, when I spoke about the Japanese treatment of our prisoners, and it was suggested that the Soviet Government might be asked to make representations to the Japanese Government on behalf of these prisoners. I communicated later with his Majesty's Ambassador in Moscow and he recently approached the Soviet Government and explained to them our anxiety. There were three points on which we particularly wanted satisfaction from the Japanese Government.

They were, first of all, that the right should be recognized of a protecting Power, in this case Switzerland, and of the International Red Cross, to visit all the camps wherein British subjects were held and report freely and frankly on conditions prevailing. [An hon. Member: And civilians?] Yes. Secondly, we should be given complete lists of our prisoners of war and internees in their hands, together with a list of those who had died; and, thirdly, the Japanese Government should agree to receive Red Cross supplies which would be sent at regular intervals in neutral ships to Japanese ports and facilities should be given to distribute those supplies. The Soviet Government replied that while these matters fell directly within the competence of the protecting Power, they were nevertheless prepared to approach the Japanese Government in regard to them, and they have now done so, and I want to thank them and to express the thanks of the Government for their action. I ought to add that this action does not in any way express any lack of confidence in Switzerland as the protecting Power. We know that our Swiss friends have done everything in their power, and we hope this additional action may assist them in their work in this connection and in what they will do for us hereafter.

My time is nearly up. I want to say a word on economic affairs. I want to tell my hon. Friends that it is true that the Foreign Office has taken over certain fresh activities in the economic field. We have not snatched them, as an hon. Gentleman suggested—the Foreign Office never snatches—but we have negotiated. We have these additional opportunities now. We shall need them, I am confident, and perhaps in a later Debate I may be able to describe the set-up for dealing with these activities to anybody else, either to the United States or anybody. We maintain our organization in that respect. As a result of this arrangement we shall receive at the Foreign Office now the economic intelligence which used to go to the Ministry of Economic Warfare. That will be of great value to us in our political work; and also, a new Department which I am setting up will be able to make use of the economic intelligence that we receive. There will be, as a result, a closer relation between our political and economic policies as a whole, and I hasten to add, it does not mean that I am attempting to take any duties away from my right hon. Friend the President of the Board of Trade or my right hon. Friend, the Chancellor of the Exchequer. But it is the truth that foreign policy and economic policy are now more closely related; or perhaps, what is more probable, there is a better understanding now than there used to be of how closely they are related. But however we express it, there is no doubt of the need for an organization such as I have described and which I would like to describe more fully at a later time. . . .

I want for a few minutes . . . to look in to the future, as some of the hon. Members have done. There has been much said about the League of Nations, where it succeeded, and where it failed. I am not going to argue that now. There is not time, and even if there were it would take many hours of discussion, and there would be many divergent opinions. The Prime Minister explained yesterday that we do not want to impose upon others in detail whatever our ideas may be; at the same time we are entitled to say what our general ideas are about world organization.

I would like to leave with the Committee just a few principles on which we suggest this future organization should be based. They are these: first, that the world organization must be designed in the first instance to prevent a recurrence of aggression by Germany and Japan and must be fully equipped with Forces to meet the purpose; secondly, that to ensure this, there must be close political and military co-operation between the United States, the Soviet Union, the British Commonwealth and China . . . and other Powers; thirdly, that the responsibility in any future world organization must be related to power, and consequently the world organization should be constructed on and around the four great Powers I have mentioned and all other peace-loving States should come in to play their part in the structure; fourthly, that the world organization should be flexible and not rigid, that is to say it should grow by practice and not try straight away to work to a fixed and rigid code or rule; and, fifthly, all Powers great and small, included in the world organization, should strive for economic as well as for political collaboration.

I understand only too well the difficulties in any attempt to translate into practical experience the principles I have outlined. What I can say is that we have already begun informal conversations with other Powers about these propositions and I hope that in coming months we shall be able to make more progress with them. At least, we are convinced that it is only by translating into the period of peace the confidence which we have built up and the machinery we have built up for collaboration as Allies in war that we can hope to save the world from a repetition of those conflicts which twice in our generation have caused so much misery to mankind. I have tried to give the Committee some account of our policy, and I can only repeat as I began that, despite the difficulties to which the hon. Members have referred, we shall persist in our course and do so with a greater measure of hope as a result of the meetings of the Prime Ministers held in London in these last weeks.

DECLARATION BY GREEK PRIME MINISTER GEORGE PAPANDREOU, AT CAIRO, ON GREEK MINISTRIES OF DEFENSE

May 27, 1944 [1]

As the Greek Communist Party and the EAM are still conferring with the guerrillas in the mountains of Greece about the persons who will participate

[1] Greek Government Office of Information.

in the government of national unity on their behalf, we consider it was necessary to complete immediately in the meantime the ministry of national defense so that the reorganization of our armed forces may start quickly.

The War Ministry has two main aims: First the reorganization of the military forces in the Middle East to enable them to face the enemy as soon as possible and fulfill their national mission and second, the reorganization of our guerrilla forces, their unification and the creation of a national army which will belong only to the fatherland and will obey the government's orders.

The task of the Air Ministry is easier because our Air Force has the great advantage of having remained almost untouched during the recent sad events.

In our Navy the work of reorganization which, under the command of Admiral Voulgaris, is going well will continue unimpeded and the whole government will support it.

The new Minister of the Navy, Mr. Alexander Mylonas, made the following declaration after taking the oath:

Leaving the shores of Greece we were accompanied by the Hellenic wish for national unity. The happy agreement of Lebanon is being fulfilled. The Greek people united at the side of the Allies are frantic upholders of their liberty and are united in condemning the sad events in Egypt. I myself am also inspired by the conscience of national necessity of restoring as soon as possible our armed forces and especially our glorious Navy to the outstanding position which it occupied at the side of our Allies and I undertake the weighty function of Minister of the Navy with the determination, in collaboration with the distinguished chief of our fleet, to succeed in effacing a sad page by new achievements of heroism and glorious activity.

JUNE

Secretary of State Cordell Hull pledged that the rights and position of the small nations would be safeguarded in the new world security organization planned by the United States, Soviet Russia, Great Britain and China.

2

Pope Piux XII declared that those who insisted upon complete victory or complete destruction were only helping to prolong the war. He prayed for an early peace and praised "the heralds of wisdom and moderation."

4

The American Fifth Army captured Rome, the British Eighth Army joining it in close pursuit of the fleeing Germans.

In an encircling move the Japanese Army increased its threat to Changsha.

5

King Victor Emmanuel III, although retaining his throne, yielded his "royal prerogatives" to his son Crown Prince Umberto (Humbert).

The American Fifth Army entered Rome in triumph amidst great jubilation of the population.

General Eisenhower announced complete agreement between himself and the French Committee of National Libration on military problems for the invasion of France.

6

The Allied invasion of western Europe began by British, American and Canadian troops under command of Gen. Sir Bernard L. Montgomery on the Normandy coast of France.

A sky train of transport planes and gliders fifty miles long crossed the Channel to reinforce and resupply the Allied invasion troops in the Cherbourg Peninsula.

Chinese troops cut the Burma Road so that it was no longer available to the Japanese.

7

Upon the completion of the first day of the invasion of western Europe the German Atlantic Wall was successfully breached; the battle was centered in Caen.

8

Allied troops captured Bayeux and cleared the beaches as Nazi resistance stiffened.

9

Former Premier Ivanoe Bonomi was chosen by all Italian anti-fascist parties as Premier of Italy.

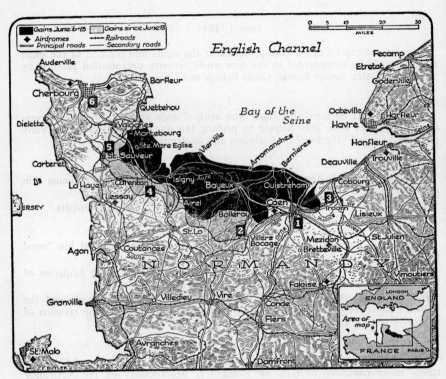

Courtesy New York Times

Six Critical Points in the 2nd Week of the Normandy Invasion
June, 1944

Legislation to extend price, wage and rent controls for eighteen months beyond June 30th was voted by the Senate, but with cotton price rise amendments.

10

American invasion troops smashed a third of the way across the Cherbourg peninsula.

American Central Pacific task forces struck a crippling blow in the Mariana Islands, destroying 140 Japanese aircraft and sinking 13 ships.

11

The Red Army launched a full offensive against Finland, on the Karelian Isthmus.

Chinese troops took from the Japanese the city of Lungling, the second most important Japanese base in Yunnan Province.

12

The Vichy authority was reported disintegrating before French patriot risings.

Invading Japanese troops pounded incessantly at besieged Changsha on the Canton-Hankow railway line.

13

The Senate passed a $3,920,602,200 appropriation bill for Lend-Lease and U. S. participation in the UNRRA program.

14

Gen. Charles de Gaulle visited the battlefields of Normandy, four years after he had raised the standard of French resistance to the Germans.

15

American amphibious forces stormed the strategic island of Saipan in the Marianas.

B-29 Superfortresses made a heavy assault on Japanese home territory.

17

General Eisenhower said that the French underground had seriously disrupted German communications.

18

The greatest air-sea battle since Midway was fought off the Marianas when an American carrier task force supporting the ground attack on Saipan shot down 300 Japanese planes.

Marshal Tito and Dr. Ivan Subasitch, Yugoslav Prime Minister, reached an accord.

19

The U. S. Ninth Infantry Division fought its way to the west coast of the Cherbourg Peninsula, isolating Cherbourg.

The Allied powers approved the Italian Government headed by Premier Ivanoe Bonomi.

20

Vice-President Wallace arrived in Chungking to confer with Generalissimo Chiang Kai-shek.

21

Changsha, capital of Hunan Province, fell to the Japanese.

22

Commenting on the initial successes of German robot "revenge" planes, Dr. Goebbels wrote: "When we state that retaliation has but begun we believe British plutocracy will be forced definitely to abandon its habit of minimizing our threats."

23

The Red Army opened its summer offensive on the Eastern Front.

26

The Republican National Convention opened in Chicago.

27

Wendell Willkie attacked the proposed Republican foreign policy plank as ambiguous. He stated: "The net result would be no international organization. No effective international force for the suppression of aggression. No peaceful world. Another world war fought in vain. And the youth of America once more betrayed."

The Finnish Government announced its decision to fight on by the side of Germany after a visit by German Foreign Minister Ribbentrop.

Cherbourg was captured by American troops.

28

Governor Thomas E. Dewey of New York was chosen by the Republican Convention as its Presidential candidate; Governor John W. Bricker of Ohio won the nomination for Vice-President.

French guerrillas, disguised as policemen, executed the collaborationist Vichy Minister of Propaganda Philippe Henriot.

29

Gen. George C. Marshall, Admiral Ernest J. King and Gen. H. H. Arnold, in a report to President Roosevelt, denounced the optimism on the home front which considered that the war was already as good as over.

30

Secretary of State Cordell Hull announced that the U. S. Government had severed diplomatic relations with Finland because it was conclusively proved that it was a puppet of Germany.

POPE PIUS XII'S ADDRESS TO THE COLLEGE OF CARDINALS, PLEADING FOR THE SAFETY OF ROME AND FOR PEACE

June 2, 1944 [1]

It is a full year, venerable brethren, since we had the consolation of receiving for the fifth time, on the feast day of our holy patron and predecessor, from the lips of the much-loved and venerated cardinal dean whom we are sorry not to see in our midst today, your devoted congratulations, your offering of prayers, the promise of your complete dedication of yourselves to the evergrowing tasks and to the grave responsibilities of the apostolic ministry,

[1] *New York Times.*

and the reiterated pledge of your unfailing participation in the cares and anxieties that weigh on the Father of Christendom.

A year has gone, a brief span of time, and yet so filled with hate and mournful happenings and unmeasured unspeakable suffering; for the terrible tragedy of the World War, as it unfolds itself before and around us, has reached a pitch and kind of frightfulness which smite and shock every Christian and human sense.

That is why, as this our feast day comes around and we see you gathered here once again, we feel the need of confiding to you the intimate anguish of our soul and of deploring, with you, the rampant and sanguinary accumulation of destruction, ruin and carnage, so vast that what a year ago many might have thought impracticable or impossible is now, alas! a reality.

The Eternal City, mother cell of civilization, and even holy ground around the Tomb of St. Peter, have had to learn by experience how far the spirit inspiring present day methods of warfare, for a variety of reasons becoming ever more ferocious, has departed from those abiding norms which were once hailed as inviolable laws.

On the other hand, amidst so much suffering, we do not wish to overlook the fact that threat of air raids on districts not beyond the outer parts of Rome has given way in fact to conduct that shows greater regard.

We nourish hope that this more equitable and moderate trend will prevail over the opposing considerations of seeming utility and so-called military exigencies or needs, and that the Eternal City, in every eventuality and at all costs, may be saved from becoming a theatre of war.

We therefore do not hesitate to repeat once again, with complete impartiality and due firmness: Whoever dared raise a hand against Rome would be guilty of matricide in the eyes of the civilized world and in the eternal judgments of God.

If we now pass on to consider the present state of affairs throughout the world, we find ourselves confronted with events which, in their spiritual and material issues, fill our soul with justifiable anxiety.

The bitter dissensions and quarrels between children of the same people, while carrying with them the germs of more serious consequences, create an atmosphere in which authority of the Church (which stands above all earthly and passing currents of thought) finds itself drawn by both sides into a vortex of controversies which not infrequently creates lack of essential clarity of ideas and true balance of judgment.

Thus it is that the heavy responsibility that weighs on our weak shoulders, increases and intensifies to a degree unknown in other times and demands from us, from day to day and from hour to hour, an indefatigable largeness of heart, open to all souls who seek sincerely the true and the good.

[The Pope referred to the activity of the Apostolic See in defense of justice and in relief of want.]

Here we may aptly appeal to the thoughts expressed in 449 by an eastern Bishop, Eusebius of Dorileus, in a better to Pope Leo the Great.

"The apostolic throne," he writes, "has been from the beginning accustomed to defend those who suffered injustice, to relieve, as far as it could, the prostrate: you indeed commiserate all men. The reason is that you are inspired by the sense of right and keep inviolate the faith toward our Lord Jesus Christ, as you also portray a genuine charity toward all the brethren and toward everyone who is called in the name of Christ."

These noble words, which pay tribute to the constant defense of truth and right by this Apostolic See, and to its practical charity toward all who suffer and are oppressed, were inspired by the experience of the first centuries of Christendom. But the Roman Church thanks and praises our Lord for having maintained, with the help of the divine assistance, this holy custom in successive ages also.

Thus it is that one of the best-known historians of the nineteenth century, a man who certainly is under no suspicion of being favorable to the See of Peter, did not hesitate to make this confession at the end of his work on the city of Rome in the Middle Ages:

"History has not sufficient titles for heroes with which to indicate even approximately the world-wide activity, the great achievements and the imperishable glory of the Popes." [Indication reference work of Ferdinand Gregorvius.]

Following therefore the example of our predecessors we, too, venerable brethren, in this period of unparalleled want and poverty, deem it our sacred duty to devote our pastoral care to an extent hitherto scarcely surpassed or reached, to the indigence which surrounds us on every side and calls for help.

It is not that the Church, least of all at the present moment, aspires in any way after earthly advantage or human glory; for our thoughts, day and night, are bent on one only purpose: how we may be able to meet this bitter trial, helping all without distinction of nationality or race, and how we may help toward restoring peace at last to tortured mankind. [Referring to his anxiety about the serious situation in Rome.]

If at the moment our anxiety is especially for Rome it is because such sentiments are evoked by the pitiable conditions in which so large a part of the population of the city—which is also our diocese—finds itself.

It is certainly not the first time that the storm has smitten the Eternal City. Christian Rome, in the course of its history, has known other very bitter calamities: occupation and sackings, from that of Alaric to the terrible sack of 1527; internal party strife as in the tenth century; dereliction as in the Avignon period and at the time of the great western schism; pests, as in the calamitous days of St. Gregory and under Pope Sixtus IV; starvation and famine from natural causes, as during the reign of Clement XIII in the years 1763 and 1764.

During this last public calamity the famished crowds also flocked to Rome from all the states of the Church and even from Tuscany and Naples, and the provision of food and lodging for them demanded the greatest exertion. The Pope, with untiring and generous hand, succeeded in averting a catastrophe.

But what were the 6,000 refugees of that occasion, joined to the less than 160,000 Romans—the whole of the Papal States numbered a little more than 2,000,000 souls—what were they, we say, in comparison with the situation of today with the sum of the population, with the want, the risks, the worries, the separations, the sufferings of all kinds by which they are stricken and intimidated?

In few parts of Italy, not to say of the world, is there experienced at the present moment as extensively as in Rome and its environs, the want of the necessities of life and the danger that this want may culminate in an all-but incalculable impoverishment of whole masses of the people.

On the other hand, the force of the attraction which the Eternal City exerts on many war victims, who come here in search of shelter and help, brings those who provide for their housing and feeding face to face with problems which are at times almost insoluble.

In spite of laudable zeal of public authorities and charitable associations, the army of poor grows from day to day. With ever-greater anxiety these unfortunate ones turn their gaze, and with ever-greater insistence outhold their hands to the common Father; many now constrained to seek that charity which but yesterday they themselves generously dispensed.

To the very utmost limit of our means and our powers, helped and supported by the offerings of generous souls, by the organizing activity of provident and industrious experts, by the courage and self-sacrifice of upright and capable workers (to all of whom we wish to express our lively gratitude), we have often been able to send into the gloom of direst misery and cruelest abandonment a comforting ray of light in the form of practical paternal charity; it has not, alas! always been adequate to the vast need or to the deeper promptings of our heart.

Without shirking any sacrifice, neither losing courage because of any refusal nor fearful before any violation of our rights, we have contributed uninterruptedly as far as we could toward providing the population of Rome and the country around it with at least the most urgent and essential food.

We have also initiated negotiations in order to secure the transport of food by sea in papal ships. But we are still waiting for the consent of one of the belligerents to this undertaking, which would provide a really efficacious remedy for the immense evil.

In any event, we shall not, for our part, diminish our efforts to surmount obstacles and to overcome opposition in order that this, our native city and our episcopal see, which today as at no other period, counts within its walls sons and daughters of every region of Italy, may be spared as far as possible, in one of the gravest moments in her history, so rich in glory and sorrow, from having to apply to itself the words of the prophet: "All her people sigh, they seek bread (Lamentations 1:2), the little ones have asked for bread and there was none to break it unto them (Lamentations 4:4)."

[The Pope then passed to consideration of the primacy of the Roman Church.]

But above such external cares and those of particular duties imposed by the contingencies of time and place, there stands, venerable brethren, our supreme and paramount duty from whose full and conscientious fulfillment no human power can detach us, no external crisis distract us; it is the unquestioning obedience to the commandment of our Lord: "Feed my lambs: feed my sheep" (John 21:15-17).

This divine command, which from the first Peter has passed down through the long line of Roman Pontiffs, even to us, their unworthy successor, entails in the confused and torn world of today an even vaster multitude of responsibilities, and meets with obstacles and opposition which demand that the Church, in her visible head and in her members, be ever more on the alert and vigilant.

Today, in fact, more than ever before, is to be seen by any clear-sighted and honest observer the sadly deficient balance sheet which cleavages from the Church in the course of centuries have effected for Christendom. In a turbulent and afflicted age like ours, when mankind is engaged in reaping the consequences of a spiritual decadence that has hurled it into the abyss, and when in every nation voices are raised to insist that, for the gigantic work of restoring order anew, not only external guarantees but the essential juridical and moral foundations be secured, it is of vital importance to know what influence the current of Christian ideas and of Christian moral standards can exert on the content and on the spirit of such a future reconstruction, and what influence it can have to prevent false and dangerous tendencies again predominating.

Mother Church, Catholic, Roman, she who has remained faithful to the constitution received from her divine founder, and who even today stands firmly on the solid rock on which He willed to found her, possesses in the primacy of Peter and of his legitimate successors, the assurance, guaranteed by divine promises, of maintaining and transmitting whole and inviolate, through centuries and tens of centuries, even to the end of time, the whole body of truth and grace contained in the redemptive mission of Christ.

And while she finds in the stimulating and comforting consciousness of this double possession, her force to conquer all the darkness of error and all moral deviations, she exerts her activity to the advantage not only of Christendom but of the entire world, inspiring sentiments of justice and of genuine fraternal charity in those great divergencies in which blessings and calamities, abundant harvests and poor gleanings often are to be found side by side.

But how much more potent and efficacious would be the influence of Christian thought and Christian life on the moral substructure of the future plans for peace and social reconstruction, if there were not this vast division and dispersal of religious confessions, that in the course of time have detached themselves from Mother Church! Who today can fail to recognize what substance of faith, what a genuine power of resistance to anti-religious influences is lost in many groups as a result of that separation.

A striking proof—among many others—of this painful reality, is afforded by the history of Rationalism and Naturalism in the past two centuries. In those quarters where the office of "confirming his brethren" (Luke 22:32), committed to him who is invested with the primacy, cannot exercise and exert its preservative and protective activity, the cockle of Rationalism has penetrated in a thousand different forms, with its stalks and baneful offshoots, into the thought and mentality of many souls who call themselves Christian, and has poisoned what was still left in them of the divine seed of revealed truth, spreading everywhere darkness, schism and growing abandonment of faith in the divinity of Christ.

Between Christ and Peter there reigns, from the day of the promise near Cesare Phillippi and that of the fulfillment by the Sea of Tiberias, a mysterious but eminently real bond which was effected once in time but which draws its roots from the eternal counsels of the Almighty.

The Eternal Father, who revealed to Simon Bar Jona the mystery of the divine sonship of Christ and thus rendered him capable of answering with an open and ready confession the question of our Redeemer, had from all eternity predestined the fisherman of Bethsaida for his singular office. And Christ Himself only fulfilled the will of His Father when, promising and conferring the primacy, He used expressions which were to fix forever the uniqueness of Peter's privileged position.

Those therefore, who—as was said (or better, repeated) some time ago by representatives of religious confessions who profess themselves Christian —declare that there is no vicar of Christ on earth because Christ Himself promised to remain with His church as its head and Lord to the end of time, besides depriving the whole episcopal office of its foundation, are ignoring and misinterpreting the profound meaning of papal primacy, which is not the negation but the fulfillment of that promise.

For if it be true that Christ in the fulness of His divine power disposes of the most varied forms of enlightenment and sanctification, in which He is really with those who confess Him, it is no less certain that He wished to entrust to Peter and to his successors the guidance and government of the universal church and the treasures of truth and grace of His work of redemption.

The words of Christ to Peter leave no doubt as to their meaning: that was recognized by West and East in times that cannot be questioned and with marvelous harmony. To try to create an opposition between Christ as head of the Church and his vicar, to see in the affirmation of one the negation of the other, means distorting the clearest and most luminous pages of the Gospel.

It means closing one's eyes to the most ancient and venerable testimonies of tradition, and depriving Christendom of that precious heritage, the correct knowledge and appreciation of which, at the moment known only to God and by the light of grace which He alone gives, can instill into the separated brethren the longing to return to their Father's house, and the efficacious will to come back to it.

Every year when, on the eve of the Feast of the Prince of the Apostles, we visit our patriarchal Vatican basilica, to implore at the tomb of the first Peter the strength to serve the flock committed to us according to the designs and purposes of the Eternal and Supreme Priest, from the majestic architrave of that lofty temple there appear before our gaze in glittering mosaic the words of power with which Christ manifested his intention of founding the Church on the rock of Peter; and they remind us of our insistent duty to keep intact that incomparable heritage of our divine Redeemer.

Then as we see glistening before us the "Gloria" of Bernini, and above the chair, held aloft by the giant figures of Ambrose and Augustine, Athanasius and John Chrysostom, behold refulgent and supreme, the symbol of the Holy Spirit, we are deeply conscious of all the sacred character, all the superhuman mission, which the will of our Lord with the assistance of the Spirit whom He promised and sent, has conferred on this central point of the Church of the Living God, "the pillar and ground of truth" (Timothy 1:3–15).

And in this octave of Pentecost there breaks forth from our heart and our lips the invocation to the Creator Spirit that He may arouse in our separated brethren the desire to return to the unity they desire.

Would that all those who are counted Christians could understand what an unsurpassed field of action would be open to Christianity at the present moment if, in full unity of faith and purpose, they were to dedicate their activity to saving the human family and preparing it for a better future!

One thing that has contributed significantly toward making men open their hearts to the hope of this air and more peaceful morrow is the fact that, while the instruments of destruction have reached a potency never before known, and while the world finds itself on the eve of still more dramatic and, according to some, decisive events, the discussion of the fundamental outlook and of the detailed guiding principles of the future peace attracts more and more participants; the numbers and the interest of those joining in that discussion grow from hour to hour.

Yet beside the heralds of wisdom and moderation there are not wanting others who scarcely dissimulate their program of violence or who openly espouse vengeance. While the former follow the suggestion of that Greek leader, of whom we read that he reckoned that victory outstanding in which clemency prevailed over cruelty, the latter, on the contrary, recall vividly the saying of Cicero that victory is essentially insolent and overbearing.

In many is thus born the impression or the fear that there may not be, even for the peoples and nations as such, any alternative but this: A complete victory or complete destruction. When once this sharp dilemma has entered men's minds, its baneful influence is a stimulant toward prolonging the war. Even among those who by natural impulse or for realistic considerations would be disposed to a reasonable peace, the spectre of that alternative and the conviction of a real or supposed will of the enemy to destroy national life to the very roots, smothers all other reflections and instills into many the courage of desperation.

Those who are under the domination of such feelings go on, as in a hypnotic sleep, through abysses of unspeakable sacrifice and constrain others to a war of extermination that drains their life blood, a war whose economic, social and spiritual consequences threaten to become the scourge of the age to come.

It is, therefore, of the greatest importance that this fear should give way to a well-founded expectation of honorable solutions; solutions that are not ephemeral or carry the germs of fresh turmoil and dangers to peace, but are true and durable; solutions that start from the principle that wars, today, no less than in the past, cannot easily be laid to the account of peoples, as such.

You, venerable brethren, know well how, in fulfillment of the serious obligation imposed by our apostolic ministry, we have already on several occasions, in concrete form, outlined the essential fundamentals, according to Christian thought, not only with regard to peaceful relations and international collaboration among men, but also with regard to the internal order of state and peoples.

Today we limit ourselves to observing that any right solution of the world conflict must take into consideration and treat as quite distinct two grave and complex questions: the guilt of beginning and of prolonging the war on the one hand and, on the other, the kind of peace and its maintenance; it is a distinction which naturally leaves untouched the demands for a just expiation of acts of violence, not really called for by the conduct of the war, committed against persons or things, as well as the guarantees necessary for the defense of right against possible attempts of violence.

These two different aspects of the formidable problem have been widely echoed in the conscience of peoples, and in the public declaration of competent authorities has been expressed the resolution and decision to give to the world, at the end of the armed conflict, a peace that all nations can bear.

We desire and hope that the prolongation of the war, together with the progressive harshening of the methods of warfare and the resulting heightening of tension and exasperation of spirit, do not end by lessening and extinguishing these healthy sentiments and along with them, the readiness to subordinate the instincts of vengeance and anger which is the enemy of counsel, to the majesty of justice and equanimity.

In any war where one of the belligerents succeeded only through the power of the sword and other means of irresistible coercion, in reaching a clean and unquestioned victory, it would find itself in the position of being physically able to dictate an inequitable peace imposed by force. But it is certain that nobody, whose conscience is illumined by the principles of true justice, could recognize in such a precarious solution of character of assured and prudent wisdom.

Although in the nature of things, it may be that the period of transition that runs from the termination of hostilities and the formal conclusion of peace, to the attainment of normal social stability, is determined, in large

part, by the power of the victor over the vanquished, nevertheless, wise, and
hence moderate political skill, never forgets or fails to give the losing side the
hope—we should like to say confidence—that even to their people and its
vital necessities a worthy place be prepared and juridically assigned. We
should, therefore, wish that Governments and peoples should keep before their
minds, at least as an ideal at which to aim, the words spoken in compliment
to Marcus Claudius Marcellus by the most distinguished orator of ancient
Rome: "To conquer oneself, to curb anger, to spare the vanquished, to
raise the fallen enemy—a man who does this I shall not compare with the
greatest of men, but will deem as most like to a god."

We nourish the hope that all our sons and daughters scattered over the
earth may have a lively consciousness of their collective and individual share
in the responsibility for the setting up and organization of a public order con-
formable to the fundamental exigencies of the human and Christian conscience, being always mindful of the fact that for those who glory in the
name of Christian, every peace proposal is always made under the unerring
standard: "To reject all that is hostile to that name and to promote that
which is consonant with it."

With the fervent wish that the grace of Almighty God may cause to break
soon over the hills of the Eternal City and over the whole world the dawn
of such a peace, we express to you, venerable brethren, our sincere gratitude
for the good wishes so kindly offered us through your eminent vice dean,
while we impart from our heart on you and on all those especially dear to
you in the Lord our apostolic benediction.

ALLIED STATEMENT ON THE SPARING OF ROME

June 3, 1944 [1]

Allied military authorities, confronted by the ruthless enemy in Italy, are
interested solely in the destruction and elimination of German forces in that
country.

They have taken and will continue to take every possible precaution
during the course of their campaign to spare innocent civilians and cultural
and religious monuments of permanent value to civilization.

In particular they are deeply conscious of the unique position occupied by
Rome as one of the chief historical religious and cultural centers of the world
and of the fact that Rome is the seat of His Holiness, the Pope, and contains
the neutral State of the Vatican City.

It is therefore the firm intention of Allied Governments and of Allied military authorities to continue to take every precaution in their power, consistent with essential military requirements, to safeguard the population of
Rome and its historical and religious monuments.

The Allies have only taken and will only take military action against
Rome in so far as the Germans use the city, railways and roads for their military purposes. If the Germans choose to defend Rome the Allies will be
obliged to take appropriate military measures to eject them. It therefore is
the sincere hope of His Majesty's Government and the United States Government that the enemy will not make such an ill-considered choice.

[1] *New York Times.*

GENERAL ALEXANDER'S BROADCAST TO THE PEOPLE OF ROME

June 4, 1944 [1]

The Allied armies are approaching Rome. The liberation of the Eternal City is at hand.

You citizens of Rome must act together to preserve your city from destruction and to defeat our common enemy—the Germans and Fascists. These instructions, from the headquarters of General Alexander, Commander in Chief of the Allied armies in Italy, and from Marshal Badoglio are in your interest as much as that of the Allies:

Do all in your power to prevent the destruction of your city. Prevent the enemy from blowing up charges he may have placed under bridges, government offices, ministries and public and other buildings in the capital.

Protect telegraph, telephone exchanges, radio stations and all communications lines. Guard for your own use all public-utility services, such as water, electricity and gas. Protect railways and railway installations and all other public transport services, such as trams and buses.

Hide your stocks of food from the enemy.

Take note where the enemy places mines or booby-traps as he withdraws and inform the Allied advance patrols where they are. Remove all obstacles, barricades and other obstructions from the streets.

Keep squares and thoroughfares free for the passage of military vehicles. It is vital that Allied troops be able to pass through Rome without delay in order to continue the destruction of the German armies farther north.

Citizens of Rome, this is not the time for demonstrations. Do what we tell you and continue with your daily work. Rome is yours. Your job is to save the city. Ours is the destruction of the enemy.

Citizens of Rome, you have your instructions. The future of Rome is in your hands.

PRESIDENT ROOSEVELT'S BROADCAST ON THE LIBERATION OF ROME

June 5, 1944 [2]

Yesterday, June fourth, 1944, Rome fell to American and Allied troops. The first of the Axis capitals is now in our hands. One up and two to go!

It is perhaps significant that the first of these capitals to fall should have the longest history of all of them. The story of Rome goes back to the time of the foundations of our civilization. We can still see there monuments of the time when Rome and the Romans controlled the whole of the then known world. That, too, is significant, for the United Nations are determined that in the future no one city and no one race will be able to control the whole of the world.

[1] *New York Times.*
[2] White House news release.

In addition to the monuments of the older times, we also see in Rome the great symbol of Christianity, which has reached into almost every part of the world. There are other shrines and other churches in many places, but the churches and shrines of Rome are visible symbols of the faith and determination of the early saints and martyrs that Christianity should live and become universal. And now it will be a source of deep satisfaction that the freedom of the Pope and of Vatican City is assured by the armies of the United Nations.

It is also significant that Rome has been liberated by the armed forces of many nations. The American and British armies—who bore the chief burdens of battle—found at their sides our own North American neighbors, the gallant Canadians. The fighting New Zealanders from the far South Pacific, the courageous French and the French Moroccans, the South Africans, the Poles and the East Indians—all of them fought with us on the bloody approaches to Rome.

The Italians, too, forswearing a partnership in the Axis which they never desired, have sent their troops to join us in our battles against the German trespassers on their soil.

The prospect of the liberation of Rome meant enough to Hitler and his generals to induce them to fight desperately at great cost of men and materials and with great sacrifice to their crumbling Eastern line and to their Western front. No thanks are due to them if Rome was spared the devastation which the Germans wreaked on Naples and other Italian cities. The Allied generals maneuvered so skilfully that the Nazis could only have stayed long enough to damage Rome at the risk of losing their armies.

But Rome is of course more than a military objective.

Ever since before the days of the Caesars, Rome has stood as a symbol of authority. Rome was the Republic. Rome was the Empire. Rome was the Catholic Church, and Rome was the capital of a united Italy. Later, unfortunately, Rome became the seat of Fascism—one of the three capitals of the Axis.

For a quarter century the Italian people were enslaved and degraded by the rule of Mussolini from Rome. They will mark its liberation with deep emotion. In the north of Italy, the people are still dominated and threatened by the Nazi overlords and their Fascist puppets.

Our victory comes at an excellent time, while our Allied forces are poised for another strike at Western Europe—and while armies of other Nazi soldiers nervously await our assault. And our gallant Russian allies continue to make their power felt more and more.

From a strictly military standpoint, we had long ago accomplished certain of the main objectives of our Italian campaign—the control of the sea lanes of the Mediterranean to shorten our combat and supply lines, and the capture of the airports of Foggia from which we have struck telling blows on the Continent.

It would be unwise to inflate in our own minds the military importance of the capture of Rome. We shall have to push through a long period of greater effort and fiercer fighting before we get into Germany itself. The Germans have retreated thousands of miles, all the way from the gates of Cairo, through Libya and Tunisia and Sicily and southern Italy. They have suffered heavy losses, but not great enough yet to cause collapse.

Germany has not yet been driven to surrender. Germany has not yet been driven to the point where she will be unable to recommence world conquest a generation hence.

Therefore, the victory still lies some distance ahead. That distance will be covered in due time—have no fear of that. But it will be tough and it will be costly.

In Italy the people had lived so long under the corrupt rule of Mussolini that, in spite of the tinsel at the top, their economic condition had grown steadily worse. Our troops have found starvation, malnutrition, disease, a deteriorating education, and lowered public health—all by-products of the Fascist misrule.

The task of the Allies in occupation has been stupendous. We have had to start at the very bottom, assisting local governments to re-form on democratic lines. We have had to give them bread to replace that which was stolen out of their mouths by the Germans. We have had to make it possible for the Italians to raise and use their own local crops. We have to help them cleanse their schools of Fascist trappings.

The American people as a whole approve the salvage of these human beings, who are only now learning to walk in a new atmosphere of freedom.

Some of us may let our thoughts run to the financial cost of it. Essentially it is what we can call a form of relief. At the same time we hope that this relief will be an investment for the future—an investment that will pay dividends by eliminating Fascism and ending any Italian desires to start another war of aggression in the future. They are dividends which justify such an investment, because they are additional supports for world peace.

The Italian people are capable of self-government. We do not lose sight of their virtues as a peace-loving nation.

We remember the many centuries in which the Italians were leaders in the arts and sciences, enriching the lives of all mankind.

We remember the great sons of the Italian people—Galileo and Marconi, Michelangelo and Dante—and that fearless discoverer who typifies the courage of Italy, Christopher Columbus.

Italy cannot grow in stature by seeking to build up a great militaristic empire. Italians have been overcrowded within their own territories, but they do not need to try to conquer the lands of other peoples in order to find the breath of life. Other peoples may not want to be conquered.

In the past Italians have come by the millions to the United States. They have been welcomed, they have prospered, they have become good citizens, community and governmental leaders. They are not Italian-Americans. They are Americans—Americans of Italian descent.

Italians have gone in great numbers to the other Americas—Brazil and the Argentine, for example—and to many other nations in every continent of the world, giving of their industry and their talents, and achieving success and the comfort of good living.

Italy should go on as a great mother nation, contributing to the culture and progress and goodwill of all mankind—and developing her special talents in the arts, crafts, and sciences, and preserving her historic and cultural heritage for the benefit of all peoples.

We want and expect the help of the future Italy toward lasting peace. All the other nations opposed to Fascism and Nazism should help give Italy a chance.

The Germans, after years of domination in Rome, left the people in the Eternal City on the verge of starvation. We and the British will do everything we can to bring them relief. Anticipating the fall of Rome, we made preparations to ship food supplies to the city, but it should be borne in mind that the needs are so great and the transportation requirements of our armies so heavy that improvement must be gradual. We have already begun to save the lives of the men, women, and children of Rome.

This is an example of the efficiency of your machinery of war. The magnificent ability and energy of the American people in growing the crops, building the merchant ships, making and collecting the cargos, getting the supplies over thousands of miles of water, and thinking ahead to meet emergencies—all this spells, I think, an amazing efficiency on the part of our armed forces, all the various agencies working with them, and American industry and labor as a whole.

No great effort like this can be a hundred per cent perfect, but the batting average is very, very high.

I extend the congratulations and thanks of the American people to General Alexander, who has been in command of the whole Italian operation; to General Clark and General Leese of the Fifth and the Eighth Armies; to General Wilson, the Supreme Allied Commander of the Mediterranean theater, and General Devers, his American Deputy; to General Eaker; to Admirals Cunningham and Hewitt; and to all their brave officers and men.

May God bless them and watch over them and over all of our gallant, fighting men.

DECREE OF KING VICTOR EMMANUEL III OF ITALY YIELDING ROYAL PREROGATIVES TO HIS SON, CROWN PRINCE HUMBERT

June 5, 1944 [1]

I, Victor Emmanuel III, by the grace of God and by the will of the nation, King of Italy, in collaboration with the President of the Council of Ministers and with the agreement of the Council, have ordered and order as follows:

My beloved son, Humbert of Savoy, Prince of Piedmont, is nominated our Lieutenant General. In collaboration with responsible Ministers he will in our name superintend all matters of administration and exercise all royal prerogatives without exception, signing royal decrees which will be countersigned and authenticated in the usual way.

We order all concerned to observe this decree and to see that it is observed as the law of the State.

Given at Ravello June 5, 1944.

VICTOR EMMANUEL
(Countersigned) PIETRO BADOGLIO

COMMUNIQUÉ NO. 1 ON THE INVASION OF FRANCE

June 6, 1944 [2]

Under the command of General Eisenhower, Allied naval forces, supported by strong air forces, began landing Allied armies this morning on the northern coast of France.

[1] *New York Times.*
[2] *Ibid.*

GENERAL EISENHOWER'S ORDER OF THE DAY TO THE ALLIED TROOPS INVADING FRANCE

June 6, 1944 [2]

Soldiers, sailors and airmen of the Allied Expeditionary Force: You are about to embark upon a great crusade, toward which we have striven these many months. The eyes of the world are upon you. The hopes and prayers of liberty-loving people everywhere march with you.

In company with our brave allies and brothers in arms on other fronts you will bring about the destruction of the German war machine, the elimination of Nazi tyranny over the oppressed peoples of Europe, and security for ourselves in a free world.

Your task will not be an easy one. Your enemy is well trained, well equipped and battle-hardened. He will fight savagely.

But this is the year 1944. Much has happened since the Nazi triumphs of 1940–41. The United Nations have inflicted upon the Germans great defeats in open battle, man to man. Our air offensive has seriously reduced their strength in the air, and their capacity to wage war on the ground.

Our home fronts have given us an overwhelming superiority in weapons and munitions of war, and placed at our disposal great reserves of trained fighting men.

The tide has turned. The free men of the world are marching together to victory. I have full confidence in your courage, devotion to duty and skill in battle. We will accept nothing less than full victory. Good luck.

Let us all beseech the blessing of Almighty God, upon this great and noble undertaking.

GENERAL MONTGOMERY'S MESSAGE TO HIS INVASION TROOPS

June 6, 1944 [2]

The time has come to deal the enemy a terrific blow in western Europe. The blow will be struck by the combined sea, land, and air forces of the Allies, together constituting one great Allied team under the supreme command of General Eisenhower.

On the eve of this great adventure, I send my best wishes to every soldier in the Allied team. To us is given the honor of striking a blow for freedom which will live in history, and in the better days that lie ahead men will speak with pride of our doings. We have a great and a righteous cause. Let us pray that the Lord, mighty in battle, will go forth with our armies and that His special providence will aid us in the struggle.

I want every soldier to know that I have complete confidence in the successful outcome of the operations that we are now about to begin. With stout heart and with enthusiasm for the contest, let us go forward to victory, and,

[1] *New York Times.*
[2] *Ibid.*

as we enter the battle, let us recall the words of a famous soldier, spoken many years ago. These are the words he said:

"He either fears his fate too much.
Or his deserts are small.
That dares not put it to the touch
To gain or lose it all."

Good luck to each one of you and good hunting on the mainland of Europe! [The quotation is from James Graham, Marquis of Montrose.]

PRESIDENT ROOSEVELT'S PRAYER DURING THE FIRST LANDING OF ALLIED TROOPS IN FRANCE

June 6, 1944 [1]

My Fellow-Americans:

Last night when I spoke with you about the fall of Rome I knew at that moment that troops of the United States and our Allies were crossing the Channel in another and greater operation. It has come to pass to success thus far.

And so in this poignant hour, I ask you to join with me in prayer:

Almighty God: Our sons, pride of our nation, this day have set upon a mighty endeavor, a struggle to preserve our Republic, our religion and our civilization, and to set free a suffering humanity.

Lead them straight and true; give strength to their arms, stoutness to their hearts, steadfastness in their faith.

They will need Thy blessings. Their road will be long and hard. For the enemy is strong. He may hurl back our forces. Success may not come with rushing speed, but we shall return again and again; and we know that by Thy grace, and by the righteousness of our cause, our sons will triumph.

They will be sore tried, by night and by day, without rest—until the victory is won. The darkness will be rent by noise and flame. Men's souls will be shaken with the violences of war.

For these men are lately drawn from the ways of peace. They fight not for the lust of conquest. They fight to end conquest. They fight to liberate. They fight to let justice arise, and tolerance and goodwill among all Thy people. They yearn but for the end of battle, for their return to the haven of home.

Some will never return. Embrace these, Father, and receive them, Thy heroic servants, into Thy kingdom.

And for us at home—fathers, mothers, children, wives, sisters and brothers of brave men overseas, whose thoughts and prayers are ever with them— help us, Almighty God, to rededicate ourselves to renewed faith in Thee in this hour of great sacrifice.

Many people have urged that I call the nation into a single day of special prayer. But because the road is long and the desire is great, I ask that our people devote themselves in a continuance of prayer. As we rise to each new day, and again when each day is spent, let words of prayer be on our lips, invoking Thy help to our efforts.

Give us strength, too—strength in our daily tasks, to redouble the con-

[1] *New York Times.*

tributions we make in the physical and the material support of our armed forces.

And let our hearts be stout, to wait out the long travail, to bear sorrows that may come, to impart our courage unto our sons wheresover they may be.

And, O Lord, give us faith. Give us faith in Thee; faith in our sons; faith in each other; faith in our united crusade. Let not the keenness of our spirit ever be dulled. Let not the impacts of temporary events, of temporal matters of but fleeting moment—let not these deter us in our unconquerable purpose.

With Thy blessing, we shall prevail over the unholy forces of our enemy. Help us to conquer the apostles of greed and racial arrogances. Lead us to the saving of our country, and with our sister nations into a world unity that will spell a sure peace—a peace invulnerable to the schemings of unworthy men. And a peace that will let all men live in freedom, reaping the just rewards of their honest toil.

Thy will be done, Almighty God.
Amen.

GENERAL EISENHOWER'S BROADCAST TO THE PEOPLES OF WESTERN EUROPE

June 6, 1944 [1]

People of western Europe! A landing was made this morning on the coast of France by troops of the Allied Expeditionary Force. This landing is part of the concerted United Nations plan for the liberation of Europe, made in conjunction with our great Russian Allies. I have this message for all of you. Although the initial assault may not have been made in your own country, the hour of your liberation is approaching.

All patriots, men and women, young and old, have a part to play in the achievement of final victory. To members of resistance movements, whether led by national or outside leaders, I say, "follow the instructions you have received." To patriots who are not members of organized resistance groups I say, "continue your passive resistance, but do not needlessly endanger your lives until I give you the signal to rise and strike the enemy. The day will come when I shall need your united strength. Until that day, I call on you for the hard task of discipline and restraint."

Citizens of France! I am proud to have again under my command the gallant forces of France. Fighting beside their Allies, they will play a worthy part in the liberation of their homeland. Because the intial landing has been made on the soil of your country, I repeat to you with even greater emphasis my message to the peoples of other occupied countries in western Europe. Follow the instructions of your leaders. A premature uprising of all Frenchmen may prevent you from being of maximum help to your country in the critical hour. Be patient. Prepare.

As supreme commander of the Allied Expeditionary Force, there is imposed on me the duty and responsibility of taking all measures necessary to the prosecution of the war. Prompt and willing obedience to the orders that I shall issue is essential. Effective civil administration of France must

[1] *New York Times.*

be provided by Frenchmen. All persons must continue in their present duties
unless otherwise instructed. Those who have common cause with the enemy
and so betrayed their country will be removed. As France is liberated from
her oppressors, you yourselves will choose your representatives, and the
government under which you wish to live.

In the course of this campaign for the final defeat of the enemy you may
sustain further loss and damage. Tragic though they may be, they are part
of the price of victory. I assure you that I shall do all in my power to mitigate
your hardships. I know that I can count on your steadfastness now, no less
than in the past. The heroic deeds of Frenchmen who have continued their
struggle against the Nazis and their Vichy satellites, in France and throughout the French Empire, have been an example and an inspiration to all of us.

This landing is but the opening phase of the campaign in western Europe.
Great battles lie ahead. I call upon all who love freedom to stand with us.
Keep your faith stanch—our arms are resolute—together we shall achieve
victory.

GENERAL CHARLES DE GAULLE'S INVASION MESSAGE TO FRANCE

June 6, 1944 [1]

The supreme battle has begun. After so much struggling, bickering and
suffering, here is the decisive, the much hoped-for clash. It is, of course,
the battle of France and France's battle. Immense means of attack, to us
means of rescue, have been unleashed from the shores of old England. On this
last bastion of Western Europe, not so long ago, the tide of German oppression was stopped. This bastion is today the starting point for liberty's offensive. For years submerged, but neither defeated nor conquered, France is on
her feet to take part in the fight. Sons of France, wherever you are, whoever
you may be, it is your simple but sacred duty to fight on with all the means
at your disposal. We must destroy the enemy, the enemy who has crushed
and sullied our motherland, the hated enemy, the dishonored enemy.

The enemy will make every effort to escape his fate. Obstinately, he will
try to hold on to our land as long as possible. But for a long time now, he
has been nothing but a tracked beast. From Stalingrad to Tarnopol, from
the shores of the Nile to the shores of Bizerte, from Tunis to Rome, the
enemy is getting used to defeat.

France will fight this battle with fury, but France will also fight it with
discipline. This is the way we have won our victories in the past 1,500 years.
This is how we shall win this one.

There is no problem for our land, sea and air forces; they have never been
more resolute, more skillful, better disciplined. In Africa, in Italy, on the
seas and in the air, they have proven their strength and renascent glory.
Their native land will see them tomorrow.

As for the nation, bound hand and foot as it is, fighting against an oppressor
armed to the teeth, the good conduct of the battle imposes several conditions.
The first is that the directives given by the French Government and the
French chiefs it has qualified, locally and nationally, be carefully followed,
in letter and in spirit.

[1] French Press and Information Service.

The second is that the fight which we conduct behind enemy lines be co-ordinated as closely as possible with the frontal attacks of the Allied and French armies. Everybody must be prepared for a long, hard struggle. This means that the part played by the forces of Resistance must be continued and go on increasing until the moment of the German army's rout.

The third condition is that all who are capable of taking part in any action, either as combatants, informers, or through the refusal to work for the enemy, must do everything possible not to be taken prisoners. All of them must take measures to avoid imprisonment or deportation, no matter how great the difficulties. Anything is better than being put out of the fight without fighting.

The battle of France has begun. The Nation, the Empire, the fighting forces have but one single will, one single and identical hope. Behind the heavy cloud of our blood and tears, the sun of our greatness shines again.

PRIME MINISTER WINSTON CHURCHILL'S STATEMENT IN COMMONS ON THE LIBERATION OF ROME AND THE LANDINGS IN FRANCE

June 6, 1944 [1]

I must apologise to the House for having delayed them, but Questions were gone through rather more rapidly than usual. The House should, I think, take formal cognisance of the liberation of Rome by the Allied Armies under the Command of General Alexander, with General Clark of the United States Service and General Oliver Leese in command of the Fifth and Eighth Armies respectively. [HON. MEMBERS: "Hear, hear."] This is a memorable and glorious event, which rewards the intense fighting of the last five months in Italy. The original landing, made on 22nd January at Anzio, has, in the end, borne good fruit. In the first place, Hitler was induced to send to the south of Rome eight or nine divisions which he may well have need of elsewhere. Secondly, these divisions were repulsed, and their teeth broken, by the successful resistance of the Anzio bridgehead forces in the important battle which took place in the middle of February. The losses on both sides were heavy—the Allies losing about 20,000 men, and the Germans about 25,000 men. Thereafter, the Anzio bridgehead was considered by the enemy to be impregnable.

Meanwhile, the great regrouping of the main Army had to take place before the attacks could be renewed. These attacks were at first unsuccessful, and Cassino still blocked the advance. On 11th May, General Alexander began his present operation and after unceasing and intense fighting by the whole of the Armies, broke into the enemy's lines and entered the Liri Valley. It is noteworthy that, counting from right to left, the whole of the Polish, British Empire, French and United States Forces broke the German lines in front of them by frontal attack. That has an important bearing on other matters, which I shall come to before I sit down.

At what was judged the right moment the bridgehead force, which by this time had reached a total of nearly 150,000 men, fell upon the retreating

[1] Parliamentary Debates.

enemy's flank and threatened his retreat. The junction of the main Armies with the bridgehead forces drove the enemy off his principal lines of retreat to the north, forcing a great part of his army to retire in considerable disorder with heavy losses, especially in material, through mountainous country. The Allied Forces, with great rapidity were re-grouped, with special emphasis on their left flank, which soon deployed against Rome after cutting the important highway. The American and other Forces of the Fifth Army broke through the enemy's last line and entered Rome, where the Allied troops have been received with joy by the population. This entry and liberation of Rome mean that we shall have the power to defend it from hostile air attack, and to deliver it from the famine with which it was threatened. However, General Alexander's prime object has never been the liberation of Rome, great as are the moral, political and psychological advantages of that episode. The Allied Forces with the Americans in the van, are driving ahead, northwards, in relentless pursuit of the enemy. The destruction of the enemy army has been, throughout, the single aim and they are now being engaged at the same time along the whole length of the line as they attempt to escape to the north. It is hoped that the 20,000 prisoners already taken will be followed by further captures in future, and that the condition of the enemy's army, which he has crowded into southern Italy, will be decisively affected.

It would be futile to attempt to estimate our final gains at the present time. It is our duty, however, to pay the warmest tribute of gratitude and admiration to General Alexander for the skill with which he has handled this Army of so many different States and nations, and for the tenacity and fortitude with which he has sustained the long periods when success was denied. In General Clark the United States Army has found a fighting leader of the highest order and the qualities of all Allied troops have shone in noble and unjealous rivalry. The great strength of the air forces at our disposal, as well as the preponderance in armour, has undoubtedly contributed in a notable and distinctive manner to the successes which have been achieved. We must await further developments in the Italian theatre before it is possible to estimate the magnitude or quality of our gains, great and timely though they certainly are.

I have also to announce to the House that during the night and the early hours of this morning the first of the series of landings in force upon the European Continent has taken place. In this case the liberating assault fell upon the coast of France. An immense armada of upwards of 4,000 ships, together with several thousand smaller craft, crossed the Channel. Massed airborne landings have been successfully effected behind the enemy lines and landings on the beaches are proceeding at various points at the present time. The fire of the shore batteries have been largely quelled. The obstacles that were constructed in the sea have not proved so difficult as was apprehended. The Anglo-American Allies are sustained by about 11,000 first line aircraft, which can be drawn upon as may be needed for the purposes of the battle. I cannot, of course, commit myself to any particular details. Reports are coming in in rapid succession. So far the Commanders who are engaged report that everything is proceeding according to plan. And what a plan! This vast operation is undoubtedly the most complicated and difficult that has ever occurred. It involves tides, wind, waves, visibility, both from the air and the sea standpoint, and the combined employment of land, air and sea forces in the highest degree of intimacy and in contact with conditions which could not and cannot be fully foreseen.

There are already hopes that actual tactical surprise has been attained, and we hope to furnish the enemy with a succession of surprises during the course of the fighting. The battle that has now begun will grow constantly in scale and in intensity for many weeks to come and I shall not attempt to speculate upon its course. This I may say, however. Complete unity prevails throughout the Allied Armies. There is a brotherhood in arms between us and our friends of the United States. There is complete confidence in the supreme commander, General Eisenhower, and his lieutenants, and also in the commander of the Expeditionary Force, General Montgomery. The ardour and spirit of the troops, as I saw myself, embarking in these last few days was splendid to witness. Nothing that equipment, science or forethought could do has been neglected and the whole process of opening this great new front will be pursued with the utmost resolution both by the commanders and by the United States and British Governments whom they serve.

GENERAL EISENHOWER'S REPORT TO PRESIDENT ROOSEVELT ON ALLIED MILITARY OPERATIONS IN EUROPE

June 13, 1944 [1]

On June 6th we initiated the first vital step leading to the decisive battle of Europe. The first great obstacle has been surmounted—that is the breaching of the beach defenses that the enemy by lavish employment of enslaved labor had installed in forest-like density along the entire lateral of northwest Europe. Gallantry, fortitude and skill were called for, and these, in abundant measure, the entire Allied force has displayed since the opening day of the battle. A particularly satisfying feature of the fighting has been the fine performance of troops—American, British, and Canadian—committed to battle for the first time. Just as they did and are still doing in the Mediterranean, these untried Allied units have conducted themselves in a manner worthy of their more experienced comrades who conquered the German in Africa, Sicily and Italy.

What is more important, complete unity between the air, ground and naval services has prevailed.

Satisfactory as is the progress of this battle to date, in magnitude it is but a mere beginning to the tremendous struggles that must follow before final victory is achieved. Although the cross-channel landing operation was attended by hazards and difficulties greater, I believe, than have ever before faced an invading army, this initial success has given us only a foothold upon northwestern France. Through the opening thus made, and through others yet to come, the flood of our fighting strength must be poured. Our operations, vast and important as they are, are only part of the far larger pattern of a combined assault against the fortress of Germany by the great Russian armies from the East and our forces from the Mediterranean.

The Nazis will be forced to fight throughout the perimeter of their stronghold, daily expending their dwindling resources until overwhelmed by the hopelessness of their position. To this end we need every man, every weapon, and all the courage and fortitude of our respective peoples. The Allied soldier will do his duty.

DWIGHT D. EISENHOWER

[1] White House news release.

GENERAL EISENHOWER'S MESSAGE TO ALLIED INVASION TROOPS IN FRANCE

June 13, 1944 [1]

One week ago this morning there was established, through your coordinated efforts, our first foothold in northwestern Europe.

High as was my pre-invasion confidence in your courage, skill and effectiveness in working together as a unit, your accomplishments in the first seven days of this campaign have exceeded my brightest hopes.

You are truly a great Allied team, a team which in each part gains its greatest satisfaction in rendering maximum assistance to the entire body and in which each individual member is justifiably confident in all others.

No matter how prolonged or bitter the struggle that lies ahead you will do your full part toward the restoration of Free France, the liberation of all European nations under Axis domination and the destruction of the Nazi military machine.

I truly congratulate you upon a brilliantly successful beginning to this great undertaking. Liberty loving people everywhere would like to join me in saying to you:

I am proud of you.

MARSHAL JOSEPH STALIN'S STATEMENT EXTOLLING THE ALLIED INVASION OF FRANCE

June 13, 1944 [2]

In adding up the results of the seven-day battles by the Allied troops of liberation who invaded northern France, one may say without hesitation that the large-scale forcing of the English Channel and the mass landing of troops of the Allies in northern France have fully succeeded. This is undoubtedly a brilliant success of our Allies. One must admit that the history of wars does not know any such undertaking so broad in conception and so grandiose in its scale and so masterly in execution.

As we know, the "invincible" Napoleon shamefully failed in his own time with his plans to force the Channel and capture the British Isles. Hitler, the hysteric, who boasted for two years that he would carry out a crossing of the Channel, did not even risk making an attempt to carry out his threat.

Only the British and American troops succeeded in honorably fulfilling the grandiose plan of crossing the Channel and landing troops in mass. History will write this down as an achievement of the highest order.

[1] *New York Times.*
[2] *Ibid.*

PRESIDENT MANUEL L. QUEZON'S BROADCAST TO THE PHILIPPINES

June 14, 1944 [1]

My countrymen: On this day, wherever you may be, pause a moment in silent prayer—a prayer of thanksgiving and petition.

Today, June 14, is the day set aside by the President of the United States for the honoring not only of the flag of America but the flags of all the United Nations who fight for liberty. Today, June 14, is also the second anniversary of my signing the Declaration of United Nations on behalf of the Philippines. By that simple fact, the Philippines joined herself with thirty-four sovereign nations of the world in the fight against aggression.

In the midst of your sufferings—and I share them to the full—let us turn our thoughts today to our flag of the Sun and Three Stars, the flag that our heroes followed in unnumbered battles for freedom. Let us renew our pledge that our hopes for it will not be dimmed, nor our faith in it fettered, nor our love for it weakened by the invader, but that each returning sun will make us more determined in our resolve that, as in honor we inherited it from our fathers, in honor we must bequeath it to our sons. That honor is the badge that only free men can wear.

Two years ago today, our Flag was unfurled side by side with that of the other United Nations in the fight for liberty and democracy. I do not have to stress the transcendental significance of our having been admitted as signatory to the declaration of the nations fighting Germany and Japan, as an independent government. When I signed it for the Filipino people and subscribed to the principles set forth in the Atlantic Charter, I knew that I was expressing our nation's determination never to be cowed by the Japanese invader. Your courageous resistance has shown the world the Filipinos can suffer and die for the cause of freedom.

Let us give thanks for the friendship of America and our other Allies in our common struggle against the enemy, and for the victories of the armed forces of the United Nations, in Italy, in Russia, and in the Southwest Pacific. Let us be grateful that the forces of liberation are coming ever closer to our beloved shores. And today, let us humbly petition the Almighty for the continued success of our arms, and beseech Him to hasten the glorious day of liberation for all peoples all over the world.

AGREEMENT BETWEEN THE ROYAL JUGOSLAV GOVERNMENT AND THE NATIONAL COMMITTEE OF LIBERATION

June 16, 1944 [2]

The National Committee of Liberation of Jugoslavia and the Prime Minister of the Royal Jugoslav Government have agreed to the following:

[1] Department of Information and Public Relations of the Commonwealth of the Philippines.
[2] Royal Jugoslav Information Service.

1. The Royal Jugoslav Government shall be formed from those progressive democratic forces which have not compromised themselves in the struggle against the National Liberation Movement. The main task of this Government is to render all possible aid to the National Liberation Army as well as to all others who from now on fight with equal determination against the common enemy of our fatherland, but on condition that the latter join the single national front. It will also be the duty of this Government to ensure the supply of foodstuffs to the Jugoslav population and to see that the work of our representative bodies abroad and of our representatives on international commissions has due care for our national rights for the needs of our people and for the national liberation struggle within Jugoslavia.

2. The National Committee of Liberation of Jugoslavia and the Royal Jugoslav Government of Dr. Subasitch will appoint the organs which will co-ordinate the collaboration in the struggle against the enemy in the task of reconstruction of the country and in conduct of foreign policy, thus facilitating as soon as possible the creation of a single representation of the state.

3. The National Committee of Liberation considers that it is not necessary to give prominence and exacerbate at the moment the question of the King and the Monarchy as this does not at present constitute an obstacle to the collaboration between the National Committee of Liberation of Jugoslavia and the Government of Dr. Subasitch, for it has been mutually agreed that final solution of the organization of the state shall be decided by the people after liberation of the whole country.

4. Dr. Subasitch's Government will make a declaration: Recognizing the national and democratic achievements of the Jugoslav peoples during their three-year struggle by which the foundations of a democratic federal organization of our federal state have been laid and a temporary administration of the country set up by the Anti-Fascist Council of the National Liberation Army of Jugoslavia and the National Liberation Committee of Jugoslavia and its executive organ; giving full recognition to the fighting forces of the people organized in the National Army of Liberation under the command of the Marshal of Jugoslavia, Josip Broz Tito, and condemning all traitors of the people who have collaborated with the enemy, either openly or secretly; addressing an appeal to the whole nation for all fighting forces to join up with the National Army of Liberation in a single front.

5. On his part, the Marshal of Jugoslavia, Josip Broz Tito, as the president of the National Liberation Committee of Jugoslavia, will issue a declaration of collaboration with the Government of Dr. Subasitch and will also once again make it clear that the National Liberation Committee of Jugoslavia will not raise the question of the final organization of the Jugoslav state during the war.

On liberated Jugoslav territory, June 16, 1944.

For the National Committee of Liberation of Jugoslavia,

President Marshal of Jugoslavia,

(Signed) J. B. Tito

For the Prime Minister of the Royal Jugoslav Government,

(Signed) Dr. Ivan Subasitch

JOINT STATEMENT BY PRESIDENT CHIANG KAI-SHEK AND VICE-PRESIDENT HENRY A. WALLACE IN CHUNGKING

June 24, 1944 [1]

During his visit in Chungking Vice-President Wallace has had an opportunity to discuss with President Chiang and officials of the Chinese Government—in an informal, frank and friendly atmosphere—matters of common interest and concern. They have exchanged views to mutual advantage and found themselves in agreement in basic principles and objectives.

Prosecution of the war against Japan in Asia is an urgent job and mutual assistance in every possible way to get that job done quickly and efficiently is fundamental in Chinese-American relations.

The objective of victory in the Pacific is the establishment of a democratic peace based on political and social stability deriving from government devoted to the welfare of peoples.

Enduring peace in the Pacific will depend upon (1) effective permanent demilitarization of Japan; (2) understanding, friendship and collaboration between and among the four principal powers in the Pacific area—China, the Soviet Union, the United States and the British Commonwealth of Nations —and among all United Nations willing to share in the responsibilities of postwar international order; and (3) recognition of the fundamental right of presently dependent Asiatic peoples to self-government and the early adoption of measures in the political, economic and social fields to prepare those dependent peoples for self-government within a specified practical time limit.

Cognizance was taken of the cornerstone position of China in Asia and of the importance of China in any structure for peace in the Pacific area. It was assumed as axiomatic that essential to such a peace structure would be continuation of the ties of friendship that have characterized American-Chinese relations for over a century, and the maintenance of relations on a basis of mutual understanding between China and the Soviet Union, China's nearest great neighbor, as well as between China and her other neighbors. No balance of power arrangement would serve the ends of peace.

Seven years of resistance to Japan—during the last three of which China has been virtually cut off from physical contact with the outside world— has resulted in serious economic and financial difficulties in Free China. The Chinese people are facing these difficulties with fortitude, confident of their ability to stand the strain until greater material assistance from abroad becomes feasible.

The Chinese people and the Government are determined to implement and make real the Three People's Principles of Sun Yat-Sen. The first of these principles—National Sovereignty—is now a reality. The second—Democracy—is implicit in plans being formulated for the establishment of a Constitution to guarantee individual rights and freedom and to establish representative government. Concrete consideration of the third—the People's Livelihood—is inherent in plans for economic reconstruction.

With regard to the People's Livelihood, the fundamental importance of agricultural reconstruction in any plans for economic or industrial reconstruction was recognized. The lifelong interest of Vice-President Wallace in

[1] Chinese News Service.

agricultural development gave him a special understanding of China's agrarian problem and enabled him to discuss with President Chiang realistic solutions. Vice-President Wallace was confident that President Chiang would find among the American people a willingness to co-operate in every practical way with the Chinese people in solving agricultural and related problems posed in Chinese plans for economic reconstruction, implementation of which would mean trade relations between Chinese and American businessmen on a mutually advantageous basis.

President Chiang and Vice-President Wallace were continually mindful of the fact that the fundamental purpose of their governments is the promotion of the security and welfare of the peoples of China and the United States, respectively, and were in agreement in believing that pursuit of the broad objectives which they had discussed would be in line with accomplishment of that purpose.

PLATFORM ADOPTED BY THE REPUBLICAN NATIONAL CONVENTION

June 27, 1944 [1]

The tragedy of wars is upon our country as we meet to consider the problems of government and our people. We take this opportunity to render homage and enduring gratitude to those brave members of our armed forces who have already made the supreme sacrifice, and to those who stand ready to make the same sacrifice that the American course of life may be secure. Mindful of the solemn hours and humbly conscious of our heavy responsibilities, the Republican party in convention assembled presents herewith its principles and makes these covenants with the people of our nation.

The War and the Peace

We pledge prosecution of the war to total victory against our enemies in full cooperation with the United Nations and all-out support of our Armies and the maintenance of our Navy under the competent and trained direction of our General Staff and Office of Naval Operations without civilian interference and with every civilian resource.

At the earliest possible time after the cessation of hostilities we will bring home all members of our armed forces who do not have unexpired enlistments and who do not volunteer for further overseas duty.

We declare our relentless aim to win the war against all our enemies: (1) for our own American security and welfare; (2) to make and keep the Axis powers impotent to renew tyranny and attack; (3) for the attainment of peace and freedom based on justice and security.

We shall seek to achieve such aims through organized international cooperation and not by joining a world state.

We favor responsible participation by the United States in post-war cooperative organization among sovereign nations to prevent military aggression and to attain permanent peace with organized justice in a free world.

Such organization should develop effective cooperative means to direct peace forces to prevent or repel military aggression. Pending this, we pledge

[1] *New York Times.*

continuing collaboration with the United Nations to assure these ultimate objectives.

We believe, however, that peace and security do not depend upon the sanction of force alone, but should prevail by virtue of reciprocal interests and spiritual values recognized in these security agreements. The treaties of peace should be just; the nations which are the victims of aggression should be restored to sovereignty and self-government; and the organized cooperation of the nations should concern itself with basic causes of world disorder. It should promote a world opinion to influence the nations to right conduct, develop international law and maintain an international tribunal to deal with justiciable disputes.

We shall seek, in our relations with other nations, conditions calculated to promote world-wide economic stability, not only for the sake of the world, but also to the end that our own people may enjoy a high level of employment in an increasingly prosperous world.

We shall keep the American people informed concerning all agreements with foreign nations. In all of these undertakings we favor the widest consultation of the gallant men and women in our armed forces, who have a special right to speak with authority in behalf of the security and liberty for which they fight. We shall sustain the Constitution of the United States in the attainment of our international aims; and pursuant to the Constitution of the United States any treaty or agreement to attain such aims made on behalf of the United States with any other nation or any association of nations shall be made only by and with the advice and consent of the Senate of the United States, provided two-thirds of the Senators present concur.

We shall at all times protect the essential interests and resources of the United States.

Western Hemisphere Relations

We shall develop Pan-American solidarity. The citizens of our neighboring nations in the Western Hemisphere are, like ourselves, Americans. Cooperation with them shall be achieved through mutual agreement and without interference in the internal affairs of any nation. Our policy should be a genuine good neighbor policy commanding their respect, and not one based on the reckless squandering of American funds by overlapping agencies.

Post-War Preparedness

We favor the maintenance of post-war military forces and establishments of ample strength for the successful defense and the safety of the United States, its possessions and outposts, for the maintenance of the Monroe Doctrine, and for meeting any military commitments determined by Congress.

We favor the peacetime maintenance and strengthening of the National Guards under State control with Federal training and equipment as now provided in the National Defense Act.

Domestic Policy

We shall devote ourselves to re-establishing liberty at home.

We shall adopt a program to put men to work in peace industry as promptly as possible and with special attention to those who have made sacrifice by serving in the armed forces. We shall take Government out of competition with private industry and terminate rationing, price fixing and all other emergency powers. We shall promote the fullest stable employment through private enterprise.

The measures we propose shall avoid federalization of Government activities, to the end that our States, schools and cities shall be free, shall avoid delegation of legislative and judicial power of administrative agencies, to the end that the people's representatives in Congress shall be independent and in full control of legislative policy; and shall avoid, subject to war necessities, detailed regulation of farmers, workers, business men and consumers, to the end that the individual shall be free. The remedies we propose shall be based on intelligent cooperation between the Federal Government, the States and local government and the initiative of civic groups, not on the panacea of Federal cash.

Four years more of New Deal policy would centralize all power in the President, and would daily subject every act of every citizen to regulation by his henchmen; and this country could remain a republic only in name. No problem exists which cannot be solved by American methods. We have no need of either the communistic or the fascist technique.

Security

Our goal is to prevent hardship and poverty in America. That goal is attainable by reason of the productive ability of free American labor, industry and agriculture, if supplemented by a system of social security on sound principles.

We pledge our support of the following:

1. Extension of the existing old-age insurance and unemployment insurance systems to all employes not already covered.

2. The return of the public employment-office system to the States at the earliest possible time, financed as before Pearl Harbor.

3. A careful study of Federal-State programs for maternal and child health, dependent children, and assistance to the blind, with a view to strengthening these programs.

4. The continuation of these and other programs relating to health, and the stimulation by Federal aid of State plans to make medical and hospital service available to those in need without disturbing doctor-patient relationship or socializing medicine.

5. The stimulation of State and local plans to provide decent low-cost housing properly financed by the Federal Housing Administration, or otherwise, when such housing cannot be supplied or financed by private sources.

Labor

The Republican party is the historical champion of free labor. Under Republican Administrations American manufacturing developed, and American workers attained the most progressive standards of living of any workers in the world. Now the nation owes those workers a debt of gratitude for their magnificent productive effort in support of the war.

Regardless of the professed friendship of the New Deal for the workingman, the fact remains that under the New Deal American economic life is being destroyed.

The New Deal has usurped selfish and partisan control over the functions of Government agencies where labor relationships are concerned. The continued perversion of the Wagner act by the New Deal menaces the purposes of the law and threatens to destroy collective bargaining completely and permanently.

The long series of Executive Orders and bureaucratic decrees reveal a deliberate purpose to substitute for contractual agreements of employers and employes the political edicts of a New Deal bureaucracy. Labor would thus remain organized only for the convenience of the New Deal in enforcing its orders and inflicting its whims upon labor and industry.

We condemn the conversion of administrative boards, ostensibly set up to settle industrial disputes, into instruments for putting into effect the financial and economic theories of the New Deal.

We condemn the freezing of wage rates at arbitrary levels and the binding of men to their jobs as destructive to the advancement of a free people. We condemn the repeal by Executive Order of the laws secured by the Republican party to abolish "contract labor" and peonage. We condemn the gradual but effective creation of a labor front as but one of the New Deal's steps toward a totalitarian state.

We pledge an end to political trickery in the administration of labor laws and the handling of labor disputes; and equal benefits on the basis of equality to all labor in the administration of labor controls and laws, regardless of political affiliation.

The Department of Labor has been emasculated by the New Deal. Labor bureaus, agencies and committees are scattered far and wide, in Washington and throughout the country, and have no semblance of systematic or responsible organization. All Governmental labor activities must be placed under the direct authority and responsibility of the Secretary of Labor. Such labor bureaus as are not performing a substantial and definite service in the interest of labor must be abolished.

The Secretary of Labor should be a representative of labor. The office of the Secretary of Labor was created under a Republican President, William Howard Taft. It was intended that a representative of labor should occupy this Cabinet office. The present Administration is the first to disregard this intention.

The Republican party accepts the purposes of the National Labor Relations Act, the Wage and Hour Act, the Social Security Act and all other Federal statutes designed to promote and protect the welfare of American working men and women, and we promise a fair and just administration of these laws.

American well-being is indivisible. Any national program which injures the national economy inevitably injures the wage-earner. The American labor movement and the Republican party, while continuously striving for the betterment of labor's status, reject the communistic and New Deal concept that a single group can benefit while the general economy suffers.

Agriculture

We salute the American farmers, their wives and families for their magnificent job of wartime production and their contribution to the war effort, without which victory could not be assured. They have accomplished this in spite of labor shortages, a bungled and inexcusable machinery program and confused, unreliable, impractical price and production administration.

Abundant production is the best security against inflation. Governmental policies in war and in peace must be practical and efficient, with freedom from regimentation by an impractical Washington bureaucracy in order to assure independence of operation and bountiful production, fair and equitable market prices for farm products, and a sound program for conservation and use of our soil and natural resources. Educational progress and the social and economic stability and well-being of the farm family must be a prime national purpose.

For the establishment of such a program we propose the following:

1. A Department of Agriculture under practical and experienced administration free from regimentation and confusing Government manipulation and control of farm programs.

2. An American market price to the American farmer and the protection of such price by means of support prices, commodity loans, or a combination thereof, together with such other economic means as will assure an income to agriculture that is fair and equitable in comparison with labor, business and industry. We oppose subsidies as a substitute for fair markets.

3. Disposition of surplus war commodities in an orderly manner without destroying markets or continued production and without benefit to speculative profiteers.

4. The control and disposition of future surpluses by means of (a) new uses developed through constant research, (b) vigorous development of foreign markets, (c) efficient domestic distribution to meet all domestic requirements, and (d) arrangements which will enable farmers to make necessary adjustments in production of any given basic crop only if domestic surpluses should become abnormal and exceed manageable proportions.

5. Intensified research to discover new crops, and new and profitable uses for existing crops.

6. Support of the principle of bona fide farmer-owned and farmer-operated cooperatives.

7. Consolidation of all Government farm credit under a non-partisan board.

8. To make life more attractive on the family-type farm through development of rural roads, sound extension of rural electrification service to the farm and elimination of basic evils of tenancy wherever they exist.

9. Serious study of and search for a sound program of crop insurance with emphasis upon establishing a self-supporting program.

10. A comprehensive program of soil, forest, water and wildlife conservation and development, and sound irrigation projects, administered as far as possible at State and regional levels.

Business and Industry

We give assurance now to restore peacetime industry at the earliest possible time, using every care to avoid discrimination between different sections of the country, (a) by prompt settlement of war contracts with early payment of Government obligations and disposal of surplus inventories, and (b) by disposal of surplus Government plants, equipment and supplies, with due consideration to small buyers and with care to prevent monopoly and injury to existing agriculture and industry.

Small business is the basis of American enterprise. It must be preserved. If protected against discrimination and afforded equality of opportunity throughout the nation, it will become the most potent factor in providing employment. It must also be aided by changes in taxation, by eliminating excessive and repressive regulation and Government competition, by the enforcement of laws against monopoly and unfair competition, and by providing simpler and cheaper methods for obtaining venture capital necessary for growth and expansion.

For the protection of the public, and for the security of millions of holders of policies of insurance in mutual and private companies, we insist upon strict and exclusive regulation and supervision of the business of insurance by the several States where local conditions are best known and where local needs can best be met.

We favor the re-establishment and maintenance, as early as military considerations will permit, of a sound and adequate American merchant marine under private ownership and management.

The Republican party pledges itself to foster the development of such strong privately owned air transportation systems and communications systems as will best serve the interests of the American people.

The Federal Government should plan a program for flood control, inland waterways and other economically justifiable public works, and prepare the necessary plans in advance so that construction may proceed rapidly in emergency and in times of reduced employment. We urge that States and local governments pursue the same policy with reference to highways and other public works within their jurisdiction.

Taxation and Finance

As soon as the war ends the present rates of taxation on individual incomes, on corporations and on consumption should be reduced as far as is consistent with the payment of the normal expenditures of Government in the post-war period. We reject the theory of restoring prosperity through Government spending and deficit financing.

We shall eliminate from the budget all wasteful and unnecessary expenditures and exercise the most rigid economy.

It is essential that Federal and State tax structures be more effectively coordinated to the end that State tax sources be not unduly impaired.

We shall maintain the value of the American dollar and regard the payment of Government debt as an obligation of honor which prohibits any policy leading to the depreciation of the currency. We shall reduce that debt as soon as economic conditions make such reduction possible.

Control of the currency must be restored to Congress by repeal of existing legislation which gives the President unnecessary and dangerous powers over our currency.

Foreign Trade

We assure American farmers, livestock producers, workers and industry that we will establish and maintain a fair protective tariff on competitive products so that the standards of living of our people shall not be impaired through the importation of commodities produced abroad by labor or producers functioning upon lower standards than our own.

If the post-war world is to be properly organized, a great extension of world trade will be necessary to repair the wastes of war and build an enduring peace. The Republican party, always remembering that its primary obligation, which must be fulfilled, is to our own workers, our own farmers and our own industry, pledges that it will join with others in leadership in every cooperative effort to remove unnecessary and destructive barriers to international trade. We will always bear in mind that the domestic market is

America's greatest market and that tariffs which protect it against foreign competition should be modified only by reciprocal bilateral trade agreements approved by Congress.

Relief and Rehabilitation

We favor the prompt extension of relief and emergency assistance to the peoples of the liberated countries without duplication and conflict between Government agencies.

We favor immediate feeding of the starving children of our Allies and friends in the Nazi-dominated countries and we condemn the New Deal Administration for its failure, in the face of humanitarian demands, to make any effort to do this.

We favor assistance by direct credits in reasonable amounts to liberated countries to enable them to buy from this country the goods necessary to revive their economic systems.

Bureaucracy

The National Administration has become a sprawling, overlapping bureaucracy. It is undermined by executive abuse of power, confused lines of authority, duplication of effort, inadequate fiscal controls, loose personnel practices and an attitude of arrogance previously unknown in our history.

The times cry out for the restoration of harmony in Government, for a balance of legislative and executive responsibility, for efficiency and economy, for pruning and abolishing unnecessary agencies and personnel, for effective fiscal and personnel controls, and for an entirely new spirit in our Federal Government.

We pledge an Administration wherein the President, acting in harmony with Congress, will effect these necessary reforms and raise the Federal service to a high level of efficiency and competence.

We insist that limitations must be placed upon spending by Government corporations of vast sums never appropriated by Congress, but made available by directives, and that their accounts should be subject to audit by the General Accounting Office.

Two-Term Limit for President

We favor an amendment to the Constitution providing that no person shall be President of the United States for more than two terms of four years each.

Equal Rights

We favor submission by Congress to the States of an amendment to the Constitution providing for equal rights for men and women. We favor job opportunities in the post-war world open to men and women alike without discrimination in rate of pay because of sex.

Veterans

The Republican party has always supported suitable measures to reflect the nation's gratitude and to discharge its duty toward the veterans of all wars.

We approve, have supported and have aided in the enactment of laws which provide for re-employment of veterans of this war in their old positions, for mustering-out-pay, for pensions for widows and orphans of such veterans killed or disabled, for rehabilitation of disabled veterans, for temporary unemployment benefits, for education and vocational training, and for assisting veterans in acquiring homes and farms and in establishing themselves in business.

We shall be diligent in remedying defects in veterans' legislation and shall insist upon efficient administration of all measures for the veteran's benefit.

Racial and Religious Intolerance

We unreservedly condemn the injection into American life of appeals to racial or religious prejudice.

We pledge an immediate Congressional inquiry to ascertain the extent to which mistreatment, segregation and discrimination against Negroes who are in our armed forces are impairing morale and efficiency and the adoption of corrective legislation.

We pledge the establishment by Federal legislation of a permanent Fair Employment Practice Commission.

Anti-Poll Tax

The payment of any poll tax should not be a condition of voting in Federal elections, and we favor immediate submission of a Constitutional amendment for its abolition.

Anti-Lynching

We favor legislation against lynching and pledge our sincere efforts in behalf of its early enactment.

Indians

We pledge an immediate, just and final settlement of all Indian claims between the Government and the Indian citizenship of the nation. We will take politics out of the administration of Indian affairs.

Problems of the West

We favor a comprehensive program of reclamation projects for our arid and semi-arid States, with recognition and full protection of the rights and interests of those States in the use and control of water for present and future irrigation and other beneficial consumptive uses.

We favor (a) exclusion from this country of livestock and fresh and chilled meat from countries harboring foot and mouth disease or rinderpest; (b) full protection of our fisheries whether by domestic regulation or treaties; (c) consistent with military needs, the prompt return to private ownership of lands acquired for war purposes; (d) withdrawal or acquisition of lands for establishment of national parks, monuments and wild life refuges, only after due regard to local problems and under closer controls to be established by the Congress; (e) restoration of the long established public land policy which provides opportunity of ownership by citizens to promote the highest land use; (f) full development of our forests on the basis of cropping and sustained yield; cooperation with private owners for conservation and fire protection; (g) the prompt reopening of mines which can be operated by miners and workers not subject to military service and which have been closed by bureaucratic denial of labor or material; (h) adequate stock-piling of war minerals and metals for possible future emergencies; (i) continuance, for tax purposes, of adequate depletion allowances on oil, gas and minerals; (j) administration of laws relating to oil and gas on the public domain to encourage exploratory operations to meet the public need; (k) continuance of present Federal laws on mining claims on the public domain, good faith administration thereof, and we state our opposition to the plans of the Secretary of the Interior to substitute a leasing system; and (l) larger representation in the Federal Government of men and women especially familiar with western problems.

Hawaii

Hawaii, which shares the nation's obligations equally with the several States, is entitled to the fullest measure of home rule looking toward Statehood; and to equality with the several States in the rights of their citizens and in the application of all our national laws.

Alaska

Alaska is entitled to the fullest measure of home rule looking toward Statehood.

Puerto Rico

Statehood is a logical aspiration of the people of Puerto Rico who were made citizens of the United States by Congress in 1917; legislation affecting Puerto Rico, in so far as feasible, should be in harmony with the realization of that aspiration.

Palestine

In order to give refuge to millions of distressed Jewish men, women and children driven from their homes by tyranny, we call for the opening of Palestine to their unrestricted immigration and land ownership, so that in accordance with the full intent and purpose of the Balfour Declaration of 1917 and the resolution of a Republican Congress in 1922, Palestine may be constituted as a free and democratic commonwealth. We condemn the failure of the President to insist that the mandatory of Palestine carry out the provision of the Balfour Declaration and of the mandate while he pretends to support them.

Free Press and Radio

In times like these, when whole peoples have found themselves shackled by Governments which denied the truth, or, worse, dealt in half-truths or withheld the facts from the public, it is imperative to the maintenance of a free America that the press and radio be free and that full and complete information be available to Americans. There must be no censorship except to the extent required by war necessity.

We insistently condemn any tendency to regard the press or the radio as instruments of the Administration and the use of Government publicity agencies for partisan ends. We need a new radio law which will define, in clear and unmistakable language, the role of the Federal Communications Commission.

All channels of news must be kept open with equality of access to information at the source. If agreement can be achieved with foreign nations to establish the same principles, it will be a valuable contribution to future peace.

Vital facts must not be withheld.

We want no more Pearl Harbor reports.

Good Faith

The acceptance of the nominations made by this convention carries with it, as a matter of private honor and public faith, an undertaking by each candidate to be true to the principles and program herein set forth.

Conclusion

The essential question at trial in this nation is whether men can organize together in a highly industrialized society, succeed, and still be free. That is the essential question at trial throughout the world today.

In this time of confusion and strife, when moral values are being crushed on every side, we pledge ourselves to uphold with all our strength the Bill of Rights, the Constitution and the law of the land. We so pledge ourselves that the American tradition may stand forever as the beacon light of civilization.

GOVERNOR THOMAS E. DEWEY'S SPEECH ACCEPTING THE REPUBLICAN NOMINATION FOR PRESIDENT

June 28, 1944 [1]

Mr. Chairman and Fellow Americans:

I am profoundly moved by the trust you have placed in me at this grave hour in our nation's history. I feel deeply the responsibility which goes with your nomination for President of the United States.

That I have not sought this responsibility, all of you know. I told the people of my State, two years ago, that it was my intention to devote my full time as Governor exclusively to their service. You have decided otherwise. In accordance with the principles of our Republican form of government you have laid upon me the highest duty to which an American can be called. No one has a right to refuse such a call. With the help of God I shall try to be worthy of the trust. I accept the nomination.

I am happy and proud to be associated in this great effort with my good friend the distinguished Governor of the State of Ohio, John W. Bricker. For many months John Bricker has gone from State to State in these United States telling the people what the issues are and telling them the great need our country has for better government, for the sound principles of government and for the leadership which will come to it with the Republican party's election this year. Never before in the history of our party did any man display

[1] *New York Times.*

such fine statesmanship and good sportsmanship as he did this morning, and I'm proud to be associated with him.

I come to this great task a free man. I have made no pledges, promises or commitments, expressed or implied, to any man or woman. I shall make none, except to the American people.

These pledges I do make:

To men and women of the Republican party everywhere I pledge my utmost efforts in the months ahead. In return, I ask for your support. Without it, I cannot discharge the heavy obligation you lay upon me.

To Americans of every party I pledge that on Jan. 20 next year our Government will again have a Cabinet of the ablest men and women to be found in America. The members of that Cabinet will expect and will receive full delegation of the powers of their respective offices. They will be capable of administering their powers. They will each be experienced in the task to be done and young enough to do it. This election will bring an end to one-man Government in America.

To Americans of every party I pledge a campaign dedicated to one end above all others—that this nation under God may continue in the years ahead a free nation of free men.

At this moment on battlegrounds around the world Americans are dying for the freedom of our country. Their comrades are pressing on in the face of hardship and suffering. They are pressing on for total victory and for the liberties of all of us.

Everything we say or do today and in the future must be devoted to the single purpose of that victory. Then, when victory is won, we must devote ourselves with equal unity of purpose to rewinning at home the freedom they have won at such desperate cost abroad.

To our Allies let us send from this convention one message from our hearts: the American people are united with you to the limit of our resources and our manpower, devoted to the single task of victory and the establishment of a firm and lasting peace.

To every member of the Axis Powers let us send this message from this convention: By this political campaign which you are unable to understand, our will to victory will be strengthened, and with every day you further delay surrender the consequences to you will be more severe.

That we shall win this war none of us and few of our enemies now have any doubt. But how we win this war is of major importance for the years ahead. We won the last war, but it didn't stay won. This time we must also win the purposes for which we are fighting.

Germany must never again nourish the delusion that she could have won. We must carry to Japan a defeat so crushing and complete that every last man among them knows that he has been beaten. We must not merely defeat the armies and the navies of our enemies. We must defeat, once and for all, their will to make war. In their hearts as well as with their lips, let them be taught to say: "Never again."

The military conduct of the war is outside this campaign. It is and must remain completely out of politics. General Marshall and Admiral King are doing a superb job. Thank God for both of them. Let me make it crystal clear that a change of Administration next January cannot and will not involve any change in the military conduct of the war. If there is not now any civilian interference with the military and naval commands, a change in Administration will not alter that status. If there is civilian interference, the new Administration will put a stop to it forthwith.

But the war is being fought on the home front as well as abroad. While all of us are deeply proud of the military conduct of the war, can we honestly say that the home front could not bear improvement? The present Administration in Washington has been in office for more than eleven years.

Today it is at war with Congress, and at war with itself. Squabbles between Cabinet members, feuds between rival bureaucrats and bitterness between the President and his own party members, in and out of Congress, have become the order of the day. In the vital matters of taxation, price control, rationing, labor relations, manpower, we have become familiar with the spectacle of wrangling, bungling and confusion.

Does any one suggest that the present National Administration is giving either efficient or competent government? We have not heard that claim made, even by its most fanatical supporters. No, all they tell us is that in its young days it did some good things. That we freely grant. But now it has grown old in office. It has become tired and quarrelsome. It seems that the great men who founded this nation really did know what they were talking about when they said that three terms were too many.

When we have won the war we shall still have to win the peace. We are agreed, all of us, that America will participate with other sovereign nations in a cooperative effort to prevent future wars. Let us face up boldly to the magnitude of that task. We shall not make secure the peace of the world by mere words. We cannot do it simply by drawing up a fine-sounding treaty. It cannot be the work of any one man or of a little group of rulers who meet together in private conferences. The structure of peace must be built.

It must be the work of many men. We must have as our representatives in this task the ablest men and women America can produce, and the structure they join in building must rest upon the solid rock of a united American public opinion.

I am not one of those who despair of achieving that end. I am utterly confident we can do it. For years we have had men in Washington who were notoriously weak in certain branches of arithmetic but who specialized in division. They have played up minor differences of opinion among our people until the people of other countries might have thought that America was cleft in two.

But all the while there was a large, growing area of agreement. Recently the overwhelming majesty of that broad area of agreement has become obvious. The Republican party can take pride in helping to define it and broaden it. There are only a few, a very few, who really believe that America should try to remain aloof from the world. There are only a relatively few who believe it would be practical for America or her Allies to renounce all sovereignty and join a superstate.

I certainly would not deny those two extremes the right to their opinions; but I stand firmly with the overwhelming majority of my fellow-citizens in that great wide area of agreement. That agreement was clearly expressed by the Republican Mackinac declaration and was adopted in the foreign policy plank of this convention.

No organization for peace will last if it is slipped through by stealth or trickery or the momentary hypnotism of high-sounding phrases. We shall have to work and pray and be patient and make sacrifices to achieve a really lasting peace. That is not too much to ask in the name of those who have died for the future of our country. This is no task to be entrusted to stubborn men, grown old and tired and quarrelsome in office. We learned that in 1919.

The building of the peace is more than a matter of international cooperation. God has endowed America with such blessings as to fit her for a great role in the world. We can only play that role if we are strong and healthy and vigorous as nature has equipped us to be.

It would be a tragedy after this war if Americans returned from our armed forces and failed to find the freedom and opportunity for which they fought. This must be a land where every man and woman has a fair chance to work and get ahead. Never again must free Americans face the specter of long-continued, mass unemployment. We Republicans are agreed that full employment shall be a first objective of national policy. And by full employment I mean a real chance for every man and woman to earn a decent living.

What hopes does the present National Administration offer here? In 1940, the year before this country entered the war, there were still ten million unemployed. After seven years of unequaled power and unparalleled spending, the New Deal had failed utterly to solve that problem. It never solved that problem. It was left to be solved by war. Do we have to have a war to get jobs?

What are we now offered? Only the dreary prospect of a continued war economy after the war, with interference piled on interference and petty tyrannies rivaling the very regimentation against which we are now at war.

The present Administration has never solved this fundamental problem of jobs and opportunity. It can never solve this problem. It has never even understood what makes a job. It has never been for full production. It has lived in chattering fear of abundance. It has specialized in curtailment and restriction. It has been consistently hostile to and abusive of American business and industry, although it is in business and industry that most of us make our living.

In all the record of the past eleven years is there anything that suggests that the present Administration can bring about high-level employment after this war? Is there any reason to believe that those who have so signally failed in the past can succeed in the future? The problem of jobs won't easily be solved; but it will never be solved at all unless we get a new, progressive Administration in Washington—and that means a Republican Administration.

For 150 years America was the hope of the world. Here on this great broad continent we had brought into being something for which men had longed throughout all history. Here all men were held to be free and equal. Here government derived its just powers from the consent of the governed. Here men believed passionately in freedom, independence—the God-given right of the individual to be his own master.

Yet, with all of this freedom—I insist—because of this freedom—ours was a land of plenty. In a fashion unequaled anywhere else in the world, America grew and strengthened; our standard of living became the envy of the world. In all lands, men and women looked toward America as the pattern of what they, themselves, desired.

And because we were what we were, good-will flowed toward us from all corners of the earth. An American was welcomed everywhere and looked upon with admiration and regard.

At times, we had our troubles; made our share of mistakes; but we faltered only to go forward with renewed vigor. It remained for the past eleven years, under the present national administration, for continuing unemployment to be accepted with resignation as the inevitable condition of a nation past its prime.

It is the New Deal that tells us that America has lost its capacity to grow. We shall never build a better world by listening to those counsels of defeat.

Is America old and worn out, as the New Dealers tell us? Look to the beaches of Normandy for the answer. Look to the reaches of the wide Pacific —to the corners of the world where American men are fighting. Look to the marvels of production in the war plants in your own cities and towns. I say to you: Our country is just fighting its way through to new horizons. The future of America has no limit.

True, we now pass through dark and troubled times. Scarcely a home escapes the touch of dread anxiety and grief; yet in this hour the American spirit rises, faith returns—faith in our God, faith in our fellow-men, faith in the land our fathers died to win, faith in the future, limitless and bright, of this, our country.

In the name of that faith we shall carry our cause in the coming months to the American people.

PRESIDENT ROOSEVELT'S STATEMENT ON JOINT RESOLUTIONS OF CONGRESS RESPECTING THE PHILIPPINES

June 29, 1944 [1]

I have signed today two joint resolutions of Congress respecting the Philippines. The first of these resolutions lays down a policy for the granting of independence, and for the acquisition of bases adequate to provide for the mutual protection of the United States and the Philippine Islands.

In that resolution it is declared to be the policy of "the Congress that the United States shall drive the treacherous, invading Japanese from the Philippine Islands, restore as quickly as possible the orderly, free democratic processes of government to the Filipino people, and thereupon establish the complete independence of the Philippine Islands as a separate self-governing nation." The measure makes it possible to proclaim independence as soon as practicable after constitutional processes and normal functions of government have been restored in the Philippines.

It is contemplated that as soon as conditions warrant, civil government will be set up under constitutional officers. It will be their duty forthwith to take emergency measures to alleviate the physical and economic hardships of the Philippine people and to prepare the Commonwealth to receive and exercise the independence which we have promised them. The latter includes two tasks of great importance: Those who have collaborated with the enemy must be removed from authority and influence over the political and economic life of the country; and the democratic form of government guaranteed in the Constitution of the Philippines must be restored for the benefit of the people of the islands.

On the problem of bases, the present organic act permitted acquisition only of naval bases and fueling stations, a situation wholly inadequate to meet the conditions of modern warfare. The measure approved today will permit the acquisition of air and land bases in addition to naval bases and fueling stations. I have been informed that this action is most welcome to Commonwealth authorities and that they will gladly cooperate in the establishment and maintenance of bases both as a restored Commonwealth and as an independent nation. By this we shall have an outstanding example of cooperation

[1] White House news release.

designed to prevent a recurrence of armed aggression and to assure the peaceful use of a great ocean by those in pursuit of peaceful ends.

The second joint resolution signed today brings into effect the joint economic commission first ordained in the present organic act, and enlarges its scope to include consideration of proposals for the economic and financial rehabilitation of the Philippines.

We are ever mindful of the heroic role of the Philippines and their people in the present conflict. Theirs is the only substantial area and theirs the only substantial population under the American flag to suffer lengthy invasion by the enemy. History will attest the heroic resistance of the combined armies of the United States and the Philippines in Luzon, Cebu, Iloilo, and other islands of the archipelago. Our character as a nation will be judged for years to come by the human understanding and the physical efficiency with which we help in the immense task of rehabilitating the Philippines. The resolution creates the Philippine Rehabilitation Commission whose functions shall be to study all aspects of the problem and, after due investigation, report its recommendations to the President of the United States and the Congress, and to the President and the Congress of the Philippines.

THE UNITED STATES' SEVERANCE OF DIPLOMATIC RELATIONS WITH FINLAND

June 30, 1944 [1]

On June 30 the following note was delivered to Mr. Alexander Thesleff, Chargé d'Affaires of Finland:

JUNE 30, 1944.

SIR:

On June 27, 1944, the Finnish Government made the following announcement:

"The German Foreign Minister von Ribbentrop has concluded his visit to the Finnish Government.

"During this visit questions of interest to Finland and Germany were discussed, especially Finland's expressed desire with respect to military aid. The German Government has declared itself prepared to comply with this wish of the Finnish Government.

"The discussions which were conducted between the President of the Finnish Republic Ryti and Foreign Minister Ramsay on one side and the German Foreign Minister on the other, are sustained by the spirit which has its roots in the comradeship in arms between the armies and the existing friend ship between the two peoples.

"Complete agreement and understanding were reached on all points between the Finnish Government and the German Government."

The Finnish Government has thus formally admitted to the world that it has now entered a hard and fast military partnership with Nazi Germany irrevocable throughout the war, for the purpose of fighting the Allies of the United States, in alliance with the enemies of the United States. This action was taken without recourse to the established democratic procedure of Finland, and responsibility for the consequences must rest solely on the Finnish Government.

[1] State Department Bulletin.

The American Government is not unaware of the fact that the infiltration of German troops into Finland, with the consent of the Finnish Government and German infiltration into the councils of the Finnish Government have deprived Finland of liberty of action and reduced the Government of the Republic of Finland to the condition of a puppet of Nazi Germany.

This necessarily changes the status of the Finnish Government. The United States, up to the present, has taken every opportunity, publicly and through diplomatic representations, to warn the Finnish Government of the inevitable consequences of continuing its association with Nazi Germany. These warnings have been ignored, and the partnership is now complete.

The Government of the United States must take into account the fact that at this decisive stage in the combined operations of the military, naval and air forces of the United States and the other United Nations, the Finnish operations have a direct bearing on the success of the Allied effort. Notwithstanding the esteem in which the American people have held the people of Finland, further relations between the Government of the United States and the Government of Finland are now impossible.

The American Chargé d'Affaires in Helsinki has therefore been instructed to request passports for himself and for the members of his staff and their families.

The American Government is requesting the Swiss Government to assume immediately the representation of American interests in Finland.

Accept [etc.]

CORDELL HULL

JULY

The Japanese launched an offensive northward in the Canton area.

3

Danish trade unionists paralyzed Copenhagen with a general strike, erecting street barricades and defying Nazi rule.

4

The Red Army captured the White Russian capital of Minsk, the last major enemy bastion in Russia on the way to Warsaw.

Nazi military authorities capitulated to Danish workers' demands that the Quislingist Schalburg Corps be withdrawn from Copenhagen.

5

Secretary of War Henry L. Stimson received a private audience from Pope Pius XII in the course of which they discussed the problems of peace.

Adolf Hitler urged the German people "not to capitulate to difficulties no matter how great."

6

Generalissimo Chiang Kai-shek, speaking on the seventh anniversary of China's war with Japan, admitted that the military situation for his country was very grave.

Hitler ordered Field Marshal Gen. Guenther von Kluge to replace Field Marshal Gen. von Rundstedt as Supreme Commander of the German forces in the West.

Gen. Charles de Gaulle arrived in the United States and was received by President Roosevelt and his Cabinet at the White House.

Japanese forces began a general retreat on the Hunan and Honan fronts of the China war theatre.

7

The Allies authorized Premier Ivanoe Bonomi to move his government from Naples to Rome.

Premier Ivan Subasitch formed a new Yugoslav Cabinet with two representatives of Marshal Tito in it.

Chinese troops smashed through Japanese encirclement around vital Hengyang and took the initiative on all sectors in Hunan Province.

Superfortresses attacked the great Japanese naval base of Sasebo and the steel center of Yawata.

8

Dr. Joseph Goebbels warned the German people: "The country, the nation, the people is in danger—terrible danger . . . because our adversaries, if we do

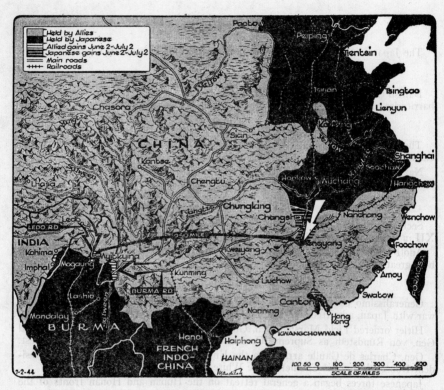

Courtesy New York Times

The East Asia Theatre of War
July, 1944

not throw them back now, will erase Germany and everything German from the face of the globe."

9

Admiral Chester W. Nimitz announced: "Our forces have completed the conquest of Saipan."

10

President Roosevelt agreed to run for a fourth term, stating: "If the people elect me, I will serve."

11

President Roosevelt announced that the United States had granted to the French Committee of National Liberation the status of a "de facto authority" in French civil affairs in liberated territory.

13

German broadcasts said that before the Russian "peril" could penetrate the Reich's borders the Nazis would "turn this continent into a maelstrom of destruction where only one cry is heard—the cry of blood."

14

In compliance with the direction of Congress, an Army and Navy board was named to investigate the facts regarding the Pearl Harbor attack of Dec. 7, 1941.

The Red Army captured Pinsk, vital rail junction in the Pripet marshes, and Volkovysk, a Nazi stronghold shielding Bialystok.

President Roosevelt, in a Bastille Day message to the French people, said he looked forward to the celebration of July 14, 1945 in a liberated France.

17

Admiral Shigetaro Shimada was replaced as Japanese Navy Minister by Admiral Naokuni Nomura "in view of the grave war situation."

18

Premier Gen. Hideki Tojo was relieved as Chief of Staff of the Japanese Army because, in his own words, "imperial Japan has come to face an unprecedentedly great national crisis."

19

Premier Gen. Hideki Tojo's entire Cabinet resigned, the official reason being: "By utilizing all means available the present Cabinet was not able to achieve its objective."

Lieut. Gen. Edmund Hoffmeister, former German tank corps commander captured by the Russians, denounced Hitler from Moscow, blaming him for "gross mistakes in German strategy" and for his personal ban on strategic retreats.

20

President Roosevelt was nominated by the Democratic Party for a fourth term.

Gen. Kuniaki Koiso arrived from Korea to join Admiral Mitsumasa Yonai in the formation of a new "critical decisive wartime" Cabinet by "command" of Emperor Hirohito.

Adolf Hitler had a narrow escape from death by assassination at his secret headquarters when a bomb injured thirteen members of his military staff, one fatally. Hitler told the German people later: ". . . you shall hear the details about a crime that has no equal in German history." Immediately after, Hitler appointed Gestapo

Chief Heinrich Himmler in absolute command within the Reich. He also replaced Field Marshal Gen. Keitel with Col. Gen. Guderian as Chief of Staff.

21

Senator Harry S. Truman of Missouri won the Democratic nomination for Vice-President over Vice-President Henry A. Wallace on the second ballot.

22

Premier Koiso of Japan, in taking office, declared that his new government would "work for thoroughgoing realization of the principles of the Greater East Asia Joint Declaration, thereby carrying out this sacred war to complete victory, thus setting the Imperial mind at ease."

Adolf Hitler, two days after the assassination attempt on him and after he first announced the German Army revolt, addressed a plea to the German Army: "I know that as hitherto you will fight with exemplary obedience and loyalty until victory is ours in spite of all."

25

Adolf Hitler promulgated a decree ordering the total mobilization of Germany and of the occupied countries. He named Propaganda Minister Joseph Goebbels "Reich Plenipotentiary for the Total War Effort."

The Soviet Government entered into an agreement with the Polish Committee of National Liberation for the civil administration of Polish territory liberated by the Red Army.

27

Admiral Chester W. Nimitz proclaimed the reestablishment of American sovereignty on Guam.

28

Soviet troops captured Brest-Litovsk and Przemysl.

29

Red Army artillery began shelling the suburbs of Warsaw.

Premier Stalin cabled Prime Minister Churchill a notification of his willingness to discuss Russian-Polish problems in Moscow with Premier Mikolajczyk of the Polish Government-in-Exile.

30

Mohandas K. Gandhi agreed to meet Mohammed Ali Jinnah, President of the Moslem League, in Bombay on August 8th to try and reach a compromise settlement on Moslem autonomy in India.

Gen. Bradley's army broke the back of eight German divisions in Normandy.

31

Dr. Joseph Goebbels told the Reich Cabinet Ministers that "we must reckon with closing down whole branches of public services," in order to be able to throw every ounce of strength into the war effort.

SECRETARY OF TREASURY HENRY MORGENTHAU, JR.'S ADDRESS OPENING THE UNITED NATIONS MONETARY AND FINANCIAL CONFERENCE AT BRETTON WOODS, N. H.

July 1, 1944 [1]

Fellow delegates and members of the conference:

You have given me an honor and an opportunity. I accept the presidency of this conference with gratitude for the confidence you have reposed in me. I accept it also with deep humility. For I know that what we do here will shape to a significant degree the nature of the world in which we are to live— and the nature of the world in which men and women younger than ourselves must round out their lives and seek the fulfillment of their hopes. All of you, I know, share this sense of responsibility.

We are more likely to be successful in the work before us if we see it in perspective. Our agenda is concerned specifically with the monetary and investment field. It should be viewed, however, as part of a broader program of agreed action among nations to bring about the expansion of production, employment and trade contemplated in the Atlantic Charter and in Article VII of the Mutual Aid Agreements concluded by the United States with many of the United Nations. Whatever we accomplish here must be supplemented and buttressed by other action having this end in view.

President Roosevelt has made it clear that we are not asked to make definite agreements binding on any nation, but that proposals here formulated are to be referred to our respective governments for acceptance or rejection. Our task, then, is to confer and to reach understanding and agreement upon certain basic measures which must be recommended to our governments for the establishment of a sound and stable economic relationship among us.

We can accomplish this task only if we approach it not as bargainers but as partners—not as rivals but as men who recognize that their common welfare depends, in peace as in war, upon mutual trust and joint endeavor. It is not an easy task that is before us; but I believe, if we devote ourselves to it in this spirit, earnestly and sincerely, that what we achieve here will have the greatest historical significance. Men and women everywhere will look to this meeting for a sign that the unity welded among us by war will endure in peace.

Through cooperation we are now overcoming the most fearful and formidable threat ever to be raised against our security and freedom. In time, with God's grace, the scourge of war will be lifted from us. But we shall delude ourselves if we regard victory as synonymous with freedom and security. Victory in this war will give us simply the opportunity to mold, through our common effort, a world that is, in truth, secure and free.

We are to concern ourselves here with essential steps in the creation of a dynamic world economy in which the people of every nation will be able to realize their potentialities in peace; will be able, through their industry, their inventiveness, their thrift, to raise their own standards of living and enjoy, increasingly, the fruits of material progress on an earth infinitely blessed with natural riches.

This is the indispensable cornerstone of freedom and security. All else

[1] *New York Times.*

must be built upon this. For freedom of opportunity is the foundation for all other freedoms.

I hope that this conference will focus its attention upon two elementary economic axioms. The first of these is this: that prosperity has no fixed limits. It is not a finite substance to be diminished by division. On the contrary, the more of it that other nations enjoy, the more each nation will have for itself.

There is a tragic fallacy in the notion that any country is liable to lose its customers by promoting greater production and higher living standards among them. Good customers are prosperous customers. The point can be illustrated very simply from the foreign-trade experience of my own country. In the pre-war decade about 20 per cent of our exports went to the 47,000,000 people in the highly industrialized United Kingdom; less than 3 per cent went to the 450,000,000 people in China.

The second axiom is a corollary of the first. Prosperity, like peace, is indivisible. We cannot afford to have it scattered here or there among the fortunate or to enjoy it at the expense of others. Poverty, wherever it exists, is menacing to us all and undermines the well-being of each of us. It can no more be localized than war, but spreads and saps the economic strength of all the more favored areas of the earth.

We know now that the thread of economic life in every nation is inseparably woven into a fabric of world economy. Let any thread become frayed and the entire fabric is weakened. No nation, however great and strong, can remain immune.

All of us have seen the great economic tragedy of our time. We saw the world-wide depression of the Nineteen Thirties. We saw currency disorders develop and spread from land to land, destroying the basis for international trade and international investment and even international faith. In their wake, we saw unemployment and wretchedness—idle tools, wasted wealth. We saw their victims fall prey, in places, to demagogues and dictators. We saw bewilderment and bitterness become the breeders of fascism, and, finally, of war.

In many countries controls and restrictions were set up without regard to their effect on other countries. Some countries, in a desperate attempt to grasp a share of the shrinking volume of world trade, aggravated the disorder by resorting to competitive depreciation of currency.

Much of our economic ingenuity was expended in the fashioning of devices to hamper and limit the free movement of goods. These devices became economic weapons with which the earliest phase of our present war was fought by the fascist dictators. There was an ironic inevitability in this process. Economic aggression can have no other offspring than war. It is as dangerous as it is futile.

We know now that economic conflict must develop when nations endeavor separately to deal with economic ills which are international in scope. To deal with the problems of international exchange and of international investment is beyond the capacity of any one country, or of any two or three countries.

These are multilateral problems, to be solved only by multilateral cooperation. They are fixed and permanent problems, not merely transitional considerations of the post-war reconstruction. They are problems not limited in importance to foreign exchange traders and bankers but are vital factors in the flow of raw materials and finished goods, in the maintenance of high levels of production and consumption, in the establishment of a satisfactory standard of living for all the people of all the countries on this earth.

Throughout the past decade the Government of the United States has sought in many directions to promote joint action among the nations of the world. In the realm of monetary and financial problems this Government undertook, as far back as 1936, to facilitate the maintenance of orderly exchanges by entering into the tri-partite agreement with England and France, under which they, and subsequently Belgium, the Netherlands and Switzerland, agreed with us to consult on foreign exchange questions before important steps were taken. This policy of consultation was extended in the bilateral exchange arrangements which we set up, starting in 1937, with our neighbors on the American continents.

In 1941 we began to study the possibility of international cooperation on a multilateral basis as a means of establishing a stable and orderly system of international currency relationships and to revive international investment. Our technical staff—soon joined by the experts of other nations—undertook the preparation of practical proposals, designed to implement international monetary and financial cooperation.

The opinions of these technicans, as reported in the joint public statement which they have issued, reveal a common belief that the disruption of foreign exchanges can be prevented, and the collapse of monetary systems can be avoided, and a sound currency basis for the balanced growth of international trade can be provided, if we are forehanded enough to plan ahead of time—and to plan together.

It is the consensus of these technical experts that the solution lies in a permanent institution for consultation and cooperation on international monetary, finance and economic problems. The formulation of a definite proposal for a stabilization fund of the United and Associated Nations is one of the items on our agenda.

But provision for monetary stabilization alone will not meet the need for the rehabilitation of war-wrecked economies. It is not, in fact, designed toward that end. It is proposed, rather, as a permanent mechanism to promote exchange stability. Even to discharge this function effectively, it must be supplemented by many other measures to remove impediments to world trade.

For long-range reconstruction purposes international loans on a broad scale will be imperative. We have in mind a need wholly apart from the problem of immediate aid which is being undertaken by the United Nations relief and Rehabilitation Administration.

The need which we seek to meet through the second proposal on our agenda is for loans to provide capital for economic reconstruction, loans for which adequate security may be available and which will provide the opportunity for investment, under proper safeguards, of capital from many lands. The technicians have prepared the outline of a plan for an international bank for postwar reconstruction which will investigate the opportunities for loans of this character, will recommend and supervise them and, if advisable, furnish to investors guaranties of their payment.

I shall not attempt here to discuss these proposals in detail. That is the task of this conference. It is a task the performance of which calls for wisdom, for statesmanship, above all for good-will.

The transcendent fact of contemporary life is this—that the world is a community. On battlefronts the world over the young men of all our united countries have been dying together—dying for a common purpose. It is not beyond our powers to enable the young men of all our countries to live together—to pour their energies, their skills, their aspirations into mutual enrichment and peaceful progress.

Our final responsibility is to them. As they prosper or perish, the work which we do here will be judged. The opportunity before us has been bought with blood. Let us meet it with faith in one another, with faith in our common future, which these men fought to make free.

PRIME MINISTER WINSTON CHURCHILL'S SPEECH IN COMMONS ON ROBOT BOMB ATTACKS

July 6, 1944 [1]

I consider that His Majesty's Government were right in not giving out a great deal of information about the flying bombs until we knew more about them and were able to measure their effect. The newspapers have in an admirable manner helped the Government in this, and I express my thanks to them. The time has come, however, when a fuller account is required and a wider field of discussion should be opened, and in my opinion such a discussion is no longer hampered by the general interest. I would at the same time enjoin upon hon. Members and the public outside to watch their step in anything they say, because a thing which might not strike one as being harmful at all might give some information to the enemy which would be of use to him and a detriment to us. Still, a very wide field of discussion will be open henceforth.

Let me say at the outset that it would be a mistake to under-rate the serious character of this particular form of attack. It has never been under-rated in the secret circles of the Government. On the contrary, up to the present time the views which we formed of the force and extent of the danger were considerably in excess of what has actually happened. The probability of such an attack has, among other things, been under continuous intense study and examination for a long time. During the early months of 1943 we received, through our many and varied Intelligence sources, vague reports that the Germans were developing a new long-range weapon with which they proposed to bombard London. At first our information led us to believe that a rocket weapon would be used. Just over a year ago the Chiefs of Staff proposed to me that the Joint Parliamentary Secretary to the Minister of Supply, my hon. Friend the Member for Norwood (Mr. Sandys), should be charged with the duty of studying all the intelligence as it came in and reporting what truth, if any, there was in these reports and advising the Chiefs of State and the War Cabinet as to counter measures. Long before this time my right hon. Friend the Home Secretary, whose vigilance has been unceasing, had begun to strengthen the street shelters generally, and he now intensified this work so that these shelters are by no means ill adapted to withstand the blast effects of the bombs at present being used.

The House will realise that the enemy took all possible precautions to conceal his designs from us. Nevertheless, as the result of searching investigations by agents and by reconnaissance, we had by July, 1943, succeeded in locating at Peenemunde, on the Baltic, the main experimental station both for the flying bomb and the long-range rocket. In August last the full strength of Bomber Command was sent out to attack those installations.

[1] Parliamentary Debates.

The raids were costly, on account of the great distances into Germany which had to be flown, but very great damage was done to the enemy and his affairs, and a number of key German scientists, including the head scientist, who were all dwelling together in a so-called Strength-Through-Joy establishment, were killed. This raid delayed by many months the development and bringing into action of both these weapons.

About this time we had also located at Watten, in the Pas de Calais, the first of the large structures which appeared to be connected with the firing of a long-range rocket. This site was very heavily attacked as long ago as September, and has been under continual treatment since by the heaviest weapons carried by the British and American Air Forces. We also carried out a most thorough air reconnaissance of the whole of North-West France and Belgium. This was an immense task, and not without its cost, but in the result we discovered in October last that in addition to the large structures of the Watten type other structures, in greater numbers, were being erected all along the French coast between Havre and Calais. I meditated at that time whether I should make a statement to the House in Secret Session on the subject, but on the whole, everything being in such a hypothetical condition, I thought that might cause needless alarm and that we had better proceed step by step till we had greater assurances as to what we could say.

The reconnaissance which we carried out was an immense task, but it yielded very important information. Eventually we found that about 100 of these rather smaller sites all along the French coast between Havre and Calais were being erected, and we concluded that they would be the firing points for a jet-propelled projectile much smaller than the rocket to which our thoughts had first been turned. All these hundred firing points were continuously bombed since last December, and every one of them was destroyed by the Royal Air Force, with the wholehearted assistance of the growing United States air power. If it had not been for our bombing operations in France and Germany, the counter-preparations in which we indulged, the bombardment of London would no doubt have started perhaps six months earlier and on a very much heavier scale. Under the pressure of our countermeasures, the enemy, who felt, among other impulses, the need of having something to boast about and to carry on a war of nerves in order to steady the neutrals and satellites and assuage his own public opinion, developed a new series of prefabricated structures which could be rapidly assembled and well camouflaged, especially during periods of cloudy weather. It is from those comparatively light and very rapidly erected structures that the present attack is being made.

What is the scale of this attack? The hundred firing sites which were destroyed, assuming that the enemy's production of the missiles was adequate, could have delivered a vastly greater discharge of H.E. on London per day than what we have now. I think it is only just to the British and American Air Forces to record that diminution in the scale of attack to which we are now exposed by their untiring and relentless efforts. The new series of firing points, like the first, have been heavily and continuously bombed for several months past. As new sites are constructed or existing ones repaired, our bombing attacks are repeated. Every effort is used to destroy the structures and also to scatter the working parties and to deal with other matters concerned with the smooth running of this system of attack. The total weight of bombs so far dropped on flying bomb and rocket targets in France and Germany, including Peenemunde, has now reached about 50,000 tons, and the number of reconnaissance flights now totals many thousands. The scrutiny and interpretation of the tens of thousands of air photographs obtained for this purpose have alone been a stupendous task discharged by the Air Reconnaissance and Photographic Interpretation Unit of the R.A.F.

These efforts have been exacting to both sides, friend and foe. Quite a considerable proportion of our flying power has been diverted for months past from other forms of offensive activity. The Germans, for their part, have sacrificed a great deal of manufacturing strength which would have increased their fighter and bomber forces working in conjunction with their hard-pressed armies on every front. It has yet to be decided who has suffered and will suffer the most in the process. There has, in fact, been in progress for a year past an unseen battle into which great resources have been poured by both sides. This invisible battle has now flashed into the open, and we shall be able, and indeed obliged, to watch its progress at fairly close quarters.

To the blood-curdling threats which German propaganda has been making in order to keep up the spirit of their people and of their satellites, there have been added the most absurd claims about the results of the first use of the secret weapon. I minimise nothing. I assure the House, but I think it right to correct those absurdities by giving some actual facts and figures, knowledge of which, although they may not be known to the enemy, will do him very little good, in my opinion and in the opinion of my advisers. Between 100 and 150 flying bombs, each weighing about one ton, are being discharged daily, and have been so discharged for the last fortnight or so from the firing points in France. Considering the modest weight and small penetration power of these bombs, the damage they have done by blast effect has been extensive. It cannot at all be compared with the terrific destruction by fire and high explosives with which we have been assaulting Berlin, Hamburg, Cologne and scores of other German cities and other war manufacturing points in Germany.

This form of attack is, no doubt, of a trying character, a worrisome character, because of its being spread out throughout the whole of the twenty-four hours, but people have just got to get used to that. [HON. MEMBERS: "Hear, hear"] Everyone must go about his duty and his business, whatever it may be—every man or woman—and then, when the long day is done, they should seek the safest shelter that they can find and forget their cares in well-earned sleep. We must neither under-rate nor exaggerate. In all up to six a.m. to-day, about 2,750 flying bombs have been discharged from the launching stations along the French coast. A very large proportion of these have either failed to cross the Channel or have been shot down and destroyed by various methods, including the great deployment of batteries, aircraft and balloons which has been very rapidly placed in position. [AN HON. MEMBER: "Improvising"] Well, batteries move to any position in which they are required and take up their positions rapidly, but once on the site great improvements can be made in the electrical connections and so forth; and the Air Force, confronted with the somewhat novel problem of chasing a projectile, have found new methods every day.

Therefore, I say, a very large proportion of those that were discharged from the other side has been shot down and destroyed by various methods. Sometimes shooting them down means that they explode upon the ground. Therefore the places where they should be shot down are better chosen where successful hits do not necessarily mean explosions in a built-up area. I am very careful to be vague about areas. The weather, however, during the month of June has been very unfavourable to us for every purpose. In

Normandy it has robbed us in great part of the use of our immense superiority. These battles in Normandy are being waged without that extraordinary and overwhelming, exceptional aid of the vast Air Force we had collected for the purpose. When the weather improves a new great reinforcement will come into play. In Britain the bad weather has made more difficult the work and combination of the batteries and aircraft. It has also reduced the blows we strike at every favourable opportunity at the launching stations or suspicious points on the other side of the Channel.

Nevertheless, the House will, I think, be favourably surprised to learn that the total number of flying bombs launched from the enemy's stations have killed almost exactly one person per bomb. That is a very remarkable fact, and it has kept pace roughly week by week. Actually the latest figures are 2,754 flying bombs launched and 2,752 fatal casualties sustained. They are the figures up to six o'clock this morning. Well, I am bound to say I was surprised when, some time ago, I perceived this wonderful figure. This number of dead will be somewhat increased by people who die of their injuries in hospital. Besides these there has been a substantially larger number of injured, and many minor injuries have been caused by splinters of glass. A special warning of this danger was issued by the Ministries of Home Security and Health, and in giving wide publicity to the recommendations for reducing this risk the newspapers have also rendered a most useful service.

As this battle—for such it is—may be a somewhat lengthy affair, I do not propose to withhold the number of casualties. I will give the number because I believe the exaggerated rumours and claims that are made are more harmful than the disclosure of the facts. I will now give the casualties up to date and, thereafter, they will be given in the usual form, at monthly intervals, by my right hon. Friend the Minister of Home Security. The total number of injured detained in hospital is about 8,000. This does not include minor injuries treated at first-aid posts and out-patients' departments of hospitals not needing to be detained at the hospital even for a single day. Of those detained in hospital a large proportion has, in fact, been discharged after a few days. Here let me say that the casualty and first-aid services of Greater London are working excellently. This machine has been well tested in the past, and it has been continually reviewed, kept up to date and improved in the light of experience. It is not at all strained beyond its capacity and, naturally, we draw from other parts of the country which are not affected to strengthen the central machine.

So far as hospital accommodation is concerned, we prepared for so many more casualties in the Battle of Normandy than have actually occurred so far that we have, for the present, a considerable immediate emergency reserve in which to disperse patients. The injured are speedily transferred to hospitals in safer districts, and I am glad to say that penicillin, which up to now has had to be restricted to military uses, will be available for the treatment of all flying bomb casualties. Here, I must say a word about our American friends and Allies in London, from the highest official to the ordinary soldier whom one meets, who have, in every way, made common cause with us and been forthcoming as helpers, wardens and assistants of every kind. No one can visit a bombed site where an explosion has recently taken place without seeing how very quickly they are, in many numbers, on the scene and running any risk to give a helping hand to anyone in distress. And the same is true of the great headquarters under General Eisenhower, where they are conducting this great battle and where, apart from that, every conceivable assistance is given to our Forces and aid services. It will be another tie, I think, between our two peoples to see something of what we go through in London and to take a generous part in facing this burden. A very high proportion of these casualties I have mentioned—somewhere around 10,000—not always severe or mortal, have fallen upon London, which presents to the enemy—now I have mentioned it the phrase "Southern England" passes out of currency—a target eighteen miles wide by, I believe, over twenty miles deep, and it is, therefore, the unique target of the world for the use of a weapon of such gross inaccuracy.

The flying bomb, Mr. Speaker, is a weapon literally and essentially indiscriminate in its nature, purpose and effect. The introduction by the Germans of such a weapon obviously raises some grave questions upon which I do not propose to trench to-day.

Slight repairs to buildings are being done as quickly as possible. As a temporary measure these are usually rough protective repairs to roofs and windows. A large force of building workers is engaged on this work. Copious reinforcements have been brought in, and are being brought in, from the provinces by my right hon. Friend the Minister of Labour, and are arriving here daily. Repairs to a very large number of houses have already been carried out, but there are areas where the blast damage is at present somewhat ahead of our growing repair forces. This will be remedied as time goes on.

As to evacuation, as I have said, everyone must remain at his post and discharge his daily duty. This House would be affronted if any suggestion were made to it that it should change its location from London. Here we began the war, and here we will see it ended. We are not, however, discouraging people who have no essential work to do from leaving London at their own expense if they feel inclined to do so by the arrangements they make. In fact, they assist our affairs by taking such action at their own expense. We do not need more people in London than are required for business purposes of peace and war. For people of small means, who are not engaged in war work and wish to leave, registers have been opened and arrangements will be made for their transfer as speedily as possible to safer areas. Children are already being sent——

MR. BELLENGER: At Government expense?

THE PRIME MINISTER: Certainly. Children are already being sent at their parents' wish out of the danger areas, which are by no means exclusively confined to the Metropolis. There is, of course, the bomb highway over which the robots all pass before reaching that point of Southern England which I have ventured to particularise this morning. Children are being sent if their parents wish out of the danger areas and, in all cases, mothers with small children, or pregnant women, will be given full facilities by the State. And we do not propose to separate the mother from the child except by her wish, but a terrible thing happened last time. Mothers were separated from children of two or three years of age, and, after a period, when they had saved up money and got time to go down and see them, the children hardly knew them. I hope now with our growing strength, reserves and facilities for removal, we shall be able to say to a mother with three or four children, "If you wish to leave, it is perfectly possible. Arrangement will be made to take you into the country with your children. If you wish them to go by themselves and you wish to stay here with your husband, or because of your job, then arrangements can be made that way too." We do not consider that the scale of attack under which we lie at present justifies Governmental compulsion in any case. In order to speed these arrangements, my Noble Friend the Minister of War Transport, Lord Leathers, has arranged that the railways should provide a larger service of trains from the London stations.

All these matters, Sir, and many others are reviewed daily, or almost daily, certainly whenever necessary, by the Civil Defence Committee over which my right hon. Friend the Minister of Home Security has so long presided. He has presided over it since those dark days when he took over the care of London, especially, which he knew so well, in the old original blitz. Upon this Committee sit either the heads or the representatives of every single Department concerned, and the War Cabinet is always available to confirm any decision which involves high policy. There is no delay. Matters are settled with very great speed, but a very great power is given to this Committee, and the question about what I may call the social side of the flying bomb, the social reactions, should be addressed either to my right hon. Friend, who will answer them himself, or to the Minister of Health, who has a great sphere of responsibility.

MR. BELLENGER: Can questions be asked?

THE PRIME MINISTER: A good many questions can be asked, but the House, I am sure, would wish to have a check-up on them beforehand, because a perfectly innocent and proper question might have some connection which would tell the enemy more than we need tell him. After all, the Germans keep large Intelligence services, always prying about and trying to find out everything they can, and really we ought to leave them something to do. I can see lots of questions that could well be discussed here, and if there were some particular kind of question we wanted to talk over among ourselves such procedure is always available to the House. I am not going to attempt to parade to the House the many difficult questions that have been settled. I have mentioned a good many of them. I could give a complete list, and if I have left anything out, that is a matter that can be reserved for a future day. We can with confidence leave our civil organisation to do their work under the watchful supervision of the House of Commons. We have had many periods in the war in which the Government have relied on the House of Commons to keep them in close touch with the people and the population affected and from whom we have welcomed helpful suggestions. I think that we can have great confidence in our civil organisation, for they have immense experience and have handled machinery which has stood far greater strains than this.

On the operational side, a Special Committee has been set up to review, concert and advise upon all counter-measures, both offensive and defensive, to deal with the flying bomb. This Committee consists of my hon. Friend the Joint Parliamentary Secretary to the Ministry of Supply as Chairman; Air Marshal Hill, who is in charge of A.D.G.B.; General Pile, who has been our highly competent Commander-in-Chief of the Ack-Ack Command since the beginning of the war; the Deputy Chief of the Air Staff; and a representative of the Deputy Allied Commander, Air Marshal Tedder. This Committee have at their disposal a great number of able scientists and engineers who are studying from the technical standpoint the improvement of our counter-measures. The Committee report to me personally, to the Chiefs of Staff, and, finally, to the War Cabinet. There is an organisation for getting quick decisions from all the authorities concerned.

The House will ask, What of the future? Is this attack going to get worse, or is it going to be beat like the magnetic mine, or beat like the attempted destruction of Britain by the aeroplane, or beat like the U-boat campaign was beat? Will new developments, on the other hand, of a far more formidable character come upon us? Will the rocket bomb come? Will improved explosives come? Will greater ranges, faster speeds and larger war-heads come upon us? I can give no guarantee that any of these evils will be entirely prevented before the time comes, as come it will, when the soil from which these attacks are launched will be finally liberated from the enemy's grip. In the meanwhile I can only say that when I visited various scenes of bomb explosions on Saturday, only one man of many hundreds whom I saw asked a question. The question was, "What are you going to do about it?" I replied, "Everything in human power, and we have never failed yet." He seemed contented with the reply. That is the only promise I can make.

I must, however, make it perfectly plain—I do not want there to be any misunderstanding on this point—that we shall not allow the battle operations in Normandy or the attacks we are making against special targets in Germany to suffer. They come first, and we must fit in our own domestic arrangements in the general scheme of war operations. There can be no question of allowing the slightest weakening of the battle in order to diminish in scale injuries which, though they may inflict grievous suffering on many people and change to some extent the normal, regular life and industry of London, will never stand between the British nation and their duty in the van of a victorious and avenging world. It may be a comfort to some to feel that they are sharing in no small degree the perils of our soldiers overseas and that the blows which fall on them diminish those which in other forms would have smitten our fighting men and their Allies. But I am sure of one thing, that London will never be conquered and will never fail and that her renown, triumphing over every ordeal, will long shine among men.

VICE PRESIDENT HENRY A. WALLACE'S BROADCAST FROM SEATTLE, WASHINGTON

July 9, 1944 [1]

Since I left the skies above America seven weeks ago, I have visited two great countries—Soviet Asia and China. I have not stood upon the threshold of these countries like a stranger. I have been honored with the confidence of those who are working to shape their countries' destinies. I have been privileged to look behind the scenes.

Today I want to tell you something of my experiences of the past weeks.

In the first place, I am today more than ever an American. The more I examine other countries, the more convinced I am that the American way of life is the best way for us. In the second place, we can and should fit our own way of life to cooperation with other nations and other peoples whose way of life is different from ours but who need our cooperation quite as much as we need theirs, and are not only willing but eager to cooperate with us.

In the third place, I am convinced that a main area of new development after this war—new enterprise, new investment, new trade, new accomplishments—will be in the new world of the North Pacific and Eastern Asia.

This will give to our Pacific coast an importance greater than it has ever had before, and I am glad, returning from Soviet Asia and China, that

[1] Office of the Vice President.

Seattle is my port of entry. No city is more American in spirit and action than Seattle. But no city has shown itself more alive to the importance of our relations with other areas of the North Pacific. This spirit is well exemplified, not only in your active peace-time trade with Asia, but also in the University of Washington, where for several years you have worked on integrating the study of the languages, cultures, history, politics and economics of the Pacific.

We shall need all our resources of knowledge and all our American readiness to think out new ways of tackling new problems when we have won the war in the Pacific.

The day will come when the Pacific will be cleared of Japs and our boys, coming home from Tokyo, will land at Seattle, Portland, San Francisco and Los Angeles. Then we shall think more and more of our West as a link with the East of Asia. Those who say that East is East and West is West and that the two shall never meet are wrong. The East of Asia, both Chinese and Russian, is on the move in a way which is easy for any American to understand who sees these great areas at first-hand for himself. The rapid agricultural and industrial development of this great area means so much to the peace and prosperity of the postwar world that I am glad on my return to America to give my impressions of the manifest destiny of the West of America and the East of Asia.

Here in Northwest United States we were long held back by unfair freight rates and by failure to develop the power inherent in the great rivers. But more and more we are perceiving the importance of strengthening our West and especially our Northwest. Thanks to men like Norris, McNary, Bone and Roosevelt, the Northwest during the past ten years has rapidly expanded. This expansion must continue to the limit of its agricultural, industrial and commercial potentialities. This includes Alaska, which has not yet begun to measure up to its possibilities. Our growth must be not merely in terms of ourselves, but also in terms of Asia. Vigorous two-way trade with Soviet Asia and China will greatly increase the population and prosperity of our Northwest.

All of this I knew in a theoretical way before going to Asia. After having seen as much of the industry and agriculture of East Asia as any American has seen in such a short time, I am more than ever convinced that we are entering upon what might be called the "Era of the Pacific." One characteristic of the Pacific Era will be the building of great airports in parts of the world now very thinly inhabited. The extent to which the Russians have already developed runways and servicing for airplanes in East Asia amazed me. We landed at perhaps a dozen airports in Soviet Asia, the names of which not one in a thousand Americans ever heard. It is quite possible that for fifteen or twenty years after this war the air route to Asia via Fairbanks, Alaska, will not be a money-making one. But it is also certain that our national future requires that we, in cooperation with Russia and the Chinese, maintain such a route.

Soviet Asia during the past fifteen years has more than doubled in population. It is quite possible that the next fifty years will see a further increase of more than thirty million people. I am convinced from what I saw of the Amur River region that in the Southern part of *that* area there will be a great increase in population. Russia, as a result of her experience with this war, will certainly shift much of her industry east of the Urals. Most of the people who moved to Siberia with their factories will stay there.

Everywhere, from Magodan on the Pacific Ocean to Tashkent in Central

Asia, I found the Russian people producing to the limit in the factory and on the farm. About two-thirds of the work on farm, and one-third of the work in the factories is being done by women. In the factories everywhere I found American machinery, some purchased before the war but most of it obtained under Lend-Lease.

The way in which American industry through Lend-Lease has helped Russia to expand production in Soviet Asia has given me an increased admiration for both the United States and Russia.

I found American flour in the Soviet Far East, American aluminum in Soviet airplane factories, American steel in truck and railway repair shops, American machine tools in shipbuilding yards, American compressors and electrical equipment on Soviet naval vessels, American electric shovels in open-cut coal mines, American core drills in copper mines of Central Asia, and American trucks and planes performing strategic transportation functions in supplying remote bases. I found the people, both in positions of management and at the work benches, appreciative of the aid rendered by the United States and other Allies. While it is misleading to make any comparison between the huge Soviet industrial effort and the amount of Lend-Lease aid we have been able to give the USSR, I am convinced from what I saw in Siberia and Central Asia that Lend-Lease has helped the Russians in many difficult and even critical situations on the industrial front, as well as on the military front.

On the rich irrigated land of Central Asia a strong cotton industry is being rapidly developed. At Tashkent, a city of a million people, I found experimental work in cotton which for its originality and practical effectiveness compares most favorably with the best in the United States. Modern industry was also flourishing at this ancient seat of Eastern culture.

From Tashkent, my farthest point west, we turned east to Alma Ata, my last stop before entering China. There I found not only excellent scientific work with apples, but also the beginnings of a moving picture industry which may make Alma Ata the Hollywood of Central Asia. Located at the foot of the Tien Shan—Heavenly Mountains—the city is blessed with a superb climate—*almost* as good as that of southern California.

China is totally different from Soviet Asia. While she is eager and anxious to enter the machine age, she has not yet been able to turn out, in either modern war materials or heavy goods, more than a small fraction of her needs. This situation should not long continue. China, with her 450 million people and her great resources, should sooner or later produce a large portion of her requirements in the way of heavy and light industrial goods and also consumer goods. But to modernize her industry and train her people China needs help. We have thousands of technical and business men in the United States who are able to furnish that help. But the business men in particular want to be sure of one thing. They want to be certain, before they lay the foundations and make the necessary outlay, that there is no foreseeable likelihood of conflict within China or between China and the USSR.

I am glad to say that I found among those with whom I talked an outspoken desire for good understanding; and personally I am convinced that China and the USSR will take the necessary steps to insure continuing peace and to promote cultural and commercial exchanges among the nations of the Pacific to the benefit of all.

Asia is the center of the greatest land and population masses of the world. It is our business to be friends with both Russia and China and exchange with both Russia and China the goods and information which will raise the standard of living of all our peoples. I found the leaders in both Soviet Asia and China anxious for the most friendly relationship with the United States and expressing the utmost confidence in the leadership of President Roosevelt. Living standards can be raised. Causes of war can be removed. Failure to concern ourselves with problems of this sort after World War I is costing us today hundreds of billions of dollars and a terrible toll of human life.

To avoid a recurrence of the scourge of war, it is essential insofar as the Pacific basin is concerned, that relations among the four principal powers in the Pacific—China, the Soviet Union, the British Commonwealth, and the United States—be cordial and collaborative.

Postwar stability in China is dependent upon economic reconstruction—agricultural as well as industrial—and reconstruction in China is dependent upon trade. It became clear to me during my vist to China that reconstruction is going to depend in large measure on imports from abroad. It will require technical and material assistance from us given on a businesslike basis.

We hear much about industrial reconstruction in China. I found the Chinese anxious for industrialization. China should be industrialized. But any industrialization of China must be based upon agricultural reconstruction —agrarian reform—because China is predominately a nation of farmers. They are good farmers, as I observed during my stay there, but they need a break —a new deal!

China should make the necessary reform but we can help by furnishing technicians and scientific information and, on the trade level, by selling the Chinese agricultural implements, fertilizers and insecticides. Ultimately, of course, China should make these products for herself.

China should be self-sufficient in foods but I can foresee that for many years the Chinese will continue to import food products from our West— wheat, flour and fruits for instance. In fact, it is not unreasonable to anticipate that, with an increase in the standard of living of China's consumers, a healthy exchange of food products peculiar to China and our West will develop and endure.

Northwest lumber should play an important part, in the China of the future as it has in the China of the past.

The industrialization of China will require machines, and the materials of which machines are made. During recent years our West has been developing facilities for the production of steel and machinery. These will be in demand in China to produce the consumer goods which will be needed by the masses of East Asia.

Machines for land, sea, and air transportation will also be needed. Our West is in a particularly strategic position to produce for the East of Asia airships and sea ships, and the timber, steel and aluminum of which they are made.

Trade is not a one-way affair—it is a swap, sometimes direct and sometimes complicated. It seems evident that credits will have to be employed to finance economic development in East Asia. But those credits must be repaid, and the most satisfactory way to repay is with goods. So, speaking particularly of China, we should plan to buy as well as to sell. Such typical commodities as wood oil, silks, tea, hides, and metals, which formed the bulk of China's exports to us before the war should form the basis of an expanding Chinese export to the United States after the war.

There is a great future for trade between East Asia and ourselves. To bring this to pass will take only a sympathetic understanding of each other's conditions and a far-sighted determination to make trade what it should be—a mutually beneficial transaction.

Day after tomorrow I hope to report to President Roosevelt certain definite facts which I am not at liberty to discuss here. But I can say that everywhere I went in Eastern Asia I found rapid changes. Even in Mongolia, one of the most remote regions of the world, I found that the changes of the past twenty years had been very great. The United States, together with Russia and Great Britain, has a profound interest in the rapid, peaceful change of Eastern Asia to the more fruitful use of her vast natural and human resources.

Here is a great new frontier to which Seattle can furnish much in the way of leadership. Our scientists must cooperate with Russian and Canadian scientists in learning how to lick the problem of the permanently frozen ground of Alaska, Canada and the north of Siberia. We must exchange agricultural and weather information. I have found a splendid disposition on the part of Russian scientists to cooperate in agricultural matters and a frank readiness on the part of Chinese administrators to consider America's position as well as China's in discussing future economic cooperation. This gives me great hope for the long future.

The American business man of tomorrow should have a broad world outlook. I have faith that American economic leadership will confer on the Pacific region a great material benefit and on the world a great blessing. The new frontier extends from Minneapolis via the Coast States and Alaska through Siberia and China all the way to Central Asia. Here are vast resources of minerals and manpower to be developed by democratic, peaceful methods—the methods not of exploitation, but on the contrary the more profitable method of creating higher living standards for hundreds of millions of people.

It was a wonderful trip. I am grateful to the President for giving me an opportunity to talk with people in every walk of life in Asia who are aiding us in winning this war. With victory we can continue to work together in peace. We want a higher standard of living in America. We want full production, jobs for our boys who come home, and peacetime jobs for those who are now employed. Trade with Russia and China will help keep the factories of America busy in the days that lie ahead. We are on our way!

PRESIDENT ROOSEVELT'S LETTER TO ROBERT E. HANNEGAN ON WILLINGNESS TO ACCEPT RENOMINATION

July 11, 1944 [1]

DEAR MR. HANNEGAN:

You have written me that in accordance with the records a majority of the delegates have been directed to vote for my renomination for the office of President, and I feel that I owe to you, in candor, a simple statement of my position.

If the convention should carry this out, and nominate me for the Presidency, I shall accept. If the people elect me, I will serve.

Every one of our sons serving in this war has officers from whom he takes

[1] *New York Times.*

his orders. Such officers have superior officers. The President is the Commander in Chief and he, too, has his superior officer—the people of the United States.

I would accept and serve, but I would not run, in the usual partisan, political sense. But if the people command me to continue in this office and in this war, I have as little right to withdraw as the soldier has to leave his post in the line.

At the same time, I think I have a right to say to you and to the delegates to the coming convention something which is personal—purely personal.

For myself, I do not want to run. By next spring, I shall have been President and Commander in Chief of the armed forces for twelve years—three times elected by the people of this country under the American constitutional system.

From the personal point of view, I believe that our economic system is on a sounder, more human basis than it was at the time of my first inauguration.

It is perhaps unnecessary to say that I have thought only of the good of the American people. My principal objective, as you know, has been the protection of the rights and privileges and fortunes of what has been so well called the average of American citizens.

After many years of public service, therefore, my personal thoughts have turned to the day when I could return to civil life. All that is within me cries out to go back to my home on the Hudson River, to avoid public responsibilities, and to avoid also the publicity which in our democracy follows every step of the nation's Chief Executive.

Such would be my choice. But we of this generation chance to live in a day and hour when our nation has been attacked, and when its future existence and the future existence of our chosen method of government are at stake.

To win this war wholeheartedly, unequivocally and as quickly as we can is our task of the first importance. To win this war in such a way that there be no further world wars in the foreseeable future is our second objective. To provide occupations, and to provide a decent standard of living for our men in the armed forces after the war, and for all Americans, are the final objectives.

Therefore, reluctantly, but as a good soldier, I repeat that I will accept and serve in this office, if I am so ordered by the Commander in Chief of us all—the sovereign people of the United States.

Very sincerely yours,

FRANKLIN D. ROOSEVELT

PLATFORM ADOPTED BY THE DEMOCRATIC NATIONAL CONVENTION

July 20, 1944 [1]

I

The Democratic party stands on its record in peace and in war.

To speed victory, establish and maintain peace, guarantee full employment and provide prosperity—this is its platform.

We do not here detail scores of planks. We cite action.

[1] *New York Times.*

II

Beginning March, 1933, the Democratic Administration took a series of actions which saved our system of free enterprise.

It brought that system out of collapse and thereafter eliminated abuses which had imperiled it.

It used the powers of government to provide employment in industry and to save agriculture.

It wrote a new Magna Carta for labor.

It provided social security, including old age pensions, unemployment insurance, security for crippled and dependent children and the blind. It established employment offices. It provided Federal bank deposit insurance, flood prevention, soil conservation and prevented abuses in the security markets. It saved farms and homes from foreclosure and secured profitable prices for farm products.

It adopted an effective program of reclamation, hydroelectric power and mineral development.

It found the road to prosperity through production and employment.

We pledge the continuance and improvement of these programs.

III

Before war came, the Democratic Administration awakened the nation, in time, to the dangers that threatened its very existence.

It succeeded in building, in time, the best-trained and equipped Army in the world, the most powerful Navy in the world, the greatest Air Force in the world, and the largest merchant marine in the world.

It gained for our country, and it saved for our country, powerful allies.

When war came, it succeeded in working out with those allies an effective grand strategy against the enemy.

It set that strategy in motion, and the tide of battle was turned.

It held the line against wartime inflation.

It ensured a fair share-and-share-alike distribution of food and other essentials.

It is leading our country to certain victory.

The primary and imperative duty of the United States is to wage the war with every resource available to final triumph over our enemies, and we pledge that we will continue to fight side by side with the United Nations until this supreme objective shall have been attained and thereafter to secure a just and lasting peace.

IV

That the world may not again be drenched in blood by international outlaws and criminals, we pledge:

To join with the other United Nations in the establishment of an international organization based on the principle of the sovereign equality of all peace-loving States, open to membership by all such States, large and small, for the prevention of aggression and the maintenance of international peace and security;

To make all necessary and effective agreements and arrangements through which the nations would maintain adequate forces to meet the needs of preventing war and of making impossible the preparation for war and which would have such forces available for joint action when necessary.

Such organization must be endowed with power to employ armed forces when necessary to prevent aggression and preserve peace.

We favor the maintenance of an international court of justice of which the United States shall be a member and the employment of diplomacy, conciliation, arbitration and other like methods where appropriate in the settlement of international disputes.

World peace is of transcendent importance. Our gallant sons are dying on land, on sea, and in the air. They do not die as Republicans. They do not die as Democrats. They die as Americans. We pledge that their blood shall not have been shed in vain. America has the opportunity to lead the world in this great service to mankind. The United States must meet the challenge. Under divine Providence, she must move forward to her high destiny.

V

We pledge our support to the Atlantic Charter and the Four Freedoms, and the application of the principles enunciated therein to the United Nations and other peace-loving nations, large and small.

We shall uphold the Good Neighbor policy, and extend the trade policies initiated by the present Administration.

We favor the opening of Palestine to unrestricted Jewish immigration and colonization, and such a policy as to result in the establishment there of a free and democratic Jewish commonwealth.

We favor legislation assuring equal pay for equal work regardless of sex.

We recommend to Congress the submission of a Constitutional amendment on equal rights for women.

We favor Federal aid to education administered by the States without interference by the Federal Government.

We favor Federal legislation to assure stability of products, employment, distribution and prices in the bituminous coal industry to create a proper balance between consumer, producer and mine worker.

We endorse the President's statement recognizing the importance of the use of water in arid land States for domestic and irrigation purposes.

We favor non-discriminatory transportation charges and declare for the early correction of inequalities in such charges.

We favor enactment of legislation granting the fullest measure of self-government for Alaska, Hawaii and Puerto Rico and eventual Statehood for Alaska and Hawaii.

. We favor the extension of the right of suffrage to the people of the District of Columbia.

VI

We offer these post-war programs:

A continuation of our policy of full benefits for ex-service men and women with special consideration for the disabled. We make it our first duty to assure employment and economic security to all who have served in the defense of our country.

Price guarantees and crop insurance to farmers with all practical steps:

To keep agriculture on a parity with industry and labor;

To foster the success of the small independent farmer;

To aid the home ownership of family-sized farms;

To extend rural electrification and develop broader domestic and foreign markets for agricultural products.

Adequate compensation for workers during demobilization.

The enactment of such additional humanitarian, labor, social and farm legislation as time and experience may require, including the amendment or repeal of any law enacted in recent years which has failed to accomplish its purpose.

Promotion of the success of small business.

Earliest possible release of war-time controls.

Adaptation of tax laws to an expanding peacetime economy, with simplified structure and wartime taxes reduced or repealed as soon as possible.

Encouragement of risk capital, new enterprise, development of natural resources in the West and other parts of the country and the immediate reopening of the gold and silver mines of the West as soon as manpower is available.

We reassert our faith in competitive private enterprise, free from control by monopolies, cartels, or any arbitrary private or public authority.

VII

We assert that mankind believes in the Four Freedoms.

We believe that the country which has the greatest measure of social justice is capable of the greatest achievements.

We believe that racial and religious minorities have the right to live, develop and vote equally with all citizens and share the rights that are guaranteed by our Constitution. Congress should exert its full constitutional powers to protect those rights.

We believe that without loss of sovereignty, world development and lasting peace are within humanity's grasp. They will come with the greater enjoyment of those freedoms by the peoples of the world, and with the freer flow among them of ideas and goods.

We believe in the world right of all men to write, send and publish news at uniform communication rates and without interference by governmental or private monopoly and that right should be protected by treaty.

To those beliefs the Democratic party subscribes.

These principles the Democratic party pledges itself in solemn sincerity to maintain.

Finally, this convention sends its affectionate greetings to our beloved and matchless leader and President, Franklin Delano Roosevelt.

He stands before the nation and the world, the champion of human liberty and dignity. He has rescued our people from the ravages of economic disaster. His rare foresight and magnificent courage have saved our nation from the assault of international brigands and dictators. Fulfilling the ardent hope of his life, he has already laid the foundation of enduring peace for a troubled world and the well-being of our nation. All mankind is his debtor. His life and service have been a great blessing to humanity.

That God may keep him strong in body and in spirit to carry on his yet unfinished work is our hope and prayer.

PRESIDENT ROOSEVELT'S ACCEPTANCE SPEECH UPON RENOMINATION FOR PRESIDENT

July 20, 1944 [1]

Mr. Chairman, ladies and gentlemen of the convention, my friends:

I have already indicated to you why I accept the nomination that you have offered me, in spite of my desire to retire to the quiet of private life.

You in this convention are aware of what I have sought to gain for the nation, and you have asked me to continue.

It seems wholly likely that within the next four years our armed forces, and those of our Allies, will have gained a complete victory over Germany and Japan, sooner or later, and that the world once more will be at peace, under a system, we hope, that will prevent a new world war. In any event, whenever that time comes new hands will then have full opportunity to realize the ideals which we seek.

In the last three elections the people of the United States have transcended party affiliation. Not only Democrats but also forward-looking Republicans and millions of independent voters have turned to progressive leadership, a leadership which has sought consistently, and with fair success, to advance the lot of the average American citizen who had been so forgotten during the period after the last war. I am confident that they will continue to look to that same kind of liberalism, to build our safer economy for the future.

I am sure that you will understand me when I say that my decision, expressed to you formally tonight, is based solely on a sense of obligation to serve if called upon to do so by the people of the United States.

I shall not campaign, in the usual sense, for the office. In these days of tragic sorrow, I do not consider it fitting. And besides in these days of global warfare, I shall not be able to find the time. I shall, however, feel free to report to the people the facts about matters that concern them and especially to correct any misrepresentations.

During the past few days I have been coming across the whole width of the continent to a naval base where I am speaking to you now from the train.

As I was crossing the fertile lands and the wide plains and the Great Divide, I could not fail to think of the new relationship between the people of our farms and cities and villages and the people of the rest of the world overseas, on the islands of the Pacific, in the Far East, in the other Americas, in Britain and Normandy, and Germany and Poland and Russia itself.

For Oklahoma and California, for example, are becoming a part of all these distant spots as greatly as Massachusetts and Virginia were a part of the European picture in 1776. Today, Oklahoma and California are being defended in Normandy and on Saipan; and they must be defended there, for what happens in Normandy and Saipan vitally affects the security and the well-being of every human being in Oklahoma and California.

Mankind changes the scope and the breadth of its thought and vision slowly indeed. In the days of the Roman Empire eyes were focused on Europe, on the Mediterranean area. The civilization in the Far East was barely known of. The American continents were unheard of. And even after the people of Europe began to spill over to other continents

[1] *New York Times.*

the people of North America in colonial days knew only their Atlantic sea-board and a tiny portion of the other Americas, and they turned most for trade and international relationship to Europe. Africa at that time was considered only as the provider of human chattels. Asia was essentially unknown to our ancestors.

During the Nineteenth Century, during that era of development and expansion on this continent we felt a natural isolation, geographic, economic and political, an isolation from the vast world which lay overseas. Not until this generation, roughly this century, have people here and elsewhere been compelled more and more to widen the orbit of their vision to include every part of the world. Yes, it has been a wrench perhaps, but a very necessary one.

It is good that we are all getting that broader vision. For we shall need it after the war. The isolationists and the ostriches who plagued our thinking before Pearl Harbor are becoming slowly extinct. The American people now know that all nations of the world, large and small, will have to play their appropriate part in keeping the peace by force, and in deciding peacefully the disputes which might lead to war.

We all know how truly the world has become one, that if Germany and Japan, for example, were to come through this war with their philosophies established and their armies intact, our own grandchildren would again have to be fighting in their day for their liberties and their lives.

Some day soon we shall all be able to fly to any other part of the world within twenty-four hours. Oceans will no longer figure as greatly in our physical defense as they have in the past. For our own safety and for our own economic good, therefore, if for no other reason, we must take a leading part in the maintenance of peace and in the increase of trade among all the nations of the world.

And that is why your Government for many, many months has been laying plans, and studying the problems of the near future, preparing itself to act so that the people of the United States may not suffer hardships after the war, may continue constantly to improve its standards, and may join with other nations in doing the same.

They are even now working toward that, and the best staff in all our history, men and women of all parties and from every part of the nation. I realize that planning is a word which in some places brings forth sneers, but, for example, before our entry into the war it was planning which made possible the magnificent organization and the equipment of the Army and Navy of the United States which are fighting for us and for our civilization today.

Improvement through planning is of necessity the order of the day. Even in military affairs things do not stand still. An army or a navy trained and equipped and fighting according to a 1932 model would not have been a safe reliance in 1944, and if we are to progress in our civilization improvement is necessary in other fields, in the physical things that are part of our daily lives, and also in the concepts of social justice at home and abroad.

I am now at this naval base in the performance of my duties under the Constitution. The war waits for no elections. Decisions must be made, plans must be laid, strategy must be carried out. They do not concern merely a party or a group. They will affect the daily lives of Americans for generations to come.

What is the job before us in 1944? First, to win the war, to win the war fast and to win it overpoweringly. Second, to form world-wide international organizations, and to arrange to use the armed force of the sovereign nations of the world to make another war impossible within the foreseeable future. And third, to build an economy for our returning veterans and for all Americans which will provide employment and provide decent standards of living.

The people of the United States will decide this fall whether they wish to turn over this 1944 job, this world-wide job, to inexperienced or immature hands, to those who opposed lend-lease and international cooperation against the forces of aggression and tyranny, until they could read the polls of popular sentiment; or whether they wish to leave it to those who saw the danger from abroad, who met it head-on, and who now have seized the offensive and carried the war to its present stages of success; to those who, by international conferences and united actions have begun to build that kind of common understanding and cooperative experience which will be so necessary in the world to come.

They will also decide, these people of ours, whether they will entrust the task of post-war reconversion to those who offered the veterans of the last war breadlines and apple-selling, and who finally led the American people down to the abyss of 1932; or whether they will leave it to those who rescued American business, and agriculture, and industry, and finance and labor in 1933, and who have already planned and put through much legislation to help our veterans resume their normal occupations in a well-ordered reconversion process.

They will not decide these questions by reading glowing words or platform pledges, the mouthings of those who are willing to promise anything and everything, contradictions, inconsistencies, impossibilities, anything which might snare a few votes here and a few votes there.

They will decide on the record, the record written on the seas, on the land, in the skies.

They will decide on the record of our domestic accomplishments in recovery and reform since March 4, 1933.

And they will decide on the record of our war production and food production, unparalleled in all history, in spite of the doubts and sneers of those in high places who said it cannot be done.

They will decide on the record of the International Food Conference, of UNRRA, the Relief Organization, of the International Labor Conference, of the International Education Conference, of the International Monetary Conference.

And they will decide on the record written in the Atlantic Charter, at Casablanca, at Cairo, at Moscow and at Teheran.

We have made mistakes. Who has not?

Things have not always been perfect. Are they ever perfect in human affairs?

But the objective, the objective at home and abroad, has always been clear before us. Constantly we have made steady, sure progress toward that objective. The record is plain, plain and unmistakable as to that, a record for every one to read.

The greatest wartime President in our history, after a wartime election which he called "the most reliable indication of public purpose in this country," set a goal for the United States, a goal in terms as applicable today as they were in 1865, terms which the human mind cannot improve.

"* * * With firmness in the right, as God gives us to see the right, let us strive on to finish the work we are in, to bind up the nation's wounds, to care for him who shall have borne the battle, and for his widow, and his orphan, to do all which may achieve and cherish a just and lasting peace among ourselves, and with all nations."

CHANCELLOR ADOLF HITLER'S RADIO SPEECH AFTER ATTEMPT ON HIS LIFE

July 20, 1944 [1]

German men and women: I do not know how many times an attempt on my life has been planned and carried out. If I address you today I am doing so for two reasons: first, so that you shall hear my voice and know that I personally am unhurt and well and, second, so that you shall hear the details about a crime that has no equal in German history.

An extremely small clique of ambitious, unscrupulous and at the same time foolish, criminally stupid, officers hatched a plot to remove me and, together with me, virtually to exterminate the staff of the German High Command. The bomb that was placed by Col. Graf von Stauffenberg exploded two meters [slightly more than two yards] away from me on my right side. It wounded very seriously a number of my dear collaborators. One of them has died. I personally am entirely unhurt apart from negligible grazes, bruises or burns.

This I consider to be confirmation of the task given to me by Providence to continue in pursuit of the aim of my life, as I have done hitherto. For I may solemnly admit before the whole nation that since the day I moved into the Wilhelmstrasse I have been imbued with one thought only: to do my duty to the best of my knowledge and ability. Also since it became clear to me that war was inevitable and could no longer be postponed I lived practically only in work and worry throughout countless days and sleepless nights.

At an hour in which the German army is waging a very hard struggle there has appeared in Germany a very small group, similar to that in Italy, that believed that it could thrust a dagger into our back as it did in 1918. But this time they have made a very great mistake. The assertion of these usurpers that I was no longer alive is disproved at this moment, as I am talking to you, my dear German fellow-countrymen. The circle that comprises these usurpers is extremely small. It has nothing to do with the German armed forces, and particularly nothing with the German army.

It is a very small clique of criminal elements, which will now be exterminated quite mercilessly.

I order, therefore, at this moment that no civilian authority has to accept any order from an authority that these usurpers arrogantly assume. Secondly, that no military authority and no leader of troops and no soldier should obey any order by these usurpers; that on the contrary everyone is in duty bound either to arrest a person bearing or issuing such an order or to kill him immediately if he offers resistance.

To create order at last, I have appointed Reich Minister Himmler to be commander of the army at home. Into the General Staff I have called Colonel General Guderian to replace the chief of the General Staff, who had to retire for health reasons, and I have summoned another proved leader of the eastern front to be his assistant. In all other Reich authorities there is no change.

I am convinced that by stamping out this very small clique of traitors and

[1] New York Times.

conspirators we will now at last create that atmosphere in the rear, at home, that the fighting front needs, for it is impossible that in the front line hundreds of thousands and millions of honest men offer their utmost, while at home a very small clique of miserable, ambitious types constantly attempts to sabotage this.

This time we will settle accounts in such a manner as we National Socialists are wont.

I am convinced that every decent officer and every brave soldier will understand at this hour what fate would have overtaken Germany if the attempt today had succeeded. Only very few, perhaps, are capable of visualizing the consequences. I myself thank providence and the Lord, not because I have been spared—my life is only care and work for my people—I thank them that I shall be allowed in the future also to carry this burden and to carry on with my work to the best of my abilities, as I have to answer for it with my conscience and before my conscience.

Therefore every German, whoever he may be, has a duty (shouting) to counter these elements at once and with ruthless determination and either to arrest them at once or—should they offer resistance anywhere—to wipe them out at once. Apppropriate orders have been issued to all troops. They are being strictly carried out with the obedience typical of the German Army.

Once more I may greet with joy especially you, my old fighting comrades, now that I have been again spared a fate that did not contain horrors for me personally, but that would have brought horror over the German people. But we also see here a clear sign of providence that I must carry on with my work and that I shall carry on with it.

SPEECH BY GRAND ADMIRAL KARL DOENITZ

July 20, 1944 [1]

Men of the German Navy:
Sacred anger and unbounded fury is in us in face of the criminal attempt that was designed to take the life of our beloved Fuehrer. Providence has determined differently; she has guarded and protected our Fuehrer and thereby not abandoned our German fatherland in its fateful struggle.

A mad small clique of generals that has nothing in common with our brave Army has in cowardly disloyalty instigated this murder to commit a most base betrayal of the Fuehrer and the German people. If these rascals and henchmen of our enemies, whom they served with unprincipled, dastardly and false cleverness—in reality their stupidity is unlimited—believe that by removal of the Fuehrer they can free us from our hard but inexorable and fateful struggle, they do not see in their fearful and blind limitation that their criminal act would have thrown us into terrible chaos and would deliver us unarmed into the hands of our enemies. Extermination and enslavement of our men and hunger and unbelievable misery would be the consequences.

Unspeakable unhappiness would be the lot of our people—infinitely more cruel and more difficult than even the hardest days that the present war may entail.

We will get even with these traitors. The German Navy stands fast in

[1] *New York Times.*

allegiance to its oath and in well-tried loyalty to the Fuehrer. Our devotion to duty and readiness for battle are unconditional.

You will accept orders only from me as Commander in Chief of the German Navy and from your own military commanders so as to prevent any misleading by forged instructions. You will ruthlessly annihilate any person who should turn out to be a traitor.

Long live our Fuehrer, Adolf Hitler!

SPEECH BY REICHSMARSHAL HERMANN GOERING

July 20, 1944 [1]

Comrades of the Luftwaffe:

An incredible, mean attempt at murder was today committed against our Fuehrer by a colonel, Count Stauffenberg, acting on orders of a miserable clique of former generals who had to be chased from their posts for a leadership that was cowardly as it was incompetent.

The Fuehrer was saved miraculously by the working of an almighty Providence. These criminals are now trying to spread confusion among the troops by issuing false orders, be it as a new Government of the Reich or as usurpers.

I, therefore, have given the following order:

Colonel General Stumpf assumes on my order the leadership of all formations of the Luftwaffe inside Reich territory as commander in chief of the Luftwaffe of the Reich.

Only my and his orders are to be obeyed. When in doubt, confirm by telephone. Reich leader of the S.S. Himmler is, if requested, to be given every assistance by all commands of the Luftwaffe. Dispatch flights can be carried out only with my or his permission.

Officers and soldiers, whatever your rank, and also civilians: wherever these criminals appear or approach you and try to draw you into their contemptible plans, they are to be arrested at once and to be shot.

Where you yourselves are being employed for the extermination of these traitors you are to proceed ruthlessly. These are the self-same curs who tried to betray and sabotage the front. All officers who have abetted in these crimes have put themselves outside the pale of the nation, outside the army and outside all military honor, and outside their oath and loyalty.

Their extermination will give us new strength. Against this treason the Luftwaffe pits the loyalty that it has sworn and its ardent love to the Fuehrer and unreserved application of all its strength to victory.

Long live our Fuehrer, whom Almighty God has today blessed so manifestly!

JAPANESE (DOMEI) STATEMENT ON RESIGNATION OF TOJO CABINET

July 22, 1944 [2]

The Tojo Cabinet's resignation en bloc cannot be interpreted as a general retreat of Gen. Hideki Tojo's policies. As stated in the Board of Informa-

[1] *New York Times.*
[2] Office of War Information.

tion's anouncement, the Tojo Cabinet tendered its resignation in order to infuse (new) life into our people, and fully cope with the present war situation.

Insofar as its internal policies were concerned, the Tojo Cabinet had many policies which it was unable fully to translate into action. However, responsibility for it should not be placed upon Premier Tojo alone. Herein lies the cause of the Cabinet's wholesale resignation. At the outset, Premier Tojo attempted to remedy this defect through particular reorganization of the Cabinet, but the majority of opinion within and without the Cabinet favored the Cabinet's total resignation to give way to a new Cabinet which will carry out more (vigorously) the policies which the Tojo Cabinet tried its best to continue and enforce. Thereupon Premier Tojo altered his original intention and decided to (words missing).

Under these circumstances, there can be absolutely no material change in Japan's internal or external policies as a result of the Imperial command on Gen. Kuniaki Koiso and Admiral Mitsumasa Yonai to jointly form a new Cabinet. As to Japan's firm determination to prosecute the war to a successful consummation, it is superfluous to say that it remains immutable. The significance of the present change of Cabinet lies in the pronounced stress laid on vigorous translation into action of national policies. In this sense, the new Cabinet may be called a continuance of the Tojo Cabinet.

As a matter of fact, the new Cabinet includes such members of the Tojo Cabinet as Foreign Minister Mamoru Shigemitsu, Finance Minister Sotaro Ishiwata, and Minister Without Portfolio Ginjiro Fujiwara. Since Foreign Minister Mamoru Shigemitsu holds in the new Cabinet the concurrent post of Minister of Greater East Asiatic Affairs, he will enhance his position as the driving force of Japan's foreign policy and strive his utmost to materialize Japan's policies for enabling all nations to (coerce) and co-prosperity. That he who drafted the Greater East Asia Joint Declaration occupies such important key posts in the new Cabinet attests to the fact that Japan's foreign policies remain unchanged despite the change in Cabinet.

Reappointment of Sotaro Ishiwata to the post of Finance Minister means that, insofar as the finnancial policies of the new Cabinet are concerned, the policies of the Tojo Cabinet will be followed. Since Ginjiro Fujiwara served in the Tojo Cabinet as Minister Without Portfolio and conducted a number of administrative inspections of war plants, his appointment to the post of Munitions Minister in the new Cabinet signifies that the war production policies of the Tojo Cabinet will be more vigorously enforced under his direction.

Moreover, those who know how much former Premier Tojo cooperated during the course of the three days of Cabinet formation in order to facilitate its formation as early as possible, fully recognize the strong close tie between the Tojo Cabinet and the Koiso-Yonai coalition Cabinet.

OFFICIAL JAPANESE STATEMENT ON THE FOREIGN POLICY OF THE NEW KOISO GOVERNMENT

July 22, 1944 [1]

Katsuo Okazaki, Spokesman of the Foreign Office, declared in a press interview today that Mamoru Shigemitsu's reappointment as Foreign Minister

[1] Office of War Information.

in the new Cabinet and his concurrent assumption of the portfolio of Greater East Asiatic Affairs, are the most conclusive indication that Japan's foreign policy, in general, and East Asiastic, in particular, will remain absolutely unchanged under the new Government headed by Gen. Kuniaki Koiso.

He declared that the fact that Shigemitsu remained as Foreign Minister in the new Cabinet should be taken as a clear cut indication of the line of foreign policy that will be pursued by Premier Koiso's Government. Namely, the policy looking to further strengthening of close relations between Japan, Germany, and other Allies, with a view to successful prosecution of the current war in close cooperation with these friendly powers; while toward Japan's neighboring countries and neutral powers, the policy of friendship and good neighborliness, which Shigemitsu clarified before the recent 84th session of the Japanese Diet, will be vigorously propelled.

Meanwhile, authoritative quarters disclosed that complete agreement of views was reached between Shigemitsu. Yamamoto lengthily conferred with Shigemitsu immediately after the latter's appointment as Minister of Greater East Asiatic Affairs concurrently as Foreign Minister. According to the same quarters, Yamamoto is expected to be largely responsible for the execution of Shigemitsu's administrative duties as Minister of Greater East Asiatic Affairs.

It was understood that in the course of today's (July 22) conference between Shigemitsu and Yamamoto, they discussed general outlines of the Ministry's policy which is fundamentally based on the Joint Declaration of Greater East Asiatic Nations and also examined the continental policy, as well as programs for the Southern Regions, to be pursued under the new Minister.

Their conference ended in complete agreement on views of these lines of policy. These quarters also revealed that both Shigemitsu and Yamamoto agreed that one of the Ministry's important policies is to lay special stress on strengthening the network of communications and transportation lines covering the whole area of Greater East Asia, with particular emphasis on that linking the Japanese mainland and the continent.

SECRETARY OF THE TREASURY MORGENTHAU'S FINAL ADDRESS AT THE UNITED NATIONS MONETARY AND FINANCIAL CONFERENCE AT BRETTON WOODS

July 22, 1944 [1]

I am gratified to announce that the Conference at Bretton Woods has successfully completed the task before it.

It was, as we knew when we began, a difficult task, involving complicated technical problems. We came here to work out methods which would do away with the economic evils—the competitive currency devaluation and destructive impediments to trade—which preceded the present war. We have succeeded in that effort.

The actual details of an international monetary and financial agreement may seem mysterious to the general public. Yet at the heart of it lie the most elementary bread-and-butter realities of daily life. What we have done here

[1] United Nations Monetary and Financial Conference news release.

in Bretton Woods is to devise machinery by which men and women everywhere can freely exchange, on a fair and stable basis, the goods which they produce through their labor. And we have taken the initial steps through which the nations of the world will be able to help one another in economic development to their mutual advantage and for the enrichment of all.

The representatives of the forty-four nations faced differences of opinion frankly and reached an agreement which is rooted in genuine understanding. None of the nations represented here has altogether had its own way. We have had to yield to one another not in respect to principles or essentials but in respect to methods and procedural details. The fact that we have done so, and that we have done it in a continuing spirit of good-will and mutual trust, is, I believe, one of the hopeful and heartening portents of our times. Here is a sign blazoned upon the horizon, written large upon the threshold of the future—a sign for men in battle, for men at work in mines and mills, and in the fields, and a sign for women whose hearts have been burdened and anxious lest the cancer of war assail yet another generation—a sign that the peoples of the earth are learning how to join hands and work in unity.

There is a curious notion that the protection of national interests and the development of international cooperation are conflicting philosophies—that somehow or other men of different nations cannot work together without sacrificing the interests of their particular nations. There has been talk of this sort—and from people who ought to know better—concerning the international cooperative nature of the undertaking just completed at Bretton Woods. I am perfectly certain that no delegation to this Conference has lost sight for a moment of the particular national interests it was sent here to represent. The American delegation, which I have had the honor of leading, has at all times been conscious of its primary obligation—the protection of American interests. And the other representatives here have been no less loyal or devoted to the welfare of their own people.

Yet none of us has found any incompatibility between devotion to our own countries and joint action. Indeed, we have found on the contrary that the only genuine safeguard for our national interests lies in international cooperation. We have come to recognize that the wisest and most effective way to protect our national interests is through international cooperation—that is to say, through united effort for the attainment of common goals. This has been the great lesson taught by the war and is, I think, the great lesson of contemporary life—that the peoples of the earth are inseparably linked to one another by a deep, underlying community of purpose. This community of purpose is no less real and vital in peace than in war, and cooperation is no less essential to its fulfilment.

To seek the achievement of our aims separately through the planless, senseless rivalry that divided us in the past, or through the outright economic aggression which turned neighbors into enemies, would be to invite ruin again upon us all. Worse, it would be once more to start our steps irretraceably down the steep, disastrous road to war. That sort of extreme nationalism belongs to an era that is dead. Today the only enlightened form of national self-interest lies in international accord. At Bretton Woods we have taken practical steps toward putting this lesson into practice in the monetary and economic field.

I take it as an axiom that after this war is ended no people—and therefore no government of the people—will again tolerate prolonged and wide-spread unemployment. A revival of international trade is indispensable if full employment is to be achieved in a peaceful world and with standards of living which will permit the realization of men's reasonable hopes.

What are the fundamental conditions under which commerce among the nations can once more flourish?

First, there must be a reasonably stable standard of international exchange to which all countries can adhere without sacrificing the freedom of action necessary to meet their internal economic problems.

This is the alternative to the desperate tactics of the past—competitive currency depreciation, excessive tariff barriers, uneconomic barter deals, multiple currency practices, and unnecessary exchange restrictions—by which governments vainly sought to maintain employment and uphold living standards. In the final analysis, these tactics only succeeded in contributing to world-wide depression and even war. The International Fund agreed upon at Bretton Woods will help remedy this situation.

Second, long-term financial aid must be made available at reasonable rates to those countries whose industry and agriculture have been destroyed by the ruthless torch of an invader or by the heroic scorched-earth policy of their defenders.

Long-term funds must be made available also to promote sound industry and increase industrial and agricultural production in nations whose economic potentialities have not yet been developed. It is essential to us all that these nations play their full part in the exchange of goods throughout the world.

They must be enabled to produce and to sell if they are to be able to purchase and consume. The Bank for International Reconstruction and Development is designed to meet this need.

Objections to this Bank have been raised by some bankers and a few economists. The institutions proposed by the Bretton Woods Conference would indeed limit the control which certain private bankers have in the past exercised over international finance. It would by no means restrict the investment sphere in which bankers could engage. On the contrary, it would greatly expand this sphere by enlarging the volume of international investment and would act as an enormously effective stabilizer and guarantor of loans which they might make. The chief purpose of the Bank for International Reconstruction and Development is to guarantee private loans made through the usual investment channels. It would make loans only when these could not be floated through the normal channels at reasonable rates. The effect would be to provide capital for those who need it at lower interest rates than in the past and to drive only the usurious money-lenders from the temple of international finance. For my own part I cannot look upon this outcome with any sense of dismay.

Capital, like any other commodity, should be free from monopoly control and available upon reasonable terms to those who will put it to use for the general welfare.

The delegates and technical staffs at Bretton Woods have completed their portion of the job. They sat down together, talked as friends, and perfected plans to cope with the international monetary and financial problems which all their countries face. These proposals now must be submitted to the legislatures and the peoples of the participating nations. They will pass upon what has been accomplished here.

The result will be of vital importance to everyone in every country. In the last analysis, it will help determine whether or not people have jobs and the amount of money they are to find in their weekly pay envelopes. More important still, it concerns the kind of world in which our children are to grow to maturity. It concerns the opportunities which will await millions of young men when at last they can take off their uniforms and come home and roll up their sleeves and go to work.

This monetary agreement is but one step, of course, in the broad program of international action necessary for the shaping of a free future. But it is an indispensable step and a vital test of our intentions.

Incidentally, tonight we had a dramatic demonstration of these intentions. Tonight the Soviet Government informed me, through Mr. Stepanov, chairman of its delegation here in Bretton Woods, that it has authorized an increase in its subscription to the International Bank for Reconstruction and Development to $1,200,000,000. This was done after a subscription of $900,000,000 had been agreed upon unanimously by the Conference. By this action, the Union of Soviet Socialist Republics is voluntarily taking a greatly increased responsibility for the success of this Bank in the post-war world. This is an indication of the true spirit of international cooperation demonstrated throughout this Conference.

We are at a crossroads, and we must go one way or the other. The Conference at Bretton Woods has erected a signpost—a signpost pointing down a highway broad enough for all men to walk in step and side by side. If they will set out together, there is nothing on earth that need stop them.

SECRETARY OF STATE HULL'S SUMMARY OF BRETTON WOODS AGREEMENTS

July 24, 1944 [1]

The successful completion of the important work of the Bretton Woods Conference is another step toward the goal of the United Nations and nations associated with them in the war for a peaceful, secure, and happy world in which all peace-loving nations will cooperate for their mutual benefit. Once again these nations have met and discussed in a most friendly spirit problems vital to the economic security of each and every one of us. The faith expressed in my address to Congress on the Moscow Conference has never diminished. I was therefore not surprised by the splendid cooperation of the U.S.S.R. and all the other countries in the work of the Conference and by their willingness to contribute to its success. The results of the Bretton Woods Conference are another demonstration of the fact that the nations which love peace are working together, every day and every hour, without fanfare or drums, to provide opportunities and create facilities for the attainment by all of an increasing measure of security and prosperity.

SUMMARY OF AGREEMENTS [2]

This Conference at Bretton Woods, representing nearly all the peoples of the world, has considered matters of international money and finance which are important for peace and prosperity. The Conference has agreed on the problems needing attention, the measures which should be taken, and the forms of international cooperation or organization which are required. The

[1] State Department Bulletin.
[2] Annex C of the Final Act.

agreement reached on these large and complex matters is without precedent in the history of international economic relations.

I. *The International Monetary Fund*

Since foreign trade affects the standard of life of every people, all countries have a vital interest in the system of exchange of national currencies and the regulations and conditions which govern its working. Because these monetary transactions are international exchanges, the nations must agree on the basic rules which govern the exchanges if the system is to work smoothly. When they do not agree, and when single nations and small groups of nations attempt by special and different regulations of the foreign exchanges to gain trade advantages, the result is instability, a reduced volume of foreign trade, and damage to national economies. This course of action is likely to lead to economic warfare and to endanger the world's peace.

The Conference has therefore agreed that broad international action is necessary to maintain an international monetary system which will promote foreign trade. The nations should consult and agree on international monetary changes which affect each other. They should outlaw practices which are agreed to be harmful to world prosperity, and they should assist each other to overcome short-term exchange difficulties.

The Conference has agreed that the nations here represented should establish for these purposes a permanent international body, *The International Monetary Fund*, with powers and resources adequate to perform the tasks assigned to it. Agreement has been reached concerning these powers and resources and the additional obligations which the member countries should undertake. Draft Articles of Agreement on these points have been prepared.

II. *The International Bank for Reconstruction and Development*

It is in the interest of all nations that post-war reconstruction should be rapid. Likewise, the development of the resources of particular regions is in the general economic interest. Programs of reconstruction and development will speed economic progress everywhere, will aid political stability and foster peace.

The Conference has agreed that expanded international investment is essential to provide a portion of the capital necessary for reconstruction and development.

The Conference has further agreed that the nations should cooperate to increase the volume of foreign investment for these purposes, made through normal business channels. It is especially important that the nations should cooperate to share the risks of such foreign investment, since the benefits are general.

The Conference has agreed that the nations should establish a permanent international body to perform these functions, to be called *The International Bank for Reconstruction and Development*. It has been agreed that the Bank should assist in providing capital through normal channels at reasonable rates of interest and for long periods for projects which will raise the productivity of the borrowing country. There is agreement that the Bank should guarantee loans made by others and that through their subscriptions of capital all countries should share with the borrowing country in guaranteeing such loans. The Conference has agreed on the powers and resources which the Bank must have and on the obligations which the member countries must assume, and has prepared draft Articles of Agreement accordingly.

The Conference has recommended that in carrying out the policies of the institutions here proposed special consideration should be given to the needs of countries which have suffered from enemy occupation and hostilities.

The proposals formulated at the Conference for the establishment of the Fund and the Bank are now submitted, in accordance with the terms of the invitation, for consideration of the governments and people of the countries represented.

STATEMENT ON THE SOVIET UNION'S RELATIONS WITH POLAND

July 25, 1944 [1]

The People's Commissariat of Foreign Affairs of the USSR has been entrusted by the Soviet Government to make the following statement:

The Red Army, successfully advancing, has reached the State frontier between the Soviet Union and Poland.

Pursuing the retreating German armies, Soviet troops, together with the Polish Army operating on the Soviet-German front, have crossed the Western Bug River, have crossed the Soviet-Polish frontier and have entered the limits of Poland. Thus a beginning of the liberation of our long-suffering brother Polish people from German occupation has been made.

Soviet troops have entered the limits of Poland filled with one determination: to rout the enemy German armies and to help the Polish people in the task of its liberation from the yoke of the German invaders and of the restoration of an independent, strong and democratic Poland.

The Soviet Government declares that it considers the military operations of the Red Army on the territory of Poland as operations on the territory of a sovereign, friendly, allied state. In connection with this, the Soviet Government does not intend to establish on the territory of Poland organs of its own administration, considering this the task of the Polish people.

It has decided, in view of this, to conclude with the Polish Committee of National Liberation an agreement on relations between the Soviet Command and the Polish Administration.

The Soviet Government declares that it does not pursue aims of acquiring any part of Polish territory or of a change of social structure in Poland, and that the military operations of the Red Army on the territory of Poland are dictated solely by military necessity and by the striving to render the friendly Polish people aid in its liberation from German occupation.

The Soviet Government expresses its firm confidence that the fraternal people of the USSR and Poland will jointly bring to a conclusion the struggle of liberation against the German invaders and will lay a firm foundation for friendly Soviet-Polish collaboration.

[1] Information Bulletin, Embassy of the U.S.S.R.

SPEECH BY GENERAL CHARLES DE GAULLE BEFORE
THE FRENCH PROVISIONAL CONSULTATIVE
ASSEMBLY ON THE FUTURE
OF FRANCE

July 25, 1944 [1]

Gentlemen: After years of indescribable trials, no one can any longer doubt that we are making huge strides toward victory. Such has been the course of events that for France, as for the other European nations overwhelmed by the tide of German invasion, liberation, for so long a time no more than a dream of indomitable hope, is today an impending realization. Liberation has indeed begun on a small portion of Metropolitan territory. Today, therefore, our country is no longer in that period when, as you know, we could but treat vast problems as eventualities, but well on in that phase when these problems must be progressively and effectively solved. The destiny of the nation depends, literally, on the manner in which she solves these problems, on the spirit in which she solves them, on the order she produces. This shows the magnitude of the task devolving upon the government, one which is, I believe, without precedent in our history.

I shall outline to the Assembly the policy the Government plans to follow to accomplish its task as liberation proceeds. In so doing I believe I shall answer the questions and suggestions raised by the speakers who participated in this great debate. Although the various aspects of this policy are obviously interrelated, for the sake of clarity I shall treat them in order. In doing this I shall indicate the course we are following and shall continue to follow with respect to the war effort, with respect to internal reorganization of the country, and lastly with respect to her place and role in the world.

More than ever the Government is convinced that the conflict must be definitely settled by force of arms, and that despite the plight into which invasion and treason have thrown our country, it is vitally important that France participate in the great battle of Europe with all the forces at her command. It is no less important that the role played by our forces be a truly French role. And finally it is essential that all our efforts, whether within or without the country constitute a whole, a single collected effort of the nation under the sole authority of the State.

For geographical reasons the western powers have had to divide their operations in Europe between two theaters, that of the north and that of the Mediterranean. The Government felt that it was best to concentrate the main effort of our armies in the Mediterranean. This was done not only for practical reasons, for most of our combat units originated in Africa, but also for reasons of national interest. It is indeed fitting that French military power, largely constrained within the Empire by a temporary defeat in Europe and in Metropolitan France, wage battles from the Empire for the liberation of France and Europe. In this regard, it must be emphasized that the French military effort, since the tragic days of June, 1940, has been uninterrupted. Our participation in the battles of Tunisia, Italy, as well as the liberation of our Corsica by ourselves and the conquest of the Isle of Elba by our troops, were nothing more than the extension by ever increasing means of what we did before in Eritrea, in Libya and in the Fezzan. Since the so-called armistice

[1] French Press and Information Service.

signed by the men of Vichy, the French Forces fighting outside Metropolitan France have lost under enemy fire a total of 61,000 casualties in killed, wounded and missing. They have taken prisoner close to 100,000 enemy soldiers. It is worth emphasizing that despite incredible misfortunes, the constant activity of France has been maintained, and shall be maintained, in the military as in other domains.

Now, therefore, we are exerting our main efforts in the Mediterranean theater. This policy has led us to participate extensively, and, I believe, gloriously, in the battle of Italy. It is true that because of this, the participation of our Forces of the Interior in the battle of Normandy has thus far, been limited to the brilliant and effective action of certain air and naval forces and some landing and airborne elements. I can guarantee, without mentioning any date or route of course, that the liberation of our Metropolitan territory shall be accomplished with the combined efforts of all French Forces of land, sea and air equipped to fight on modern battlefields. That is the very principle of our co-operation with our Allies. May I add that just as was done in the recent operations in Italy, the strategic plans for the battle of France were made known to the French Government and High Command in good time, that the participation of the French Forces was decided upon in agreement with us, and that our appropriate staff officers regularly take part in the preparation of plans for the use of inter-Allied forces which include our own. Without in any way questioning the unity of command to which we have agreed, and considering the relative strength of troops and matériel of the United States, Great Britain and France, now in action, the Government can state that our military effort is directed toward the service of national interests. And this is, moreover, the best practical way of serving the military interests of the coalition.

Nothing could be a better illustration of this principle than the powerful action being carried on at present by our Forces of the Interior to aid in the common battle. Moreover, we are pleased to note that the Inter-Allied High Command recognized the value of this action as soon as its importance in co-ordinated operations became clear. The result has been that our Forces of the Interior have been somewhat better supplied with arms. The Assembly will be glad to hear that the amount of equipment received by the Forces of the Interior during June and July was seven times as much as in the best month before the battle of France began.

I must also tell you that, at the same time, the number of men who have been, or could be engaged, has more than tripled in the last three months, and at present amounts to several hundred thousand men of whom only a third are provided with suitable arms. This shows how much still remains to be done in order to equip these Forces, and also what an extremely important part they are capable of playing during later operations if we judge by what they have already accomplished.

You will all understand that the mobile and scattered nature of the fight waged by our Forces of the Interior prohibits the use of ordinary methods of command. It is obvious that directives must be given mainly on a local scale. The initial impulse which is provided, of course, by the Government and the organizations responsible within the system of the Inter-Allied Command, consists in outlining a general plan to be observed by the FFI according to the ways in which the various phases of the battle develop, and the opportunities provided for setting them certain principal objectives; in organizing relief and communications, in stimulating the initiative of various groups and their leaders, and keeping them informed. In this way during the first phase marked by the Allies' landing and the establishment of a bridgehead on the Saint-Lô-Caen line, instructions were given to the FFI through contacts previously established, to cut enemy communications at designated centers and advanced points and to attack isolated enemy units in all regions, either in their camps or on the highways, without being drawn into large scale or prolonged engagements.

At the same time, the FFI, while continuing the fight, had to complete their organization arrangements in view of the increasing numbers of men who were joining them, the weapons delivered to them, the arrival of specially trained officers, and the supplies sent them from outside.

Gentlemen, the results already obtained have been all that the Government expected and much greater than certain experts had hoped for. It is literally true that since the beginning of June the entire network of railroad communications in France has been, and remains, disrupted by our forces, and that through this the arrival of certain detachments of German reserve troops has been seriously delayed, sometimes for more than a week, as in the case of the "Das Reich" Division which was mentioned a little while ago. Besides this, certain areas, sometimes entire departments, were at times completely in the hands of French Forces operating in the open. This happened in Ain, Drôme, Ardêche, Aveyron, Dordogne, Isère, the Hautes-Alpes, the Basses-Alpes, Vaucluse, the Haute-Loire, Corrèze, Cantal, Creuse, Haute-Vienne, Lot, the Hautes- Pyrénées, Haute-Garonne, Bretagne intérieure, Vosges, Vienne, and Franche-Comté. The enemy in the Vercors, Ain, Ardèche, Savoie, Dauphinè and Haute-Provence has had to start powerful military offensives to try to re-establish his hold there. At this very moment he is attacking the Vercors Massif with considerable forces, tank troops supported by several planes. According to indisputable reports, the Germans have already lost in this fight, at least eight thousand men, more than two thousand prisoners and great quantities of matériel.

The Germans have been compelled to use the equivalent of at least seven or eight divisions against our Forces on French soil. In spite of the savage cruelty with which they treat the defenseless populations, they have not yet succeeded in gaining control of the situation.

We have reason to believe that such losses and difficulties will continue and multiply as a result of our attacks being gradually intensified, and of the increasing sabotage of everything the enemy uses, through strikes in factories working for them, and finally because of thousands of small hostile acts that are occurring daily in every corner of our towns and countrysides, and which all contribute to lessen German power and break down German morale. France knows that this type of warfare has to be paid for in human lives and material destruction. The Government has to see that losses are kept as far as possible proportionate to results. But it also has to act in such a way that the enemy will remember for generations how much it cost to invade the land of our fathers. That is why I give my word that our effort inside France will grow ever greater as an essential contribution to the liberation of the country, until the day of a general revolt when the whole nation will rise under the leadership of the Government of the Republic, and together with its own and the Allied Armies, will act so that the only Germans left on French soil will be imprisoned or dead.

But as the zones of our territory emerge from the smoke of battle and the darkness of oppression we can see the problems that accompany national restoration. Our task shall be multifold: to re-establish the State, to feed the nation, and to establish favorable conditions for thorough reforms which will be the basis of the restoration of France. This task will have to be accomplished under the most difficult conditions. We do not hesitate to state in advance that many measures that we shall adopt, just as many that we have already adopted, cannot always be completely satisfactory to everyone. Before going any further, let me say that we expect perfection neither in men nor in things. If there were time, I would undertake now to draw up a list of probable criticisms that could be made as re-establishment progresses, but I feel that such a list would fill several dictionaries. Despite all the obstacles and deficiencies already met, and those that still have to be met, the Government is confident of its ability to complete its task in the service of the nation, because it has established its aims and its procedure, and because it is assured of the fervent and reasoned co-operation of the huge mass of the French people, to the very end.

I said re-establish the State. We have chosen a policy. We have chosen democracy and the republic. The right of free speech shall be returned to the people; in other words, we must establish, as soon as possible, the liberty, order and dignity essential to a National Popular Election, which will give us our great Constituent Assembly. This is our aim. In the meantime, however, we shall continue in accordance with our decision; in other words, a more representative Consultative Assembly shall meet, and later on if the occasion arises, an elected Representative Assembly, in order that the Government be kept informed as thoroughly as possible on public opinion. Moreover, we shall proceed with reorganization, then the re-election of Councils General, and of Municipal Councils whose role is absolutely essential during this period of confusion.

We must also restore the justice of the State and place under its equitable jurisdiction those who betrayed our country. And finally we must restore both in the Government and locally, the French Administration without whose labors and devotion there will be nothing but disorder and confusion.

On this question I must tell you that if the Government expects to proceed in Metropolitan France as it has elsewhere, with necessary dismissals; if it intends to draw or is already drawing replacements from among the very able organizations of the Resistance; if it wants to put into effect certain reforms which are essential in a selection of several if not of all categories of officials, it has no intention whatsoever of suddenly dismissing the great majority of State officials most of whom during the terrible years of occupation and usurpation, did try as best they could to serve the public cause. Disparagement of such and such members and of such and such categories of the French Governmental service is easy, but all too often unjust and exaggerated. Moreover the public officials have assistants worthy of them and it is by themselves giving the example of competence, disinterestedness and a sense of responsibility that public officials are more likely to be served as they should be.

The staunchness of public officials from the highest to the lowest positions in the State is the more important as we find ourselves suddenly confronted with serious problems concerning the very existence of the Nation. A country in ruins, deprived by losses in battle, by imprisonment in Germany, and by mobilization of a great portion of her active citizens, pillaged of all her food stocks and raw materials, stripped of transportation facilities and industrial and agricultural equipment, undermined in health, inevitably taxed by the help given the Allied Armies now on her soil, that is what victorious France will be at first.

In agreement with the Assembly, the Government has outlined in advance a course of action to re-establish and maintain activity in the Nation's arteries and at the same time strictly to regulate production, consumption and distribution, in order to provide the proper conditions for our renaissance. By rationing, price control, monetary control, import and export control, credit control, fixing the salaries at reasonable, certainly more equitable levels, but without any upheaval, without permitting inflation or the disappearance of commodities, the Government expects to achieve a situation in which production and the development of foreign trade will have reached a level at which supply meets demand. Meanwhile, the co-operation of our Allies, especially that of the Americans, has been agreed upon and the assistance provided by our overseas territory will help us cope with these great difficulties. But I must reiterate that liberation will not bring an immediate state of well being. However, I am convinced that the great French people is fully aware of this and that it is resolved steadfastly to support the burdens of the present, in order to establish at the earliest moment and for a long future its domestic harmony, its economic strength, and its social welfare.

In the last analysis there is a broader problem. If, on rising from the abyss we were shamefully to restore the failings which weakened, divided, and demoralized us, or if we were to allow ourselves to tumble into ruinous upheavals, it will indeed have been in vain that we exerted this extraordinary effort which has brought us to the portals of liberty and grandeur. No! No! No! The French Nation has decided on the course of her restoration. Clearly the great reforms which will give France her new élan especially with respect to her democracy, her economic activity, her social structure and the manner of association of the peoples linked to her destiny, cannot and must not be achieved save by the Nation itself. In other words, by the representatives we will have freely chosen. But it is the duty of the Government to take measures which are in a sense measures of conservation, without which certain established abuses would, if accepted by us become strong enough to prevent the accomplishment of certain necessary reforms. By the use of sequestration and requisition, the law gives us the means necessary to place at the disposition of the Nation the great sources of national wealth and to prevent the intrigue of those great combinations which overburdened the State and citizens. At the same time we shall have to take up the great problem of the birth rate and of public health which is for France—and this must be clear to all—a question of life or death.

Gentlemen, if no nation can henceforth live isolated in a world where distances are reduced, France, geographically, intellectually and morally is and will remain the least isolated of all. It follows, then, that the future of humanity will largely depend upon the attitude she adopts toward others, and theirs in regard to her. When we say that our foreign policy is aimed at restoring France to her place in the world in conditions that will allow her to maintain it, we are convinced that we are serving the interests of a great number of men as well as of our own country. I may add that we are strengthened in this opinion by realization of what the invasion of France by the enemy has cost the camp of Liberty strategically and politically, or the stupefaction and terror that the possibility of her disappearance caused in every continent, and finally of the vibrant enthusiasm aroused in the masses by the proof of her reappearance. Therefore, the French Government clearly states its policy which consists in maintaining French sovereignty intact everywhere that it is legally exercised; in obtaining for our country real conditions of security, for lack of which three invasions in the space of one man's lifetime, have almost destroyed her; in playing a part in the forefront of the reorganization of Europe, and finally, in participating in the first rank of international co-operation.

The visits I had occasion to make to Great Britain last month, and recently to the United States were for our part primarily intended as a tribute from France to these two great and valiant Allies, whose magnificent war effort will have counted so much toward a joint victory and the liberation of our own country. These visits were also meant on both sides as an opportunity to settle our mutual relationship, to clarify the situation and, in this way serve the common interests of the democracies. I had the most comprehensive and frankest conversations with members of His Majesty's Government. There is a distinct community of European and world interests between Britain and ourselves that can never again be disunited by any outdated rivalry in any part of the world. There is an identity of ideals and an instinctive and reasoned friendliness between the United States and ourselves, which ought, in my opinion to be essential factors in the work of joint reorganization of the world. I add that the very friendly attitudes adopted toward us since a long time by Marshal Stalin and the Government of the Soviet Union whose gigantic part in the war will have made it of capital importance in the peace, gives us grounds to hope that France and Russia will soon be able to settle between them what their methods of close collaboration shall be. Upon this, there rests, I believe, the future security and balance of Europe.

I cannot omit speaking of the audience granted me by His Holiness Pope Pius XII. I cannot omit mentioning the most cordial conversations I had in London with the Chiefs of State or of the Governments of the Netherlands, Belgium, Luxembourg, Poland, Czechoslovakia, Norway, as well as the extremely cordial welcome given me by the Government and the people of Canada. I cannot neglect to say that our relations with Marshal Chiang Kai-shek and the Chinese Government so invaluable to us, have become completely normal. How many European States, enlightened by trial, are prepared to accept France for what she is worth, and by that I mean a natural friend, particularly understanding, disinterested, equipped by the experience of a thousand years to evaluate and support a state of stability in the old continent as well as in the world!

The indisputable improvement of France's international position will be marked very soon, we hope, by the conclusion of practical agreements with London and Washington concerning the co-operation in liberated Metropolitan territory between French Governmental agencies and the Allied Armies which has so long been a subject of controversy. As is essential, this accord will assure full respect for both the sovereignty of France and the authority of her Government and for the recognized right of the High Command to receive from us all possible co-operation and facilities it may require, in order to lead the brave soldiers of our Allies, as well as our own, to victory.

In the interest of all we hope that such an accord will mark the beginning of better organized co-operation between our Allies and ourselves. This is all the more urgent because questions absolutely vital to us may arise at any moment such as the armistice to be imposed on conquered Germany, which will contain the seed of her destiny and consequently of ours.

To achieve the future she desires, France will still have to fight bitter battles, accept hard sacrifices, exert a vast effort. The enemy is tottering. It remains to crush him. Whatever aspect Germany may assume we can have no assurance unless she has been completely and irredeemably beaten. Therefore, let us redouble our efforts side by side with all our dear and valiant Allies! Let us direct our thoughts and our confidences toward our armies, within and without the country, burning to unite in the decisive battle. Let us be steadfast, firm and united! All together, let us in fraternity draw from our great trials, great lessons and great plans.

It is for us to make a new glory out of that tempest that almost carried France away.

HITLER'S "TOTAL WAR" DECREE TO THE GERMAN PEOPLE

July 25, 1944 [1]

Fuehrer's headquarters: On July 25, 1944, the Fuehrer has issued a decree on total war for the area of the Greater German Reich and, accordingly, for the incorporated and occupied territories. The essential regulations have the following text:

The war situation makes incumbent the exhaustive use of all resources for the armed forces and armament. Therefore I decree:

1. Reich Marshal Hermann Goering, President of the Ministerial Council for Reich Defense, is to adapt the whole of public life to the requirements of total war in every respect. To carry out this task he will propose to me a "Reich Plenipotentiary for Total War."

2. The plenipotentiary will be specially charged with seeing that all public acts are in accordance with the aims of total war and in no way keep manpower from the armed forces and armaments.

He is to examine the entire State organization, including Reich railways, Reich post and all public institutes, organizations and enterprises with the aim of releasing the maximum of manpower for the armed forces and armaments by complete rational employment of men and means, by closing down or restricting the tasks of lesser importance to the war, and by simplifying their organization and their procedure. For this purpose he can demand information from supreme Reich authorities and can issue instructions to them.

Legal instructions by competent supreme Reich authorities and fundamental administrative instructions will be issued in agreement with the Reich Minister and chief of the Reich chancellery, the head of the party chancellery and the delegate general for Reich administration.

The head of the party chancellery will actively support measures decreed by me by directing the party effort according to the full powers given him.

By reason of this decree, the Fuehrer, acting on the recommendation of Reich Marshal Hermann Goering, chairman of the Ministerial Council for Reich Defense, has appointed Reich Minister Dr. Goebbels to be "Reich Plenipotentiary for the Total War Effort."

[1] *New York Times.*

STATEMENT BY THE STATE DEPARTMENT ON THE NON-RECOGNITION OF THE ARGENTINE REGIME

July 26, 1944 [1]

I. *The Basic Issues*

1. The American republics jointly with all of the United Nations are engaged in a war of unprecedented magnitude for the protection and preservation of the liberties of each and all of them against the most powerful aggressors in history. In this war the United States has over eleven million of its own men under arms. Our men are fighting the enemy on every battle-front in the world, and tens of thousands of them will never return to partake of the privileges of that liberty for which they are now fighting. For generations to come our people will be called upon to discharge a debt of over two hundred billion dollars which represents our material contribution to the defeat of the enemy. To this common cause all but one of the American nations have been giving full and wholehearted support.

2. At this most critical moment in the history of the American republics, the Government of one great Republic, Argentina, has seen fit to take two steps which have resulted in tremendous injury to the Allied cause, to wit: (1) it has deliberately violated the pledge taken jointly with its sister republics to cooperate in support of the war against the Axis powers, and in thus deserting the Allied cause has struck a powerful blow at the whole system of hemispheric cooperation; (2) it has openly and notoriously been giving affirmative assistance to the declared enemies of the United Nations.

3. These are the fundamental issues which are now brought to a head by the actions of the present regime in Argentina. They relate immediately to the prosecution of the war. The enemies of American cooperation and the friends of Axis aggression would of course wish, and are indeed recommending, that the Argentine course of action be approved by the American republics through the establishment of full and normal relations with the Farrell regime. This would have the effect of a public proclamation of complete approval of the Argentine action. For the American republics to take such a course would be seriously to damage the Allied cause and to undermine the principles which the united organization of the nations of this hemisphere has been resolutely supporting in the war against the Axis powers. The free republics of America are honor-bound to preserve the integrity of those principles and that organization, and to do so they must stand firm in their common fight against the Axis enemy.

II. *Multilateral Agreements of the American Republics for the Defense of the Hemisphere*

During the eight years prior to Pearl Harbor the American republics devoted their best efforts to perfect and strengthen the system of inter-American cooperation, so that if the wave of world aggression should reach this hemisphere they would be ready to act together for the common defense of their heritage. Great progress was achieved and a spirit of solidarity and unity was developed which justified the hope that any external threat to the

[1] State Department Bulletin.

peace and security of the hemisphere would meet a common and united resistance.

At the Eighth International Conference of American States in Lima in 1938 the American governments reaffirmed their solidarity and proclaimed their intention to make that solidarity effective in the event that the peace, security, or territorial integrity of any American nation were threatened. By so doing they provided the spiritual foundation for the belief that in the event of aggression, the supreme test of unity would be fully met by each one of the twenty-one republics. The Meeting of Foreign Ministers of the American Republics at Panamá in 1939, upon the outbreak of war in Europe, was animated by the same spirit. Immediately following the occupation of France by Germany, the determination of the American republics to maintain their solidarity and unity of action in the face of the threatened spread of Axis aggression to this hemisphere was unanimously proclaimed by the Foreign Ministers at Habana in July 1940 in the solemn pledge:

"That any attempt on the part of a non-American State against the integrity or inviolability of the territory, the sovereignty or the political independence of an American State shall be considered as an act of aggression against the States which sign this declaration."

On the binding bases for continental defense thus established, the American Foreign Ministers, meeting at Rio de Janeiro in January 1942, after Axis aggression had reached this hemisphere, were enabled quickly to agree on uniform measures to be taken by each nation in the political, economic, and military fields for the collective security of all of them. The measures adopted at Rio provided for an integrated total defense against the total attack of the Axis aggressors.

Firm adherence to the principles of these inter-American agreements by all of the republics would have created an unshakable tradition of hemispheric unity the benefits of which would have been felt for generations to come by all of our peoples. But when the real test came, the Government of one of those republics, Argentina, chose to pursue a divergent and separate course. The fact that even the most urgent considerations of the national security and independence of each of the American republics, including Argentina itself, have not influenced the Argentine Government to practice unity in time of war, completely invalidates any suggestion that the other American governments should recognize it on the assumption that such action would contribute to hemispheric unity after the war.

Efforts have been made to confuse the issue by charging that the policy followed by the American republics and their associates among the United Nations constitutes a departure from the normal rules and procedure with regard to recognition and amounts to intervention in the internal affairs of Argentina. This contention disregards completely the foundation on which the policy of non-recognition rests, namely, the defense and security of the hemisphere. Furthermore, it overlooks the fact that this policy was adopted after full and free consultation among the American republics and that it is the logical outgrowth of the multilateral agreements which all of them accepted in order to make that defense effective. The American republics have expressly declared that this policy does not affect, and has nothing to do with, the ordinary rules and procedure for recognition in time of peace. The problem involves the fundamental question of whether the American republics are to endorse the action of one republic which has undermined their unity and strength and given aid to the Axis enemy. It is not, as has sometimes been asserted, merely a question of relations between the United States and Argentina.

III. *Developments During Four Months Between Overthrow of Ramírez Government and Recall of Ambassador Armour*

The government of General Ramírez announced the break of relations with Germany and Japan on January 26, 1944. It based its action on the criminal espionage activities which it declared were directly chargeable to the Axis governments and which, it asserted, "infringe the national sovereignty, compromise the foreign policy of this Government, and threaten the security of the continent." Repeated assurances were given by President Ramírez, the Foreign Minister, General Gilbert, and other responsible members of the Argentine Government, in public statements as well as private conversations, that immediate, energetic measures would be taken to suppress subversive Axis activities and in other ways to give effect to the severance of relations. Very soon, however, it became clear that powerful forces within the Government were determined to oppose those measures and render the break valueless. General Gilbert, who had played a leading role in the decision to break relations and the efforts thereafter to implement it, resigned as Foreign Minister on February 15. Ten days later General Ramírez "delegated" his authority as President to General Farrell and a few days thereafter submitted his resignation.

In view of these sudden developments nearly all of the American governments determined to abstain from normal relations with the Farrell regime in order to ascertain the reasons for this change and the attitude of the new regime toward the Axis. It has since been established that extremist, pro-Axis elements were responsible for the elimination of General Ramírez and his principal collaborators from the Government because of their decision to break relations.

The Farrell government firmly refused to commit itself to implementation of the break with the Axis. It implicitly disavowed any intention to honor the rupture with the Axis by insisting repeatedly that it was due to foreign pressure.

This attitude was confirmed by its actions. The freedom of the country was extended to Axis diplomatic and consular officers. Affirmative assistance was given to Axis firms, both through large official contracts and through requisitioning of critical materials from firms friendly to the democratic cause. Immediately following the break of relations police activity and arrests of Axis agents were briefly stimulated by the Ramírez government, but under the new regime numerous Axis spies and agents were set at liberty. As a result Axis espionage again flourished. Such pro-Axis newspapers as *El Federal, Cabildo,* and *La Fronda* enjoyed governmental support and assistance in obtaining newsprint and carried on a bitter propaganda campaign against the United Nations and on behalf of the Axis. A commentary by *La Fronda* on the Allied landings in France exemplified this propaganda:

"It is most comforting that all the peoples of the Continent are closely grouped under the brilliant leadership of Hitler, who has been supernaturally transformed by developments into . . . more than an intrepid defender of Germany, he is the defender of Europe."

Nevertheless, from time to time certain elements in the Farrell government professed a desire to see the rupture implemented. Were such an attempt to be made, however, these same elements admitted that they would be eliminated as were Ramírez and Gilbert by the extremist forces within the Government. That the dominant power in Argentina was, and continues to be, in the hands of pro-Axis elements determined to impose their desires is strikingly revealed by this situation. Furthermore, it is significant that these same elements control the most important ministries and agencies of the National Government as well as the governments of the provinces and have rapidly and energetically implanted a domestic totalitarian system that fully complements and supports their pro-Axis foreign policy, through control of the press, the courts, the schools, and other key institutions. The basic civil rights have been either nullified or so modified as to have no real meaning. Every effort was made to stamp out democratic opposition to the Government's totalitarian program. A striking demonstration of the nature of this program was afforded in the declarations of the Minister of War on June 10 when he said that military re-armament is the objective to which the entire economy of the country and the life of all of its people must be dedicated. The Minister admitted in so many words that the keystone of Argentina's international policy is to be military force, when he stated that in addition to the use of diplomacy to achieve political objectives it possessed the power of its armed forces.

Shortly after the Farrell regime came into power various of its members undertook to arrange interviews with members of the diplomatic corps in Buenos Aires through intermediaries. Ambassador Armour participated in two informal discussions of this kind, one with the Foreign Minister and the other with the Ministers of Foreign Relations, War and Navy. The Ambassador reported to this Department, and likewise informed his colleagues of the American diplomatic corps, that little or nothing was accomplished at either meeting, since the Foreign Minister insisted that recognition be accorded before implementation of the break with the Axis on the basis of Argentine promises of future action. Ambassador Armour was recalled, and a full statement of this Government's position was transmitted to the other American republics and to the Government of Great Britain on June 22.

IV. *Developments Since the Recall of Ambassador Armour*

We have reexamined the entire Argentine situation in the light of developments since our recall of Ambassador Armour.

Practically all of the other republics have expressed unqualified agreement with the position and statement of facts sets forth in the Department's communication of June 22. The chiefs of mission of most of the American republics as well as the British Ambassador have been recalled for consultation.

The Chilean Chargé in Washington has informally made available to the Department two memoranda by the Farrell government, one dated June 30 and the other July 10, which profess to summarize the action taken by the Castillo administration, the government of General Ramírez and the present regime, ostensibly in aid of the United Nations and in implementation of the break in relations with the Axis. The memorandum of July 10, which is the more comprehensive of the two documents, convincingly establishes the principle conclusion of our statement of June 22. That memorandum demonstrates that potentially significant anti-Nazi measures were adopted as incidents of the break in relations by the Ramírez government and that almost immediately after these measures were adopted the government was overthrown in circumstances and for reasons which are now well known. A mere notation of the dates of the decrees cited in the memorandum demonstrates that as soon as the new regime took power the program of implementation was sharply stopped. Save for the departure of the German diplomats, who enjoyed the freedom of the country for almost six months (and thus had ample time and opportunity to reorganize the Nazi espionage system), the sentencing of four Germans for espionage, and the suspension for a few days of one of several pro-Nazi papers, the Farrell regime has done little or nothing to implement the action of the Ramírez government. Thus the memoranda reinforce the conclusion that the extremist pro-Nazi elements of the present regime, which were largely responsible for the overthrow of the Ramírez government, have been able to block any efforts that might have been made to proceed vigorously and adequately against Axis activities. The basic facts with regard to political and economic defense measures remain as set forth in our statement. Furthermore, extremely important problems of Axis control were either not mentioned in the memoranda or were touched upon by carefully qualified promises of future action.

The net effect of the position of the Farrell regime is firm adherence to the thesis that recognition should be accorded on the basis of a few acts of the overthrown Ramírez government and mere promises of future performance. A declared determination to collaborate fully and decisively with the rest of the hemisphere has been and continues to be studiously avoided. The memorandum of June 30 states that, *"At the proper time* the Argentine Government *will* take the necessary steps to make public the measures which it *may* adopt in consequence of its position of rupture."* This is precisely the position of procrastination and evasion adopted by the Argentine Government immediately after the Conference of Rio de Janeiro in January 1942 and maintained ever since.

At the very time that the Farrell regime was protesting its intention to collaborate with the United Nations this Government was receiving reports of actions conclusively establishing that a contrary policy was being pursued. The Department is in possession of irrefutable evidence that as late as the middle of June of this year the Argentine authorities required firms friendly to the United Nations to receive bids as subcontractors from Nazi firms on contracts calling for materials imported from the United Nations. It is definitely established that during the past three months large government contracts for public works were given to firms that were either of enemy origin or actively cooperating with the enemy. As late as July 4 the Ministry of Finance placed display advertisements in Axis papers *Deutsche La Plata Zeitung, Il Mattino d'Italia, El Federal,* and *La Fronda.* The June issue of the scurrilous Nazi publication *Clarinada* contained a full-page advertisement by the Ministry of Interior. Within the past two weeks newsprint imported under grant of Allied navicerts has been supplied with the aid of the Farrell government to the four papers mentioned, which day after day have been viciously attacking the United Nations while enthusiastically supporting the Axis cause and furthering Axis propaganda.

Although the Argentine memoranda refer to economic defense measures, the irrefutable fact is that internal controls over Axis firms are non-existent and that the Farrell government has in truth been aiding those firms. During the past three years representative Axis firms in Argentina have been able to double, and in some cases to treble, their normal peacetime profits. The prosperity of these powerful commercial firms, which have been geared according to the well-known pattern into the espionage and propaganda machine of the

Nazi party, is the result not merely of passive failure of the Argentine Government to implement the Rio agreements but of positive aid from that Government.

There is, of course, nothing new in these developments. They merely demonstrate the futility of any effort to decide the issue of recognition by reference to isolated acts of apparent implementation of the break in relations. Since the day of Axis aggression against this hemisphere Argentina has protested its solidarity and unity with its sister republics. But during two and one-half years it has persisted in an open, notorious, and contrary course of action which has given constant aid and comfort to the enemies of those republics. Spasmodic token gestures of cooperation have been made. In almost all instances, however, they have been designed to do no more than foster the false hope that Argentina might yet be prepared to honor her solemn pledge of hemisphere solidarity.

In the same manner, the superficial anti-Axis gestures of recent weeks have been calculated to weaken the collective determination of the non-recognizing governments. They have been part of an effort to induce those governments to accord recognition in exchange for promises of action which Argentina has long been pledged to take. Expediency in a desperate effort to achieve recognition, rather than a change of Argentine foreign policy to support the Allied cause in good faith, has inspired these actions of the Farrell regime.

The suggestion has been made that the recent gestures of the Farrell regime offer a basis for negotiation. Bargaining or negotiating with regard to action which Argentina has long since agreed to take would be a serious error. The principles for which the free nations of the world are today contributing the full measure of their human and material resources cannot be the subject of a bargain. The controlling issue is support in good faith of the Allied cause.

The injury to the solidarity of the Continent and to the war effort of the United Nations by the continuing acts and utterances of the Farrell regime is abundantly clear. It is the judgment of this Government that the American republics and their associates among the United Nations should firmly adhere to the present policy of non-recognition of the Farrell regime until by unequivocal acts it is conclusively demonstrated that there has been a fundamental change of Argentine policy in favor of the cause against the Axis and in support of inter-American unity and common action.

AGREEMENT BETWEEN THE GOVERNMENT OF THE USSR AND THE POLISH COMMITTEE OF NATIONAL LIBERATION

Concerning Relations Between the Soviet Commander-in-Chief and the Polish Administration after the Entry of Soviet Troops to the Territory of Poland

July 26, 1944 [1]

In the course of the past few days negotiations took place between the Government of the USSR and the Polish Committee of National Liberation on the conclusion of an agreement concerning relations between the Soviet

[1] Information Bulletin, Embassy of the U.S.S.R.

Commander-in-Chief and the Polish Administration after the entry of Soviet troops to the territory of Poland.

As a result of these negotiations, which took place in an atmosphere of cordiality and friendly mutual understanding, on July 26 an agreement was signed in Moscow between the Government of the Union of Soviet Socialist Republics and the Polish Committee of National Liberation concerning relations between the Polish Administration and the Soviet Commander-in-Chief after the entry of Soviet troops to the territory of Poland. The agreement was signed in the Kremlin on behalf of the Government of the USSR by the People's Commissar of Foreign Affairs, Molotov, and on behalf of the Polish Committee of National Liberation by the President and Director of the Department of Foreign Affairs of the Committee, Ossubka-Morawski.

Present at the signing of the agreement were:

On the part of the USSR—Chairman of the Council of People's Commissars of the USSR STALIN; Deputy People's Commissar of Foreign Affairs of the USSR VYSHINSKY; Member of the Collegium of the People's Commissariat of Foreign Affairs of the USSR PAVLOV, and Marshal ZHUKOV.

On the part of the Polish Committee of National Liberation—Vice President and Director of the Department of Agriculture and Agrarian Reform, WITOS; Director of the Department of National Defense, Colonel General ROLA-JIMERSKI; Director of the Department of Protection of Labor, Social Insurance and Health Protection, Doctor DROBNER.

Text of Agreement

The Government of the Union of Soviet Socialist Republics and the Polish Committee of National Liberation, desiring that relations between the Soviet Commander-in-Chief and the Polish Administration on the territory of the Polish Republic after the entry of Soviet troops to the territory of Poland be resolved in a spirit of friendship, have concluded the present agreement to the following effect:

ARTICLE I

In the zone of military operations on the the territory of Poland after the entry of Soviet troops, supreme power and responsiblity in all affairs relating to the conduct of the war for the time necessary for the execution of military operations shall be concentrated in the hands of the Commander-in-Chief of the Soviet troops.

ARTICLE II

On Polish territory liberated from the enemy, the Polish Committee of National Liberation: (a) Sets up and directs in conformity with the laws of the Polish Republic administrative organs which the latter establishes; (b) Carries out measures for the further organization, formation and replenishment of the Polish Army; (c) Insures active assistance of organs of the Polish Administration to the Soviet Commander-in-Chief in the execution of military operations by the Red Army and in meeting its requirements and needs during its stay on Polish territory.

ARTICLE III

Polish military units which are formed on the territory of the USSR shall operate on the territory of Poland.

ARTICLE IV

Contact between the Soviet Commander-in-Chief and the Polish Committee of National Liberation shall be maintained through the Polish Military Mission.

ARTICLE V

In the zone of direct military operations, contact between Polish administrative organs and the Soviet Commander-in-Chief shall be maintained through the delegate of the Polish Committee of National Liberation.

ARTICLE VI

As soon as any part of the liberated territory of Poland ceases to be a zone of direct military operations, the Polish Committee of National Liberation shall fully assume the direction of all affairs of civil administration.

ARTICLE VII

All personnel of Soviet troops on the territory of Poland shall be under the jurisdiction of the Soviet Commander-in-Chief. All personnel of the Polish Armed Forces shall be subordinated to Polish military laws and regulations. The civilian population on Polish territory shall also be under the latter jurisdiction, even in cases of crimes committed against Soviet troops, with the exception of crimes committed in the zone of military operations, which shall be under the jurisdiction of the Soviet Commander-in-Chief. In disputable cases the question of jurisdiction shall be decided by mutual agreement between the Soviet Commander-in-Chief and the delegate of the Polish Committee of National Liberation.

ARTICLE VIII

For the entire duration of joint military operations of Soviet troops and the Polish Armed Forces, the latter shall be subordinated operationally to the Supreme Command of the USSR, and in matters relating to organization and personnel to the Chief Command of the Polish Armed Forces.

ARTICLE IX

A special agreement shall be concluded as regards financial and economic problems relating to the stay of Soviet troops on the territory of Poland, also relating to Polish armed forces which are being formed on the territory of the USSR.

ARTICLE X

The present agreement takes effect immediately after it is signed. The agreement is made in two copies, each in the Russian and Polish languages. Both texts are equally valid.

(*Signed*)

On behalf of the Government of the Union of Soviet Socialist Republics

MOLOTOV

On behalf of the Polish Committee of National Liberation

OSSUBKA-MORAWSKI

Moscow,
July 26, 1944

PROPAGANDA MINISTER JOSEPH GOEBBELS' BROADCAST DESCRIBING PLOT TO ASSASSINATE HITLER

July 26, 1944 [1]

MY FELLOW-GERMANS:

I owe the German people an accounting of the events of July 20 and the conclusions to be drawn from them. By innumerable letters from the whole country I have been asked to do so. But, nevertheless, I thought I should wait a few days until the last elements of the background of these disgraceful events had been discovered.

That is now the case. There is nothing more to be kept silent or to be extenuated in them. The events speak such a clear and unmistakable language that one can safely leave them to speak for themselves. I want to do that in a sober and unembellished report of the facts.

The German people have every reason to derive therefrom a strengthened certainty of the coming victory of our cause, which is just and under the protection of God.

Even our enemies will hardly be able to flatter themselves with the hope that this mean and cunning blow that was struck against the Fuehrer and his staff has brought their own cause even the slightest profit. I am convinced that there is no misfortune and no danger at all that will not in the end unfold to our advantage.

When I was informed at noon last Thursday by a telephone call from the Fuehrer's headquarters of the horrible crime that shortly before had been undertaken against the Fuehrer and his closest military collaborators, I had the same reaction as probably all Germans had when a few hours later the news came over the radio.

For a moment I had the feeling as if the ground under me was tottering. With my inner eye I saw apocalyptic pictures of a historic possibility that might have been the result of this cowardly and base plot for our people, yes —even for the whole of Europe.

Over untold millions of German peasants and workers, soldiers and intellectuals, a completely unimaginable disaster would have come under such circumstances, caused by the hand of a common criminal, who, on the order of an ambitious, unscrupulous small clique of fortune hunters and gamblers, had raised his hand to put an end to the life that is most valuable in the world to all of us.

But then my heart was filled with an almost religious, devout gratitude. I had experienced often, but never as visibly and unequivocally as in this case, that the Fuehrer performs his work under the protection of Providence, that no baseness or vileness would suffice to hinder or even stop him, and that thereby also a divine fate ruling over all human life and deeds gives us a hint that this work—even if it encounters the greatest possible difficulties— is to be completed, can be completed and will be completed.

Two of my ministerial colleagues were just with me for a discussion when the news arrived from the Fuehrer's headquarters. At once I saw clearly that none of the construction laborers working at the Fuehrer's headquarters could have committed this crime.

[1] *New York Times.*

Why should a decent German be interested at all in lifting his hand against the Fuehrer, who is the hope of our nation and to whose life and work we owe everything? This insidious attack could only have been carried out by an infinitely bad and despicable person, and I knew in which circle he was to be looked for. At four o'clock in the afternoon, as we had expected, the small clique of traitors standing behind him began with their machinations.

The man who carried out the attack, a certain Count Stauffenberg, had in the meantime arrived in Berlin on board a courier plane and had brought along the false report that the Fuehrer had died as a result of the attack and that now those ambitious criminals were free to act.

For they had carried out the attack to free the German Wehrmacht from the obligation of its oath and then, as they believed they could in their blind delusion, to draw the German armed forces over to their side without difficulty in the artificially created confusion and to use it for their abominable plans.

Under the pretext of having to protect the political leadership of the Reich, they, who, even if for only a very short time, were in possession of the apparatus in Bendler Street, ordered the Berlin Guard Battalion to the Government district—and here already ended all rebellious activity on their part worthy of mention at all.

For they had forgotten that the Berlin Guard Battalion consists of fanatical National Socialists, as do all units of the German armed forces, and that its commander, Major Remer, who by virtue of his lightning-like smashing of this anti-national activity of this clique, which forgot about its oath and about loyalty, has won great merit, came to me as quickly as possible to be enlightened as to the situation.

Thereby the entire felonious action was already practically finished at the end of scarcely an hour. Major Remer could immediately be connected with the Fuehrer from my desk and received from him at once clear and unequivocal orders as to what he was to do from then on.

This telephone conversation is one of the most gripping experiences of my life. A young officer of the German Army, who has proved himself at the front and has been decorated with oak leaves to the Knight's Cross, has the honor of receiving direct orders from the lips of his Fuehrer and commander in chief, and that at an hour when it counts most to act independently, in cold blood, and with lightning speed.

The orders were to smash this clique of traitors immediately and to strike down the criminals.

In a few minutes the Guard Battalion is recalled from its post in the government district and gathered together in my garden. At the request of Major Remer I speak to the assembled men, explain the state of events to them and experience an outbreak of fury and indignation such as I had until then never seen.

I shall never forgot that hour. Immediately after the end of my speech officers and soldiers take up their machine pistols and rifles to get them ready to settle accounts.

From all sides I am assailed to leave to no formation but this one the honor of washing out the disgrace that the clique of traitors is trying to inflict on the German soldier's uniform with the blood of the traitors themselves.

Meanwhile, from Berlin itself and from the near-by and more distant surroundings, the commanders of the troop formations stationed here, of infantry and tank schools, of flak and fighter groups, of armed SS, police and other units report, and none wants to let another have precedence in wiping out the nest of traitors.

The Guard Battalion gets the assignment. The Bendler block is occupied without a shot being fired, since in it itself everyone has already risen up against the group of traitors.

They are already disarmed and are crowded together, completely helpless and deserted, into one office and are trying desperately to play government.

One general, who hitherto had distinguished himself in command only by sabotaging every big decision, is the leader. A colonel general, who had had to be relieved and pensioned years ago because at the slightest burden he had nervous breakdowns and sobbing fits, is to take over the civilian leadership of the Reich. For that reason he came in civilian clothes, the only expert requirement he brings for his new office.

Another colonel general, who some time ago was dismissed from the Wehrmacht and deprived of the right to wear the uniform because of a cowardly retreat on the Eastern Front, is chosen to lead the German Army.

The criminal would-be murderer, Count Stauffenberg, plays the political adviser.

To these are added a few unimportant bit players and extras, who are arrested without making a trace of resistance.

A drumhead court-martial called on the spot condemns the obviously guilty to death. The others are taken into safekeeping.

A platoon of the Guard Battalion immediately undertakes the execution down in the courtyard. The criminals who broke their oath suffer the death they have deserved. And thus the whole incident is over.

Spare me having to tell you further details. They are so shaming for the participants in the plot that they could only confuse the facts.

It seems essential to me that a putsch attempt of a number of criminal, ambitious men, who want to besmirch the memory of their fallen comrades and attack the fighting front from the rear, is crushed by the army itself.

No soldier and no officer need be ashamed because he wears the same uniform that these gamblers wore or were unworthy of wearing. A profession is not discredited because it harbors a few criminals in its ranks.

The uniform of the German Army is represented by hundreds of thousands of German soldiers who died a heroic death in it for Fuehrer and people, and by millions of others who daily and hourly risk their lives at the front for the life of the nation, not by these ambitious men.

On the whole, on that Thursday afternoon and evening I made the acquaintance of so many good and deeply loyal National Socialist officers and soldiers of the army that I believe I can give a competent opinion also with regard to this point.

No unit of the armed forces, neither at the front nor in the homeland, in those critical hours had wavered, even for a moment, in its loyalty to the Fuehrer, to the regime and to the German people. All of them, officers and soldiers, only competed in the greatest endeavor to wipe out the disgrace, to strike down the unfaithful clique of traitors.

It need hardly be stressed, especially that the deserved punishment will be meted out to that clique of traitors in so far as this is not already the case. The German people demand this, but, above all, also the German Army.

It now wants to be freed also from the last meager left-overs of a reactionary backwardness, from those doubtful persons who are still living with the conceptions of the seventeenth century; those persons who do not wish to understand our people's State, nor can understand it; who never forgave the Fuehrer because he has opened also to the sons of the people the road to the officers' career; that the soldier receives the same decorations for bravery as the officer, that in our regime everybody is measured only by his accomplishments and not by name, birth and wealth.

In so far as they cannot give up this point of view, they do not belong at the helm of the people, not even in the military sector. If they raise their hand against our new state, which has arisen from the National Socialist revolution, or even touch the life of the Fuehrer, they will be destroyed in the name of the people.

We owe this also to a front that now for five years has fulfilled its hard duty, bravely and valiantly, and sets to the whole nation a practical example of the National Socialist community. The front has a right to protection in the rear by the whole of the German people.

This indeed would be the limit: that the front fights against the enemy and that, behind it, the homeland is seduced by political bankrupt frauds to cowardice and weakness.

How little danger there is of such a development has been proved again by the twentieth of July. Already for months I had noticed that the enemy press pointed out at regular intervals that they had been saving up a special trump for their conduct of the war, which they would play one day when the time had come.

Over and over again the assertion was made in London, Washington and Moscow that an opposition existed in certain circles of the body of generals in Germany, and over and over again certain names were mentioned that now —in the attempted putsch of July 20—made their appearance.

This is not the only evidence that these criminals conspired with the enemy and acted on his orders. Does not also the fact that an English explosive was used in the attempt on the Fuehrer point to it?

The assassin was related to the English high aristocracy and, after the attempt became known, the London press expressed its vivid hope that the events of July 20 would now soon lead to a collapse of the Reich. And yet it was an attempt originating from the camp of the enemy, even if creatures bearing a German name were willing to carry it out.

But all of them had miscalculated. They miscalculated in their estimation of the German people, of the German soldier and above all also of the National Socialist movement. After all, they can't play Badoglio with us. And as for the Fuehrer, he is in God's hands.

I have just returned from a several days' visit to the Fuehrer's headquarters. I have heard all the reports and accounts given by the eye-witnesses. I have inspected the room in which the attack took place.

And I can only say that if the salvation of the Fuehrer from extreme danger to his life was no miracle, then there just are no miracles at all.

The perpetrator had been sent by one of the arrested generals to the daily discussion of the situation for a pseudo-consultation. He brought the explosive in a briefcase to the room where the daily situation was being discussed and under the pretext of wanting to set it down had pushed it directly in front of the feet of the Fuehrer at an unguarded moment.

Colonel General Korten, who was standing directly behind the Fuehrer, was severely wounded in the attack and died of his wounds on Saturday. Participants in the discussion were thrown through the window for a distance of many meters by the force of the explosion and their uniforms were torn to shreds.

In the entire room there was, within the area affected by the enormous wave of the detonation caused by the explosive, only one single spot that remained comparatively untouched by it. That was the spot on which the Fuehrer was sitting at the map table.

The map table itself was thrown through the room by the explosion, but the Fuehrer himself remained entirely unhurt with the exception of slight bruises, burns and scratches on his forehead.

I am not ashamed to confess that I am a man who believes in history; that is, I believe that history has meaning and logic, even though the latter may at times be able to be recognized only at some future date.

It is this belief that protects me from the danger of doubting, even if only now and then, that in spite of all difficulties we will gain final victory in this war. My belief in the deep meaning of history has again been confirmed for me on July 20.

Realistic historians may smile at this, but nevertheless I am firmly convinced that Providence had taken the Fuehrer under its gracious protection in that tragic hour, because it wants to keep him ready for a great future. And I feel that also our people in their entirety are of the same conviction. How else would it be possible that such a dark day could give such a tremendous uplift to a people?

Two days after July 20 the enemy papers were still writing that the rebels were gradually running short of ammunition and that the danger existed that they would soon have to capitulate, a fact over which the population of Berlin was allegedly very sad. In fact, however, one single prayer of thanks had risen up to the Almighty from Berlin and from the entire country—thanks for having protected and saved the Fuehrer.

Out in the world they will not understand this at all, and because of this they always appraise us so wrongly. The fact that the traitorous camarilla did likewise is another proof that it completely misjudged our people and had no inner connections with it at all. To believe that at any time at all the people would leave the Fuehrer in the lurch, or would follow a traitorous clique that wanted to do away with him by force, is absolutely absurd.

July 20 represents the opposite of an indication of deteriorating morale on the part of our people. From many thousands of letters I have learned that countless persons, who did not know each other personally at all, embraced each other in the streets and on public transportation facilities when they heard that the Fuehrer had remained unhurt in the attack.

Not one has concluded from his miraculous escape that we now should let up in our war effort or weaken in it. But all realize that we have to regard that day as a token of fate and that no effort can be too great to make it available for the fight of our life.

And thus I come to the conclusions we have drawn from the events that are now behind us:

At the fronts we are opposing a world of enemies, filled with hatred, who do not hesitate to use any means, not even the most insidious or the basest ones, to defeat us. The events of July 20 have again proved this to be true. In this fight the Fuehrer is truly to be compared to the well-known Knight Against Death and the Devil, depicted by Albrecht Dürer.

We must pass through this hell of resistance, difficulties and dangers before we can come out into the open again at the end of the war and can again breathe fresh air. There can be no doubt that we will succeed in this.

But we must succeed, or else all of us are lost. It is clear that we must not spare our strength in the least in this fateful fight for our life and that, on the contrary, we must employ it unlimitedly and unconditionally—to an extent to which it is humanly possible at all.

And the entire people want to do that. They are prepared to give their last and, if necessary, their very last, in this war to an extent that deserves only admiration. It is the task of the leadership, however, to transform this willingness into action and to create the organizational and legal prerequisites so that the burdens are distributed justly and each one carries as much of them as he can possibly carry.

There is no doubt that this is still not entirely the case. We have in the country itself a tremendous potential of strength that is being utilized to a considerable extent, it is true, but not entirely. That must not be. The war demands our total strength. But if we employ this total strength, then victory is assured us.

In his midnight speech on July 20 the Fuehrer announced to the German people that he has entrusted to Party Member Reich Minister Heinrich Himmler the leadership of the reserve army, to get the strong army forces in the homeland to the front in a well-trained condition and to set up and train in their place numerous new divisions.

We do not doubt one moment that Party Member Himmler will solve this task with his customary energy in the most prudent and comprehensive way. He has all the prerequisites for it and a wealth of experience.

Our manpower strength at the front will likewise be filled out very quickly, and thus the front itself will again receive the stability and offensive strength it urgently needs for the next few months. The problems connected with this are now being attacked with National Socialist energy. Success can and will not fail to result.

The Reich Minister for Armament and War Production, Party Member Albert Speer, by his untiring work and by an ideal simplification process invented and planned by him, has increased German armament production to an extent that is astonishing.

Enemy air raids have not been able to inflict any serious damage on our war production. On the contrary, they were not even able to prevent the production of arms and ammunition being increased enormously from month to month. This intensification process goes on unhampered and has by no means reached its height.

It is true that we need for it large numbers of workers, above all Germans, who of course always form the backbone of the armament industry.

In addition, the young men going from the armament industry to the Wehrmacht must be replaced, for the strengthening of the front with soldiers and arms must go hand in hand if success is to be assured. Therefore it is necessary to utilize and to employ the strength of the German homeland to an even much greater extent than has been the case hitherto. That goes without saying.

The air emergency areas every day prove how many superfluous things we can do without, without damaging our working strength and our readiness to serve. They must serve the whole people as examples of what can be done and what must be done.

I do not believe that our enemies will rejoice and see in these measures a sign that we are going downhill. It makes no difference to us. Total war is the order of the hour. It will free so many people in the country for the front, as well as for the armament industry, that it should not be too hard for us to master in sovereign fashion the difficulties that the war situation will again and again bring on. How little reason the enemy has to triumph will be shown by the next few months.

Under yesterday's date the Fuehrer signed a decree that has today been published in the press. It decrees that the whole State machinery, including the Reich railroad and the Reich postoffice, as well as all public institutions, establishments and concerns, are to be scrutinized with the aim of freeing a maximum number of people for the Wehrmacht and for the armament industry by even more rationalized employment of the workers, by the closing down or reduction of less war-important tasks and by the simplification of organization and procedure.

In addition, according to this decree, all public life is to adapt itself in every respect to the demands of total war. All public performances are to be adapted to the aim of total war, and especially are to take no forces from the Wehrmacht or from the armament industry. In a word, total war thus becomes a practical reality.

The extensive tasks connected with this mighty change are placed in the hands of a Reich Plenipotentiary for the Total War Effort. To carry out his assignment, he receives comprehensive powers from the Fuehrer. At the suggestion of the Reich Marshal [Goering], the Fuehrer entrusted this task to me and thereby appointed me Reich Plenipotentiary for the Total War Effort.

Of course, I realize very well the difficulties that await me in the execution of this assignment from the Fuehrer, but I do not shun them and do not shrink from them. I know that in them I will have the aid of the whole people.

It would be premature if I should try to develop my program today, even though it is now ready in outline in my ideas and plans. I shall attack my task with sober objectivity and take my measures without consideration of person and rank, serving only the high purpose connected therewith.

I hope and wish that I bring to it the necessary actual knowledge, but also the necessary imagination and ability to improvise. There are so many forces yet to be saved among us that I am not worried about the success of my work.

I have been leading the Reich capital, which since the heavy air raids of last November has a standard of living much simplified compared to its former one, without having lost anything of energy, enthusiasm for work, war morale and even humor. No one froze or starved among us. All have their work, their bed and their roof over their heads, even if the rain comes through once in a while.

I flatter myself that with my fellow-workers I have carried out this comprehensive process of simplification without any dangerous friction. My experience here has shown that we can save enormously if we want to and, above all, if we have to.

I will use my powers to distribute the burdens of war justly and to hold to war-important work everyone who is at all in a position to do it.

From laws and decrees it is to become clear what the individual has to do and to leave undone and what his duty to the Fatherland is. I do not believe that thereby our war morale will sink, but rather that it will rise enormously.

I know that innumerable millions throughout the country will answer this sentence, in the moment that I speak it, with an enthusiastic "Yes." There must be justice, above all in war. If all participate equally in the burdens of this difficult time, they say to themselves, "Only thus will we be a real national community that today together bears the burdens of the war and that in the end together will harvest the fruits of victory."

I promise the German people to leave nothing untried in order in a few weeks to make Germany fit for war in every connection. Some things will take a little long, some things even longer, but with the aid of all we will master even the last and the greatest difficulties.

Thereby I rely especially on the support of the party. The Fuehrer entrusted the head of the party chancellery, Reichsleiter Party Member Martin

Bormann, with the task of energetically supporting the measures ordered by him with the efforts of the party on the basis of the powers given him. Party Member Bormann and I have long agreed on how that is to be done.

The party will be the motor of the entire process of reorganization. It will, from now on, principally serve the task of freeing soldiers for the front and workers for the production of armaments. It will fill this task with its usual energy and with its old revolutionary élan. I know that a race will start among the gaus, districts and local groups to see who will be on the top.

While our enemies believe that we are at our end, they will soon have to admit, to their own horror, that we are now no more than starting in many a field.

The situation on the fronts, and especially on the East Front, will soon change because of these measures, and substantially so, to our advantage. The war will take on a new aspect and the triumphant shouting of our enemies will stop dead in their throats.

They believed they could give us an annihilating stab by what happened on July 20. All they did was to wake us up. And it is not we, but they, who will get to feel the consequences.

It has been so every time when the foes of national socialism played their last trumps. In August, 1930, a hireling of the Prussian Ministry of the Interior staged a revolt in the party. Three weeks later, Sept. 14, we advanced in the Reichstag elections from twelve to 107 seats.

In November and December, 1932, again a traitor tried to split the party. Eight weeks later we were in power. In February, 1938, a great personnel crisis broke out in the structure of our State. Five weeks later the Ostmark returned to the Reich.

Every time our foes believed the end of national socialism and of the Fuehrer was here. Every time they experienced a cruel disappointment. With us such difficulties have always been symptoms of recovery and not of disease. Thus it will be here again.

I not only feel it, I know it. I read it in the eyes of the many people I meet. All of us have the feeling that things will go up from now on, and not by some accident, but by virtue of their own strength.

And there is something else. When realizing a temporary technical superiority of the enemy in certain fields, we have had to start from the beginning. For a long time it has been clear to us that we can beat the adversary, not by besting him in his own, but only by the creation of new types and possibilities in technical warfare.

Therefore it was not a question of merely catching up with the advantage they had gained, but rather of surpassing it. This has been achieved in the various spheres of military techniques during the last two years. The results of this trenchant development will become gradually more and more apparent on the battle field.

The employment of the V-1 weapon is the first step in this direction, as it were. The decisive element in this development is the fact that it takes place in a completely new sphere, and that therefore it may be rightly expected that it will confront the enemy with entirely novel facts and that thus the enemy will find himself rather unprepared.

It is, therefore, quite natural that now the British public cries for means of defense against our V-1 weapon, because the most important advantage of this weapon is not so much in the fact that the flying bomb flies without a crew, but rather in the fact that it completely upsets the entire system of protection and defense of the enemy.

It will be similiar with other novel weapons that we are soon going to employ in the most varied spheres. Thus we have here not only caught up with, but even surpassed, an advantage the enemy had enjoyed on this or the other sector of military techniques.

The results of this development are only to a small extent still in an experimental phase. To the greater extent they are already in a state of production.

I should be ashamed to talk in this way if I were not justified by the facts. I saw lately modern German weapons at the sight of which my heart did not start beating more rapidly, but stood still for a moment. This I do not say to boast or to bluff.

I have always been, and particularly in the critical phases of this war, absolutely certain of the justice, and hence of the final success, of our cause. None of us really needs to be convinced by the power of the proof furnished by techniques to make us convinced of the certainty of the coming victory. We believe in it because we believe in the German nation.

In addition to this, there are a number of historic reasons that relieve us of the danger of ever doubting the final success. It is, however, entrancing to see such firmness of opinions and views confirmed by real facts.

In the sphere of our armament production this is true today in more than one case. German inventive genius has passed its test. The world had to wait a long time until it made itself heard again. Soon this will be the case.

But the decisive circumstance is the fact that our production is in a position to manufacture the technical inventions in sufficient quantities and make them available to the front. Here it is necessary to make all imaginable preparations to prevent any hitch anywhere.

Without the help of the whole nation this is impossible. If the nation in its entirety puts forth a powerful effort, all these problems can be mastered without difficulty. Our enemies are not "over the hill," as their leader claims again and again, but they are still in front of it.

This will be again evident from the developments in the next weeks and months. In any case, after the measures that have been taken, and those that are yet to be taken, we can face them with complete composure.

Naturally it would be disastrous and completely at variance with the sense and purpose of my explanations if the German nation were to base its hopes for the coming victory of our arms exclusively, or even only in the main, on the here-indicated developments. That could lead to a weakening, rather than a strengthening of our national efforts.

I shall not become tired repeating my conception of this world-wide struggle—a conception I expressed already at its very beginning—that the war is a historic event that cannot be mastered solely by means of techniques or solely by military, political or economic effort, or solely by morale. It is rather the cooperation of all these forces, in a total exertion embracing the entire nation, that brings success.

Never yet has a single weapon alone decided the outcome of a war. Weapons, hands and hearts have to be employed to assure success.

Even though we welcome with great relief the favorable development of our military technics just referred to, and even though we are willing to get up enough patience to wait a certain length of time until this development shall have been completely realized, this must be no reason for letting up on all our other war efforts, even to the least possible extent, but we must increase them in every case and, if possible, to double them. And our entire people are absolutely willing to do this.

Not only must they survive steadfastly against the present difficult time in which we have to defend ourselves against the joined assault of almost the entire world and draw from it even additional strength, but they must prepare themselves for the difficult time that is to follow.

Our enemies will leave nothing untried in their attempt to strike us down. Nothing, therefore, must be left untried by us in our efforts to prevent this and to strike at them wherever we can and not to wince at any blow that we receive doing so.

We must strive to surpass each other in regard to attitude, morale, work, fighting spirit and steadfastness. Then our virtues, along with our weapons, will win the victory. The more difficult it is made for us, that much more firmly will we believe in this, and that much more fanatically will we fight for it.

This, on the whole, is the balance sheet of July 20. I believe that the German people had more reason to be satisfied with it than had their enemies. As always, the Fuehrer stands at the helm of our state and steers the people and the nation through all storms and tempests of this war with a steady hand.

Our people are brave, good and industrious and are dominated only by the thought of fighting and working so that victory may be ours. They thank the Almighty that He has taken the Fuehrer into His gracious protection and ask Him to continue to do so.

All of us, however, want to surpass one another in our love and loyalty to him, in the belief in his historic mission. The task of giving a new turn to the war in a short time lies without our hands. The prerequisites for it are at hand. Let us seize them.

The Almighty will never again reveal Himself more distinctly to us than in His miraculous salvation of the Fuehrer. He desires that we should continue to earn our victory, so that one day He will be able to hand us the laurels.

And so let us go to work, with eyes looking toward a future that will be ours.

AUGUST

August 1, 1944

Following the resignation of President Risto Ryti of Finland, Field Marshal Baron Carl Gustav Mannerheim was appointed his successor.

Manuel Quezon, President of the Philippine Commonwealth, died at Saranac Lake, N. Y. Sergio Osmena, the Vice-President, was sworn in as his successor in Washington, D. C.

2

Turkey broke off diplomatic and economic relations with Germany at the request of Britain, backed by the United States.

American troops entered Brittany and the French plains, their drive carrying them thirteen miles southwest of Avranches.

3

President Roosevelt ordered the Army to take over the Philadelphia transit system after that city had been paralyzed by a strike for two days.

President Roosevelt paid a surprise visit to an Aleutian island base en route from Honolulu.

4

Berlin announced that Hitler had ordered a "ruthless purge" of the German Army and had appointed a "court of honor" headed by Field Marshals Rundstedt and Keitel to initiate an inquiry.

Myitkyina, largest town in northern Burma, was captured by General Stilwell's Chinese and American forces.

6

Premier Mikolajczyk of the Polish Government-in-Exile sat down with leaders of the Polish Committee of National Liberation in Moscow to work out a solution of the internal Polish problem and of the Soviet-Polish difficulties.

Adolph Hitler told Nazi Party leaders that the "criminal clique" that made the bombing attempt on his life on July 20th was "limited in numbers but important in influence."

7

The American Army overran Brittany in four days and turned its left flank eastward on two main roads leading directly to Paris.

8

Premier General Kuniaki Koiso of Japan told his people that the Allies intended "to strike at our homeland in a single blow."

After a two-day blitz trial eight high German officers were hanged, including Marshal von Witzleben, for their alleged part in the plot to assassinate Hitler.

Courtesy New York Times

August, 1944

9

B-29 Superfortresses struck the Japanese in Nagasaki and Sumatra.

In a joint statement President Roosevelt and Prime Minister Churchill announced that the German U-boat drives were becoming ineffective, and that since the war began more than 500 Nazi submarines had been sunk.

10

Three Allied Armies joined the battle along the 250-mile line in France in a coordinated offensive to clear the entire area north of the Loire River and southwest of the Seine up to Paris.

Returning to London from his conferences in the Kremlin, Premier Mikolajczyk of the Polish Government-in-Exile declared that "the Russian Government wants full unity among all the Polish people except such Poles as are fascist-minded." He hoped that his discussions in Moscow would be resumed shortly in liberated Warsaw.

The Red Army renewed its full-scale battle for Warsaw by launching two big assaults to outflank the city and split the Nazi lines.

12

General Koenig, commander of the French Forces of the Interior, called on all underground units in eighteen French departments "to strike hard now" to prevent reinforcements from reaching the fighting fronts.

13

The Soviet Government disclaimed all responsibility for the ill-fated Polish insurrection in Warsaw, stating: "No attempts to notify and coordinate any events with the Soviet Command were even made by Polish emigrant circles."

Admiral Chester W. Nimitz said that the Allies might force Japan to surrender without invading her homeland islands.

Prime Minister Churchill conferred in Rome with Marshal Tito and Premier Subasitch of Yugoslavia.

14

Soviet Russia proposed to the United States and Britain the creation of a world security organization backed by an "international military air corps" which would warn and punish future aggressors.

War Production Board Chairman Donald M. Nelson issued an order permitting the manufacture of hundreds of long-unobtainable civilian articles on the basis of local material and labor conditions.

15

American and French troops swarmed on the south coast of France on a broad front between Marseilles and Nice.

16

The Berlin Foreign Office declared that a third world war was inevitable unless Germany and Japan received a "compromise" peace by negotiation.

17

President Roosevelt stated that Germany would not escape full occupation at the end of World War II as she did in 1918.

19

American Third Army tanks smashed their way into the suburbs of Paris.

20

The citizens of Paris rose to oust the Germans.

22

King Michael of Rumania ordered the armed forces of his country to surrender unconditionally to the Allies.

Unity talks between the Chungking Government and the representatives of the Chinese Communists broke down.

The United States, Great Britain and Soviet Russia outlined their proposals for an international security organization at the Dumbarton Oaks Conference.

23

Wendell L. Willkie urged Republicans to support the proposal giving the President power to use U. S. military forces to preserve world peace without prior approval of Congress.

Marseilles, the second largest French city, and Grenoble fell before French troops.

After four days of hard fighting by the populace of Paris, aided by 50,000 resistance troops, the French metropolis was liberated from the Germans.

Premier Koiso appealed for an intensification of Japan's war effort because of the "unprecedentedly grave national crisis."

Prime Minister Churchill and Pope Pius XII conferred on peace and on the future of Italy.

24

Dr. Joseph Goebbels issued decrees ending all amusements for the German people except the radio and the movies. Also, all students were mobilized for war work and a sixty-hour week was established.

Great Britain proposed in a memorandum to the United States and Soviet Russia the formation of a United Nations Military Staff Committee to be established under a world security council to help prevent and repel aggression.

25

The new Rumanian Government declared war on the Reich.

26

Moscow announced that Bulgaria had agreed to withdraw from the war on the side of Germany and disarm the Nazis.

Gen. Charles de Gaulle escaped death when French fascists opened fire on him during the great liberation parade in Paris.

29

American troops crossed the Marne for the second time in history and captured Chateau-Thierry.

30

Advancing at twenty-five miles a day, American forces crossed the Aisne River at Soissons and the Marne near Châlons.

The Red Army captured the great Rumanian oil refinery city of Ploesti and with it the richest oil fields in Europe.

31

The State Department appointed Robert D. Murphy to the staff of Gen. Eisenhower "as a political adviser with the personal rank of Ambassador in the machinery that will be set up for the military government of Germany."

After defeating the enemy south of the Ploesti oil fields, Soviet troops entered Bucharest.

PRIME MINISTER WINSTON CHURCHILL'S SPEECH IN COMMONS ON THE WAR SITUATION

August 2, 1944 [1]

I have, upon the whole, a good report to make to the House. On every battle front all over the world the arms of Germany and Japan are recoiling. They are recoiling before the armed forces of the many nations which in various groupings form the Grand Alliance. In the air, on the sea and under the sea, our well-established supremacy increases with steady strides. The losses by U-boats since the beginning of 1944, compared to former years, are almost negligible. The vast fleets of the Allies have sailed the seas and oceans from January to June with less than half the losses we have inflicted upon the small, dwindling and largely immobile naval resources of the enemy, both in the East and in the West. It is always possible that there may be a return of the U-boat war. There is talk of Germany trying to make U-boats faster under the water: there are various talks, and it is never well to discount these matters. It is always possible that the Germans may gain some temporary relative advantage in their aircraft. For these reasons we must be very careful not to relax unduly either our precautions or our exertions in order to turn our strength to other channels. Naturally, we wish to turn our strength increasingly to other channels: when one danger is removed a new opportunity presents itself; but we must be very careful, in view of the possibility of unexpected and usually unpleasant things turning up in future. But at this moment, throughout the world there is no theatre in which Allied mastery has not become pronounced.

At Washington in January, 1942, it was decided that Germany was the prime enemy, and that only the minimum of forces necessary for the safeguarding of vital interests should be diverted to operations against Japan. Our joint resources, British and American, however, increased so rapidly that it became possible to wage the two wars simultaneously with offensive vigour. In the Pacific the immense armadas of the United States, equipped with aircraft and every conceivable form of craft needed on the sea for amphibious warfare, all on the largest scale, armed with science and led with commanding skill both on sea and on land, under both Admiral Nimitz and General MacArthur, who commands not only American but also the powerful Australian and New Zealand Forces, have gained important and expanding success. New Guinea has been dominated, the Marshalls and Saipan have been taken, the fleets and other forces of the United States have already advanced through the far-flung outer defences of Japan, and in some parts they have pierced through the inner defences, thus opening to us the prospect of a much more speedy climax in the Far East. Many scores of thousands of Japanese have been by-passed, and are starving to death in islands and jungles, with only such aid from Japan as can be given by submarines which have to be diverted from their normal warlike use.

[1] Parliamentary Debates.

The reverberations of these events in Japan, the sense of growing weakness on the sea and in the air, the sense of the vain dispersal of their forces and of economic tribulation at home, have produced the fall of Admiral Tojo, the chief war leader of Japan, whose accomplice and close colleague Admiral Yamamato, declared at one time that he would dictate his terms of peace to the United States in Washington. It is not easy for us here to measure the character of the seismic forces which have produced this remarkable political and military convulsion in Japan, but it can hardly arise from a conviction among the Japanese that Admiral Yamamato's programme is being realised as fully as he and Admiral Tojo had expected. I must repeat that I am increasingly led to believe that the interval between the defeat of Hitler and the defeat of Japan will be shorter—perhaps much shorter—than I at one time had supposed.

In the Indian theatre, coming a step nearer home in this long distance war, the campaign in Burma has been difficult to follow in detail because of the ceaseless fighting and the intricate character of the country. Broadly speaking it may be said that at Quebec last year we planned advances into Northern Burma with the object of giving greater security to the immense American air highway into China. I may mention that the American highway carries far more tonnage than was ever delivered, or likely to be delivered in a measurable time, over the old Burma Road. It carries it over what is called the hump— the vast mountain range of the Himalayas—and deals with an immense tonnage every month. This of course is of the greatest assistance to General Chiang Kai-shek and the Chinese in their long and hard-driven struggle. The House may imagine what a vast effort this achievement by the United States, indispensable to the life of China, has involved.

We placed our hopes at Quebec in the new supreme commander, Admiral Mountbatten, and in his brilliant lieutenant Major-General Wingate, who alas has paid the soldier's debt. There was a man of genius who might well have become also a man of destiny. He has gone, but his spirit lives on in the long-range penetration groups and has underlain all these intricate and daring air operations and military operations based on air transport and on air supply.

This forward move which had been decided on at Quebec involved rather more than 250,000 British and Imperial troops, with many more upon the long and precarious communications stretching back into India. This move met at an early stage a Japanese movement in the opposite direction, which had for its object the invasion of India and the cutting of the American air highway. Thus these two opposing forces came together in collision at many points along a 1,200-mile front, in the early part of February, and they have been locked in engagements of intense fierceness ever since, with the result that the Japanese have been flung backward at every point. At the same time important centres in the north of Burma were captured by brilliant operations conducted by General Stilwell from the North, with the participation of Chinese troops and with the invaluable support of the British long-range penetration groups operating against the enemy's rear. The thanks of the country should go out to the British 14th Army which has done some of the hardest service in the whole of this war and must not be forgotten because of the violence and vividness of larger and nearer events at home.

But there are many others besides the 14th Army whom we should not forget. When we think of the Fighting Forces we naturally think first of all of those who are fighting on the main war fronts, but we should be wrong not to remember all those men who loyally serve our cause in distant lands and remote garrisons all over the world, whose steady and unspectacular work does not often get into the newspapers, men who in many cases have not had the stimulus of engagement in battle, men who have not seen their families or their homes for four years or five years, or more. They may be far away, but their work is an essential part of the pattern of victory, and, as such, it rests for ever in our hearts.

To return to Burma, Admiral Mountbatten and his commanders fought a successful and vigorous campaign in these unprofitable jungles and swamps in which our duty lies. The Japanese, everywhere driven back, sustained losses far exceeding our own. India has been successfully defended from invasion for another year, the air line to China strengthened and maintained and danger warded further off its necessary bases. In addition, Admiral Somerville, now at the head of a powerful British Eastern fleet, which includes fine French and Dutch units, has shown enterprise in his attack upon Sebang and Sourabaya and other Japanese points in the Dutch East Indies. Our Fleet in Eastern waters will be greatly strengthened at the end of the year. It is probable, however, that the Japanese Navy will have its time fully taken up with the Navy of the United States, which is already double the size of the fleet of that presumptuous, ambitious and treacherous Oriental Power. I thought it right to bring the Burma scene before the House, because our men out there are cheered by the fact that the House of Commons follows with attentive eyes their fortunes and their achievements.

Now I come to a larger matter. A volume would be required to recount the story of the crossing of the Channel and the landing of the Armies of Liberation upon the soil of France. I have only a few minutes, and therefore I must practise the selective art as far as possible. In April, 1943, General Morgan, of the British Army, became the head of the British and American Planning Staff, which surveyed the whole project by the decision of the Combined Chiefs of Staff Committee. They made a plan, which I took with me last year to Quebec, where it was submitted to the President and the Combined British and American Chiefs of Staff. This plan selected the beaches for the attack and presented the outlines of the scheme, together with a mass of detail to support it. It received, in principle, complete agreement. It is rather remarkable that a secret of this character, which had to be entrusted from the beginning, to scores, very soon to hundred and ultimately to thousands, of people, never leaked out either in these Islands or the wide expanses of the United States.

At Teheran, we promised Marshal Stalin we would put this plan, or something like it, into operation at the end of May or the beginning of June, and he for his part promised that the whole of the Russian Armies would be thrown, as indeed they have been, into general battle in the East. In January of this year, the commanders were appointed. The Mediterranean had a British commander, General Wilson, and General Eisenhower assumed the command of the Expeditionary Force gathered in Britain. No man has ever laboured more skilfully or intensely for the unification and goodwill of the great forces under his command than General Eisenhower. He has a genius for bringing all the Allies together and is proud to consider himself an ally as well as a United States Commander. The names of all the distinguished commanders are already familiar to the House and the country.

General Eisenhower forthwith appointed the Commander-in-Chief of the British Expeditionary Army, General Montgomery, to the command of all the invading troops, British and American. For more than a year past, American stores, equipment and men have been moving steadily into these Islands, and we ourselves have selected from the British Armies here, an expeditionary force which was practically as large as that of the United States in the opening stage. Great reinforcements which flow in from America have already altered, and will continually alter that balance but in the great adventure we were practically equal. The training of all these troops was undertaken in a most strenuous fashion. The plan also provided for the successive landings which were to be made in relation to the major thrust. The great episode seemed to every one to be the crossing of the Channel, with its stormy waters, swift currents and eighteen-foot rise and fall of the tide, and above all the changes of weather, which when an operation as big as this has to be undertaken might easily cut a portion of the Army off upon the shore for several days without anyone being able to get to them to reinforce them or even to withdraw them, and thus leave them at the mercy of a superior enemy. That was the element, this possible change in the weather, which certainly hung like a vulture poised in the sky over the thoughts of the most sanguine.

In all these matters, the work of the Combined Operations Headquarters, founded in 1940 under Admiral Keyes for the purpose of amphibious warfare, and developed since 1942 by Admiral Mountbatten, proved its value. As is well-known, I was opposed to making this great invasion across the Channel in 1942, and thereafter it was plainly impossible in 1943, owing to our having chosen the Mediterranean and our amphibious resources all being concentrated there. Now we were all agreed, and the Commanders took the vast mass of knowledge which had been accumulated and put their own stamp upon it, improving the plans in many ways and animating and training their troops to fit in to its different phases and features.

I do not believe myself that this vast enterprise could have been executed earlier. We had not the experience. We had not the tackle. But, before we launched the attack in 1944 we had made five successful opposed landings in the Mediterranean, and a mass of wonderful craft of all kinds have been devised by our services and by our United States colleagues on the other side of the ocean. The bulk of these had to be constructed in the United States, although our yards were strained and gorged to the utmost. There are more than sixty variants of these landing craft and escort vessels, and they provide for the landing, not only of an Army, but for everything that an Army can need.

For instance, I myself saw a few days after the landing was complete six of these large landing craft—I should say, medium landing craft, vessels of considerable size—charge up in line together till they were stopped by the sloping sandy beach; down fell their drawbridges, out poured their vehicles, and in five minutes an entire heavy battery was drawn up in column of route ready for immediate, or almost immediate action. I had this timed, because I certainly thought it would be a matter of hours, but in less than fifteen minutes these heavy craft had pushed themselves off the shore and were returning to England for another consignment. This is a new atmosphere, a new light upon the possibility of an invasion across the Channel, which I hope will not be altogether lost upon our own people in the days when many of us have handed over our burdens to others. The marvellous American invention spelt D.U.K.W., is a heavy lorry which goes at between forty and fifty miles per hour along the road, and can plunge into the water and swim out for miles to sea in quite choppy weather, returning with a load of several tons, coming ashore and going off to wherever it is specially needed.

An immense system of harbours, breakwaters and landing stages was also prepared which, as soon as the foothold was gained, could be disposed in their appropriate places to give large sheltered water space. In less than a month, harbours had been created compared with which Dover seems small. At these harbours, and on the beaches they protect, a very large Army, with the entire elaborate equipment of modern armies, which have about one vehicle for every four or five men, was landed, and by the end of June, in spite of the worst June gale for forty years, a solid base had been created which gave us the certainty of being able to conduct an offensive campaign on the largest scale against any Forces which, according to our calculations, the enemy was likely to bring.

These operations were protected and supported by a considerable British Fleet, assisted by a strong detachment of the American Fleet, the whole under Admiral Ramsay. In spite of gales, in spite of mines, in spite of more than 100 German submarines waiting baffled in the Biscay Ports, and a swarm of E-boats and other marauders, ceaseless traffic has been maintained over the 100-miles stretch of channel, and General Eisenhower, with his lieutenant, General Montgomery, now stands at the head of a very large and powerful Army, equipped as no Army has ever been equipped before.

Overwhelming air power was, of course, as indispensable as sea power to the carrying out of such an operation. The strategic bombing by the combined British and American Bomber Forces, and the use of the medium bomber and fighter forces, was the essential prelude to our landing in Normandy. Preparations definitely began for the battle in April, and, not only at the point of attack for that would have revealed much, but necessarily impartially all along the coast and far in the rear. Thus when our ships crossed the Channel, unseen and unmolested, half the guns that were to have blown them out of the water were already dismantled or silent, and when the counter-attack began on the land and under the sea, the Tactical and Coastal air forces held it back while our foothold on shore and our sea-lanes were being firmly established.

These deeds of the Air Force were not done without losses, which, in killed and in proportion to the number of flying personnel, far exceeded those of any branch of the Services. If we take 1st April as the opening of the air campaign and from then till 30th June, over 7,000 men of the Home Command from the R.A.F. alone have been killed or are missing. United States losses are also most severe. The devotion of the pilots and the air crews of both countries was sublime.

Since those days we have been in constant battle, General Omar Bradley, clearing the Cherbourg Peninsula and General Dempsey occupying the area around Caen. We have inflicted losses on the enemy which are about double those we have suffered ourselves. It is remarkable considering we were the challengers, and unusual compared with the experiences of the last war. We have been hampered continually by the most unseasonable weather, which by its early mists and low clouds has day after day put off operations by rendering impossible the avalanche of fire and steel with which our air power prepares for an attack. Now at last we are gaining that space in which to deploy which is necessary for armies of the size that we are using.

I must confess that the latest news seems to me extremely good. The first American Army advancing down the Atlantic coast has reached the line of the River Selune and may well be approaching the important railway centre of Rennes, about halfway across the base of the Brest Peninsula. Further to the East the Americans have by-passed the town of Villedieu-le-Poeles and have captured Brecey. The British attack has also made very great progress and has advanced in the centre about twelve miles. On the Canadian front South of Caen we attacked yesterday and heavy fighting is in progress. We are largely superior to the enemy in men, in armour and in the air, and I have little doubt in mobility also once the front is widened out.

It is the wish and also the desire of General Eisenhower that the battle for Normandy should be viewed as a whole and as one single set of operations conducted by an Allied Force, linked in brotherhood and intermingled in every manner that may seem convenient. But this should certainly not prevent the British House of Commons from expressing its unstinted admiration for the splendid and spectacular victories gained by the United States troops under General Bradley both at Cherbourg and in the southward march, now become almost a gallop down the peninsula. The Germans have certainly had remarkable opportunities of revising the mocking and insulting estimate which they put upon the military value of the American Army at the time they declared war upon the great Republic.

We British and Canadians too have taken our full share in these fierce and prolonged conflicts. We have fulfilled the indispensable part which was assigned to us by the Supreme Commander and, under him, by General Montgomery. If General Eisenhower as supreme Commander or General Montgomery, as his lieutenant in the field, had ever in the slightest degree to consider whether they would employ British or American or Canadian troops in this way or in that, here or there, on any grounds other than military those officers would have been hampered in a most grievous manner. But lest our enemies should suggest upon their wireless that the burden of the struggle has been unfairly shared or make invidious comparisons of any kind, let me say that the losses of the British and Canadian Forces together are about equal to those of the larger United States Army in proportion to their relative strength. It has been share and share alike, in good fortune and bad, all along the front.

So far as it has gone, this is certainly a glorious story, not only liberating the fields of France after atrocious enslavement but also uniting in bonds of true comradeship the great democracies of the West and the English speaking peoples of the world. That is all I wish to say of the actual operations across the Channel to-day. Members would be well advised to follow them with the closest attention. Very full and excellent accounts are given in the Press. Very often they are ahead of the official news, and they are not incorrect, because more care has to be taken about anything that is said officially. A most lively and true picture is given by the Press at the present time, by the accounts we have of this fighting so near home.

MR. GALLACHER (Fife, West): A pat on the back for the "Daily Worker."

THE PRIME MINISTER: Yes, I have no doubt. Lots of things are happening which will cause the hon. Gentleman pleasure, and the paper of which he is certainly an admirer. I promised some weeks ago to refer to the question of the British tanks before the end of the Session, and, with the permission of the House, I will make a short divagation from my theme, as this is the last opportunity.

I have told the House how at the time of the fall of Tobruk the President gave the first 350 Sherman tanks which had already been issued to the American army and we know that they played a key part in the Battle of El Alamein. When I went back to America a year after, I found that there was an ample supply of these tanks, formerly so precious and rare from the flow of American mass production which had got into its stride, and they were able to offer us 3,000 or 4,000 more of those invaluable weapons. This was of great advantage to us. We were able to carry through the further redisposition of our tank programme and to reduce the scale of our production, thus releasing man-power and materials for making other instruments of war which we urgently required. We were able also to carry through the development of the Cromwell, the Churchill and other types in an orderly manner freed from fear of a shortage of tanks in the hands of the troops. The Sherman tank has maintained its reputation gained in Africa at every stage in the battles in Italy and Normandy. It is of course essentially a cruiser tank, like the Cromwell, which is the largest type of British cruiser tank. Both these tanks are reported to be excellent and trustworthy for the purposes for which they were designed. As the House knows, we succeeded in mounting the seventeen-pounder gun in the Sherman, a remarkable feat, and many hundreds of these are either in action in Normandy or moving thither in a steady stream.

General Montgomery has written as follows about the recent battle:

"In the fighting to date we have defeated the Germans in battle and we have no difficulty in dealing with the German army once we had grasped the problem. In this connection British armour has played a notable part. The Panther and Tiger tanks are unreliable mechanically and the Panther is very vulnerable from the flank. Our seventeen-pounder guns will go right through them. Provided our tactics are good we can defeat them without difficulty."

Well, they say the customer is always right.

The Cromwell, of course, possesses superior speed which will be specially effective when and if we come as we may into more open country. As to the Sherman, I saw with my own eyes last week an example of the work of the seventeen-pounder. It was on the approaches to Caen. There was an expanse of large fields of waving corn out of which a grey stone village rose. Generals Montgomery and Dempsey brought me to this spot and invited me to count the broken-down Panther tanks which were littered about. I counted nine in the space of about 1,000 yards square. The general then told me that all these nine had been shot with a seventeen-pounder from one single British Sherman tank from the side of the village wall. One cannot help being impressed by these things when one sees them with one's own eyes. Of course you will never get the same armour in a thirty-ton tank as you will in one of sixty-tons. But mobility, speed and manoeuvrability also count high, and when the seventeen-pounder gun is added to all these qualities, no one has the right to say that these lighter tanks are not fitted in every way for their task and are not a wise and far-seeing employment of our war power.

I am afraid all this must be causing pain and sorrow to the hon. Member for Ipswich (Mr. Stokes).

MR. STOKES: That is not the whole story.

THE PRIME MINISTER: The hon. Member had better pull himself together, because there is worse to come. The notorious Churchill tank, the most thick-skinned weapon in Europe, also won commendation. This tank was originally conceived in 1940, for fighting in the lanes and in the enclosed country of this island, and in spite of every form of abuse as well as the difficulty inherent upon haste, in design and construction, it is now once again coming into its own as it did for a short while in Northern Tunisia in 1942. It is coming into its own because the conditions of the war in France and in parts of Italy in which we are now fighting are extremely suitable to its climbing and manoeuvrable qualities and heavy armour. No particular type can be perfect. The Tiger and the Panther are, essentially, weapons of defence, whereas the

Cromwell and Sherman belong to the offensive. The Churchill can be either defensive or offensive as circumstances may require. I pass from these technical details. General Oliver Leese reports as follows about the fighting in Italy:

"It may interest you to know of the fine performance of the Churchill tanks, which supported the Canadian Corps when they attacked and broke through the Adolf Hitler line last month. They stood up to a lot of punishment from heavy anti-tank guns. Several tanks were hard hit without the crews being injured. They got across some amazingly rough ground. Their six-pounder guns made good penetration and were quick to load and aim."

I saw also that in the recent fighting in France similar distinction has been gained by these weapons in the assault in some of these wooded hills and in this very thickly enclosed country in which our centre is now moving.

But there is one more general feature which has emerged in the fighting in Normandy to which I must draw the attention of the House. No new tank weapon or type of ammunition has been employed by the enemy. They have brought out nothing new so far whereas we have put into operation for the first time in these operations the Sherman tank mounting the seventeen-pounder, the latest Churchill tank, the new Cromwell tank and we have also a number of interesting variants of very great ingenuity, which I cannot tell the House about to-day, because we do not know whether the enemy have had an opportunity of testing them and tasting them. It is only when I know they know, that the secrets can be unfolded. One has to be very careful because people object very much indeed if anything is revealed which seems to take away any chance that our troops may enjoy in this country and with our Allies.

In leaving this subject of equipment, I am going to do something that has never been done before, and I hope the House will not be shocked at the breach of precedent. I am going to make public a word of praise for the War Office. In all the forty years I have served in this House I have heard that Department steadily abused before, during, and after our various wars. And if my memory serves me aright I have frequently taken part in the well-merited criticism which was their lot. But when I last saw General Montgomery in the field he used these words which he authorised me to repeat if I chose. He said: "I doubt if the British War Office has ever sent an Army overseas so well equipped as the one fighting now in Normandy." That is what he said, and I must say I think it is a well-justified statement.

The punctual movement and supply of our large armies in so many varied theatres, the high standard of training imparted to the troops, the smoothness with which arrangements of all kind are fitted together, the meticulous care bestowed upon equipment in all its forms, the efficiency of the hospitals, the large share taken by officers in the Army in the devising of every instrument of amphibious warfare, the whole manner in which the affairs of the millions of men now with the Colours at home and abroad have been handled, reflect high credit upon the War Office with all its innumerable branches and its enormous staff, military and civilian. They all deserve credit, and none more than the Chief of the Imperial General Staff, that great officer Field Marshal Sir Alan Brooke, and also my right hon. Friend the Secretary of State for War. Indeed I may say that not only in the War Office, but throughout the Service departments, the whole method and execution of war policy stand, I believe, at this moment at a higher level than they have ever reached before, and at a level which compares not unfavourably with similar organisations in any other country, whether friend or foe. War is a hard school, but the British, once compelled to go there, are attentive pupils. To say this is by no means inconsistent with any criticisms that it may be necessary to put forward from time to time.

I must now turn to the campaign of General Alexander in Italy. When I spoke about this in February, how different was the scene? The army seemed to be frustrated, dammed up in the defiles and caves of Cassino; the landing force which we had at Anzio and which we had hoped would resolve the deadlock was itself pennned in and had, indeed, to fight for its very existence and on the turn of a card depended the life of that strong force; our very heavy losses; other operations apparently being delayed; the capture of Rome continuously delayed; the enemy sending reinforcements down, and so forth—an effect of standstill. Criticisms came, as they do wherever success is absent, of those responsible. But now the scene is changed. By a series of very rapid and brilliant manoeuvres based upon a victory of sheer hard fighting, sheer dogged ding-dong fighting, the whole scene is changed. The Army rapidly advanced; it made contact with the Anzio bridgehead; it flung its encircling claws round Rome, protecting the city from all danger. It is absolutely free from all danger now. The Air Force guards it from attack from without. General Alexander's army rolled forward, rapidly pushing the enemy before it, taking 50,000 or 60,000 prisoners, up the whole of the long leg of Italy, and now stands before Florence. It has gained the valuable ports of Leghorn and Ancona as well as bringing forward its railhead in the centre into much closer proximity.

We have had, of course, to move up this Italian peninsula with very unsatisfactory lines of supply, but with the command of the sea and the ports and the advance of the railhead, the position of that army becomes very greatly strengthened. We may hope that operations of the utmost vigour will be continued by General Alexander and his army throughout the summer and autumn. What an extraordinary army it is! There has never been anything like it, and there is nothing which could so bring home to one how this is a war of the United Nations. You have the British and the United States troops, the New Zealanders, the American Japanese troops, who have fought with great vigour, the Greeks are coming—some are already there—a Brazilian force is already beginning to take its place upon the field, the French are there, the South Africans are there, the Poles have greatly distinguished themselves, and, of course, bearing a most important part, our gallant Indian troops. There are also powerful Canadian forces. I was not reading this out from a list, but it is really a most extraordinary parade of all the nations advancing to cleanse the Italian soil. There are Italians also, because respectable Italian forces, in strength, have been fighting well, and we are going to increase their numbers.

MR. GALLACHER: Some of the respectables are Communists.

THE PRIME MINISTER: The hon. Gentleman may sometimes conceivably be biased. He wants good guidance to show him not to push his bias too far. Things are going very well in Italy. I must say that in talking about all these various campaigns that are going on at once all over the world, I have left the obvious, essential fact till this point, namely, that it is the Russian armies who have done the main work in tearing the guts out of the German army. In the air and on the oceans we could maintain our place, but there was no force in the world which could have been called into being, except after several more years, that would have been able to maul and break the German army unless it had been subjected to the terrible slaughter and manhandling that has fallen to it through the strength of the Russian Soviet armies.

I salute Marshal Stalin, the great champion, and I firmly believe that our twenty years' treaty with Russia will prove to be one of the most lasting and durable factors in preserving the peace and the good order and the progress of Europe. It may well be that the Russian success has been somewhat aided by the strategy of Herr Hitler—of Corporal Hitler. Even military idiots find it difficult not to see some faults in some of his actions. Here he now finds himself with perhaps ten divisions in the North of Finland and twenty or thirty divisions cut off in the Baltic States, all of which three or four months ago could have been transported with their material and their weapons to stand between Germany and the Russian advance. Do not tell him how to do it. It is far too late for him to achieve that at the present time. Altogether, I think it is much better to let officers rise up in the proper way.

I have tried to give the House what cannot be more than a sweeping glance of this world-wide war as it approaches the end of its fifth year, and also as it approaches perhaps its closing phase. I naturally end my military survey at home here in famous and might London—in London which, with the surrounding counties, particularly those upon what may be called the bomb-highway, has now been under almost continual bombardment for seven weeks. In all, by our calculations—and I procured the latest for the House—5,735 of these robots have been launched upon us, killing 4,735 persons, with 14,000 more or less seriously injured. There are also many slightly injured. The result has been a sad tale of human sorrow and suffering, and a wholesale destruction of homes, with all the difficult circumstances attaching to that for people who have lost all the little articles on which their memories and affections centre. We are sure that our defences are gaining in power. We press to the utmost our counter-offensive measures. The patience and courage of our people at a time when they might have thought that for London her trials were past has been wonderful. We are sure that the people will continue to the end.

I fear greatly to raise false hopes but I no longer feel bound to deny that victory may come perhaps soon. If not we must go on till it does. How long it will be we do not know, but there will be unfading honour for all the brave hearts that never failed. The working of all the Civil Defence services, men and women, has been a model. About 17,000 houses have been totally destroyed and about 800,000 have received damage. One can judge the efficiency and vigour of the measures taken by the Ministries involved—Labour, Health and Works—and the strength of our building and repair resources throughout the country from which volunteers have come forward in large numbers, by the fact that three-quarters, or upwards of 600,000, have already been made at least habitable again, and in the last two weeks the rate at which repairs have been overtaking new damage has very sensibly increased.

Nearly a million people who have no war business here, among them 225,000 mothers with children, have been encouraged and assisted to leave London and, thanks to the hospitality and kindness of those in areas not affected, have been welcomed and comforted. There have been a few exceptions but they are not worth recording beside the good spirit which has prevailed. They are not worth recording except for the purpose of reprobation. A large number of extra trains were laid on to meet this considerable outward move. It is remarkable, as showing the outlook of the people of this country, that many of these trains—including sometimes the extra relief trains—have come back to London nearly as full as they went out. While a daring and adventurous spirit is to be commended, this kind of needless risk and movement will be discouraged in every way. I only mention it now because it gives the lie in the most effective manner to the fantastic German stories of London being in panic under a perpetual pall of smoke and flames. If the Germans imagine that the continuance of this present attack—which has cost them dear in many ways in other branches of production—will have the slightest effect upon the course of the war, or upon the resolve of the nation or the morale of the men, women and children who are under fire, they will only be making another of those psychological blunders for which they have so long been celebrated.

The only result of the use of this indiscriminate weapon, as far as they are concerned, will be that the severity of the punishment which they will receive after their weapons have been struck from their hands by our fighting men will be appreciably increased. There is no question of diverting our strength from the extreme prosecution of the war, or of allowing this particular infliction to weaken in any way our energetic support of our Allies. Every effort in human power is being made to prevent and mitigate the effects of this bombardment. Hundreds of the best expert brains we have are constantly riveted upon the problem. My hon. Friend was not right when, in an earlier discussion, he threw out the suggestion that it was all makeshift and improvisation. Very careful plans had been prepared, for instance, for the artillery—the great gun belt—but it is not always possible to foresee accurately what form the attack will take or how things will go.

At the same time as these preparations were made, a quite different disposition of the guns had to be made to guard the invasion ports from which our convoys to France were to start, and we expected that very likely the flying bombs would begin at the same time as we landed in order to cheer up the German people. But there was a slight interval, and it was convenient in that interval that we were able to make a quick redistribution of the batteries. It was a very complicated matter, and I am so glad that Members of the House have attended the various meetings addressed by the Home Secretary and by the Joint Parliamentary Secretary to the Ministry of Supply, and have been able to ask them questions. Here, I must say that I cannot understand why anybody should say that there is any constitutional issue involved in any Member or any number of Members taking a Committee Room and talking to each other on any conceivable subject. It is likely that a grave constitutional issue would arise if Members were to be hampered and obstructed in taking counsel with one another. I think it would be unfortunate if a kind of gulf were made between Ministers and other Members, as if they were a sort of elite of the House and had no right to mingle with their Parliamentary colleagues. I think there are a good many arguments I could use to free us of the charge of having infringed the constitution. As I was saying, hundreds of the best brains we have are riveted on the problem, but I can hold out no guarantee that it will be completely solved until we have occupied the region from which these bombs are launched, as we shall no doubt do before the unconditional surrender of the enemy has been received. But even that will be good enough.

As long ago as 22nd February, I warned the House that Hitler was preparing to attack this country by new methods, and it is quite possible that attempts will be made with long-range rockets containing a heavier explosive charge than the flying bomb, and intended to produce a great deal more mischief. London, we may expect, will be the primary target on account of the probable inaccuracy of the rocket weapon. We, therefore, advise the classes for whom evacuation facilities have been provided by the Government, and others with no war duties here who can make their own arrangements, to take the opportunity of leaving the capital in a timely, orderly and gradual manner. It is by no means certain that the enemy has solved the difficult technical problems connected with the aiming of the rockets, but none the less I do not wish to minimise the ordeal to which we may be subjected, except to say that I am sure it is not one we will not be able to bear.

I have finished with this, and as a grim comment on all I have said this fact must be added. The hon. Member for Eye (Mr. Granville) put a Question to my right hon. Friend the Secretary of State for Air, the answer to which I thought might come in here so he kindly consented to defer his Question. I think it makes a grim comment upon what I have just been saying. The weight of flying bombs launched against this country from the night of 15th June to the night of 31st July is estimated to be some 4,500 tons. During the same period the Allied Air Forces dropped approximately 48,000 tons of high explosive bombs on Germany. Of course we try in the main to aim at important military objectives and consequently it may be that there is less loss of life in particular places than when a weapon is used which has no other object than the indiscriminate slaughter of the civilian population.

I have trespassed a good deal on the House—[HON. MEMBERS: "Go on."] —but I think I must take a little more time, especially in view of the decision to which the House has properly come to have an interval in our labours. I now approach, not without natural anxiety the delicate subject of Foreign Affairs. I still hold to the view which I expressed last time that as the war enters its final phase it is becoming, and will become increasingly less ideological. Confusion was caused in some minds by mixing ideology with idealism, whereas in fact there is quite a notable difference between them. While I cherish idealism as a cheerful light playing over the thoughts and hopes of men and inspiring noble deeds, ideology too often presents itself as undue regimentation of ideas and may very likely be incompatible with freedom. I have rejoiced to see the Fascist ideology overthrown, and I look forward to its complete extirpation in Italy.

I rejoice in the prospect, now becoming sure and certain, that the Nazi ideology enforced in a hideous manner upon a vast population, will presently be beaten to the ground. These facts and manifestations, which I see taking place continually as the world war crashes onwards to its close, make me increasingly confident that when it is won, when the hateful aggressive Nazi and Fascist systems have been laid low, and when every precaution has been taken against their ever rising again, there may be a new brotherhood among men which will not be based upon crude antagonisms of ideology but upon broad, simple, homely ideals of peace, justice and freedom. Therefore, I am glad that the war is becoming less an ideological war between rival systems and more and more the means by which high ideals and solid benefits may be achieved by the broad masses of the people in many lands and ultimately in all.

Since I spoke last on the general position to the House, marked improvements have occurred in several quarters. Foreign affairs are powerfully influenced by the movements of the war situation. The successes I have been recounting to the House have carried all our affairs into a more favourable condition. Among the first of these is the great improvement in the relations of the French National Committee headed by General de Gaulle with that of the Government of the United States. This arose in part from the careful spadework done over here by my right hon. Friend the Foreign Secretary and by the great success which attended General de Gaulle's visit to the President of the United States. In these last four years I had many differences with General de Gaulle, but I have never forgotten, and can never forget, that he stood forth as the first eminent Frenchman to face the common foe in what seemed to be the hour of ruin of his country and, possibly, of ours, and it is only fair and becoming that he should stand first and foremost in the days when France shall again be raised, and raise herself, to her rightful place among the great Powers of Europe and of the world. For forty years I have been a consistent friend of France and its brave Army; all my life I have been grateful for the contribution France has made to the culture, glory and above all the sense of personal liberty and the rights of man which have radiated from the soul of France. But these are not matters of sentiment or personal feeling. It is one of the main interests of Great Britain that a friendly France should regain and hold her place among the major Powers of Europe and the world. Show me a moment when I swerved from this conception and you will show me a moment when I have been wrong.

I must confess that I never liked Trotsky, but there is one thing he said at the time of the brutal German treaty of Brest-Litovsk, which stuck in my mind. He said to the German bullies:

"The destiny of a great nation has never yet been settled by the temporary condition of its technical apparatus."

So it will be with France, struck down in a few weeks of agony, and deprived thereafter of the power of self-expression and almost of the right of existence. But the soul of France did not die. It burned here and there with exceptional brightness. It burned over wider areas with a dim but unquenchable flame.

Our landing in Normandy, the course of the war, the whole tide of events show quite clearly that we shall presently once again have to deal with the problem of France and Germany along the Rhine, and from that discussion France can by no means be excluded. It is evident from what I have said that I look forward to the closest association of the British Empire, the United States and the Russian and French representatives in the settlement of these important European problems. We are an alliance of united, peace-loving nations who have been forced to take up arms to defend our fundamental rights, and we must not fail in the hour of victory to make the arrangements necessary to continue the peace that we shall have so dearly bought. I must pay my tribute to the House for the wise forbearance that it exercised seven weeks ago in discouraging the Debate on British, French and American relations. That was a time much more critical than this and the fact that the House, which is all-powerful in these matters, deliberately abstained from discussing a question in which interest ran high on all sides was extremely helpful to the conduct of affairs by my right hon. Friend, and I think furthered the smooth deployment of our policy.

Everyone should bear in mind the unusual complexities which attend the foreign policy of this Island in the world coalition of which we are members. We have first the Dominions to consider and consult, and then there are the three great Powers. We have two valiant and trusted Allies who are larger and in some respects more powerful than we are. We all mean the same thing on fundamentals and essentials but to reach precise agreement from day to day on diplomatic tactics and details is necessarily an elaborate business. Here we enter a field of triangular diplomacy where we all have to telegraph to each other and, when two are agreed, the third often has further Amendments to propose, and when all are agreed very often the subject has ceased to be of interest. How would you have it otherwise, with all the different viewpoints, characteristic, historic and national, from which these matters have to be approached? I have said before that, if the heads of the three Governments could meet once a month, there would be no problems between us which would not be swiftly and I trust sensibly solved. Geographical and locomotion difficulties thrust their obstructive hands between us and such constant reunions and correspondence however faithfully conceived is not a substitute for meeting round a table. The three principal Allies have to deal from day to day with all kinds of burning issues arising in eight or ten vanquished, occupied or neutral States, two or three of which have quite healthy civil wars either in prospect or in progress. When I recall or survey all the complexities of arriving together at united agreements, I must say I think the Governments of the United States, Great Britain and Soviet Russia have done pretty well. But great patience and an unceasing desire to understand each other's point of view are necessary between the great Powers, and the House of Commons can help everyone by taking a broad and tolerant view.

This in my opinion is a hopeful moment for Poland, for whose rights and independence we entered the war against Germany. We therefore did our best, my right hon. Friend and I and others late into the night to promote the visit of M. Mikolajczyk and other members of his Cabinet to Moscow, where Marshal Stalin was willing to receive them. The President of the United States was also favourable. How could it be otherwise in these matters considering his deep interest in the Polish question? The Russian Armies now stand before the gates of Warsaw. They bring the liberation of Poland in their hands. They offer freedom, sovereignty and independence to the Poles. They ask that there should be a Poland friendly to Russia. This seems to me very reasonable considering the injuries which Russia has suffered through the Germans marching across Poland to attack her. The Allies would welcome any general rally or fusion of Polish Forces, both those who are working with the Western Powers and those who are working with the Soviet. We have several gallant Polish Divisions fighting the Germans in our Armies now and there are others who have been fighting in Russia. Let them come together. We desire this union and it would be a marvellous thing if it could be proclaimed, or at least its foundations laid, at the moment when the famous capital of Poland, which so valiantly defended itself against the Germans, has been liberated by the bravery of the Russian Armies.

Conditions in Yugoslavia have sensibly improved since I last dealt with this topic in the House. The lawful King of Yugoslavia, who came to us under our advice in his distress, has gathered round him under the Ban of Croatia, a Government in friendly contact with Marshal Tito. Representatives of the fighting administration of the partisans have taken their seat in the new Government, and we have General Velebit, a remarkable and accomplished soldier and thinker, who is the liaison between the King's Government and the Forces led by Marshal Tito. We are working for unity here and elsewhere for one purpose alone—namely, the gathering together of the whole united strength of Yugoslavia—Serbians, Croats, Slovenes—and the cleansing of their soil from the foul German invader. This union and this hurling out, I can assure the House, have good chances of being accomplished before long.

The Foreign Secretary made a statement last week about Greece which had the full assent of the War Cabinet and marks the line that we are taking in Greece. On this line we intend to fight, so far as may be needful, in the House. By fight in this case I mean argue and then, if necessary, vote. We have a clear view of the policy we intend to pursue and we shall do our best to carry it through even if we have not the satisfaction of unanimous agreement. In the Eastern Mediterranean it has fallen to us to handle most of the business. We lost about 30,000 men in Greece. We have unbreakable ties with that historic land. We keep our Allies constantly informed of everything that we do and we endeavour, and with good fortune in the main, to carry them with us. A measure of success has, I think, attended our recent handling of events. The Greek Navy is once again at sea. A Greek brigade will soon take its place in the line of battle in Italy. The Greek air squadrons are also doing useful work. The Government of M. Papandreou is broadly representative of all the main forces of Greece and this new figure who has sprung upon the stage seems to recall in many ways the vigour and courage which won such wide acclaim in the personality of the great Venizelos, whose son is also associated with the Greek Government.

It seems to me that Rumania must primarily make its terms with Russia, whom they have so outrageously assaulted and at whose mercy they will soon lay. Russia has offered generous terms to Rumania, and I have no doubt they would be accepted with gratitude by the Rumanian people, if only the Rumanian leaders had not got a Prussian automatic pistol pressed pretty closely against their breast or at the nape of their neck. The same applies to Bulgaria. Thrice thrown into wars on the wrong side by a miserable set of criminal politicians, who seem to be available for their country's ruin generation after generation, three times in my life has this wretched Bulgaria subjected a peasant population to all the pangs of war and chastisements of defeat. For them also, the moment of repentance has not passed, but it is passing swiftly. The whole of Europe is heading, irresistibly, into new and secure foundations. What will be the place of Bulgaria at the judgment seat, when the petty and cowardly part she has played in this war is revealed, and when the entire Yugoslav and Greek nations, through their representatives, will reveal at the Allies' armistice table the dismal tale of the work the Bulgarian Army has done their countries as the cruel lackeys of the fallen Nazi power.

In the Mediterranean theatre of war, I mentioned that we have recently had the satisfaction of welcoming as our comrades in arms, a finely-equipped expeditionary force from Brazil, and there are more legions to come from this great land which, for a long time, has been rendering valuable war service to the Allied cause both in the air and on the sea. As an Englishman, I may be pardoned at this moment for thinking of another South American country with which we have had close ties of friendship and mutual interest since her birth to liberty and independence. I refer to Argentina. We all feel deep regret and also anxiety as friends of Argentina, that in this testing time for nations she has not seen fit to declare herself unmistakably and with no reserve or qualification upon the side of freedom, and has chosen to dally with the evil, and not only with the evil, but with the losing side. I trust that my remarks will be noted, because this is a very serious war. It is not like some small wars in the past where all could be forgotten and forgiven. Nations must be judged by the part they play. Not only belligerents, but neutrals, will find that their position in the world cannot remain entirely unaffected by the part they have chosen to play in the crisis of the war.

When I last spoke I made some observations about Turkey which the House may perhaps remember. I have a great regard for the Turks and there is a current tradition in the British Army of sympathy and alliance with them. In the last war they were turned against us by the influence of a handful of men and the arrival of a single ship-of-war. We must not forget that Turkey declared her alliance with us before the present war when our arms were weak and our policy pacific. I visited Turkey in February of last year and had a lengthy conference with President Inonu and his Prime Minister, Mr. Sarajoglu. We had further conferences after Teheran when we met near the Pyramids. I am well aware of the difficulties of Turkey. When the war began she felt herself a strong military power. She looked out on the ranks of her brave army, her unrivalled infantry and cavalry, and she felt herself a strong military power and was resolute in her goodwill towards England and France.

Presently there appeared an entirely new set of weapons—aircraft, tanks, self-propelled artillery and mechanisation in every form, which altered the relative strength of Armies and seemed to be the only means by which victory could be procured. The Turkish Army was by no means modern. It was very much as it had come out of the last war or series of wars. I understand plainly the feelings of military prudence which made the action of Turkey less strong when these new facts were apparent to them all of a sudden at the opening of great battles. These difficulties have to a considerable extent been repaired. The German power is falling under the mighty Allied flail, and with the contribution we and the United States are making in Italy and France, and with the advance of Russia in the region of the Black Sea, I feel that the Turks are in a more secure position than they have ever been since the war began and that they will not be committing themselves to dangers against which they have no shield if they come forward on the side of their friends.

I have the authority of the Turkish Government to announce here to-day in the House of Commons that on the basis of the Anglo-Turkish Alliance Turkey has broken off all relations with Germany. This act infuses new life into the Alliance. No one can tell whether Germany or Bulgaria will attack Turkey. If so, we shall make common cause with her and shall take the German menace as well as we can in our stride. Turkish cities may receive the kind of bombardment we have never shrunk from here. Herr von Papen may be sent back to Germany to meet the blood bath he so narrowly escaped at Hitler's hands in 1934. I can take no responsibility for that. It was the policy of Mustapha Kemal to bring about close unity of action between the Russian and Turkish people. The elements are all there and he endeavoured to bring about an end to antagonism of centuries. I hope this new step will contribute to the friendship between Turkey and Russia.

Sir Hugh O'Neill (Antrim): Does that mean that Turkey is coming into the war on our side?

The Prime Minister: My right hon. Friend is surely well aware of the distinction between breaking off relations and declaring war. What the other Power may do, I cannot pretend to guess.

The ordeal of the House is very nearly at an end, and I hesitate to inflict myself on it any further, but there are so many important things to say that if you start to give an account of what is going on in this war and leave out anything important, great complaints are made.

Mr. Shinwell: Meet next week again.

The Prime Minister: At the present time, no speech by a prominent politician in any of the victorious countries could be deemed complete without a full exposition of the future organisation of the world. I was severely reproached last time for not having dealt methodically with this considerable topic. One of my difficulties is that it does not rest with me to lay down the law for all our Allies. If that was the general wish, I could certainly make one or two suggestions; but, odd as it may seem, countries like the United States and Soviet Russia might wish to have their say in the matter and might not look on it from exactly the same angle or express it in exactly the same terms as would gain the loudest applause in this House. I am sorry about this, because nothing would have given me greater pleasure than to devote a couple of hours in giving my personal ideas about the general lay out; but it would be very troublesome to all of us here if I made a great pronouncement on this subject and found myself contradicted and even repudiated by our most powerful Allies. From time to time a great many very eloquent statements are made on the future organisation of the world by the most eminent people. In spite of all urges that we should take the lead in laying down the law, I personally should prefer to hear the opinions of other powerful nations before committting our country to too many details.

Can we not be content with the broad declaration upon which we are all agreed, that there is to be a World Council to preserve peace which will, in the first instance, be formed and guided by the major Powers who have gained the war, and that thereafter other Powers, and eventually all Powers, will be offered their part in this world organisation? Can we not be content with that, and concentrate our efforts on winning a victory, bearing ourselves so prominently in the conflict that our words will receive honoured consideration when we come to the organisation of the peace?

In the meanwhile, as the House will be aware, important discussions on the official level are shortly to begin in Washington, and when those are completed we shall have a very much better idea where we stand. As I have said, it is vain and idle for any one country to try to lay down the law on this subject or to try to trace frontiers or describe the intricate instruments by which those frontiers will be maintained without further bloodshed; it is vain, and it is even unwise. The man who sold the hyena's skin while the beast lived was killed in hunting it—if I might venture to make a slight emendation of the poet's words.

Not only are those once proud German armies being beaten back on every front and by every one of the many nations who are in fighting contact with them, every single one, but, in their homeland in Germany, tremendous events have occurred which must shake to their foundations the confidence of the people and the loyalty of the troops. The highest personalities in the German Reich are murdering one another, or trying to, while the avenging armies of the Allies close upon the doomed and ever-narrowing circle of their power. We have never based ourselves on the strength of our enemy but only on the righteousness of our cause. Therefore, potent as may be these manifestations of internal disease, decisive as they may be one of these days, it is not in them that we should put our trust, but in our own strong arms and the justice of our cause.

Let us go on, then, to battle on every front. Thrust forward every man who can be found. Arm and equip the Forces in bountiful supply. Listen to no parley from the enemy. Vie with our valient Allies to intensify the conflict. Bear with unflinching fortitude whatever evils and blows we may receive. Drive on through the storm, now that it reaches its fury, with the same singleness of purpose and inflexibility of resolve as we showed to all the world when we were all alone.

PREMIER KUNIAKI KOISO'S BROADCAST TO THE JAPANESE PEOPLE

August 7, 1944 [1]

The World War has now developed into a conflict of exceptionally gigantic proportions. In all its recorded history, mankind has never witnessed anything so massive in scale. Our Empire also has come to be confronted by national difficulties of unprecedented seriousness.

Having unexpectedly been commanded by the Throne to organize a Cabinet at such a time in cooperation with Admiral Yonai, I undertook, in humble obedience to the august will of His Majesty, the task of forming a Cabinet. In reading in humility the Imperial Rescript, we cannot help but feel deeply moved by the profundity and graciousness of His Imperial council. It is as clear as day that if we translate into action these instructions so graciously granted to us, our victory in the war is inevitable.

In the two years and nine months since the outbreak of the war, the enemy, deeply distressed by profound difficulties of their own and by pressing internal and external developments, have encroached upon the Marianas in an attempt to obtain a quick decision in the war and to present appearances as if to strike at our homeland in a single blow. In the New Guinea area too, they have made gradual advances and have revealed their plan to threaten our lines of communication with the Southern Region. The time has now come when military operations by our Imperial Forces on a grand and bold scale are expectantly awaited, and at the same time, when our 100,000,000 people must arm themselves and in obedience to the Imperial Rescript, must combine our total strength to strike against the enemy and destroy their evil designs.

Reading in humility the Imperial Rescript on this occasion, I desire, in company with my fellow countrymen, especially to renew our consciousness of the real aim of the War of Greater East Asia, and reinforce still further our immutable faith in our certain victory. When we fully grasp the fundamental principles and significance of the national policy of our Empire, we know that the Rescript shows that our country must, with unity of spirit and matter and with oneness of the Sovereign and the people, completely ensure the defense of our Empire against the encroachment of external foes and thereby assure forevermore the glory of the Imperial Throne along with the eternity of heaven and earth.

We fully know also, that for 2,600 years since the founding of our Empire, successive Imperial ancestors leading our ancestors and their local subjects carried forward the task bequeathed by their Imperial ancestors; and that our present Sovereign, who is the living incarnation of the Imperial virtues, has constantly been solicitous of carrying forward the bequeathed task of ancestors and has endeavored earnestly to establish everlasting peace in East Asia. (They were) prevented, however, by the evil designs of the U. S. and Britain who think only in egotistic terms, and have been confronted by a situation in which not only has the attainment of the Imperial wish been rendered difficult, but even the homeland of our Empire cannot be made secure against the encroachment of the enemy.

Such developments having come to pass, there is but one conclusion, and

[1] Office of War Information.

that is, as indicated by the Imperial Rescript on Defense granted by the Imperial ancestors and as manifested by the Imperial Rescript declaring the present war, to consolidate resolutely our total strength to overcome all difficulties and thus win the war.

The way to win the war, too, is clearly indicated in the Imperial Rescript: "Officers and men of Our Army and Navy shall do their utmost in prosecuting the war, Our public servants of various departments shall perform faithfully and diligently their appointed tasks, and all other subjects of Ours shall pursue their respective duties; the entire Nation, with united will, shall mobilize their total strength so that nothing will miscarry in the attainment of our war aims." Will there be any among our 100,000,000 people who, in reading these gracious Imperial words and calmly reflecting, will not be thoroughly ashamed of himself, regardless of his occupation? We, subjects of His Majesty, obedient to the gracious counsel of Amaterasu Omikami on the unity of the Sovereign and the people, have faith in the absoluteness of the grand task of His Majesty and believe firmly that the mission to be performed respectively by us in our own fields of endeavor also is absolute.

When we hold fast to this faith and conviction and demonstrate the combined strength of the whole Nation, then there will result a power that will pervade throughout the universe and will serve to assist powerfully the destiny of the Imperial Throne coeval with heaven and earth. This power will bring about our complete victory and lead to the permanent security of our Empire. When the fighting services, Government officials, and the people in general, dedicate all they have and are in service to His Majesty in obedience to the Imperial Rescript and in great harmony and unity demonstrate their absolute strength in performing their respective duties, then will the supreme justice and righteousness of mankind be firmly established, the necessary quantity of materials for victory naturally will be acquired together with Divine help, large scale and bold military operations to crush the enemy will be further strengthened, and thus may we confidently expect ultimate victory in the War of Greater East Asia.

This, I believe, is the prime essential of our faith in the sure victory which I propose with all my heart that my fellow countrymen will fully grasp. The war is now extremely intense, and difficult situations arise in various parts of our front lines. This I believe to be a trial which has been assigned to us by the hallowed spirits of our Imperial ancestors in order that we may further gain in strength. And only when we hold fast to this faith in certainty of our victory, and triumph over this trial, then only shall Divine help be bestowed upon us. Until that Divine help comes, we must endure every hardship and do everything in our power to overcome this trial.

It goes without saying that the Government will concentrate all their measures on the point of attaining complete victory in the war. We are determined, with the recently established Supreme Council for the Direction of the War as a basis, to bring about not only the rapid expansion of our armed strength but also the stabilization and further brightening of the people's livelihood, for all of which no efforts will be spared.

Fellow countrymen, the winning of the war is the only way to safeguard our glorious Empire. Let us meet all our difficulties as a God-given trial, let us overcome them, and with faith in God and consecrating our all to His Imperial Majesty, let us devote all of our efforts to the winning of complete victory. Let me repeat the passage in the Imperial Rescript which says, "We rely upon the loyalty and courage of Our subjects."

The time has now come when, in coordination with bold and large-scale operations of the Imperial Forces, our entire Nation should all arm themselves, consolidate their total power, and vigorously march forward together to destroy the evil designs of the enemy. The war situation which we now face is indeed of the greatest importance in which we must respond heart and soul to the gracious trust of His Imperial Majesty in us. The opportunity for which the supreme efforts of our 100,000,000 people should be made is now at hand, and will, I believe, never come again.

FIRST ADDRESS BY PRESIDENT SERGIO OSMENA OF THE PHILIPPINES TO HIS CABINET

August 10, 1944 [1]

GENTLEMEN OF THE CABINET:

Nine days ago when I performed the painful duty of announcing the passing of our beloved leader, President Manuel L. Quezon, I said, in part:

President Quezon's death is a great loss to the freedom loving world. No champion of liberty fought for such a noble cause with more determination and against greater odds. His whole life was dedicated to the achievement of his people's freedom, and it is one of the sad paradoxes of fate that with the forces of victory fast approaching the Philippines, he should pass away now and be deprived of seeing the culmination of his labors—the freedom of his people.

President Quezon was a champion of freedom in war and in peace. The plains and hills of Bataan where the brave Filipino and American soldiers faced with heroism the overwhelming power of the Japanese invader were also his field of action during the Revolutionary Days. The city of Washington where his body temporarily rests was the scene of his early appeals and peaceful efforts for Philippine freedom. It was here, almost thirty years ago, where he secured from Congress the promise of independence which is contained in the preamble of the Jones Law. Here, again, eighteen years later, he succeeded in obtaining the passage of the Tydings-McDuffie Act—a re-enactment with some slight amendments of the Hare-Hawes-Cutting Law which was rejected previously by the Philippine Legislature. Pursuant to the provisions of the Tydings-McDuffie Law, which was accepted by the Filipino people, we drafted our Constitution and established the present Commonwealth of the Philippines, and elected Manuel L. Quezon as its first President.

When the war came and it became necessary to evacuate Manila, President Quezon, frail and sick as he was, moved with his Cabinet to Corregidor where he shared with the soldiers the rigors of tunnel life and from there braved the hazards of a perilous journey to the Visayas, Mindanao, Australia and America, in order to continue the fight for the freedom of his people. Here, in Washington, with his War Cabinet, he functioned as the legitimate Government of the Filipino people and served as the symbol of their redemption.

It was largely through his untiring efforts that the Philippines was made a member of the United Nations and accorded a seat in the Pacific War Council. It was through his initiative that negotiations were held, resulting in the introduction of Senate Joint Resolutions 93 and 94. By the terms of Senate Joint Resolution 93, the advancement of the date of independence prior to July 4, 1946, was authorized and the pledge given to the Filipino people by President

[1] United Nations Review.

Roosevelt in 1941—that Philippine independence will not only be established but also protected—was sanctioned by Congress. His efforts to secure the rehabilitation of the Philippines from the ravages of war resulted in the enactment by Congress of Senate Joint Resolution 94 which provides for the physical and economic rehabilitation of the Philippines. Even before Congress definitely acted on this resolution, he had already created the Postwar Planning Board, entrusting it, together with his Cabinet, with the task of making studies and submitting recommendations looking toward the formulation of a comprehensive rehabilitation program for the Philippines.

In the last few moments before his martyrdom, the great Rizal lamented that he would not be able to see the dawn of freedom break over his beloved country, but he prophesied that his countrymen would see that day. "I have sown the seeds," he said, "others are left to reap." Quezon, more fortunate than Rizal, died with the comforting thought that the freedom of the Philippines was already an incontestable reality, awaiting only the certain defeat of the enemy for its full expression.

The immediate duty, then, of those of us who, under the mandate of the Constitution and the laws of the Philippines, are charged with the mission of continuing President Quezon's work, is to follow the course he has laid, to maintain and strengthen our partnership with America, and to march forward with the United Nations with unwavering faith and resolute determination until complete victory is won.

The tide of the war which rose high against us in the early stages of the struggle has turned in our favor. The forces of victory are on the march everywhere—in Europe, in India, and China, and in the Pacific. Normandy and Brittany have been occupied by the Anglo-American forces. Poland is half reconquered by our great Russian ally. Two thirds of the Italian peninsula are in our hands, while thousands and thousands of planes continue to batter and destroy German communication and production centers, bringing the war to the German homeland.

In the Pacific, the progress of the war has been equally impressive. Most of the Japanese strongholds in the Bismark archipelago, in New Guinea, in the Gilberts and in the Marshalls, have fallen. The Japanese bastion of Saipan is in Allied hands; so is Tinian. The reconquest of Guam is almost completed. B-29's, the American super-fortresses, are already penetrating the Japanese inner defenses, causing destruction in the enemy's vital centers of production. General MacArthur's forces are hammering the enemy's outposts only 250 miles from the Philippines; while the United States Navy, maintaining mastery in the central Pacific, is relentlessly attacking Palau, Yap, Ponape and the Bonin Islands, in its steady advance towards the Philippines, China and Japan.

The size and strength of the Allied landings in Europe, supported by thousands of planes and using thousands of ships, surpasses the imagination. It is no wonder that before them the most formidable defenses of the enemy are crumbling. I believe that when our D-Day comes the same pattern will be followed, and the mighty Allied forces will join our brave loyal countrymen in an epic victory.

But the forces of freedom will not land in the Philippines with guns and tanks alone. They will also bring with them food, medical supplies and clothing which are so much needed by our suffering people. 30,000,000 pesos have already been set aside for the requisition of these supplies which will be sent to the front as soon as possible for distribution to our civilian population. As the war progresses and as more troops are landed in the Philippines, increasing quantities of these supplies will be made available. Philippine relief will be prompt and adequate.

As Philippine territory is wrested from the enemy, civil government will promptly follow military occupation so that the orderly processes of self-government may be established under the Constitution. Red Cross units, both Filipino and American, will follow the armies of freedom to help alleviate the sufferings of the people. Hospitals, health and puericulture centers will be re-established. All the schools in operation before the war will be reopened in order to resume an education of patriotism, democracy and humanitarianism.

The veterans of our wars for independence, and all those who supported our struggle for freedom, will receive for their labors and sacrifices the full recognition expected of a grateful nation. War widows and orphans will be provided for. Ample compensation will be made for the destruction of public and private properties. Roads and bridges destroyed by the enemy will be rebuilt. Disrupted communications by land, sea and air, will be repaired and improved. Towns and cities which either were destroyed or suffered damages because of the war will be reconstructed under a systematic and scientific town planning program. In this program, the towns of Bataan and Zambales will receive preferential attention. Bataan, the historic battleground where our brave soldiers, Americans and Filipinos, faced the enemy until death, will be made a national shrine.

In providing for the reconstruction of our industries and the rehabilitation of our agriculture, immediate attention will be given to factory workers and farm hands throughout the Philippines, and full and generous assistance will be given to the small farmers who, because of the war, have lost with their nipa hut, their work animals and farm implements.

We are making preparations to meet the manifold problems arising from the closing and insolvency of our banks, insurance and credit institutions, the adulteration of our currency with unsound enemy issues, the impairment of the basis of taxation and the initial difficulty of tax collection. Moreover, we are formulating a long-range economic program with a view to securing that sound economic foundation which will give our independence stability and permanence.

In the gigantic task of rehabilitation and reconstruction, we are assured of America's full assistance and support. The joint Filipino-American Rehabilitation Commission, created by Congress is already functioning. This Commission is under the chairmanship of a staunch friend of the Filipino people, Senator Tydings of Maryland. To it is entrusted the task of studying and recommending to the United States and Philippine Governments measures calculated to secure the complete physical and economic rehabilitation of the Philippines and the re-establishment as soon as possible of such commercial relations between the two countries as will assure us a reasonable level of public and private prosperity.

In the preparation and execution of the Filipino rehabilitation program, America's support and assistance are essential. But there are responsibilities which we as a people must undertake ourselves, and which can be assumed only if we are faithful to our ideals, principles and commitments.

We are a Christian people and the faith that we imbibed sprang from our contacts with nations of Occidental civilization. We embraced Christianity a century before the Pilgrim Fathers landed at Plymouth. For more than 400 years we have kept that faith. We cannot now turn back and be a pagan people.

For centuries we have been a law-abiding people. We believe in and practice democracy. That is the reason why Section III, Article II of our Constitution provides that we renounce war as an instrument of national policy and adopt the generally accepted principles of international law as a part of the law of the nation. It is repugnant to our Christian traditions and democratic ideals to be the satellite of a conquering power or to be allied with the masters of brute force, whether in Asia, Europe or elsewhere.

The mutual relationship between the American and Filipino peoples for half a century has revealed to the Filipinos the high ideals of the American nation and the good faith that has always animated the United States in its dealings with us. Out of this association have arisen mutual understanding and continuous co-operation between the two countries, resulting in great national progress for the Philippines, progress that is without parallel in history. In the Epic of Bataan where the American and Filipino soldiers fought together, the enduring friendship of our two peoples was sealed.

In this war between a free world and a slave world, the Philippines has freely and voluntarily taken side with the defenders of liberty and democracy. In the same manner as the enemy is resorting to every means to attain his evil ends, the United Nations are exerting their utmost to achieve complete victory. Pledged in this war to the finish, we will continue doing our best to help the war effort. Every commitment made by us in this respect will be fulfilled.

The Filipino people, with their wisdom in peace and gallantry in war, have established their right to take a place in the family of nations as a full and sovereign member. We cannot renounce this right nor its obligations and responsibilities. We shall, as a free and self-respecting nation, fulfill our duties not only to ourselves but also to the entire freedom-loving world by participating in the establishment and preservation of a just peace for the benefit of mankind.

Our path of duty is clear. It is the path of national honor, dignity and responsibility. It was laid out for us by the great heroes of our race—Rizal, Bonifacio and Quezon. We shall move forward steadily to reach our goal, maintaining our faith in the United States and fully co-operating with her.

In the fulfillment of my duties as President of the Philippines, I ask in all humility but in all earnestness the co-operation of all my countrymen in the United States, Hawaii, in the homeland and elsewhere in the world. With their full and unstinted co-operation and support, and God helping me, I shall not fail.

PRESIDENT ROOSEVELT'S BROADCAST AT THE PUGET SOUND NAVY YARD, ON THE WAR IN THE PACIFIC

August 12, 1944 [1]

LADIES AND GENTLEMEN, OFFICERS AND MEN OF THE PUGET SOUND NAVY YARD:

I am glad to be back here in well-known surroundings, for, as you know, I have been coming here off and on ever since I was Assistant Secretary of the Navy in 1913, and that's over thirty years ago.

[1] White House news release.

It's nearly about four weeks ago since I left Washington, but, of course, at all times I have been in close touch with the work there and also in daily communication with our forces in the European and Far Eastern theatres of war.

Since my visit here at Bremerton nearly two years ago I have been happy at all times to know of the splendid progress that is being maintained—kept up—both here and at many other places on the Coast, progress in turning out ships and planes and munitions of almost every other kind and in the training of men and women for all of the armed forces.

So I have thought that you would be interested in an informal summary of the trip I have just taken to Hawaii and from there to the Aleutian Islands and Alaska, from which, when I get across the Sound, I am about to step foot on the shore of the continental United States again.

When I got to San Diego three weeks ago I spent three days before going on shipboard, and I had the opportunity at the southern end of the Pacific Coast to visit many of the patients in the large hospitals there, a large number of these patients having just come back from the fighting in the Marshall Islands and the Marianas.

And I also witnessed a large practice landing operation on the beaches of Southern California, between Los Angeles and San Diego.

It's a kind of warfare that has been most successfully developed by us during the past two years. It's a warfare of a wholly new type calling for all kinds of new equipment and new training.

And I think I can safely say that no other nation in the world has worked it out as successfully as we have—the way we have shown it within the past few weeks in the capture of Saipan and Tinian and the recapturing of Guam, an effort which is resulting in new threats against Japan itself and against all of their operations in the Southwest Pacific.

You know, it takes a personal observation—you've got to see things with your own eyes, such as I saw from a high bluff right on the coast overlooking the shore below—to understand how well the application of experience in war is being carried out.

The landing craft, a wholly new type of ship, one we didn't dream of two years and a half ago, came to the beach from the transports that were lying offshore under cover of a fog.

They came on in waves, the marines and the infantry getting the first toehold, followed by other waves and then by all manner of equipment, ammunition and wire and tanks, all protected by air coverage and preceded theoretically—because I wouldn't be here today if it was real—by a devastating bombardment from heavy ships lying offshore.

When the beachhead was obtained to a depth of a mile or two there followed the unloading of great quantities of supplies and stores of all kinds, including tanks and trucks and jeeps.

Timing—that's why we have to practice this—timing is of the utmost importance. Any operation of this kind has to be carried out click-click-click, right on schedule, together with instantaneous communication both the radio, the written kind and the voice from the shore to the ships and to the planes themselves.

Here was demonstrated the perfect cooperation between all the services—Army and Navy and Marines, and to this should be added the teamwork for the immediate care of the wounded—in the case I saw it was the theoretically wounded—and the quick transfer of them back to the hospital ships.

We in our comfortable homes, I think, ought to realize more than we do that to all troops and Marines who are to conduct a new landing expedition on some far distant island in the Pacific, as well as on the coast of France, this amphibious training is being given at a number of places in the United States before the expedition ever starts.

Hundreds of instructors are required, nearly all men who have participated in actual combat operations beforehand, and many of these instructors, most of them, indeed, will, of course, accompany the troops in the actual operation of the future landings.

The cruiser, which is on her way to another place, the cruiser on which I went from San Diego to Honolulu, is one of a number of what we call post-treaty cruisers, much larger, more powerful and faster than the pre-war cruisers, which were limited by the old treaties to 10,000 tons.

This particular ship on which I voyaged joined the Pacific Fleet less than a year ago in the Western and Southwestern Pacific. Hers is a magnificent record. Her skipper and crew have brought her through all of these many offensive missions unscathed, fifteen of them, fifteen battles.

And because of the experience that she has gained and that they have gained she is an even more powerful weapon than she was the day that she joined the fleet.

Well, the voyage was uneventful and we arrived at Pearl Harbor on July 26. At this moment may I just add a word of appreciation to the press and the radio of our country. You know we have a voluntary censorship, purely voluntary. I want to thank them for the protection and the security which they gave to me and to my party at a time on this trip when nearly all the time I was within easy reach of enemy action.

The press associations and some of the newspapers actually refused to publish the facts which they got from local friends who had heard of my arrival and my trip around the Hawaiian Islands—or from local friends whose sons out there had written home about it—and the newspapers didn't print it. That is a modern marvel.

Well, I got there on the twenty-sixth of July and what an amazing change since my visit there ten years ago: as big and bigger a change than a comparison between the Puget Sound Navy Yard of today with what this was ten years ago.

But out there—the change! At that time Pearl Harbor had maintained a steady growth as this yard has, so that today it is capable of making repairs to the heaviest ships, and employs a force nearly ten times as great as it did then. And, incidentally, very many of that force came straight there during the past two years and a half from the West Coast.

All of the battleships and smaller craft that were sunk or damaged in the attack on Pearl Harbor on the seventh of December, 1941, have been raised with the exception of the Arizona. In her case, because of the explosion in her forward magazine, salvage was impossible. But again in her case, her main battery of heavy guns was removed and remounted and now forms a part of the coastal defenses on the island of Oahu.

All of the other ships are afloat, most of them having been put back into commission here at Puget Sound, and nobody will ever forget that.

And, incidentally, the ships that you put back into commission, what you did to them in the process, has made of them vastly more powerful ships, better ships, with more gun power than they had before they were sunk.

And that's one thing that I'll never forget, the way that sunken fleet was set afloat again and has gone over the world in actually carrying out the plans of this war.

They've been in service, they've been in action, in the Pacific and elsewhere. Indeed, one of them, I think it is the Nevada, took part in the bombardment of the coast of Normandy during and after the landing operations there on the sixth of June of this year.

I spent three days on the Island of Oahu, and everywhere, as at the Navy Yard, the war activities have multiplied almost beyond belief.

On the afternoon of my arrival my old friend General Douglas MacArthur arrived by air from New Guinea and we began a series of extremely interesting and useful conferences, accompanied by Admiral Nimitz and by my own Chief of Staff, Admiral Leahy, who stands beside me now, and General Richardson, the commanding general of the Army forces in the Hawaiian area and Admiral Halsey, commander of the Third Fleet.

In the three days we were there we talked about Pacific problems and the best methods of conducting the Pacific campaign in the days to come. These discussions developed complete accord both in the understanding of the problem that confronts us and in the opinion as to the best methods for its solution.

All of us must bear in mind the enormous size of the Pacific Ocean, the Pacific area, keeping a mental map of the world constantly in mind. The distances are greater there than anywhere else on earth.

In the old days the Hawaiian Islands used to be considered an outpost. We were not allowed to fortify Guam, nor did we fortify Wake, or Midway or Samoa.

Today the Hawaiian Islands are no longer a mere outpost. They constitute a major base from which, and from the Pacific coast, front-line operations are being conducted twice as far away as the distance between the coast and Hawaii itself.

The Hawaiian Islands have helped to make possible the victories at Guadalcanal and New Guinea and the Marshalls and the Marianas. The islands will make possible future operations in China—will make possible the recapture and independence of the Philippines and make possible the carrying of war into the home islands of Japan itself and their capital city of Tokyo.

In a few minutes I think it will interest you if you will let me say a few additional words about the future of the Pacific.

But first, during the rest of my stay in Hawaii, I visited the many activities, including the great airfields, the hospitals and an ambulance plane at Hickam Field which had just flown in with wounded men from Saipan. I reviewed the Seventh Division, which has made such a splendid record.

I saw a large Army group that was going through a complete course in jungle warfare—they have to do it there because we haven't got any jungles around here—jungle warfare, an art which we have developed so expertly that our troops are more than a match in the jungle for any Japanese whom we have met yet. And I am proud of all of this basic training and the final training of our sons—all that they're getting both at home and when they get near the front.

After rejoining our ship we headed for the Aleutian Islands. I had read about them—heard about them—but I'd never been there before.

Arriving four days later at Adak, which is one of the more westerly islands of the group, there again I found intense activity at what might be called a nearly completed advance base. It was from there that a great part of the expeditions for the recapture of Attu and Kiska started. Adak two years ago was a bleak and practically uninhabited spot which with the other

Aleutian Islands seemed relatively unimportant in the plans for the security of our own continent.

You here can well realize the commotion that followed the Japanese occupation of Attu and Kiska. You've dreamt of Japanese marching up the streets of Bremerton or Seattle tomorrow morning. You may have thought that the Chiefs of Staff in Washington were not paying enough attention to the threat against Alaska and the coast. We realized, of course, that such a Japanese threat could become serious if it was unopposed. But we knew also that Japan did not have the naval and air power to carry the threat into effect without greater resources and a longer time to carry it out.

Preparation to throw the Japanese from their toehold, very skimpy toehold, had been laid even before the Japs got there, and the rest of the story you know.

It took great preparations and heavy fighting to eject them from Attu and by the time the great expedition to recapture Kiska got there the Japanese had decided that discretion was the better part of valor. They decided that retirement and retreat was better for them than hara-kiri and so they abandoned the Aleutians.

The climate at Adak is not the most inviting in the world, but I want to say a word of appreciation to the thousands of officers and men of all the services who have built up this base and other bases, many other bases, in the extreme northwest of the American Continent, built them up in such a short time to a point where the people of our Pacific Coast, the people of British Columbia and of Alaska, can feel certain that we are safe against Japanese invasion on any large scale.

We were delayed by fog and rain as almost everybody is up in those parts; we had to give up putting in at Dutch Harbor but we did stop at Kodiak, a large island off the end of the Alaskan Peninsula. Here, also, the three services completed a very excellent, though smaller, base. The first little town really that we built in those parts, and there's actually a small community there, the first that we saw in Alaskan waters and the first trees that we saw, because the outer Aleutians just don't have trees. That town and those trees made me think of the coasts of Maine and Newfoundland.

We were told that a number of officers and men at this place and other posts are considering settling in Alaska after the war is over. I do hope that this is so because the development of Alaska has only been scratched and it is still the country of the pioneers, and in one sense every American is a descendant of pioneers.

Only a small part of Alaska's resources have been explored and there is, of course, an abundance of fish and game and timber, together with great possibilities for agriculture. I could not help remembering that the climate and the crops and other resources are not essentially different from northern Europe—Norway and Sweden, Finland—for the people of these countries in spite of the cold and in winter darkness have brought their civilizations to a very high and very prosperous level. On my return to Washington I am going to set up a study of Alaska and the Aleutian Islands as a place to which many veterans of this war, especially those who do not have strong home roots, can go to become pioneers. Alaska is a land with a very small population, but I am convinced that it has great opportunities for those who are willing to work and to help build up all kinds of new things in new lands.

So this trip has given me a chance to talk over the social and economic future of the Hawaiian group with Governor Stainback and the future of the people of Alaska with Governor Gruening. By the way, he asked me to assure you that the tan which I have acquired in Alaska in a week has come from the bright sunlight of Alaska. Near Juneau one afternoon, when we were nearly fogged out, I played hookey for three hours. I went fishing and I caught one halibut and one flounder.

Speaking again of the future, of the future of the defense of the Pacific and the use of its strong points in order to prevent attacks against us.

You who live in the Pacific Northwest have realized that a line for sea and air navigation following the Great Circle course from Puget Sound to Siberia and China passes very close to the Alaskan coast and thence westward along the line of the Aleutian Islands.

From the point of view of national defense, therefore, it is essential that our control of this route shall be undisputed. Everybody in Siberia and China knows that we have no ambition to acquire land on the Asiatic continent.

We as a people are utterly opposed to aggression and sneak attacks. But we as a people are insistent that other nations must not under any circumstances through the foreseeable future commit such attacks against the United States. Therefore, it is essential that we be fully prepared to prevent them for all time to come.

The word and the honor of Japan cannot be trusted. That is a simple statement from the military and naval and air point of view. But with the end of a Japanese threat, soon we hope, there is an excellent outlook for a permanent peace in the whole of the Pacific area.

It is therefore natural and proper for us to think of the economic and the commercial future. It is logical that we should foresee a great interchange of commerce between our shores and those of Siberia and China.

And in this commercial development Alaska and the Aleutian Islands become automatic stepping stones for trade, both by water and by cargo planes. And this means the automatic development of transportation on the way there, including the Puget Sound area.

It is as long as ten years, I think, that I talked with Mr. Mackenzie King, Prime Minister of Canada, in regard to the development of highways, in regard to air routes and even a railroad via the northwest and British Columbia and the Yukon. Great interest in both nations was aroused but it took the war to get quick action.

Today the Alcan Highway is practically completed and an air route to Fairbanks enables us to deliver thousands of planes to our ally Russia by way of Alaska and Bering Straits and Siberia. These planes are an important factor in the brilliant and brave advance of the Russian armies on their march to Berlin. And I might observe also that our close relations, our true friendship with Canada during these years has proved to be an illustrious example of working hand in hand with your neighbor for the general good.

South of this northern route, Alaska and the Aleutians, the use of other island groups must also be thought of for defense and for commerce in getting to and from the Asiatic and the American Continents. We understand at last the importance of the Hawaiian Islands. It is important that we have other bases, forward bases nearer to Japan than Hawaii lies.

The same thing, we have to remember, holds true in regard to the defense of all the other American Republics, twenty others, from Mexico down past the Panama Canal and all the way down to Chile. There are hundreds of islands in the South Pacific that bear the same relation to South America and Central America and the Panama Canal as Hawaii bears to North America.

These islands are mostly in the possession of the British Empire and the French. They are important commercially just as they are from the defense point of view because they lead to New Zealand, and Australia, and the Dutch Islands and the Southern Philippines. With all these places we undoubtedly are going to have a growing trade.

We have no desire to ask for any possessions of the United Nations. But the United Nations who are working so well with us in the winning of the war will, I am confident, be glad to join us in protection against aggression and in machinery to prevent aggression. With them and with their help I am sure that we can agree completely so that Central and South America will be as safe against attack—attack from the South Pacific—as North America is going to be very soon from the North Pacific as well.

The self-interest of our Allies is going to be affected by fair and friendly collaboration with us. They too will gain in national security. They will gain economically. The destinies of the peoples of the whole Pacific will for many years be entwined with our own destiny. Already there are stirring among hundreds of millions of them a desire for the right to work out their own destinies and they show no evidence in this Pacific area to overrun the earth —with one exception.

That exception is and has been for many, many years that of Japan and the Japanese people—because whether or not the people of Japan itself know and approve of what their war lords and their home lords have done for nearly a century, the fact remains that they seem to be giving hearty approval to the Japanese policy of acquision of their neighbors and their neighbors' lands and a military and economic control of as many other nations as they can lay their hands on.

It is an unfortunate fact that other nations cannot trust Japan. It is an unfortunate fact that years of proof must pass by before we can trust Japan and before we can classify Japan as a member of the society of nations which seeks permanent peace and whose word we can take.

In removing the future menace of Japan to us and to our continent we are holding out the hope that other people in the Far East can be freed from the same threat.

The people of the Philippines never have wished and never will wish to be slaves of Japan. Of the people of Korea, that ancient kingdom which was overrun by the Japanese half a century ago, the same is true. The peoples of Manchuria and all the rest of China, feel the same.

The same thing is true of the peoples of Indo-China and Siam, the peoples of Java and even the most primitive peoples of New Guinea and the so-called mandated islands which I am glad to say we are in the splendid process of throwing the Japs out from.

I am glad to have the opportunity of taking this short trip, first, for the conferences with General MacArthur and Admiral Nimitz and, secondly, for the first hand view of certain bases that are of vital importance to the ending of the war and to the prevention in the future of any similar attack.

More than a million of our troops are today overseas in the Pacific. The war is well in hand in this vast area, but I cannot tell you, if I knew, when the war will be over, either in Europe or in the Far East or the war against Japan itself.

It will be over sooner, if the people of this country will maintain the making of the necessary supplies of ships and planes and all the things that go with them. By so doing we shall hasten the day of the peace. By so doing we will save our own pocketbooks and those of our children. And by so doing we will stand a better chance of substantial unity not only at home but among the United Nations in laying so securely what we all want, the foundation of a lasting peace.

GENERAL EISENHOWER'S ORDER OF THE DAY TO THE ALLIED ARMIES IN FRANCE

August 13, 1944 [1]

Allied soldiers, sailors and airmen: Through your combined skill, valor and fortitude, you have created in France a fleeting but definite opportunity for a major Allied victory, one whose realization will mean notable progress toward the final downfall of our enemy. In the past I have in moments of unusual significance made special appeals to the Allied forces it has been my honor to command. Without exception the response has been unstinted and the result beyond my expectations.

Because the victory we can now achieve is infinitely greater than any it so far has been possible to accomplish in the west, and because this opportunity may be grasped only through the utmost in zeal, determination and speedy action, I make my present appeal to you more urgent than ever before.

I request that every airman make it his direct responsibility that the enemy is blasted unceasingly by day and by night and denied safety either in fight or in flight.

I request that every sailor make sure that no part of the hostile forces can either escape or be reinforced by sea, and that our comrades on land want nothing that guns and ships and the ships' companies can bring to them.

I request every soldier to go forward to his assigned objective with the determination that the enemy can survive only through surrender; let no foot of ground once gained be relinquished nor a single German escape through a line once established.

With all of us resolutely performing our special tasks we can make this week a momentous one in the history of this war—a brilliant and fruitful week for us and a fateful one for the ambitions of the Nazi tyrants.

CALL TO ARMS BY THE FRENCH COMMITTEE OF NATIONAL LIBERATION, BROADCAST TO THE PEOPLE OF FRANCE

August 14, 1944 [2]

Frenchmen, your duty has been outlined to you in an appeal from General de Gaulle to the people of France. We repeat:

There is no Frenchman who does not feel or know that it is his simple and sacred duty to participate immediately in the supreme war effort of his

[1] *New York Times.*
[2] *Ibid.*

country. In the fields, in the factories, in the work shops, in the offices, at home and on the streets, whether he is under arrest, deported, or a prisoner of war, every Frenchman can harass the enemy or prepare to harass him. The French resistance movement is active everywhere. You will have only to join it and follow its orders.

The national uprising in Brittany has contributed largely to the liberation of that region. The French Forces of the Interior in all regions of France have received their battle orders. All Frenchmen who want to join them and all those who already have joined the fighting units must comply with the following instructions which will guarantee the success of the national uprising:

All Frenchmen in Brittany must cooperate with the French Forces of the Interior to annihilate enemy groups and isolated garrisons trying to reach enemy-held ports or trying to escape eastward.

In the regions north of the Loire Frenchmen should seize weapons from the enemy and arrest collaborators.

Form small, mobile groups and join the formations of the French Forces of the Interior. Attack the enemy. Take prisoners.

Workmen in factories working directly or indirectly for the enemy: Go on strike and remain on strike until the arrival of the Allies will allow you to resume work.

Officials: Take your orders from authorities trusted by the resistance movement. They are representatives of the Provisional Government of the French Republic.

Patriots in the region between the Loire and Garonne: Join the French Forces of the Interior. Harass enemy formations which might try to go northward in the direction of Paris or eastward. Destroy small enemy garrisons and SS elements.

In the Pyrenees: The patriotic population will try to prevent, at all cost, collaborators from crossing the Pyrenees, the authorities of the so-called Vichy Government, enemy agents, military men, officers and soldiers of the Wehrmacht trying to find refuge abroad.

Special instructions will be given for Paris and its suburbs.

Frenchmen, the hour of liberation has struck. Join the Forces of the Interior. Follow the orders of their leaders. The national uprising will be the signal of liberation.

Frenchmen, arise! To arms!

HULL, GROMYKO, CADOGAN STATEMENTS AT OPENING OF DUMBARTON OAKS CONFERENCE

August 21, 1944 [1]

Remarks by the Secretary of State

On behalf of President Roosevelt and on my own behalf, I welcome you to Washington. In the name of both of us, I desire to offer some brief remarks on the opening of this important meeting.

[1] State Department Bulletin.

The series of conversations which we initiate today marks another step toward establishing a lasting system of organized and peaceful relations among nations. We meet at a time when the war is moving toward an overwhelming triumph for the forces of freedom. It is our task here to help lay the foundations upon which, after victory, peace, freedom, and a growing prosperity may be built for generations to come.

The very character of this war moves us to search for an enduring peace— a peace founded upon justice and fair dealing for individuals and for nations. We have witnessed—and are witnessing today—the sweep of forces of savagery and barbarism of the kind that civilized men hoped and believed would not rise again. Armed with the weapons of modern science and technology and with equally powerful weapons of coercion and deceit, these forces almost succeeded in enslaving mankind because the peace-loving nations were disunited. During the years while these aggressors made their preparations for attack, the peace-loving nations lacked both unity and strength because they lacked a vigilant realization of the perils which loomed before them. These forces of evil now face utter defeat because, at long last, their intended victims attained the unity and armed power which are now bringing victory to us.

The lessons of earlier disunity and weakness should be indelibly stamped upon the minds and hearts of this generation and of generations to come. So should the lessons of unity and its resultant strength achieved by the United Nations in this war.

Unity for common action toward common good and against common peril is the sole effective method by which, in time of peace, the nations which love peace can assure for themselves security and orderly progress, with freedom and justice. In the face of what modern war means to the physical and moral being of man, the maintenance of such unity is a matter of the highest and most enlightened self-interest. In the final analysis it is, first and foremost, a thing of the spirit.

Peace, like liberty, requires constant devotion and ceaseless vigilance. It requires willingness to take positive steps toward its preservation. It requires constant cooperation among the nations and determination to live together as good neighbors in a world of good neighbors. Peace requires an acceptance of the idea that its maintenance is a common interest so precious and so overwhelmingly important that all differences and controversies among nations can and must be resolved by resort to pacific means.

But peace also requires institutions through which the will to peace can be translated into action. The devising of such institutions is a challenge to the wisdom and ingenuity of men and women everywhere. That is why the United Nations, in the midst of a relentless prosecution of the war, have been working together to create the institutional foundations for a just and enduring peace.

These foundations must support arrangements for peaceful settlement of international disputes and for the joint use of force, if necessary, to prevent or suppress threats to the peace or breaches of the peace. They must also support arrangements for promoting, by cooperative effort, the development of conditions of stability and well-being necessary for peaceful and friendly relations among nations and essential to the maintenance of security and peace. These are basic problems of international organization.

Substantial progress has already been achieved through the Food and Agriculture Conference, the Conference on Relief and Rehabilitation, and the Financial and Monetary Conference. These and other similar steps are indicative of the profound desire of the United Nations to act together for advancing the well-being of their peoples. They have been achieved by united effort of more than 40 nations, large and small.

The governments represented here are fully agreed in their conviction that the future maintenance of peace and security—the supreme objective of international cooperation—must be a joint task and a joint responsibility of all peace-loving nations, large and small. They solemnly proclaimed this conviction in a declaration of their Foreign Ministers at Moscow on October 30, 1943. It cannot be emphasized too often that the principle of the sovereign equality of *all* peace-loving states, irrespective of size and strength, as partners in a system of order under law, must constitute the foundation of any future international organization for the maintenance of peace and security.

In the Moscow Declaration each Government also assumed its share of responsibility for leadership in bringing about the creation of an international organization for this purpose through joint action by all peace-loving nations. Success or failure of such an organization will depend upon the degree to which the participating nations are willing to exercise self-restraint and assume the responsibilities of joint action in support of the basic purposes of the organization. There must be agreement among all whereby each can play its part to the best mutual advantage and bear responsibility commensurate with its capacity.

It is generally agreed that any peace and security organization would surely fail unless backed by force to be used ultimately in case of failure of all other means for the maintenance of peace. That force must be available promptly, in adequate measure, and with certainty. The nations of the world should maintain, according to their capacities, sufficient forces available for joint action when necessary to prevent breaches of the peace.

For a long time before the Moscow Conference, and especially during the months which have elapsed since that Conference, each of our Governments has been making diligent preparations for an effort to reach the agreement to which I have just referred. We have committed our tentative thoughts to writing, and each of us has had an opportunity to study the results of the work done by the others. All this should make easier the task which is now before you of reaching a consensus of views which you can jointly recommend to your respective Governments.

It is the intention of the Government of the United States that after similar consultations with the Government of China the conclusions reached will be communicated to the Governments of all the United Nations and of other peace-loving nations.

It is our further thought that as soon as practicable these conclusions will be made available to the peoples of our countries and of all countries for public study and debate. We are fully aware that no institution—especially when it is of as great importance as the one now in our thoughts—will endure unless there is behind it considered and complete popular support. The will to peace must spring from the hearts and minds of men and women everywhere if it is to achieve enduring peace.

For us in the United States it is as natural as it is desirable that we gather around a table with the representatives of other nations to devise means for maintaining peace and security. No passion runs deeper in the thoughts of the people of this country than the belief that all men should enjoy liberty under law. It has been our faith from the beginning of our nation, it is our dream for the future, that every individual and every nation should attain freedom and the security to enjoy it. The people of this country are now united as never before in their determination that the tragedy which today is sweeping the earth shall not recur.

The people of all the United Nations are hoping and praying for the opportunity to build anew toward a system of decent and just relationships among nations. Their noblest capacities and their highest skills have been diverted from the creative pursuits of peace to the grim and terrible tasks of battle. They see the destruction of their homes and the resources of their lands. They will not be content with a precarious peace. Their sacrifices can only be rewarded by the fulfillment of their reasonable hopes.

It is the sacred duty of the governments of all peace-loving nations to make sure that international machinery is fashioned through which the peoples can build the peace they so deeply desire. The President is confident, and I share his view, that this thought will govern the deliberations which you are now undertaking.

Remarks by Ambassador Gromyko

The present meeting is the first meeting of exploratory discussions between representatives of the United States, Great Britain, and the Soviet Union on the establishment of an international security organization. I fully share the thoughts expressed by Secretary Hull in regard to the importance of · the present discussions. The peoples of our countries are waging a life-and-death struggle against the worst enemy of humanity—Hitlerite Germany. This struggle has already cost our countries, as well as many other freedom-loving countries of the world, heavy human and material sacrifices. Waging a struggle for its freedom and independence, the peoples of our three great nations are also saving the freedom and independence of other freedom-loving peoples of the world. As a result of the combined efforts of the Allies, our common foe—Nazi Germany—is nearing its inevitable catastrophe. Our brave warriors are squeezing the enemy from the east, west, and south. As a result of the latest offensive of the Red Army, military operations are already being carried to enemy soil. The time is not far off when the combined efforts of the freedom-loving countries of the world, and, first of all, the efforts of our nations, will bring a complete and decisive victory and will force Nazi Germany to her knees.

In view of the heavy destruction and countless sacrifices which the present war has brought to humanity, the freedom-loving peoples of the world are naturally looking for means to prevent repetition of a similar tragedy in the future. They have shed too much blood and made too many sacrifices to be indifferent to their future. That is why they are striving to establish an international organization which would be capable of preventing the repetition of a similar tragedy and of guaranteeing for the peoples peace, security, and prosperity in the future. Members of such an organization can be, as it is said in the Four Nations Declaration signed at the Moscow Conference on October 30, 1943, all big and small freedom-loving countries of the world. All of us are glad that one of the distinguished participants of the Moscow Conference, Secretary Hull, is among us at the present meeting.

It goes without saying that in order to maintain peace and security it is not enough to have the mere desire to harness the aggressor and the desire to apply force against him if it should be demanded by circumstances. In order to guarantee peace and security it is absolutely necessary to have resources with the aid of which aggression could be prevented or suppressed and international order maintained.

In the light of the above, it becomes clear what responsibility falls to the nations, members of the future security organization, and especially to the nations which bear the main brunt of the present war and which possess the necessary resources and power to maintain peace and security. That is why all those to whom freedom and independence are dear cannot but draw the conclusion that this freedom and independence can be preserved only if the future international security organization will in the interests of the freedom-loving peoples of the world use effectively all resources in possession of members of the organization and, first of all, the resources of such great nations as the Soviet Union, and United States, and Great Britain.

The unity displayed by these countries in the present struggle against Hitlerite Germany and its vassals gives ground for certainty that after final victory is achieved these nations will cooperate in maintaining peace and security in the future as they are cooperating at the present time in saving humanity from enslavement by the Fascist barbarians. In this noble striving our countries naturally cannot but find support on the part of the other United Nations, big and small, which will be participants of the international security organization, which will be based on the principle of the sovereign equality of all freedom-loving countries and which will bear joint responsibility for the maintenance of peace.

The unity of the Allies displayed in the struggle against the common foe and their striving to maintain peace in the future is a guarantee that the present exploratory discussions will bring positive results. They are the first step leading to the erection of a building in the foundation of which all freedom-loving peoples of the world are interested—for an effective international organization on maintenance of peace and security.

In closing I consider it necessary to note the initiative taken by the Government of the United States in calling the present conference. The Soviet delegation is glad to begin discussions with the American delegation headed by Edward R. Stettinius, with whom I have had the pleasure since 1941 of meeting and discussing at different times various matters of mutual interest, and also with the British delegation headed by Sir Alexander Cadogan. I have no doubt that in the course of the present discussions the representatives of the three nations will conduct their work in a spirit of mutual understanding and in a friendly atmosphere which cannot but add to the successful outcome of the discussions.

Remarks by Sir Alexander Cadogan

The discussions which open today arise out of article 4 of the Declaration of Moscow, in the framing of which Mr. Hull played such a notable and prominent part. We have listened with admiration to the wise and powerful words with which he has initiated our labours, and we are, I know, all profoundly grateful to him for his indefatigable efforts in the cause of international understanding. Of him it may well be said that he embodies in his own thought and person the qualities which have been responsible for the creation and the development of the country which he represents.

To the Soviet Government too we all have reason to be grateful. It was, I think, on M. Molotov's initiative that the decision to hold these discussions was taken; and it was evident from their attitude at the time of the Moscow Conference that the Soviet Government attached the highest importance to the establishment of a system designed to prevent a recurrence of Nazi and Fascist aggression.

My Government, for their part, have from the outset favoured such discussions as these and have done their best to facilitate them. We have expressed our provisional views in the papers which have been circulated and are most happy to find that in the papers of all three Governments there is such a large measure of agreement.

There seems, in fact, to be a general will on the part of what are at present the three most powerful states in the world to achieve some kind of world organization, and, what is more, to achieve it soon. That should itself be a good augury for the success of our labours.

Chinese statesmen also have declared their wish to join in the establishment of such an organization, and I am confident that the subsequent discussions with the Chinese delegation will show that there is a community of aim on the part of the most populous and ancient of our civilizations. We shall thus, I hope, be able to achieve agreement on principles between officials from states comprising about half the inhabitants of the globe, and from states moreover whose combined power and determination is now playing so prominent a part in overthrowing the sinister forces of evil which only a few years ago came near to dominating all mankind.

The victory of the United Nations, whenever it comes, must be complete, the military defeat of the aggressors must be made clear beyond all doubt, and most of all to the German people themselves, and those responsible for the wanton outrages that have horrified the civilized world must receive their just retribution. On that basis we may hope to build more securely for the future. In 1919 there was a widespread feeling in many western countries that force was in itself an immoral thing: now there is a much more widespread conviction that it is only by the victors' remaining both strong and united that peace can be preserved. We have, I believe, learnt many salutary lessons during the last few years.

We are met here to plan a system which will enable individual nations to cooperate effectively for the common good. Individual nations, small and great, must be the basis of our new world organization; and our problem is to construct a machine which will give to each of them the responsibilities commensurate with its power. This is no light task, but it can be accomplished. No one wishes to impose some great-power dictatorship on the rest of the world, but it is obvious that unless the great powers are united in aim and ready to assume and fulfil loyally their obligations, no machine for maintaining peace, however perfectly constructed, will in practice work. On the other hand, even Hitler has surely learnt by now, what we have ourselves long known, that it is not by riding roughshod over the smaller powers that the vital interests of the larger can in the long run best be protected.

Another lesson I submit we may learn from experience is that we should not attempt too closely to define what is perhaps undefinable. As I have already said, no machine will work unless there is, at any rate on the part of the great powers, a will to work it; and equally even an imperfect machine may function satisfactorily provided such a will exists. We might do well, therefore, to concentrate on certain guiding principles and on certain basic institutions, rather than on a set of detailed regulations, which, however ingeniously drafted, will probably have to be revised in the light of subsequent experience.

Again, if there is a danger in excessive legalism, there is also a danger in believing, or at any rate in giving the impression, that because we may be able to agree, first as between ourselves and later as between all the United Nations, on some theoretically perfect organization for maintaining peace, peace will therefore indefinitely and automatically be maintained.

One other consideration I would put before you: we must remember that peace, in the negative sense of absence of war, is not enough. No world system can endure unless it permits of growth and unless it tends to promote the well-being of humanity as a whole. Hence, however we may fit the various non-political world organizations into our general system, we must attempt to discover means whereby the expanding force of modern scientific discoveries is turned into constructive rather than into destructive channels. For this reason we must arrange for at least a measure of coordination between the various functional organizations now created or to be created and in some way gear them to our world international machine. All I would emphasize here is that we should always recognize that, if there is acute political instability, no economic or social organizations will function successfully; and, on the other hand, let us never forget that acute discomfort in the economic and social field will constantly hamper the smooth operation of the best political plans. In other words, freedom from fear and freedom from want must, so far as human agency can contrive it, move forward simultaneously.

In conclusion; I must for my part emphasize that the working party from the United Kingdom is recruited from the humble official level. From that it follows that, so far as we are concerned, these talks are necessarily exploratory and non-committal. Within these limitations we will make the best contribution we can, and I can pledge every one of us to devote his best energies and such knowledge and experience as he possesses to the search for agreed recommendations for submission by our Governments, if they approve them, to all the other United Nations. We may take comfort in the fact that, as will be seen from the memoranda already circulated, there is already much common ground.

Let us also not forget the time factor. Events are moving fast, and peace may come sooner than some expect. It would be folly to delay the construction of at least some framework of future international cooperation until the problems of peace confront us with all their insistency. Moreover, the time even of officials is limited. If therefore we are to establish the points on which there seems to be provisional agreement, we must work fast and well.

Much depends on our efforts, and some give-and-take will probably be required. Let us go forward with a full sense of our responsibilities, not only to our own nations, but to the world at large. Let us go forward above all with the determination to produce a scheme worthy of the men and women of the United Nations who are giving their all to make possible the construction of a better world.

PRESIDENT ROOSEVELT'S REMARKS TO THE DELEGATES TO THE DUMBARTON OAKS CONFERENCE

August 23, 1944 [1]

Gentlemen, this is an informal occasion. I have not prepared any speech. This is merely a feeling on my part that I would like to shake hands with you. I should like to be able to go out to Dumbarton Oaks, to take a part in your discussions.

A conference of this kind always reminds me of an old saying of a gentle-

[1] White House news release.

man called Alfred E. Smith, who used to be Governor of New York. He was very, very successful in settling any problem between capital and labor, or anything that had to do with the State government in which there was a controversy. He said if you can get the parties into one room with a big table and make them take their coats off and put their feet up on the table, and give each one of them a good cigar, you can always make them agree. Well, there was something in the idea.

You have a great responsibility. In a way, it is a preliminary responsibility. But after all we learn from experience, and what I hope is that in planning for the peace that is to come we will arrive at the same good cooperation and unity of action as we have in the carrying on of the war. It is a very remarkable fact that we have carried on this war with such great unanimity.

I think that often it comes down to personalities. When, back in 1941, at the time of the Atlantic Charter, just for example, I did not know Mr. Churchill at all well. I had met him once or twice very informally during the first World War. I did not know Mr. Eden. But up there in the North Atlantic—three or four days together, with our two ships lying close together —we got awfully fond of each other. I got to know him, and he got to know me. In other words, we met, and you cannot hate a man that you know well.

Later on Mr. Molotov came here and we had a grand time together. Then during the following year, at Teheran, the Marshal and I got to know each other. We got on beautifully. We cracked the ice, if there ever was any ice; and since then there has been no ice. And that's the spirit in which I know you are going about your work.

I was just talking with the Secretary of War, Mr. Stimson. He was saying that one of the tasks we face is making this conference of ours—and the successor conferences—something that will last, last a long time. He said that unfortunately in Germany the young people, the young Nazis, favor an idea which will be dangerous to the peace of the world just as long as they have anything to say about it. The prisoners of 17, 18, 20 that we are capturing now—both the French front and the Soviet front—these German prisoners of that age are even worse in their Nazism than the prisoners of 40 or 45. And, therefore, as long as these young men have anything to say about it, the peril of Nazism will always be before us.

And we have got to make not merely a peace but a peace that will last, and a peace in which the larger nations will work absolutely in unison in preventing war by force. But the four of us have to be friends, conferring all the time—the basis of getting to know each other—"putting their feet up on the table."

And so I am very hopeful that it can be done because of the spirit that has been shown in the past in getting together for the winning of the war. But that is the spirit that we have learned so well in the last few years. It is something new, this close relationship between the British Empire and the United States. This great friendship between the Russian people and the American people—that is new. Let's hang on to both friendships, and by spreading that spirit around the world we may have a peaceful period for our grandchildren to grow up in.

All I can do is to wish you every possible success in this great task that you have undertaken. It will not be a final task, but at least it gives us something to build on, so that we can accomplish the one thing that humanity has been looking forward to for a great many hundreds of years.

It is good to see you. Good luck.

PROCLAMATION BY KING MICHAEL OF RUMANIA, ACCEPTING FOR HIS COUNTRY THE ALLIED ARMISTICE TERMS

August 23, 1944 [1]

Rumanians! In this most difficult hour of my duty and in complete understanding with my people, I have considered that there is only one path for the salvation of the fatherland from total catastrophe: relinquishing of our alliance with the Axis power and immediate cessation of hostilities with the United Nations.

A new Government of National Union has been entrusted with the task of fulfilling the determined will of the country and of concluding peace with the United Nations.

Rumania has accepted an armistice offered by the Soviet Union, Great Britain and the United States.

From this moment all hostilities and other activities against the Soviet armies as well as the state of war with Great Britain and the United States cease. I accept with confidence the call of those nations.

The United Nations have guaranteed the independence of Rumania and her internal affairs. They have recognized the injustice of the Vienna Dictate by which Transylvania was torn from us.

Rumanians! Our people wish to be masters on their own soil. Anyone opposing the decision which we have taken of our own free will and anyone taking justice into his own hands is an enemy of our nation against whom I order the army and the whole nation to fight with all means and at the price of any sacrifice. All Rumanians must rally around the throne and the Government for the salvation of the fatherland. Whoever disobeys the Government and resists the will of the nation is a traitor to the country.

Rumanians! The dictatorship has ended, and with it all oppression ceases. A new Government represents the beginning of a new era in which the rights and liberties of all citizens are guaranteed and respected.

At the side of the Allied Armies and with their help I mobilize all forces of the nation, and we shall cross the frontiers unjustly imposed upon us at Vienna so as to liberate our Transylvania from enemy occupation.

Rumanians! The future of our country depends on the courage with which we, with weapons in our hands, defend our independence against any attempt to encroach on our right to decide our own fate.

Let us have faith in the future of the Rumanian nation and in the dawn of a free, strong and happy Rumania! (Signed) Michael I, King of Rumania.

GENERAL CHARLES DE GAULLE'S SPEECH ON THE LIBERATION OF PARIS, DELIVERED AT THE HÔTEL DE VILLE IN PARIS

August 25, 1944 [2]

There is no point in hiding the fact that joy overwhelms us all, men and women, here in Paris as it rises to liberate itself and as it wins its freedom by

[1] *New York Times.*
[2] French Press and Information Service.

its own efforts. No, we shall not conceal our deep and sacret feelings; there are moments, we know, that are ageless and beyond the scope of our mortal lives.

Paris! Paris ravaged! Paris crushed! Paris martyred! But Paris free!

Liberated by ourselves, liberated by her people with the help of the Armies of France, with the help and co-operation of all of France, and by that I mean the true France, the fighting France, France the eternal.

Now that Paris is free, now that the enemy has surrendered into our hands, France is returning home to Paris. She returns bloody but well-determined; her return is lighted by the fires of destruction, but she is more certain than ever of her duties and of her rights.

I shall speak first of her duties, and I shall express all of them at one stroke in saying that her duties are war itself. The enemy is tottering, but the enemy is not yet defeated. He is still on our soil and it will not be enough that with the aid of our dear and courageous Allies, we drive him from our land. After what has happened we shall not be satisfied until, as is fitting, we shall have entered his territory as conquerors.

That is why the vanguard of the French Army has entered Paris, accompanied by the sound of guns firing, that is why the French Army of Italy that landed in the Midi is advancing so rapidly northward in the Rhône Valley. And that is why our brave and loyal Forces of the Interior want to be modern and regular units. To be revenged, and for that vengeance and at the same time justice, we shall fight to the last hour, to the hour of complete and total victory. Every man here, every man throughout France, who is listening to us, well knows that this duty to fight carries with it other duties and that the supreme duty is to maintain our national unity.

The Nation in her present plight cannot countenance destruction of her unity. The Nation well knows that to conquer, to flourish, to be great she must have the co-operation of all her children. The Nation well knows that her sons and her daughters, all her sons and all her daughters, save those miserable traitors who joined the enemy and have herded others over to the enemy and who know and shall know the severity of the law, save these, all sons all daughters of France are marching and shall march together hand in hand toward victory.

This is the great and noble conduct the Government demands of all her citizens. But this great and noble national unity does not blind the Nation to the awareness of her rights. I say this now for after what happened in 1940, after France relinquished her sovereignty, after her Government was hatefully usurped, there is no other practical and acceptable way for the people to be heard than by free and universal suffrage for all French men and women. As soon as conditions permit the people shall be sovereign.

As to the rights of France, I mean her internal rights, those which concern all her children, and which therefore vitally concern her, we shall never again as long as it lies within our power, allow any man or any woman to fear hunger or the misery of a tomorrow. We want French men and French women to be worthy of themselves and of the Nation. We want, for every person in France, living conditions of such quality as every man and woman has a right to demand.

Moreover, France has rights abroad. France is a great nation. She has proved it at the time when there was but the sea about us. We were aware of this, and now we stand, our forces joined, beside the victors. But that is not all. France, this great nation, shall command respect for herself and her rights. She has a right to insist she never again be invaded by an enemy who so often invaded her. She has a right to be in the first line among the great nations who are going to organize the peace and the life of the world. She has a right to be heard in all four corners of the world.

France is a world power. She knows it and will act so that others may know it because this is of supreme interest—that is the interest of humanity.

This is what we must achieve, standing by the Government: war, unity, grandeur. This is our program. I have only to look at you to know that your determination to fulfill this task is shared by all Frenchmen. Onward everyone.

We shall be faced with many difficulties, especially in Paris.

It is not overnight that we shall restore yesterday's wealth, abundance, ease of living to Paris and to France. And it is not today that we shall restore to the face of our Nation the peaceful look that was hers for centuries.

We shall have to surmount many an obstacle, we shall have to overcome many a difficulty. The Government shall fulfill its duty. The entire Nation will require that it do so. Thus we shall look toward happier days . . .

(The last words of the address were not audible on account of transmission difficulties.)

PRIME MINISTER WINSTON CHURCHILL'S MESSAGE FROM ROME TO THE PEOPLE OF ITALY

August 28, 1944 [1]

On leaving the shores of Italy after a profoundly interesting and instructive visit I should like to send a few words of encouragement and hope to the Italian people.

I am most deeply touched by the extraordinary kindness with which I was welcomed in all the villages and small towns through which I have driven in traversing the entire front. There is no doubt that in the zone of the armies the relations of the Italians with the British, American, and other Allies are of a most friendly and co-operative character.

Of course, owing to the hard conditions of war and the disorganization caused by the demolitions of the enemy and the shortage of shipping and transport, much hardship may arise in particular places. I have given directions to the British representatives in the various international bodies concerned to do their utmost, in harmony with their colleagues, to meet these difficulties, and I am sure these efforts will be warmly supported by our Allies.

Italy suffered a long period of governmental tyranny under the Fascist regime, which terminated in the frightful disaster and most cruel suffering which has befallen the Italian people. She would be very unwise to let herself again fall into the clutches of this Fascist totalitarian system in any guise in which it might present itself.

Such systems of governmental tyranny breed in conditions of social dislocation, economic hardship, and moral depression which follow in the wake of war and defeat. It is in such a crisis in their history that peoples should be most on their guard against unscrupulous parties seeking after power and most zealous in the preservation of their liberties.

[1] British Speeches of the Day.

When a nation has allowed itself to fall into a tyrannical regime it cannot be absolved from the faults due to the guilt of that regime, and naturally we cannot forget the circumstances of Mussolini's attack on France and Great Britain when we were at our weakest, and people thought that Great Britain would sink forever—which, in fact, she has not done.

But in the main, speaking for the British—although the other victorious Allies would have a say in this—I believe that the British nation will be happy to see the day when Italy, once again free and progressive, takes her place among all the peace-loving nations.

It has been said that the price of freedom is eternal vigilance. The question arises, "What is freedom?" There are one or two quite simple, practical tests by which it can be known in the modern world in peace conditions, namely:

Is there the right to free expression of opinion and of opposition and criticism of the Government of the day?

Have the people the right to turn out a Government of which they disapprove, and are constitutional means provided by which they can make their will apparent?

Are their courts of justice free from violence by the Executive and free of all threats of mob violence and all association with any particular political parties?

Will these courts administer open and well-established laws which are associated in the human mind with the broad principles of decency and justice?

Will there be fair play for poor as well as for rich, for private persons as well as Government officials?

Will the rights of the individual, subject to his duties to the State, be maintained and asserted and exalted?

Is the ordinary peasant or workman earning a living by daily toil and striving to bring up a family free from the fear that some grim police organization under the control of a single party, like the *Gestapo*, started by the Nazi and Fascist parties, will tap him on the shoulder and pack him off without fair or open trial to bondage or ill-treatment?

These simple practical tests are some of the title deeds on which a new Italy could be founded.

The first duty of all is to purge the soil of Italy from the foul German taint. This can only be done by hard fighting. I rejoice that large new Italian Forces will soon join the Allied armies.

Hard work, a strong resolve, high inspirations, and above all true unity will all be needed if Italy is to nourish her people and resume her place among the leading Powers of Europe. Political excitement and the clash of many parties will not achieve those simple joys and rights which the mass of the people so desire. Italy must recapture the ideals of freedom which inspired the Risorgimento.

May this thought rest with you through your trouble, and may your friends, both in England and across the ocean, see their hopes rewarded.

STATEMENT BY THE PEOPLE'S COMMISSARIAT OF FOREIGN AFFAIRS OF THE USSR ON THE NECESSITY FOR AN INDEPENDENT RUMANIA

August 29, 1944 [1]

In connection with the events in Rumania, the Soviet Government considers it again necessary to confirm its statement made in April of this year that the Soviet Union does not have any intention of acquiring any part of Rumanian territory or of changing the existing social order in Rumania or of infringing in any way the independence of Rumania.

On the contrary, the Soviet Government considers it necessary to establish, together with the Rumanians, the independence of Rumania by liberating Rumania from the German-fascist yoke.

The Soviet Supreme Command considers that if the Rumanian troops will cease military action against the Red Army and if they will pledge, hand in hand with the Red Army, to carry on the liberation war against the Germans for the independence of Rumania, or against the Hungarians for the liberation of Transylvania, then the Red Army will not disarm them and will preserve fully to them all armaments, and with all means will help them to fulfill this honorable task.

However, the Red Army may cease military action on the territory of Rumania only after the German troops in Rumania, which are carriers of suppression and slavery for the Rumanian people, will be liquidated.

The aid of Rumanian troops to the troops of the Red Army in the matter of the liquidation of German troops is the only means to the speedy cessation of military action on the territory of Rumania and to the conclusion of an armistice between Rumania and the Allied coalition.

GENERAL CHARLES DE GAULLE'S BROADCAST TO THE FRENCH PEOPLE ON LIBERATION

August 29, 1944 [2]

Four days ago the Germans who held Paris capitulated to the French. Four days ago Paris was liberated. An immense joy, a mighty pride have swept over the nation. The entire world thrilled when it heard that Paris had emerged from the abyss and that its light was to shine again.

France pays tribute to all those whose services contributed to the victory of Paris. To the people of Paris, first, who, in their secret souls, never faltered, never accepted defeat and humiliation; to the brave people, men and women who long and actively conducted the resistance to the oppressor before helping to rout him.

And to the soldiers of France who beat him and subdued him: warriors who came from Africa, and after what combats! To those valiant fighters

[1] Information Bulletin, Embassy of the U.S.S.R.
[2] New York Times.

grouped in the units of the interior—spontaneously, above all and most of all, to those men and women who have given their lives for their country on the field of battle and before the firing squads.

But France renders equal homage to the brave and good Allied armies and to their leaders, whose irresistible offensive made possible the liberation of Paris and is making certain the liberation of the entire territory by crushing, with us, the German force. As the abominable tide recedes, the nation breathes with delight the air of victory and of liberty, and a wonderful unity is revealed in its depths. The nation feels that the future offers it now not merely the hope but the certitude of being once and for all a victorious nation.

France now faces the prospect of a flaming rebirth, the opportunity of taking again in the world the place that she always held—that is to say, in the ranks of the greatest.

But the nation knows also what distance separates it from the goal that it wants to and can reach. It is aware of the necessity to act in such a way that the enemy will be completely and irretrievably beaten and that the French part in the final triumph may be the largest possible one. It realizes the extent of the ravages that it has suffered in its soil and in its flesh. It appreciates the extreme difficulties of supply, of transport, of armament, of equipment under which it labors and that hamper the battle effort and the productive effort of its liberated territories.

If the certainty of the triumph of our cause, which is at the same time that of all mankind, justifies our joy and our pride, it does not bring us bliss; on the contrary, we understand what hard labors, what painful distances still separate us from our goal. The French are resolved to endure this toil. They endure the constraints because this is the price added to so many ordeals to which they had to submit for their salvation, their liberty and their greatness.

The French, a people that has grown wise in 2,000 years of its history, have decided by instinct and by reason to fulfill the two conditions without which nothing great and powerful is ever accomplished; order and ardor—republican order under the sole valid authority, that of the state; the ardent zeal that makes possible the creation of new life in a spirit of lawfulness and brotherliness. ["Ardor consecrated to the rebirth of the French Republic," the National Broadcasting Company translation read.]

This is what is meant by the acclamations of our towns and villages finally cleansed of the enemy. This is what we hear in the great voice of liberated Paris.

STATEMENT BY UNDER-SECRETARY OF STATE EDWARD R. STETTINIUS, JR., EXPLAINING THE POLICY OF SECRECY ADOPTED FOR THE DUMBARTON OAKS CONFERENCE

August 29, 1944 [1]

There has been some misunderstanding about the reasons for reticence in regard to our joint discussions at Dumbarton Oaks concerning an international organization to prevent war and secure peace.

The preliminary discussions which are now taking place there are explora-

[1] *New York Times.*

tory and designed to reach a common understanding. Embarrassment would ensue to the conferring governments if piecemeal reports of expressions of views advanced from day to day were construed as representing unalterable positions or as having a binding effect. I am sure that anyone who gives the subject careful consideration will understand this.

It has always been recognized, throughout the whole history of the United States, that an expression of opinions in confidence is an indispensable prerequisite to successful procedure in the preliminary work involved in reaching agreements.

From the time of the Constitutional Convention of 1787 right down to the present, private discussions have always preceded public announcements.

In our national political conventions the committees hold public hearings, but they go into executive sessions to draft the platforms of the parties.

In the halls of the Congress matters are referred to committees, which hold public hearings and obtain the views of various elements, but the committees then go into executive session and draft documents which are submitted to the appropriate Houses of Congress. Such is the practice of the Foreign Relations Committee, of the Foreign Affairs Committee, of the Appropriations Committees, of the Ways and Means Committee, and of all the committees of each House of Congress.

The object of this procedure is to obtain a calm exchange of views as a contributing factor to eventual agreement expressive of the ideas upon which those responsible have been able to formulate a concurrence.

The conversations at Dumbarton Oaks are no different in this respect from any other conference, except that in this instance it is a matter of international as well as of domestic concern.

The representatives of the other agencies of our Government invested by this Constitution with authority over these matters have been and are being consulted and kept thoroughly informed of developments.

It has been agreed that the heads of the three delegations will join in issuing statements which will carry information about the progress of the discussions. These statements will necessarily be general in form. To go beyond this and describe the discussions in detail would be not only discourteous but improper, in view of the fact that the representatives of the other governments represented at the conference must enjoy the opportunity to consult their own governments before "meeting of minds" can be arrived at.

It needs to be kept in mind that there remain to be held the impending conversations with the Chinese.

It should be obvious that in giving full considerations to all suggestions which may be advanced by the several Governments engaged at this stage in the formulating of the common proposals, the participants in the present conversations should continue to discuss with the Chinese delegation the approach of their Government to the subject and to bring the views of all the delegations into a common alignment.

Before any binding commitments are made there will be full opportunity for public discussion. As Secretary of State Cordell Hull said so well at the opening of the conversations:

"It is the intention of the Government of the United States that after similar consultations with the Government of China the conclusions reached will be communicated to the Governments of all the United Nations and of other peace-loving nations.

"It is our further thought that as soon as practicable these conclusions will be made available to the peoples of our countries and of all countries for public study and debate."

SEPTEMBER

September 1, 1944

The First United States Army crossed the Meuse and drove the Germans headlong before them, reaching Sedan and Charleville, ten miles from Belgium.

The British Second Army, advancing sixty miles in two days, captured Amiens, crossed the Somme and headed for Pas-de-Calais, center of German flying bomb operations.

2

The Allied offensive in France swept to the Belgian border. Among the strongholds that fell were historic Verdun, Arras, Saint-Mihiel and Dieppe.

Finland abandoned her ally Germany and became the third of Germany's satellites to capitulate to the Allies in ten days. Premier Antti V. Hackzell stated that he had requested the German troops in Finland to withdraw by September 15th according to the Soviet terms for the beginning of armistice negotiations.

3

Former Senator George W. Norris, the dean of American liberals, died at the age of eighty-three.

4

Finland ended its three-year war against the Soviet Union with a cease-firing order, while German troops, scattered throughout south Finland from Karelia to Helsinki, began their evacuation.

5

Sweden announced that it would not grant asylum to war criminals and traitors.

Lieut. Gen. Kurt Dittmar, Nazi military spokesman, told the German people their army was being defeated and it was up to the "third line" reserves being mobilized to halt the Allies at the borders of the Reich.

6

American forces probed the outer defenses of the Siegfried Line from the border of Luxembourg to south of Nancy. General Patton's Third Army fought its way across the Moselle River. The First Army was driving toward Liège and Aachen. The British Second Army was in the Netherlands nearing Ghent in Belgium.

Sofia announced that all German troops in Bulgaria had been interned.

7

Japanese Premier Gen. Kuniaki Koiso told the Japanese Diet and the Japanese people that they could expect intensified American air raids on the mainland and warned them not to overlook the "possibility" of a "landing on our home soil."

Secretary of State Cordell Hull charged that Argentina was the headquarters of the Fascist movement in the Western Hemisphere.

September, 1944

397

Joseph Goebbels, Reich Plenipotentiary for Total War, conscripted Germany's school children and Red Cross workers for war service in the "fight for our very lives."

8

The U. S. First Army captured Sedan, the famous French frontier fortress town. Three Allied Armies wheeled eastward through northern France and Belgium in the first phase of the battle for the Siegfried Line.

9

Mohandas K. Gandhi, leader of the Indian National Congress, and Mohammed Ali Jinnah, head of the rival Moslem organization, met in Bombay in an attempt to establish all-India unity.

The American First Army seized the fortress city of Liège in eastern Belgium.

Argentina withdrew from the Emergency Advisory Committee for the Political Defense of the Continent in Montevideo.

Russia's four-day war with Bulgaria ended with the announcement from Moscow that armistice terms were being drawn up by the United States, Britain and the Soviet Union. An anti-Fascist government, headed by Kimon Georgieff, was installed in Sofia.

10

Marshal Tito's Partisans captured Dr. Ante Pavelitch, quisling dictator of Croatia.

11

President Roosevelt and Prime Minister Churchill opened their second Quebec Conference.

The U. S. First Army stormed across the Luxembourg border into Germany and drove five miles into the heart of the Siegfried Line north of Trier.

12

A second American column invaded Germany from Lammersdorf, thirty-nine miles from Cologne.

13

Troops of the U. S. First Army captured the railroad village of Roetgen, the first German town ever to fall to American soldiers.

An armistice with Rumania was concluded by Russia, Great Britain and the United States on behalf of the United Nations.

14

A National War Labor Board inquiry found the increased cost of living a justification for the revision of the Little Steel wage formula.

Soviet Republics signed agreements with the Polish Committee of National Liberation for the voluntary transmigration of minority groups.

Marshal Tito demanded a place for Yugoslavia at the peace table.

Anthony Eden arrived unexpectedly to participate in the second Roosevelt-Churchill Quebec Conference.

15

American infantry broke through the main Siegfried Line at Aachen.

American troops invaded Palau Island near the Philippines.

16

The Red Army entered Sofia, capital of Bulgaria, in its drive toward Yugoslavia.

17

President Roosevelt and Prime Minister Churchill closed their second conference at Quebec with the pledge to launch the final crushing blow at Japan as soon as Europe is freed from "the corroding heel of Nazism."

The U. S. Fourteenth Air Force destroyed its air bases near Kweilin in Kwangse province in the face of the Japanese advance which threatened, not only to split China in two, but the whole structure of the American military effort in that country.

18

The Red Army arrested ten Rumanian and German military and political leaders, including Gen. Ion Antonescu, former Fascist dictator of Rumania, and Dr. Karl Clodius, Nazi economic expert. All were to be tried as war criminals.

19

President Roosevelt ordered all Government agencies to plan for the earliest demobilization of the civilian war machine.

21

Jefferson Caffery was named U. S. envoy to France.

24

The French Forces of the Interior (FFI) were incorporated into the regular French Army.

26

Prime Minister Winston Churchill assured the House of Commons that war criminals would not escape.

27

In a radio address War Mobilization Director James F. Byrnes demanded that the war-time controls of prices and wages be not relaxed until the danger of inflation was passed.

Allied forces invaded Albania and the Adriatic Islands of Yugoslavia.

Mohandas K. Gandhi and Mohammed Ali Jinnah, leader of the Indian Moslems, broke off negotiations, the former appealing to the public to exert pressure to bring about a settlement of their conflicting views.

30

The German radio reported that Marshal Henri-Philippe Pétain, head of the Vichy Government, had fled to Germany before the advancing Allied armies.

President Roosevelt accepted the resignation of Donald M. Nelson as chairman of the War Production Board, announcing at the same time his appointment to an unspecified "high post of major importance . . . laying the groundwork for post-war economic cooperation with other nations."

REPORT TO PRESIDENT ROOSEVELT BY
WILLIAM PHILLIPS, UNITED STATES
AMBASSADOR TO INDIA

September 2, 1944 [1]

May 14, 1943.

DEAR MR. PRESIDENT:

May I add a few words to what I said to you on Tuesday afternoon when I had the pleasure of giving you an oral report on my impressions of the Indian situation.

Assuming that India is known to be an important base for our future operations against Burma and Japan, it would seem to be of highest importance that we should have around us a sympathetic India rather than an indifferent and possibly a hostile India. It would appear that we will have the prime responsibility in the conduct of the war against Japan. There is no evidence that the British intend to do more than give token assistance. If that is so, then the conditions surrounding our base in India become of vital importance.

At present, the Indian people are at war only in a legal sense, as for various reasons the British Government declared India in the conflict without the formality of consulting Indian leaders or even the Indian Legislature. Indians feel they have no voice in the Government and therefore no responsibility in the conduct of the war. They feel that they have nothing to fight for, as they are convinced that the professed war aims of the United Nations do not apply to them.

The British Prime Minister, in fact, has stated that the provisions of the Atlantic Charter are not applicable to India, and it is not unnatural therefore that Indian leaders are beginning to wonder whether the charter is only for the benefit of white races. The present Indian army is purely mercenary and only that part of it which is drawn from the martial races has been tried in actual warfare and these martial soldiers represent only thirty-three per cent of the army.

General Stilwell has expressed his concern over the situation and in particular in regard to the poor morale of the Indian officers.

The attitude of the general public toward the war is even worse. Lassitude and indifference and bitterness have increased as a result of the famine conditions, the growing high cost of living and continued political deadlock.

While India is broken politically into various parties and groups, all have one object in common—eventual freedom and independence from British domination.

There would seem to be only one remedy to this highly unsatisfactory situation in which we are unfortunately but nevertheless seriously involved, and that is to change the attitude of the people of India toward the war, make them feel that we want them to assume responsibilities to the United Nations and are prepared to give them facilities for doing so and that the voice of India will play an important part in the reconstruction of the world. The present political conditions do not permit of any improvement in this respect.

Even though the British should fail again, it is high time that they should make an effort to improve conditions and re-establish confidence among the

[1] *New York Times.*

Indian people that their future independence is to be granted. Words are of no avail. They only aggravate the present situation.

It is time for the British to act. This they can do by a solemn declaration from the King Emperor that India will achieve her independence at a specific date after the war and as a guarantee of good faith in this respect a provisional representative coalition government will be re-established at the center and limited powers transferred to it.

I feel strongly, Mr. President, that in view of our military position in India, we should have a voice in these matters. It is not right for the British to say this is none of your business when we alone presumably will have the major part to play in the struggle with Japan.

If we do nothing and merely accept the British point of view that conditions in India are none of our business, then we must be prepared for various serious consequences in the internal situation in India which may develop as a result of the despair and misery and anti-white sentiments of hundreds of millions of subject people.

The peoples of Asia—and I am supported in the opinion by other diplomatic and military observers—cynically regard this war as one between fascist and imperialist powers.

A generous British gesture to India would change this undesirable political atmosphere. India itself might then be expected more positively to support our war effort against Japan. China, which regards the Anglo-American bloc with misgivings and mistrust, might then be assured that we are in truth fighting for a better world.

And the colonial people conquered by the Japanese might hopefully feel that they have something better to look forward to than simply a return to their old masters.

Such a gesture, Mr. President, will produce not only a tremendous psychological stimulus to flagging morale through Asia and facilitate our military operations in that theatre, but it will also be proof positive to all peoples— our own and the British included—that this is not a war of power politics, but a war for all we say it is.

Sincerely yours,

WILLIAM PHILLIPS

DIRECTIVE ISSUED BY GENERAL GEORGE C. MARSHALL, U. S. CHIEF OF STAFF, RELATING TO THE POST-WAR ARMY

September 2, 1944 [1]

1. Preliminary assumptions.

A. It is assumed that for some time after the defeat of the Axis powers the United States will maintain such temporary military forces, in cooperation with its Allies, as may be necessary in order to lay the foundations for a peaceful world order. The plans for a permanent peace establishment, referred to in this circular, relate to a later period when the future world order can be envisaged.

B. It is also assumed, for purposes of planning, that the Congress will enact

[1] New York Times.

(as the essential foundation of an effective national military organization) that every able-bodied young American shall be trained to defend his country; and that for a reasonable period after his training (unless he volunteers for service in the regular establishment of the armed forces) he shall be incorporated in a reserve, all, or any necessary part, of which shall be subject to active military duty in the event of an emergency requiring reinforcement of the Regular Army.

2. Types of military organization. There are two types of military organization through which the manpower of a nation may be developed.

A. (1) One of these is the standing-Army type. In this type the men of the nation are drawn into the Army to serve in the lower grades. The function of the common citizen is ordinarily to be a private soldier or, at most, a non-commissioned officer in war. Reserve officers are drawn from the better educated classes, but are generally employed in the lower grades and in subordinate capacities. Under this system, leadership in war and the control of military preparations and policy in peacetime are concentrated largely and necessarily in a special class or caste of professional soldiers.

(2) This is the system of Germany and Japan. It produces highly efficient armies. But it is open to serious political objections. In a nation maintaining such a system, intelligent opinion as to military policy (and the international political policy associated therewith) is concentrated in a special class. Under such a system, the people themselves are competent to exert only a limited intelligent influence on the issues of war and peace.

Under such a system, only the brawn of a people is prepared for war, there being no adequate provision for developing the latent military leadership and genius of the people as a whole. It therefore has no place among the institutions of a modern democratic state based upon the conception of government by the people.

B. (1) The second type of military institution through which the national manpower can be developed is based upon the conception of a professional peace establishment (no larger than necessary to meet normal peacetime requirements) to be reinforced in time of emergency by organized units drawn from a citizen army reserve, effectively organized for this purpose in time of peace; with full opportunity for competent citizen soldiers to acquire practical experience through temporary active service and to rise by successive steps to any rank for which they can definitely qualify; and with specific facilities for such practical experience, qualification, and advancement definitely organized as essential and predominating characteristics of the peace establishment.

(2) An army of this type has, among others, the following advantages:

(a) First—While, as in all effective military systems, the efficiency of this system depends primarily upon expert professional control, its leadership is not exclusively concentrated in a professional soldier class. All citizen soldiers after their initial training are encouraged to develop their capacity for leadership to such an extent as may be consistent with their abilities, their tastes, and their civil obligations.

(b) Second—As a great majority of the leaders of the war army are included in the civil population in time of peace, an intelligent and widespread public opinion is provided as the basis for the determination of all public questions relating to military affairs.

(c) Third—As with a properly organized citizen army reserve, no officers or men need be maintained in the Regular Army to perform duties which can be performed effectively and in time by reserve officers and reservists, the dimensions and cost of the peace establishment, under such a system, are necessarily reduced to a determinable minimum.

(d) And, finally, as all our great wars have been fought in the main by citizen armies, the proposal for an organized citizen army reserve in time of peace is merely a proposal for perfecting a traditional national institution to meet modern requirements which no longer permit extemporization after the outbreak of war.

This is the type of army which President Washington proposed to the First Congress as one of the essential foundations of the new American Republic. This is the type of army, which, in the absence of effective peacetime organization, had to be extemporized to meet our needs in World War I and World War II.

(3) Details of military organization change with changes in weapons, modes of transportation, and international relations. But the type of our military institutions was determined in the beginning by the form of our Government and has not changed since Washington's administration. It will therefore be made the basis for all plans for a post-war peace establishment.

U. S. WAR DEPARTMENT PLAN FOR DEMOBILIZATION AFTER DEFEAT OF GERMANY

September 6, 1944 [1]

The Army has adopted a plan for the readjustment of military personnel after the defeat of Germany and prior to the defeat of Japan calling for a partial and orderly demobilization from its present peak strength.

When the war against Germany has ended, the military might of the United States will be shifted from the European area to the Pacific area. Military requirements in the European and American areas will be drastically curtailed, while tremendous increases will be essential in the Pacific.

To defeat Japan as quickly as possible, and permanently, the United States will have to assemble, readjust and streamline its military forces in order to apply the maximum power. Our military requirements to achieve this end, involving men, weapons, equipment and shipping, have been set forth by the combined chiefs-of-staff. These requirements are the determining factors of the readjustment and demobilization plan adopted by the War Department.

Military necessity decrees that sufficient men suited to the type of warfare being waged in the Pacific must remain in service as long as they are essential. Certain units of the Army also, of necessity, will have to be retained in the various theatres where action has ceased in order to fulfill such occupation duties as are necessary. Other elements, no longer needed in the theatre in which they are assigned, will be transferred to other areas, reorganized and redesignated to meet current military requirements in the theatre, or they will be inactivated.

Within each element of the Army thousands of individuals may become surplus to the needs of the theatre or major command in which they are serving. But more thousands will be required for further military service.

First priority in this readjustment program will be the transfer of elements

[1] *New York Times.*

from theatres no longer active to the Pacific war zone, or from the United States to the Pacific war zone. All available transportation will be utilized for this tremendous undertaking.

The readjustment and demobilization plan developed by the War Department after months of study takes into account all of these variable factors.

Briefly, the plan for the return of non-essential soldiers to civilian life will start with the assembly in the United States of men declared surplus to the needs of each overseas theatre and to the major commands in the United States. From among these men some will be designated essential, and a substantial number will be designated as non-essential to the new military needs of the Army and will be returned to civilian life according to certain priorities.

As an example, the commanding general of the European theatre of operations will be informed by the War Department of the types and numbers of his units which will be needed in the Pacific, and the types and numbers of his units which will remain as occupation troops, and the types and numbers of his units which are surplus.

The simplest plan of demobilization would have been to return these surplus units to this country and discharge their personnel intact. Such a method, however, would operate with great unfairness to many individuals who have had long and arduous service but are not assigned to one of the units declared surplus.

If only units in Europe were considered, this basis of expediency would work unfairly to units long in the Pacific or at outpost bases in the American theatre. It would operate unfairly to men who have seen extended combat service both in Europe and the Pacific and have been returned to this country for reassignment. It would release men only recently assigned as replacements to units long in combat and would discriminate against veterans of many campaigns in units not selected for return.

Consequently, it was determined that the fairest method to effect partial demobilization would be through the selection of men as individuals, rather than by units, with the selection governed by thoroughly impartial standards.

For the standards, the War Department went to the soldiers themselves. Experts were sent into the field to obtain a cross-section of the sentiments of enlisted men. Thousands of soldiers, both in this country and overseas, were interviewed to learn their views on the kind of selective process they believed should determine the men to be returned first to civilian life. Opinions expressed by the soldiers themselves became the accepted principles of the plan.

As finally worked out, the plan accepted by the War Department as best meeting the tests of justice and impartiality will allow men who have been overseas and men with dependent children to have priority of separation. Ninety per cent of the soldiers interviewed said that that is the way it should be.

As part of the plan adopted, an "adjusted service rating card" will be issued to all enlisted personnel after the defeat of Germany. On this card will be scored the following four factors that will determine priority of separation:

1. Service Credit—Based upon the total number of months of Army service since Sept. 16, 1940.

2. Overseas Credit—Based upon the number of months served overseas.

3. Combat Credit—Based upon the first and each additional award to the individual of the Medal of Honor, Distinguished Service Cross, Legion of Merit, Silver Star, Distinguished Flying Cross, Soldier's Medal, Bronze Star Medal, Air Medal, Purple Heart, and Bronze Service Stars (battle participation stars).

4. Parenthood Credit—Which gives credit for each dependent child under eighteen years up to a limit of three children.

The value of the point credits will be announced after the cessation of hostilities in Europe. In the meantime, the point values will be kept under continuous study. The total score will be used to select surplus men from the theatres overseas and in the United States. The score also will be used when a certain portion of all these surplus men will be declared non-essential and returned to civilian life.

In all cases, however, the demands of military necessity and the needs of the war against Japan must first be met. Regardless of a man's priority standing, certain types of personnel can never become surplus as long as the war against Japan continues.

As an example of how the plan will work, assume that there are four infantry divisions in the European theatre. One is declared surplus. Men in all four divisions are rated according to the priority credit scores. The top fourth is selected and those not essential for retention in service by reason of military necessity are designated as surplus.

Men in the surplus division who are marked for retention by reason of military necessity are then shifted into the active divisions, all of the men designated as surplus are shifted into the surplus divisions, which now will serve as a vehicle for eventually returning them to the United States.

No man in a unit that remains in service can become surplus until a qualified replacement is available. If military necessity should entail the immediate transfer of a unit to the Pacific, there may conceivably be no time to apply the plan to men of that unit before the emergency transfer is made. Consideration will be given these men when they arrive in the new theatre.

The active units needed against Japan will be shipped to the Pacific. Those units required for occupation duty in Europe will be sent to their stations, and surplus units will be returned to the United States as quickly as possible.

In the United States, the men of these surplus units will revert to a surplus pool in the Army Ground Forces, Army Service Forces and Army Air Forces. These surplus pools will include surplus men from all overseas theatres and surplus men from the continental United States.

From these surplus pools the reduction of various types of Army personnel will be made. The number to be returned to civilian life as no longer essential to over-all Army needs will be chosen from among those with the highest priority credit scores.

It is emphasized that the rate of return of surplus men from overseas will depend upon the number of ships available. Thousands of ships will be required to supply the Pacific theatre. The Pacific theatre will have No. 1 priority. All else must wait. To it will be transported millions of fighting men, millions of tons of landing barges, tanks, planes, guns, ammunition and food, over longer supply lines than those to Europe.

This means that most of the ships and planes that were used to supply the European theatre will be needed to supply the Pacific theatre. The majority of ships proceeding to Europe will continue on to the Pacific laden with troops and supplies for that distant campaign. Very few will turn around and come back to the United States. The Army, therefore, will not be able to return all surplus men to the United States immediately. It may take many months.

While the process of selecting and returning men from the European theatre is taking place, the plan for readjustment and partial demobilization also will be applied in active theatres like the Southwest Pacific. Individuals in those theatres will be declared surplus to the extent that replacements can be provided.

Naturally, since the Pacific will be the only active theatre, there will be no surplus units of any type. Military requirements there will demand an increase rather than a decrease in fighting units. Nevertheless, troops in the Pacific area will benefit by the reduction of the Army, not as units, but as individuals.

Commanders in the Pacific area will be told the number and types of men who can be replaced. They then will select these men, using the same standards as apply in inactive theatres and in the United States. These men then will be returned to the United States as rapidly as replacements of the same type become available and as the military situation permits.

As an example: Normally there will be a great flow of men needed to build up and maintain an offensive against Japan, but say that several thousand men, over and above the required number, can be shipped to the Pacific each month. Then, a corresponding number of men in the Pacific with the highest priority credit scores can be declared surplus and returned to the United States, where their scores and military necessity will determine whether they are among the personnel no longer essential to the Army.

Simultaneously with the selection and return of men in the overseas theatres, the same selective formula will be applied among troops stationed in the continental United States. Troops in the United States, however, will serve as the main reservoir of replacements for the overseas theatres; for in general their priority scores will be lower than the scores of men who have served overseas and have seen combat duty.

Any man who may have been declared non-essential under this plan who wishes to remain in the Army, provided he has a satisfactory record, will not be forced out of the Army if he can be usefully employed.

In the case of officers, military necessity will determine which ones are non-essential. These will be released as they can be spared.

Priority of release for members of the Women's Army Corps will be determined in the same way as for the rest of the Army, but treating the corps as a separate group. However, in the case of all female personnel of the Army, those whose husbands have already been released will be discharged upon application.

The plan as now adopted will provide some reduction in the Army's ground forces and initially considerably less in the service forces and in the air forces.

Following Germany's defeat, the air forces will have to move combat groups and supporting ground units from all over the world to the Pacific areas. The nature of the Pacific area dictates that service forces personnel will be needed in great numbers to carry the war to Japan. Long supply lines, scattered bases, jungles, primitive country, all contribute to the importance and necessity for service forces personnel. Therefore the reduction in its strength will be slow at first.

As replacements become available from the ground forces and from new inductees, the air forces and the service forces will discharge a fair share of men proportionate with the ground forces.

Surplus individuals declared non-essential to the needs of the Army will be discharged from the service through separation centers. Five Army separation centers are already in operation and additional ones will be set up when the need develops. A total of eighteen in all parts of the country are contemplated. Their wide distribution will enable us to discharge soldiers close to their homes.

The readjustment and demobilization plan applies only to readjustment and demobilization and in the period between the defeat of Germany and prior to the defeat of Japan. It sets forth the principles and responsibilities involved during that period. Theatre commanders and commanders of all other major commands of the Army will put the plan into operation in as simple a manner as possible based on those principles and responsibilities.

The War Department has determined that the successful operation of the plan requires that the troops themselves, as well as the public, be kept fully informed.

The size of the military establishment that will be needed after the defeat of Germany has been calculated with the same exactness as the size of the Army needed up to now. No soldier will be kept in the military service who is not needed to fulfill these requirements. No soldier will be released who is needed.

It must be borne in mind always that the war will not be won, nor the peace enjoyed, until Japan has been completely crushed.

GOVERNOR THOMAS E. DEWEY'S OPENING CAMPAIGN SPEECH IN PHILADELPHIA

September 7, 1944 [1]

Governor Martin, Governor Edge, fellow Americans:

Tonight we open a campaign to decide the course of our country for many years to come. The next national Administration will take office Jan. 20, 1945, and will serve until 1949. Those years, 1945 to 1949, will be largely —and we pray wholly—peacetime years.

For nearly three years our nation has been engaged in a world war. Today our armed forces are winning victory after victory. Total, smashing victory is in sight. Germany and Japan shall be given the lessons of their lives— right in Berlin and Tokyo.

America—our America which loves peace so dearly—is proving once again than it can wage war mightily. That it can crush any aggressor who threatens the freedom which we love even more than peace. The American people have risen to the challenge. The war is being won on the battlefronts. It is also being won in the factory, the office, the farm, the mine and the home.

Yes, we are proving that we can wage war. But what are the prospects of success as a nation at peace? The answer depends entirely on the outcome of this election.

At the very outset I want to make one thing clear. This is not merely a campaign against an individual or a political party. It is not merely a campaign against an individual or a political party. It is not merely a campaign to displace a tired, exhausted, quarreling and bickering Administration with a fresh and vigorous Administration.

This is a campaign against an Administration which was conceived in defeatism, which failed for eight straight years to restore our domestic economy, which has been the most wasteful, extravagant and incompetent

[1] *New York Times.*

Administration in the history of the nation and, worst of all, one which has lost faith in itself and in the American people.

This basic issue was clearly revealed in the recent announcement by the Director of Selective Service in Washington. He said that when Germany and Japan have been defeated it will still be necessary to demobilize the armed forces very gradually. And why? Because, he said, "We can keep people in the Army about as cheaply as we could create an agency for them when they are out."

Let me repeat that. He said we can keep people in the Army about as cheaply as we could create an agency for them when they are out.

For six months we have been hearing statements from the New Deal underlings in Washington that this was the plan. Now it is out in the open. They have been working up to it. Because they are afraid of peace. They are afraid of a continuance of their own failures to get this country going again. They are afraid of America.

I do not share that fear. I believe that our members of the armed forces should be transported home and released at the earliest moment practicable after victory. I believe that the occupation of Germany and Japan should very soon be confined to those who voluntarily choose to remain in the Army when peace comes. I am not afraid of the future of America—either immediate or distant. I am sure of our future, if we get a National Administration which believes in the United States of America.

The New Deal was founded on the philosophy that our frontiers are behind us and that all we have left to do is to quarrel among ourselves over the division of what we have. Mr. Roosevelt himself said in 1932:

"Our industrial plant is built, * * * our task is not * * * necessarily producing more goods. It is the soberer, less dramatic business of administering resources and plants already in hand."

The New Deal operated on that philosophy for seven straight peacetime years with unlimited power and unlimited money. At the end of that time, in 1939, the New Deal gave its own official verdict on its failure by this cold admission: "The American economic machine is stalled on dead center."

The Administration knows that the war, with all its tragic toll of death, debt and destruction, is the only thing that saved it. They are deadly afraid that they will go back to resumption of their own failures. That is why they are afraid to let men out of the Army. That is why they say it is cheaper to keep men in the Army than to let them come home when peace has been won.

Now let us get another point straight for the records right here at the beginning. In the last hundred years we have had eleven periods during which business and employment were well below normal. During that period the average depression lasted two years. In the entire hundred years the longest depression of all was five years and the next longest was four years—up to the last one.

When this Administration took office the depression was already over three years old. Then what happened? In 1934, when the depression was then five years old—that's longer than any other depression in a whole century, we still had 12,000,000 unemployed in America. By 1940 the depression was almost eleven years old. This Administration had been in power for more than seven straight years and there were still 10,000,000 Americans unemployed.

It took a world war to get jobs for the American people.

Let's get one thing clear and settled. Who was President of the United

States during the depression that lasted from 1933 until some time in 1940, when war orders from all over the world began to bring us full employment again? It was the New Deal that kept this country in a continuous state of depression for seven straight years. They lived on a depression. It was the New Deal that made, that managed to make a three-year depression last eleven straight years—over twice as long as any other depression in a whole century.

And now Washington is getting all set for another depression. They intend to keep the young men in the Army. The New Deal spokesmen are daily announcing that reconversion will be difficult, if not impossible. They say that relief rolls will be enormous. They drearily promise us that we shall need to prepare for an army of unemployed bigger than the armies we have put in the field against the Germans and the Japanese. That's what's wrong with the New Deal. That's why it's time for a change.

The reason for this long continued failure is twofold. First, because there never was a worse job of running the Government of this country in all its history. When one agency fails, the New Deal just piles another one on and we pay for both. When both fail they invent a third and we pay for all three. When men quarrel, there isn't anybody to put a stop to it in our Government. When agencies get snarled up there is no one in authority to unsnarl them. Meanwhile, the people's business goes to pot and the people are the victims.

Right in the final crisis of this war, the most critical of all war agencies—the War Production Board—fell apart right before our eyes. This is also the board, and don't forget it, this is also the board in charge of reconversion and jobs. Yet we have seen quarreling, disunity and public recriminations day after day, as one competent man after another resigned and the head of the board was sent to China. This isn't a new experience; others have been sent to China. And we have seen this very thing happen to agency after agency. The cost of the war effort, to the country, can never be calculated. And it's time the people put an end to it, because no one else will.

When the WPB fell apart, so did your chance under this Administration for jobs after this war is over. For now the New Dealers have moved in, and their handiwork, their promise for America has never been jobs—but the dole.

The other reason for this long continued failure—the reason why they are now dismally preparing for another depression—is because this Administration has so little faith in the United States. They believe in the defeatist philosophy that our industrial plant is built, that our task is not to produce more goods but to fight among ourselves over what we have.

I believe that we have not even begun to build our industrial plant. We have not exhausted our inventive genius. We have not exhausted our capacity to produce more goods for our people. No living man has yet dreamed of the limit to which we can go if we have a Government which believes in the American economic system and in the American people.

This Administration is convinced that only, only by surrendering a little bit of freedom for every little bit of security can we achieve social security. That is exactly what our enemies thought. So their people first lost their freedom and then they lost their security. I cannot accept that course for America. I believe—I know—that if we achieve real social security, we can achieve it only if we do keep our freedom.

There can be—there must be—jobs and opportunity for all, without discrimination on account of race, creed, color or national origin. There must be jobs in industry, in agriculture, in mines, in stores, in offices, at a high level of wages and salaries. There must be opportunity and incentive for men and women to go into business for themselves.

The war has proved that despite the New Deal, America can mightily increase its frontiers of production. With competent government America can produce mightily for peace. And the standard of living of our people is limited only by the amount of goods and services we are able to produce.

The New Deal prepares to keep men in the Army because it is afraid of a resumption of its own depression. They can't think of anything for us to do once we stop building guns and tanks. But to those who believe in America there's lots to do.

Why, just take housing, for example. If we simply build the homes the American people need in order to be decently housed, it will keep millions of men employed for years. After twelve years of the New Deal the housing of the American people has fallen down so badly that just to come up to the standards of 1930 we shall need to build a million homes a year for many years to come. And this does not include the enormous need for farm housing repairs and alterations.

Why by the end of this year we shall have an immediate need for 6,000,000 automobiles just to put the same number of cars back on the road that were there in 1941. We shall need after the war 3,500,000 vacuum cleaners, 7,000,000 clocks, 23,000,000 radio sets, 5,000,000 refrigerators, 3,000,000 washing machines, and millions of other household appliances.

There are 600 different articles made of steel and iron which have not been manufactured since 1942. All of this means production and production means jobs. But that kind of production, that kind of jobs, are beyond the experience and beyond the vision of the New Deal.

Why, the transportation industry—the railroads, the whole moving, growing aircraft industry and the motor—is just waiting to get going, and to burst into production such as we've never seen in the history of our country.

The mighty energy we found lying dormant and unused in this country at the beginning of the war must be turned from destruction to creation. There can and must be jobs for all who want them and a free, open door for every man who wants to start out in business for himself.

We know from long experience that we shall not provide jobs and restore small business by the methods of the New Deal. We cannot keep our freedom and at the same time continue experimentation with a new policy every day by the national Government. We cannot succeed with a controlled and regulated society under a Government which destroys incentive, chokes production, fosters disunity and discourages men with vision and imagination from creating employment and opportunity.

The New Deal really believes that unemployment is bound to be with us permanently and it says so. They will change this twelve-year-old tune between now and election. They do it every time. But they always come back to it after election. The New Deal really believes that we cannot have good social legislation and also have good jobs for all. I believe with all my heart and soul that we can have both.

Of course we need security regulation. Of course we need bank deposit insurance. Of course we need price support for agriculture. Of course the farmers of this country cannot be left to the hazards of a world price while they buy their goods at an American price. Of course we need unemployment insurance and old-age pensions and also relief whenever there are not enough jobs. Of course the rights of labor to organize and bargain collectively are fundamental. My party blazed the trail in that field by passage of the Railway Labor Act in 1926.

But we must also have a Government which believes in enterprise and Government policies which encourage enterprise. We must see to it that a man who wants to start a business is encouraged to start it, that the man who wants to expand a growing business is encouraged to expand it. We must see to it that the job-producing enterprises of America are stimulated to produce more jobs. We must see to it that the man who wants to produce more jobs is not throttled by the Government—but knows that he has a Government as eager for him to succeed as he is himself.

We cannot have jobs and opportunity if we surrender our freedom to Government control. I say we do not need to surrender our freedom to Government control in order to have the economic security to which we are entitled as free men. I say we can have both opportunity and security within the framework of a free society. That is what the American people will say at the election next November.

With the winning of the war in sight, there are two overshadowing problems. First, the making and keeping of the peace of the world so that your children and my children shall not face this tragedy all over again. This great objective, to which we are all so deeply devoted, I shall talk about at Louisville tomorrow night on the radio.

The other problem is whether we shall replace the tired and quarrelsome defeatism of the present Administration with a fresh and vigorous Government which believes in the future of the United States, and knows how to act on that belief.

Such action involves many things: tax policies, regulatory policies, labor policies, opportunity for small business, the bureaucracies which are attempting to regulate every detail of the lives of our people and these are all of major importance. I will discuss each of them in detail before this campaign is over. I will discuss them in plain English and say what we propose to do about them, so that there shall be no misunderstanding.

I am interested—desperately interested in bringing to our country a rebirth of faith in our future. I am deeply interested in bringing a final end to the defeatism and failure of this Administration in its domestic policies. I am deeply devoted to the principle that victory in this war shall mean victory for freedom and for the permanent peace of the world. Our place in a peaceful world can and shall be made secure. But nothing on earth will make us secure unless we are strong, unless we are productive and unless we have faith in ourselves. We can and we will recover our future and go forward in the path of freedom and security. I have unlimited faith that the American people will choose that path next November.

EMPEROR HIROHITO'S MESSAGE TO OPENING OF EIGHTY-FIFTH DIET

September 7, 1944 [1]

Imperial Rescript—We hereby conduct the ceremony opening the Imperial Diet, and so announce to the members of the House of Peers and the House of Representatives. The warriors (who represent us) are fighting bravely

[1] Office of War Information.

and strenuously, and by crushing numerous (word missing), are enhancing their military prestige. In the same manner, the construction of G.E.A. is progressing step by step, and the bond of alliance with our allied countries is growing stronger. We deeply rejoice over this.

However, the counteroffensive of the enemy is becoming increasingly fierce and the war situation is finally becoming more intense. Truly, today, is the time for Imperial Japan to decide victory by massing her total strength. We look forward to you guardsmen standing before the people to crush the inordinate ambition of the enemy countries by renewing your intense vigor and strengthening your solidarity, thereby guarding and maintaining the prosperity of the Imperial Throne through eternity.

We have ordered the State Ministers to present to the Imperial Diet emergency bills concerning the present situation in particular, and expect that you will deliberate on them in harmony in accordance with our wishes, thereby fulfilling your duty by giving your approval.

PREMIER KUNIAKI KOISO'S ADDRESS AT OPENING OF EIGHTY-FIFTH DIET

September 7, 1944 [1]

To have been given this opportunity of expressing the views of the Government at this eighty-fifth session of the Imperial Diet is a source of gratification to me.

The gracious message of His Majesty the Emperor upon the evening of this Diet today (Sept. 7) leaves us deeply impressed. I, with all of you, in obedience to His Majesty's command, desire to faithfully fulfill our duties as warriors; swiftly achieve the war aims; and bring peace to the mind of His Majesty.

At this critical time, when the rise or fall of our Nation is in the balance, I have been given the responsibility of guiding the Nation. I believe that the time in which we must defend this incomparable Empire, which has grown under the divine spirit of our Imperial ancestors, and when we must write a brilliant and eternal page in history faces us today.

Holding to a firm conviction in certain victory with their 100,000,000 compatriots, and concentrating their entire strength in harmony and unity, our Imperial Forces are about to take a course of action to annihilate the U. S. and Great Britain. I hope that in cooperation with this gallant undertaking, all national affairs may be carried out to the end of attaining the objective of this war.

The war situation at present is truly grave and the rise or fall of our Empire hinges on the developments today. In order to break through these critical conditions, the basic operations of our national administration must be unified toward the sole goal of the prosecution of the G.E.A. War.

Through the close coordination of the civil and military, and the Supreme Command and the national affairs, it is to be expected that a strong unshakable war leadership will result. This is one of the principal reasons which lead to the formation of the Supreme Council for the Direction of the war, and the execution of national administration in the future will be decided

[1] Office of War Information.

by the basic policies of this Council which unifies Supreme Command and the national affairs.

All other plans and matters will also follow this wartime pattern. The primary consideration of our wartime policy is to uplift the fighting spirit and to establish a national wartime structure for victory. It is needless to say at this time, that in order to enhance the fighting spirit, the spirit of national consciousness must be thoroughly brought home to the people. This war, in which we are trying to surmount all difficulties to defend the structure of a nation unexcelled, is in other words, a fight with the will to win an ultimate victory. A strong national consciousness is therefore the greatest fighting power. Moreover, the enhancing of fighting spirit is, on one hand, impossible without the execution of the people's will.

The Government, in facing the decisive stage of the war, intends to inform the people of the actual conditions at home and abroad, have them re-realize the mutual responsibilities of the war, and share with them the spirit of patriotism; and by deeply trusting their loyalty, I believe the 100,000,000 people will continue to meet the national crisis.

There are many measures to be undertaken in order to establish a sure-victory national structure. First of all, in order to break all bottlenecks obstructing production, it is the intention of the Government to carry out effective and appropriate measures one after another. Thus, by unifying the hearts of the people, obtain their total cooperation. Furthermore, I would like to pay one great attention to the manifestation of the people's moral principles.

Moreover, in answer to the call for unstinting efforts by our peoples, those in Chosen (Korea) and Taiwan (Formosa) have responded by contributing their parts as members of our Empire in order to aid in the prosecution of the war and the enhancement of the Empire. Their young men have been serving in the Army and the Navy as special volunteers, while recently a conscription was instituted. Already many of our compatriots are participating in this Holy War showing the true spirit of service and patriotism. This is fortunate for our Nation, and also at this time, I believe that we must give full consideration to their treatment.

The second measure is the expansion of fighting strength. All national power which can be mobilized to increase war strength should be concentrated, especially in the development of air power. The solution to the problem of seizing the initiative and turning the approaching of war to our advantage lies in the above measure. There is nothing greater which demands the aroused action of our fellow-compatriots engaged in the munition production than this (word missing).

In other words, the emphasis in all plans must be placed on this objective. Manpower, materials, money, and all else are being directed towards the swift materialization of these aims. I believe that it is absolutely necessary to divert all installations and production activities at present not contributing to the war effort to war production.

Many such measures have already been carried out. In order to increase fighting power, especially air power, it is necessary to augment the production of arms and munitions and ensure land and sea transportation. The Government will do all in its power to eliminate bottlenecks.

The third important measure is the ensuring of increased food production and stabilization of the people's livelihood. Needless to say, in this present war, it is very essential to guarantee the minimum standard of living. Up to now, the people, bearing fairly uncomfortable conditions, have devoted themselves to the prosecution of the war, for which I am very grateful.

The fourth important measure is labor and the national mobilization. In this crucial time, we cannot tolerate any slacker and bystander, regardless of age and sex. The 100,000,000 people, taking their battle stations to victory, giving their everything in their mission, are, in other words, awaiting divine aid by giving all.

Enterprisers, office workers, technicians, industrial workers, farmers, and fishermen, with the spirit of every man a soldier and with the readiness of those answering the call for armed service, must give their total efforts and develop maximum efficiency. It is only then that we are worthy of being Imperial subjects along with those officers and men of the armed forces who are sacrificing their lives in the rain of bullets. The administration is working hard to smooth out difficulties of labor conscription system and labor management, and is determined to mobilize all possible labor by working out every possible means.

The fifth important measure is a stronger home defense setup. Recently, when enemy planes raided the western part of our homeland, officials and the people unitedly served in their duties of defense and minimized the damages, and again I feel very much reassured. I ask you officials and the people to defend with all your might, no matter how often the enemy may raid our country. Strengthening of the defense of essential industries and important cities is a present pressing problem.

The sixth important measure is the mobilization and utilization of scientific technique. The war has now assumed all aspects of a scientific warfare. Therefore, the Government has brought about the unification of the Army and Navy in the operation of scientific technique; and, in order to streamline scientific technique representative of our country to fit the phase of the war situation, and further, to realize speedy and smooth large scale production of armaments necessary for a decisive war, the Government has established special facilities and has encouraged the people to invent new weapons. Through these actions, national scientific technique has been speedily converted into fighting power, and the people have been enabled to cooperate fully in the prosecution of the war. The Government anticipated much in results.

In conclusion I wish to state that, paralleling the aforementioned domestic policy, Japan's foreign policy will be to ever strengthen our ties with our ally, Germany, and collaborate with our allies in G.E.A., to continue prosecuting this war. At the same time, Japan will strive to maintain friendly relations with neutrals.

Under extremely difficult circumstances, our ally, Germany, continues to fight with a firm conviction in ultimate victory. We cannot help admiring her. We believe that the day is not so far off when she will surmount all obstacles, and manifesting her potential might, turn the fortune of war favorably on her side. We pray for her success.

The various nations of the G.E.A., and their peoples show no sign of wavering despite the war, rather, more conscious of their mission in the reconstruction of G.E.A., fully cooperating with Japan and determined to fight it out to the bitter end together, they are intensifying their efforts to that end. It is most reassuring.

It is needless for me to repeat the indivisible relationship between Japan and Manchukuo. The unity between China and Japan is also ever enhanced by the pact of alliance. For the past seven years and more our Imperial

Army has fought bravely on the continent, to free China from the yoke of Anglo-American tyranny of over 100 years, and to mutually establish a G.E.A. based on justice. As the true intention permeates among the people of China, Sino-Japanese coalition will become ever increasingly firm.

A change in the Thailand Cabinet took place some time ago. The new Cabinet under Abhaiwong is adhering to the policy of prosecuting the war in accordance with the alliance pact. Even though expected, this bears testimony to the solidarity of the G.E.A. Sphere.

Burma has already celebrated the first anniversary of her independence. Under the inspiring leadership of Adipadi Ba Maw, surmounting innumerable difficulties, she is progressing steadily. Ardently determined to prosecute the war until the final victory is achieved, she has proven herself a most reliable ally.

The Philippines, also, will soon greet the anniversary of their independence. Under President Laurel's leadership, the Filipinos have successfully solved their wartime food problem, as well as that of maintaining public peace and order. They are now streamlining their war effort. The Philippine nation is indeed, a very reassuring and friendly ally.

Subhas Chandra Bose, head of the Provisional Government of Free India, and his followers are carrying on their struggle to obtain the independence of India. We pay them due tribute. Japan, as a matter of course, will give her utmost cooperation to help them achieve their goal of independence.

Next, in the East Indies, Japan has since last year, in compliance with the wishes of the inhabitants, instituted measures for the participation of these native peoples in local government. The East Indian natives have contributed greatly toward the execution of the G.E.A. War. In view of these facts, Japan will grant these people their independence to establish their permanent happiness and well-being.

In the future, Japan will adhere to her G.E.A. policy and put forth every effort to develop the spirit of the joint G.E.A. Declaration. She will do everything in her power to keep the trust that the G.E.A. countries have placed in her. Thus, with Japan as the core, all G.E.A. countries will unite more firmly than ever in confidence in victory. All manpower and materials will be mobilized to prosecute the war in order to bring about the renaissance of G.E.A. I am certain that we shall succeed in crushing the inordinate ambitions of America and Britain.

GENERAL EISENHOWER'S WARNING TO THE PEOPLE OF THE RHINELAND AND THE RUHR

September 12, 1944 [1]

The battle of Germany is about to begin.

On the 26th of August I addressed a warning to German civilians in the Duchy of Luxembourg, the French Province of Alsace-Lorraine, and in Germany west of the Rhine. The swift advance of the Allied armies and the disintegration of the German armies in the west have brought you within the scope of that warning.

I am repeating it now to the inhabitants of the Ruhr and the Rhineland.

[1] New York Times.

The areas in which you live are already today in the rear area of military operations. Very soon they may become a theatre of war.

In view of these facts I am giving you the following warning:

1. The rear communications of the remnants of the German Army retreating into Germany will be subjected to bombing as devastating as that which preceded and accompanied the Allied campaign in Normandy. Civilians are hereby warned that everyone who lives or works in the vicinity of road, railroad and canal communications; of military depots, camps and installations, or factories working for the Nazi war machine, must from now on reckon that they will not be saved from high level and low level air attack at any hour of the day or night.

2. Particularly emergency earthworks and fortifications will be areas of special danger. Civilians are warned that all who work on these military targets do so at their own peril.

To prevent useless civilian casualties all civilians are advised during the coming weeks to evacuate the danger areas enumerated above and to take refuge in the countryside as far as possible from such areas.

3. Civilians are further warned that the perpetrators of all atrocities committed against non-Germans in these areas will be brought to trial for their crimes. Evidence as to these crimes will be accepted by the Allied judicial authorities from German and non-German witnesses.

ALLIED ARMISTICE TERMS FOR RUMANIA

September 12, 1944 [1]

Following are the terms of the Rumanian armistice agreement which has been signed in Moscow:

Agreement Between the Governments of the United States of America, the Soviet Union, and the United Kingdom on the One Hand, and the Government of Rumania on the Other Concerning an Armistice:

The Government and High Command of Rumania, recognizing the fact of the defeat of Rumania in the war against the Union of Soviet Socialist Republics, the United States of America, and the United Kingdom, and the other United Nations, accept the armistice terms presented by the Governments of the above mentioned three Allied Powers, acting in the interests of all the United Nations.

On the basis of the foregoing the representative of the Allied (Soviet) High Command, Marshal of the Soviet Union, R. Y. Malinovski, duly authorized thereto by the Governments of the United States of America, the Soviet Union, and the United Kingdom, acting in the interests of all the United Nations, on the one hand, and the representatives of the Government and High Command of Rumania, Minister of State and Minister of Justice L. Patrascanu, Deputy Minister of Internal Affairs, Adjutant of His Majesty the King of Rumania, General D. Damaceanu, Prince Stirbey, and Mr. G. Popp, on the other hand, holding proper full powers, have signed the following conditions:

1. As from August 24, 1944, at four a.m., Rumania has entirely discontinued military operations against the Union of Soviet Socialist Republics on

[1] State Department Bulletin.

all theaters of war, has withdrawn from the war against the United Nations, has broken off relations with Germany and her satellites, has entered the war and will wage war on the side of the Allied Powers against Germany and Hungary for the purpose of restoring Rumanian independence and sovereignty, for which purpose she provides not less than twelve infantry divisions with corps troops.

Military operations on the part of Rumanian armed forces, including naval and air forces, against Germany and Hungary will be conducted under the general leadership of the Allied (Soviet) High Command.

2. The Government and High Command of Rumania undertake to take steps for the disarming and interning of the armed forces of Germany and Hungary on Rumanian territory and also for the interning of the citizens of both states mentioned who reside there. (See Annex to Article Two)

3. The Government and High Command of Rumania will ensure to the Soviet and other Allied forces facilities for free movement on Rumanian territory in any direction if required by the military situation, the Rumanian Government and High Command of Rumania giving such movement every possible assistance with their own means of communications and at their own expense on land, on water and in the air. (See Annex to Article Three)

4. The state frontier between the Union of Soviet Socialist Republics and Rumania, established by the Soviet-Rumanian Agreement of June 8, 1940, is restored.

5. The Government and High Command of Rumania will immediately hand over all Soviet and Allied prisoners of war in their hands, as well as interned citizens and citizens forcibly removed to Rumania, to the Allied (Soviet) High Command for the return of these persons to their own country.

From the moment of the signing of the present terms and until repatriation the Rumanian Government and High Command undertake to provide at their own expense all Soviet and Allied prisoners of war, as well as forcibly removed and interned citizens, and displaced persons and refugees, with adequate food, clothing and medical service, in accordance with hygienic requirements, as well as with means of transport for the return of all those persons to their own country.

6. The Rumanian Government will immediately set free, irrespective of citizenship and nationality, all persons held in confinement on account of their activities in favor of the United Nations or because of their sympathies with the cause of the United Nations, or because of their racial origin, and will repeal all discriminatory legislation and restrictions imposed thereunder.

7. The Rumanian Government and High Command undertake to hand over as trophies into the hands of the Allied (Soviet) High Command all war material of Germany and her satellites located on Rumanian territory, including vessels of the fleet of Germany and her satellites located in Rumanian waters.

8. The Rumanian Government and High Command undertake not to permit the export or expropriation of any form of property (including valuables and currency) belonging to Germany, Hungary or to their nationals or to persons resident in their territories or in territories occupied by them without the permission of the Allied (Soviet) High Command. They will keep this property in such manner as may be prescribed by the Allied (Soviet) High Command.

9. The Rumanian Government and High Command undertake to hand over to the Allied (Soviet) High Command all vessels belonging or having belonged to the United Nations which are located in Rumanian ports, no

matter at whose disposal these vessels may be, for the use of the Allied (Soviet) High Command during the period of the war against Germany and Hungary in the general interests of the Allies, these vessels subsequently to be returned to their owners.

The Rumanian Government bear the full material responsibility for any damage or destruction of the aforementioned property until the moment of the transfer of this property to the Allied (Soviet) High Command.

10. The Rumanian Government must make regular payments in Rumanian currency required by the Allied (Soviet) High Command for the fulfillment of its functions and will in case of need ensure the use on Rumanian territory of industrial and transportation enterprises, means of communication, power stations, enterprises and installations of public utility, stores of fuel, fuel oil, food and other materials, and services in accordance with instructions issued by the Allied (Soviet) High Command.

Rumanian merchant vessels, whether in Rumanian or foreign waters, shall be subject to the operational control of the Allied (Soviet) High Command for use in the general interest of the Allies. (See Annex to Article Ten)

11. Losses caused to the Soviet Union by military operations and by the occupation by Rumania of Soviet territory will be made good by Rumania to the Soviet Union, but, taking into consideration that Rumania has not only withdrawn from the war, but has declared war and in fact is waging war against Germany and Hungary, the parties agree that compensation for the indicated losses will be made by Rumania not in full but only in part, namely to the amount of three hundred million United States dollars payable over six years in commodities (oil products, grain, timber products, seagoing and river craft, sundry machinery, et cetera).

Compensation will be paid by Rumania for losses caused to the property of other Allied states and their nationals in Rumania during the war, the amount of compensation to be fixed at a later date. (See Annex to Article Eleven)

12. The Rumanian Government undertakes within the periods indicated by the Allied (Soviet) High Command to return to the Soviet Union in complete good order all valuables and materials removed from its territory during the war, belonging to state, public and cooperative organizations, enterprises, institutions or individual citizens, such as: factory and works equipment, locomotives, railways trucks, tractors, motor vehicles, historic monuments, museum valuables and any other property.

13. The Rumanian Government undertakes to restore all legal rights and interests of the United Nations and their nations on Rumanian territory as they existed before the war and to return their property in complete good order.

14. The Rumanian Government and High Command undertake to collaborate with the Allied (Soviet) High Command in the apprehension and trial of persons accused of war crimes.

15. The Rumanian Government undertakes immediately to dissolve all pro-Hitler organizations (of a Fascist type) situated in Rumanian territory, whether political, military or para-military, as well as other organizations conducting propaganda hostile to the United Nations, in particular to the Soviet Union, and will not in future permit the existence of organizations of that nature.

16. The printing, importation and distribution in Rumania of periodical and non-periodical literature, the presentation of theatrical performances and films, the work of wireless stations, post, telegraph and telephone shall be

carried out in agreement with the Allied (Soviet) High Command. (See Annex to Article Sixteen)

17. Rumanian Civil Administration is restored in the whole area of Rumania separated by not less than fifty-one hundred kilometers (depending upon conditions of terrain) from the front line, Rumanian administrative bodies undertaking to carry out, in the interests of the reestablishment of peace and security, instructions and orders of the Allied (Soviet) High Command issued by them for the purpose of securing the execution of these armistice terms.

18. An Allied Control Commission will be established which will undertake until the conclusion of peace the regulation of and control over the execution of the present terms under the general direction and orders of the Allied (Soviet) High Command, acting on behalf of the Allied Powers. (See Annex to Article 18)

19. The Allied Governments regard the decision of the Vienna award regarding Transylvania as null and void and are agreed that Transylvania (or the greater part thereof) should be returned to Rumania, subject to confirmation at the peace settlement, and the Soviet Government agrees that Soviet forces shall take part for this purpose in joint military operations with Rumania against Germany and Hungary.

20. The present terms come into force at the moment of their signing.

Done in Moscow, in four copies, each in the Russian, English and Rumanian languages, the Russian and English texts being authentic. *September 12, 1944.*

By authority of the Governments of the United States of America, the Union of Soviet Socialist Republics and the United Kingdom.

By authority of the Government and High Command of Rumania.

Annex to the Armistice Agreement between the Governments of the United States of America, the Soviet Union, and the United Kingdom on the one hand and the Government of Rumania on the other hand.

A. Annex to Article 2.

The measures provided for in Article 2 of the agreement regarding the internment of citizens of Germany and Hungary now in Rumanian territory do not extend to citizens of those countries of Jewish origin.

B. Annex to Article 3.

Under cooperation of the Rumanian Government and High Command of Rumania, mentioned in Article 3 of the Agreement, is understood the placing at the disposal of the Allied (Soviet) High Command for use at its discretion during the armistice all Rumanian military, air and naval constructions and installations, ports, harbors, barracks, warehouses, airfields, means of communication, meteorological stations which might be required for military needs in complete good order and with the personnel required for their maintenance.

C. Annex to Article 10.

The Rumanian Government will withdraw and redeem within such time limits and on such terms as the Allied (Soviet) High Command may specify, all holdings in Rumanian territory of currencies issued by the Allied (Soviet) High Command, and will hand over currency so withdrawn free of cost to the Allied (Soviet) High Command.

D. Annex to Article 11.

The basis for settlements of payment of compensation provided for in Article 11 of the present Agreement will be the American dollar at its gold parity on the day of signing of the Agreement, i.e. thirty-five dollars for one ounce of gold.

E. Annex to Article 16.

The Rumanian Government undertakes that wireless communication, telegraphic and postal correspondence, correspondence in cypher and courier correspondence, as well as telephonic communication with foreign countries of Embassies, Legations and Consulates situated in Rumania, will be conducted in the manner laid down by the Allied (Soviet) High Command.

F. Annex to Article 18.

Control over the exact execution of the armistice terms is entrusted to the Allied Control Commission to be established in conformity with Article 18 of the Armistice Agreement.

The Rumanian Government and their organs shall fulfill all instructions of the Allied Control Commission arising out of the Armistice Agreement.

The Allied Control Commission will set up special organs or sections entrusting them respectively with the execution of various functions. In addition, the Allied Control Commission may have its officers in various parts of Rumania.

The Allied Control Commission will have its seat in the City of Bucharest.

Moscow: *September 12, 1944.*

GENERAL EISENHOWER ANNOUNCES ESTABLISHMENT OF ALLIED MILITARY GOVERNMENT (AMG) TO RULE OCCUPIED GERMANY

September 18, 1944 [1]

1. The Allied Military Government is established in the theatre under my command to exercise in occupied German territory the supreme legislative, judicial and executive authority vested in me as Supreme Commander, Allied Expeditionary Force, and as Military Governor.

2. The immediate task of the Allied Military Government during the course of military operations will be to secure the lines of communication of the Allied armies and to suppress any activities in the occupied areas of Germany that would impair the speedy conclusion of the war.

3. Simultaneously, the Allied Military Government will begin the task of destroying National Socialism. It will remove from responsible posts all members of the Nazi party and of the SS (Elite Guard) and others who have played a leading part in the National Socialist regime. This process begins immediately on the arrival of the Allied armies in each area and the inauguration of the Allied Military Government.

4. The civilian population will as far as possible continue in the normal occupations. Detailed instructions to them will be issued by the Allied Military Government in each area.

[1] *New York Times.*

ARMISTICE TERMS GRANTED TO FINLAND
BY THE ALLIES

September 20, 1944 [1]

In view of the fact that the Government of Finland has accepted the preliminary terms of the Soviet Government relating to the break with Germany and to the withdrawal of German troops from Finland, and taking into account the fact that the conclusion of the future peace agreement will be facilitated by the inclusion of some of the terms of the peace agreement in the armistice agreement, the Government of the Union of Soviet Socialist Republics and the Government of His Majesty in the United Kingdom and Northern Ireland, acting on behalf of all the United Nations that are in a state of war with Finland, on the one side, and the Government of Finland on the other side decided to conclude the present armistice agreement, the carrying out of which will pass under the control of the Soviet High Command, which is also acting on behalf of the United Nations that are in a state of war with Finland, and which is to be known further as the Allied (Soviet) High Command.

On the basis above mentioned, the representative of the Allied (Soviet) High Command, Col. Gen. Zhdanoff, and representatives of the Government of Finland, Minister for Foreign Affairs, Mr. Carl Enckell; Minister for Defense, Infantry Gen. Rudolf Walden; Chief of the General Staff, Infantry Gen. Erick Heinrichs, and Lieut. Gen. Oscar Enckell, empowered with due authority, have signed the following terms:

1. In connection with the cessation of military operations by Finland from Sept. 4, 1944, and by the Soviet Union from Sept. 5, 1944, Finland undertakes to withdraw her troops beyond the line of the Soviet-Finnish frontier of 1940 in an order provided for in an appendix of the present agreement. (See appendix to Article 1.)

2. Finland undertakes to disarm German land, naval and air forces who have remained in Finland after Sept. 15, 1944, and to hand over their personnel to the Allied (Soviet) High Command as prisoners of war. In this, the Soviet Government will aid the Finnish Army. The Government of Finland also undertakes to intern German and Hungarian citizens on Finnish territory. (See appendix to Article 2.)

3. Finland undertakes on the request of the Allied (Soviet) High Command to put at their disposal airdromes on the south and southwestern coast of Finland, together with their installations, to be used as bases for Soviet planes for a period required by military operations in the air against German troops in Estonia and against the German Navy in the northern part of the Baltic Sea. (See appendix to Article 3.)

4. Finland undertakes to transfer her army to a peacetime footing within two and a half months from the day of the signing of this agreement. (See appendix to Article 4.)

5. Having broken off relations with Germany, Finland also undertakes to break off relations with the satellite states of Germany. (See appendix to Article 5.)

6. The validity of the peace treaty concluded between the Soviet Union

[1] *New York Times.*

and Finland in Moscow on March 12, 1940, is restored with alterations following from the present agreement.

7. Finland will return to the Soviet Union the area of Petsamo (Pechenga), which had been ceded voluntarily by the Soviet States by the peace agreement of Oct. 14, 1920, and March 12, 1940, within boundaries described in the appendix to the present agreement and shown on the map. (See appendix to Article 7 and map scale one to 500,000.)

8. The Soviet Union renounces its rights to the lease of Hangoe Peninsula, which had been granted to her by the Soviet-Finnish peace agreement of March 12, 1940. Finland, on the other hand, undertakes to lease to the Soviet Union territory and a sea area for the establishment of a military base in the area of Porkkala Udd. The boundaries of the territory and the sea area of the Porkkala Udd base are defined in the appendix to this article and shown on the map. (See appendix to Article 8 and map scale one to 100,000.)

9. The validity of the agreement on the Aaland Islands, concluded between Finland and the Soviet Union Oct. 11, 1940, is fully restored.

10. Finland undertakes to hand over at once all Soviet and Allied prisoners of war whom she holds, as well as Soviet and Allied internees and citizens taken to Finland by force, to the Allied (Soviet) High Command for repatriation of these persons. From the moment of the signing of the present agreement, and until their repatriation, Finland undertakes to supply at her own expense all Soviet and Allied prisoners of war, as well as internees and citizens who had been carried away by force, with sufficient food, clothing and medical attention in accordance with health requirements, as well as with means of transport for repatriation of all these persons. Simultaneously, Finnish prisoners of war and internees in territories of the Allied States will be handed over to Finland.

11. Finland undertakes to compensate the Soviet Union for damages caused by Finland through military operations and occupation of Soviet territory by the sum of $300,000,000, to be paid in the course of six years in kind—timber, paper, cellulose, sea and river ships and various machine equipment. Further provision will be made for compensation by Finland of damages caused to the property of other Allied States and to their citizens in Finland during the war. The sum of compensation will be established separately. (See appendix to Article 11.)

12. Finland undertakes to reestablish all lawful rights and interests of the United Nations and their citizens on Finnish territory as they existed before the war and also to return their property intact.

13. Finland undertakes the obligation of collaborating with the Allied powers in the task of the detention of persons accused of war crimes, and the trials of such persons.

14. Finland undertakes to return intact to the Soviet Union within a period fixed by the Allied (Soviet) High Command all valuable articles and material that had been removed to Finland from Soviet territory during the war and that belong to state, public and cooperative organizations, enterprises, offices or individual citizens, such as equipment of factories and works, locomotives, railway carriages, ships, tractors, motor vehicles, historic monuments, museum pieces and all other goods.

15. Finland undertakes to hand over as booty for disposal by the Allied (Soviet) High Command the entire military equipment of Germany and of its satellites that is at present on Finnish territory, including military and merchant vessels that belong to the above-mentioned countries and are in her possession.

16. Finland undertakes not to allow the export or expropriation of any kinds of goods, including valuables and currency, belonging to Germany, Hungary or to their citizens, or to persons residing on their territory, or on territory occupied by them, without the permit of the Allied (Soviet) High Command.

17. A control of the Allied (Soviet) High Command must be established over Finnish merchant ships, excluding those that are already under Allied control, for their use in the common interest of the Allies.

18. Finland undertakes to hand over to the Allied (Soviet) High Command all ships belonging to the United Nations stationed in the ports of Finland, at whose disposal the ships are to be utilized by the Allied (Soviet) High Command during the war against Germany in the common interest of the Allies, with the subsequent return of these ships to their owners.

19. Finland will deliver such materials and manufactured goods as the United Nations may require for purposes connected with the war.

20. Finland undertakes to set free immediately, irrespective of citizenship and nationality, all persons who are under detention in connection with their activities in favor of the United Nations or for their sympathy with the cause of the United Nations or because of their racial origin, as well as to annul discriminating legislation of any kind and the limitation resulting therefrom.

21. Finland undertakes to dissolve immediately on her territory all pro-Hitlerite organizations of a fascist type, political, military and paramilitary, as well as other organizations that indulge in hostile propaganda against the United Nations, and in particular against the Soviet Union, and not to allow the existence of organizations of this kind in the future.

22. An Allied Control Commission is to be set up that, up to the time when peace shall be concluded with Finland, will assume the regulation and control of the fulfillment of present conditions under the general direction and instructions of the Allied (Soviet) High Command, acting on behalf of the Allied Powers.

23. The present agreement becomes valid from the moment of its signing.

Prepared in Moscow, Sept. 19, 1944, one copy of which will be handed over to the Government of the U.S.S.R. for safekeeping, Russian-English, Finnish-Russian and English texts being authentic.

Endorsed copies of the present agreement, with appendixes and maps, will be handed by the Government of the U.S.S.R. to every other Government on behalf of the whole when present agreement is signed.

On behalf of the Governments of the U.S.S.R. and the United Kingdom.

ZDHANOFF

On behalf of the Government of Finland.

ENCKELL, WALDEN, HEINRICH *and* ENCKELL

APPENDIXES

Following are excerpts from an unofficial translation of the appendix to the Finnish armistice terms as they were reported by the Federal Communications Commission from a Moscow domestic radio broadcast:

Appendix to Article 1. The withdrawal of the Finnish troops to the state border, and the advance of the Red Army troops to it, is to begin at 9 A.M., Sept. 21, 1944, simultaneously along the entire line of the front. The withdrawal of the Finnish troops is to be effected through daily marches of not less than fifteen kilometers a day, whereas the advance of the Red Army troops is to be effected in such a manner as to keep a distance of fifteen kilometers between rear units of the Finnish troops and forward units of the Red Army. The withdrawing Finnish troops are to take along with them only the portable reserves of ammunition, food fodder, fuel and grease. All the other reserves are to be left where they are and surrendered to the Red Army.

Appendix to Article 2. The Finnish Government undertakes, as soon as the withdrawal of German troops from Finland is complete, to stop their postal communications as well as all radio, telegraph and telephone-correspondence and telephone communications with abroad by legations and consulates in Finland.

The Finnish military command shall hand over to the Allied (Soviet) High Command within a period fixed by the latter all information at its disposal regarding the German armed forces and plans of the German military command for the development of military operations against the Union of Soviet Socialist Republics and other United Nations and also charts and maps and all operational documents relating to military operations of the German armed forces.

The Finnish Government shall instruct its appropriate authorities regularly to supply the Allied (Soviet) High Command with meteorological information.

Appendix to Article 3. In accordance with Article 3 of the agreement, the Allied (Soviet) High Command will indicate to the Finnish Military Command what airdromes it will be necessary to put at the disposal of the Allied (Soviet) Command and what installations must remain on the airdromes, and will likewise lay down in what manner these airdromes are to be used. The Finnish Government will secure for the Soviet Union the use of railway lines, water routes, highroads and airlines necessary for the transport of personnel and cargoes dispatched from the Soviet Union to areas where the above mentioned airdromes are situated. Up to cessation of hostilities with Germany, Allied warships and merchant vessels will have the right to sail in territorial waters and use ports, harbors and anchorages in Finland. The Finnish Government will render all necessary help in material and technical servicing.

Appendix to Article 4. In accordance with Article 4 of the agreement, the Finnish military command shall immediately make available to the Allied (Soviet) High Command full information regarding the composition, armament and location of all land, sea and air forces of Finland and shall come to an agreement with the Allied (Soviet) High Command regarding the manner of placing the Finnish Army on a peace footing within the period fixed by the agreement.

All Finnish naval vessels, merchant ships and aircraft for the period of war against Germany must be returned to their bases, ports and airdromes and must not leave them without obtaining the requisite permission to do so from the Allied (Soviet) High Command.

Appendix to Article 5. Severance by Finland of relations with Germany and her satellites referred to in Article 5 of the agreement must be interpreted to mean also the severance of all diplomatic, consular and other relations as well as severance of Finland's postal, telegraph and telephone communications with Germany and Hungary.

Appendix to Article 8. In accordance with Article 8 of the agreement, the territory and waters in the area of Porkkala Udd shall be transferred by Finland to the Soviet Union within ten days from the moment of the signature of the armistice agreement for the organization of a Soviet naval base on lease, to be used and controlled for a period of fifty years, the Soviet Union making an annual payment of 5,000,000 Finnish marks.

The Finnish Government undertakes to enable the Soviet Union to make use of railways, waterways, roads and air routes necessary for the transport of personnel and freight dispatched from the Soviet Union to the naval base at Porkkala Udd. The Finnish Government shall grant to the Soviet Union the right of unimpeded use of all forms of communication between the U.S.S.R. and the territory leased in the area of Porkkala Udd.

Appendix to Article 11. The exact description and types of goods to be delivered by Finland to the Soviet Union in accordance with Article 11 of the agreement, and the detailed timing of these deliveries, year by year, will be established by separate agreement between the two Governments. Calculation of payment and compensation provided for in Article 11 of this agreement is to be based on the American dollar at its gold parity on the day of the signing of this agreement; viz. thirty-five dollars equaling one ounce of gold.

Appendix to Article 22. The Allied Control Commission is an organ of the Allied (Soviet) High Command, to which it is directly subordinated. The Control Commission will be the liaison between the Allied (Soviet) High Command and the Finnish Government, through which the government commission will carry on all its relations with Finnish authorities.

The chief task of the Control Commission is to see to the punctual and accurate fulfillment by the Finnish Government of Articles 2, 3, 4, 10, 12, 13, 14, 15, 16, 17, 18, 20 and 21 of the armistice agreement.

The Control Commission shall have the right to receive from the Finnish authorities all information it requires for the fulfillment of the above-mentioned task.

In the event of discovery of any violation of the above-mentioned articles of the armistice agreement the Control Commission shall make appropriate representations to the Finnish authorities in order that proper steps may be taken.

The Control Commission may, through its officers, make the necessary investigations and the collection of information it requires.

The Control Commission shall be established in Helsinki.

Members of the Control Commission, and equally its officers, shall have the right to visit without let or hindrance any institution, enterprise or port, and to receive there all information necessary for their functions.

The Control Commission shall enjoy all diplomatic privileges, including the inviolability of person, property and archives, and it shall have the right of communication by means of cipher and diplomatic courier.

The Control Commission shall have at its disposal a number of aircraft, for use of which the Finnish authorities shall grant all necessary facilities.

PRESIDENT ROOSEVELT'S OPENING CAMPAIGN SPEECH AT DINNER OF INTERNATIONAL BROTHERHOOD OF TEAMSTERS

September 23, 1944 [1]

Well, here we are together again—after four years—and what years they have been! I am actually four years older—which seems to annoy some people. In fact, millions of us are more than eleven years older than when we started in to clear up the mess that was dumped in our laps in 1933.

[1] White House news release.

We all know certain people who make it a practice to depreciate the accomplishments of labor—who even attack labor as unpatriotic. They keep this up usually for three years and six months. But then, for some strange reason, they change their tune—every four years—just before election day. When votes are at stake, they suddenly discover that they really love labor, and are eager to protect it from its old friends.

I got quite a laugh, for example—and I am sure that you did—when I read this plank in the Republican platform adopted at their National Convention in Chicago last July:

"The Republican party accepts the purposes of the National Labor Relations Act, the Wage and Hour Act, the Social Security Act and all other Federal statutes designed to promote and protect the welfare of American working men and women, and we promise a fair and just administration of these laws."

Many of the Republican leaders and Congressmen and candidates, who shouted enthusiastic approval of that plank in that Convention Hall would not even recognize these progressive laws, if they met them in broad daylight. Indeed, they have personally spent years of effort and energy—and much money—in fighting every one of those laws in the Congress, in the press, and in the courts, ever since this Administration began to advocate them and enact them into legislation. That is a fair example of their insincerity and of their inconsistency.

The whole purpose of Republican oratory these days seems to be to switch labels. The object is to persuade the American people that the Democratic party was responsible for the 1929 crash and depression, and that the Republican party was responsible for all social progress under the New Deal.

Imitation may be the sincerest form of flattery—but I am afraid that in this case it is the most obvious common or garden variety of fraud.

There are enlightened, liberal elements in the Republican party, and they have fought hard and honorably to bring the party up to date and to get it in step with the forward march of American progress. But these liberal elements were not able to drive the Old Guard Republicans from their entrenched positions.

Can the Old Guard pass itself off as the New Deal?

I think not.

We have all seen many marvelous stunts in the circus, but no performing elephant could turn a hand-spring without falling flat on his back.

I need not recount to you the centuries of history which have been crowded into these four years since I saw you last.

There were some—in the Congress and out—who raised their voices against our preparations for defense—before and after 1939—as hysterical war mongering, who cried out against our help to the Allies as provocative and dangerous. We remember the voices. They would like to have us forget them now. But in 1940 and 1941 they were loud voices. Happily they were a minority and—fortunately for ourselves, and for the world—they could not stop America.

There are some politicians who kept their heads buried deep in the sand while the storms of Europe and Asia were headed our way, who said that the lend-lease bill "would bring an end to free government in the United States," and who said "only hysteria entertains the idea that Germany, Italy or Japan contemplate war upon us." These very men are now asking the

American people to intrust to them the conduct of our foreign policy and our military policy.

What the Republican leaders are now saying in effect is this: "Oh, just forget what we used to say, we have changed our minds now—we have been reading the public opinion polls about these things, and we now know what the American people want. Don't leave the task of making the peace to those old men who first urged it, and who have already laid the foundations for it, and who have had to fight all of us inch by inch during the last five years to do it—just turn it all over to us. We'll do it so skillfully—that we won't lose a single isolationist vote or a single isolationist campaign contribution."

There is one thing I am too old for—I cannot talk out of both sides of my mouth at the same time.

This government welcomes all sincere supporters of the cause of effective world collaboration in the making of a lasting peace. Millions of Republicans all over the nation are with us—and have been with us—in our unshakeable determination to build the solid structure of peace. And they too will resent this campaign talk by those who first woke up to the facts of international life a few short months ago—when they began to study the polls of public opinion.

Those who today have the military responsibility for waging this war in all parts of the globe are not helped by the statements of men who, without responsibility and without knowledge of the facts, lecture the Chiefs of Staff of the United States as to the best means of dividing our armed forces and our military resources between the Atlantic and Pacific, between the Army and the Navy, and among the Commanding Generals of the different theatres of war.

When I addressed you four years ago, I said: "I know that America will never be disappointed in its expectation that labor will always continue to do its share of the job we now face, and do it patriotically and effectively and unselfishly."

Today we know that America has not been disappointed. In his Order of the Day when the allied armies first landed in Normandy General Eisenhower said: "Our home fronts have given us overwhelming superiority in weapons and munitions of war."

I know that there are those labor baiters among the opposition who, instead of calling attention to the achievements of labor in this war, prefer to pick on the occasional strikes which have occurred—strikes which have been condemned by every responsible national labor leader—every national leader except one. And that one labor leader, incidentally, is certainly not among my supporters.

Labor-baiters forget that, at our peak, American labor and management have turned out airplanes at the rate of 109,000 per year; tanks—57,000 per year; combat vessels—573 per year; landing vessels—31,000 per year; cargo ships—19 million tons per year; and small arms ammunition—23 billion rounds per year.

But a strike is news, and generally appears in shrieking headlines—and, of course, they say labor is always to blame. The fact is that, since Pearl Harbor, only one-tenth of one per cent of man-hours have been lost by strikes.

But even those candidates who burst out in election-year affection for social legislation and for labor in general still think you ought to be good boys and stay out of politics. And above all, they hate to see any working man or woman contribute a dollar bill to any wicked political party. Of course, it is all right for large financiers and industrialists and monopolists to contribute tens of thousands of dollars—but their solicitude for that dollar which the men and women in the ranks of labor contribute is always very touching.

They are, of course, perfectly willing to let you vote—unless you happen to be a soldier or sailor overseas, or a merchant seaman carrying the munitions of war. In that case they have made it pretty hard for you to vote— for there are some political candidates who think they may have a chance if only the total vote is small enough.

And while I am on the subject of voting let me urge every American citizen —man and woman—to use your sacred privilege of voting, no matter which candidate you expect to support. Our millions of soldiers and sailors and merchant seamen have been handicapped or prevented from voting by those politicians and candidates who think they stand to lose by such votes. You here at home have the freedom of the ballot. Irrespective of party you should register and vote this November. That is a matter of good citizenship.

Words come easily, but they do not change the record. You are old enough to remember what things were like for labor in 1932.

You remember the closed banks and the breadlines and the starvation wages; the foreclosures of homes and farms, and the bankruptcies of business; the "Hoovervilles," and the young men and women of the nation facing a hopeless, jobless future; the closed factories and mines and mills; the ruined and abandoned farms; the stalled railroads and the empty docks; the blank despair of a whole nation—and the utter impotence of our Federal Government.

You remember the long hard road, with its gains and its setbacks, which we have traveled together since those days.

Now there are some politicians, of course, who do not remember that far back, and some who remember but find it convenient to forget. But the record is not to be washed away that easily.

The opposition has already imported into this campaign the propaganda technique invented by the dictators abroad. The technique was all set out in Hitler's book—and it was copied by the aggressors of Italy and Japan. According to that technique, you should never use a small falsehood; always a big one, for its very fantastic nature will make it more credible—if only you keep repeating it over and over again.

For example, although I rubbed my eyes when I read it, we have been told that it was not a Republican depression, but a Democratic depression from which this nation has been saved—that this Administration is responsible for all the suffering and misery that the history books and the American people always thought had been brought about during the twelve ill-fated years when the Republican party was in power.

Now, there is an old and somewhat lugubrious adage which says: "Never speak of rope in the house of one who has been hanged." In the same way, if I were a Republican leader speaking to a mixed audience, the last word in the whole dictionary that I think I would use is that word "depression."

For another example, I learned—much to my amazement—that the policy of this Administration was to keep men in the Army when the war was over, because there might be no jobs for them in civil life.

Why, the very day that this fantastic charge was first made, a formal plan for the method of speedy discharge from the Army had already been announced by the War Department—a plan based upon the wishes of the soldiers themselves.

This callous and brazen falsehood about demobilization was an effort to stimulate fear among American mothers, wives and sweethearts. And, incidentally, it was hardly calculated to bolster the morale of our soldiers and sailors and airmen fighting our battles all over the world.

Perhaps the most ridiculous of these campaign falsifications is the one that this Administration failed to prepare for the war which was coming. I doubt whether even Goebbels would have tried that one. For even he would never have dared hope that the voters of America had already forgotten that many of the Republican leaders in the Congress and outside the Congress tried to thwart and block nearly every attempt which this Administration made to warn our people and to arm this nation. Some of them called our 50,000 airplane program fantastic. Many of those very same leaders who fought every defense measure we proposed are still in control of the Republican Party, were in control of its National Convention in Chicago, and would be in control of the machinery of the Congress and of the Republican Party in the event of a Republican victory this Fall.

These Republican leaders have not been content with attacks upon me, or my wife, or my sons—they now include my little dog, Fala. Unlike the members of my family, he resents this. Being a Scottie, as soon as he learned that the Republican fiction-writers had concocted a story that I had left him behind on an Aleutian Island and had sent a destroyer back to find him— at a cost to the taxpayers of two or three or twenty million dollars—his Scotch soul was furious. He has not been the same dog since. I am accustomed to hearing malicious falsehoods about myself—such as that old, worm-eaten chestnut that I have represented myself as indispensable. But I think I have a right to object to libellous statements about my dog.

But we all recognize the old technique. The people of this country know the past too well to be deceived into forgetting. Too much is at stake to forget. There are tasks ahead of us which we must now complete with the same will and skill and intelligence and devotion which have already led us so far on the road to victory.

There is the task of finishing victoriously this most terrible of all wars as speedily as possible and with the least cost in lives.

There is the task of setting up international machinery to assure that the peace, once established, will not again be broken.

And there is the task which we face here at home—the task of reconverting our economy from the purposes of war to the purposes of peace.

These peace-building tasks were faced once before, nearly a generation ago. They were botched by a Republican Administration. That must not happen this time. We will not let it happen this time.

Fortunately, we do not begin from scratch. Much has been done. Much more is under way. The fruits of victory this time will not be apples to be sold on street corners.

Many months ago, this Administration set up the necessary machinery for an orderly peace-time demobilization. The Congress has now passed legislation continuing the agencies needed for demobilization—with additional powers to carry out their functions.

I know that the American people—business and labor and agriculture— have the same will to do for peace what they have done for war. And I know that they can sustain a national income which will assure full production and full employment under our democratic system of private enterprise, with government encouragement and aid whenever and wherever it is necessary.

The keynote of all that we propose to do in reconversion can be found in the one word—"jobs."

We shall lease or dispose of our government-owned plants and facilities and our surplus war property and land, on the basis of how they can best be operated by private enterprise to give jobs to the greatest number.

We shall follow a wage policy which will sustain the purchasing power of labor—for that means more production and more jobs.

The present policies on wages and prices were conceived to serve the needs of the great masses of the people. They stopped inflation. They kept prices on a stable level. Through the demobilization period, policies will be carried out with the same objective in mind—to serve the needs of the great masses of the people.

This is not the time in which men can be forgotten as they were in the Republican catastrophe which we inherited. The returning soldiers, the workers by their machines, the farmers in the field, the miners, the men and women in offices and shops, do not intend to be forgotten.

They know they are not surplus. Because they know that they are America.

We must set targets and objectives for the future which will seem impossible to those who live in and are weighted down by the dead past.

We are even now organizing the logistics of the peace just as Marshall, King, Arnold, MacArthur, Eisenhower and Nimitz are organizing the logistics of this war.

The victory of the American people and their Allies in this war will be far more than a victory against fascism and reaction and the dead hand of despotism and of the past. The victory of the American people and their Allies in this war will be a victory for democracy. It will constitute such an affirmation of the strength and power and vitality of government by the people as history has never before witnessed.

With that affirmation of the vitality of democratic government behind us, that demonstration of its resilience and its capacity for decision and for action—with that knowledge of our own strength and power—we move forward with God's help to the greatest epoch of free achievement by free men the world has ever known or imagined possible.

GENERAL EISENHOWER'S STATEMENT COVERING ACTIVITIES OF THE ALLIED MILITARY GOVERNMENT IN GERMANY

September 23, 1944 [1]

Allied Military Government detachments went into action in German towns immediately after Allied combat troops had driven out the Nazi defenders.

Acting under the powers of General Eisenhower as supreme authority in occupied Germany, one of the first duties of the Military Government officers was to display proclamations, orders and laws addressed to the German inhabitants.

Some details of these proclamations, under which Military Government detachments operate in German towns occupied by the forces under command of General Eisenhower, were made known at Supreme Headquarters today. They amplify the initial announcement made by a SHAEF spokesman in a

[1] *New York Times.*

broadcast to the people of western and southwestern Germany Monday evening, Sept. 18.

Before all else, while military operations are in progress, comes the immediate task of Military Government detachments everywhere to secure the lines of communications of Allied armies and to suppress any activities in occupied areas which could impair the speedy conclusion of the war.

Other orders and laws of the Military Government are designed with the following objectives:

To promote the safety and health of the occupying troops, to eliminate nazism, to maintain public order, to establish a suitable civil government in occupied territory in so far as it is necessary to support military operations, to apprehend war criminals, to care for and repatriate Allied prisoners of war and displaced persons—the latter estimated to number at least 8,000,000—to protect the property of the Allied and United Nations and to control transfers of certain property in Germany, including foreign exchange assets.

One of the Military Government laws decrees the immediate dissolution of Nazi organizations, both political and military, within an area controlled by the supreme commander. German laws involving discrimination on the grounds of race, religion or political opinion are abrogated.

German residents of occupied territory must surrender all firearms of every sort and also must surrender all wireless transmitting equipment. German civilian activity in general is under rigid control, with travel within the country and across borders allowed only at the discretion of military authorities.

So far as the Nazi party is concerned, the Military Government will take into custody all party funds, property, records and equipment, from party administrative officers who are being directed to remain at their posts until the exchange is effected, upon penalty of death.

Law No. 1, as promulgated by the Military Government, abolished fundamental German laws underlying the privileged position of the National Socialist party and its members. The German decree placing the Nazi party above the authority of law is dissolved; the law for "protection of German blood and honor," one of the infamous, discriminatory Nuremburg racial laws, is abrogated; the Reich citizenship law of 1935, denying citizenship to those not of German blood, is dissolved.

The Hitler Youth law requiring membership in that organization is abrogated, and the laws protecting Nazi symbols, Nazi uniforms and the Nazi flag are swept aside. Similarly the law which penalizes any attempt to establish or maintain political parties other than the National Socialist party is abrogated.

The Military Government's law No. 2 temporarily suspends the regular civil, criminal and administrative courts in occupied Germany, and at the same time dissolves all special Nazi party courts. It is proposed that regular courts, when purged of Nazi influences, be reopened as soon as conditions permit.

German courts have no authority, however, over members of the armed forces or nationals of the United Nations, or in cases arising out of suspension of German laws by the Military Government, or in cases involving money claims against the German Government.

Still another law established Allied military marks as legal tender for all purposes in Germany.

Control of the Reich's posts, telephones, telegraph and radio establishments is provided for in another Military Government decree, and a system of censorship for all civilian communications is provided.

Various ordinances promulgated by the Military Government establish the death penalty for any German who acts as a spy for the enemy, who aids the Nazis in any way, who engages in looting or pillaging, who is guilty of sabotage or theft of Allied war material, or who deliberately misleads the Allied forces.

One of the ordinances establishes English as the official language in all official matters relating to the Military Government.

GENERAL EISENHOWER'S INSTRUCTIONS TO ORGANIZED CELLS OF FOREIGN WORKERS IN GERMANY

September 25, 1944 [1]

The hour for action has come!

Note carefully the following instructions:

The organized cells of foreign workers within the Reich will take immediate action according to the prearranged plan. Members of organized cells will refrain from all unorganized resistance and useless provocation of the Gestapo. They will obey the orders of their leaders precisely.

Foreign workers who are not members of organized cells and who have not already carried out my instructions to go into hiding in the towns or—preferably—on the land will do so at once.

I have already warned them that they are in gravest danger if they remain in the factories. Their safest course is to disappear from the towns and cities and to seek shelter and employment on the land.

In certain areas of Germany workers of the organized cells are today being provided with means for active resistance. These instruments will not be effective if they are used thoughtlessly or without purpose. Those of you who find them should immediately read the instructions that are provided and memorize them. Then destroy the instructions. Hide the instruments in a safe place. Determine carefully where and how the instruments can be used most effectively. Work out your plan of action. After your plan is complete in every detail—and only then—put the instruments to the use for which they are designed.

Bear in mind, while deciding on your plans, that foodstuffs and crops in Germany will be needed after the defeat of Hitler.

Act wisely. Do not underrate the power of the Gestapo. However, remember that today the Gestapo stands in fear of the 12,000,000 foreign workers who, by acting now, can seal the fate of the Third Reich.

GOVERNOR THOMAS E. DEWEY'S OKLAHOMA CITY CAMPAIGN SPEECH

September 25, 1944 [2]

Senator Moore, Governor Schoeppel, My Friend and Next Senator from Oklahoma Bill Otjen, fellow Americans everywhere:

For two and a half weeks I have been laying before our people the program

[1] *New York Times.*
[2] *Ibid.*

I believe we must adopt if we are to win at home the things for which our American men are fighting abroad. In six major speeches I have set forth a part of that program. There is much more to come.

In doing this I have been deeply conscious that this campaign is being waged under the most difficult circumstances and at the most trying time in the history of our nation. Our national unity for war and for the cause of lasting peace must be strengthened as a result of this campaign. I believe the conduct of the campaign on our side has greatly strengthened that unity.

I had assumed that every American joined me in hoping that would be the spirit of this campaign. Last July, Franklin Roosevelt, in accepting his party's nomination for a fourth term said, and I quote: "I shall not campaign, in the usual sense . . . in these days of tragic sorrow, I do not consider it fitting . . .," he said.

Last Saturday night the man who wants to be President for sixteen years made his first speech of this campaign. Gone was the high-sounding pledge. Forgotten were these days of tragic sorrow. It was a speech of mud-slinging, ridicule and wisecracks. It plumbed the depths of demagogy by dragging into this campaign the names of Hitler and Goebbels; it descended to quoting from "Mein Kampf" and to reckless charges of "fraud" and "falsehood."

Let me make one thing entirely clear. I shall not join my opponent in his descent to mud-slinging. If he continues in his desire to do so, he will be all alone.

I shall not use the tactics of our enemies by quoting from "Mein Kampf." I will never divide America. Those tactics also I leave to my opponent.

I shall never make a speech to one group of American people inciting them to hatred and distrust of any other group. In other nations the final product of such discord has been communism or fascism. We must never reap that harvest in America.

The winning of this war and the achievement of a people's peace are too sacred to be cast off with frivolous language. I believe that Americans whose loved ones are dying on the battlefronts of the world—men and women who are praying daily for the return of their boys—want the issues which vitally affect our future discussed with the utmost earnestness. This I shall continue to do with full consciousness of the solemn obligation placed upon me by my nomination for President of the United States.

My opponent, however, has chosen to wage his campaign on the record of the past and has indulged in charges of fraud and falsehood. I am compelled, therefore, to divert this evening long enough to keep the record straight. He has made the charges. He has asked for it. Here it is.

My opponent describes as, and I quote him, a "fantastic charge" the statement that his Administration plans to keep men in the Army when the war is over and that it intends to keep them there because it fears there will be no jobs for them in civil life. Well, who brought that up?

Here is the statement of a high official of the Administration as reported on Aug. 23, 1944, in the publication of the United States Army, The Stars and Stripes. He said:

"We can keep people in the Army about as cheaply as we could create an agency for them when they are out."

Now, who said that? It was the National Director of Selective Service appointed by Mr. Roosevelt and still in office.

But, says Mr. Roosevelt, the War Department thereafter issued a plan for what he called "speedy discharges." You can read that plan from now until doomsday and you cannot find one word about "speedy discharges." It is, in fact, a statement of the priority in which men will be discharged after the war. It does not say whether they are to be retained in service a month or years after victory. That will be up to the next Administration. The present Administration, with its record of peacetime failure, is afraid to bring men home after victory. That's why it's time for a change.

Now why does my opponent first describe what is a matter of record as a "fantastic charge" and then try to laugh off the problem of jobs after the war? He jokes about depressions—about the seven straight years of unemployment of his Administration. But he cannot laugh away the record.

In March, 1940, Mr. Roosevelt had been in office seven years. Yet the depression was still with us. We still had ten million Americans unemployed. Those are not my figures—those are the figures of the American Federation of Labor.

Is that fraud or falsehood? If so, let Mr. Roosevelt tell it to the American Federation of Labor.

By waging relentless warfare against our job-making machinery, my opponent succeeded in keeping a depression going eleven long years—twice as long as any previous depression in our history, and the somber, tragic thing is that today he still has no better program to offer. That is why the New Deal is afraid of peace, that's why it resorts to wisecracks and vilification—when our people want victory followed by lasting peace in the world—and jobs and opportunity here at home. That's why it's time for a change.

Now I had not intended in this campaign to rake over my opponent's sad record of failing to prepare the defenses of this country for war. It's all in the past—a very tragic past. It has cost countless American lives; it has caused untold misery.

But my opponent has now brought that subject up. In his speech of Saturday night he seized violently upon the statement that we were not prepared for war when it came. He calls that a "falsification" which not "even Goebbels" would" have attempted.

Now, were we prepared for war, or were we not? It's a perfectly simple question of fact.

In 1940, the year after the war began in Europe, the United States was in such a tragic condition that it couldn't put into the field as a mobile force more than 75,000 men. The Army was only "twenty-five per cent ready." Now, Mr. Roosevelt, did those statements come from Goebbels? Was that fraud or falsification? Those are the words of Gen. George C. Marshall, Chief of Staff of the United States Army, under oath.

I quote again: "Dec. 7, 1941, found the Army Air Forces equipped with plans but not with planes." Did that come from Goebbels? That statement was made in an official report on Jan. 4 of this year by H. H. Arnold, commanding general of the Army Air Forces of the United States of America.

Does my opponent still desire to use the words "falsification" and "Goebbels"? Does he still claim we were prepared? If so, let's go further.

Four months before Pearl Harbor, there was a debate in the United States Senate. The chairman of a Senate committee described on the floor of the Senate the shocking state of our defense program. Senator Vandenberg asked the chairman where the blame should be laid, and the chairman replied, "There is only one place where the responsibility can be put." Then Senator Vandenberg said, "Where is that—the White House?" and the chairman of that committee replied, "Yes, sir."

Who was the committee chairman? It was Harry Truman, the New Deal candidate for Vice President of the United States.

Again, in a magazine article in November, 1942, this statement appeared: "The reasons for the waste and confusion, the committtee found, were everywhere the same: the lack of courageous, unified leadership and centralized direction at the top." Again, on the floor of the Senate in May, 1943, these words were uttered: "After Pearl Harbor we found ourselves woefully unprepared for war." Was that Dr. Goebbels on the floor of the Senate?

The very words my opponent calls a falsification came from the mouth of his running mate, Harry Truman, the Democratic nominee for Vice President.

Now listen to this: "When the treachery of Pearl Harbor came we were not ready." Mr. Roosevelt, was that from Dr. Goebbels? The man who said that was Alben Barkley, your majority leader of the United States Senate. And where do you suppose Alben Barkley said when the treachery of Pearl Harbor came we were not ready. Right in his speech nominating Mr. Roosevelt for a fourth term.

Now, why is it we were not ready when we were attacked? Let's look at my opponent's own words. In a message to Congress in 1935, he said: "There is no ground for apprehension that our relations with any nation will be otherwise than peaceful."

In 1937 he said, and I quote: "How happy we are that the circumstances of the moment permit us to put our money into bridges and boulevards . . . rather than into huge standing armies and vast implements of war."

But war came just two years later. It was in January of 1940 that I publicly called for a two-ocean Navy for the defense of America. It was that statement of mine which Mr. Roosevelt called, and I quote his words: "Just plain dumb." Then as now we got ridicule instead of action.

The war rose in fury. When Hitler's armies were at the gates of Paris, Mr. Roosevelt once again soothed the American people with the jolly comment: "There is no need for the country to be discomboomerated."

The simple truth is, of course, that my opponent's record is desperately bad. The price the American people have had to pay for that record is desperately high. This is not a record on which any man should seek the confidence of the American people.

My opponent now announces his desire to be President for sixteen years. Yet in his speech of Saturday night he called it a "malicious falsehood" that he had ever represented himself to be "indispensable."

Let's look at these closely supervised words of his hand-picked candidate for Vice President. Mr. Truman said of my opponent, and I am quoting him: "The very future of the peace and prosperity of the world depends upon his re-election in November." Now I have not heard Mr. Truman repudiated by Mr. Roosevelt as yet. He usually waits to shed his Vice Presidents until they have served at least one term.

Here are the words of Boss Kelly of the Chicago machine, who was the manager of that fake third-term draft of 1940, you remember? He said: "The salvation of this nation rests in one man." Was that statement ever repudiated by my opponent? No, it was rewarded by increased White House favors. So it was repeated again by the same man at the same time in the same city and for the same purpose this year: "The salvation of this nation rests in one man."

And was it a falsehood that one of the first acts of Mr. Roosevelt's newly selected national chairman was to announce last May that he was for a fourth term and—that he was looking forward toward a fifth term?

Let's get this straight. The man who wants to be President for sixteen years is, indeed, indispensable. He is indispensable to Harry Hopkins, to

Mme. Perkins, to Harold Ickes, he's indispensable to a host of other political job holders. He's indispensable to America's leading enemy of civil liberties—the Mayor of Jersey City. He's indispensable to those infamous machines, in Chicago—in the Bronx—and all the others. He's indispensable to Sidney Hillman and the Political Action Committee, he's indispensable to Earl Browder, the ex-convict and pardoned Communist leader.

Shall we, the American people, perpetuate one man in office for sixteen years? Shall we do that to accommodate this motley crew? Shall we expose our country to a return of the seven years of New Deal depression because my opponent is indispensable to the ill-assorted, power-hungry conglomeration of city bosses, Communists and career bureaucrats which now compose the New Deal? Shall we submit to the counsel of despair that in all the great expanse of our nation there is only one man capable of occupying the White House?

The American people will answer that question in November. They will see to it that we restore integrity to the White House, so that its spoken word can be trusted once again.

On battlefronts and at home Americans have won the admiration of the world. Under the stress of war, we have thrown off the stupor and despair that seemed in the decade of the Nineteen Thirties to have settled permanently upon the land.

Today we know our strength and we know our ability. Shall we return to the philosophy that my opponent proclaimed when he said our industrial plant is built? Shall we go back to the seven straight years of unemployment? Shall we go back to the corroding misery of leaf-raking and doles? Shall we continue an administration which invokes the language of our enemies and recklessly hurls charges of falsehood concerning things it knows to be the truth?

I say the time has come to put a stop to everything that is summed up in that phrase "the indispensable man."

If any man is indispensable, then none of us are free. But America, America hasn't lost its passionate belief in freedom. America has not lost its passionate belief in opportunity. It need never lose those beliefs. For here in this country of ours there is plenty of room for freedom and for opportunity, and we need not sacrifice security to have both freedom and opportunity.

To achieve these objectives we must have integrity in our Government. We need a new high standard of honesty in the Government of the United States. We need a singleness of purpose, a devotion to the people of this country and to the gigantic problems we face at home after this war. We need a whole-souled devotion to the building of a people's peace that will last far beyond the lives and friendships of any individuals.

We need humility and courage. With the help of Almighty God we shall achieve the spiritual and physical strength to preserve our freedom in the pursuit of happiness for all.

JOINT STATEMENT BY PRESIDENT ROOSEVELT AND PRIME MINISTER CHURCHILL ON PROBLEMS IN ITALY

September 26, 1944 [1]

The Italian people, freed of their Fascist and Nazi overlordship, have in these last twelve months demonstrated their will to be free, to fight on the side of the democracies, and to take a place among the United Nations devoted to principles of peace and justice.

We believe we should give encouragement to those Italians who are standing for a political rebirth in Italy, and are completing the destruction of the evil Fascist system. We wish to afford the Italians a greater opportunity to aid in the defeat of our common enemies.

The American and the British people are of course horrified by the recent mob action in Rome, but feel that a greater responsibility placed on the Italian people and on their own government will most readily prevent a recurrence of such acts.

An increasing measure of control will be gradually handed over to the Italian Administration, subject of course to that Administration's proving that it can maintain law and order and the regular administration of justice. To mark this change the Allied Control Commission will be renamed "The Allied Commission."

The British High Commissioner in Italy will assume the additional title of Ambassador. The United States representative in Rome already holds that rank. The Italian Government will be invited to appoint direct representatives to Washington and London.

First and immediate considerations in Italy are the relief of hunger and sickness and fear. To this end we instructed our representatives at the UNRRA Conference to declare for the sending of medical aids and other essential supplies to Italy. We are happy to know that this view commended itself to other members of the UNRRA Council.

At the same time, first steps should be taken toward the reconstruction of an Italian economy—an economy laid low under the years of the misrule of Mussolini, and ravished by the German policy of vengeful destruction.

These steps should be taken primarily as military aims to put the full resources of Italy and the Italian people into the struggle to defeat Germany and Japan. For military reasons we should assist the Italians in the restoration of such power systems, their railways, motor transport, roads and other communications as enter into the war situation, and for a short time send engineers, technicians and industrial experts into Italy to help them in their own rehabilitation.

The application to Italy of the Trading with the Enemy Acts should be modified so as to enable business contacts between Italy and the outside world to be resumed for the benefit of the Italian people.

We all wish to speed the day when the last vestiges of Fascism in Italy will have been wiped out, and when the last German will have left Italian soil, and when there will be no need of any Allied troops to remain—the day when free elections can be held throughout Italy, and when Italy can earn her proper place in the great family of free nations.

[1] White House news release.

PRIME MINISTER WINSTON CHURCHILL'S SPEECH
IN COMMONS ON THE WAR

September 28, 1944 [1]

Little more than seven weeks have passed since we rose for the summer
vacation, but this short period has completely changed the face of the war
in Europe. When we separated, the Anglo-American Armies were still penned
in the narrow bridgehead and strip of coast from the base of the Cherbourg
Peninsula to the approaches to Caen, which they had wrested from the enemy
several weeks before. The Brest Peninsula was untaken, the German Army
in the West was still hopeful of preventing us from striking out into the fields
of France, the Battle of Normandy, which had been raging bloodily from the
date of the landing, had not reached any decisive conclusion. What a transformation now meets our eyes! Not only Paris, but practically the whole of
France, has been liberated as if by enchantment. Belgium has been rescued,
part of Holland is already free, and the foul enemy, who for four years
inflicted his cruelties and oppression upon these countries, has fled, losing perhaps 400,000 in killed and wounded and leaving in our hands nearly half a
million prisoners. Besides this, there may well be 200,000 cut off in the
coastal fortresses or in Holland whose destruction or capture may now be
deemed highly probable. The Allied Armies have reached and in some places
crossed the German frontier and the Siegfried Line.

All these operations have been conducted under the supreme command of
General Eisenhower, and were the fruit of the world-famous battle of Normandy, the greatest and most decisive single battle of the entire war. Never
has the exploitation of victory been carried to a higher perfection. The chaos
and destruction wrought by the Allied Air Forces behind the battle front
have been indescribable in narrative and a factor of the utmost potency in
the actual struggle. They have far surpassed, and reduce to petty dimensions all that our Army had to suffer from the German Air Force in 1940.
Nevertheless, when we reflect upon the tremendous fire power of modern
weapons and the opportunity which they give for defensive and delaying
action, we must feel astounded at the extraordinary speed with which the
Allied Armies have advanced. The vast and brilliant encircling movement
of the American Armies will ever be a model of military art, and an example
of the propriety of running risks not only in the fighting—because most of
the armies are ready to do that—but even more on the Q. side, or, as the
Americans put it, the logistical side. It was with great pleasure that all of us
saw the British and Canadian Armies, who had so long fought against heavy
resistance by the enemy along the hinge of the Allied movement, show themselves also capable of lightning advances which have certainly not been surpassed anywhere.

Finally, by the largest airborne operation ever conceived or executed, a
further all-important forward bound in the north has been achieved. Here
I must pay a tribute, which the House will consider due, to the superb feat
of arms performed by our First Airborne Division. Full and deeply moving
accounts have already been given to the country and to the world of this
glorious and fruitful operation, which will take a lasting place in our military
annals and will, in succeeding generations, inspire our youth with the highest

[1] Parliamentary Reports.

ideals of duty and of daring. The cost has been heavy; the casualties in a single division have been grievous; but for those who mourn there is at least the consolation that the sacrifice was not needlessly demanded nor given without results. The delay caused to the enemy's advance upon Nijmegen enabled their British and American comrades in the other two airborne divisions, and the British Second Army, to secure intact the vitally important bridges and to form a strong bridgehead over the main stream of the Rhine at Nijmegen. "Not in vain" may be the pride of those who have survived and the epitaph of those who fell.

To return to the main theme, Brest, Havre, Dieppe, Boulogne and Antwerp are already in our hands. All the Atlantic and Channel ports, from the Spanish frontier to the Hook of Holland, will presently be in our possession, yielding fine harbours and substantial masses of prisoners of war. All this has been accomplished by the joint exertions of the British and American Armies, assisted by the vehement and widespread uprising and fighting efforts of the French Maquis. While this great operation has been taking its course, an American and French landing on the Riviera coast, actively assisted by a British airborne brigade, a British Air Force and the Royal Navy, has lead with inconceivable rapidity to the capture of Toulon and Marseilles, to the freeing of the great strip of the Riviera coast and to the successsful advance of General Patch's Army up the Rhone Valley. This army, after taking over 80,000 prisoners, joined hands with General Eisenhower, and has passed under his command. When I had the opportunity on 15th August of watching— alas, from afar—the landing at Saint Tropez, it would have seemed audacious to hope for such swift and important results. They have, however, under the spell of the victories in the north, already been gained in superabundance and in less than half the time prescribed and expected in the plans which were prepared beforehand. So much for the fighting in France.

Simultaneously with that, very hard and successful fighting on a major scale has also proceeded on the Italian Front. General Alexander, who commands the armies in Italy with complete operational discretion, has under him the Fifth and Eighth Armies. The Fifth Army, half American and half British, with whom are serving the fine Brazilian Division, some of whose troops I had the opportunity of seeing—a magnificent band of men—is commanded by the United States General Clark, an officer of the highest quality and bearing, with a proud record of achievements behind him and his troops. The Eighth Army, under General Oliver Leese, whose qualities are also of the highest order, comprises the Polish Corps which fought so gallantly under General Anders, and a Greek Brigade which in happier surroundings has already distinguished itself in the forefront of the battle. There are also fighting on this Front a strong force of Italians, who are ardent to free their country from the German grip and taint. This force will very soon be more than double in strength. The Lieutenant of the Realm is often with these troops.

The largest mass of all the troops on the Italian Front come, of course from the United Kingdom. Not far short of half the divisions on the whole front are from this island. Joined with them are New Zealand, Canadian, South African and Indian Divisions, or perhaps I should say British-Indian Divisions, because, as is sometimes forgotten, one-third of them are British. The British Army in Italy includes also Palestinian units; and here I would mention the announcement, which hon. Members may have read, and which I think will be appreciated and approved, that the Government have decided to accede to the request of the Jewish Agency for Palestine that a Jewish

Brigade group should be formed to take part in active operations. I know there are vast numbers of Jews serving with our Forces and the American Forces throughout all the Armies, but it seems to me indeed appropriate that a special Jewish unit, a special unit of that race which has suffered indescribable torments from the Nazis, should be represented as a distinct formation amongst the forces gathered for their final overthrow, and I have no doubt they will not only take part in the struggle but also in the occupation which will follow.

A very hard task lies before the Army in Italy. It has already pierced at several points the strong Gothic line by which Kesselring has sought to defend the passage of the Apennines. I had an opportunity of watching and following the advance of the Eighth Army across the Metauro River, which began on 26th August. The extraordinary defensive strength of the ground held by the enemy was obvious. The mountain ridges rise one behind the other in a seemingly endless succession, like the waves of the sea, and each had to be conquered or turned by superior force and superior weapons. The process was bound to be lengthy and costly, but it is being completed, has, in fact, been practically completed. At the same time, General Clark's Fifth Army, advancing from the Florence area, has pierced deep into the mountain ranges, and, having broken the enemy's centre, now stands on the northern slopes of the Apennines at no great distance from Bologna, a place of definite strategic importance. General Alexander has now definitely broken into the basin of the Po, but here we exchange the barriers of mountain ridges for the perpetual interruption of the ground by streams and canals. Nevertheless, conditions henceforward will be more favourable for the destruction or rout of Kesselring's Army, and this is the objective to which all British and Allied Forces will be unceasingly bent. Further than that, it is not desirable to peer at the present moment.

I am now going to give a few facts and figures about the operations in Europe. These have been very carefully chosen to give as much information as possible to the House and to the public, while not telling the enemy anything he does not already know, or only telling him too late for it to be of any service to him. The speed with which the mighty British and American Armies in France were built up is almost incredible. In the first twenty-four hours a quarter of a million men were landed, in the teeth of fortified and violent opposition. By the twentieth day 1,000,000 men were ashore. There are now between 2,000,000 and 3,000,000 men in France. [An Hon. Member: "Good old War Office."] Certainly the progress in the power of moving troops and landing troops has vastly increased since the early days, when we had to plunge into the war with no previous experience. But the actual number of soldiers was only part of the problem of transportation. These armies were equipped with the most perfect modern weapons and every imaginable contrivance of modern war, and an immense artillery supported all their operations. Enormous masses of armour of the highest quality and character gave them extraordinary offensive power and mobility. Many hundreds of thousands of vehicles sustained their movements, many millions of tons of stores have already been landed—the great bulk of everything over open beaches or through the synthetic harbours which I described when last I spoke to the House.

All this constitutes a feat of organisation and efficiency which should excite the wonder and deserve the admiration of all military students, as well as the applause of the British and American nations and their Allies. I must pay my tribute to the United States Army, not only in their valiant and ruthless battle-worthy qualities, but also in the skill of their commanders and the excellence of their supply arrangements. When one remembers that the United States four or five years ago was a peace-loving Power, without any great body of troops or munitions, and with only a very small regular Army to draw their commanders from, the American achievement is truly amazing. After the intense training they have received for nearly three years, or more than three years in some cases, their divisions are now composed of regular professional soldiers whose military quality is out of all comparison to hurriedly raised war time levies. These soldiers, like our own from Great Britain who have been even longer under arms, are capable of being placed immediately on landing in the battle line, and have proved themselves more than a match for the so-called veteran troops of Germany who, though fighting desperately, are showing themselves decidedly the worse for wear. When I think of the measureless output of ships, munitions and supplies of all kinds with which the United States has equipped herself and has sustained all the fighting Allies in generous measure, and of the mighty war she is conducting, with troops of our Australian and New Zealand Dominions, over the spaces of the Pacific Ocean, this House may indeed salute our sister nation as being at the highest pinnacle of her power and fame.

I am very glad to say that we also have been able to make a worthy contribution. Some time ago, a statement was made by a Senator to the effect that the American public would be shocked to learn that they would have to provide eighty per cent of the Forces to invade the Continent. I then said that at the outset of the invasion of France the British and American Forces would be practically equal, but that thereafter the American build-up would give them steadily the lead. I am glad to say that after 120 days of fighting we still bear, in the cross-Channel troops, a proportion of two to three in personnel and of four to five-an-a-half in fighting divisions in France. Casualties have followed very closely the proportions of the numbers. In fact, these troops fight so level that the casualties almost exactly follow the numbers engaged. We have, I regret to say, lost upwards of 90,000 men, killed, wounded and missing, and the United States, including General Patch's Army, over 145,000. Such is the price in blood paid by the English-speaking democracies for the actual liberation of the soil of France.

When this view is extended to cover the entire European scene and the campaigns both in France and Italy, it will be a source of satisfaction to the House to know that after more than five years of war, we still maintain almost exactly the same number of divisions, taking both theatres together, in full action against the enemy as the United States have, by all the shipping resources which can be employed, yet been able to send to Europe. Considering that the population of the Empire—of British race—is only 70,000,000, and that we have sustained many losses in the early years of the war, it certainly is a remarkable effort and one which was most fully and cordially recognised by our American colleagues, the Chiefs of Staff and others at the recent Conference at Quebec.

In thus trying to do justice to the British and American achievements, we must never forget, as I reminded the House before we separated, the measureless services which Russia has rendered to the common cause, through long years of suffering, by tearing out the life of the German military monster. The terms in which Marshal Stalin recently, in conversation, has referred to our efforts in the West have been of such a generous and admiring character that I feel, in my turn, bound to point out that Russia is holding and beating far larger hostile forces than those which face the Allies in the West, and has through long years, at enormous loss, borne the brunt of the struggle on land. There is honour for all. It is a matter of rejoicing that we, for our part and in our turn, have struck resounding blows, and it is right that they should be recorded among the other feats of arms so loyally performed throughout the Grand Alliance.

I must again refer to the subject of the campaign in Burma on which I touched in my last statement to the House. I was somewhat concerned to observe from my reading of the American Press, in which I indulged during my stay on the other side, that widespread misconception exists in the public mind, so far as that is reflected by the newspapers, about the scale of our effort in Burma and the results to date of Admiral Mountbatten's campaign. Many important organs of United States' opinion seem to give the impression that the British campaign in Burma of 1944 had been a failure, or at least a stalemate, that nothing much had been done, and that the campaign was redeemed by the brilliant capture of Myitkyina—which I may say is spelt "Myitkyina" but pronounced "Michynaw"—by General Stilwell at the head of an American Regiment of very high class commando troops and with the assistance of the Chinese. That is the picture, but I must, therefore, set matters in their true light. It is well known that the United States has been increasingly engaged in establishing an air route to China capable of carrying immense supplies, and, by astounding efforts and at vast cost, they are now sending over the terrible Himalayas, or the Hump as it is called in the Army, I will not say how many times as much as the Burma Road has ever carried in its palmiest days, or will carry for several years to come; an incredible feat of transportation—over mountains 20,000 or 22,000 feet high in the air, over ground where an engine failure means certain death to the pilot—has been performed by a main effort which the United States made in their passionate desire to aid the resistance of China. Certainly no more prodigious example of strength, science and organisation in this class of work has ever been seen or dreamed of.

Along the Eastern Frontier of India stands the 14th British Imperial Army comprising the main war effort of India, including some of the most famous Indian Divisions from the Middle East and a substantial proportion of United Kingdom troops and Divisions, together with some excellent Divisions from Africa—native Divisions from Africa, West Africa principally. This Army under Admiral Mountbatten—amounting to between 250,000 and 300,000 men, apart from rearward services which, in that theatre of extraordinary long and precarious communications, are very great—has by its aggressive operation guarded the base of the American air line to China and protected India against the horrors of a Japanese invasion. Once again, India and her vast population have reposed serenely among the tumults and hurricanes of the world behind the Imperial shield. The fact should sometimes be noted that under British rule in the last eighty years incomparably fewer people have perished by steel or firearms in India than in any similar area or community on the globe.

MR. MCGOVERN (Glasgow, Shettleston): Many perished of hunger.

THE PRIME MINISTER: As the population has increased by 50,000,000 in the last ten years it is evident that the famine, which was caused by military conditions last year affecting transport, is by no means representative of the administration under which the broad peninsula and triangle of India has met an increase in population exceeding the speed of any increase in any other country throughout the whole world. I think it a very remarkable fact that India has received this shelter and has been this vast harbour of peace, protected by the arms and policy of Great Britain, protected also by the care and attention of this House. In this the brave fighting races of India have at all times borne a most honourable and memorable part.

I regret to say the fighting on the Burma Front throughout the year has been most severe and continuous, and there were times when the issue in particular localities appeared to hang in doubt. However, the ten Japanese Divisions which were launched against us with the object of invading India and cutting the air line have been repulsed and largely shattered as the result of a bloody and very costly campaign which is still being continued in spite of the monsoon conditions. How costly this campaign has been in disease may be judged from the fact that in the first six months only of this present year the 14th British Imperial Army sustained no fewer than 237,000 cases of sickness which had to be evacuated to the rear over the long, difficult communications and tended in hospital. More than ninety per cent of these cases returned within six months, but the ceaseless drain upon the Army and the much larger numbers required to maintain a fighting strength, in spite of this drain, in the neighbourhood of a quarter of a million may well be imagined. When you have a loss and drain like that going on, much larger numbers are needed to maintain your limited fighting strength. In addition, there were over 40,000 battle casualties in the first six months, that is to say, to the end of June, and the number has certainly increased by now.

I think these facts ought to be known; I think they ought to be given wide publicity, as I am sure they will now that I have stated them, because the campaign of Admiral Mountbatten on the Burma Frontier constitutes—and this is a startling fact—the largest and most important ground fighting that has yet taken place against the armies of Japan. Far from being an insignificant or disappointing stalemate, it constitutes the greatest collision which has yet taken place on land with Japan, and has resulted in the slaughter of between 50,000 and 60,000 Japanese and the capture of several hundred prisoners. The Japanese Army has recoiled before our troops in deep depression and heavily mauled. We have often, too, found circles of their corpses in the jungle where each one had committed suicide in succession, the officer, who had supervised the proceedings, blowing out his own brains last of all. We did not ask them to come there, and it is entirely their own choice that they find themselves in this difficult position.

We must expect, however, a renewal of the Japanese offensive as soon as the monsoon is over, and every preparation is being made to meet it with the utmost vigour. Nelson said, "If in doubt a captain cannot do wrong if he places his ship alongside one of the enemy." The engagement of the Japanese on the largest possible scale on land—and certainly not less in the air—is part of the official wearing down process which marks the present phase of the war against Japan, and this function our 14th Army has certainly discharged with the utmost fidelity and success in spite of the inordinately heavy toll of disease. I trust that this toll will be markedly reduced in future operations. We have discovered many preventives of tropical disease, and, above all, against the onslaught of insects of all kinds, from lice to mosquitoes and back again.

The excellent D.D.T. powder, which has been fully experimented with and found to yield astonishing results, will henceforward be used on a great scale by the British forces in Burma and by American and Australian forces in the Pacific and, indeed, in all theatres, together with other remedies constantly improving, and these will make their effect continually manifest. The Japanese, I may mention, also suffer from jungle diseases and malaria which are an offset against the very heavy losses which are suffered by our Indian and white and African troops. These remedies will be a help to all the Allies; indeed, they have been a help. The eradication of lice in Naples by the strict hygienic measures taken may be held to have averted a very grievous typhus epidemic in that city and neighbourhood when we occupied it. I can assure the House that the war against the Japanese and other diseases of the jungle will be pressed forward with the utmost energy.

I must here note with keen regret that in spite of the lavish American help that has been poured into China, that great country, worn by more than seven years of war, has suffered from severe military reverses involving the loss of valuable airfields upon which the American squadrons of General Chennault were counting. This, of course, is disappointing and vexatious. When we survey the present state of the European and Asiatic wars as a whole, the House will, I am sure, wholeheartedly acclaim the skill and enterprise of the generals and the tireless courage and fighting qualities of the troops, and they may even feel disposed to view without any special mark of disapprobation the management, combination and design which it reveals on the part of the Allied staffs, and even on the part of the Governments concerned.

But we must not forget that we owe a great debt to the blunders—the extraordinary blunders—of the Germans. I always hate to compare Napoleon with Hitler, as it seems an insult to the great Emperor and warrior to connect him in any way with a squalid caucus boss and butcher. But there is one respect in which I must draw a parallel. Both these men were temperamentally unable to give up the tiniest scrap of any territory to which the high water-mark of their hectic fortunes had carried them. Thus, after Leipzig in 1813, Napoleon left all his garrisons on the Rhine, 40,000 men in Hamburg. He refused to withdraw many other vitally important elements of his armies, and he had to begin the campaign of 1814 with raw levies and a few seasoned troops brought in a hurry from Spain. Similarly, Hitler has successfully scattered the German armies all over Europe, and by obstinating at every point from Stalingrad and Tunis down to the present moment, he has stripped himself of the power to concentrate in main strength for the final struggle.

He has lost, or will lose when the tally is complete, nearly 1,000,000 men in France and the Low Countries. Other large armies may well be cut off in the Baltic States, in Finland and in Norway. Less than a year ago, when the relative weakness of Germany was already becoming apparent, he was ordering further aggressive action in the Aegean and the re-occupation of the islands which the Italians had surrendered, or wished to surrender. He has scattered and squandered a very large army in the Balkan Peninsula, whose escape will be very difficult; twenty-seven divisions, many of them battered, are fighting General Alexander in Northern Italy. Many of these will not be able to re-cross the Alps to defend the German Fatherland. Such a vast frittering away and dispersal of forces has never been seen, and is, of course, a prime cause of the impending ruin of Germany.

When Herr Hitler escaped his bomb on 20th July he described his survival as providential; I think that from a purely military point of view we can all agree with him, for certainly it would be most unfortunate if the Allies were to be deprived, in the closing phases of the struggle, of that form of warlike genius by which Corporal Schickelgruber has so notably contributed to our victory. There is a great deal more mopping up to be done in the Low Countries and in some of the French Atlantic ports, and the harbours have to be cleared and developed on the greatest scale possible before the winter gales. Problems of supply have to be resolved on the morrow of the prodigious British and American advances, and I deprecate very much people being carried away into premature expectations of an immediate cessation of the fighting. It is very hard not to be, when, each day, the papers are filled—rightly filled—with the news of the captures of important places and of advances of the armies; but there is still a great deal to be done in the military sense.

Hitherto, as I have said, during the first four critical months in Europe, we have managed to be an equal, or almost equal, partner with the United States, but now, of course, the great flow of their well-trained divisions from across the Atlantic will, step by step, carry them decisively into the leading position, and, unless organised German resistance collapses in the near future, enormous additional United States forces will be brought to bear in the final struggle. I shall certainly not hazard a guess—it could be no more—as to when the end will come. Many persons of the highest technical attainments, knowledge and responsibility have good hopes that all will be over by the end of 1944. On the other hand, no one, and certainly not I, can guarantee that several months of 1945 may not be required.

There is also a possibility that after the organised resistance of the German army and State is completely broken, fierce warfare may be maintained in the forests and mountains of Germany by numbers of desperate men, conscious of their own guilt and impending doom. These of course, would, at a certain stage, deserve the treatment which the Germans have so ruthlessly meted out to guerrilla movements in other countries. It may be necessary for the Allies to declare at a certain date that the actual warfare against the German State has come to an end and that a period of mopping up of bandits and war criminals has begun. No one can foresee exactly what form the death agony of Nazidom will take. For us, the important decision will be to choose the moment when substantial forces can be withdrawn from Europe to intensify the war against Japan. We certainly do not consider that the declared date of the ending of the war against Germany must necessarily be postponed until the last desperado has been tracked down in his last lair.

There is no doubt that surpassing victories gained in common make a very agreeable foundation for inter-Allied Conferences like that which has just finished. It is really very much better and very much more pleasing to share victories than it is to share disasters. We have shared both, and I can tell the House that the former is in every way a more exhilarating process. I took occasion to associate Canadian, Australian and New Zealand representatives with our work. I have also, with our Chiefs of Staff, attended a meeting of the Dominion of Canada Cabinet and have received both from Mr. Mackenzie King and Mr. Curtin the most cordial expressions of satisfaction at the manner in which our affairs were conducted and of agreement in the decisions taken. I have also been in very full correspondence, as I often am, with Field-Marshal Smuts and also with Mr. Fraser. Certainly when the President and I with our respective staffs met at Quebec, we had behind us a record of successful war which justified feelings of solemn satisfaction, and warmed the glow of our brotherhood in arms.

It is now two years almost to a day since Rommel's final offensive against Cairo was repulsed by the newly appointed Generals Alexander and Montgomery, a month before their decisive victory at Alamein, and since that time our affairs all over the world, and the affairs of our mighty ally Russia, have proceeded without a single reverse of any kind, except only the loss of Leros and Cos in the Aegean, and even those will ultimately turn out to be a loss to Hitler rather than to the Allies. Such a long and mounting tide of victory is unexampled in history. The principal Governments of the Allies have every right to claim the confidence of the United Nations in the new efforts that will be required from all of us and in the further designs which have been conceived and shaped and have still to be unfolded in action. Complete agreement on every point was reached at Quebec by the Combined Chiefs of Staff. The President and I have both pursued a policy of making no changes other than those enforced by death, as in the lamented loss of Admiral Pound, in the Chiefs of Staff charged with the conduct of the war.

In this country there have been none of those differences between the professional and the political elements such as were evident in a large measure in the former war. We have worked together in perfect harmony. Our confidence in the Chiefs of Staff—British confidence and the confidence of the War Cabinet—has steadily grown. In consequence of the fact that there have been no changes, the men who met together at Quebec knew each other well, were united in bonds of comprehension and friendship, and had the whole picture and sequences of the war ingrained in their minds and in their very being. When you have lived through all these things you do not have to turn up musty files to remember what happened on particular occasions. Men's minds are shaped from day to day by what they live through; and the discussions on that level between these high officers is very very quick and swift.

Obviously, our discussions were concerned with the successful winding up of the war in Europe by bringing about the unconditional surrender of Germany at the earliest moment, and also with the new phase of the war against Japan which will dominate all minds and command all resources from the moment when the German war is ended. On behalf of His Majesty's Government, nearly two years ago, I assured the President that Great Britain would pursue the war against Japan with all her strength and resources to the very end. As I explained to Congress when I last addressed them, we have losses to repair and injuries to repay on the Japanese account at least equal to, if not indeed greater than, those suffered by the United States. We owe it to Australia and New Zealand to help them to remove for ever the Japanese menace to their homelands; and as they have helped us on every front in the fight against Germany, we will certainly not be behindhand in giving them effective aid.

Our perseverance in this quarrel is not to be doubted. I offered some time ago to embody this undertaking in a definite treaty, but the President made the courteous reply that the British word was enough. That word we shall certainly make good. Accordingly, we offered to the United States the fine, modern British Fleet, and we asked that it should be employed in the major operations against Japan. This offer was at once cordially accepted. A large portion of this fleet is already gathered in the Indian Ocean. For a year past, our modern battleships have been undergoing a further measure of modernisation and tropicalisation to meet the rapid war-time changes in technical apparatus. We have already, nine months ago, begun the creation of an immense Fleet train, comprising many vessels, large and medium, specially fitted as repair ships, recreation ships for personnel, provision and munition ships and many modern variants, in order that our Fleet may have a degree of mobility which for several months together will make them largely independent of main shore bases. A substantial portion of the vessels which we shall use for this purpose have been building in Canada, for it is found better and more economical to adapt new merchant ships while they are building to the exact purpose they have to fulfil than to convert existing vessels, although that process has also been carried very far. Thus we hope to place in the Pacific a fleet capable in itself of fighting a general action with the Japanese Navy and which, added to the far greater United States Naval power, should give a Naval command in all these vast ocean spaces and seas of the most complete and decisive character.

One must certainly contemplate that a phase in the war against Japan will be the severe, intense, prolonged and ever-increasing air bombardment to which the Japanese mainland installations and munitions centres will be subjected. In this also we shall bear our part to the utmost limit which the bases will allow. As for the land or amphibious operations which the British Empire will conduct, these must rightly be veiled in mystery. Suffice it to say that the scale of our effort will be limited only by the available shipping. In this however we may presently receive a magnificent addition. The end of the U-boat war, when it comes, will allow us to go out of convoy in the Western hemisphere, thus adding at a bound at least twenty-five per cent to the efficient carrying capacity of our Mercantile Marine, and a larger percentage to the carrying capacity of tankers.

I must, however, add a word of caution about taking too optimistic views of the speed at which this great transference of forces can be made from one side of the world to the other. Not only will the Allied shipping, vast as it is and far greater as it is than at the beginning of the war, be a limiting factor, but the development of bases, the accumulation of stores and supplies and the construction and protection of airfields all impose restraints upon those vivid, imaginative strategists who carry fleets and armies across the globe as easily as they would help themselves to a plate of soup. The huge distances, the tropical conditions and other physical facts added to the desperate resistance of the enemy, make the war against Japan an enterprise of the first magnitude, and it will be necessary to use to the full the resources of machinery and science to enable our armies to do their work under the most favourable conditions and with the least sacrifice of Allied life. When all these aspects are considered the House may rest assured that the entire brain and technical power of Great Britain and the United States will be ceaselessly employed, and having regard to the results already obtained in so many directions, one may feel good confidence that it will not be employed in vain.

I have now reached the close of the military aspect of what I have to say, and it might be convenient for the House, it certainly would be an indulgence to, I must not say the speaker, but the orator, if we could have an interlude for lunch, and I would respectfully ask, I will not say the Leader of the Opposition but my right hon. Friend opposite, whether he would be in accord with such proceedings?

Mr. ARTHUR GREENWOOD (Wakefield): The House would be only too delighted to grant my right hon. Friend the facilities he needs at this stage.

Mr. SPEAKER: The Sitting will be suspended, and I will take the Chair again at two o'clock exactly.

Sitting suspended.

On resuming,

2.1 P.M.

THE PRIME MINISTER: When we were last assembled here I had completed a review of the military situation which, although not by any means complete or exhaustive, yet, I trust, gave the general outline of our position at the present time from the point of view of one who has special opportunities of seeing things in their broad perspective. The foreign situation has responded to military events. Never was the alliance against Germany of the three great Powers more close or more effective. Divergencies of view and interest there must necessarily be, but at no time have these been allowed to affect in any way the majestic march of events in accordance with the decisions and agreements at Teheran. One by one, in rapid succession, the satellite States have writhed or torn themselves free from the Nazi tyranny, and, as is usual in such cases, the process has not been one from alliance with Germany to neutrality, but from alliance with Germany to war. This has taken place in Roumania and Bulgaria. Already there is fighting between the Finns and the Germans. The Germans, in accordance with their usual practice and character, are leaving a trail of burnt and blackened villages behind them, even in the land of their unhappy Finnish dupes.

Hungary is still in the Nazi grip, but when, as will happen, that grip is broken by the steel hammer blows of war, or when it relaxes by reason of the internal lesions and injuries of the tyrant, the Hungarian people will turn their weapons, with all their remaining strength, against those who have led them through so much suffering to their present ruin and defeat. The armistice terms agreed upon for Finland and Rumania bear, naturally, the imprint of the Soviet will—and here I must draw attention to the restraint which has characterised the Soviet treatment of these two countries, both of which marched blithely behind Hitler in his attempted destruction of Russia, and both of which added their quota of injuries to the immense volume of suffering which the Russian people have endured, have survived, and have triumphantly surmounted.

The Bulgarian armistice terms have not yet been signed. The Soviet intervention in this theatre was at once startling and effective. Their sudden declaration of war against Bulgaria was sufficient to induce Bulgaria to turn her catiff armies against the German intruders. Britain and the United States have long been at war with Bulgaria and have now joined with the Soviets in framing suitable armistice conditions. The Bulgarian people have been plunged by their leaders in the last thirty-five years into three wrongful, forlorn and disastrous wars, and in this last war we cannot forget the many acts of cruelty and wickedness for which they have been responsible both to Greece and Yugoslavia. They have suffered nothing themselves. No foot has been set upon their soil. Apart from some air bombardment, they have suffered nothing. Some of the worst war criminals are Bulgarians. The conduct of their troops in harrying and trying to hold down, at Hitler's orders, their two sorely-pressed small neighbours, Greece and Yugoslavia, is a shameful page for which full atonement must be exacted. They may want to be treated as co-belligerents. So far as Great Britain is concerned, they must work their passage for a long time and in no uncertain fashion before we can accord them any special status, in view of the injuries that our Allies Greece and Yugoslavia have sustained at their hands. In the meantime, let them march and destroy all the Germans they can find in enemy lands. We do not want them in those of our Allies. This is the only path which will serve them and their interests. The more vigour with which they fall upon the Germans, the more they will be likely to draw the attention of the victorious nations in arms from their previous misdeeds.

It would be affectation to pretend that the attitude of the British and, I believe, the United States Governments towards Poland is identical with that of the Soviet Union. Every allowance must be made for the different conditions of history and geography which govern the relationship of the Western democracies on the one hand and of the Soviet Government on the other with the Polish nation. Marshal Stalin has repeatedly declared himself in favour of a strongly, friendly Poland, sovereign and independent. In this our great Eastern Ally is in the fullest accord with His Majesty's Government and also, judging from American public statements, in the fullest accord with the United States. We in this island and throughout our Empire who drew the sword against mighty Germany, we who are the only great unconquered nation which declared war on Germany on account of her aggression against Poland, have sentiments and duties towards Poland which deeply stir the British race. Everything in our power has been and will be done to achieve, both in the letter and in the spirit, the declared purposes towards Poland of the three great Allies.

Territorial changes on the frontiers of Poland there will have to be. Russia has a right to our support in this matter, because it is the Russian armies which alone can deliver Poland from the German talons; and after all the Russian people have suffered at the hands of Germany they are entitled to safe frontiers and to have a friendly neighbour on their Western flank. All the more do I trust that the Soviet Government will make it possible for us to act unitedly with them in the solution of the Polish problem, and that we shall not witness the unhappy spectacle of rival Governments in Poland, one recognised by the Soviet Union and the other firmly adhered to by the Western Powers. I have fervent hopes that M. Mikolajczyk, the worthy successor of General Sikorski, a man firmly desirous of friendly understanding and settlement with Russia, and his colleagues may shortly resume those important conversations at Moscow which were interrupted some months ago.

It is my duty to impress upon the House the embarrassment to our affairs and the possible injury to Polish fortunes which might be caused by intemperate language about Polish and Russian relations in the course of this Debate. It is my firm hope, and also my belief, that a good arrangement will be achieved and that a united Polish Government will be brought into being, which will command the confidence of the three great Powers concerned and will assure for Poland those conditions of strength, sovereignty and independence which we have all three proclaimed as our aim and our resolve. Nothing is easier than to create by violent words a prospect far less hopeful than that which now opens before us. Hon. Members will take upon themselves a very grave responsibility if they embroil themselves precipitately in these controversies and thus mar the hopes we cherish of an honourable and satisfactory solution and settlement. We recognise our special responsibilities towards Poland, and I am confident that I can trust the House not to engage in language which would make our task harder.

We must never lose sight of our prime and overwhelming duty, namely, to bring about the speediest possible destruction of the Nazi power. We owe this· to the soldiers, who are shedding their blood and giving their lives in the cause at this moment. They are shedding their blood in the effort to bring this fearful struggle in Europe to a close; and that must be our paramount task. Every problem—and there are many; they are as legion; they crop up in vast array—which now faces the nations of the world will present itself in a far easier and more adaptable form once the cannons have ceased to thunder in Europe and once the victorious Allies gather round the table of armistice or peace. I have every hope that wise and harmonious settlements will be made, in confidence and amity, between the great Powers thus affording the foundations upon which to raise a lasting structure of European and world peace. I say these words on the Polish situation; and I am sure that our friends on both sides will realise how long and anxious has been the study which the Cabinet have given to this matter, how constantly we see representatives of the Poles, how frequent and intimate our correspondence is with Russia on this subject.

I cannot conceive that it is not possible to make a good solution whereby Russia gets the security which she is entitled to have, and which I have resolved that we shall do our utmost to secure for her, on her Western Frontier, and, at the same time, the Polish Nation have restored to them that national sovereignty and independence, for which, across centuries of oppression and struggle, they have never ceased to strive.

Turning to another difficult and tangled problem, the House will already have read the joint statement by the President and myself which we drafted together, embodying a very definite and distinct improvement and mitigation in our relationships with the Italian Government. During my visit to Italy, I had an opportunity of seeing the leaders of all parties, from the extreme Right to the extreme Communist. All the six parties represented in the Italian Government came to the British Embassy, and I had the pleasure of making the acquaintance of all the different Ministers who are working together, as well as they can, in conditions necessarily difficult and depressing. I had conversations with the Prime Minister, Signor Bonomi, and also talked with him and Marshal Badoglio together. They are friends. The Marshal has very faithfully observed the conditions imposed by the armistice a year ago. He has done his best to send all Italian forces, particularly naval forces, into the struggle against Germany, and he has worked steadfastly for the improvement of relations between Italy and Britain and between Italy and the Allies. His behaviour on leaving office, in giving cordial support to his successor, is also creditable. Finally, I had the advantage of an interview with the Lieutenant of the Realm, whose sincerity and ardour in the Allied cause and whose growing stature in Italian eyes are equally apparent. [*Interruption.*] I give my opinion, and I dare say it will weigh as much as a mocking giggle.

What impressed and touched me most in my journey through Italy was the extraordinary goodwill to the British and American troops everywhere displayed by the Italian people. As I drove through the small towns and villages behind the line of the armies day after day, the friendliness and even enthusiasm of the peasants, workmen and shopkeepers, indeed, of all classes, was spontaneous and convincing. I cannot feel—I make my confession—any sentiments of hostility towards the mass of the misled or coerced Italian people. Obviously, no final settlement can be made with them or with their Government until the North of Italy and its great cities have been liberated and the basis on which the present Government stands has been broadened and strengthened. There are good hopes that this will be achieved, I might say soon, but it would be safer to say in due course. Indeed, it would be a miserable disaster if the Italian people, after all their maltreatment by their former Allies and by the Fascist remnants still gathered round Mussolini, were to emerge from the European struggle only to fall into violent internal feuds. It was for that reason, on leaving Rome, that I tried to set before the Italian nation some of those broad simple, Liberal safeguards and conceptions which are the breath of our nostrils in this country—so much so that we scarcely notice them—and which sustain the rights and freedoms of the individual against all forms of tyranny, no matter what liveries they wear or what slogans they mouth.

We were, all of us, shocked by the horrible lynching outrage which occurred in the streets of Rome a week or so ago. Every measure of precaution and authority must be taken to prevent outbreaks of mob vengeance, however great the provocation may have been, and, for this, responsibility rests, not only with the Italian Government, but ultimately with the Allied military power. Punishment for criminals who have committed most cruel, barbarous acts under the orders of the Germans, of men who have made themselves the agents of the betrayal of the 300 or 400 hostages shot *en masse* in the catacombs of Rome—punishment for them there must certainly be, but it must be the punishment of courts of justice, with the strictest adherence to the forms and principles of justice. This shameful incident has been a baffling factor in the Italian scene. Nevertheless, it has not deterred us from issuing the joint statement to which I have already referred, and which, so far as Great Britain is concerned, was, of course, approved by the War Cabinet before I gave my agreement to it.

I turn from the Italian scene. Nothing has given the British nation and the King's Dominions all over the world more true joy than the wonderful spectacle of the rescue of France by the British and American arms, of the rescue of France from the horrible oppression of the Hun under which she has writhed or languished for four hideous years. It is now nearly forty years since I first became convinced that the fortunes of Great Britain and France were interwoven, and that their military resources must be combined in the most effective manner, by alliance and agreement and plan, and I think I can claim to have pursued this object through all the changing scenes we have witnessed, not only before and during the last war, but in the uneasy interval between the two wars, and not only in years of success, but during the period of blackest disaster, and also during periods when there was friction on other grounds between the two countries.

Bearing in mind some mistakes in our own policy between the wars; bearing in mind also the failure of the League of Nations, in consequence, largely, of the falling out of America, and other weaknesses for which other Powers are responsible, to give general security to the world; bearing in mind the withdrawal of the United States from the Anglo-American guarantee against German aggression promised by President Wilson, on the strength of which France relinquished her claims on the Rhine frontier; bearing in mind, above everything, the loss of nearly 2,000,000 men which France, with her small and declining population, sustained in bearing the brunt, as she bore it, of the last war, and the terrible effect of this unexampled blood-letting upon the whole heartbeat, the life heart beat, of France; bearing all this, and much else, in mind, I have always felt the liveliest sympathy for the French in the years when we watched, supinely, the dreadful and awe-inspiring growth of the German power.

It will be remembered that we told the French Government that we would not reproach them for making a separate peace in the fearful circumstances of June, 1940, provided they sent their Fleet out of the reach and power of the Germans. The terms of the Cabinet offer to France in this tragical hour are also on record. I, therefore, have never felt anything but compassion for the French people as a whole who found themselves deprived of all power of resistance and could not share the good fortune of those who, from our shores or in the French Empire, had the honour and opportunity to continue the armed struggle. What could a humble, ordinary man do? He might be on the watch for opportunity, but he might be rendered almost powerless. The Maquis have shown one way in which, at the end, and after much suffering, and having overcome all the difficulties of getting weapons, free men may strike a blow for the honour and life of their country; but that is given to the few, to the young and active, those who can obtain weapons.

For my part, I have always felt that the heart of the French nation was sound and true, and that they would rise again in greatness and power, and that we should be proud to have taken a part in aiding them to recover their place in the van of the nations and at the summit of the cultural life of the world. Long have we looked forward to the day when British and American troops would enter again the fields of France, and, regardless of loss and sacrifice, drive the foe before them from towns and cities famous in history, and often sacred to us for the memories of the last war and of the dear ones, whose memories abide with us and who rest in French soil. Often have we longed to receive, and dreamed of receiving, the gratitude and blessings of the French people as our delivering Armies advanced. This has been given to us in unstinted measure, and it has been, indeed, a glorious experience to witness and a glorious experience for the Armies to enjoy this marvellous transformation of scene, and for us to feel that we have acted up to our duties as a faithful Ally to the utmost limit of our strength.

I have repeatedly stated that it is the aim, policy and interest of His Majesty's Government, of this country of Great Britain, and of the Commonwealth and Empire to see erected once more, at the earliest moment, a strong, independent and friendly France. I have every hope that this will soon be achieved. The French people, working together as they must do for their lives and future, in unity of purpose, with sincerity and courage, have a great chance of building a new and undivided France who will take her rightful place among the leading nations of the world.

In my last statement to the House, I spoke of the importance of including representatives of France in all the discussions affecting the Rhine frontier and a general settlement of W. Germany. Hitherto, by force of circumstances, the French Algiers Committee could not be a body representative of France as a whole. Now, however, progress has been made. Naturally, that body has new elements, especially amongst those who formed the Maquis and resistance movements and among those who raised the glorious revolt in Paris, which reminded us of the famous days of the Revolution, when France and Paris struck a blow that opened the path broadly for all the nations of the world. Naturally, we, and, I believe, the United States and the Soviet Union, are most anxious to see emerge an entity which can truly be said to speak in the name of the people of France—the whole people of France. It would now seem possible to put into force the decree of the Algiers Committee whereby, as an interim stage, the Legislative Assembly would be transformed into an elected body, reinforced by the addition of new elements drawn from inside France. To this body, the French Committee of National Liberation would be responsible. Such a step, once taken, when seen to have the approval of the French people, would greatly strengthen the position of France and would render possible that recognition of the Provisional Government of France, and those consequences thereof, which we all desire to bring about at the earliest moment. I close no doors upon a situation which is in constant flux and development. The matter is urgent, however, for those, of whom I am one, who desire to see France take her place at the earliest moment in the high councils of the Allies. We are now engaged in discussing these matters both with the French and with other Allied governments, and I am hopeful that, in the near future, a happy settlement will be reached to the satisfaction of all concerned.

I should like to take this opportunity to express our gratification and pride at the part played by British troops in the liberation of Belgium. The House will have read of the tumultuous welcome with which our troops were everywhere greeted by the Belgian people. This also I regard as a happy augury for the maintenance and strengthening of the ties of friendship between our two countries. Many hundreds of thousands of our dead sleep on Belgian soil, and the independence of that country has always been a matter sacred to us as well as enjoined by our policy. I should like to acknowledge in this House the many agreeable things that were said about this country in the Belgian Parliament when it re-assembled last week. I trust that the day is not far distant when our Forces will also have completed their task of liberating the territory of our staunch and sorely tried friends and allies in Holland—allies in the war of the Spanish Succession and in all the struggles for the establishment of freedom in Europe. They are also very near to us in thought and sympathy and their interests at home, and also abroad, command British support and are largely interwoven with our own fortunes.

I have had to deal with these countries one by one. I now come to the broader aspect, as far as I can touch upon it today, which can only be in a very tentative and partial manner. Since 21st August conversations between representatives of this country, the United States and the Soviet Union have been taking place at Dumbarton Oaks, in the United States, on the future organisation of the world for preventing war. It is expected that similar conversations will follow between the United Kingdom and the American delegations with the representatives of China. These conversations have been on the official level only and do not in any way bind the Governments represented. There has, however, been assembled a body of principles and the outline of the kind of structure which in one form or another it is the prime purpose of the Allies to erect after the unconditional surrender and total disarmament of Germany have been accomplished. His Majesty's Government could have had no abler official representative than Sir Alexander Cadogan, and there is no doubt that a most valuable task has been discharged. The whole scene has been explored and many difficulties have been not merely discovered, but adjusted. There are, however, still some important questions outstanding, and we ought not to be hurried into decisions upon which united opinion by the various Governments responsible is not at present ripe. It would not be prudent to press in a hurry for momentous decisions governing the whole future of the world. The House must realise—and I am sure it does realise, I can see by the whole attitude of the House to-day that it fully realises—that it is one thing for us here to form and express our own opinions on these matters and another to have them accepted by other Powers as great as we are.

There is another warning which I would venture to give to the House, and that is, not to be startled or carried away by sensational reports and stories which emanate from the other side of the Atlantic. There is an election on, and very vivid accounts of all kinds of matters are given by people who cannot possibly have any knowledge of what has taken place at secret conferences. The United States is a land of free speech; nowhere is speech freer, not even here where we sedulously cultivate it even in its most repulsive form. But when I see some of the accounts given of conversations that I am supposed to have had with the President of the United States, I can only recall a Balfourian phrase at which I laughed many years ago, when he said that the accounts which were given bore no more relation to the actual facts than the wildest tales of the Arabian Nights do to the ordinary incidents of domestic life in the East. I may say that everything depends on the agreement of the three leading European and world Powers. I do not think satisfactory agreement will be reached—and unless there is agreement nothing can be satisfactory—until there has been a further meeting of the three heads of Government assisted as may be necessary by their Foreign Secretaries. I must say that I think it is well to suspend judgment and not to try to form or express opinions on what can only be partial and incomplete accounts. I earnestly hope it may be possible to bring about such a meeting before the end of the year. There are great difficulties but I hope they may be overcome. The fact that the President and I have been so closely brought together at the Quebec Conference and have been able to discuss so many matters bearing upon the course of the war and on the measures to be taken after the Germans surrender and also for the broad future, makes it all the more necessary that our third partner, Marshal Stalin, who has, of course, been kept informed, should join with us in a tripartite conference as soon as the military situation renders this possible. The future of the whole world, and certainly the future of Europe, perhaps for several generations, depends upon the cordial, trustful and comprehending association of the British Empire, the United States and Soviet Russia, and no pains must be spared and no patience grudged which are necessary to bring that supreme hope to fruition.

I may say at once, however, that it will not, in my opinion, be possible for the great Powers to do more, in the first instance, than act as trustees for the other States, great or small, during the period of transition. Whatever may be settled in the near future must be regarded as a preliminary, and only as a preliminary, to the actual establishment in its final form of the future world organisation. Those who try in any country to force the pace unduly will run the risk of overlooking many aspects of the highest importance, and also by imprudence they can bring about a serious deadlock. I have never been one of those who believe that all the problems of the immediate future can be solved while we are actually engaged in a life and death struggle with the German and Nazi Power and when the course of military operations and the development of the war against Japan must increasingly claim the first place in the minds of those in Britain and the United States, upon whom the chief responsibility rests.

To shorten the war by a year, if that can be done, would in itself be a boon greater than many important acts of legislation. To shorten this war, to bring it to an end, to bring the soldiers home, to give them a roof over their heads, to re-establish the free life of our country, to enable the wheels of commerce to revolve, to get the nations out of their terrible frenzy of hate, to build up something like a human world and a humane world—it is that that makes it so indispensable for us to struggle to shorten, be it even by a day, the course of this terrible war.

It is right to make surveys and preparations beforehand and many have been made and are being made, but the great decisions cannot be taken finally, even for the transition period, without far closer, calmer, and more searching discussions than can be held amid the clash of arms. Moreover, we cannot be blind to the fact that there are many factors, at present unknowable, which will make themselves manifest on the morrow of the destruction of the Nazi regime. I am sure this is no time for taking hard and fast momentous decisions on incomplete data and at breakneck speed. Hasty work and premature decisions may lead to penalties out of all proportion to the issues immediately involved. That is my counsel to the House, which I hope they will consider. I hope that the House will notice that, in making my statement to-day, I have spoken with exceptional caution about Foreign Affairs, and, I hope, without any undue regard for popular applause. I have sedulously avoided the appearance of any one country trying to lay down the law to its powerful allies or to the many other States involved. I hope, however, that I have given the House some impression of the heavy and critical work that is going forward and will lie before us even after the downfall of our principal enemy has been effected. I trust that what I have said may be weighed with care and goodwill not only in this House and in this country but also in the far wider circles involved.

PRESIDENT ROOSEVELT'S STATEMENT ON UNITED STATES POLICY TOWARD ARGENTINA

September 29, 1944 [1]

I have been following closely and with increasing concern the development of the Argentine situation in recent months. This situation presents the extraordinary paradox of the growth of Nazi-Fascist influence and the increasing application of Nazi-Fascist methods in a country of this hemisphere, at the very time that those forces of oppression and aggression are drawing ever closer to the hour of final defeat and judgment in Europe and elsewhere in the world.

The paradox is accentuated by the fact, of which we are all quite aware, that the vast majority of the people of Argentina have remained steadfast in their faith in their own free, democratic traditions and in their support of the nations and peoples who have been making such great sacrifices in the fight against the Nazis and Fascists. This was made clear beyond all doubt by the great spontaneous demonstration of public feeling in Argentina after word was received of the liberation of Paris.

The policy of the Government of the United States toward Argentina as that policy has been developed in consultation with the other American republics, has been clearly set forth by Secretary Hull. There is no need for me to restate it now.

The Argentine Government has repudiated solemn inter-American obligations on the basis of which the nations of this hemisphere developed a system of defense to meet the challenge of Axis aggression.

Unless we now demonstrate a capacity to develop a tradition of respect for such obligations among civilized nations, there can be little hope for a system of international security, theoretically created to maintain principles for which our peoples are today sacrificing to the limit of their resources, both human and material.

In this connection I subscribe wholeheartedly to the words of Prime Minister Churchill in the House of Commons on Aug. 2, when he declared that: "This is not like some small wars in the past where all could be forgotten and for-given. Nations must be judged by the part they play. Not only belligerents, but neutrals, will find that their position in the world cannot remain entirely unaffected by the part they have chosen to play in the crisis of the war."

I have considered it important to make this statement of the position of the Government of the United States at this time because it has come to my attention that the Nazi radio beamed to Latin America, the pro-Nazi press

1 *New York Times.*

in Argentina, as well as a few irresponsible individuals and groups in this and certain other republics, seek to undermine the position of the American republics and our associates among the United Nations by fabricating and circulating the vicious rumor that our counsels are divided on the course of our policy toward Argentina.

STETTINIUS—GROMYKO—CADOGAN REMARKS AT CONCLUSION OF THE FIRST PHASE OF THE DUMBARTON OAKS CONVERSATIONS

September 29, 1944 [1]

Remarks by Under Secretary of State Stettinius

Mr. Ambassador, Sir Alexander, Gentlemen: Nearly six weeks have elapsed since we began these important conversations. In this brief period of time we have accomplished a great deal, more than many thought possible. In large measure, our achievements have been made possible by the cordial cooperation of my fellow chairmen, Ambassador Gromyko and Sir Alexander Cadogan, and all who have worked with us. I wish to express my deep personal appreciation and thanks for this cooperation, which has resulted in the splendid spirit of harmony and good-will which has prevailed throughout the conversations.

We have every reason for satisfaction with what has been accomplished. We have developed in the brief period of six weeks a wide area of agreement on the fundamental and necessary principles for an international organization to maintain peace and security. These principles will be of vital importance in guiding our Governments at every step that must yet be taken to bring into existence the organization which we have here envisaged.

The peace-loving peoples of the world will be heartened and encouraged by what we have accomplished at Dumbarton Oaks. They will await with eager hope the early completion of the task. We must not fail them and I confidently anticipate that the spirit of cooperation which has united our nations in war and which has prevailed throughout our deliberations here will lead to early agreement among the governments of all peace-loving nations.

Remarks by Ambassador Gromyko

The three delegations have sat together from August 21 until now discussing a number of important questions of the establishment of an international security organization. Today we have ground to state that the conversations have undoubtedly been useful. On behalf of the Soviet Delegation, I wish to express appreciation of the friendly atmosphere in which the delegates carried on their work. I believe I will express the opinion of all present if I thank Mr. Stettinius for his able chairmanship. I also wish to thank the United States Government, and in this I am sure I express the appreciation of every one of us for the hospitality that we have received.

[1] State Department Bulletin.

Remarks by Sir Alexander Cadogan

I should like to thank you, Mr. Chairman, for what you have said on behalf of all of us. I agree that much useful work has been done here which will contribute to ultimate success in the later stages of the discussions.

I wish to say a word about the manner in which Mr. Stettinius has conducted the conversations. He knew how to combine energy with courtesy and patience, and thus, as chairman, he has hastened our passage over the smooth parts of the road and has helped to iron out the asperities. A large part of such success as we have achieved is due to him.

I do not, of course, use the word "asperities" in its more sinister sense. There was never anything of that. Sometimes we found ourselves in disagreement in our discussion, but I believe that we disagreed amiably and reasonably. It was the experience of each of us at some time to be in opposition to the other two delegations, but even if we considered the views of the other two peculiar, we recognized that they were sincerely held, and therefore worthy of respect. I believe this is a good augury for the future.

I wish to add my thanks to the secretariat. They have been prompt, efficient, and helpful. I also wish to express our indebtedness to the United States Government for their hospitality. They have given us every facility in this wonderful setting. They have filled, in fact almost over-filled, our scanty leisure hours. We will go home with the most agreeable memories and a deep sense of gratitude.

Joint Statement by Heads of American, British and Soviet Delegations

Conversations between the United States, United Kingdom, and Soviet Union Delegations in Washington regarding the establishment of a World Security Organization have now been completed. These conversations have been useful and have led to a large measure of agreement on recommendations for the general framework of the Organization, and in particular for the machinery required to maintain peace and security. The three Delegations are making reports to their respective Governments who will consider these reports and will in due course issue a simultaneous statement on the subject.

HULL—CADOGAN—KOO REMARKS AT OPENING OF SECOND PHASE OF THE DUMBARTON OAKS CONVERSATIONS

September 29, 1944 [1]

Remarks by Secretary of State Hull

In opening this phase of our conversations, it is my pleasure to bring to you the cordial greetings of President Roosevelt and to extend to you the best wishes of both of us for the complete success of your labors.

We are particularly happy to welcome here the distinguished Delegation from the Republic of China. The great wisdom and experience in inter-

[1] State Department Bulletin.

national affairs which is represented by your Delegation reflects not only the high importance which your Government attaches to this subject, but assures that the Chinese contribution to the conversations will reflect mature and practical considerations.

All of us are constantly mindful of the tremendous hardships and sacrifices which the Chinese people have suffered over the long years since the cruel and barbarous enemy first launched upon its course of conquest. Nor can we ever forget with what patience and courage the great Chinese people have fought on when almost every avenue of assistance seemed closed. Happily for all of us their dauntless faith in ultimate victory and their unyielding belief in human freedom have been steadfastly maintained. Their heroic efforts, together with our efforts and those of our other gallant Allies, have brought to all of us the assurance of complete victory.

It is of the highest importance, therefore, that we prepare with vigor, determination, and expedition for the new day which is dawning.

The preceding phase of the conversations has been carried out in this spirit. I wish to take this opportunity, on behalf of the President as well as on my own behalf, to express again our deep appreciation of the significant contribution which the Governments of the United Kingdom and the Soviet Union have made through their able representatives, Sir Alexander Cadogan and Ambassador Gromyko and their associates. I am fully convinced that the excellent work already done, and that which we are about to undertake, will carry us a long way toward complete understanding among our Governments and toward the wider understanding which the peace-loving peoples of the world so ardently desire.

We all realize that the successful conclusion of these exploratory conversations will constitute only the first step in the formation of the international organization which we seek to establish. Other steps must be taken as quickly as possible if we are to be prepared for the peace. The joint recommendations to be made by the representatives of our Governments will, upon the conclusion of this phase of the conversations, be made available promptly to our peoples and to the peoples of other peace-loving nations for full public discussion. The strength of the organization which we propose to establish can be no greater than the support given to it by an informed public opinion throughout the world.

It is also our hope that a full United Nations conference may be convened at an early date to bring to fruition the work which has been initiated in these conversations.

In all these deliberations we must never forget that millions of people throughout the world are struggling for an opportunity to live in freedom and security. Our great objective must be to create conditions which will make for the maintenance of international peace and security and for the advancement of human welfare, and to establish an organization for the effective realization of these high purposes.

Remarks by Sir Alexander Cadogan

In opening our discussions with our Chinese friends we are gratefully conscious that there is already a very large measure of agreement between them and us. We are all, I am sure, well aware of the importance and complexity of the problems which we have set out to resolve, but we know that the Chinese Delegation will bring all their ability and all their good-will to their solution. We look forward with pleasure to consultation with representatives of the oldest civilisation in the world, which throughout many trials, as severe as any nation has endured, has kept intact the moral ideals which are the foundations of its unique culture and way of life.

The Chinese Delegation will, I am confident, make a large contribution to the establishment of a world organisation for the maintenance of peace and security. China has shown herself ready to assume the responsibilities which her position in history, her vast and industrious population, and the heroic conduct of her armies in a seven-year struggle against a cruel and implacable enemy have placed upon her. As a signatory of the Moscow Declaration she has declared her intention to join in setting up at the earliest practicable date a world organisation in which all peace-loving states can take part.

The papers that have been exchanged between us have shown not only that we are agreed on the main objectives, but that there is a very large measure of agreement even in detail on the methods by which these objectives shall be reached. We all desire to see set up an Assembly of all peaceful states, with a smaller Council of great and small states, together with an efficient secretariat and an international court of justice. We are all anxious to give the new organisation life by basing it on the moral ideas on which our civilisations are founded. We all also recognise that responsibility should be commensurate with power. It is for us to find the methods by which power may be rightly applied in the best interests of all nations. The horror and suffering that the world has endured should give us the will and energy to overcome all the tremendous difficulties which history shows have confronted those who apply themselves to such a task.

No people has suffered more than the Chinese. They, like the peoples of the British Commonwealth, have known what it is to stand alone on the brink of disaster. Now we are all conscious of the terrible danger that threatened not only this nation or that but the whole future of the world on which the happiness and well-being of every man and woman depends. We hope, therefore, that the memory of the danger that we have escaped, as well as of the sufferings which we have endured, will bring a unity to the world such as it has never before had. If we can agree to work together to this end we shall be able to devise, in the light of a common experience, institutions necessary to carry out our purpose. Without such common purpose and practice no institutions however well devised have the necessary strength when the moment for action comes.

Remarks by Ambassador V. K. Wellington Koo

It is a matter for congratulation that the Government of the United States has arranged the present series of preliminary consultations for the establishment of an international system of peace and security. This is the great object set forth in the Four Nations Declaration of October 30th, 1943 at Moscow, and these discussions constitute another significant step towards the realization of our high purpose. One part of the consultations has already taken place and yielded fruitful results. Today's meeting marks the beginning of another part which will complete the first place in seeking an agreed set of proposals for approval by the Governments of the four signatory States to the above-mentioned declaration, and for recommendation to the other United Nations.

We of China, like you, Mr. Secretary of State, and like our British and American colleagues, attach the greatest importance to the work lying ahead of us, and we shall participate in it with the guiding thought of contributing to its success. The lack of security which has been responsible for the present world catastrophe made my country its first victim. Just as the long years of resistance to invasion with all its attendant sufferings and sacrifices have been singularly painful for China, so the prospect of a new international organization rising to effectively maintain peace and justice is particularly welcome to us.

Our desire to see it come into existence is all the keener, not only because our appeals and warnings in the past did not always meet with the response they deserved, but also because, loyal to our traditional sentiment of peace, we have ever believed in the need and the wisdom of collective effort to ensure the peace and security of nations. Our common experience has made it clear to us all that the unity of purpose and the spirit of unreserved cooperation which have together yielded such striking results in our joint struggle against the forces of tyranny and barbarism, are equally essential in our striving to build a system of durable peace.

All nations which love peace and freedom, whatever their size and strength, have a part to play in any security organization which is to be set up. We believe that such an organization should be universal in character, and that eventually all nations should be brought into it. In order to achieve full and permanent success, the new institution requires such general participation in its membership. The responsibility of member states in safeguarding international peace and security may vary according to their respective resources, but sovereign equality as reaffirmed by the Four Nations Declaration of Moscow should remain a guiding principle of the new organization.

There is a consensus of opinion among the freedom-loving peoples of the world that all disputes between nations should be settled solely by pacific means. Resort to force by any member state should be proscribed except when authorized by the new organization and acting in its name in accordance with its declared purposes and principles. Any breach of or threat to the peace should be stopped or forestalled by the application of measures which may, if necessary, take the form of military action. Since peace is the supreme interest of the world, vital for the well-being of all peoples, we think no effort should be spared in ensuring its maintenance. But to be able to carry out this primary duty, we firmly believe that the proposed structure should have at its disposal an adequate force which it can promptly use whenever and wherever it may be needed.

In the light of past experience, we believe that plans for the application of necessary measures should be worked out beforehand by appropriate agencies and reviewed from time to time, taking into account changed and changing conditions in the world. In our view it is important that such measures, to serve as an effective deterrent to actual or potential aggression, must have certainly definiteness and promptness of execution. Provision should therefore be made to obviate the necessity of consultation and debate at the last minute, which, in the light of experience, would invariably cause delay and thereby lead to an aggravation of a situation already critical.

However, the world does not stand still; and international life, like life in other domains, must grow and develop. We should, therefore, make it possible to bring about such adjustments by peaceful means as may be required by new conditions. In order to facilitate the necessary pacific settlement, full provision should be made in the basic instrument of the new institution.

This is also true of international law. As the intercourse between peoples grows in complexity and the common interests of nations multiply and become more varied, principles and rules of conduct for their guidance need elucidation, revision, and supplementation. For such work I can think of no more authoritative or better qualified body than the proposed new institution.

One more point I wish to bring forward before I conclude. While the safeguarding of international security is an essential condition to the general welfare and peaceful development of humanity, positive and constructive efforts are also required to strengthen the foundation of peace. This can only be achieved by mitigating the causes of international discord and conflict. It is therefore our belief that the new organization should also concern itself in the study and solution of economic and social problems of international importance. It should be able to recommend measures for adoption by member states, and should also play a central role in the directing and coordinating of international agencies devoted to such purposes. With the continuous revelation of the wonders of science and the unending achievements of technology, a systematic interchange of ideas and knowledge will be invaluable in the promotion of the social and economic welfare of the peoples of the world. Similarly common effort should be made to advance international understanding and to uproot the causes of distrust and suspicion amongst nations by means of educational and cultural collaboration.

The few observations which I have just presented reflect the general views of the Government and people of China. I hope they are largely in harmony with your sentiments. We have come to take part in the consultations not merely to present our own views, but also to hear with an open mind the opinions of the other delegations. Above all, we are animated by the spirit of cooperation and by the desire to promote the success of our joint task.

The establishment of an effective international peace organization is the united hope and aspiration of all the freedom-loving peoples who have been making such heroic sacrifices in life, blood, and toil. We owe it to them as well as to humanity at large to subordinate all other considerations to the achievement of our common object. We of the Chinese Delegation felicitate ourselves upon the opportunity afforded us of exploring this all-important problem with the eminent representatives of the United States and Great Britain. We are confident that with a common will to cooperate, with faith in our ideal, and with determination to share the responsibility, we cannot fail in our undertaking.

OCTOBER

October 1, 1944

Canadian troops captured the bomb-torn port of Calais.

In a speech at Lille, Gen. Charles de Gaulle explicitly committed himself and his Government to the creation of a new economic system in France based on a planned economy under Government direction.

3

After sixty-three days of vain resistance, the Polish underground forces in Warsaw under the command of General Bor surrendered, their losses estimated above 300,000 in dead alone.

4

The U. S. First Army cracked the Siegfried Line near Aachen.

German Propaganda Minister Goebbels and Gestapo chief Himmler ordered the German people to fight the advancing Allied armies as guerrillas.

5

British troops landed in Greece, taking the important port of Patras. The ELAS and the EAM, cooperating with Premier Papandreou's Government, proved of great help to the Allies' small forces.

7

The Four-power conversations for a world security organization ended at Dumbarton Oaks.

The American First Army broke through Westwall defenses north of Aachen.

8

Wendell L. Willkie died suddenly.

9

Prime Minister Churchill and Foreign Secretary Eden, accompanied by a large staff of the highest British military leaders, arrived in Moscow for a series of war conferences with Marshal Stalin and Foreign Commissar Molotoff.

10

At a luncheon given in honor of Prime Minister Churchill and Foreign Minister Eden, Marshal Stalin spoke about the need for future cooperation among the Allies to insure continued world peace and to avoid the mistakes of the past.

11

Bulgaria accepted preliminary armistice terms from the U. S., Britain and Russia.

The National War Labor Board, by a vote of 8 to 4, with the labor members dissenting, refused to ask President Roosevelt to modify the Little Steel formula.

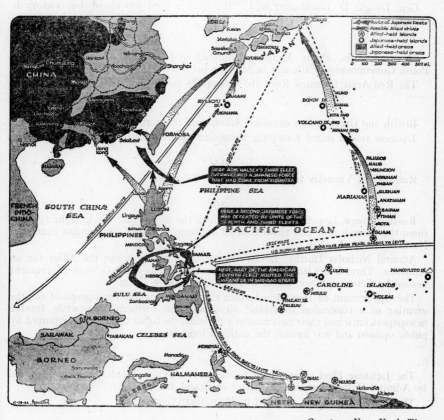

The Battle of the Philippine Sea
October, 1944

12

In his first speech in German since the liberation of Rome, Pope Pius XII said that he would "follow developments of post-war Germany with love and if necessary, will give her his help."

Premier Mikolajczyk of the Polish Government-in-Exile, and two associates, reached Moscow in an attempt to come to an agreement with leaders of the Polish Committee of National Liberation.

Gen. Dwight D. Eisenhower said: "We have a hard job ahead, but victory is certain."

13

Marshal Stalin, Prime Minister Churchill and Premier Mikolajczyk of the Polish Government-in-Exile met in Moscow for a solution of the Polish conflict.

The Red Army liberated Riga, the metropolis and capital of Latvia.

14

British and Greek troops occupied Athens and the port of Piraeus.

Japanese troops seized Kweiping, increasing the disaster for Chinese armies.

15

Russian and Yugoslav troops stormed into Belgrade.

16

Russian troops, launching an offensive along the main Polar Circle highway, captured the Finnish post and naval base of Petsamo, splitting the German armies in Northern Finland.

Admiral Nicholas Horthy, fascist Regent of Hungary, asked the Allies for an armistice. Three hours later Budapest was seized by a new pro-German government headed by Ferenc Szalasy, leader of the Fascist Arrow Cross.

The Government of Iran turned down the Soviet Government's proposal for the granting of a concession to exploit oil deposits in northern Iran, while Iranian newspapers criticized their government's decision, declaring it was not supported by public opinion and was against the national interest.

17

The Japanese Fleet came out of hiding to engage the Third American Fleet led by Admiral Halsey, but thought better of it and fled.

The Vichy Government set itself up in southern Germany.

18

A tentative understanding was reached in Moscow between the Polish Committee of National Liberation and Premier Mikolajczyk of the Polish Government-in-Exile.

The exiled Greek Government under Premier George Papandreou returned to Athens receiving the full cooperation of the National Liberation Front (EAM).

19

The Red Army crossed into German territory for the first time by invading East Prussia.

20

Aachen, the first German city to fall in this war, was captured by American troops under General Hodges' command.

Gen. Douglas MacArthur officially proclaimed the invasion of the Philippines.

21

With synchronization of air, sea and land power, involving an American army of 225,000 men, the invasion of the Philippines proceeded from steadily enlarging beachheads.

23

American invasion forces, in full control of the Leyte coastal road, drove the Japanese into the hills.

The United States, the U.S.S.R. and Great Britain formally recognized the de Gaulle regime as the Provisional Government of France.

Skirmishes took place along the French-Spanish frontier between Spanish Republican guerrillas and regular army troops of General Franco.

25

Britain and the United States resumed diplomatic relations with Italy, the first such action with a former enemy of World War II.

The Brazilian Government formally agreed to permit the United States to use its naval and air bases in northern Brazil against the Japanese.

Dr. William Temple, Archbishop of Canterbury and Primate of all England, died.

27

In a broadcast to the German nation, Propaganda Minister Goebbels declared that the Germans would "go on fighting until a peace is possible that guarantees our people's right to live, our national independence and expansion of the basis of our existence."

28

American troops, aided by Philippine guerrillas, overran Samar, the third largest island in the Philippines.

Bulgaria, Germany's satellite, signed an armistice with the United Nations in Moscow.

U. S. warships and planes sank two Japanese battleships and four carriers in the Battle of the Philippines, increasing Japanese naval losses in the Western Pacific of the preceding week to forty-eight ships sunk or damaged.

29

General Charles de Gaulle, saying the "period of insurrection is over," ordered the Resistance movement to surrender its arms. Its members were invited to join any authorized military organization.

The Soviet Union announced that it would not participate in the civil air conference in Chicago because neutrals with anti-Soviet policies had also been invited.

31

President Roosevelt confirmed reports that Gen. Joseph W. Stilwell had been relieved of his command in China, Burma and India in response to a demand from Generalissimo Chiang Kai-shek.

PRESIDENT ROOSEVELT'S CAMPAIGN BROADCAST
FROM THE WHITE HOUSE

October 5, 1944 [1]

My fellow Americans—I am speaking to you tonight from the White House. I am speaking particularly on behalf of those Americans who, regardless of party, very much hope that there will be recorded a large registration and a large vote this fall. I know from personal experience how effective precinct workers of all parties throughout the nation can be in assuring a large vote.

We are holding a national election despite all the prophecies of some politicians and a few newspapers who have stated, time and again in the past, that it was my sinister purpose to abolish all elections and to deprive the American people of the right to vote.

These same people, caring more for material riches than human rights, try to build up bogies of dictatorship in this Republic, although they know that free elections will always protect our nation against any such possibility.

Nobody will ever deprive the American people of the right to vote except the American people themselves—and the only way they could do that is by not voting.

The continuing health and vigor of our democratic system depends on the public spirit and devotion of its citizens which find expression in the ballot box.

Every man and every woman in this nation—regardless of party—who have the right to register and to vote, and the opportunity to register and to vote, have also the sacred obligation to register and to vote. For the free and secret ballot is the real keystone of our American constitutional system.

The American Government has survived and prospered for more than a century and a half, and it is now at the highest peak of its vitality. This is primarily because when the American people want a change of Government—even when they merely want "new faces"—they can raise the old electioneering battle-cry of "throw the rascals out!"

It is true that there are many undemocratic defects in voting laws in the various States; and some of these produce injustices which prevent a full and free expression of public opinion.

The right to vote must be open to our citizens irrespective of race, color or creed—without tax or artificial restriction of any kind. The sooner we get to that basis of political equality, the better it will be for the country as a whole.

Candidates in every part of the United States are now engaged in running for office.

All of us are actuated by a normal desire to win. But, speaking personally, I should be very sorry to be elected President of the United States on a small turnout of voters. And by the same token, if I were to be defeated, I should be much happier to be defeated in a large outpouring of voters. Then there could not be any question of doubt in anybody's mind as to which way the masses of the American people wanted this election to go.

The free and full exercise of our sacred right and duty to vote is more important than the personal hopes or ambitions of any candidate for any office in the land.

The administration which must cope with the difficult problems of winning

1 White House news release.

the war, and of peace and reconstruction should be chosen by a clear majority of all the people and not a part of the people.

In the election of 1920—one of the most fateful elections in our history— only forty-nine per cent of the potential voters actually voted.

Thus more than one-half of American voters failed to do their basic duty as citizens.

We can be gratified that in recent years the percentage of potential voters in national elections who actually voted has been steadily going up.

In 1940, it was sixty-two and a half per cent.

But that still is not nearly good enough.

This year for many millions of our young men in the armed forces and the merchant marine and similar services, it will be difficult in many cases—and impossible in some cases—to register and vote.

I think the people will be able to fix the responsibility for this state of affairs, for they know that during this past year there were politicians who quite openly worked to restrict the use of the ballot in this election, hoping selfishly for a small vote.

It is, therefore, all the more important that we here at home must not be slackers on Registration Day or Election Day.

I wish to make a special appeal to the women of the nation to exercise their right to vote. Women have taken an active part in this war in many ways— in uniform, in plants and ship yards, in offices and stores and hospitals, on farms and on railroads and buses—that they have become more than ever a very integral part of our national effort.

I know how difficult it is, especially for the many millions of women now employed, to get away to register and vote. Many of them have to manage their households as well as their jobs. A grateful nation remembers that.

But all women whether employed directly in war jobs or not—women of all parties and those not enrolled in any party—this year have a double obligation to express by their votes what I know to be their keen interest in the affairs of government—their obligation to themselves as citizens, and their obligation to their fighting husbands, sons, brothers and sweethearts.

It may sound to you repetitious on my part but it is my plain duty to reiterate to you that this war for the preservation of our civilization is not won yet.

In the war our forces and those of our Allies are steadily, relentlessly carrying the attack to the enemy.

The Allied Armies under General Eisenhower have waged during the past four months one of the most brilliant campaigns in military history—a campaign which has carried us from the beaches of Normandy and of Southern France into the frontiers of Germany itself.

In the Pacific, our naval task forces have advanced to attack the Japanese, more than five thousand miles west of Pearl Harbor.

But German and Japanese resistance remains as determined—as fanatical— as ever.

The guns of Hitler's Gestapo are silencing those German officers who have sense enough to know that every day that the fighting continues means that much more ruin and destruction for their beaten country. We shall have to fight our way across the Rhine—we may have to fight every inch of the way to Berlin.

But we Americans and our British and Russian and French and Polish Allies—all the massed forces of the United Nations—will not stop short of our final goal.

Nor will all of our goals have been achieved when the shooting stops. We must be able to present to our returning heroes an America which is stronger and more prosperous, more deeply devoted to the ways of democracy, than ever before.

"The land of opportunity"—that's what our forefathers called this country. By God's grace, it must always be the land of opportunity for the individual citizen—ever broader opportunity.

We have fought our way out of economic crisis—we are fighting our way through the bitterest of all wars—and our fighting men and women—our plain, everyday citizens—have a right to enjoy the fruits of victory.

Of course all of us who have sons on active service overseas want to have our boys come home at the earliest possible moment consistent with our national safety. And they will come home and be returned to civilian life at the earliest possible moment consistent with our national safety.

The record is clear on this matter and dates back many months.

Bills to provide a national program for demobilization and postwar adjustment were introduced by Senator George and Senator Murray last February.

This legislation, since May 20, 1944, has contained the following provision: "The War and Navy Departments shall not retain persons in the armed forces for the purpose of preventing unemployment or awaiting opportunities for employment."

This provision was approved by the War Department and by this Administration.

On June twelfth, the Director of War Mobilization, Justice Byrnes, made a public statement in behalf of this bill. He said: "Our fighting men are entitled to first consideration in any plan of demobilization. Their orderly release at the earliest possible moment consistent with the effective prosecution of the war, has ever been the primary consideration of both the President and the Joint Chiefs of Staff."

On September sixth the War Department issued its plan for speedy demobilization, based upon the wishes of the soldiers themselves.

The George Bill has been passed by the Congress, signed by me, and is now the law.

That law is there, for all Americans to read—and you do not need legal training to understand it.

It seems a pity that reckless words, based on unauthoritative sources, should be used to mislead and to weaken the morale of our men on the fighting fronts and the members of their families here at home.

When our enemies are finally defeated, we all want to see an end at the earliest practicable moment to wartime restrictions and wartime controls.

Strict provisions for the ending of these inconveniences have been written into our wartime laws. Those who fear that wartime measures, like price and rent control and rationing, for example, might be continued indefinitely into peacetime, should examine these laws. They will find that they are all temporary—to expire either at an early fixed date, or at the end of the war, or six months after the war, or sooner if the Congress or the President so determines.

The American people do not need, and no national administration would dare to ask them, to tolerate any indefinite continuance in peacetime of the controls essential in war time.

The power of the will of the American people expressed through the free ballot is the surest protection against the weakening of our democracy by "regimentation" or by any alien doctrines.

It is a source of regret to all decent Americans that some political propagandists are now dragging red herrings across the trail of this national election.

For example, labor baiters and bigots and some politicians use the term "communism" loosely, and apply it to every progressive social measure and to the views of every foreign-born citizen with whom they disagree.

They forget that we in the United States are all descended from immigrants (all except the Indians); and there is no better proof of that fact than the heroic names on our casualty lists.

I have just been looking at a statement by Representative Anderson, Chairman of the House Committee on Campaign Expenditures, about a document recently sent free, through the mails, by one Senator and twelve Representatives—all of them Republicans. They evidently thought highly of this document, for they had more than three million copies printed by the Government Printing Office—requiring more than eighteen tons of scarce and expensive paper—and sent them through the mails all over the country at the taxpayers' expense.

Now—let us look at this document to see what made it so important to thirteen Republican leaders at this stage of the war when many millions of our men are fighting for freedom.

Well—this document says that the "Red spectre of communism is stalking our country from East to West, from North to South"—the charge being that the Roosevelt Administration is part of a gigantic plot to sell our democracy out to the communists.

This form of fear propaganda is not new among rabble rousers and fomenters of class hatred—who seek to destroy democracy itself. It was used by Mussolini's black shirts and by Hitler's brown shirts. It has been used before in this country by the silver shirts and others on the lunatic fringe. But the sound and democratic instincts of the American people rebel against its use, particularly by their own Congressmen—and at the taxpayers' expense.

I have never sought, and I do not welcome the support of any person or group committed to communism, or fascism, or any other foreign ideology which would undermine the American system of government or the American system of free competitive enterprise and private property.

That does not in the least interfere with the firm and friendly relationship which this nation has in this war, and will, I hope, continue to have with the Soviet Union. The kind of economy that suits the Russian people is their own affair. The American people are glad and proud to be allied with the gallant people of Russia, not only in winning this war but in laying the foundations for the world peace which will follow the war—and in keeping that peace.

We have seen our civilization in deadly peril. We successfully met the challenge, due to the steadfastness of our Allies, to the aid we were able to give to our Allies, and to the unprecedented outpouring of American manpower, American productivity and American ingenuity—and to the magnificent courage and enterprise of our fighting men and our military leadership.

What is now being won in battle must not be lost by lack of vision or by lack of faith or by division among ourselves and our Allies.

We must and we will continue to be united with our Allies in a powerful world organization which is ready and able to keep the peace—if necessary by force.

To provide that assurance of international security is the policy, the effort and the obligation of this Administration.

We owe it to our posterity, we owe it to our heritage of freedom, we owe it to our God, to devote the rest of our lives and all of our capabilities to the building of a solid durable structure of world peace.

STETTINIUS—KOO—HALIFAX STATEMENTS AT CONCLUSION OF THE SECOND PHASE OF THE DUMBARTON OAKS CONVERSATIONS

October 7, 1944 [1]

Remarks by Under Secretary of State Stettinius

During the past week we have had opportunity to consider the document of proposals with our colleagues from China. Our thoughtful reexamination of these proposals in plenary session, in the formulation group, and in the Steering Committee has been most fruitful. We have benefited greatly from the close study which Dr. Koo and his associates have given the document and from their penetrating observations and their new perspectives. I am deeply gratified that the members of the Chinese group have found in the proposals, based as they are upon the documents submitted by all four participating groups, an acceptable body of principles for an international organization to maintain peace and security. Out of our discussions during this phase have emerged many points to which we shall all want to give consideration in preparations for a full conference.

It has been rightly said of war-makers that they destroy in days that which has taken generations to build. Our task has happily been to construct. I sincerely hope it may sometime be said that the men of peace who have sat around *this* table have reached agreement in days upon principles which strengthen the promise of security and peace for generations.

The common understanding we have achieved and the agreements we have reached in so brief a period have been possible because of the great qualities of statesmanship of my fellow chairmen, Dr. Koo and Lord Halifax, and of the constructive spirit of cooperation which has prevailed among all who have worked with us. I wish to express my deep appreciation and that of the American group for the cordiality and the wisdom which our British and Chinese colleagues have brought to the task and for the spirit of harmony which has prevailed in our deliberations.

The peace-loving peoples of the world will soon have opportunity to judge what we have accomplished here. They will appraise our work critically, for they are deeply earnest in their search for means to rid the world of the horrors of war and insecurity under which they have suffered so cruelly and so long. I am fully confident that the proposals upon which we have agreed will meet the test of their scrutiny. Within these proposals are contained the more important principles for an organization that will make possible, in our era, effective international cooperation for peace and security.

As we conclude this final phase of our conversations at Dumbarton Oaks I am deeply conscious of the bonds of friendship and common purpose which

[1] Department of State Bulletin.

join us with China and with the United Kingdom in our common struggle to defeat the Japanese and German aggressors. I anticipate with full confidence that the unity which the United Nations have achieved in war, and which has so richly manifested itself in our present conversations, will strengthen in peace. The four nations which have participated in these conversations will, I am sure, take early steps to complete the task we have begun at Dumbarton Oaks and thereby make possible in the not-distant future the calling of a general conference for the establishment of the organization which we have projected here and which is so devoutly desired by the peace-loving peoples of the world.

Remarks by Ambassador Koo

MR. CHAIRMAN, GENTLEMEN:

I have listened with deep appreciation to the generous tribute which you, Mr. Chairman, have paid to the Chinese Delegation and the fair appraisal which he has made of the work of the second phase of the Dumbarton Oaks conversations. I wish to say how grateful we of the Chinese Delegation feel toward you, Mr. Chairman, for having acted as chairman of our meetings, over which you have presided with such marked ability and unfailing courtesy. We wish also to express our thanks for the hospitality of the Government of the United States, which left nothing to be desired in affording facilities for our meetings and comfort for the delegates. The efficient secretariat provided by the State Department has also been a very great help to us in our work.

In our deliberations, we found the achievement of the first phase of the conversations excellent groundwork. The set of proposals which has now received the endorsement of the different participating delegations furnishes a preliminary and concrete plan for the formation of an international organization to maintain peace and security. We hope that the fruits of our labor will contribute in the end to the strengthening of the foundation of this new structure to be reared.

From the outset we were animated by an earnest desire to promote the success of our joint task. We are glad and delighted to be able to say that our spirit of collaboration was fully reciprocated by our colleagues on the American and British Delegations. At all the meetings we had, whether of the plenary session, the Steering Committee, the formulation group, or of the military experts, an atmosphere of frankness and cordiality prevailed. The learning and wisdom of our American and British colleagues made a deep impression on us. All this made our deliberations and participation both pleasant and profitable.

We believe that this important series of conversations initiated by the United States Government has accomplished its purpose. The set of agreed proposals, when approved by the four governments and finally embodied in a more complete form, will constitute a most valuable instrument for consideration and adoption by all the interested nations at a general conference. It is our hope that this conference can be held in the near future so that the ardent wish of all the peace-loving peoples to see the establishment of a universal organization to safeguard international peace and security after the achievement of victory over our common enemy in the East and in the West can find its early fulfillment.

Remarks by the Earl of Halifax

MR. STETTINIUS, AND DR. KOO, AND LADIES AND GENTLEMEN:

The conversations just concluded under your able chairmanship have in my own view and in that of all the members of the British Delegation made a great contribution to the eventual establishment of the International Organisation that we seek. The Chinese Delegation I have no doubt feel with us that we have owed much to the rare personal qualities that you, Sir, have brought to your duties in the Chair, and to the large-minded participation of the whole American team. We have throughout the consideration of these problems been much influenced by the views which the Chinese Delegation were good enough to place before us at an early date, and we were much encouraged by finding that the line of approach which we ourselves favoured was very similar to that advocated by our Chinese friends. On most questions of the first importance we found ourselves in close agreement with them.

Thus, the plan which we have worked out together at Dumbarton Oaks owes much to the wise and consistent thinking of the Chinese Delegation. Dr. Wellington Koo has, as always, given to us freely and candidly the results of his long experience of international affairs, and the exchanges which we have had with him and with his colleagues have been both searching and constructive. The large measure of agreement that we have reached shows that there is no barrier between the East and the West on these questions, which mean so much to the future of the world.

We have all recognised the common interest in the solution of these large issues, and, if we have not resolved all of them, that is because some of them require more prolonged and intense study than we have been able here to give. But a great deal has been accomplished, and I can say frankly that when the suggestion was first made that these conversations should take place, I had no expectation that we should have been able to go so far at this stage. That we have done so, Mr. Chairman, is of good augury for the future.

We must all be very conscious of the difficulty of the problems that confront us, but if we handle them with the same spirit of good-will and common sense which has shown itself at all our meetings in these hospitable quarters, I am certain that we can find answers for them which all peace-loving nations can accept, and thus make possible the creation of an international society in which mankind can find the opportunity to reach a higher level of civilization than has previously existed.

A great Greek philosopher said that the State came into existence in order that men might live, but that its justification was to be found only if men lived nobly. So (and I believe that in this thought I have the full agreement of all those who have taken part in these conversations), the International Organisation should be brought into existence in order that nations may be saved from destruction; but it also will only be justified if through the years all humanity is enabled by it to find the way to a better and a nobler life.

Joint Statement by Heads of American, British, and Chinese Delegations

Conversations between the United States, the United Kingdom, and the Chinese Delegations in Washington regarding the establishment of a World Security Organisation have now reached a satisfactory conclusion. Rapid progress has been made possible because of the work accomplished at the first phase of the Dumbarton Oaks discussions and because the three delegations had earlier exchanged written memoranda on the subject. These conversations have afforded the delegations the opportunity of a full and frank exchange of views and have resulted in an agreed set of proposals for the general framework of an international organization and the machinery required to maintain peace and security which the three delegations are now reporting to their respective governments. The three governments will issue a statement on the subject in the near future.

ROOSEVELT—HULL—STETTINIUS STATEMENTS ON DUMBARTON OAKS CONVERSATIONS

October 9, 1944 [1]

Statement by President Roosevelt

I wish to take this opportunity to refer to the work of the Dumbarton Oaks Conversations between the delegations of the United States, the United Kingdom, the Soviet Union, and China on the plans for an international organization for the maintenance of peace and security.

The conversations were completed Saturday, October 7, 1944, and proposals were submitted to the four Governments for their consideration. These proposals have been made public to permit full discussion by the people of this country prior to the convening of a wider conference on this all-important subject.

Although I have not yet been able to make a thorough study of these proposals, my first impression is one of extreme satisfaction, and even surprise, that so much could have been accomplished on so difficult a subject in so short a time. This achievement was largely due to the long and thorough preparations which were made by the Governments represented, and in our case, was the result of the untiring devotion and care which the Secretary of State has personally given to this work for more than two and a half years— indeed for many years.

The projected international organization has for its primary purpose the maintenance of international peace and security and the creation of the conditions that make for peace.

We now know the need for such an organization of the peace-loving peoples and the spirit of unity which will be required to maintain it. Aggressors like Hitler and the Japanese war lords organize for years for the day when they can launch their evil strength against weaker nations devoted to their peaceful pursuits. This time we have been determined first to defeat the enemy, assure that he shall never again be in position to plunge the world into war, and then to so organize the peace-loving nations that they may through unity of desire, unity of will, and unity of strength be in position to assure that no other would-be aggressor or conqueror shall even get started. That is why from the very beginning of the war, and paralleling our military plans, we have begun to lay the foundations for the general organization for the maintenance of peace and security.

It represents, therefore, a major objective for which this war is being fought, and as such, it inspires the highest hopes of the millions of fathers and mothers whose sons and daughters are engaged in the terrible struggle and suffering of war.

[1] State Department Bulletin.

The projected general organization may be regarded as the keystone of the arch and will include within its framework a number of specialized economic and social agencies now existing or to be established.

The task of planning the great design of security and peace has been well begun. It now remains for the nations to complete the structure in a spirit of constructive purpose and mutual confidence.

Statement by Secretary of State Cordell Hull

The proposals for an international organization for the maintenance of international peace and security, upon which the representatives of the United States, the United Kingdom, the Soviet Union, and China have agreed during the conversations at Dumbarton Oaks, have been submitted to the four Governments and are today being made generally available to the people of this Nation and of the world.

All of us have every reason to be immensely gratified by the results achieved at these conversations. To be sure, the Proposals in their present form are neither complete nor final. Much work still remains to be done before a set of completed proposals can be placed before the peace-loving nations of the world as a basis of discussion at a formal conference to draft a charter of the projected organization for submission to the governments. But the document which has been prepared by the able representatives of the four participating nations and has been agreed to by them as their recommendation to their respective Governments is sufficiently detailed to indicate the kind of an international organization which, in their judgment, will meet the imperative need of providing for the maintenance of international peace and security.

These proposals are now being studied by the four Governments which were represented at the Washington Conversations and which will give their urgent attention to the next steps which will be necessary to reach the goal of achieving the establishment of an effective international organization.

These proposals are now available for full study and discussion by the peoples of all countries.

We in this country have spent many months in careful planning and wide consultation in preparation for the conversations which have just been concluded. Those who represented the Government of the United States in these discussions were armed with the ideas and with the results of thinking contributed by numerous leaders of our national thought and opinion, without regard to political or other affiliations.

It is my earnest hope that, during the time which must elapse before the convocation of a full United Nations conference, discussions in the United States on this all-important subject will continue to be carried on in the same non-partisan spirit of devotion to our paramount national interest in peace and security which has characterized our previous consultations. I am certain that all of us will be constantly mindful of the high responsibility for us and for all peace-loving nations which attaches to this effort to make permanent a victory purchased at so heavy a cost in blood, in tragic suffering, and in treasure. We must be constantly mindful of the price which all of us will pay if we fail to measure up to this unprecedented responsibility.

It is, of course, inevitable that when many governments and peoples attempt to agree on a single plan the result will be in terms of the highest common denominator rather than of the plan of any one nation. The organization to be created must reflect the ideas and hopes of all the peace-loving nations which participate in its creation. The spirit of cooperation must manifest itself in mutual striving to attain the high goal by common agreement.

The road to the establishment of an international organization capable of effectively maintaining international peace and security will be long. At times it will be difficult. But we cannot hope to attain so great an objective without constant effort and unfailing determination that the sacrifices of this war shall not be in vain.

Report to Secretary of State Hull Submitted by the Chairman of the American Delegation, Edward R. Stettinius, Jr.

I take great pleasure in submitting to you the results of the exploratory conversations on international organization held in Washington between representatives of the Governments of the United States, the United Kingdom, the Soviet Union, and China. The first phase of the conversations, between representatives of the United States, the United Kingdom, and the Soviet Union, took place from August 21 to September 28; the second phase, between representatives of the United States, the United Kingdom, and China, was held from September 29 to October 7. The results of the work accomplished in both phases are embodied in the following Proposals which each of the four delegations is transmitting to its respective Government as the unanimously agreed recommendations of the four delegations.

I am happy to report that the conversations throughout were characterized by a spirit of complete cooperation and great cordiality among all participants, the proof of which is evident in the wide area of agreement covered in the Proposals. The few questions which remain for further consideration, though important, are not in any sense insuperable, and I recommend that the necessary steps for obtaining agreement on these points be taken as soon as possible.

It is proper to emphasize, at the conclusion of these preliminary conversations, that the Proposals as they are now submitted to the four Governments comprise substantial contributions from each of the delegations. It is my own view, which I believe is shared by all the participants, that the agreed Proposals constitute an advance over the tentative and preliminary proposals presented by each delegation. This has resulted from a single-minded effort of all the delegations at Dumbarton Oaks to reach a common understanding as to the most effective international organization capable of fulfilling the hopes of all peoples everywhere.

I wish to take this opportunity to express my grateful recognition of the contribution to the successful outcome of these conversations made by the members of the American delegation and to commend the advisers and the staff for their most helpful assistance. Above all, I wish to express my profound appreciation to the President and to you, Mr. Secretary, for the constant advice and guidance without which our work could not have been accomplished with such constructive and satisfactory results.

STATEMENT ISSUED SIMULTANEOUSLY BY THE PARTICIPATING GOVERNMENTS ON THE DUMBARTON OAKS PROPOSALS FOR AN INTERNATIONAL ORGANIZATION

October 9, 1944 [1]

The Government of the United States has now received the report of its delegation to the conversations held in Washington between August 21 and October 7, 1944, with the delegations of the United Kingdom, the Union of Soviet Socialist Republics, and the Republic of China on the subject of an international organization for the maintenance of peace and security.

There follows a statement of tentative proposals indicating in detail the wide range of subjects on which agreement has been reached at the conversations.

The Governments which were represented in the discussions in Washington have agreed that after further study of these proposals they will as soon as possible take the necessary steps with a view to the preparation of complete proposals which could then serve as a basis of discussion at a full United Nations conference.

Proposals for the Establishment of a General International Organization

There should be established an international organization under the title of The United Nations, the Charter of which should contain provisions necessary to give effect to the proposals which follow.

CHAPTER I

PURPOSES

The purposes of the Organization should be:

1. To maintain international peace and security; and to that end to take effective collective measures for the prevention and removal of threats to the peace and the suppression of acts of aggression or other breaches of the peace, and to bring about by peaceful means adjustment or settlement of international disputes which may lead to a breach of the peace;

2. To develop friendly relations among nations and to take other appropriate measures to strengthen universal peace;

3. To achieve international cooperation in the solution of international economic, social and other humanitarian problems; and

4. To afford a center for harmonizing the actions of nations in the achievement of these common ends.

CHAPTER II

PRINCIPLES

In pursuit of the purposes mentioned in Chapter I the Organization and its members should act in accordance with the following principles:

1. The Organization is based on the principle of the sovereign equality of all peace-loving states.

[1] Department of State Bulletin.

2. All members of the Organization undertake, in order to ensure to all of them the rights and benefits resulting from membership in the Organization, to fulfill the obligations assumed by them in accordance with the Charter.

3. All members of the Organization shall settle their disputes by peaceful means in such a manner that international peace and security are not endangered.

4. All members of the Organization shall refrain in their international relations from the threat or use of force in any manner inconsistent with the purposes of the Organization.

5. All members of the Organization shall give every assistance to the Organization in any action undertaken by it in accordance with the provisions of the Charter.

6. All members of the Organization shall refrain from giving assistance to any state against which preventive or enforcement action is being undertaken by the Organization.

The Organization should ensure that states not members of the Organization act in accordance with these principles so far as may be necessary for the maintenance of international peace and security.

CHAPTER III

MEMBERSHIP

1. Membership of the Organization should be open to all peace-loving states.

CHAPTER IV

PRINCIPAL ORGANS

1. The Organization should have as its principal organs:
   a. A General Assembly;
   b. A Security Council;
   c. An international court of justice; and
   d. A Secretariat.

2. The Organization should have such subsidiary agencies as may be found necessary.

CHAPTER V

THE GENERAL ASSEMBLY

SECTION A
COMPOSITION

All members of the Organization should be members of the General Assembly and should have a number of representatives to be specified in the Charter.

SECTION B
FUNCTIONS AND POWERS

1. The General Assembly should have the right to consider the general principles of cooperation in the maintenance of international peace and security, including the principles governing disarmament and the regulation of armaments; to discuss any questions relating to the maintenance of international peace and security brought before it by any member or members of the Organization or by the Security Council; and to make recommendations with regard to any such principles or questions. Any such questions on which

action is necessary should be referred to the Security Council by the General Assembly either before or after discussion. The General Assembly should not on its own initiative make recommendations on any matter relating to the maintenance of international peace and security which is being dealt with by the Security Council.

2. The General Assembly should be empowered to admit new members to the Organization upon recommendation of the Security Council.

3. The General Assembly should, upon recommendation of the Security Council, be empowered to suspend from the exercise of any rights or privileges of membership any member of the Organization against which preventive or enforcement action shall have been taken by the Security Council. The exercise of the rights and privileges thus suspended may be restored by decision of the Security Council. The General Assembly should be empowered, upon recommendation of the Security Council, to expel from the Organization any member of the Organization which persistently violates the principles contained in the Charter.

4. The General Assembly should elect the non-permanent members of the Security Council and the members of the Economic and Social Council provided for in Chapter IX. It should be empowered to elect, upon recommendation of the Security Council, the Secretary-General of the Organization. It should perform such functions in relation to the election of the judges of the international court of justice as may be conferred upon it by the statute of the court.

5. The General Assembly should apportion the expenses among the members of the Organization and should be empowered to approve the budgets of the Organization.

6. The General Assembly should initiate studies and make recommendations for the purpose of promoting international cooperation in political, economic and social fields and of adjusting situations likely to impair the general welfare.

7. The General Assembly should make recommendations for the coordination of the policies of international economic, social, and other specialized agencies brought into relation with the Organization in accordance with agreements between such agencies and the Organization.

8. The General Assembly should receive and consider annual and special reports from the Security Council and reports from other bodies of the Organization.

Section C

VOTING

1. Each member of the Organization should have one vote in the General Assembly.

2. Important decisions of the General Assembly, including recommendations with respect to the maintenance of international peace and security; election of members of the Security Council; election of members of the Economic and Social Council; admission of members, suspension of the exercise of the rights and privileges of members, and expulsion of members; and budgetary questions, should be made by a two-thirds majority of those present and voting. On other questions, including the determination of additional categories of questions to be decided by a two-thirds majority, the decisions of the General Assembly should be made by a simple majority vote.

Section D

PROCEDURE

1. The General Assembly should meet in regular annual sessions and in such special sessions as occasion may require.

2. The General Assembly should adopt its own rules of procedure and elect its President for each session.

3. The General Assembly should be empowered to set up such bodies and agencies as it may deem necessary for the performance of its functions.

CHAPTER VI

THE SECURITY COUNCIL

SECTION A

COMPOSITION

The Security Council should consist of one representative of each of eleven members of the Organization. Representatives of the United States of America, the United Kingdom of Great Britain and Northern Ireland, the Union of Soviet Socialist Republics, the Republic of China, and, in due course, France, should have permanent seats. The General Assembly should elect six states to fill the non-permanent seats. These six states should be elected for a term of two years, three retiring each year. They should not be immediately eligible for reelection. In the first election of the non-permanent members three should be chosen by the General Assembly for one-year terms and three for two-year terms.

SECTION B

PRINCIPAL FUNCTIONS AND POWERS

1. In order to ensure prompt and effective action by the Organization, members of the Organization should by the Charter confer on the Security Council primary responsibility for the maintenance of international peace and security and should agree that in carrying out these duties under this responsibility it should act on their behalf.

2. In discharging these duties the Security Council should act in accordance with the purposes and principles of the Organization.

3. The specific powers conferred on the Security Council in order to carry out these duties are laid down in Chapter VIII.

4. All members of the Organization should obligate themselves to accept the decisions of the Security Council and to carry them out in accordance with the provisions of the Charter.

5. In order to promote the establishment and maintenance of international peace and security with the least diversion of the world's human and economic resources for armaments, the Security Council, with the assistance of the Military Staff Committee referred to in Chapter VIII, Section B, paragraph 9, should have the responsibility for formulating plans for the establishment of a system of regulation of armaments for submission to the members of the Organization.

SECTION C

VOTING

(Note: The question of voting procedure in the Security Council is still under consideration.)

SECTION D

PROCEDURE

1. The Security Council should be so organized as to be able to function continuously and each state member of the Security Council should be permanently represented at the headquarters of the Organization. It may hold meetings at such other places as in its judgment may best facilitate its work. There should be periodic meetings at which each state member of the Security Council could if it so desired be represented by a member of the government or some other special representative.

2. The Security Council should be empowered to set up such bodies or agencies as it may deem necessary for the performance of its functions including regional subcommittees of the Military Staff Committee.

3. The Security Council should adopt its own rules of procedure, including the method of selecting its President.

4. Any member of the Organization should participate in the discussion of any question brought before the Security Council whenever the Security Council considers that the interests of that member of the Organization are specially affected.

5. Any member of the Organization not having a seat on the Security Council and any state not a member of the Organization, if it is a party to a dispute under consideration by the Security Council, should be invited to participate in the discussion relating to the dispute.

Chapter VII

AN INTERNATIONAL COURT OF JUSTICE

1. There should be an international court of justice which should constitute the principal judicial organ of the Organization.

2. The court should be constituted and should function in accordance with a statute which should be annexed to and be a part of the Charter of the Organization.

3. The statute of the court of international justice should be either (a) the Statute of the Permanent Court of International Justice, continued in force with such modifications as may be desirable or (b) a new statute in the preparation of which the Statute of the Permanent Court of International Justice should be used as a basis.

4. All members of the Organization should *ipso facto* be parties to the statute of the international court of justice.

5. Conditions under which states not members of the Organization may become parties to the statute of the international court of justice should be determined in each case by the General Assembly upon recommendation of the Security Council.

Chapter VIII

ARRANGEMENTS FOR THE MAINTENANCE OF INTERNATIONAL PEACE AND SECURITY INCLUDING PREVENTION AND SUPPRESSION OF AGGRESSION

Section A

PACIFIC SETTLEMENT OF DISPUTES

1. The Security Council should be empowered to investigate any dispute, or any situation which may lead to international friction or give rise to a dispute, in order to determine whether its continuance is likely to endanger the maintenance of international peace and security.

2. Any state, whether member of the Organization or not, may bring any such dispute or situation to the attention of the General Assembly or of the Security Council.

3. The parties to any dispute the continuance of which is likely to endanger the maintenance of international peace and security should obligate themselves, first of all, to seek a solution by negotiation, mediation, conciliation, arbitration or judicial settlement, or other peaceful means of their own choice.

The Security Council should call upon the parties to settle their dispute by such means.

4. If, nevertheless, parties to a dispute of the nature referred to in paragraph 3 above fail to settle it by the means indicated in that paragraph, they should obligate themselves to refer it to the Security Council. The Security Council should in each case decide whether or not the continuance of the particular dispute is in fact likely to endanger the maintenance of international peace and security, and, accordingly, whether the Security Council should deal with the dispute, and, if so, whether it should take action under paragraph 5.

5. The Security Council should be empowered, at any stage of a dispute of the nature referred to in paragraph 3 above, to recommend appropriate procedures or methods of adjustment.

6. Justiciable disputes should normally be referred to the international court of justice. The Security Council should be empowered to refer to the court, for advice, legal questions connected with other disputes.

7. The provisions of paragraph 1 to 6 of Section A should not apply to situations or disputes arising out of matters which by international law are solely within the domestic jurisdiction of the state concerned.

SECTION B

DETERMINATION OF THREATS TO THE PEACE OR ACTS OF AGGRESSION AND ACTION WITH RESPECT THERETO

1. Should the Security Council deem that a failure to settle a dispute in accordance with procedures indicated in paragraph 3 of Section A, or in accordance with its recommendations made under paragraph 5 of Section A, constitutes a threat to the maintenance of international peace and security, it should take any measures necessary for the maintenance of international peace and security in accordance with the purposes and principles of the Organization.

2. In general the Security Council should determine the existence of any threat to the peace, breach of the peace or act of aggression and should make recommendations or decide upon the measures to be taken to maintain or restore peace and security.

3. The Security Council should be empowered to determine what diplomatic, economic, or other measures not involving the use of armed force should be employed to give effect to its decisions, and to call upon members of the Organization to apply such measures. Such measures may include complete or partial interruption of rail, sea, air, postal, telegraphic, radio and other means of communication and the severance of diplomatic and economic relations.

4. Should the Security Council consider such measures to be inadequate, it should be empowered to take such action by air, naval or land forces as may be necessary to maintain or restore international peace and security. Such action may include demonstrations, blockade and other operations by air, sea or land forces of members of the Organization.

5. In order that all members of the Organization should contribute to the maintenance of international peace and security, they should undertake to make available to the Security Council, on its call and in accordance with a special agreement or agreements concluded among themselves, armed forces, facilities and assistance necessary for the purpose of maintaining international peace and security. Such agreement or agreements should govern the numbers and types of forces and the nature of the facilities and assistance to be pro-

vided. The special agreement or agreements should be negotiated as soon as possible and should in each case be subject to approval by the Security Council and to ratification by the signatory states in accordance with their constitutional processes.

6. In order to enable urgent military measures to be taken by the Organization there should be held immediately available by the members of the Organization national air force contingents for combined international enforcement action. The strength and degree of readiness of these contingents and plans for their combined action should be determined by the Security Council with the assistance of the Military Staff Committee within the limits laid down in the special agreement or agreements referred to in paragraph 5 above.

7. The action required to carry out the decisions of the Security Council for the maintenance of international peace and security should be taken by all the members of the Organization in cooperation or by some of them as the Security Council may determine. This undertaking should be carried out by the members of the Organization by their own action and through action of the appropriate specialized organizations and agencies of which they are members.

8. Plans for the application of armed force should be made by the Security Council with the assistance of the Military Staff Committee referred to in paragraph 9 below.

9. There should be established a Military Staff Committee the functions of which should be to advise and assist the Security Council on all questions relating to the Security Council's military requirements for the maintenance of international peace and security, to the employment and command of forces placed at its disposal, to the regulation of armaments, and to possible disarmament. It should be responsible under the Security Council for the strategic direction of any armed forces placed at the disposal of the Security Council. The Committee should be composed of the Chiefs of Staff of the permanent members of the Security Council or their representatives. Any member of the Organization not permanently represented on the Committee should be invited by the Committee to be associated with it when the efficient discharge of the Committee's responsibilities requires that such a state should participate in its work. Questions of command of forces should be worked out subsequently.

10. The members of the Organization should join in affording mutual assistance in carrying out the measures decided upon by the Security Council.

11. Any state, whether a member of the Organization or not, which finds itself confronted with special economic problems arising from the carrying out of measures which have been decided upon by the Security Council should have the right to consult the Security Council in regard to a solution of those problems.

SECTION C

REGIONAL ARRANGEMENTS

1. Nothing in the Charter should preclude the existence of regional arrangements or agencies for dealing with such matters relating to the maintenance of international peace and security as are appropriate for regional action, provided such arrangements or agencies and their activities are consistent with the purposes and principles of the Organization. The Security Council should encourage settlement of local disputes through such regional arrangements or by such regional agencies, either on the initiative of the states concerned or by reference from the Security Council.

2. The Security Council should, where appropriate, utilize such arrange-

ments or agencies for enforcement action under its authority, but no enforcement action should be taken under regional arrangements or by regional agencies without the authorization of the Security Council.

3. The Security Council should at all times be kept fully informed of activities undertaken or in contemplation under regional arrangements or by regional agencies for the maintenance of international peace and security.

CHAPTER IX

ARRANGEMENTS FOR INTERNATIONAL ECONOMIC AND SOCIAL COOPERATION

SECTION A

PURPOSE AND RELATIONSHIPS

1. With a view to the creation of conditions of stability and well-being which are necessary for peaceful and friendly relations among nations, the Organization should facilitate solutions of international economic, social and other humanitarian problems and promote respect for human rights and fundamental freedoms. Responsibility for the discharge of this function should be vested in the General Assembly and, under the authority of the General Assembly, in an Economic and Social Council.

2. The various specialized economic, social and other organizations and agencies would have responsibilities in their respective fields as defined in their statutes. Each such organization or agency should be brought into relationship with the Organization on terms to be determined by agreement between the Economic and Social Council and the appropriate authorities of the specialized organization or agency, subject to approval by the General Assembly.

SECTION B

COMPOSITION AND VOTING

The Economic and Social Council should consist of representatives of eighteen members of the Organization. The states to be represented for this purpose should be elected by the General Assembly for terms of three years. Each such state should have one representative, who should have one vote. Decisions of the Economic and Social Council should be taken by simple majority vote of those present and voting.

SECTION C

FUNCTIONS AND POWERS OF THE ECONOMIC AND SOCIAL COUNCIL

1. The Economic and Social Council should be empowered:
   a. to carry out, within the scope of its functions, recommendations of the General Assembly;
   b. to make recommendations, on its own initiative, with respect to international economic, social and other humanitarian matters;
   c. to receive and consider reports from the economic, social and other organizations or agencies brought into relationship with the Organization, and to coordinate their activities through consultations with, and recommendations to, such organizations or agencies;
   d. to examine the administrative budgets of such specialized organizations or agencies with a view to making recommendations to the organizations or agencies concerned;
   e. to enable the Secretary-General to provide information to the Security Council;
   f. to assist the Security Council upon its request; and

g. to perform such other functions within the general scope of its competence as may be assigned to it by the General Assembly.

SECTION D

ORGANIZATION AND PROCEDURE

1. The Economic and Social Council should set up an economic commission, a social commission, and such other commissions as may be required. These commissions should consist of experts. There should be a permanent staff which should constitute a part of the Secretariat of the Organization.

2. The Economic and Social Council should make suitable arrangements for representatives of the specialified organizations or agencies to participate without vote in its deliberations and in those of the commissions established by it.

3. The Economic and Social Council should adopt its own rules of procedure and the method of selecting its President.

CHAPTER X

THE SECRETARIAT

1. There should be a Secretariat comprising a Secretary-General and such staff as may be required. The Secretary-General should be the chief administrative officer of the Organization. He should be elected by the General Assembly, on recommendation of the Security Council, for such term and under such conditions as are specified in the Charter.

2. The Secretary-General should act in that capacity in all meetings of the General Assembly, of the Security Council, and of the Economic and Social Council and should make an annual report to the General Assembly on the work of the Organization.

3. The Secretary-General should have the right to bring to the attention of the Security Council any matter which in his opinion may threaten international peace and security.

CHAPTER XI

AMENDMENTS

Amendments should come into force for all members of the Organization, when they have been adopted by a vote of two-thirds of the members of the General Assembly and ratified in accordance with their respective constitutional processes by the members of the Organization having permanent membership on the Security Council and by a majority of the other members of the Organization.

CHAPTER XII

TRANSITIONAL ARRANGEMENTS

1. Pending the coming into force of the special agreement or agreements referred to in Chapter VIII, Section B, paragraph 5, and in accordance with the provisions of paragraph 5 of the Four-Nation Declaration, signed at Moscow, October 30, 1943, the states parties to that Declaration should consult with one another and as occasion arises with other members of the Organization with a view to such joint action on behalf of the Organization as may be necessary for the purpose of maintaining international peace and security.

2. No provision of the Charter should preclude action taken or authorized

in relation to enemy states as a result of the present war by the Governments having responsibility for such action.

NOTE

In addition to the question of voting procedure in the Security Council referred to in Chapter VI, several other questions are still under consideration.
WASHINGTON, D. C.
October 7, 1944

GOVERNOR THOMAS E. DEWEY'S ST. LOUIS CAMPAIGN SPEECH

October 16, 1944 [1]

Fellow Americans:

I am happy to come again to Missouri to carry on the battle for honest and competent government in Washington. I am happy also to salute your fine present and future Mayor Kaufmann. I am happy to salute your next Governor, Jean Paul Bradshaw, and your distinguished present Governor, who, next January, will become United States Senator, Forrest C. Donnell.

It's clear to everybody by now that the New Deal has been taken over by a combination of corrupt big city bosses, Communists and fellow-travelers. But the people of Missouri have shown their independence before by throwing off the rule of the corrupt Pendergast machine. In the light of that record, I am sure they will never permit men who are the products of that machine to succeed in their current attempt to take over our national Government.

The war in Europe is drawing to a close. But hard tasks remain. We must speed the drive for final victory. We must put behind our fighting men the backing of a competent, effective government at home. We must make sure that when total victory is won those fighting men are brought home and promptly. We must take the leadership in bringing about effective international cooperation to prevent a future war.

We in America face a mighty decision. Ten million heroes will be coming home, entitled to the fruits of victory—a prospering country with security and opportunity to get ahead. Millions of workers in war plants will demand their right to a good job in peace industry at good wages with security and stable employment. The farmers of America have a right to know that their tremendous efforts in the face of inadequate help and machinery will be rewarded by a new future of freedom from regimentation with stable and good prices for the fruits of their labor.

Is the New Deal, the tired and quarrelsome New Deal, all America has to offer? Must we go back to leaf-raking and doles? Must our returning heroes go on the same old WPA? Must our farmers go back to detailed control by a host of New Deal agents, with falling prices to boot?

These questions will all be decided in this election. Never in its history was it so important that we have a Government which will be respected at home and respected abroad. Never was it so important that we choose a Government which can restore our job-making machinery. Jobs and oppor-

[1] *New York Times.*

tunity for every American and our chance for a lasting peace in the world —all depend on this election.

Now, what kind of an administration do we need for the mighty problems we shall face after this war? That's right. We'll need a Government that meets these simple tests:

1. Is it honest?
2. Are the people who run it trained and competent for their jobs?
3. Is it a Government with faith in the future of America and a whole-hearted determination to make our system work?

Let's apply these simple tests to what we now have so that we can find out whether it's time for a change.

For twelve years the New Deal has treated us to constant bickering, quarreling and back-biting by the most spectacular collection of incompetent people who ever held public office at the same time. We must not trust our future to such people as Harry Hopkins, Madam Perkins and Harold Ickes. Certainly America can do better than these. I propose that we will do better.

But we can never do better under the New Deal. The scars of its failures and its own quarrels are too deep. Going right back to its beginning, if it wasn't a free-for-all fight in the NRA, it was Messrs. Ickes and Hopkins fighting over who got four billion borrowed dollars to spend on PWA or WPA. It was Henderson and Ickes squabbling over the right to be gasoline czar or a fight between the rubber director and the Under-Secretary of War.

If it wasn't the OPA fighting within itself, it was Mr. Ickes denouncing the War Labor Board for its part in what he called a "black—and stupid—chapter in the history of the home front * * *."

The most disgraceful performance came when the Vice President accused Secretary of Commerce Jones of having, and I am quoting, "done much to harass the * * * effort to help shorten this war * * *," and Mr. Jones charged the Vice President with "malice, innuendo, half truths and no truths at all * * *."

What kind of Government is this that even a war can't make it sober down and go to work? Little men rattling around in big jobs. Our country can't afford the wasteful luxury of incompetent people in high places who spend their time fighting with each other.

Even Mr. Roosevelt finally publicly confessed on Aug. 21, 1942, that these conflicts within his own Administration have been, and I quote his words, "a direct and serious handicap to the prosecution of the war." How costly they have been to our people we will never know. But we do know one thing. Twelve years of this kind of Government are too long and sixteen years would be intolerable.

This Administration has lived on conflict. And that's no accident. They plan it that way. Listen to the President's Executive Order No. 9334. It says in part: "The Secretary of Agriculture and the War Food Administrator * * * shall each have authority to exercise any and all of the powers vested in the other." * * *

In other words, Mr. Roosevelt gives two men the same powers and then turns them loose to fight about it. He has been doing that for twelve straight years and it is one of the major reasons the New Deal has failed. It failed in peacetime and would fail again if it got a chance. We can't stand this kind of deliberately planning, noisy chaos, bungling and confusion in the days ahead. The future welfare and happiness of the American people require that it come to an end. That's why it's time for a change.

Now, there is another important reason why this New Deal administration has been one long chapter of quarreling and confusion. That reason is the consistent practice of everybody evading responsibility. High officials issue statements. Nobody rebukes or removes them. But when the statements later prove embarrassing they are lightly disavowed or turned aside as unauthoritative.

Last month, for example, I challenged a statement by the National Director of Selective Service in which he said, and I'm quoting him: "We can keep people in the Army about as cheaply as we could create an agency for them when they are out." Those are his words.

Mr. Roosevelt was quite upset when I called attention to that statement. In fact, he spoke about "reckless words, based on unauthoritative sources. * * *" And last Saturday he handed out from the White House a letter from the general in which the general said the idea was all his own.

Now, is Mr. Roosevelt quite accurate when he calls his own appointee, the general, unauthoritative? The fact is that the Director of Selective Service is charged by law with the duty of helping to get jobs for returning veterans. If anybody is an authority on that subject, he is the man.

But where did General Hershey get this idea that fighting men ought not to come home after victory is won? I'll tell you. He got it from another one of those White House releases put out by Mr. Roosevelt himself. It was a report submitted by Mr. Roosevelt's own uncle, Frederic A. Delano, chairman of the National Resources Planning Board. It was the report of the conference on post-war readjustment of civilian and military personnel, appointed by my opponent.

It discussed the pros and cons of speedy demobilization. After saying that good reasons exist for desiring a rapid rate of demobilization, the report goes on to say, and I'm quoting him:

"Despite * * * compelling reasons for rapid military demobilization, the prospects of economic and industrial dislocation at the close of the war are so grave and the social consequences are so far-reaching that a policy of orderly, gradual, and, if necessary, delayed military demobilization has been strongly advocated." Mind you, I'm reading from report released by Mr. Roosevelt himself. "The following reasons," this report goes on to say, "have been advanced.

"Rapid demobilization might throw into the labor market large numbers of men just at the time when the industries might be least able to absorb them. It might create unemployment and depression. Those in the services," this report continues, "will constitute the only large group of persons over whom the nation could, in the event of economic crisis, exercise any degree of direct control." * * * Then it says: "The economic and social costs of retaining men in the services would be less than those involved in dealing with an unemployment depression through civilian relief." * * *

So this idea of keeping our men in the Army for fear that they won't get jobs after the war was in a report made public last year by Mr. Roosevelt himself. The New Deal had it in mind right along.

Now let my opponent try to pass the buck to one of his assistants. They can slip and squirm in this New Deal, but when my opponent uses the word "falsification," as he did on the radio in the teamsters' speech, it comes home to haunt him.

And let me add that as long ago as last April, Mr. Roosevelt remained silent while his director of Selective Service in a public speech in New York said he saw no purpose in letting men out of the Army "into some kind of a WPA." I do not see any such purpose either. Our fighting men ought to be brought home from the armed services at the earliest possible moment after victory and to jobs and opportunity when they get here. And that will be done when we get a new, an honest and a responsible Administration in Washington.

The truth is the New Deal has been afraid all along that when the time came to let men out of the Army there wouldn't be any jobs for them. There would be a case of back to normalcy under the New Deal with 10,000,000 unemployed.

When the New Deal took office on March 4, 1933, the world-wide depression was already nearly four years old. In its first seven years the New Deal spent nearly $58,000,000,000. Yet the official figures of the League of Nations prior to the outbreak of the World War show that among the major nations of the world the United States had almost the poorest recovery of all. Out of twenty-two leading industrial nations of the world, nineteen had made greater recovery than the United States in the ten years following the crash of 1929. All but five had exceeded the 1929 level of production, but not America under the New Deal.

It was Winston Churchill who, late in 1937, said, and I quote him: "The Washington Administration has waged so ruthless a war on private enterprise that the United States * * * is actually at the present moment leading the world back into the trough of depression."

Then Mr. Churchill solemnly added, and this, too, was in 1937: "Those who are keeping the flag of peace and free government flying in the Old World have almost the right to ask that their comrades in the New World should * * * set an example of strength and stability."

But Mr. Roosevelt ignored the warning. He went on with his war on business and employment, his experimentation—his quarrels and his chaos. So in 1940 we ended up with 10,000,000 unemployed and it took a war to get jobs under the New Deal.

The record of this Administration at home is one long chapter of failure. But some people still tell us: "We agree that the New Deal is a failure at home, but its foreign policies are very good." Let me ask you: Can an Administration which is so disunited and unsuccessful at home be any better abroad? Can an Administration which is filled with quarrelling and back-biting where we can see it be any better abroad where we cannot see it? Well, the answer to that question seeps through the thick wall of censorship.

For example, on Feb. 11, 1943, while we were seeking vital war materials in Brazil, an article in The New York Times told how that conflict to which I referred between Vice President Wallace and Secretary Jones was being echoed among our representatives in Brazil. It went on to say that dissension among the scores of agency representatives from America had actually, and I am quoting, "led the Americans to participate in departmental rows among agencies of the Brazilian Government itself."

Last year a special committee of United States Senators was sent to our war theatres overseas. Listen to what a Democratic Senator, Richard B. Russell, said in a report to the Senate on Oct. 28, 1943. These are his words: "Our civil agencies abroad are numerous, but too often they are either working at cross purposes or, worse to relate, in some cases have no apparent purpose at all."

Here is a report from the July 30, 1943, issue of The United States News. It says, and I quote it: "In North Africa * * * field agents of half a dozen agencies—the Treasury, BEW, lend-lease, State Department and others—are reported to have brought confusion to the brink of chaos."

Now, why is it that our representation in the vital areas abroad is on the brink of chaos? The answer is the same abroad as it is at home.

In addition to the duly constituted officers of the State Department and the Army and Navy, there are now operating all over the world the following agencies of this Administration:

The FEA, RFC, WFA, OCIAA, OSS, OWI, WSA, WRB, OAPC, OC, OWN, PWRCB, OFAR, FRC and the ACPSAHMWA.

There are more, but I won't read the rest.

It's really serious. Our country has a very important role to play in the world in the years to come. We can never achieve our objectives under an Administration too tired and worn out to bring order out of its own chaos, either at home or abroad.

This nation of ours can be an inspiration to all the world. We can be a steadying influence for freedom and for peace. But first we must have peace in our own Government. We must set our own house in order. That can never be done by a weary and worn-out Administration. It can and must be done by a fresh and vigorous Administration which will restore honesty and competence to our national Government.

These things we pledge to you:

An administration devoted to public service instead of public bickering.

An administration working in harmony with the Congress of the United States.

An administration in which the Cabinet is restored as a responsible instrument of government.

An administration in which you will not have to support three men to do one man's job.

An administration which will root out waste and bring order out of present chaos.

An administration which will give the people of this country value received for the taxes they pay.

An administration made up of the ablest men and women in America who will receive from the President full authority to do their jobs and will be let alone to do them.

An administration free from the influence of Communists and the domination of corrupt big city machines.

An administration in which the Constitution is respected so that the liberties of our people shall again be secure.

An administration with a conscience and a sincere devotion to broad and secure social security.

An administration which will devote itself to the single-minded purpose of jobs and opportunity for all.

My distinguished associate, John W. Bricker, and I are united in our determination to these ends. We know that they can be achieved.

We are united by these objectives and a firm determination, under God, to achieve them. America must never go back to the insecurity, unemployment and chaos of this New Deal. Because she must, America can and will go forward once again.

CHANCELLOR ADOLF HITLER'S DECREE SETTING UP THE GERMAN HOME ARMY

October 18, 1944 [1]

After five years of the most bitter fighting the enemy, due to the defections of all our European Allies, stands on several fronts before, or on, the German borders.

He is straining every nerve to crush our German Reich and to destroy the German people and its social order. His ultimate goal is the elimination of the German race.

Just as in the fall of 1939, we stand again alone on the front against our enemies. In a few years we succeeded then, in a first enormous effort of our German people's strength, in solving the most important military problems, in securing the existence of the Reich, and thus of Europe, for years to come.

While our enemy now believes he is able to start out for the final blow, we are determined to accomplish the second great total effort of our entire people. We must and we shall succeed in breaking the destructive will of our foes, just as in 1939–1941, trusting only in our own power; but more: We will throw them back and keep them away from the Reich until such time when a peace is secured that will guarantee the future of Germany and of her Allies and thus of Europe.

Against the total destructive will of our Jewish international enemies we set the total effort of all Germans.

For the strengthening of the active forces of our Wehrmacht and, especially, for the conduct of an inexorable fight against the foe wherever he wants to enter German soil, I therefore summon all able-bodied German men to a total fighting effort.

I order:

1. In all Gaus (districts) of the Greater German Reich a Volkssturm will be formed from all those men between sixteen and sixty who are able to carry arms. This Home Army will defend the home soil by means and weapons suitable to that purpose.

2. In the various Gaus, the Gauleiter (district leader) will be in charge of the formation and leadership of the German Volkssturm. To carry out this task they will call upon the most capable organizers and leaders of such proved party institutions as the SA (Storm Troops), SS (Elite Guards), NSKK (National Socialist Motor Corps) and the HJ (Hitler Youth).

3. I appoint the Chief of Staff of the SA, Schepmann, inspector for the shooting instruction, and the corps leader of the NSKK, Strauss, inspector for the motor-technical instruction of the Volkssturm.

4. The members of the German Volkssturm, during the time of their service, are soldiers in the meaning of the Army Law.

5. The members of the Volkssturm will continue to be members of the non-professional organizations. However, service in the Volkssturm will take precedence over service in any other organization.

6. The Reich leader of the SS (Heinrich Himmler), as commander of the Reserve Army, is responsible for the military organization, the instruction, the arming and the equipment of the German Volkssturm.

7. The German Volkssturm will join the battle under my orders through

[1] *New York Times.*

the Reich leader of the SS in his capacity as commander of the Reserve Army.

8. As commander of the Reserve Army, Reich Leader of the SS Himmler will issue the detailed military orders; Reich Leader Bormann, on my behalf, will issue the organizational and political directives.

9. The National Socialist party, by making its organization the main fighter in this battle, is fulfilling its noblest duty of honor before the German people.

INVASION COMMUNIQUÉ BY GENERAL DOUGLAS MacARTHUR, ANNOUNCING AMERICAN LANDINGS IN THE PHILIPPINES

October 20, 1944 [1]

In a major amphibious operation we have seized the eastern coast of Leyte Island in the Philippines, 600 miles north of Morotai and 2,500 miles from Milne Bay from whence our offensive started nearly sixteen months ago.

The landing in the Visayas is midway between Luzon and Mindanao and at one stroke splits into two Japanese forces in the Philippines. The enemy expected the attack on Mindanao.

Tacloban was secured with small casualties. The landing was preceded by heavy air and naval bombardment which was devastating in effect. Our ground troops are already extending their hold.

JOINT COMMUNIQUÉ ON THE MOSCOW MEETINGS OF PRIME MINISTER CHURCHILL AND MARSHAL STALIN

October 21, 1944 [2]

Meetings were held at Moscow from Oct. 9 to 18 between Mr. Churchill and Mr. Eden, representing the United Kingdom, and Marshal Stalin and Mr. Molotoff, assisted by their political and military advisers.

The unfolding of military plans agreed upon at Teheran was comprehensively reviewed in the light of recent events and conclusions of the Quebec conference on the war in western Europe. Utmost confidence was expressed in the future progress of Allied operations on all fronts.

Free and intimate exchange of views took place on many political questions of common interest. Important progress was made toward solution of the Polish question, which was closely discussed between the Soviet and British Governments.

They held consultations both with the Prime Minister and Minister for Foreign Affairs of the Polish Government and with the president of the National Council and chairman of the Committee of National Liberation at Lublin.

These discussions have notably narrowed differences and dispelled misconceptions. Conversations are continuing on outstanding points.

[1] *New York Times.*
[2] *Ibid.*

The march of events in southeast Europe was fully considered and agreement was reached on main points in the Bulgarian armistice terms.

The two Governments agreed to pursue a joint policy in Yugoslavia de-designed to concentrate all energies against the retreating Germans and bring about a solution of Yugoslav internal difficulties by a union between the Royal Yugoslav Government and the National Liberation movement.

The right of the Yugoslav people to settle their future Constitution for themselves after the war is of course recognized as inalienable.

The meeting took place with the knowledge and approval of the United States Government, which was represented at the conversations by the United States Ambassador at Moscow, Mr. Averell Harriman, acting in the capacity of observer.

PRESIDENT ROOSEVELT'S CAMPAIGN ADDRESS BEFORE THE FOREIGN POLICY ASSOCIATION IN NEW YORK

October 21, 1944 [1]

Tonight I am speaking as a guest of the Foreign Policy Association—a distinguished organization composed of Americans of all shades of political opinion.

I am going to talk about our American foreign policy.

I am talking without rancor or snap judgment.

I am speaking without losing my temper or losing my head.

When the first World War was ended, I believed—I believe now—that enduring peace in the world has not a chance unless this nation is willing to cooperate in winning it and maintaining it. I thought then—I know now—that we have to back our words with deeds.

A quarter of a century ago we helped to save our freedom but we failed to organize the kind of world in which future generations could live in freedom. Opportunity knocks again. There is no guarantee that it will knock a third time.

Today, Hitler and the Nazis continue the fight—desperately, inch by inch, and may continue to do so all the way to Berlin.

And we have another important engagement in Tokyo. No matter how long or hard the road we must travel, our forces will fight their way there under the leadership of MacArthur and Nimitz.

All of our thinking about foreign policy in this war must be conditioned by the fact that millions of our American boys are today fighting, many thousands of miles from home, for the defense of our country and the perpetuation of our American ideals. And there are still many hard and bitter battles to be fought.

The leaders of this nation have always held that concern for our national security does not end at our borders. President Monroe and every American President following him were prepared to use force, if necessary, to assure the independence of other American nations threatened by aggressors from across the seas.

The principle has not changed, though the world has. Wars are no longer fought from horseback, or from the decks of sailing ships.

[1] White House news release.

It was with recognition of that fact that in 1933 we took, as the basis for our foreign relations, the Good Neighbor policy—the principle of the neighbor who, resolutely respecting himself, equally respects the rights of others.

We and the other American republics have made the Good Neighbor policy real in this hemisphere. It is my conviction that this policy can be, and should be, made universal.

At inter-American conferences, beginning at Montevideo in 1933, and continuing down to date, we have made it clear to this hemisphere that we practice what we preach.

Our action in 1934 with respect to Philippine independence was another step in making good the same philosophy which animated the Good Neighbor policy.

As I said two years ago: "I like to think that the history of the Philippine Islands in the last forty-four years provides in a very real sense a pattern for the future of other small nations and peoples of the world. It is a pattern of what men of good will look forward to in the future."

I cite another early action in the field of foreign policy of which I am proud. That was the recognition in 1933 of Soviet Russia.

For sixteen years before then the American people and the Russian people had no practical means of communicating with each other. We re-established those means. And today we are fighting with the Russians against common foes—and we know that the Russian contribution to victory has been, and will continue to be, gigantic.

However, certain politicians, now very prominent in the Republican Party, have condemned our recognition.

I am impelled to wonder how Russia would have survived against German attack if these same people had had their way.

After the last war—in the political campaign of 1920—the isolationist Old Guard professed to be enthusiastic about international cooperation.

While campaigning for votes in 1920, Senator Harding said that he favored with all his heart an Association of Nations "so organized and so participated in as to make the actual attainment of peace a reasonable possibility."

However, after President Harding's election, the Association of Nations was never heard of again.

One of the leading isolationists who killed international cooperation in 1920 was Senator Hiram Johnson. In the event of Republican victory in the Senate this year—1944—that same Senator Johnson would be Chairman of the Senate Foreign Relations Committee. I know the American voters will bear that in mind.

During the years which followed 1920, the foreign policy of the Republican Administrations was dominated by the heavy hand of isolationism.

Much of the strength of our Navy was scuttled;—and some of the Navy's resources were handed over to friends in private industry—as in the unforgettable case of Teapot Dome.

Tariff walls went higher and higher—blocking international trade.

There was snarling at our former Allies and at the same time encouragement was given to American finance to invest two and one-half billion dollars in Germany, our former enemy.

All petitions that this nation join in the World Court were rejected or ignored.

After this Administration took office, Secretary Hull and I replaced high tariffs with a series of reciprocal trade agreements under a statute of the

Congress. The Republicans opposed these agreements—and tried to stop the extension of the law every three years.

In 1935 I asked the Congress to join the World Court. The Democrats in the Senate voted for it forty-three to twenty. The Republicans voted against it fourteen to nine. Thus we were prevented from obtaining the necessary two-thirds majority.

In 1937 I asked that aggressor nations be quarantined—and for this I was branded by isolationists in and out of public office as an "alarmist" and "war-monger."

From that time on, as you well know, I made clear by repeated messages to the American Congress and by repeated statements to the American people the danger threatening from abroad—and the need of rearming to meet it.

In July, 1939, I tried to obtain a repeal of the Arms Embargo provisions in the Neutrality Law which tied our hands against selling arms to the European democracies for defense against Hitler.

The late Senator Borah told a group, which I called together in the White House, that his own private information from abroad was better than that of the State Department—and that there would be no war in Europe.

And it was made plain to Mr. Hull and me that, because of the isolationist vote, we could not possibly hope to attain the desired revision of the Neutrality Law.

This fact was also made plain to Adolf Hitler. A few weeks later he brutally attacked Poland—and the second World War had begun.

In 1941, this Administration proposed and the Congress passed, in spite of isolationist opposition, the Lend-Lease Law—a practical and dramatic notice to the world that we intended to help those nations resisting aggression.

These days—and I am now speaking of October, 1944—I hear voices on the air attacking me for my "failure" to prepare this nation for this war and to warn the American people of the approaching tragedy.

These same voices were not so very audible five years ago—or even four years ago—giving warning of the grave peril which we then faced.

There have been, and there still are, in the Republican Party distinguished men and women of vision and courage, both in and out of public office, who have vigorously supported our aid to our Allies and all the measures that we took to build up our national defense. And many of these Republicans have rendered magnificent services to our country in this war as members of this Administration. I am happy that one of these distinguished Americans is our great Secretary of War—Henry Stimson.

Let us remember that this very war might have been averted if Mr. Stimson's views had prevailed when, in 1931, the Japanese ruthlessly attacked Manchuria.

The majority of the Republican members of the Congress voted against the Selective Service Law in 1940; they voted against repeal of the Arms Embargo in 1939; they voted against the Lend-Lease Law in 1941 and they voted in August, 1941, against extension of Selective Service—which meant voting against keeping our army together—four months before Pearl Harbor.

I am quoting history to you. I am going by the record. And I am giving you the whole story and not merely a phrase here and half a phrase there picked out of context in such a way that they distort the facts.

I happen to believe that, even in a political campaign, we should all obey that ancient injunction—Thou shalt not bear false witness against thy neighbor.

The question of the men who will formulate and carry out the foreign policy of this country is in issue in this election—very much in issue. It is in issue not in terms of partisan application, but in terms of sober, solemn facts—the facts that are on the record.

If the Republicans were to win control of the Congress in this election, inveterate isolationists would occupy positions of commanding influence and power.

I have already spoken of the ranking Republican member of the Senate Foreign Relations Committee, Senator Hiram Johnson.

One of the most influential members of the Senate Foreign Relations Committee—a man who would also be the chairman of the powerful Senate Committee on Appropriations—is Senator Gerald P. Nye.

In the House of Representatives, the man who is the present leader of the Republicans there, and who undoubtedly would be Speaker, is Joseph W. Martin. He voted against the Repeal of the Arms Embargo, against the Lend-Lease Bill, against the extension of the Selective Service Law, against the arming of merchant ships, and against the Reciprocal Trade Agreements Act and their extensions.

The Chairman of the powerful Committee on Rules would be none other than Hamilton Fish.

There are many others like them in the Congress of the United States— and every one of them is now actively campaigning for the national Republican ticket this year.

Can anyone really suppose that these isolationists have changed their minds about world affairs? Politicians who embraced the policy of isolationism— or who never raised their voices against it in our days of peril—are not reliable custodians of the future of America.

There have been Democrats in the isolationist camp but they have been few and far between, and they have not attained positions of leadership.

And I am proud of the fact that this Administration does not have the support of the isolationist press—and I mean specifically the McCormick-Patterson-Hearst-Gannett press.

The American people have gone through great national debates in the recent critical years. They were soul-searching debates. They reached from every city to every village and to every home.

We debated our principles and our determination to aid those fighting for freedom.

Obviously, we could have come to terms with Hitler, and accepted a minor role in his totalitarian world. We rejected that!

We could have compromised with Japan, and bargained for a place in a Japanese-dominated Asia by selling out the heart's blood of the Chinese people. And we rejected that!

The decision not to bargain with the tyrants rose from the hearts and souls and sinews of the American people. They faced reality; they appraised reality; and they knew what freedom meant.

The power which this nation has attained—the moral, the political, the economic and the military power—has brought to us the responsibility, and with it the opportunity, for leadership in the community of nations. In our own best interest, and in the name of peace and humanity, this nation cannot, must not, and will not shirk that responsibility.

There are some who hope to see a structure of peace, completely set up immediately, with all the apartments assigned to everyone's satisfaction, with the telephones in, the plumbing complete, the heating system and the electric iceboxes functioning perfectly, all furnished with linen and silver—and with the rent pre-paid.

The United Nations have not yet produced such a comfortable dwelling place. But we have achieved a very practical expression of a common purpose on the part of four great nations, who are now united to wage this wage, that they will embark together after the war on a greater and more difficult enterprise—that of waging peace. We will embark on it with all the peace-loving nations of the world—large and small.

Our objective, as I stated ten days ago, is to complete the organization of the United Nations without delay and before hostilities actually cease.

Peace, like war, can succeed only where there is a will to enforce it, and where there is available power to enforce it.

The Council of the United Nations must have the power to act quickly and decisively to keep the peace by force, if necessary. A policeman would not be a very effective policeman if, when he saw a felon break into a house, he had to go to the Town Hall and call a town meeting to issue a warrant before the felon could be arrested.

It is clear that, if the world organization is to have any reality at all, our representative must be endowed in advance by the people themselves, by constitutional means through their representatives in the Congress, with authority to act.

If we do not catch the international felon when we have our hands on him, if we let him get away with his loot because the Town Council has not passed an ordinance authorizing his arrest, then we are not doing our share to prevent another World War. The people of the Nation want their Government to act, and not merely to talk, whenever and wherever there is a threat to world peace.

We cannot attain our great objectives by ourselves. Never again, after cooperating with other nations in a world war to save our way of life, can we wash our hands of maintaining the peace for which we fought.

The Dumbarton Oaks Conference did not spring up overnight. It was called by Secretary Hull and me after years of thought, discussion, preparation and consultation with our Allies. Our State Department did a splendid job in preparing for the Conference and leading it to a successful termination. It was another chapter in the long process of cooperation with other peace-loving nations—beginning with the Atlantic Charter Conference, and continuing through Conferences at Casablanca, Moscow, Cairo, Teheran, Quebec and Washington.

It is my profound conviction that the American people as a whole have a very real understanding of these things.

The American people know that Cordell Hull and I are thoroughly conversant with the Constitution of the United States and know that we cannot commit this Nation to any secret treaties or any secret guarantees which are in violation of that Constitution.

After my return from Teheran, I stated officially that no secret commitments had been made. The issue then is between my veracity and the continuing assertions of those who have no responsibility in the foreign field—or, perhaps I should say, a field foreign to them.

The peace structure which we are building must depend on foundations that go deep into the soil of men's faith and men's hearts—otherwise it is worthless. Only the unflagging will of men can preserve it.

No President of the United States can make the American contribution to preserve the peace without the constant, alert and conscious collaboration of the American people.

Only the determination of the people to use the machinery gives worth to the machinery.

We believe that the American people have already made up their minds on this great issue; and this administration has been able to press forward confidently with its plans.

The very fact that we are now at work on the organization of the peace proves that the great nations are committed to trust in each other. Put this proposition any way you will, it is bound to come out the same way; we either work with the other great nations, or we might some day have to fight them.

The kind of world order which we the peace-loving nations must achieve, must depend essentially on friendly human relations, on acquaintance, on tolerance, on unassailable sincerity and good will and good faith. We have achieved that relationship to a remarkable degree in our dealings with our Allies in this war—as the events of the war have proved.

It is a new thing in human history for Allies to work together, as we have done—so closely, so harmoniously and effectively in the fighting of a war, and—at the same time—in the building of the peace.

If we fail to maintain that relationship in the peace—if we fail to expand it and strengthen it—then there will be no lasting peace.

As for Germany, that tragic nation which has sown the wind and is now reaping the whirlwind—we and our Allies are entirely agreed that we shall not bargain with the Nazi conspirators, or leave them a shred of control—open or secret—of the instruments of government.

We shall not leave them a single element of military power—or of potential military power.

But I should be false to the very foundations of my religious and political convictions, if I should ever relinquish the hope—and even the faith—that in all peoples, without exception, there live some instinct for truth, some attraction toward justice, and some passion for peace—buried as they may be in the German case under a brutal regime.

We bring no charge against the German race, as such; for we cannot believe that God has eternally condemned any race of humanity. For we know in our own land how many good men and women of German ancestry have proved loyal, freedom-loving, peace-loving citizens.

There is going to be stern punishment for all those in Germany directly responsible for this agony of mankind.

The German people are not going to be enslaved—because the United Nations do not traffic in human slavery. But it will be necessary for them to earn their way back into the fellowship of peace-loving and law-abiding nations. And, in their climb up that steep road, we shall certainly see to it that they are not encumbered by having to carry guns. They will be relieved of that burden—we hope, forever.

The task ahead of us will not be easy. Indeed it will be as difficult and complex as any task which has ever faced an American administration.

I will not say to you now, or ever, that we of my party know all the answers. I am certain, for myself, that I do not know how all the unforeseeable difficulties can be met. What I can say to you is this—that I have unlimited faith that the job can be done. And that faith is based on knowledge gained in the arduous, practical and continuing experience of these past eventful years.

I speak to the present generation of Americans with reverent participation in its sorrows and in its hopes. No generation has undergone a greater test, or has met that test with greater heroism and greater wisdom, and no generation has had a more exalted mission.

For this generation must act not only for itself, but as a trustee for all those who fell in the last war—a part of their mission unfulfilled.

It must act also for all who have paid the supreme price in this war—lest their mission, too, be betrayed.

And finally it must act for the generations to come—which must be granted a heritage of peace.

I do not exaggerate that mission. We are not fighting for, and we shall not achieve, Utopia. Indeed, in our own land, the work to be done is never finished. We have yet to realize the full and equal enjoyment of our freedom. So, in embarking on the building of a world fellowship, we have set ourselves to a long and arduous task, which will challenge our patience, our intelligence, our imagination, as well as our faith.

That task requires the judgment of a seasoned and a mature people. And this the American people have become. We shall not again be thwarted in our will to live as a mature nation, confronting limitless horizons. We shall bear our full responsibility, exercise our full influence, and bring our full help and encouragement to all who aspire to peace and freedom.

We now are, and we shall continue to be, strong brothers in the family of mankind—the family of the children of God.

GOVERNOR THOMAS E. DEWEY'S MINNEAPOLIS CAMPAIGN SPEECH

October 24, 1944 [1]

GOVERNOR THYE, MRS. STASSEN, FELLOW AMERICANS:

It's mighty good to come back again to Minnesota, the State of that gallant leader, Comdr. Harold Stassen. As a great Governor and a bold and courageous leader of opinion, he rendered services to his country equaled only by his present service in the United States Navy.

To the people of Minnesota he gave something else very precious and too long absent from our national life. He gave teamwork government, not one-man government.

As a result, when he left for the Navy, there was a first-class man ready and able to fill his shoes. That man has so ably and successfully conducted the affairs of the State that everyone agrees that you will elect by an overwhelming majority my good friend, Edward J. Thye.

The experience of the people of Minnesota under these great Republican Administrations points the way toward the progressive, forward-looking teamwork Government the people will install in the nation next Jan. 20.

I had intended to talk tonight about some of the problems of the American farmer. I have deferred that talk so that I can without delay correct some errors and omissions in the speech of my opponent last Saturday night.

But before doing so, I want here and now to repledge my adherence to the farm program of the Republican platform which was drawn by the farm leaders themselves. The wide fluctuations of prices on farm products that followed the last war will not be tolerated.

A floor will be placed and maintained under farm prices with assurance of

1 *New York Times.*

seal-up crop loans. A proper farm program will be created and so operated that it will leave with the farmers the administration, control and operation of their program without domination or dictation from appointed bureaucrats.

I shall discuss in detail the problems of our farmers on the Farm and Home Hour next Saturday.

On three great objectives, we, the American people, are wholly agreed. We are determined to carry through this war to swift and total victory. We are determined, we are determined that the United States shall take the lead, even before victory, in the establishment of a world organization to prevent future wars. We are determined that our fighting men shall find when they return victorious a vigorous and productive America, the kind of America in which there will be jobs and opportunity for all.

It was for the very purpose of keeping our unity for peace that, last August, I lifted our peace plans wholly out of partisan conflicts—by joining hands with Secretary Hull in work on the proposed organization to prevent future wars.

In my addresses on that subject I have tried to keep it out of partisan debate.

Unhappily, however, last Saturday night my opponent once again sowed among us the seeds of disunity. He made a speech, a very long speech, on foreign affairs. We had hoped he would speak to the American people as grown-ups and tell us what our foreign policy is and where it's going.

We had also hoped to hear some word of cheer about the smaller nations, so important to the conscience of the American people—some word about the fate of Poland, some hope for the people of Italy, some assurance that the Scandinavian countries which have suffered so much, and the other small countries, might soon be admitted to their full partnership in the work for organized peace.

But Mr. Roosevelt gave us none of that. Instead, he sat by the fireside and dreamed of yesterday. He paraded before the American people the ghosts of the long-dead past. He told us a few bits of history, carefully selected, and then said in effect, "Ask me no questions—you are not entitled to know where we are going. Just leave everything to me."

Now, Mr. Roosevelt said in that speech, and I quote him: "I am giving you the whole story." Let's look at the vital events my opponent left out of what he called the whole story.

My opponent says that the heavy hand of isolationism governed our country in the Nineteen Twenties. Does he mean to apply that term to the three great Republican Secretaries of State: Charles Evans Hughes, Frank B. Kellogg and Henry L. Stimson, his own present Secretary of War? If so, I am afraid he has a very convenient memory.

It was my opponent himself who said on the day he took office, the 4th of March, 1933, and I now quote his words: "The world picture was an image of substantial peace. International consultation and widespread hope for the bettering of relations between the nations gave to all of us a reasonable expectation (he continued) that the barriers to mutual confidence, to increased trade and to the peaceful settlement of disputes could be progressively removed."

That statement about 1933 was the truth. My opponent did inherit a progressively improving structure of international cooperation from the Disarmament Conference of 1921, led by Charles Evans Hughes, through the great Kellogg-Briand Pact of 1928, in which most of the nations of the world renounced war as an instrument of national policy.

But it was on March 5, 1933, that Adolf Hitler made himself dictator of Germany. That was a fateful year. Germany walked out of the Disarmament Conference. Germany and Japan quit the League of Nations. And tragically, under the leadership of Mr. Roosevelt, America did her own bit toward the breakdown of international cooperation for peace.

Mr. Roosevelt now speaks fondly of the League of Nations. But it was he who in 1933 said this of the League, and I quote his words: "We are not members and we do not contemplate membership."

He rejected the policy of collaboration with the League which had previously been established, and in 1933 the American representative at Geneva was instructed "that we desire to follow our course independently."

Here are two parts of the story my opponent conveniently forgot. Now let's look at some more.

It was also in 1935 that, instead of the policy of consultation with other nations, an overwhelmingly Democratic Congress adopted the fruitless Neutrality Act and the President signed it.

It was in 1933 that we really had our last chance to bring order out of the chaos of international money exchange and trade. The London Economic Conference had been labored over for months by Republican Secretary of State Henry L. Stimson. Yet, as one of his early acts as President, Mr. Roosevelt deliberately scuttled that conference. That was the most completely isolationist action ever taken by an American President in our 150 years of history. It was that tragic event that led at least one European statesman to say there was nothing then ahead in Europe but war.

Year after year, our chiefs of staff reported on the utterly impoverished and pitifully small manpower of our Army. Year after year, the Budget Bureau, which is under the personal direction of the President, cut down the amounts requested. It was right in the fall of 1939, after the second World War had actually begun that Mr. Roosevelt's Budget Bureau cut out 550 million dollars of amounts certified by the Army for critical and essential items.

It was in January, 1940, that Mr. Roosevelt told the Congress that $1,800,-000,000 for national defense was in his judgment and I quote him, "a sufficient amount for the coming year," although he then admitted that it was "far less than many experts on national defense think should be spent."

It was in that month that I publicly called for a two-ocean navy, a concept which Mr. Roosevelt still later called "just plain dumb."

It was in those terrifying days of the Nazi blitz, in May of 1940, that he told us we should not become "discombobolated" (per Dewey pronunciation). Then, with France about to fall, he publicly announced on June 4, 1940, that he saw no reason for Congress to stay in session. It was an election year— so in that hour of national peril he said that a continued session of Congress would serve no useful end except, sarcastically, the laudable purpose of making speeches.

It was that American Congress which refused at that historic time to go home. It stayed in Washington and went to work.

It was that Congress which then passed the National Selective Service Act, sponsored by a Republican Congressman and an anti-New Deal Democrat. It was that Congress which stayed after it had been told to go home and ran the appropriations and authorizations for national defense up to twelve billion dollars, and it was that Congress that authorized our two-ocean Navy.

Those are a few more of the chapters of the whole story—all of which my opponent conveniently forgets. But the American people will not forget them when they go to the polls in November.

Now in his speech of last Saturday night, my opponent did remember the Washington Arms Conference by which, for the first time, we succeeded in restricting Japan to an inferior naval relationship of 5-5-3. But he forgot that he was supposed to be telling the whole story. He complained that we "scuttled" part of the strength of our Navy. But that's not what he said at the time. Then, in a magazine article, Mr. Roosevelt asked America to trust Japan and complained, and I now quote his words, "of the delay in the scrapping of United States ships as provided for and pledged in accordance with the treaty," close quote. What he also forgot last Saturday night was that as late as 1934, he called the Washington Arms Conference "a milestone in civilization."

How election times do change men's memories! If we're going to learn our lesson for future use, we have to keep the record straight.

It was in that year, 1934, that Japan served notice of termination of the limitation treaty which kept her navy inferior to ours. Yet it was in the first two administrations of the New Deal that this country sent 10,000,000 tons of scrap iron and steel to Japan, unchecked by my opponent until Oct. 16, 1940. The weight of that scrap iron alone was ten times the tonnage of the whole Japanese Navy.

Mr. Roosevelt said last Saturday night that we could have "compromised" with Japan, and I quote him, "by selling out the heart's blood of the Chinese people." Well, let's see what we did.

In addition to scrap iron, he permitted the shipment to Japan of as much as three million barrels a month of oil, the heart's blood of war, for use against China and for storage against America. That oil continued to flow until July of 1941, four months before Pearl Harbor.

Let those who claim to have exercised great foresight remember these lessons in history. And let us as a nation never forget them.

Now, my opponent in his speech actually blamed a handful of Republicans for our failure to go into the World Court in 1935.

That was when Mr. Roosevelt was still on the crest of his leadership, with three-quarters of the United States Senate Democratic. And even with the help of nine Republicans he still couldn't muster a two-thirds vote. Since then he has warred with Congress at every major turn. He has insulted its integrity publicly and its members have learned the bitter lesson that legislation asked for one purpose is twisted to another. This is a sad foundation on which to build the teamwork necessary for the future. And that's why it's time for a change.

Three times in recent months I have discussed at length what I consider the sound and successful program for lasting peace. I have emphasized that this work must be pressed forward without waiting for the end of the war. I have emphasized, as my opponent has not, that, and I am quoting, "we must make certain that our participation in the world organization is not subjected to reservations that would nullify the power of that organization to maintain peace and to halt future aggressions."

That means, of course, that it must not be subject to a reservation that would require our representative to return to Congress for authority every time he had to make a decision. Obviously Congress, and only Congress, has the constitutional power to determine what quota of force it will make available and what discretion it will give our representative to use that force.

I have not the slightest doubt that a Congress which is working in partnership with the President will achieve the result we all consider essential and grant adequate power for swift action to the American representative.

But those who would attempt to ride roughshod over the Congress and to dictate the course it should follow before it has even been acquainted with the facts are trifling with the hope of the world. They are deliberately, in my judgment, seeking to precipitate a hardening of minds. If this stubborn course is pursued, it can only result once again as in 1919, in a disastrous conflict between the President and the Congress. To that I will never be a party.

I deeply believe that we cannot build an understanding and a purpose for our future if we are to continue to have abuse from the President of the United States of the members of the Congress of the United States.

None of us has been all-wise in these matters. Individual Congressmen and Senators of both parties have made mistakes. Individual citizens have made mistakes. Every single one of us—both in and out of office—has made mistakes.

I'm not interested in the mistakes of the past by any individual in either party. I am interested—the people of this country are interested—in what the next Congress will do. We must not find ourselves after next Jan. 20, stalled on dead center as a result of this series of recriminations between my opponent and the Congress. He's already demonstrated that he cannot work with a Congress of his own party. It is unmistakably clear that our future demands that we have a new Chief Executive who can, and will, work with the new Republican Congress. We must be able to go forward harmoniously and effectively if we are to meet the mighty problems of peace.

Now who will lead the next Senate and the next House? Well, here are the acknowledged leaders today:

Wallace H. White, Jr. of Maine, Acting Minority Leader of the United States Senate.

Arthur Vandenberg of Michigan, chairman of the Senate Republican Conference Committee.

Warren R. Austin of Vermont, chairman of the Republican National Convention Foreign Relations Sub-committee.

Robert A. Taft of Ohio, chairman of the Republican Steering Committee.

Kenneth Wherry of Nebraska, Republican Senate whip.

Joseph W. Martin, Jr. of Massachusetts, the minority leader of the House of Representatives.

I hold in my hand a telegram from each of these gentlemen. Let me read you the wire from Senator Wallace H. White, the acting minority leader of the United States Senate. It reads:

"Your statements in support of a post-war organization and your vigorous leadership in developing and clarifying our country's foreign policy have my respect and approval. Your views will be accorded enthusiastic and loyal support by Republicans of the Senate and by the American people."

Now let me read a wire from Joseph W. Martin, whom my opponent last Saturday night, by the way, practically conceded will be the next Speaker of the House of Representatives. That wire reads:

"When elected President, you can count on enthusiastic support of the Republican House of Representatives to carry into effect your plan for United States leadership in organization to cooperate with other nations for world peace. I shall personally be very pleased to follow your splendid leadership in bringing this plan into reality."

The rest of these messages are in identical vein and I have made them public tonight. Here's the kind of unity we need in this country—this is the kind of unity we need so desperately in the years ahead.

From the beginning of this campaign I have insisted that organization for world peace can and must be a bipartisan effort. I shall continue to insist on that approach.

The avoidance of future wars is too important to be in the sole custody of any one man, of any one group or of any one party. It's too important to hang by the slender thread of one man's continuity in office.

Only with the unity now demonstrated by the telegrams I have read to you tonight from the next leaders of the Congress and the Senate can we achieve the kind of action necessary to preserve peace. Only with a Chief Executive who will work with the Congress in harmony can our future be assured.

Our work for future peace must and will become on Jan. 20 next a bipartisan effort, bringing to it the ablest men in our country from both political parties.

That sense of unity can also be brought to our domestic affairs. With a Congress and a President who will cooperate with each other, we need not fear the peace. For agriculture, for labor, and for business we have an unlimited future before us if we will seize it and unite to bring it about.

Certain this, this is the least we can do in the name of those who are fighting today to make that future possible. With God's help we shall unite America and go forward once again.

PRIME MINISTER WINSTON CHURCHILL'S SPEECH IN COMMONS ON THE WAR

October 27, 1944 [1]

The present stage of the war is dour and hard, and the fighting must be expected on all fronts to increase in scale and in intensity. We believe that we are in the last lap, but this is a race in which failure to exert the fullest effort to the end may protract that end to periods almost unendurable to those who now have the race in their hands after struggling so far. The enemy has two hopes. The first is that by lengthening the struggle he may wear down our resolution; the second, and more important, hope is that division will arise between the three great Powers by whom he is assailed, and whose continued union spells his doom. His hope is that there will be some rift in this alliance; that the Russians may go this way, the British and Americans that; that quarrels may arise about the Balkans or the Baltic, about Poland or Hungary, which he hopes will impair the union of our councils and, consequently, the symmetry and momentum of our converging advance. There is the enemy's great hope. It is to deprive that hope of all foundation and reality that our efforts must ceaselessly be bent.

You would not expect three great Powers, so differently circumstanced as Britain, the United States and Soviet Russia, not to have many different views about the treatment of the various and numerous countries into which their victorious arms have carried them. The marvel is that all has hitherto been kept so solid, sure and sound between us all. But this process does not arise of itself. It needs constant care and attention. Moreover, there are those problems of distance, occasion and personalities which I have so often mentioned to the House, and which make it extremely difficult to bring the

[1] Parliamentary Debates.

heads of the three principal Allies together in one place at one time. I have, therefore, not hesitated to travel from court to court like a wandering minstrel, always with the same songs to sing—or the same set of songs.

The meeting at Moscow was the sequel to Quebec. At Quebec, the President and I felt very much the absence of Russia. At Moscow, Marshal Stalin and I were deeply conscious that the President was not with us, although in this case the American observer, Mr. Averell Harriman, the accomplished Ambassador of the United States, made us feel at all times the presence of the great Republic. There was a special reason for our dual conference at Quebec. The British and American fighting forces are intermingled in the lines of battle as fighting men of two countries have never been intermingled before. Fighting men have never before mingled so closely and so easily. We must meet; we must discuss.

As to Russia, Great Britain has many problems in Eastern Europe to solve in common with Russia, and practical issues arise on all these from day to day. We must disperse misunderstandings and forestall them before they occur. We must have practical policies to deal with day to day emergencies, and, of course, we must carry with us at every stage the Government of the United States. I am satisfied that the results achieved on this occasion at Moscow have been highly satisfactory. But I am quite sure that no final result can be attained until the heads of the three Governments have met again together, as I earnestly trust they may do before this year is at its end. After all, the future of the world depends upon the united action in the next few years of our three countries. Other countries may be associated, but the future depends upon the union of the three most powerful Allies. If that fails, all fails: if that succeeds, a broad future for all nations may be assured. I am very glad to inform the House that our relations with Soviet Russia were never more close, intimate and cordial than they are at the present time. Never before have we been able to reach so high a degree of frank and friendly discussions of the most delicate and often potentially vexatious topics as we have done at this meeting from which I have returned, and about which I thought it would be only respectful to the House to make some short statement.

Where we could not agree, we understood the grounds for each other's disagreement and each other's point of view, but, over a very wide area, an astonishingly wide area considering all the different angles from which we approached these topics, we found ourselves in full agreement. Of course, it goes without saying that we were united in prosecuting the war against Hitlerite Germany to absolute victory, and in using the last and every resource of our strength and energy in combination for that purpose. Let all hope die in German breasts that there will be the slightest division or weakening among the forces which are closing in upon them, and will crush the life out of their resistance.

Upon the tangled question of the Balkans, where there are Black Sea interests and Mediterranean interests to be considered, we were able to reach complete agreement. I do not feel that there is any immediate danger of our combined war effort being weakened by divergencies of policy or of doctrine in Greece, Rumania, Bulgaria, Yugoslavia, and, beyond the Balkans, Hungary. We have reached a very good working agreement about all these countries, singly and in combination, with the object of concentrating all their efforts, and concerting them with ours against the common foe, and of providing, as far as possible, for a peaceful settlement after the war is over. We are, in fact, acting jointly, Russia and Britain, in our relations with both the Royal

Yugoslav Government headed by Dr. Subasic and with Marshal Tito, and we have invited them to come together for the common cause, as they had already agreed to do at the conference which I held with them both at Naples. How much better that there should be a joint Anglo-Russian policy in this disturbed and very complex area, than that one side should be backing one set of ideas, and the other the opposite. That is a most pernicious state of affairs to grow up in any country, as it may easily spread to corresponding differences between the great Powers themselves.

Our earnest hope and bounden duty is so to conduct our policy that these small countries do not slip from the great war effort into internal feuds of extreme bitterness. We have, as I say, invited them to come together and form a united government for the purpose of carrying on the war until the country itself can pronounce. All this is, of course, only a guide for the handling of matters from day to day, but it is so much easier to enter into arrangements by conversation than by telegram and diplomatic correspondence, however carefully phrased and however lengthily expressed, or however patiently the discussions may be conducted. Face to face, difficulties which appear really insuperable at a distance are very often removed altogether from our path. But these workaday arrangements must be looked upon as a temporary expedient to meet the emergency, and all permanent arrangements await the presence of the United States, who have been kept constantly informed of what was going forward. Everything will eventually come to review at some future conference, or at an armistice or peace table.

There were, of course, a good many serious military questions discussed. I had with me the Chief of the Imperial General Staff, General Ismay and other officers acquainted with the conduct of the whole of our military affairs and strategy, and we also had the advantage of the assistance, not only of the American Ambassador, but of the very able United States technical representative, General Deane. All these discussions were part of the process of carrying out and following up the great decisions taken nearly a year ago at Teheran, which, I think, without exaggeration may be said to have altered the face of the world war. But, naturally, I could not say anything about these discussions or decisions, except that I found them very good, and, indeed the best that could be devised to lift the cruel scourge of war from Europe at the earliest possible moment.

The most urgent and burning question was of course that of Poland, and, here again, I speak words of hope, of hope reinforced by confidence. To abandon hope in this matter would, indeed, be to surrender to despair. In this sphere there are two crucial issues. The first is the question of the Eastern frontier of Poland with Russia and the Curzon Line, as it is called, and the new territories to be added to Poland in the north and in the west. That is the first issue. The second is the relation of the Polish Government with the Lublin National Liberation Committee. On these two points, apart from many subsidiary and ancillary points, we held a series of conferences with both parties. We saw them together and we saw them separately, and, of course, we were in constant discussion with the heads of the Soviet Government. I had several very long talks with Marshal Stalin, and the Foreign Secretary was every day working on these and cognate matters with Mr. Molotov. Two or three times we all four met together without anyone else but the interpreters being present.

I wish I could tell the House that we had reached a solution of these problems. It is certainly not for want of trying. I am quite sure, however, that we have got a great deal nearer to the solution of both. I hope Mr. Mikolajczyk will soon return to Moscow, and it will be a great disappointment to all the sincere friends of Poland, if a good arrangement cannot be made which will enable him to form a Polish Government on Polish soil—a Government recognised by all the great Powers concerned, and indeed by all those Governments of the United Nations which now recognise only the Polish Government in London. Although I do not underrate the difficulties which remain, it is a comfort to feel that Britain and Soviet Russia, and I do not doubt the United States, are all firmly agreed in the re-creation of a strong, free, independent, sovereign Poland loyal to the Allies and friendly to her great neighbour and liberator, Russia. Speaking more particularly for His Majesty's Government it is our persevering and constant aim that the Polish people, after their suffering and vicissitudes, shall find in Europe an abiding home and resting place, which, though it may not entirely coincide or correspond with the pre-war frontiers of Poland, will, nevertheless, be adequate for the needs of the Polish nation and not inferior in character and quality, taking the picture as a whole, to what they previously possessed.

These are critical days and it would be a great pity if time were wasted in indecision or in protracted negotiation. If the Polish Government had taken the advice we tended them at the beginning of this year, the additional complication produced by the formation of the Polish National Committee of Liberation at Lublin would not have arisen, and anything like a prolonged delay in the settlement can only have the effect of increasing the division between Poles in Poland and also of hampering the common action which the Poles, the Russians and the rest of the Allies are taking against Germany. Therefore, as I say, I hope that no time will be lost in continuing these discussions and pressing them to an effective conclusion.

I told the House on 28th September of my hope that the re-organisation of the French Consultative Assembly on a more representative basis would make it possible for His Majesty's Government, at an early date, to recognise the then French Administration as the Provisional Government of France. The Assembly has now, in fact, been enlarged and strengthened by the addition of many fresh representatives of both the resistance organisations in France, and the old Parliamentary groups. It constitutes as representative a body as it is possible to bring together in the difficult circumstances obtaining to-day in France, and it will be holding its first session in Paris in a few days' time. This development was closely followed by a further step towards the restoration of normal conditions of government in France. The Civil Affairs Agreement concluded by France with Great Britain and the United States last August, after long and patient exertions by the Foreign Secretary, provided for the division of the country into a Forward Zone, in which the supreme Allied Commander would exercise certain over-riding powers of control considered necessary for the conduct of military operations, and an Interior Zone, where the conduct of, and responsibility for, the administration would be entirely a matter for the French authorities. For obvious reasons at the beginning, when for those anxious weeks we stood with our backs to the sea a few miles from the beaches, the whole of France had to be in the forward zone; but as the tide of battle moved up to and beyond France's eastern frontier, General Eisenhower, working in the closest and most friendly co-operation with the French civil and military authorities, found he could safely hand over his special powers, except in the areas immediately behind the battle zone, and he felt that these authorities had shown themselves fully capable of undertaking the grave responsibilities which fall to the government of any country on which a vast modern army on active service has to be based.

The French administration was, accordingly, able to announce on 20th October that, with the concurrence of the Allied High Command, it had established an Interior Zone comprising the larger part of France, including Paris. This marked the final stage of transformation of the Committee of National Liberation into a Government, exercising provisionally all the powers of the Government of France, and a Government accepted as such by the people of France in their entirety. The way was thus clear for the formal recognition of the Committee as the Provisional Government, and His Majesty's Ambassador in Paris was accordingly instructed, on 23rd October, to inform the French Minister for Foreign Affairs of the decision of His Majesty's Government in the United Kingdom, in the Union of South Africa and in New Zealand to accord such recognition. A similar communication was made by the Canadian Government, through the Canadian Ambassador in Paris, and by the Commonwealth Government, through the French representative at Canberra. The United States and Soviet Governments, with whom we had acted throughout in the closest agreements and concert in this matter, were taking similar and simultaneous action.

Some critics have asked: Why should this step not have been taken earlier? The reason is very simple. The British and American Armies had something to do with the liberation of France, and the British and United States Governments had, therefore, a responsibility at this particular moment for making sure that the French Government, emerging in part from their military action, would be acceptable to France as a whole, and would not appear to be imposed upon the country from without. It is not for us to choose the Government or rulers of France but at this particular juncture, for that very reason, we had a very special responsibility. I have been myself for some weeks past satisfied not only that the present French Government, under General de Gaulle, commands the full assent of the vast majority of the French people, but that it is the only Government which can possibly discharge the very heavy burdens which are being cast upon it, and the only Government which can enable France to gather its strength in the interval which must elapse before the constitutional and parliamentary processes, which it has declared its purpose to reinstate, can again resume their normal functions. I also made it clear in my speech on 2nd August, that France can by no means be excluded from the discussions of the principal Allies dealing with the problems of the Rhine and of Germany. This act of recognition, may, therefore, be regarded as a symbol of France's re-emergence from four dark years of terrible and woeful experience and as heralding a period in which she will resume her rightful and historic role upon the world's stage.

As I said these remarks would be in the nature of a supplement to the statement I made some time ago. I have but one other subject to mention and it is one which will cause universal rejoicing. I mean the liberation of Athens and a large part of Greece. I was able, when I visited Italy six or seven weeks ago, to arrange with General Wilson, after very careful discussion, for the necessary measures to be set in train which would enable the Royal Greek Government of Monsieur Papandreou to return to Athens at the earliest possible moment, and as a preliminary to this, I advised that Government to move from Cairo to Caserta, where they would be in the closest touch with the Commander-in-Chief. I think the arrangements were extremely well made by General Wilson, and to him we entrusted the watching for the exact moment to intervene. He found that moment with very happy discretion, so that hardly any loss of life occurred and no damage has been done to the immortal capital, which is dear to the hearts of so many nations throughout the world.

Vivid and moving accounts have appeared in the Press of the decisive events which have recently taken place, and of the fervid welcome which our Forces received throughout Greece, and above all in Athens. When we were driven out of Greece in 1941 amid so much bloodshed and disaster, with the loss of over 30,000 men, we promised to return, and the Greek people never lost faith in that promise, nor abandoned their belief in final victory. Sir, we have returned and our pledge has been redeemed. The lawful Greek Government sits in Athens. Very soon the Greek brigade which has distinguished itself in the fighting at Rimini on the Italian front, helping to drive the Germans out of Italy, will return with honour to its native land. The tide of war has rolled far to the northward in Greece. Behind the British troops, the organisation of U.N.R.R.A., in which the United States plays so great a part, is already moving to the scene. Ships having been loaded for many weeks past, and the much-needed supplies of food for the sorely-tried Greek population will soon be in process of active distribution if, indeed, that process has not begun already. We are going to do our best to assist in stabilising the Greek currency which has been a special mark of sabotage by the Germans, and highly competent officials from the Treasury are already on their way to Athens, where the Foreign Secretary is at the present time, and where he is remaining, according to my latest information, until he can confer with them and with the Greek Government on this subject.

We are doing our best in every way to bring Greece back to normal. Though, of course, we are actively aiding the Greeks in every sphere to recover from the horrible injuries inflicted on them by the Germans, and are thus adding another chapter to the story of the friendship between our countries, we do not seek to become the arbiters of their affairs. Our wish and policy is that when normal conditions of tranquillity have been restored throughout the country, the Greek people shall make, in perfect freedom, their decision as to the form of Government under which they desire to live. Pending such a decision, we naturally preserve our relations with the Greek Royal House and with the existing constitutional Government, and we regard them as the authority to whom we are bound by the alliance made at the time of the attack upon Greece in 1941. Meanwhile, I appeal to all Greeks of every party and of every group—and there is no lack of parties or of groups—to set national unity above all other causes, to cleanse their country of the remaining German forces, to destroy and capture the last of the miscreants who have treated them with indescribable cruelty, and, finally, to join hands to rebuild the strength and reduce the suffering of their famous and cherished land.

MAJOR LLOYD (Renfrew, Eastern): I have no desire to take up the time of the House, but I would be grateful to the Prime Minister if he could see his way to answer two or three questions, which, in my judgment, very many people in this country would be grateful to have answered. I realise—none better—the extremely delicate nature of the subject of Russo-Polish relations, and I do not want, and I do not think anybody in the House wants, to say one word that could possibly do anything but smooth those relations. Might I ask the Prime Minister is it still the Government's policy and wish, as previously expressed on several occasions, to defer the decisions on all territorial and boundary questions between Russia and Poland until after the cessation of hostilities? Could he also say whether the British Government is in general sympathy with the desire of the Polish Government for specific and joint guarantees from Great Britain and the other great Powers—Russia and the United States of America—in support of Poland's continued independence and completely sovereign State after the war? I would much appreciate an answer from the Prime Minister, and I assure him that the questions are not asked in any sense of causing awkwardness or controversy.

THE PRIME MINISTER: With regard to the first question, we should welcome a solution between the parties themselves, an agreement that would bring the whole matter to the Peace Conference in a form most helpful and favourable to all concerned, and also tide us over the difficult and potentially tragic period through which we are passing. With regard to the guarantee of the three Great Powers, it is certainly to be hoped that the three great Powers will guarantee the independent sovereign free Poland which will emerge from any arrangement which is made now, and ratified at the Peace Conference. As far as the Soviet Government is concerned, I understand that that will be their fixed intention, and I have not hesitated to say that His Majesty's Government will certainly conform to and themselves join in such a guarantee. It is not for me to speak of the affairs of the United States of America.

PRESIDENT ROOSEVELT'S NAVY DAY CAMPAIGN SPEECH IN SHIBE PARK, PHILADELPHIA

October 27, 1944 [1]

Today is the anniversary of the birth of a great fighting American— Theodore Roosevelt.

This day is celebrated every year as Navy Day—and I think Theodore Roosevelt would be happy and proud to know that our American fleet now is greater than all the navies of the world put together.

And when I say all the navies, I am including what was—until three days ago—the Japanese fleet.

Since Navy Day a year ago our armed forces—Army, Navy and Air Forces—have participated in no fewer than twenty-seven different D-Days —twenty-seven different landings in force on enemy-held shores.

Every one of these landings has been an incredibly complicated and hazardous undertaking, requiring months of most careful planning, flawless coordination, and split-second timing in execution. The larger operations have required hundreds of warships, thousands of smaller craft, thousands of airplanes and hundreds of thousands of men.

And every one of these twenty-seven D-Days has been a triumphant success.

It is a remarkable achievement that within less than five months we have been able to carry out major offensive operations in both Europe and the Philippines—thirteen thousands miles apart from each other.

And speaking of the glorious operations in the Philippines—I wonder— whatever became of the suggestion made a few weeks ago, that I had failed for political reasons to send enough forces or supplies to General MacArthur?

I realize that, in this political campaign, it is considered by some to be very impolite to mention the fact that there is a war on.

[1] White House news release.

But the war is still on and eleven million American fighting men know it —and so do their families. And in that war I bear a responsibility which I can never shirk and never, for one instant, forget.

For the Constitution of the United States says—and I hope you will pardon me if I quote it correctly—"The President shall be Commander in Chief of the Army and Navy of the United States."

I am not supposed to mention that, either.

But somehow or other, it seems to me that this is a matter of considerable importance to the American people.

It was due to no accident and no oversight that the framers of our Constitution put the command of our armed forces under civilian authority.

It is the duty of the Commander in Chief to appoint the Secretaries of War and Navy and the Chiefs of Staff—and I feel called upon to offer no apologies for my selection of Henry Stimson, the late Frank Knox and James Forrestal, or of Admiral Leahy, General Marshall, Admiral King and General Arnold.

Furthermore, the Commander in Chief has final responsibility for determining how our resources shall be distributed as between our land forces, sea forces and air forces, and as among the different theatres of operations, and also what portion shall be turned over to our Allies.

Our teamwork with our Allies in this war has involved innumerable intricate problems which could be settled only around the conference table by those who had final authority.

The other day, I am told, a prominent Republican orator stated that "there are not five civilians in the entire national government who have the confidence and respect of the American people."

In fact, he described your present Administration as "the most spectacular collection of incompetent people who ever held public office."

Well, now—that is pretty serious. The only conclusion to be drawn from that is that we are losing the war. If so, that will be news to most of us— and it will certainly be news to the Nazis and the Japs.

The record will show that from almost the first minute of my Administration I started to rebuild the United States Navy which had been whittled down during previous Administrations. What the Navy suffered from conspicuously during these Republican Administrations was a drastic false economy which not only scrapped ships but even prevented adequate target practice, adequate maneuvers and adequate supplies. It had reached the point that on some vessels the crews "chipped in" to buy their own brass polish to keep the bright work shining.

The record will show that—when we were attacked at Pearl Harbor—we had already made tremendous progress toward building the greatest war machine the world has ever known.

Take, for example, the ships of Admiral Halsey's powerful Third Fleet which has just given the Japanese Navy the worst licking in its history.

Every battleship in that Fleet was authorized between 1933 and 1938. Construction had begun on all of those battleships by September, 1940— well over a year before Pearl Harbor.

All but two of the great force of cruisers in Admiral Halsey's Fleet were authorized between 1933 and 1940; and construction on all but one of them had begun before Pearl Harbor.

All of the aircraft carriers in that Fleet had been authorized by the present Administration before Pearl Harbor, and half of them were actually under construction before Pearl Harbor.

There is the answer—once and for all—to a Republican candidate who said that this Administration had made "absolutely no military preparation for the events it now claims it foresaw."

Less than three months before Hitler launched his murderous assault against Poland, the Republicans in the House of Representatives voted 144 to 8 in favor of cutting the appropriations for the Army Air Corps.

I often think how Hitler and Hirohito must have laughed in those days. They are not laughing now.

In the spring of 1940, as you well remember, I called for a production of 50,000 airplanes—and that same Republican candidate spoke scornfully of such a proposal, calling it a "publicity stunt," and saying it would take four years to reach such a goal.

Nevertheless, we have since then produced more than 240,000 warplanes. We have attained a production rate of more than 9,000 per month—more than 100,000 per year.

We have trained more than 850,000 pilots, navigators, bombardiers, aerial gunners and other aerial crew members.

I admit these figures seem fantastic—but such results were not impossible for those who had real faith in America.

In 1940, we had a regular Army of approximately 250,000, and a reserve, including the National Guard, of 350,000.

Today, we have 8,000,000 in our Army, including 126,000 women. More than half of our Army is overseas.

Our Navy in 1940 had 369 combat ships and 189,000 men.

Today, we have more than 1,500 combat vessels, supported by an armada of 50,000 other ships, including landing craft. We have more than 3,500,000 men in our Navy and over 100,000 women.

Never before in history have the soldiers and sailors of any nation gone into battle so thoroughly trained, so thoroughly equipped, so well fed, and so thoroughly supported as the American soldiers and sailors fighting today in Europe, Asia and the Pacific.

In his report to the Secretary of War, in 1943, General Marshall wrote: "In matters of personnel, military intelligence, training, supply and preparation of war plans, sound principles and policies had been established in the preparation for just such an emergency as arose."

After we were attacked by the Japanese, and Hitler and Mussolini declared war on us, some people urged that we go on the defensive—that we pull in our fleet to guard this continent—that we send no forces overseas.

That policy was rejected. In my first war message to the Congress, a month after Pearl Harbor, I said:

"We cannot wage this war in a defensive spirit. As our power and our resources are fully mobilized, we shall carry the attack against the enemy— we shall hit him and hit him again wherever and whenever we can reach him. We must keep him far from our shores, for we intend to bring this battle to him on his own home grounds."

And that is the policy we have successfully followed.

In our over-all strategy, we planned our war effort in three phases:

The first phase could be called "plugging the line"—which meant stopping the Germans and Japs from expanding their conquests to such key points as Australia and the British Isles—for England then was still very vulnerable to invasion.

Within a month after Pearl Harbor, American expeditionary forces were moving across the Pacific to Australia and across the Atlantic to Northern

Ireland. Our air forces went to the Southwest Pacific, to India, China, the Middle East and Great Britain.

In this first phase we furnished arms to the British which helped them to stop the Germans in Egypt—and arms to the Russians which helped them to stop the Germans at Stalingrad.

And our own growing forces stopped the Japanese in the Coral Sea and at Midway.

The second phase was the shattering of the enemy's outer defenses—establishing bases from which to launch our major attacks.

This phase began with the operations in New Guinea, the Solomons and North Africa. It continued through all of the operations in the Marshalls, Gilberts, Aleutians, Marianas, Carolines and now the Philippines—and in Europe with the landings in Sicily and Italy and finally in France.

The war in Europe has reached the final, decisive phase—the attack on Germany itself.

But we have much longer and much farther to go in the war against Japan.

All of these operations had to be planned far in advance—and that does not mean merely drawing arrows on maps. It has meant planning in terms of precisely how many men will be needed, and how many ships—warships, cargo ships, landing craft—how many bombers and how many fighter planes —and how much equipment and what types of equipment down to the last cartridge. And it has meant getting all of them to the right place at the right moment.

It has meant establishing for our Army and Navy supply lines extending over 56,000 miles—more than twice the circumference of this earth. It has meant establishing the lines of the Aid Transport Command—150,000 miles of air supply systems running regularly.

It has meant moving supplies along these lines at the rate of almost 3,000,000 long tons a month, requiring 577 cargo ships to leave our ports with supplies every month. It has meant moving more than 14,000,000 barrels of gasoline and oil a month, requiring 156 tanker sailings a month. And those ships and those tankers were all built in American shipyards.

The production necessary to equip and maintain our vast force of fighting men on global battlefronts is without parallel.

I need not repeat the figures. The facts speak for themselves. They speak with the thunder of tens of thousands of guns on battlefields all over the world. They speak with the roar of more than 1,000,000 tons of bombs dropped by our air forces.

The whole story of our vast effort in this war has been a story of incredible achievement—the story of the job that has been done by an Administration which, I am told, is "old and tired and quarrelsome."

And while we have been doing that job we have constantly investigated and publicized our whole management of the war effort. I call particular attention to the thorough and painstaking and completely non-partisan work of that committee of the Senate which was organized and presided over by Harry Truman.

The Truman Committee has done a job which will live in history as an example of honest, efficient government at work.

There is one thing I want to say—and it cannot be told in figures.

I want to express the conviction that the greatest of our past American heroes—the heroes of Bunker Hill and Gettysburg and San Juan Hill and Manila Bay and the Argonne—would consider themselves honored to be associated with our fighting men of today.

Those boys hate war.

The average American citizen is not a soldier by choice.

But our boys have proved they can take on the best that our militaristic enemies can put forward—they can take them on and beat them. And we must never forget that our Allies, by resisting the aggressors to the last ditch, gave us time to train our men and prepare their equipment before they went into battle.

The quality of our American fighting men is not all a matter of training or of equipment or of organization. It is essentially a matter of spirit. That spirit is expressive of their faith in America.

The most important fact in our national life today is the essential fact of 11,000,000 young Americans in our Armed forces—more than half of them overseas.

When you multiply that 11,000,000 by their families and their friends, you have the whole American people personally involved in this war—a war which was forced upon us, a war which we did our utmost to avoid, a war which came upon us as inevitably as an earthquake.

I think particularly of the mothers and wives and sisters and sweethearts of the men in service. There are great numbers of these gallant women who do not have the satisfaction and distraction of jobs in war plants. They have the quiet, essential job of keeping the homes going, caring for the children or the old folks.

Mrs. Roosevelt and I hear from a great many of these women who live in loneliness and anxiety while their men are far away.

I can speak as one who knows something of the feelings of a parent with sons who are in the line of battle overseas. I know that, regardless of the outcome of this election, our sons must go on fighting for whatever length of time is necessary for victory.

When this great job in winning this war is done, the men of our armed forces will be demobilized and returned to their homes just as rapidly as possible. The War and Navy Departments are pledged to that. I am pledged to that. The very law of this land, enacted by the Congress, is pledged to that. And there are no strings attached to this pledge.

While the agony of war lasts, the families of our fighting men can be certain that their boys are being given and always will be given the best equipment, the best arms, the best food, the best medical care that the resources of this nation and the genius of this nation can provide. And I am not indulging in undue boasting when I say that that is the best in the world.

The health of our Army and Navy, Marines and Coast Guard is now better than it was in peace time. Although our forces have been fighting in all climates and exposed to all diseases, the death rate from disease has shrunk to one twentieth of one per cent—less than one seventh of the death rate from disease for men in the same age group in civilian life. The mortality rate among the wounded is less than three per cent as compared with over eight per cent in the last world war.

I have chosen Navy Day—today—to talk about the 11,000,000 Americans in uniform who with all their strength are engaged in giving us a chance to achieve peace through victory in war.

Those men could not have been armed and equipped as they are had it not been for the miracle of our production here at home.

The production which has flowed from this country to all the battle fronts of the world has been due to the efforts of American business, American labor, and American farmers—working together as a patriotic team.

The businessmen of America have had a vital part in this war. They have displayed the highest type of patriotism by their devotion, their industry, their ingenuity, their cooperation with their Government.

I am proud of the fact that in this Administration today there are a great many Republican businessmen who have placed patriotism above party.

But unfortunately there are some Republican politicians—in and out of the Congress—who are introducing a very ugly implication into this campaign—an implication of profound concern to all Americans who believe that this war must be followed by a just and lasting peace.

These politicians are stating that the Republicans in the Congress would cooperate with a Republican President in establishing a world organization for peace—clearly intimating that they would not cooperate toward the same end in the event of a Democratic victory.

That, it seems to me, is a deliberate and indefensible effort to place political advantage not only above devotion to country but also above our very deep desire to avoid the death and destruction which would be caused by future wars.

I do not think that the American people will take kindly to this policy of "Vote my way or I won't play."

May this country never forget that its power in this war has come from the efforts of its citizens, living in freedom and equality.

May this country hold in piety and steadfast faith those who have battled and died to give it new opportunities for service and growth.

May it reserve its contempt for those who see in it only an instrument for their own selfish interests.

May it marshal its righteous wrath against those who would divide it by racial struggles.

May it lavish its scorn upon the faint-hearted.

And may this country always give its support to those who have engaged with us in the war against oppression and who will continue with us in the struggle for a vital, creative peace.

God Bless the United States of America.

PRESIDENT ROOSEVELT'S CAMPAIGN SPEECH IN SOLDIERS FIELD, CHICAGO

October 28, 1944 [1]

The American people are now engaged in the greatest war in history—and we are also engaged in a political campaign.

We are fighting this war and we are holding this election—both for the same essential reason: because we have faith in democracy.

And there is no force and there is no combination of forces powerful enough to shake that faith.

As you know, I have had some previous experience in war—and I have also had a certain amount of previous experience in political campaigning.

But—I must confess—this is the strangest campaign I have ever seen.

I have listened to the various Republican orators who are urging the people

[1] White House news release.

to throw the present Administration out and put them in. And what do they say?

Well, they say in effect, just this:

"Those incompetent bunglers in Washington have passed a lot of excellent laws about social security and labor and farm relief and soil conservation— and many others—and we promise if elected not to change any of them."

And they go on to say: "These same quarrelsome tired old men have built the greatest military machine the world has ever known, which is fighting its way to victory; and, if you elect us, we promise not to change any of that, either."

"Therefore," say these Republican orators, "it is time for a change."

They also say in effect: "Those inefficient and wornout crack-pots have really begun to lay the foundations of a lasting world peace. If you elect us, we will not change any of that either." "But," they whisper, "we'll do it in such a way that we won't lose the support even of Gerald Nye or Gerald Smith—and—and this is very important—we won't lose the support of any isolationist campaign contributor. We will even be able to satisfy the *Chicago Tribune*."

Tonight, I shall talk simply about the future of America—about this land of unlimited opportunity. I shall give the Republican campaign orators some more opportunities to say—"me too."

Today everything we do is devoted to the most important job before us —winning the war and bringing our men and women home as quickly as possible.

We have astonished the world and confounded our enemies with our stupendous war production, with the overwhelming courage and skill of our fighting men—with the bridge of ships carrying our munitions and men through the seven seas—with our gigantic fleet which has pounded the enemy all over the Pacific and has just driven through for a touch-down.

The American people are prepared to meet the problems of peace in the same bold way that they have met the problems of war.

For the American people are resolved that when our men and women return home from this war, they shall come back to the best possible place on the face of this earth—to a place where all persons, regardless of race, color, creed or place of birth, can live in peace, honor and human dignity— free to speak and pray as they wish—free from want—and free from fear.

Last January, in my message to the Congress on the state of the Union, I outlined an Economic Bill of Rights on which "a new basis of security and prosperity can be established for all—regardless of station, race or creed": I repeat them now:

"The right of a useful and remunerative job in the industries, or shops or farms or mines of the nation;

"The right to earn enough to provide adequate food and clothing and recreation;

"The right of every farmer to raise and sell his products at a return which will give him and his family a decent living;

"The right of every business man, large and small, to trade in an atmosphere of freedom from unfair competition and domination by monopolies at home or broad;

"The right of every family to a decent home;

"The right to adequate medical care and the opportunity to achieve and enjoy good health;

"The right to adequate protection from the economic fears of old age, sickness, accident and unemployment;

"The right to a good education.

"All of these rights spell security. And after this war is won we must be prepared to move forward, in the implementation of these rights, to new goals of human happiness and well-being."

Some people have sneered at these ideals as well as the ideals of the Atlantic Charter and the Four Freedoms—saying they were the dreams of starry-eyed New Dealers—that it is silly to talk of them because we cannot attain these ideals tomorrow or the next day.

The American people have greater faith than that. I know that they agree with those objectives—that they demand them—that they are determined to get them—and that they are going to get them.

The American people have a habit of going right ahead and accomplishing the impossible.

And the people today who know that best are the Nazis and the Japs.

This Economic Bill of Rights is the recognition of the simple fact that, in America, the future of the worker and farmer lies in the well-being of private enterprise; and that the future of private enterprise lies in the well-being of the worker and farmer.

The well-being of the nation as a whole is synonymous with the well-being of each and every one of its citizens.

Now I have the possibly old-fashioned theory that when you have problems to solve, objectives to achieve, you cannot get very far by just talking about them.

You have got to go out and do something!

To assure the full realization of the right to a useful and remunerative employment, an adequate program must provide America with close to 60,-000,000 productive jobs.

I foresee an expansion of our peacetime productive capacity which will require new facilities, new plants and new equipment—capable of hiring millions more men.

I propose that the Government do its part in helping private enterprise to finance expansion of our private industrial plant through normal investment channels.

For example, business, large and small, must be encouraged by the Government to expand their plants and to replace their obsolete or worn out equipment with new equipment. And to that end, the rate of depreciation on these new plants and facilities for tax purposes should be accelerated. That means more jobs for the worker, increased profits for the business man, and lower cost to the consumer.

In 1933, when my Administration took office, vast numbers of our industrial workers were unemployed, our plants and businesses were idle, our monetary and banking system in ruins—our economic resources were running to waste.

By 1940—before Pearl Harbor—we had increased our employment by 10,000,000 workers. We had converted a corporate loss of $5,500,000,000 in 1932, to a corporate profit (after taxes) of nearly $5,000,000,000 in 1940.

Obviously, to increase jobs after this war, we shall have to increase demand for our industrial and agricultural production not only here at home, but also abroad.

I am sure that every man and woman in this vast gathering here tonight agree with me in my conviction that never again must we in the United States attempt to isolate ourselves from the rest of humanity.

I am confident that, with Congressional approval, the foreign trade of the United States can be trebled after the war—providing millions of more jobs.

Such cooperative measures provide the soundest economic foundation for a lasting peace. And, after this war, we do not intend to settle for anything less than lasting peace.

When we think of the America of tomorrow, we think of many things.

One of them is American homes—in our cities, in our villages and on our farms. Millions of our people have never had homes worthy of American standards—well built homes with electricity and plumbing and air and sunlight.

The demand for homes and our capacity to build them call for a program of well over a million homes a year for at least ten years. Private industry can build and finance the vast majority of these homes. Government can and will assist and encourage private industry to do this, as it has for many years. For those very low income groups that cannot possibly afford decent homes, the Federal Government should continue to assist local housing authorities in meeting that need.

In the future America we think of new highways and parkways. We think of thousands of new airports to service the new commercial and private air travel which is bound to come after the war. We think of new airplanes, new cheap automobiles with low maintenance and operation costs. We think of new hospitals and new health clinics. We think of a new merchant marine for our expanded world trade.

Think of all these vast possibilities for industrial expansion—and you will foresee opportunities for more millions of jobs.

Our Economic Bill of Rights—like the sacred Bill of Rights of our Constitution itself—must be applied to all our citizens, irrespective of race, creed or color.

In 1941, I appointed a Fair Employment Practice Committee to prevent discrimination in war industry and Government employment. The work of the Committee and the results obtained more than justify its creation.

I believe that the Congress should by law make the Committee permanent.

America must remain the land of high wages and efficient production. Every full-time job in America must provide enough for a decent living. And that goes for jobs in mines, offices, factories, stores, canneries—and everywhere where men and women are employed.

During the war we have been compelled to limit wage and salary increases for one great objective—to prevent runaway inflation. You all know how successfully we have held the line by the way your cost of living has been kept down.

However, at the end of the war there will be more goods available, and it is only good common sense to see to it that the working man is paid enough, and that the farmers earn enough, to buy these goods and keep our factories running. It is a simple fact that a greatly increased production of food and fibre on the farms can be consumed by the people who work in industry only if those people who work in industry have enough money to buy food and clothing. If industrial wages go down, farm prices will go down too. After the war, we shall of course remove the control of wages and leave their determination to free collective bargaining between trade unions and employers.

In this war, the American farmer has been called upon to do far and away the biggest food production job in history.

The American farmer has met that challenge triumphantly.

Despite all manner of war time difficulties—shortage of farm labor and of new farm machinery—the American farmer has achieved a total of food production which is one of the wonders of the world.

The American farmer is a great producer; and he must have the means to be also a great consumer. For more farm income means more jobs everywhere in the nation.

Let us look back for a moment to 1932. All of us remember the spreading tide of farm foreclosures; we remember four cent hogs, twenty cent wheat, five cent cotton.

I am going to give you some figures of recovery—and I am sure you will pardon me if I quote them correctly.

In 1932 the American farmers' net income was only $2,250,000,000.

In 1940—a year before we were attacked—farm income was more than doubled to $5,500,000,000.

This year—1944—it will be approximately $13,500,000,000.

Certainly the American farmer does not want to go back to a Government owned by the moguls of 1929—and let us bear it constantly in mind that those same moguls still control the destinies of the Republican Party.

We must continue this Administration's policy of conserving the enormous gifts with which an abundant Providence has blessed our country—our soil, our forests, our water.

The work of the Tennessee Valley Authority is closely related to our national farm program, and we look toward the similar developments which I have recommended in the valley of the Missouri—in the valley of the Arkansas—and in the Columbia River Basin.

And incidentally—and as an aside—I cannot resist the temptation to point to the gigantic contribution to our war effort made by the power generated at TVA and Bonneville and Grand Coulee.

Do you remember when the building of these great public works was ridiculed as New Deal "boondoggling"? And we are now planning developments at Grand Coulee, which will provide irrigation for many thousands of acres—providing fertile farm land for settlement—I hope—by many of our returning soldiers and sailors.

More "boondoggling"!

This Administration has put into the law of the land the farmers' long dream of parity prices.

And we propose, too, that the Government will cooperate when the weather will not—by a genuine crop insurance program.

This Administration adopted—and will continue—the policy of giving to as many farmers as possible the chance of owning their own farms.

That means something to those veterans who left their farms to fight for their country.

This time they can grow apples on their own farms instead of having to sell apples on street corners.

I believe in free enterprise—and always have.

I believe in the profit system—and always have.

I believe that private enterprise can give full employment to our people.

And if anyone feels that my faith in our ability to provide 60,000,000 peacetime jobs is fantastic, let him remember that some people said the same thing about my demand in 1940 for 50,000 airplanes.

I believe in exceptional rewards for innovation, skill, and risk-taking by business.

We shall lift production and price control as soon as they are no longer needed—encouraging private business to produce more of the things to which we are accustomed and also thousands of new things, in ever-increasing volume, under conditions of free and open competition.

This Administration has been mindful from its earliest days, and will continue to be mindful, of the problems of small business as well as large.

Small business played a magnificent part in producing thousands of items needed for our armed forces. When the war broke out, it was mobilized into war production. Money was loaned to them for machinery. Over 1,000,000 prime and subcontracts have been distributed among 60,000 smaller plants of the nation.

We shall make sure that small business is given every facility to buy Government-owned plants, equipment and inventories. The special credit and capital requirements of small business will be met.

And small business will continue to be protected from selfish and cold-blooded monopolies and cartels. Beware of that profound enemy of the free enterprise system who pays lip-service to free competition—but also labels every anti-trust prosecution as a "persecution."

This war has demonstrated that when the American business man and the American worker and the American farmer work together, they form an unbeatable team.

We know that—our Allies know that—and so do our enemies.

That winning team must keep together after the war, and it will win many more historic victories of peace for our country, and for the cause of security and decent standards of living throughout the world.

We owe it to our fighting men and to their families—we owe it to all of our people who have given so much in this war—we owe it to our children—to keep that winning team together.

The future of America, like its past, must be made by deeds—not words.

America has always been a land of action—a land of adventurous pioneering—a land of growing and building.

America must always be such a land.

The creed of our democracy is that liberty is acquired and kept by men and women who are strong and self-reliant, and possessed of such wisdom as God gives to mankind—men and women who are just, and understanding, and generous to others—men and women who are capable of disciplining themselves.

For they are the rulers and they must rule themselves.

I believe in our democratic faith and in the future of our country which has given eternal strength and vitality to that faith.

Here in Chicago you know a lot about that vitality.

And as I say good-night to you, I say it in a spirit of faith—a spirit of hope—a spirit of confidence.

We are not going to turn back the clock!

We are going forward—and—with the fighting millions of our fellow countrymen—we are going forward together.

PRIME MINISTER WINSTON CHURCHILL'S SPEECH
IN COMMONS ASKING FOR THE PRO-
LONGATION OF PARLIAMENT

October 31, 1944 [1]

In asking for a prolongation of the life of this Parliament for another year, I doubt very much whether the Parliament will last so long. There are powerful factors of uncertainty which tell in opposite directions, or from different angles. The meetings of the various parties opposing the Coalition are to take place shortly before and shortly after Christmas, and while we cannot at all forecast what will occur, we certainly cannot exclude the possibility that a desire to return to the party system will be strongly expressed. On the other hand we cannot tell when the war against Nazi Germany will be definitely ended or will fall into the guerrilla stage. I am confident that all organised parties will see that business through to the very end. This would almost certainly be the view, I believe, of the great trade union movement, where determination to finish Hitlerism is strong and invincible.

I am very clearly of opinion that the coalition of parties ought not to be broken before Nazidom is broken. This was the purpose for which we came together in the present Government, and it is still the supreme purpose which affects the safety of the nation and the Empire. As I said the other day, any attempt to estimate the date when the war with Germany can be officially declared over can be no more than a guess. A political convulsion in Germany might bring it to a speedy end at any time, but against that must be set the iron control of German life in all its forms, including the Army, which has been established by Hitler's storm troops and secret police. This exceeds anything previously known among men. Therefore, we cannot count upon any of the normal reactions of public opinion. From every quarter it seems that the civil population are plunged in a dull apathy, and certainly anyone who stirred against the police would instantly be shot or decapitated. Therefore I simply cannot place any dependence upon political uprisings in Germany.

On military grounds it seems difficult to believe that the war could be ended before Christmas, or even before Easter, although, as I have said, many high military authorities with every means to form a correct judgment have expressed themselves more hopefully, and although every effort is being made, and will be made, against the enemy. The German troops are fighting with the utmost tenacity, although cut off in many places and in defence of positions evidently forlorn. They have been counter-attacking with vigour, though as yet without success, in Holland and on the Moselle. A great deal of work has still to be done to improve the ports and build up supplies and concentrate forward the ever-growing Allied Army. In Italy the fighting is also of the most obstinate character and the weather has broken. The Eastern front has shown its main activity on the north and south flanks. Immense successes have rewarded strenuous Russian military efforts and skilful Russian and Allied diplomacy. The distances are however very large and many hostile defence positions have to be stormed or turned. In all these circumstances I certainly could not predict, still less guarantee, the end of the German war before the end of the spring, or even before we reach the early summer. It may come earlier, and no one will rejoice more than I if it should.

[1] Parliamentary Debates.

Anyhow I have no hesitation in declaring that it would be a wrongful act, unworthy of our country's fame, to break up the present governing instrument before we know where we are with Hitler's Germany. Those who forced such a disaster, even thoughtlessly, would take on themselves a measureless responsibility, and their action would be fiercely resented by the nation at large. I am thankful to say that there are no signs of any such desire in any responsible quarter.

Let us assume, however, that the German war ends in March, April or May, and that some or all the other parties in the Coalition recall their Ministers out of the Government, or wish to bring it to an end from such dates. That would be a matter of regret, both on public and on personal grounds to a great many people, but it would not be a matter of reproach or bitterness between us in this Government or in this House once Germany has been defeated.

We are told there must on no account be what is called a coupon election. By that I presume is meant an agreement between the official parties not to oppose each other in most of the seats, and to form a solid front against those who criticise or oppose us. In other words, it would mean that the present Coalition should go to the country and obtain from it a renewal of confidence. I have no doubt they would get it, but there would be some who would say it was too easy. But one must admit that many people would think this would hardly be a fair way of testing opinion in the country, and in fact it would be quite impossible to obtain party agreement to such a course. Many people feel that it would impede the electorate in expressing their free choice. Neither would it be seemly, or indeed practicable, once a dissolution had been announced, for Ministers to go all over the country expressing the utmost distaste for each other's views and records and yet be together in Cabinet discussing as colleagues all the gravest matters of the hour. Nor again would it be proper for the ministers who are also in some cases leaders and whose knowledge is needed to guide the country, to remain silent and apparently indifferent to the fortunes of their parties or of their candidates. I do not find it easy to escape from the weight and force of these arguments.

The announcement of the dissolution would therefore necessarily mark the close of the present administration. The Conservative party have a majority of more than 100 above all parties and independents in the present House, and it would therefore fall to us to make arrangements for the inevitable General Election. I cannot conceive that anyone would wish that election to be held in a violent hurry or while we were all rejoicing together and rendering thanks to God for our deliverance. There must be an interval. Moreover we have above all things to be careful that practically everybody entitled to vote has a fair chance to do so. This applies above all to the soldiers, many of whom are serving at great distances from this country. Nothing would be more shameful or more dishonourable than to deny the great mass of the soldiers, and Service men of the Air Force and of the Navy, a full opportunity of recording their votes. In my opinion they have more right to vote than anyone else in the country, and we shall all be ashamed if anything were done which prevented these men, to whom we owe almost everything, from taking their full part in deciding the immediate future of their country. That is not to say that every single man in the most remote station can be certain of being able to vote, but everything in human power will be done to give the fullest possible opportunities for the exercise of the franchise to all in the fighting Services.

It is however, in fact not legally possible, after the new electoral arrangements have come into force, as they do on the 1st December this year, for polling to take place in less than eight weeks from the issue of the writs. A minimum of six weeks must in fact elapse between the issue of the writs and the nomination of candidates alone. All this has been concerted with a general measure of assent by the House, and with the sole view of obtaining the fullest and fairest expression of the national opinion. Besides all this the partial redistribution authorised by the recent Act has to be carried through. A start will be made immediately, not waiting for the end of the German war, but the process will certainly take several months.

It may therefore be taken as certain that from the moment the King gives his consent to a dissolution a period of between two and three months would be required. This also would be fair to the political parties and candidates, who have to set about one another in the usual lusty manner. Moreover, in the interval there will undoubtedly have to be certain financial arrangements made and other matters of business wound up. It follows therefore that if events should take the course I have indicated it would seem that, roughly speaking, there is no likelihood of a General Election for from seven to nine months from now. Finally, it is contrary to precedent for Governments to hold on to office until the last moment of their legal tenure, or legally extended tenure, and it would be very unwholesome for any practice of that kind to be introduced. For these reasons we have decided not to accept any proposals or suggestions such as I have seen bruited about to reduce the period in the Bill from twelve months to six months, and I ask to-day, in introducing it, for a twelve months' prolongation of the life of the present Parliament. My right hon. Friend the Home Secretary, who will be in charge of the Bill will deal with any points of detail which may arise.

We think that we have given good reasons to the House to show that the twelve months' period would be a reasonable and proper provision to make at the present time. On the other hand we must assume that the Japanese war will have to be carried on for an indefinite period after the destruction of Nazi power. Here again there may be the possibilities of some political upheaval in Japan inducing a sudden surrender, but it would be very foolish to count upon this in a race of men of this desperate and barbarous character, whose whole constitution is dominated by the military and naval hierarchies who dragged them into their mad aggression. When the whole of the Japanese problem is examined, on military grounds alone it would certainly not be prudent to assume that a shorter period than eighteen months after the destruction of Hitler would be required for the final destruction of the Japanese will or capacity to fight, and this period must be continually revised every few months by the combined Chiefs of Staffs.

The prolongation of the life of the existing Parliament by another two or three years would be a very serious constitutional lapse. Even now, no one under thirty has ever cast a vote at a general election, or even at a by-election, since the registers fell out of action at the beginning of the war. Therefore, it seems to me that, unless all political parties resolve to maintain the present Coalition until the Japanese are defeated, we must look to the termination of the war against Nazism as a pointer which will fix the date of the General Election. I regret the break-up of the present highly efficient Government which has waged war with unsurpassed success and have shaped or carried out within the last two years a programme of reform and social progress which might well have occupied a whole Parliament under the ordinary conditions of peace for five or six years. In fact, I may say—and I will indeed be quite candid on this point—that having served for forty-two years in this House I have never seen any Government to which I have been able to give a more loyal, confident and consistent support. But while I should regret and deplore the break-up of these forces, so knit together by personal good-will, by the comradeship of fighting a great cause, and by the sense of growing success arising from that comradeship, yet I could not blame anyone who claimed that there should be an appeal to the people once the German peril is removed. Indeed, I have myself a clear view that it would be wrong to continue this Parliament beyond the period of the German war.

The foundation of all democracy is that the people have the right to vote. To deprive them of that right is to make a mockery of all the high-sounding phrases which are so often used. At the bottom of all the tributes paid to democracy, is the little man, walking into the little booth, with a little pencil, making a little cross on a little bit of paper—no amount of rhetoric or voluminous discussion can possibly palliate the overwhelming importance of that point. The people have the right to choose representatives in accordance with their wishes and feelings, and I cannot think of anything more odious than for a Prime Minister to attempt to carry on with a Parliament so aged, and to try to grapple with the perplexing and tremendous problems of war and peace, and of the transition from war to peace, without being refreshed by contact with the people or without being relieved of any special burdens in that respect.

I can assure the House that in the absence of most earnest representations by the Labour and Liberal Parties, I could not refrain from making a submission to the Crown in respect of a dissolution after the German war is effectively and officially finished. I am sure this is a straight-forward, fair and constitutional method of dealing with what is in many ways an unprecedented situation though not one which need in any way baffle our flexible British system. Meanwhile, I must confess that the position will not become increasingly easy. The odour of dissolution is in the air, and parties are inclined to look at each other across the House with an increasing sense of—

MR. KIRKWOOD (Dumbarton Burghs): Distrust?

THE PRIME MINISTER:—impending division.

MR. KIRKWOOD: Of distrust.

THE PRIME MINISTER: Well, of distrust in some aspects, and of regret for impending division in others. But we have to be specially careful in such circumstances that nothing should hamper the vigorous prosecution of the war and that, I am sure, is the resolve of all parties and also of most of those individuals who are specially interested to bring the Coalition to an end.

I thought it right as a preface to this Bill, in moving the Second Reading of it, to touch upon these matters because they are after all of very considerable importance to our constitutional procedure, but further than this I find it impossible to form an opinion. Mr. Jorrocks said of fox-hunting that it was the image of war without its gilt and one-half per cent. the danger. Something like that might be said of a General Election. It is a trial of strength between parties of which the nation is the arbiter. I have often thought that it is sometimes unwise of generals to try to foresee with meticulous exactness just what will happen after a battle has been fought. A battle hangs like a curtain across the future. Once that curtain is raised or rent we can all see how the scenery is arranged, what actors are left upon the scene and how they appear to be related to one another. In this case it will certainly be much better to wait till the new situation is fully disclosed.

Meanwhile, as we probably have a good many months of the closest comradeship and hardest work before us, and there will be ample opportunity for party oratory, which will necessarily occur between the dissolution and the poll, I should deprecate strongly the over-emphasising of party differences now, and recommend that we all bend ourselves with unflagging energy and unbroken union to the national task.

GOVERNOR THOMAS E. DEWEY'S CAMPAIGN SPEECH IN BUFFALO

October 31, 1944 [1]

Mr. Chairman, Senator Tom Curran, Fellow-Americans:

Tonight I want to ask you to look ahead into our future as a nation. Join me in looking at what our country will face the day after victory over our enemies.

But first, let me give you right now two solemn assurances prompted by the speeches of my opponent last Friday and Saturday nights.

Your next President will never use his office to claim personal or political profit from the achievements of the American people or from the sacrifices of their sons and daughters.

Your next President will never make you a promise that he does not intend with all his heart and soul to keep.

And let me add that except for the pledges I have made publicly to the American people, your next President will take office on Jan. 20, 1945, without a promise, expressed or implied, to a living soul.

There is no One Thousand Club in my party. I haven't offered the Government of the United States for sale at a $1,000 to any man and I never will to anyone at any price. Your next Administration will take office honestly, without secret promises or special privilege to any class, section or group of Americans.

Now, put your minds ahead with me, if you will, into these peacetime years ahead, these years which by the courage of our fighting men and with the help of Almighty God are now being brought closer every day.

Eleven million men and women will be coming home from this war eager for more education, for jobs, for a chance to start a business and get ahead. Twenty million war workers will want peacetime jobs and opportunity.

Last Saturday night my opponent, once again, promised jobs for every American when peacetime comes. But his own peacetime record is that at the end of eight years the New Deal had spent $58,000,000,000, it enjoyed more power than all previous Governments combined, and in March of 1940 there were still 10,000,000 Americans unemployed.

On the record his promise of jobs is worthless. It will still be worthless, even though it is repeated again and again and again.

Having discovered from my Philadelphia speech, delivered two months ago, the need for a million new homes a year, my opponent now promises that. The fact is that for years we should have been building a million homes a year just to get back up to the standards of 1930. But under the New Deal we got an average of only 380,000 new homes a year.

On the record, then, that promise, too, is no good even though it is repeated again and again and again.

My opponent now promises to free the American working man and woman

[1] *New York Times.*

from the strangling bureaucracy he himself has created. When a man promises in trying to win an election that he will reverse the course of everything he has done for twelve years, then that promise, too, on the record, is no good even though it's repeated again and again and again.

My opponent promises the farmers good prices after the war. But the farmer knows that in all the peacetime years of the New Deal he never got decent prices. Under the New Deal it took a war to get prices, just as it took a war to get jobs. On the record that promise, too, is worthless, even though it also is repeated again and again and again.

My opponent now promises to be mindful of the problems of small business. The small business men of America will know how much faith they can put in that, and I should like to talk briefly tonight about the future of small business in our country.

This is the field in which a large part of our white-color workers earn their living. This is the field of the forgotten man and woman under the New Deal.

Now, American business men know that the New Deal way of being mindful of their problems has been slowly to drown them with a rising flood of rules and regulations, questionnaires, reports and directives.

It's been bad enough for large business, but the big corporation at least has its lawyers, its accountants, clerks and statisticians. When it comes to small business the burden of Government paper work has too often meant the difference between success or failure.

Take the case of Capt. J. E. Shields, of Seattle, Wash., who is the salt codfish business. For thirty-three years his boats have gone out until last year, when the War Labor Board failed even to pass on his wage contracts. So, last year his boats couldn't go out at all.

He reports that this year he finally got clearance, after going through twenty-four different Government agencies in order to carry on one small business. In addition to the Navy Department, the Interior Department, the Commerce Department, the Treasury Department, the Immigration Service and the Maritime Commission, a partial list of the agencies he had to deal with includes WLB, WMC, OPA, WSA, FCC, USES, WPB, ODT, SS, WFA and others.

Here's another sample of what our small businessmen have had to contend with. The world trembles in the greatest war of the ages and bureaucracy puts out the following ruling which restaurants must understand and obey. Listen to it:

"Mashed potatoes offered a la carte for weekday lunches would be in the same class of food items as potatoes au gratin offered a la carte for weekday lunches, but would be in a different class than mashed potatoes offered a la carte for weekday dinners or Sunday lunches. . . ."

Well, that's the New Deal way of being mindful of the problems of small business. It's the same from restaurants to beauty parlors, from electrical shops to insurance businesses, from everything a man can start to make a living in. And that's why it's time for a change.

Yes, the New Deal pretends at election time to be the friend of small business. It pretends to be a friend of small business, but how has small business actually fared under this Administration.

The record shows that in 1942 and 1943, the most prosperous years we have had under the New Deal—because of the war—there was a net decline of five hundred thousand in the number of American small businesses. That means that a net figure of five hundred thousand, a half a million, small businesses closed their doors and died in just these two past years.

And yet my opponent has the temerity, to go on the radio and say "this Administration has been mindful from its earliest days, and will continue to be mindful, of the problem of small business. . . ."

In the light of the record that promise, too, is worthless and it will remain so even though it is repeated again and again and again.

My opponent has now read our platform and he's saying, "Me, too." Even the New Deal knows that it's time for a change.

No, we can't live on promises. We must have performance this time— before it's too late. As we keep our minds set on these peacetime years ahead, let's remember one thing: My opponent has offered no program for the peacetime years ahead except exactly the same one which failed for eight straight years of peace from 1933 to 1940.

And let me add that the figures showing that failure have been correctly quoted by me from the beginning to the end of this campaign. My opponent has insinuated, though he didn't dare say it, that some figures weren't correct. But he has never dared to point out the ones he disagreed with. Instead he says with a sneer that when he was Governor of New York he quoted figures correctly.

Now, I don't recollect his quoting figures at all when he was Governor of New York and very rarely since then—for one very good reason. In every Administration Mr. Roosevelt has headed he ended up in the red. No country can long survive under any leader who only piles up a bigger debt each year, not just in war, but in peace.

Let us as a nation relearn one simple thing. Our peacetime economic system is like a high-power motor. Every part of it must work or the engine will run badly or not at all. If one spark plug goes bad, the engine loses power. If the distributor is out of order or the fuel line gets stopped up or the carburetor goes bad, the whole tremendous power of the machine fails.

That's the thing the New Deal doesn't know and can never learn. It had to tinker first with one thing and then with another. It has changed the tax laws fifteen times in twelve years so no man could plan ahead. It fought first one part of our job-making machinery, then another. It was never willing in all its years to let all the parts of this magnificent American machine function smoothly so we could go ahead.

It's a shocking thing that my opponent, after twelve years as President, felt compelled to announce, as news, last Saturday night, that he believes in the enterprise system. Yet, in all his campaign speeches, my opponent has not indicated how he will achieve in post-war years what he so tragically failed to achieve in peacetime years.

Let me summarize, in brief, some essential parts of the program of action I have proposed in these last two months for the peacetime years ahead of us. Virtually every element of our program is something the New Deal has fought against or neglected, and cannot now, for election purposes, claim to favor.

Here is the program of my party for these peacetime years ahead:

Proposal No. 1: Direct all Government policies toward the goal of full employment through full production at a high level of wages for the worker and with an incentive for business men to make good. Your next administration will work out the problems affecting labor, agriculture and business in full consultation with all three and without discrimination against any class or section of our country or any race, color or creed.

Proposal No. 2: Adopt an entirely new tax structure which will do these things:

1. Change the personal exemption so that a man who makes as little as eleven dollars a week no longer has an income tax taken out of his standard of living.

2. Reduce personal income tax rates so that the tax law, after credit for dependents, will no longer take at least twenty-three cents out of every taxable dollar in the pay envelope.

3. Change and lower the income tax on business so that it can be encouraged to expand and help create the millions of jobs we need.

4. Overhaul the entire tax structure so that it's simple, so that every one can understand it, and then stick to it over a period of years. Only if we stick to it can we go ahead and build and create jobs. That's the only way in the world we can ever get our national income up to where it's got to go after this war. The highest our national income under this administration in peacetime has ever reached was seventy-six billion dollars, compared with eighty-nine billion dollars in the 1920's. The only way in the world we can work out is to double that New Deal best in the peacetimes to come under a decent tax structure with a system which is told by its government to go ahead and go to work and produce.

Proposal No. 3: Make our Social Security System available to every American and not to a selected part of our people. For nine long years, the New Deal has kept twenty million Americans out of our Old-Age Pension System. The right to an old-age pension has become a fundamental of our society. We can and must extend the system of old-age benefits and social security to all our people and build a society strong enough to support it.

Proposal No. 4: Establish a definite and secure floor under farm prices, one we'll know about now and next month and next year, so a man can plan ahead again. Do it by the means outlined in my speech last Saturday, together with the other elements of that program and then free the American farmer from dictation from Washington.

Proposal No. 5: Restore free collective bargaining in America. Sprawling Government agencies have now established an iron rule over the wages, hours and chance to get a job of every American worker. We shall establish the Fair Employment Practice Committee as a permanent agency with full legal authority. We will then merge the balance of these agencies in a strong and competent Department of Labor under the leadership of a man from the ranks of labor.

Proposal No. 6: Survey forthwith the millions of reports required of big and little business every year by Government and immediately abolish the greater part of them. We have done it in New York and we can do it in the nation.

Proposal No. 7: Bring a competent staff into the Department of Justice so that we can bring an end to business monopoly in this country instead of just talking about it.

Proposal No. 8: Establish an entirely new basis between the President and the Congress so that once again each shall have the respect of the other and each will be willing to work with the other in the traditional American fashion.

My opponent has continuously criticized and attempted to purge the members of the Houses of Congress elected by the people. He has so abused and insulted the Congress that his own Senate leader rebelled.

Just this year he stood up in the Senate and denounced the words of a veto message by my opponent, and I quote, "as more clever than honest" and as "a calculated and deliberate assault on the legislative integrity of every member of Congress."

That declaration was cheered to the rafters by the members of the Senate and the members of the House swarmed into the Senate chamber to congratulate the speaker.

That's what three terms of unlimited power do to a man. That's why four terms, or sixteen years, is the most dangerous threat to our freedom ever proposed by anybody. That's one reason why I believe with our great Presidents of the past that two terms must be established as the limit by Constitutional amendment.

We've seen now that a New Deal Congress no longer trusts or accepts leadership from my opponent. It's generally agreed that the House and probably the Senate will be Republican next year.

So, already Mr. Roosevelt has undertaken to insult the new leadership. In his speech of last Friday night he accused the men who will be the new leaders of placing political advantage above devotion to country just because they publicly pledged themselves to a program for lasting peace. We must not have—we cannot have—four years more of stalemate and hostility between the President of the United States and our Congress.

We can and we will restore to the White House a willingness to work out problems with the Congress as equals in the American fashion over the conference table. We must bring an end to government by abuse and by smear.

Lastly, I propose that, with an end to name calling and with unselfish devotion, we unite as a people behind the cause of a just and lasting peace through an organization with the strength to prevent future wars.

By these specific means and with a government made up of the ablest men and women in this country, we can restore honesty to our government and we can once again unite to secure the future which is our birthright.

Let us again make "getting ahead" a vital part of the American language and of the American thought. For years the New Dealers have been sneering at the old American idea of "getting ahead." Let us make sure that our children can again believe there is room for everybody to get ahead in this country. Let us nail that principle to our masthead and set out on a sure course for the future.

Let us determine that the end of this war will bring our young men and women home to the kind of an America they have earned all over the world. With high purpose and integrity and relying upon the guidance of the God of all of us we can save freedom in America and go forward once again.

I thank you.

NOVEMBER

November 1, 1944

Delegations from fifty United Nations were present at the opening of the Civil Aviation Conference in Chicago.

2

President Roosevelt asked Donald M. Nelson, former chairman of the War Production Board, to return to China and to organize there a WPB to increase the output of that country's war industries.

3

General Franco declared that Spain had never been Fascist or Nazi and never had been allied openly or secretly with the Axis powers.

4

British troops and ELAS guerrillas drove the Germans completely from Greece.

The U.S.S.R. turned down Swiss proposals for the re-establishment of diplomatic relations between the two nations after a lapse of more than twenty years because "the Swiss Government, up to now, has in no way disavowed its former policy hostile to the Soviet Union."

7

Franklin D. Roosevelt was elected to a fourth term as President of the United States by an electoral vote of 432 to 99.

Premier George Papandreou of Greece ordered the dissolution of the leftist ELAS and the rightist EDES, the two largest guerrilla organizations in the country. The order, to go into effect December 10, was issued after a conference with Lieut. Gen. Ronald Scobie, British commander in Greece. "After the complete liberation of Greece," said the Greek Premier, "our heroic resistance is ended."

8

President Roosevelt issued a statement on his re-election to the Presidency, saying: "We have again demonstrated to the world that democracy is a living, vital force; that our faith in American institutions is unshaken, that conscience and not force is the source of power in the government of man."

10

The Japanese stormed and captured the cities of Kweilin and Liuchow, former sites of U. S. air bases.

11

Former Premier Juho K. Paasikivi accepted the Premiership in a new Finnish Government.

Germany initiated a sea blockade of Sweden's Baltic coast despite the strong protest of the Swedish Foreign Office.

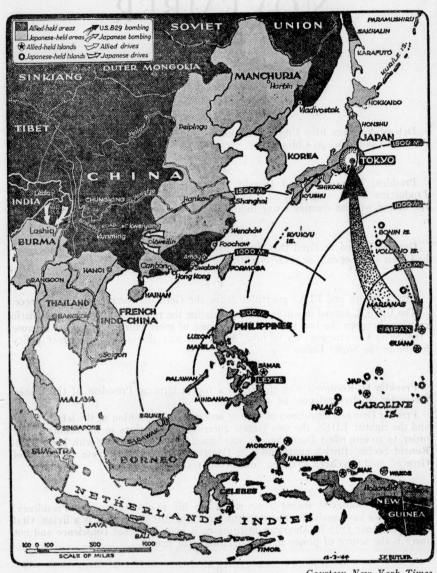

The Pacific Theatre of War
November, 1944

Prime Minister Winston Churchill, accompanied by Foreign Secretary Anthony Eden, Under-Secretary Sir Alexander Cadogan, and British Ambassador to France, Alfred Duff-Cooper, began diplomatic conversations with the leaders of the Provisional French Government in Paris.

France was formally invited to sit in the European Advisory Commission in London, in equal membership with "the big three" powers, Great Britain, the Soviet Union and the United States.

12

The Subcommittee on War Mobilization of the Senate Military Affairs Committee recommended in a report that the German munitions industry and all "primary indirect munitions industries, including the metallurgical and chemical industries," be dismantled and removed to help in the reconstruction of the devastated areas of Europe.

Prime Minister Churchill declared in Paris, after a conference with French leaders, that the British Government felt that the "establishment of a strong French Army as soon as possible is absolutely necessary to balance and sanity in Europe."

13

A deadlock between the American and British delegations to the International Civil Aviation Conference continued over the powers to be granted to the proposed international body for post-war commercial aviation.

The Government of Norway acclaimed the conduct of the Red Army in the northern Norwegian territory it liberated, indicating that there was close collaboration between the Russian and Norwegian forces.

The British Air Ministry announced that the *Tirpitz*, Germany's last big battleship, had been sunk by three six-ton bombs in Tromsoe Fjord in northern Norway.

15

Acting Secretary of State Edward R. Stettinius, Jr. said that, like Eire's, Portugal's assurances that Axis war criminals would not be given refuge in that country, were not satisfactory.

A Berlin decree ordered all German officers and non-coms who were members of the Nazi Party "to educate their men in the Nazi philosophy, to form a closer link between the Wehrmacht and the Party."

18

A special committee appointed by President Roosevelt to survey the rise in the cost of living reported to him that "the final figure for the overall increase in the cost of living from January 1941 to September 1944 would thus be found to be twenty-nine to thirty per cent."

The Albanian Army of National Liberation drove the Germans out of Tirana, the capital of Albania.

American troops stormed their way into Metz.

20

With China's military position becoming increasingly critical, Generalissimo Chiang Kai-shek reshuffled eight Cabinet posts, naming General Chen Cheng to be Minister of War in place of General Ho Ying-chin.

22

The American Ninth Army fought its way to the Roer River guarding the approaches to Cologne.

23

Setting aside a policy of five years of voluntary enlistment, the Canadian Government issued an order-in-council making 16,000 drafted men available for overseas service.

24

Superfortresses from Saipan bases bombed Tokyo for the second time in a daylight raid.

Acting Secretary of State Edward R. Stettinius announced that the European Advisory Commission, consisting of the United States, the Soviet Union and Great Britain, had agreed on a coordinated plan to occupy and administer Germany.

Premier Stanislaw Mikolajczyk of the Polish Government-in-Exile resigned his post because the Polish Cabinet refused to accept his compromise proposal for a friendly settlement with the Soviet Government. The Deputy Premier Jan Kwapinski, a Socialist, was designated by President Raczkiewicz to form another Cabinet.

J. A. Krug, chairman of the War Production Board, ordered that the output of ammunition be doubled.

25

Propaganda Minister Goebbels comforted the German people: "The Allies have once more fixed over-optimistic victory dates. We know that they are doomed to disappointment. Such disappointments are likely to increase the already widespread war weariness in the enemy camp."

The War Labor Board upheld the Little Steel formula as the keystone of the country's wage stabilization policy.

26

After ten days of fighting the American First Army broke through Huertgen Forest into the Cologne Plain.

The Italian political parties of the left forced the resignation of Premier Bonomi.

27

Conflict between the Pierlot Rightist Government of Belgium and the Resistance Movement was coming to a head with Brussels facing a general strike as a protest against the Government.

The resignation of Secretary of State Cordell Hull on account of illness was followed by the appointment of Under-Secretary of State Edward R. Stettinius, Jr. as his successor.

28

Premier Hubert Pierlot of Belgium banned parades, mass meetings, demonstrations and strikes as the Resistance Movement grew more determined in its opposition to him.

The Italian crisis was aggravated by a flat British veto of Count Carlo Sforza as Foreign Minister.

29

The American delegates to the International Civil Aviation Conference in Chicago again demanded unlimited freedom of the air, being opposed strongly by the British delegation.

30

Edward R. Stettinius, Jr. was confirmed as Secretary of State by the Senate in a roll call of 67 to 1.

A new Polish Cabinet-in-Exile took office in London under the premiership of Tomasz Arciszewski. The Peasant Party of former Premier Mikolajczyk declined to join it.

Secretary of War Stimson, pleading for increased production, disclosed that lack of ammunition compelled General Eisenhower to delay his general offensive just as the Allied troops neared the Rhine.

GOVERNOR THOMAS E. DEWEY'S BOSTON CAMPAIGN SPEECH

November 1, 1944 [1]

Governor and soon to be Senator Saltonstall, Speaker Martin, Governor Cahill, Lieut. Gov. Bradford, my Fellow-Americans:

Once in every four years, late in October, my opponent announces that he believes in the enterprise system. Then, for the remaining three years and eleven months, he wages war against the American enterprise system day in and day out. That is why there were still ten million Americans unemployed in the spring of 1940. That's why we had to have a war to get jobs and that's why it's time for a change.

Because of our magnificent military command, the heroism of our men in uniform, and the efforts of our war workers at home, victory is coming closer every day. And by installing a fresh and united administration in Washington, we can bring an end to a quarreling, bickering tired administration. We can recover the full respect of the other nations for the United States of America. Then with our great military command unhampered and backed up to the limit, we can bring ever closer the day of total victory and the prompt return of our fighting men.

Then, what do we face? As I pointed out last night at Buffalo, if we go into the post-war period with nothing better than the New Deal has offered us in the past, we can expect no better results than we had under its peacetime years before.

But if we go in with a new and vigorous administration, pledged to a program of specific constructive action, we can and we will succeed. With a government in which the President works once again in harmony and mutual respect with the Congress, we can unite America for effective leadership in a world organization for lasting peace.

And only with such new harmony can we surely take our part as we must with no reservation and with full effectiveness.

Now, one reason why the New Deal cannot provide jobs and opportunity after this war, one reason why it cannot give our country the unity we need, is because of the kind of people to whom it would owe its election. The New Deal is not a party. It is a collection of parties, all of which hate each other.

Right in my own State of New York, they hate each other so much that they won't vote unless it is under their own emblem, so Franklin Roosevelt is running on three different party lines in the State of New York.

No, the New Deal has become a collection of warring factions, tied together only by a consuming passion for power. That's why my opponent is compelled to solicit the support of bigoted reactionaries on the one hand and of Communists on the other.

[1] *New York Times.*

For twelve years the great Democratic party has been under the crushing dominance of one man. As a result, the party is weakened and divided. It is vulnerable to capture by forces hostile to every tradition for which that party has stood. Beyond that, Mr. Roosevelt, in his overwhelming desire to perpetuate himself in office for sixteen years, has put his party on the auction block—for sale to the highest bidder.

Now who will buy it? Will it be the notorious One Thousand Club, the club that sponsored and paid for Mr. Roosevelt's speech last Saturday? This is the organization, formed at Mr. Roosevelt's own suggestion, which offers, and I quote, the prospectus "special privilege," a voice "in the formulation of Administration policies" and a chance to visit with the President on Thursday afternoons, all for $1,000.

Will these purchasers of "special privilege" be the successful bidders for control of the captive Democratic party? I doubt it. The Thousand Dollar Club members are being taken in. They won't get the "special privileges" they have been offered and they think they bought. There are higher bidders on the market.

Those higher bidders are the Political Action Committee of Sidney Hillman and the Communists of Earl Browder.

In this campaign, the New Dealers attempt to smother discussion of their Communist alliance. They smear any discussions of this major question of our day. They insinuate that Americans must love communism or offend our fighting Ally, Russia. Not even the gullible believe that. In Russia, a Communist is a man who supports his government. In America, a Communist is a man who supports the fourth term so our form of government may more easily be changed.

No, the question of communism in our country has nothing whatsoever to do with our Allies any more than it has to do where a man was born. Every American—every one of us—traces his ancestry to some foreign land. As a nation, we owe our genius, our culture, our traditions, to nations all over the world.

The keystone of the arch of American freedom is our unyielding opposition to intolerance. The foundation of our American system of civil liberties is an equal respect and an equal opportunity for men of every race, creed and color and regardless of national origin. The mighty bulwark of these liberties is the Constitution of the United States.

These are the things that have given America leadership in the world. These, above all others, are what America must continue to stand for if she is to give leadership to the world once again.

The proof that communism has nothing to do with national origin is the fact that Earl Browder, the avowed leader of communism in America, was born in the United States.

Now, who is Browder? He's the man who was convicted of draft dodging in the last war. He was again convicted—this time of perjury—and pardoned by Franklin Roosevelt in time to organize the fourth-term campaign. Browder stands for everything that would destroy America.

Everyone knows that communism is for State ownership of all property, including your house, your farm and the factory and the shop and the office in which you work. It stands for absolute dictatorship, the abolition of civil rights and total political and economic bigotry. It also stands for something else.

A few years ago Mr. Browder wrote a book called "What Is Communism?" He said, and I now quote him, "We stand without any reservations for education that will root out beliefs in the supernatural . . ." He concluded, "We Communists do not distinguish between good and bad religions, because we think they are all bad for the masses."

Now, Mr. Roosevelt, in his recent speech from the White House very softly disavowed communism. But the very next day at a meeting right here in Boston, Earl Browder made a speech for Mr. Roosevelt and a collection was taken up for the fourth term. And not a voice in the entire New Deal was raised in protest. So much for Mr. Browder.

Now—who is Sidney Hillman? He has held one high post after another in the New Deal, in addition to important duties as the head of a labor union. When the fourth-term campaign came along he went to New York to concentrate on politics.

There, in the primaries this year, he organized a movement to take over the previously respectable American Labor party. And he succeeded with the help of Earl Browder's Communists.

Now, what is the American Labor party today—the party whose nomination Mr. Roosevelt has accepted and whose votes he hopes will give him sixteen years in the White House?

You don't need to take my word for what the American Labor party is today. Listen to the words of another set of my opponent's violent supporters. David Dubinsky, president of the International Ladies Garment Workers Union, was one of the founders of the American Labor party. Here is what he said last spring about that party as of today. He said: "I regard the former American Labor party as a Communist labor party. . . . Mr. Hillman can act as a front for Communists. I never did and never will."

So said David Dubinsky.

The New York Post, formerly the mouthpiece of the Labor party, says editorially that Mr. Hillman, and I quote it, "fronts for the Communists by serving as chairman for their American Labor party."

The last candidate of that party for Governor of New York, who polled 400,000 votes in 1942, is another violent supporter of my opponent. But it was he who said last spring, and I quote him:

"Political action by coercion is repugnant to our form of government. Liberals throughout the country should beware of dealing with Mr. Hillman, for he no longer comes to them with clean hands. He has set himself up as a new and dangerous type of political boss." End of quotation.

Just four months ago after that statement, just four months after that statement was issued, my opponent ordered the Democratic National Chairman to "clear everything with Sidney." The prophecy has come true. Sidney Hillman has become the biggest political boss in the United States, and in the words of David Dubinsky, Sidney Hillman is a "front for Communists."

In addition to being chairman of the Communist-controlled American Labor party, Mr. Hillman is also chairman of the Political Action Committee. This is the committee which summarized the degradation of New Deal politics in a pamphlet, two million copies of which were sent out on behalf of Franklin D. Roosevelt. That pamphlet put out by the PAC began with the words: "Politics is the science of how who gets what, when and why."

Under the cynical motto, Mr. Hillman today operates the National Citizens Political Action Committee with his lieutenants who have taken leave of absence from high Federal posts. He stalks the country squeezing dollars for the fourth-term campaign out of the working men and women of America, under threat that if they do not give the dollar they will lose their jobs.

But the working men and women of America are rising in protest all over the nation. Letters have been pouring in to me denouncing this Roosevelt poll tax imposed by Sidney Hillman. As one of them said:

"They can force my dollar out of me by threatening to take my job away, but they can't force my vote because it's secret. I'm going to vote Republican to save my own freedom."

And it's not just his freedom that man will save when he goes into the secrecy of the voting booth. He and millions of others like him will exercise their precious right of a secret ballot and will save the freedom of the whole American people.

Now, American liberty means the right of every man to believe and vote as he will, even to vote Communist. But liberty involves a corresponding duty, a duty to defend our country from what we consider evil. I have never hesitated to expose and denounce the cynical alliance of the New Deal and the corrupt big city machines which depend on the most criminal and degraded elements in our big cities. And I do not now propose to be silent when the New Deal, through Mr. Roosevelt's political lieutenant Hillman, strikes up a cynical alliance with Browder's Communists.

For a long time it has been the fashion to brush aside the Communists as of little importance because of their small numbers. The Communists themselves have cunningly played upon our respect for their civil liberties, which they themselves hold in such contempt. Yet the fact is that the Communists wield an influence far out of proportion to their numbers.

They are not themselves a political party. They are a fanatical, secret conspiracy of well-disciplined, highly trained zealots who work at their purposes every hour of the day. Falsehood, deception and smear propaganda are part of their technique.

They are adept at working behind the false front of those they contemptuously describe as "innocents." They love to fish in troubled waters. They place their members at strategic points where they can seize control of large organizations. Millions of Americans have seen this happen time after time. Liberal, intelligent organizations turn out to be Communist propaganda fronts.

Similarly, millions of workers have seen their union organizations captured by compact minorities who attend all the meetings, vote in a bloc and thereby seize the union machinery. Once in control, they cannot be dislodged. It was by just such tactics last spring that the Communists were able to seize possession of the American Labor party of New York, which in 1940 provided the balance of power that carried New York for Mr. Roosevelt.

Now, by the self-same tried and familiar tactics, the Communists are seizing control of the New Deal, through which they aim to seize control of the Government of the United States. If they should succeed, the fundamental freedom of every American would stand in the gravest of jeopardy.

Throughout the ages man's greatest struggle is the struggle to be free— free to worship God; to have a family and family life; free to educate his children; to live in economic security in his own home; to be able to have work of his own choosing; and to have a government which is his servant and not his master.

Our nation was founded by men and women who came here to achieve these things. They built their institutions in a deeply religious pattern and, by the Bill of Rights, they bound their Government to respect freedom of religion and the dignity of the individual. Because of what they did, we call America "the land of the free and the home of the brave."

But we can't take our freedom for granted, nor can we afford to stop being brave. There have always been, and there always will be, those who seek to destroy our freedoms.

Nazism and fascism are being crushed out in the world. But the totalitarian idea is very much alive and we must not slip to its other form, communism. All these concepts are enemies of freedom and we must equally reject all of them. These ideologies would make the state supreme, would give political power only to those who deny the supremacy of God and use that power to force all men to become cogs in a great materialistic machine.

Under these systems, the individual cannot worship, vote, or think as he would, or conduct his life as his own. Slavish obedience to the will of the state is the first great command, and the price of non-conformity is liquidation, either through violence or slow economic strangulation.

Today that pagan philosophy is sweeping through much of the world. As we look abroad, we see that in country after country its advocates are making a bid for power. We would be fools not to look for that same danger here. And we haven't far to look.

Even Mr. Roosevelt has felt he must say that he doesn't welcome the support of any person or group committed to communism. That is as it may be. The important facts are, first, that Mr. Roosevelt has so weakened and corrupted the Democratic party that it is readily subject to capture, and, second, that the forces of communism are, in fact, now capturing it.

That danger can be surely met only by ending a situation which leaves vast power in tired hands. The Republican party isn't perfect. But one thing at least is sure: neither the Communist group which Mr. Roosevelt professes to repudiate nor any other totalitarian group is making any effort to capture the Republican party, because they know it would be useless.

The Republican party is young and vigorous. It brought forth new leaders, brought forth new leaders all over the country like your own great Governor Saltonstall. In twenty-six of our States Republican Governors are bringing alert, progressive, competent and honest administration to the affairs of two-thirds of the American people already.

First in local governments, then in the States, the people have turned to our party. Now it is prepared to assume the responsibilities of National Government. It's rich in able leaders, every one of them steeped in the American tradition. It's close to the people. It wants to continue the American way of life and to perpetuate American institutions founded on the God-given right of individuals to be free. Millions of Democrats are voting Republican this year to save their own party and their country.

Under a Republican Administration there will be no danger that the power of government will slip through tired fingers into hands which would destroy that free America for which our sons are fighting and dying.

I have here a letter from an American soldier fighting in the Far Pacific. He says:

"When we come home there will be flags waving and people will exult in victory and cheer. But the greater effort will only begin then. We here are only securing the bridgehead of freedom. Will our generation forget that fact? If we do, this victory will be only the beginning of defeat for us and for our children."

Let us tonight resolve that we will be equal to the duty we owe that soldier and his comrades. Let us at home seize and hold that bridgehead to freedom. Let us install on Jan. 20 a government which under God will dedicate its purpose to the preservation of the individual dignity and freedom of every American.

PRESIDENT ROOSEVELT'S CAMPAIGN BROADCAST
FROM THE WHITE HOUSE

November 2, 1944 [1]

I had hoped that during the early part of this week, I could have gone in person to some of the nearer midwestern cities, such as Cleveland and Detroit, and I had hoped that I could visit some of my old friends in upstate New York.

However, on my return to Washington from Chicago, I find that I am not free to spare the time right now. Therefore, I am speaking to you from the White House.

I am disappointed about this—but, as I told the American people when I became President, I follow the principle of first things first; and this war comes first.

We have all been overjoyed by the news from the far Pacific, eight thousand miles away. Never before in all of history has it been possible successfully to conduct such massive operations with such long lanes of supply and communication.

In the Pacific Theatre, even while we are fighting a major war in Europe, our advance toward Japan is many months ahead of our own optimistic schedule.

But we must remember that any military operation conducted at such a distance is a hazardous undertaking. In any long advance, progress may be interrupted by checks or set-backs. However, ultimately our advance will stop only in Tokyo itself.

Our success has been the result of planning and organization and building; it has been the result of the hardest work and the hardest fighting of which our people are capable.

On the other side of the world, in Europe, the Allied forces under General Eisenhower are pounding the Germans with relentless force.

We do not expect to have a winter lull in Europe. We expect to keep striking—to keep the enemy on the move—to hit him again and again—to give him no rest—and to drive through to the final objective—Berlin.

In Italy, against the handicap of rugged mountain obstacles, and against bitter German resistance—the Allied Armies are steadily moving forward, wearing down the German fighting strength in a slow, hard slugging match.

In winning this war there is just one sure way to guarantee the minimum of casualties—by seeing to it that, in every action, we have overwhelming material superiority.

We have already sent to Europe—just one of our many fronts—a force greater than the entire American Expeditionary Force of 1918. American troops now are fighting along a battle-line of three hundred miles in France and about a hundred miles in Italy.

Within ten weeks after the first landings in France last June, the Allies had landed on the Normandy beaches nearly two million men, more than two million tons of supplies, and nearly half a million vehicles.

Think of all that vast mass of material for one operation—think of the war factories and ships and planes and railroads and labor required to produce and deliver the right supplies to the right place at the right time.

[1] White House news release.

Then think of the tasks that lie ahead of us—all the long, tough miles to Berlin—all the major landings yet to be made in the Pacific—and you will have a conception of the magnitude of the job that remains to be done. It is still a job requiring the all-out production efforts of all of our people here at home.

Delays in the performance of our job at home mean prolonging the war. They will mean an increase in the total price we must pay in the lives of our men.

All of our able commanders in the field know this. And so do our soldiers and sailors. And we at home must never forget it.

All Americans at home are concerned in this—the fulfillment of an obligation to our fighting men.

The women of American are most profoundly concerned.

Today, women are playing a far more direct, more personal part in the war than ever before.

First, and I think rightly first, are those women who have gone into the Wacs and the Waves and the Marines and the Coast Guard, the nursing services of the Army and Navy, the Red Cross—serving in all kinds of places, in and out of the United States—all of them performing functions which definitely relieve men for combat work.

Then there are the millions of women who have gone into war industries. They are greatly responsible for the fact that the munitions and supplies to our men at the front have gone through to them on time.

And, finally, the women who uncomplainingly have done the job of keeping the homes going—the homes with service flags in the window—service flags with blue stars or gold stars.

And we do not forget those women who have volunteered with the men in the difficult and important work of the ration board all over the nation—doing the job of apportioning the necessities of life equitably among their neighbors—rich and poor.

Everyone who has made a sacrifice in this war—and that includes one hundred and thirty-five million Americans—is determined that this must not happen again—that the disastrous mistakes of the past shall not be repeated —that this nation shall be committed to play a leading part in a world organization which shall be strong and effective and enduring.

We have been told during this political campaign that unless the American people elect the Republican Presidential choice, the Congress will not cooperate in the peace. This is a threat to build a party spite-fence between us and the peace.

I do not know who empowers these men to speak for the Congress in uttering such a threat.

Certainly the United States Senate and the House of Representatives showed no reluctance to agree with the foreign policy of this Administration when, almost unanimously last year, they passed the Connally and Fulbright Resolutions which pledged this nation to cooperate in a world organization for peace.

These are high and serious matters to those who know how greatly our victory in this war and our ability to establish a lasting peace depend on maintaining unshaken that understanding which must be the core of the United Nations.

It is heartening for me to have known and to have talked with the statesmen of the smaller nations as well as our larger Allies—men like Benes of Czechoslovakia, Mikolajczyk of Poland, Nygaardswold of Norway—and leaders of democratic thought from Yugoslavia and Greece and Denmark and Belgium and the Netherlands—and, of course, the great leaders of our neighbor countries in this Hemisphere.

I have spent many fruitful hours talking with men from the more remote nations—such as Turkey, Persia, Arabia, Abyssinia, Liberia, Siam and others —for all of them are part and parcel of the great family of nations. It is only through an understanding acquired by years of consultation, that one can get a viewpoint of their problems and their innate yearnings for freedom.

And all of them have this in common—that they yearn for peace and stability, and they look to America with hope and faith.

The world is rising from the agony of the past, the world is turning with hope to the future. It would be a sorry and cynical thing to betray this hope for the sake of mere political advantage, and a tragic thing to shatter it because of the failure of vision.

There have been some other aspects of this campaign which have been distasteful to all of us.

This campaign has been marred by even more than the usual crop of whisperings and rumorings. Some of these get into print, in certain types of newspapers; others are traded about, secretly, in one black market after another. I do not propose to answer in kind.

The voting record proves that the American people pay little attention to whispering campaigns. They have paid little attention to all the malignant rumors of enemy origin which have flooded this country during this war— and I am sure they will treat the present whispering with the same contempt.

As we approach Election Day, more wicked charges may be made with the hope that someone or somebody will gain momentary advantage.

Hysterical, last minute accusations or sensational revelations, are trumped up in an attempt to panic the people on Election Day.

But the American people are not panicked easily. Pearl Harbor proved that.

This election will not be decided on a basis of malignant murmurings—or shouts. It will be settled on the basis of the record.

We all know the record of our military achievements in this war.

And we all know the record of the tremendous production achievements of our American farmers, our American business men, and our American labor.

And we all know the record of our team-work with our Allies. Immediately after Pearl Harbor we formed with the other United Nations the greatest military coalition in world history. And we have steadily gone on from that to establish the basis for a strong and durable organization for world peace.

The America which built the greatest war machine in all history, and which kept it supplied, is an America which can look to the future with confidence and faith.

I propose the continuance of the team-work that we have demonstrated in this war.

By carrying out the plans we have made we can avoid a post-war depression—we can provide employment for our veterans and our war workers—we can achieve an orderly reconversion.

Above all, we can avoid another false boom like that which burst in 1929, and a dismal collapse like that of 1930 to 1933.

With continuance of our team-work, I look forward, under the leadership of this Government, to an era of expansion and production and employment —to new industries and increased security.

I look forward to millions of new homes, fit for decent living; to new, low-priced automobiles; new highways; new airplanes and airports; to television; and miraculous, new inventions and discoveries, made during this war, which will be adapted to the peace-time uses of a peace-loving people.

The record that we have established in this war is one of which every American has a right to be proud—today and for all time.

We do not want the later record to say that the great job was done in vain.

We do not want our boys to come back to an America which is headed for another war in another generation.

Our post-war job will be to work and to build—for a better America than we have ever known.

If in the next few years we can start that job right, then you and I can know that we have kept faith with our boys—we have helped them to win a total victory.

PRESIDENT ROOSEVELT'S BOSTON CAMPAIGN SPEECH

November 4, 1944 [1]

This is not my first visit to Boston. I shall not review all my previous visits. I should have to go on talking for several days to do that—and radio time costs a lot of money.

But I want to recall one visit, back in October, 1928, when I came here to urge you to vote for a great American named Al Smith.

And you did vote for that eternally "Happy Warrior."

The Commonwealth of Massachuetts—and your good neighbor, Rhode Island—went Democratic in 1928—four years before the rest of the Nation did.

This year—and I am making no predictions—this year we would like to welcome into the fold Maine and Vermont.

And while I am speaking of that campaign of 1928, let me remind you that, having nominated Al Smith for the second time for the Presidency, I was then running at his request for the Governorship of New York. And people were then—even then—saying that my health would not permit me to discharge the duties of public office.

I think that it is by now a pretty well established fact that I managed to survive my four years as Governor of New York.

In this connection, in 1928 Al Smith remarked publicly that the Governor of New York does not have to be an acrobat. And not many months before his untimely death, he remarked to me in my office in Washington "It is perfectly evident you don't have to be an acrobat to be President either."

When I talked here in Boston in 1928 I talked about racial and religious intolerance which was then—as it unfortunately still is—"a menace to the liberties of America."

And all the bigots were gunning for Al Smith.

Religious intolerance, social intolerance and political intolerance have no place in our American life.

Here in New England you have been fighting bigotry and intolerance for centuries. You know that all of our people—except pure-blooded Indians—are immigrants or descendants of immigrants, including even those who came here on the Mayflower.

[1] White House news release.

Today, in this war, our fine boys are fighting magnificently all over the world and among those boys are the Murphys and the Kellys, the Smiths and the Joneses, the Cohens, the Carusos, the Kowalksis, the Schultzes, the Olsens, the Swobodas, and—right in with all the rest of them—the Cabots and the Lowells.

All of these and others like them are the life-blood of America. They are the hope of the world.

It is our duty to them to make sure that, big as this country is, there is no room in it for racial or religious intolerance—and that there is no room for snobbery.

Our young men and young women are fighting not only for their existence, and their homes and their families. They also are fighting for a country and a world where men and women of all races, colors and creeds can live, work, speak and worship—in peace, freedom and security.

If we can shorten the war by one month—even by one minute—we shall have saved the lives of some of our young men and women. We must not let our comforts or conveniences, our politics or our prejudices, stand in the way of our determination to drive—to drive relentlessly and unflinchingly—over the hard road to final victory.

You and I—all of us who are war-workers—must stay on the job!

Although victory over the Nazis and the Japanese is certain and inevitable —and I for one have never had one moment's doubt of our ultimate victory —the war is still far from over. There is tough, hard and bloody fighting ahead of us.

We got into this war because we were attacked by the Japanese—and because they and their Axis partners, Hitler's Germany and Mussolini's Italy, declared war on us.

I am sure that any real American would have chosen, as this Government did, to fight when our own soil was made the object of a sneak attack. As for myself, under the same circumstances, I would choose to do the same thing—again and again and again.

When our enemies flung the gage of battle at us, we elected to fight them in the American way, which meant that we went out after them—and we started punching—and we are still punching.

One of the tyrants, Mussolini, has been knocked out. The others are getting groggier and groggier every day.

And we are made happy by the fact that the Italian people—our long-time friends—are started once again along the paths of freedom and peace.

We were better prepared for this war than for any previous war in our history.

On the day of Pearl Harbor, we had more than two million men in our armed forces.

Our war production, started a year and a half before, was rolling toward the gigantic volume of output that has been achieved.

Our Navy was building. Indeed, it had been building ever since 1933, when I first used PWA funds to start a naval building program—which included our first modern carriers. One of those carriers, authorized ten years ago, was the "Enterprise," a grand and gallant ship which has covered herself with glory all through this war and was in there fighting last week in the great victory in Philippine waters.

And—in addition to our physical preparedness—we had something far more important—spiritual preparedness.

The American people were ready for it. On the day of Pearl Harbor they

rose up as one man with a mighty shout—a shout heard 'round the world—
"Let's go!"

And we went!

The average American citizen is doing some hard thinking these days about
what sort of Government he wants during the next four years.

The memory of our people is not short. The years 1929 to 1933 are
thoroughly and grimly remembered by millions of our citizens—by workers
who lost their jobs and their homes, by farmers who lost their crops and
their farms, by families who lost their savings.

Since those dark days early in 1933, many fortifications have been erected
to protect the people of this country—just as we promised that there would be.

These fortifications have provided protection for your bank deposits and
your investments—your standard of living—your right to organize unions and
to bargain collectively with your employers.

They protect your soil and rivers and trees—your heritage of natural resources. They provide you with protection against the hazards of unemployment and old age—they protect you against inflation and runaway prices.

These fortifications are now manned by zealous defenders—and these
defenders are not Communists and they are not fossils.

Can the citizens of the Nation now afford to turn over these bulwarks to
the men who raised every possible obstacle to their original construction?

Does the average American believe that those who fought tooth and nail
against progressive legislation during the past twelve years can be trusted to
cherish and preserve that legislation?

Can it be that those who financed the bitter opposition to the New Deal
have made an about-face and are now willing and able to fight for the objectives of the New Deal?

We have all heard Republican orators in this campaign call this Administration everything under the sun and, promise that they, *if* elected—and oh, my
friends, what a big "if" that is—if elected they would institute the biggest
house-cleaning in history.

What a job that would be! It would mean, among other things, sweeping
out with my Administration the most efficient and the most patriotic Republicans that could be found in the whole country.

But—despite these campaign promises of wholesale house-cleaning—have
you heard one word of specific criticism of any of the progressive laws that
this Administration has proposed and enacted?

Have you heard any talk of sweeping out any of these laws—or sweeping
out any of the agencies which administer these laws?

Oh, no—on that subject the Republican politicians are very uncharacter-
istically silent.

This Administration has made mistakes. That I freely assert.

But our mistakes have been honestly made during sincere efforts to help
the great mass of citizens. Never have we made the inexcusable mistake of
substituting talk for action when farms were being foreclosed, homes were
being sold at auction, and people were standing in breadlines.

I thank God that it cannot be charged that at any time, under any circumstances, have we made the mistake of forgetting our sacred obligation to
the American people.

And, I might add, never will we make that kind of mistake.

Is it conceivable to you that this Administration with its record of very
deep concern for human welfare could ever be guilty of neglect of the welfare
of our fighting men?

When your sons, and my sons, come home from the battlefronts—and they are coming home just as quickly as they are no longer needed for the essential job of this war—we are going to see that they have work—honest, self-respecing jobs.

We are going to see to it that those of them seeking farms get a real chance to settle on land of their own.

We are going to see to it that those who hope to establish businesses have a legitimate and fair opportunity to do so.

The American people are quite competent to judge a political party which works both sides of the street—a party which has one candidate making campaign promises of all kinds of added government expenditures in the West while a running mate demands less government expenditures in the East.

You know—just as an aside, and I think I can speak freely to my old friends here in Boston—this is really a funny campaign.

I think I heard some campaign orator say that Secretary Hull and the rest of us had done such a fine job with the Good Neighbor policy and our plans for world peace—that it is time for a change.

I believe I heard some campaign orator say that this "incompetent" Administration had developed a program which was so good for the farmers and the businessmen and the workers of the nation—that it is time for a change.

I think I heard some campaign orator say that we have so thoroughly shifted the control over our banks from Wall Street and State Street to the Capital of the United States—that it is time for a change.

And I am quite sure I heard somebody say that this "chaotic" Administration has done such an amazing job of war production—that it is time for a change.

I think I even heard somebody say that those "tired, quarrelsome" old men—are waging such a victorious war—that it is time for a change.

Well—if it is time for a change—the way to get it in this democracy is by means of votes. Whether I win or lose, I want to see a turnout next Tuesday of the biggest vote in our American history.

And that means at least fifty million votes.

We could not find a better way to tell our boys overseas that the country they are fighting for is still going strong.

Just the other day you people here in Boston witnessed an amazing demonstration of talking out of both sides of the mouth.

Speaking here in Boston, a Republican candidate said—and pardon me if I quote him correctly—he said that "the Communists are seizing control of the New Deal, through which they aim to control the Government of the United States."

However, on that very same day that very same candidate had spoken in Worcester and he said that with Republican victory in November "we can end one-man government, we can forever remove the threat of monarchy in the United States."

Now, really—which is it—communism or monarchy?

I do not think we could have both in this country, even if we wanted either —which we do not.

We want neither communism nor monarchy. We want to live under our Constitution—which has served pretty well for 155 years. If this were a banquet hall instead of a ball park, I would propose a toast that we will continue to live under it for another 155 years.

I confess that often in this campaign, I have been tempted to speak my mind with sharper vigor and greater indignation.

Everybody knows that I was reluctant to run for the Presidency again this year. But since the campaign has developed I tell you frankly that I have become most anxious to win—for the reason that never in my lifetime has a campaign been filled with such misrepresentation, distortion, and false-hood. Never since 1928 have there been so many attempts to stimulate in America racial or religious intolerance.

When any political candidate stands up and says, solemnly, that there is danger that the Government of the United States—your Government—could be sold out to the Communists—then I say that that candidate reveals a shocking lack of trust in America.

He reveals a shocking lack of faith in democracy—in the spiritual strength of our people.

If ever there was a time in which the spiritual strength of our people was put to the test, that time was in the terrible depression of 1929 to 1933.

Then our people might have turned to alien ideologies—like communism or fascism.

But—our democratic faith was too sturdy. What the American people demanded in 1933 was not less democracy—but more democracy—and that is what they got.

The American people proved in the black days of depression—as they have again proved in this war—that there is no chink in the armor of democracy.

On this subject—and on all subjects—I say to you, my friends, what I said when first you conferred upon me the exalted honor of the Presidency: "We have nothing to fear but fear itself."

And I do not think you will ever cast your votes for fearful men.

We now face the enormous and complex problems of building with our Allies a strong world structure of peace.

In doing that historic job we shall be standing before a mighty bar of judgment—the judgment of all those who have fought and died in this war —the judgment of generations yet unborn—the very judgment of God.

I believe that we Americans will want the peace to be built by men who have shown foresight rather than hindsight.

Peace, no less than war, must offer a spirit of comradeship, a spirit of achievement, a spirit of unselfishness, and indomitable will to victory.

We have waged war against the wilderness—against the mountains and the rivers—against the droughts and the storms. We have waged war against ignorance—against oppression—against intolerance.

We have waged war against poverty—against disease.

We fought the Revolutionary War for the principle that all men are created equal—and in that war we pledged "our lives, our fortunes, and our sacred honor."

This war, which we are now fighting, has been an interruption in the story of our forward progress; but it has also opened a new chapter—a chapter which it is for us now living to begin.

At the end of this war this country will have the greatest material power of any nation in the world.

It will be a clean, shining America—richer than any other in skilled work-ers, engineers, farmers, businessmen, scientists.

It will be an America in which there is a genuine partnership between the farmer and the worker and the businessman—in which there are abundant jobs and an expanding economy of peace.

And around us we see an unfinished world—a world of awakened peoples struggling to set themselves on the path of civilization—people struggling everywhere to achieve a higher cultural and material standard of living.

I say we must wage the coming battle for America and for civilization on a scale worthy of the way we have unitedly waged the battles against tyranny and reaction and wage it through all the difficulties and disappointments that may ever clog the wheels of progress.

And I say we must wage it in association with the United Nations with whom we have stood and fought—with the association ever growing.

I say we must wage a peace to attract the highest hearts and the most competent hands and brains.

That, my friends, is the conception I have of the meaning of total victory.

And that conception is founded upon faith—faith in the unlimited destiny —the unconquerable spirit—of America.

MARSHAL JOSEPH V. STALIN'S REPORT ON THE 27TH ANNIVERSARY OF THE REVOLUTION

November 6, 1944 [1]

Comrades!

Today the Soviet people celebrate the 27th Anniversary of the triumph of the Soviet Revolution in our country. This is the fourth time that our country is observing the Anniversary of the Soviet Revolution in the midst of the Patriotic War against the German-fascist invaders.

That does not mean, of course, that the fourth year of the war does not differ from the preceding three years of the war in its results. On the contrary, there is a radical difference between them.

Whereas the preceding two years of the war were when the German forces were on the offensive and when they advanced into the interior of our country—years when the Red Army was compelled to fight defensive actions —and whereas the third year of the war was a year of radical change on our front, when the Red Army launched powerful offensive actions, smashed the Germans in a number of decisive battles, cleared the German troops out of two-thirds of the Soviet territory and compelled them to pass to the defensive while the Red Army was still waging war on the German forces single-handed without substantial support from the Allies—the fourth year of the war has been a year of decisive victories over the German forces for the Soviet Armies and the Armies of our Allies, a year in which the Germans, now compelled to fight on two fronts, found themselves flung back to the German frontiers.

In the upshot, this year has ended in the expulsion of the German forces from the Soviet Union, France, Belgium and central Italy, and the transfer of hostilities to German territory.

The decisive successes of the Red Army this year and the expulsion of the Germans from Soviet territory were predetermined by the succession of shattering blows which our troops dealt the German forces beginning as far back as last January and following then throughout the year under review.

The first blow was struck by our troops in January of this year at Leningrad and Novgorod when the Red Army broke up permanent German defenses and flung the enemy back to the Baltics. This blow resulted in the liberation of the Leningrad Region.

The second blow was struck in February and March of this year on the

[1] Information Bulletin, Embassy of the U.S.S.R.

Bug River when the Red Army routed the German forces and flung them beyond the Dniester. As a result of this blow the Ukraine west of the Dnieper was freed of the German-fascist invaders.

The third blow was struck in April and May of this year in the area of the Crimea when the German troops were flung into the Black Sea. As the result of this blow, the Crimea and Odessa were delivered from German oppression.

The fourth blow was struck in June of this year in the area of Karelia, when the Red Army routed the Finnish forces, liberated Vyborg and Petrozavodsk and flung the Finns back into the interior of Finland. This blow resulted in the liberation of the greater part of the Karelo-Finnish Soviet Republic.

The fifth blow was struck at the Germans in June and July of this year when the Red Army utterly routed the German forces at Vitebsk, Bobruisk and Mogilev; this blow culminated in the encirclement of thirty German divisions at Minsk. As a result of this blow, our forces: a) liberated the whole of the Byelorussian Soviet Republic, b) gained the Vistula and liberated a considerable part of Poland, our ally, c) gained the Niemen and liberated the greater part of the Lithuanian Soviet Republic, and d) forced the Niemen and approached the frontiers of Germany.

The sixth blow was struck in July and August of this year in the area of the Western Ukraine when the Red Army routed the German forces at Lvov and flung them beyond the San and the Vistula. As a result of this blow: a) the Western Ukraine was liberated, and b) our troops forced the Vistula and set up a strong bridgehead beyond it, west of Sandomir.

The seventh blow was struck in August of this year in the Kishinev and Jassy area when our troops utterly routed the German and Rumanian forces. It culminated in the encirclement of twenty-two German divisions at Kishinev, this number not including Rumanian divisions. As a result of this blow: a) the Moldavian Soviet Republic was liberated, b) Germany's Rumanian ally was put out of action and declared war on Germany and Hungary, c) Germany's Bulgarian ally was put out of action and likewise declared war on Germany, d) the road was opened for our troops to Hungary, Germany's last ally in Europe, and e) the opportunity arose to reach out a helping hand to Yugoslavia, our ally, against the German invaders.

The eighth blow was struck in September and October of this year in the Baltics, when the Red Army routed the German forces at Tallinn and Riga and drove them from the Baltics. As a result of this blow: a) the Estonian Soviet Republic was liberated, b) the greater part of the Latvian Soviet Republic was liberated, c) Germany's Finnish ally was put out of action and declared war on Germany, and d) over thirty German divisions found themselves cut off from Prussia and gripped in pincers between Tukums and Libava where they are now being hammered to a finish by our troops.

In October of this year the ninth blow was launched by our troops between the Tisza and the Danube in the area of Hungary; its purpose is to put Hungary out of the war and turn her against Germany. As a result of this blow which has not yet been consummated: a) our forces rendered direct assistance to our ally, Yugoslavia, in driving out the Germans and liberating Belgrade, and b) our forces receive the opportunity to cross the Carpathians and reach out a helping hand to our ally, the Czechoslovak Republic, part of whose territory has already been freed of the German invaders.

Lastly, at the end of October of this year, a blow was dealt the German forces in north Finland when the German troops were knocked out of the area of Pechenga and our troops pursuing the Germans entered the territory of Norway, our ally.

I shall not give figures of the losses in killed and prisoners which the enemy sustained in these operations, of the number of guns, tanks, aircraft, shells and machine guns captured by our troops, and so forth. You are probably acquainted with these figures from the communiqués of the Soviet Information Bureau.

Such are the principal operations carried out by the Red Army during the past year, operations which have led to the expulsion of the German forces from our country.

As a result of these operations as many as 120 divisions of the Germans and their allies have been routed and put out of action. In place of the 257 divisions that faced our front last year, of which 207 were German, we now have facing our front, after all the "total" and "super-total" mobilizations, only 204 German and Hungarian divisions, the German divisions numbering no more than 180.

It has to be admitted that in this war Hitler Germany with her fascist army has proved to be a more powerful, crafty and experienced adversary than Germany and her army were in any war of the past. It should be added that in this war the Germans succeeded in exploiting the productive forces of practically the whole of Europe and the quite considerable armies of their vassal states.

And if in spite of these favorable conditions for the prosecution of the war Germany nevertheless finds herself on the brink of imminent destruction, the explanation is that her chief adversary, the Soviet Union, has surpassed Hitler Germany in strength.

What must be regarded as a new factor in the war against Hitler Germany this past year is that this year the Red Army has not been operating against the German forces single-handed as was the case in previous years, but together with the forces of our Allies.

The Teheran Conference was not held for nothing. The decision of the Teheran Conference on a joint blow at Germany from the west, east and south began to be carried out with amazing precision. Simultaneously with the summer operations of the Red Army on the Soviet-German front, the Allied forces launched the invasion of France and organized powerful offensive operations which compelled Hitler Germany to wage war on two fronts.

The troops and navy of our Allies accomplished a mass landing operation on the coast of France that has no parallel in history for scope and organization, and overcame the German fortifications with consummate skill. Thus Germany found herself gripped in a vise between two fronts.

As was to be expected, the enemy failed to withstand the joint blows of the Red Army and the Allied forces. The enemy's resistance was broken and his troops were knocked out of central Italy, France, Belgium and the Soviet Union in a short space of time. The enemy was flung back to the German frontier.

There can be no doubt that without the opening of the second front in Europe, which holds as many as seventy-five German divisions, our troops would not have been able to break the resistance of the German forces and knock them out of the Soviet Union in such a short time.

But it is equally indubitable that without the powerful offensive operations of the Red Army in the summer of this year, which held as many as 200 German divisions, the forces of our Allies could not have coped so quickly with the German forces and knocked them out of central Italy, France and

Belgium. The thing is to keep Germany gripped in this vise between the two fronts. That is the key to victory.

If the Red Army was able to acquit itself successfully of its duty to its country and to drive the Germans from Soviet soil, it was because of the unreserved support received in the rear from our whole country, from all the peoples of our country. *Everything for the front!* has been the watchword this past year in the selfless effort of all Soviet people—workers, peasants and intelligentsia, as well as in the directing activities of our Government and Party bodies.

The past year has been marked by fresh successes in industry, agriculture and transport, by further progress in our war economy. With the war in its fourth year our factories are producing several times more tanks, aircraft, guns, mortars and ammunition than in its opening phase.

In the rehabilitation of agriculture the most difficult period has been passed. With the fertile fields of the Don and the Kuban restored to our country and the Ukraine liberated, our farming is recovering rapidly from its grave losses.

The Soviet railways have stood a strain that the transport of other countries would hardly be able to bear.

All this indicates that the economic foundation of the Soviet State proved to possess infinitely greater vitality than the economy of the enemy states. The socialist system born of the October Revolution has lent our people and our Army great and invincible strength. Despite the heavy burden of this war, despite the temporary occupation by the Germans of very large and economically important parts of the country, the Soviet State did not reduce the supply of arms and ammunition for the front as the war proceeded, but increased it from year to year. Today the Red Army has not less but more tanks, guns and aircraft than the German army. As for the quality of our war material, it is far superior to the enemy armaments in that respect.

Just as the Red Army achieved military victory over the fascist forces in its long and arduous single-handed struggle, so the workers in the Soviet rear won economic victory over the enemy in their lone fight against Hitler Germany and her associates.

The Soviet people have denied themselves many necessities, have consciously incurred serious material privations, in order to give more for the front. The unparalleled hardships of the present war have not broken but further tempered the iron will and fearless spirit of the Soviet people. Our people have rightfully won the fame of a heroic nation. Our working class is giving all its strength to the cause of victory, constantly improving the technology of production, increasing the capacity of industrial enterprises, building new factories and mills. The working class of the Soviet Union has a great labor exploit to its credit in the present war.

Our intelligentsia are striking out boldly in the field of technical and cultural innovation, successfully promoting modern science and displaying the creative spirit in applying its achievements to the production of munitions for the Red Army. By their creative work the Soviet intelligentsia have made an invaluable contribution to the enemy's defeat.

An army cannot fight and win without modern armaments. But neither can it fight and win without bread, without provisions. Thanks to the solicitude of the collective farm peasantry, the Red Army experiences no shortage of food in this fourth year of war. The men and women of the collective farms are supplying the workers and intelligentsia with foodstuffs and industry with raw materials, making it possible for factories and mills producing arms and equipment for the front to function normally. Actively and with a clear sense of duty to the country our collective farm peasantry are helping the Red Army to achieve victory over the enemy.

The matchless labor exploits of the Soviet women and of our splendid youth will go down forever in history; for it is they that have borne the brunt of the work in the factories and mills and on the collective and State farms. For the sake of their country's honor and independence Soviet women, youths and girls are displaying true valor and heroism on the labor front. They have shown themselves worthy of their fathers and sons, husbands and brothers, who are defending their homeland against the German-fascist fiends.

The labor exploits of the Soviet people in the rear, like the immortal deeds of valor of our soldiers at the front, are rooted in their fervent and life-giving spirit of Soviet patriotism. The strength of Soviet patriotism lies in the fact that it is based not on racial or nationalistic prejudices, but on the people's profound devotion and loyalty to their Soviet homeland, on the fraternal partnership of the working people of all the nationalities in our land.

Soviet patriotism blends harmoniously the national traditions of the peoples and the common vital interests of all the working peoples of the Soviet Union. Far from dividing them, Soviet patriotism welds all the nations and peoples of our country into a single fraternal family. This should be regarded as the foundation of the inviolable and ever stronger friendship among the peoples of the Soviet Union.

At the same time the peoples of the USSR respect the rights and independence of the nations of foreign countries and have always shown themselves willing to live in peace and friendship with their neighbor states. This should be regarded as the foundation of the contacts growing and gaining strength between our State and the freedom-loving nations. The reason Soviet men and women hate the German invaders is not that they are of different nationality, but that they have brought untold calamity and suffering on our people and on all freedom-loving nations. It is an old saying of our people that the wolf is not beaten for being gray but for devouring sheep.

The German fascists chose the misanthropic race theory for their ideological weapon in the expectation that by preaching bestial nationalism they would produce the moral and political conditions for the German invaders' domination over the subjugated nations. Actually, however, the policy of racial hatred pursued by the Hitlerites has proved a source of weakness for the German-fascist state internally and of its isolation internationally.

The ideology and policy of racial hatred have been a factor in the disintegration of Hitler's brigand bloc. It cannot be regarded as an accident that not only the subjugated peoples of France and Yugoslavia, Poland and Czechoslovakia, Greece and Belgium, Denmark, Norway and the Netherlands have risen against the German imperialists, but also Hitler's former vassals —the Italians and Rumanians, Finns and Bulgarians. By their savage policy the Hitler clique have set all the nations of the world against Germany, and the so-called "chosen German race" has become the object of universal hatred.

It is not only military defeat that the Hitlerites have sustained in this war, but moral and political defeat as well. The ideology of equality of all races and nations which has taken firm root in our country, the ideology of friendship among the peoples, has emerged completely victorious over the Hitlerite ideology of bestial nationalism and racial hatred.

Today when the Patriotic War is drawing to its victorious conclusion, the historic role of the Soviet people is revealed in its full greatness. It is universally acknowledged now that by their selfless struggle the Soviet people have saved the civilization of Europe from the fascist vandals. That is the great service rendered by the Soviet people to the history of mankind.

The past year has been a year of triumph for the common cause of the anti-German coalition, for the sake of which the peoples of the Soviet Union, Great Britain and the United States have joined in a fighting alliance. It has been a year of consolidation of the unity of the three main powers and of coordination of their actions against Hitler Germany.

The Teheran Conference decision on joint actions against Germany and the brilliant realization of that decision are one of the striking indications of the consolidation of the anti-Hitlerite coalition front. There are few instances in history of plans for large-scale military operations undertaken in joint actions against a common enemy being carried out so fully and with such precision as the plan for a joint blow against Germany drawn up at the Teheran Conference. There can be no doubt that without unity of opinion and coordination of actions between the three great powers, the Teheran decision could not have been put into effect so fully and with such precision. Nor, on the other hand, can there be any doubt that the successful realization of the Teheran decision was bound to serve for the consolidation of the United Nations front.

An equally striking indication of the solidity of the front of the United Nations is to be seen in the decisions of the Dumbarton Oaks Conference on postwar security. There is talk of differences between the three powers on certain security problems. Differences do exist, of course, and they will arise on a number of other issues as well. Differences of opinion are to be found even among people in one and the same party. They are all the more bound to occur between representatives of different states and different parties.

The surprising thing is not that differences exist, but that there are so few of them and that as a rule in practically every case they are resolved in a spirit of unity and coordination among the three great powers.

What matters is not that there are differences, but that these differences do not transgress the bounds of what the interests of unity of the three great powers allow, and that in the long run they are resolved in accordance with the interests of that unity. It is known that more serious differences existed between us over the opening of the second front. It is also known, however, that in the end these differences were resolved in a spirit of complete accord.

The same thing may be said of the differences at the Dumbarton Oaks Conference. What is characteristic about this conference is not that certain differences were revealed there, but that nine-tenths of the security problems were dispatched at this conference in a spirit of complete unanimity. That is why I think that the Dumbarton Oaks Conference decisions are to be regarded as a striking indication of the solidity of the front of the anti-German coalition.

The recent talks in Moscow with Mr. Churchill, the head of the British Government, and Mr. Eden, the British Foreign Secretary, are to be viewed as an even more striking indication of the consolidation of the United Nations front, held as these talks were in an atmosphere of friendship and a spirit of perfect unanimity. All through the war the Hitlerites have been making frantic efforts to cause disunion among the United Nations and set them at loggerheads, to stir up suspicion and unfriendly feeling among them, to weaken their war effort by mutual mistrust and if possible by conflict between them as well.

Ambitions like these on the part of the Hitler politicians are easy enough to understand. There is no greater danger for them than the unity of the United Nations in the struggle against Hitler imperialism, and they could achieve no greater military-political success than by dividing the Allied powers in their fight against the common foe.

It is well-known, however, how futile the efforts of the fascist politicians to disrupt the alliance of the great powers have proved. That means that the alliance between the U.S.S.R., Great Britain and the United States is founded not on casual, short-lived considerations but on vital and lasting interests. There need be no doubt that having stood the strain of over three years of war and being sealed with the blood of nations risen in defense of their liberty and honor, the fighting alliance of the democratic powers will all the more certainly stand the strain of the concluding phase of the war.

However, the past year has been not only a year of the consolidation of the anti-German front of the Allied powers, but also a year of its extension. It cannot be regarded as an accident that after Italy, other Allies of Germany —Finland, Rumania and Bulgaria—have also been put out of the war. A point to be made is that these states have not only withdrawn from the war but have broken with Germany and declared war on her, thus joining the front of the United Nations. That is certainly an extension of the United Nations front against Hitler Germany.

Without doubt Germany's last ally in Europe, Hungary, will also be put out of action in the nearest future. This will mean the complete isolation of Hitler Germany in Europe and the inevitability of her collapse.

The United Nations face the victorious conclusion of the war against Hitler Germany. The war against Germany will be won by the United Nations— of that there can no longer be any doubt today.

To win the war against Germany is to accomplish a great historical task. But winning the war is not in itself synonymous with insuring for the nations lasting peace and guaranteed security in the future. The thing is not only to win the war but also to render new aggression and new war impossible, if not forever then at least for a long time to come.

After her defeat Germany will of course be disarmed both in the economic and the military-political sense. It would however be naive to think that she will not attempt to restore her might and launch new aggression. It is common knowledge that the German chieftains are already now preparing for a new war. History reveals that a short period of time, some twenty or thirty years, is enough for Germany to recover from defeat and reestablish her might.

What means are there to preclude fresh aggression on Germany's part, and if war should start nevertheless, to nip it in the bud and give it no opportunity to develop into a big war?

The question is the more in place since history shows that aggressive nations, as the nations that attack, are usually better prepared for a new war than peace-loving nations which, having no interest in a new war, are usually behind with their preparations for it. It is a fact that in the present war the aggressive nations had an invasion army all ready even before the war broke out; while the peace-loving nations did not have even a fully adequate army to cover the mobilization.

One cannot regard as an accident such distasteful facts as the Pearl Harbor "incident," the loss of the Philippines and other Pacific islands, the loss of Hongkong and Singapore, when Japan as the aggressive nation proved to be better prepared for war than Great Britain and the United States of America, which pursued a policy of peace. Nor can one regard as an accident such a distasteful fact as the loss of the Ukraine, Byelorussia and the Baltics in the very first year of the war, when Germany as the aggressive nation proved better prepared for war than the peace-loving Soviet Union.

It would be naive to explain these facts by the personal qualities of the Japanese and the Germans, their superiority over the British, the Americans and the Russians, their foresight and so on. The reason here is not personal qualities but the fact that the aggressive nations interested in a new war, being nations that prepare for war over a long time and accumulate forces for it, are usually—and are bound to be—better prepared for war than peace-loving nations which have no interest in a new war. That is natural and understandable. If you like, this is a law of history which it would be dangerous to ignore.

It is not to be denied accordingly that in days to come the peace-loving nations may once more find themselves caught off their guard by aggression, unless of course they work out special measures right now which can avert it.

Well, what means are there to preclude fresh aggression on Germany's part, and if war should start nevertheless, to nip it in the bud and give it no opportunity to develop into a big war?

There is only one means to this end, in addition to the complete disarmament of the aggressive nations: that is, to establish a special organization made up of representatives of the peace-loving nations to uphold peace and safeguard security; to put the necessary minimum of armed forces required for the averting of aggression at the disposal of the directing body of this organization, and to obligate this organization to employ these armed forces without delay if it becomes necessary to avert or stop aggression and punish the culprits.

This must not be a repetition of the ill-starred League of Nations which had neither the right nor the means to avert aggression. It will be a new, special, fully authorized world organization having at its command everything necessary to uphold peace and avert new aggression.

Can we expect the actions of this world organization to be sufficiently effective? They will be effective if the great powers which have borne the brunt of the war against Hitler Germany continue to act in a spirit of unanimity and accord. They will not be effective if this essential condition is violated.

Comrades, the Soviet people and the Red Army are performing successfully the tasks that have confronted them in the course of the Patriotic War. The Red Army has done its patriotic duty with credit and has freed our country of the enemy.

Now and for all time our land is clear of the Hitlerite pollution. For the Red Army there now remains its last final mission: together with the Armies of our Allies to consummate the defeat of the German-fascist army, to finish off the fascist beast in his own den and hoist the flag of victory over Berlin. There is reason to expect that this task will be performed by the Red Army in the none too distant future.

Long live our victorious Red Army!
Long live our glorious Navy!
Long live the mighty Soviet people!
Long live our great homeland!
Death to the German-fascist invaders!

MARSHAL JOSEPH V. STALIN'S 27TH ANNIVERSARY ORDER OF THE DAY

November 7, 1944 [1]

Comrades Red Army men and Red Navy men, sergeants, officers and generals! Working people of the Soviet Union! Brothers and sisters forcibly driven to fascist convict labor in Germany!

On behalf of the Soviet Government and our Bolshevik Party I greet and congratulate you upon the 27th Anniversary of the Great October Socialist Revolution. We celebrate the 27th Anniversary of the October Revolution in the midst of decisive victories of the Red Army over the enemies of our homeland.

By the heroic efforts of the Red Army and the Soviet people our land has been cleared of the German-fascist invaders. This year Soviet troops incessantly rained blows on the enemy, one stronger than the other.

In the winter of 1944 the Red Army scored outstanding victories in the Ukraine, west of the Dnieper, and routed the Germans at Leningrad.

In the spring of this year the Red Army cleared the Crimea of Germans.

In the summer of 1944 our troops inflicted major defeats upon the Hitlerite army, which had as their result a radical change of the situation on the front of struggle with the German-fascist invaders.

The Red Army crushed the enemy's powerful defense in the Karelian Isthmus, also between Ladoga and Onega Lakes, and knocked Finland out of the Hitlerite brigand bloc.

In the historical battle on the Byelorussian lands, Red Army troops utterly routed the central group of German troops, which consisted of three armies, and annihilated or took prisoner 540,000 German officers and men.

In the battle in the south the Red Army surrounded and completely annihilated the group of German troops, which consisted of two armies. In this the Soviet troops wiped out or took prisoner over 250,000 German officers and men.

The Red Army smashed the Germans in Rumania, threw them out of Bulgaria, is battering the Germans on the territory of Hungary.

Our troops crushed the Baltic group of the Hitlerite army.

During the summer campaign of 1944, the Red Army fought its way from Kishinev to Belgrade—over 900 kilometers; from Zhlobin to Warsaw—over 600 kilometers; from Vitebsk to Tilsit—550 kilometers. The war has been carried now to the territory of fascist Germany.

In the course of the fighting the Red Army ejected the German-fascist invaders from the entire territory of the Soviet Ukraine and Byelorussia, the Karelo-Finnish, Moldavian, Estonian, Latvian and Lithuanian Soviet Republics.

The fascist yoke of three years on the lands of our fraternal Soviet Republics temporarily seized by the Germans has been overthrown. The Red Army restored freedom to tens of millions of Soviet people.

The Soviet state boundary treacherously violated by the Hitlerite hordes on June 22, 1941, has been reestablished throughout its length from the Black to the Barents Seas.

The past year thus has been a year of the complete liberation of the Soviet

[1] Information Bulletin, Embassy of the U.S.S.R.

land from the German-fascist invaders. After completing the liberation of its native land from the Hitlerite pollution the Red Army is now helping the peoples of Poland, Yugoslavia and Czechoslovakia to break the chains of fascist slavery and regain their freedom and independence.

In the winter and summer battles of the past year the Red Army demonstrated its grown military mastery. Red Army soldiers skilfully smashed the enemy's fortified zones, vigorously pursued, encircled and wiped out the enemy.

Efficient coordination of all Soviet arms and high skill in maneuvering have been demonstrated in offensive battles. Soviet soldiers grew steeled in battles, learned to batter and vanquish the enemy. The Red Army has grown into a redoubtable force and is superior to the enemy in military skill and fighting equipment.

The Red Army's forces are multiplied many times over by the efficient work of the Soviet rear. Workers, collective farmers and intellectuals fulfill their duty to the motherland with credit, heroically overcome wartime difficulties, uninterruptedly supply the Red Army with armaments, ammunition and provisions. The Soviet economy continuously increases its strength and renders ever-growing assistance to the front.

The Red Army and the Soviet people are ready to strike fresh crushing blows at the enemy. The days of the Hitlerite sanguinary regime are numbered. Under the blows of the Red Army the fascist bloc has finally crumbled to pieces; Hitlerite Germany has lost most of her allies.

The large-scale operations carried out with consummate skill by the Armies of our Allies in Western Europe resulted in the debacle of the German troops in France and in Belgium, and in the liberation of these countries from fascist occupation.

The Allied troops crossed Germany's western frontier. The joint blows dealt by the Red Army and the Anglo-American troops to Hitlerite Germany brought nearer the hour of the victorious termination of the war. The ring around Hitlerite Germany is closing. The den of the fascist beast has been invested on all sides, and no artifices of the enemy will save him from imminent complete defeat.

The Red Army and the Armies of our Allies have taken up initial positions for the decisive offensive on Germany's vital centers. The task now is to crush Hitlerite Germany within the shortest time by the vigorous onslaught of the Armies of the United Nations.

Comrades Red Army men and Red Navy men, sergeants, officers and generals! Working people of the Soviet Union!

In the great Patriotic War we defended our motherland from the invaders, finally eliminated the threat of enslavement of the peoples of the U.S.S.R. by the fascist fiends, and now stand on the threshold of complete victory.

To mark the historic victories of the Red Army at the front and the great achievements of the workers, peasants and intellectuals in the rear, in honor of the liberation of the Soviet land from the German-fascist invaders, I order:

Today, on the day of the 27th Anniversary of the Great October Socialist Revolution, at 8 P.M., a salute of twenty-four gun salvos be fired in Moscow, Leningrad, Kiev, Minsk, Petrozavodsk, Tallinn, Riga, Vilnius, Kishinev, Tbilisi, Sevastopol, Lvov.

Hail the 27th Anniversary of the Great October Socialist Revolution!

Long live our free Soviet country!

Long live our Red Army and Navy!

Long live the great Soviet people!
Eternal glory to the heroes who fell in the struggle for the freedom and independence of our motherland!
Death to the German invaders!

(Signed)   Supreme Commander-in-Chief,
Marshal of the Soviet Union,
JOSEPH STALIN

PRIME MINISTER WINSTON CHURCHILL'S ADDRESS AT THE LORD MAYOR OF LONDON'S LUNCHEON

November 9, 1944 [1]

When I look back over these wartime years I cannot help feeling that time is an inaccurate, even capricious, measure of the duration of it. At one time it seemed so long, and at another so short. Sometimes events are galloping forward at a breathless speed, sometimes there are long, hard pauses which we have to bear. Anniversaries like this seem to recur with extreme rapidity when you get to one and look back to the other. It seems such a very brief span, and yet the intervening months are so packed with incidents and so burdened with toil; as you retrace your steps mentally over them, you cannot believe they have been.

It is hard to remember how long ago this war began. One can never be quite sure whether it has lasted a flash or an age. I had a very shrewd suspicion, my Lord Mayor, when I received your gracious invitation, that you would probably propose the health of His Majesty's Ministers, and I must say I held myself in readiness for the task of making some reply. I thought I would see whether I should not get some hint out of what I said last year when this agreeable event and festival was also celebrated.

I saw then that I was congratulating you on the year of victory of 1943. I was congratulating the City of London on the memorable, exhilarating year of almost unbroken success, and I was recounting the long succession of places and countries which have been cleared of the enemy. All of Africa, Sardinia, Corsica and one-third of Italy were in the hands of the British and United States armies.

The mighty war which the United States were waging and are waging in the Pacific had prospered, and in Russia Marshal Stalin's armies were already rolling triumphantly forward to cleanse their native lands of the German invader. But the events of 1943 have been far surpassed by those of 1944.

Rome and Athens, Paris and Brussels all have been rescued or by their own exertions have freed themselves of German oppression. All of Hitler's satellites have turned against him. Not only have they been struck down, but they have actually turned their arms against his baleful coercion.

They who have been driven so far against their interests, against their honor, and, in many cases, their inclinations, have had a chance to turn upon their slave driver and may now wreak the vengeance which is due them, as from so many of the free countries which fought from the beginning.

Both in the east and in the west, Allied vanguards stand on German soil.

[1] *New York Times.*

The U-boat menace has for the time being been practically effaced. There was one month in which up to the last day they had not sunk a single ship. On the last day they got one, and therefore the matter was hardly of the character to be specially mentioned.

That great peril which hung over us so long and at times concentrated the whole attention of the defense organization of this country and of the United States has been effaced, and from the air there rains down upon the guilty German land a hail of fire and explosion of ever-increasing fury.

We have had our own experience, and we know how severe the ordeal may be, but I can assure you that we have not suffered one-tenth and we shall not suffer one-tenth of what is being meted out to those who first started and developed this cruel and merciless form of attack.

Such are some of the fruits of 1944, and no one can be blamed, provided he does not slacken his or her efforts for a moment, for hoping that victory may come to the Allies and peace may come to Europe in 1945.

When I was here last year I could not tell you that I was about to start for a meeting of three great Allies—the heads of three great governments—Teheran. There it was that the plans were made and agreements and decisions taken which were executed with so much precision and with a degree of combination to which Marshal Stalin referred in his wise and weighty speech of a few days ago.

Now I don't mind saying that it is high time we had another triple conference and that such a meeting might easily abridge the sufferings of mankind and the fearful process of destruction which is ravaging the earth. Prospects of such a meeting have been vastly improved by the results of the Presidential elections in the United States, and for which we waited so breathlessly on Tuesday last.

I thought, looking back on my past records, that when I was here last year I appealed to the British and American public to be very careful that election year did not in any way ruffle the good-will that exists throughout the English-speaking world and which was of so great aid to our armies. It is certainly gratifying that it should have been carried through without any disturbing of the ancient, moth-eaten controversies which are to be found in history books between Great Britain and her American kinsmen, now brothers-in-arms.

We must be very careful ourselves to avoid mixing ourselves up in American political affairs. I offer my thanks to Parliament, the press and to public men of all parties—perhaps especially to them—for the care and restraint which have made all potential indiscretions die upon their lips.

Now that that event is over and the results have been declared, there are a few things I should like to say about the American Presidential election. Let us first of all express our gratitude to both great parties for the manner in which the interests of alliance and prosecution of the war have been held high above the dust of partisanship. America has given an example to the world of how democratic institutions can be worked with the utmost vigor and freedom without injury to the permanent interests of state. We know that we in Britain have in the Republican party of the United States a vast number of friends and well-wishers and the upholding of Anglo-American friendship is cherished by tens of millions in both great parties over there.

I am sure that everybody will be moved by the sportsmanlike manner in which Governor Dewey in the moment of his defeat offered his congratulations to his opponent and pledged his party to work wholeheartedly for the world cause. What a model this would be to those States where political differences are not solvable by word and vote and where the question of who is to be in and who is to be out may be one of life and death, to be settled by violence, and where there may be but a short gap between being a ruler and being a victim.

Here in this country—foremost in all democratic and parliamentary conceptions of modern times—we in this country who are very old in the game of party politics have learned how to carry through and debate great, fiercely contested political issues without the severance of national life or even, in most cases, without severance of personal and private friendship.

However, we may regret it, it seems almost certain that this old island will have its first general election in 1945, and I am sure that it will be conducted by all concerned with all liveliness and robust vigor which will gratify the political emotions of our public without destroying that marvelous underlying unity and sense of brotherhood which has long existed in this country and which has reached its highest degree among the perils from which we have been delivered.

I said a few moments ago that we have strictly avoided any question of opinion about party issues in the United States, but at this moment, now, I feel free to express, on personal grounds, the very great joy it gives me to know that my wartime and intimate cooperation with President Roosevelt will be continued in the months that lie immediately before us. These are months profoundly interwoven with the future of both our countries, and also, we trust, the future association of our two countries will be interwoven with the peace and progress of the whole world.

We have here in General Koenig and in Burgomaster Dr. van de Meulebroeck living representatives to bring home the splendid events which have so recently taken place.

The interest of the world has been dominated by the decisive battle in Normandy in which the Anglo-American armies destroyed and pulverized the structure of German military resistance in France. A brilliant exploitation of victory enabled the Americans to sweep the enemy from France, aided by the audacious and gallant Maquis, and enabled the British to clear the Channel coast and to drive the enemy out of Belgium and out of a large portion of Holland.

How many times, when a great battle has been won, have its results been thrown away? Here we have seen the highest result, surely and firmly seized and held at every stage. There comes a time when the pursuers outstrip to the utmost limits their supplies. An enemy falling back on his own territory is enabled to once again form a front, and this shows itself very plainly by the furious and continuous fighting which has broken out on the Moselle and in that neighborhood when the Americans advanced forward with so much impetus and then came up against the hard core of recovered enemy resistance.

A pause in the Allied advance was inevitable, and during that last few months the bringing up of supplies and reinforcements and the improvement of harbors have been the main preoccupation of the Supreme Allied Command, apart from the heavy fighting I have spoken of on the Moselle. But during these last eight or ten weeks two considerable operations have been fought by armies under British command in both of which Polish and Canadian forces were represented and in both of which a large proportion of United States troops fought with their customary skill.

The largest of these two great operations was in Italy under General Alexander. They have surmounted the terrible barrier of the Apennines and the Gothic Line, and this has carried us into the Valley of the Po. The progress of the year—of the season—has brought us bad weather, quite unaccustomed weather for this time of year, and we are facing a strongly fortified line held by an army which is practically as large as our own. It was a great fall feat of arms.

The second interim victory has been in the Netherlands under Field Marshal Montgomery, and it has opened the Schelde and will very shortly place the great port of Antwerp at the disposal of the northern flank of the Allied Army which presently moves into Germany for the final struggle.

In these two operations in Italy and Holland and Belgium very great losses have been sustained, in the greatest proportion by the British and Canadian forces. In both we have been aided by our valiant Allies. In both opportunities have been offered for superb feats of heroism, and deeds have been done which, when they are known and can be studied with the attention they deserve, will long figure in song and story and will long light the martial annals of our race.

I think it is right to point out in a precise and definite manner that these two important battles, one in the Apennines and the other in the west, are only a prelude to further great operations which must be conducted in the months to come. Now we stand on the threshold of Germany, and it will take the full exertions of the three great powers and every scrap of strength they can give to crush down the desperate resistance which we must expect from this military antagonist, at last beaten back to his own lair.

Any more than on former occasions I cannot offer you an easy future on the Continent of Europe. It is always in the last lap of the race that great efforts must be forthcoming. It is no moment now to slacken. Hard as it may seem after five long years of war, every man and woman in this island must show what they are capable of doing, and I am sure our soldiers at the front will not be found incapable of that extra effort which is necessary to crown all that has been attained, and, above all, bring this frightful slaughter and devastation in Europe to an end within the shortest possible period of time.

I can assure you that that, at any rate, is the dominant thought in His Majesty's Government. Although it is our duty to work hard—and we have worked hard—to produce large schemes of social improvement and advancement, although it is our duty to make preparations for the change-over from war to peace or from war in Europe to war in Japan in far distant Asia. Although we are bound to work as hard as we can, nothing shall stand in the way of the prosecution of the war to an ultimate conclusion. If we are to fail in that we should not be worthy either of your confidence or of the kindness which has led you to drink our health this afternoon.

PRIME MINISTER WINSTON CHURCHILL'S STATEMENT IN COMMONS ON THE GERMAN USE OF V-2 LONG-RANGE ROCKETS

November 10, 1944 [1]

Last February I told Parliament that the Germans were preparing to attack this country by means of long-range rockets, and I referred again to the possibility of this form of attack in my statement in this House on July 6.

[1] *New York Times.*

For the last few weeks the enemy has been using his new weapon, the long-range rocket, and a number have landed at widely scattered points in this country. In all, the casualties and damage have so far not been heavy, though I am sure the House will wish me to express our sympathy with the victims of these attacks.

No official statement about the attack has hitherto been issued. The reason for this silence was that any announcement might have given information useful to the enemy, and we were confirmed in this course by the fact that until two days ago the enemy had made no mention of this weapon in his communiqués.

Last Wednesday an official announcement, followed by a number of highly colored accounts of attacks on this country, was issued by the German High Command. I do not propose to comment upon it except to say the statements in this announcement are a good reflection of what the German Government would wish their people to believe and of their desperate need to afford them some encouragement.

May I mention a few facts? The rocket contains approximately the same quantity of high explosive as the flying bomb. However, it is designed to penetrate rather deeper before explosion. This results in somewhat heavy damage in the immediate vicinity above the crater, with rather less extensive blast effect around it.

The rocket flies through the stratosphere, going up to sixty to seventy miles, and outstrips sound. Because of its high speed, no reliable or sufficient public warning can in present circumstances be given.

There is, however, no need to exaggerate the danger. The scale and effect of these attacks have not hitherto been significant. Some rockets have been fired at us from the Island of Walcheren. This is now in our hands. Other areas from which rockets have or can at present be fired against this country will doubtless be overrun by our forces in due course.

We cannot, however, be certain that the enemy will not be able to increase the range, either by reducing the weight of the warhead or by other methods; nor, on the other hand, can we be certain that any new launching area which he may establish farther back may not also in turn be overrun by the advancing Allied armies.

The use of this weapon is another attempt by the enemy to attack the morale of our civil population in the vain hope that he may somehow by this means stave off the defeat which faces him in the field. Doubtless the enemy had hoped by his announcement to induce us to give him information which he had failed to get otherwise. I am sure the House, the press and the public will refuse to oblige him in this respect.

CHANCELLOR ADOLF HITLER'S PROCLAMATION TO THE GERMAN PEOPLE'S ARMY, BROADCAST BY HEINRICH HIMMLER

November 12, 1944 [1]

Adolf Hitler's proclamation, as carried by DNB and reported by the Federal Communications Commission, opened with the assertion that the

[1] *New York Times.*

"requirements of total war have caused me to postpone celebrations commemorating Nov. 9 to the next available Sunday." The proclamation continued:

Work at my headquarters does not permit me to leave it at the present, even for a few days. Quite apart from this, I consider my task today to consist not so much in delivering speeches as in preparing and carrying out those measures that are necessary to wage this war to its ultimate victorious conclusion.

As in the times of crisis in 1923, I am inspired today by only one single idea dominating all other considerations: to make—now more than ever—every effort for success, which is imperative!

And as it was then possible to tell dead comrades ten years later with justification that victory had after all become theirs, so victory in the great struggle for the existence or nonexistence of our people must and will in the end belong to our nation, the fighting front, and the no less heroically battling homeland.

On many previous occasions I have pointed out how necessary it is for the nation to appreciate and honor its great men. Particularly in evil times, a despondent nation may gain courage and strength from its bearing in times gone by. How much more is this true of a people that is bearing itself with such boundless courage as the German nation. It will be able to derive from the struggle of its great men the only right lesson for the present—namely, the realization that Providence in the end helps only those who, without despairing, with stout and faithful hearts, enter the battle with adversities of the time and thus eventually become the masters of their destiny.

As far as the Almighty has opened our eyes and enabled us within the bounds of our weak human understanding to gain insight into the laws underlying His will, we can realize the incorruptible justice that life accords as its ultimate price only to him who is willing and ready to sacrifice life in order to preserve life.

It is a matter of complete indifference whether man affirms or disavows this inexorable law; he cannot change it. Hence anyone seeking to shirk the struggle for this life invalidates not this law but the underlying conditions of his own existence.

When the National Socialist movement embarked on its fight to conquer German man, every understanding individual was convinced of the internal collapse of the people and the Reich that was threatening. This was bound to result in a growing menace to our national existence, the gradual decline of our birth rate and hence in the insidious decay of our national substance that would have exacted sacrifices many times those of the World War. Such a development was in line with our enemies' aims.

The economic strangulation of the old Reich was intended to destroy the material basis of the German people's existence. Thus they hoped to achieve the fulfillment of Clemenceau's demand for the decimation of the German nation by 20,000,000 people.

The struggle of 1914–18 caused the deaths of 2,000,000 people. But there were 20,000,000 more that, according to the wishes of the democratic benefactors of mankind, were to be eliminated from our midst.

Today this demand has been increased to 40,000,000. As it does not lie within the power of man to call a halt to retarding movements in the life of a nation, nobody could say when this process of the shrinkage of our people's substance would come to an end. In this connection, another rule of nature forces itself upon us: there is no vacuum in the world.

Peoples that are too weak numerically or biologically and are no longer capable of filling their living space in a satisfactory manner receive at best a reservation commensurate to their value and their size. Other life, however, will flow into the space thus freed. Other nations—and, unfortunately, very often more primitive races—will then, acting on the command of Providence, take up the struggle for existence in the area that an old nation has lost out of cowardice and weakness, or, in other words, out of unfitness for life.

Thus, in 1919, we were faced with the realization that only the remolding of our people from top to bottom would in the long run enable it to resume its struggle for existence. Only complete negation of the phraseology of democratic disintegration of peoples and of the Bolshevik destruction of nationhood was able to bring back to our people its natural vitality, and thus the preconditions necessary to safeguard its successful self-assertion in the future. Because of this realization, the National Socialist movement entered the struggle.

Faced with these great aims, however, both the proletarian and the bourgeois class state had to lose all their significance. What the social classes, professions, religious creeds or political parties may then still have imagined to be the ideal was, in the eyes of the young movement, proved to be madness and thus a fatal poison for our people. The intention to establish for the first time in our history a people's state comprising all Germans could be realized, however, only by the mobilization of the nation's whole strength. The synthesis of Nationalist and Socialist thoughts was most suitable for the generation of that power that such a struggle demands as a prerequisite of success.

The proclamation of this young National Socialist people's state, indeed, immediately aroused the hatred of all those enemies at home and abroad who advocated the former system of German dismemberment and hence of German impotence—the hatred, that is, of parties and petty parties, of groups, estates, vocations, organizations, classes and finally of religious confessions as those most likely to derive benefit from our internal disunity, and abroad the hatred of the hostile democratic-Marxist world as the party most interested in German impotence.

The hatred generated by this conspiracy of our enemies at home and abroad has, ever since, faithfully pursued the movement throughout the years of struggle, before and after the accession to power. This hatred worked against us with all the petty tricks and all the brutality of which the system was then capable. Since the procession to the Feldherrnhalle, thousands of murdered National Socialists and tens of thousands of wounded fell victim to this, the only real aggression.

Since the accession to power our old enemies have not changed. On the contrary, they have intensified their hatred. At most, they have adapted their methods to the new situation.

As in the time of the struggle for power since the year 1933, so Jewry, as a final inspiring and impelling force, has not allowed any opportunity to pass of expressing its satanic will of persecution and destruction against the new state idea as such and against the young state born out of it. It saw in them the first dawn of the general recognition of its activity, the destroying and ruining of nations and thus eminent danger for itself.

Times have thus changed, but the essential elements of the fight forced upon us have remained. What has remained is:

1. Our own goal, the preservation of our nation, the safeguarding of its future with all available means, and,

2. The goal of our enemies, the destruction of our nation, the extirpation and therewith the termination of our existence.

That this neither was nor is the thesis of National Socialist propaganda was in the past proved by the fact of German inner disintegration and is today being confirmed by the proclamation of our enemies.

No National Socialist Minister of Propaganda could sketch the aims of our enemies more clearly than it has been done for decades, and is being done particularly today, by the Jewish press, or more clearly than enemy statesmen above all are doing in public announcements through their ministers.

The aim of our enemies has thus also been retained. Bolshevism, furthered by the democracies, once tried to destroy our movement by terror in our country. Sovietism, supported by the democracies, is endeavoring to destroy the Reich and exterminate our people. The fact that the bourgeois world, which then consciously or unconsciously acted as a handy-man for Bolshevism in the interior of our country, is approaching its own downfall in an act of blindness inflicted by God did not in the least alter the way in which it behaved.

The fact that the present democracies would be borne to their graves immediately after the victory of Bolshevism, that democratic states together with their ideas would be smashed against the wall, alters the reality of their present procedure just as little. The senselessness of their action, however incomprehensible in itself, finds its explanation the moment that one knows that behind human stupidity and weakness, that behind the lack of character on one side and the inadequacy on the other side, there is always a Jew: he is the wire-puller of democracy as he is the creator and inciter of the Bolshevik world-beast.

This danger from within had dawned on many even before National Socialism proclaimed it. Effective counter-measures, however, were taken only when these faint ideas had grown into full-blooded programmatic conception and when these ideas found a powerful executor in the National Socialist party.

Today, too, many foreign statesmen, parliamentarians and party politicians, as well as economists, have realized the necessity of saving Europe from the Bolshevik monster. Practical results, however, can be achieved only if a strong European power succeeds in organizing this common struggle for life or death, overruling all theoretical hopes, and in waging it to a successful conclusion. This can be done, and will be done, only by National Socialist Germany. Europe has always been a multitude of competing peoples and States. Nevertheless, the spiritual conception of European entity in most cases arose only in one State or in a community of related peoples. The eternal strife of European peoples among themselves certainly also has its great advantages.

As in every competitive fight, this struggle required supreme hitting power from every individual nation. But at times when all were involved in a fateful life-and-death struggle there was a great danger that the forces of this Continent would be split up in the face of the threatening onrush from the depth of the Asiatic east—that eternally latent threat to Europe.

Over long periods in Europe's history, the thesis of a European balance of power was for the narrow-minded west only too often identical with a license to side with the peril threatening Europe, in contravention of the law of European solidarity, the aim being all the more easily to throttle this or that vexatious competitor.

For centuries the old Reich had to wage its struggle against the Mongols and later on against the Turks by its own strength and with few allied resources to preserve Europe from a fate the results of which would have been just as unthinkable as would be the fact of its Bolshevization today.

Although in past centuries this struggle entailing many reserves burdened our people with very grave sacrifices, it ultimately led to success. This alone provided the requisite conditions for the birth, or existence, and for the prosperity of the European family of nations.

Moreover, conflicts of world-historic importance have necessarily the consequence that in the end those struggles, in which evidently the providence of God makes men fight to prove their supreme qualities and thus to justify their existence or fail to do so, will be decided by a tenacity not of months or years but only after long periods of time. Up-to now only the bearing of the [Nazi] movement provides the reason why the National Socialist state will not pass this historic test.

What bourgeois party could have survived the collapse of Nov. 9, 1923? What party would finally have accomplished a perfect victory after so complete a collapse, after a struggle unexampled in toughness?

Even if this struggle, measured by today's events, may appear small to a superficial observer, this merely shows the lack of ability to understand decisive values as such. For the struggle for the movement was then the struggle for Germany exactly as it is the struggle of the Reich today. It was a struggle for our people and its future that had to be decided first at home to enable us to oppose at last the enemy ideology and the will of extermination from outside.

How hopeless that struggle of the party at that time appeared to our opponents was revealed by their statements that after Nov. 9, 1923, National Socialism could be regarded as definitely dead and thus the danger to the enemies of our people was eliminated. And yet, a few years later, this party, regarded as obliterated, was already engaged in a decisive struggle for power; and, after almost a decade of unrestrained effort by many men and women and repeated through temporary setbacks, it emerged victorious in the end.

During this period the movement received and proved itself possessed of that inner spiritual bearing that enables it today to lead the nation and the Reich, and even to lead Europe. And just as we then were able to witness how the entire bourgeois world of democratic parties gradually disintegrated, how it decayed by its compromises and brought about its own downfall by cowardly renunciation, so we shall today be witnesses of the same spectacle on a large scale.

Nations, and above all their statesmen, military leaders and fighting men, at all times have easily borne days of fortune and thus of visible success. What has characterized the great personalities of world history and those nations destined for greatness has always been their steadfastness during the days of tribulation, their confidence at times when their position seemed hopeless, their defiance and their courage after reverses had been suffered.

During the time of our struggle we National Socialists have always welcomed shorter or longer periods of persecution, because they stripped the party of all those elements that in any case would have been nothing better than camp followers, although they would have certainly boasted loudest on the day of victory.

Likewise, in this most gigantic struggle of nations of all time, we witness the falling away from us of all that is small, cowardly and unfit for life. It is due to their spiritual and moral inadequacy, caused by centuries of inbreeding, that monarchs, completely misunderstanding their own position, which today has nothing but prehistoric value, should lose their courage and become traitors. Nations demand, in times like these, leaders other than ailing and decrepit old dynasties.

The fact that so-called statesmen, and generals too, allow themselves to be ensnared by a belief that they are able to decide in their favor the historical conflict for existence or non-existence by cowardly capitulations only confirms the experience gained over a period of thousands of years, that at one and the same time the earth is not inhabited by too many great men. But, wherever such capitulation has taken place, or was considered and might still be considered today, the result will not be an easy escape from a crisis of world-wide importance but, perforce, the certain eradication of the nations concerned, and with them also the annihilation of their responsible leaders.

For Bolshevik chaos and civil war within such states will be merely the first result. The second result, however, begins with the handing over of so-called "war criminals," of men who are valuable in themselves, and ends with immense columns of people who set out for the Siberian tundras to die there as victims of the weakness of the leadership of their states.

Although the military consequences of these treacheries have from the outset been very severe for Germany, a mainstay in the struggle, they have nevertheless not loosened the structure of the Reich, nor could they eliminate the spirit of resistance. On the contrary, the nation was hardened in its fighting determination and become all the more fanatical.

We are glad that, among those nations that were affected by these signs of decay, forces of resistance arose in Italy. They rallied around the creator of the new state, Benito Mussolini, as their Duce. In Hungary they gathered around Szalasy; in Slovakia, under the leadership of President Tiso; in Croatia, headed by the Poglavnik, Ante Pavelitch. In all these countries they closed their ranks behind the leaders of young nations.

We know that among other peoples, too, committees and governments have sprung up imbued with the determination of disowning capitulation and not accepting the extermination of their peoples simply because some unscrupulous weaklings failed in their honor and in their duties or because some fools fell for the mirages in which today they themselves no longer believe.

Our greatest ally, Japan, has viewed the struggle from its first day as what it really is: a decisive clash in which existence itself is at stake. And, ever since, Japan has been fighting this struggle with the courage of a real nation of heroes.

Party comrades! Fellow-countrymen! Men and women! Since the Russian armies broke through the Rumanian front on the Don in November, 1942, since the subsequent disintegration of the Italian and Hungarian formations, with all the severe consequences involved for our strategy, our people have been hit by treachery after treachery. Nevertheless, the hopes of our enemies have not come true. Again and again we succeeded in re-establishing our fronts and halting the enemy.

Thus they were left only with the one hope that they could deliver a decisive stab in the interior of our country, as was always the case when they did not know how to achieve successes against Germany in another way. Creatures devoid of all character, a blend of feudal arrogance, bourgeois inadequacy and former parliamentarian corruption, met together to break German resistance at its root in the hope that they could reap immediately the reward for this act of perjury. In one point, it is true, they were entirely correct.

As long as I am alive, Germany will not suffer the fate of European states that have been overrun by bolshevism; as long as there is a breath left in me, my body and my soul will serve only one thought—to make my people strong in defense and attack against the most mortal peril that is threatening it.

For if, in previous days, wars have been fought for dynastic or economic interests, the meaning of this war is a struggle for the survival of our very nation. Therefore the only logical consequence of all sacrifices in this war is the strengthening of the German people's state. If there are outmoded individuals who take exception to this, they cannot be helped, because this people's state will pass over them and continue its business. If individual members of subdued parties, classes or other factions of our people believe that now, perhaps, the time of their resurrection might have come, they will only experience the moment of their complete extermination.

National Socialism, once persecuted in an atrociously bloody way, showed a day after assuming power not only a truly conciliatory attitude but even generosity toward its political opponents. In this state I have either granted pensions or even called into new and higher offices innumerable men who, before National Socialism took over power, were persecutors themselves. The same Bavarian Minister of Justice under whom I was confined to the fortress for thirteen months was nevertheless appointed by me as Reich minister of Justice. Prussian Ministers and Reich Ministers who had previously been our most ardent persecutors received high pensions from me as an act of grace, although we were under no obligation to do so. I would have regarded it as unworthy of myself to plunge into misery the Social Democrats, only because when holding Ministerial offices they had been my adversaries. Judges who previously had passed sentences on us were, nevertheless, not hampered in their career and often they were even promoted.

Only those who by deed or word proclaimed their hostility to the new state were treated in accordance with law. Moreover, by the nature of my accession to power, I made it easy for every German, and for every state official and officer in particular, to fulfill his duty without coming into conflict with his conscience. For almost eighteen months the late Reich President, who, in accordance with the Constitution, made me the leader of by far the strongest party, Chancellor, was my superior and was treated by me with the esteem and high respect due to his office.

Those, however, who by no act of mine were constantly brought into conflict with their conscience and who now think fit to involve other people in conflicts with their consciences must know that this means certain death for them. As long as only I myself was the object of their persecutions, I could be magnanimous and overlook and forget their actions. Whoever today uses a dagger or bomb against Germany will be destroyed without mercy and without consideration.

A few hours were sufficient to extinguish the attempted Putsch of July 20, a few months to rout the whole clique of these Catilinian subjects who are without honor and to exterminate them completely. In the year 1934 I took the revolt of a small group inside the movement as the occasion for cleansing the party and in the same way the new revolt was the start of a thorough overhaul of the whole Government apparatus.

The time for people who like to make compromises or reservations is definitely over. The Reich war flag has become recently, as a symbol of the National Socialist idea, of the revolution and of the state, the regimental flag of the German armed forces. The German salute has been introduced. The people's grenadier divisions will, together with a stream of German youth, help the world of National Socialist ideas to final and complete victory.

There is one thing that has deeply touched me and has filled me with grateful joy after this July 20: the knowledge that the army, navy and air force—the Elite Guard can here in any case be left out of the account—in their totality had accepted the spirit of National Socialism to such an extent that there remained hardly anything to do but to expel the unworthy ones from the party, state and armed forces in order to bring about complete unity of views and the will of the party, nation, state and armed forces.

It is unfortunate that this transition had not shown itself so clearly at an earlier date. And yet, repercussions of this day have been bitter. Full of surging hopes, our enemies pulled themselves together, using all their strength in the belief that Germany could now be overrun without further ado.

I owe it to the courageous bearing of our armed forces, and above all to the courageous bearing of the German homeland, which is above praise, that they did not succeed. The response to the call for a strengthening of the Reich's defenses and mobilization for the Volkssturm [Home Guard] was only a symbol of the community of spirit among the German people in this fateful struggle for the future of our nation, a spirit that is becoming ever more evident. Thus, the soldierly homeland steps to the side of the old grenadiers, of the army soldiers, of the navy and the air force as fully equal, not only men, old men and boys, but also women and girls.

But, now that I review the sum total of unspeakable sacrifices made by our people today and all the sufferings forced on millions of human beings in our towns, I would like to ask the criminals of July 20 just one question: "With what right could such sacrifices be demanded if not the holy resolve in one's conscience of consolidating the German people's state at the end of this struggle and of building it up more and more so that eventually this, the greatest epoch of our people, may also become the birth hour of the Reich, which at last not only includes all Germans against the outside world but also gives happiness within?"

By fighting for the National Socialist German people's state, I give the only conceivable moral and ethical meaning to this greatest struggle in our history. He who in this hour too is concerned merely with interests of his own class acts not only as a criminal but at the same time as an insane egoist, insane because it requires incredible stupidity to think that one can inspire a nation for more than half a decade with enthusiasm for the fight for life or death and for the sake, perhaps, of the medieval feudal state.

Party comrades, when the year 1923 was at its close, I wrote "Mein Kampf" while in prison. All the time I had before me the aim of putting into practice the idea of the National Socialist people's state. For years we have fought for this idea and, after the accession to power, shaped it into reality. Our opponents were filled with rage and envy at the achievements that we reached in all spheres of our economic and social life, the increasing results of our cultural pursuits and the pacification of all classes. If other countries today publish so-called "plans of the future," they represent but a weak replica of what National Socialist Germany has already realized in practice.

Today I cannot do more than renew my vow to continue this work. As an old National Socialist, I shall fulfill the duties imposed on me and shall not falter for a moment in the struggle. I have not chosen these obligations; they are duties imposed on every German by destiny itself, demanding that we do everything and neglect nothing to secure the future and thus the existence of our people.

To the most severe blows of fate we shall stand up with obstinate wrath, always imbued by the conviction that destiny often punishes those that it loves best and that it tests and has to test men to reveal in just judgment their true values. In this struggle I am filled with unshakable determination to show posterity a no less laudable example than that shown by great Germans in by-gone times.

If I address you party members and the whole German people so infrequently and rarely nowadays it is because I work and toil in fulfillment of those tasks with which our age has burdened me and that must be fulfilled to bring about a turn in our fate.

For, as I have this will and as I see my people faithfully following me, I am not for a moment in doubt that the time of trials will eventually be passed successfully by us and that the hour is approaching when God Almighty will give us His blessing as he did during long periods before. We then achieved the greatest victories of world history and yet we did not become insolent. Times of reverses will never make us submit. They will, therefore, only confirm in good sense the picture of the character of the German people of today that will be handed on to posterity. I therefore believe with unshakable confidence that, as a result of our work and our sacrifice, the moment will come when success will finally crown our endeavors.

The objective of our struggle is none other than the one for which we had to fight in 1923 and for which the first sixteen martyrs of our movement went to their deaths: to save our people from distress and peril and to safeguard the lives of our children and children's children down to the most remote generations. In the shadow of our nation, there is marching Europe, which feels that today it is not Germany's fate alone that is being decided but the future of all those peoples that regard themselves as part of Europe and consciously abhor Bolshevik barbarism.

Thus I greet you from afar, my old party comrades, through the speaker of this pledge in dogged determination, with my old fighting courage unimpaired and in unshakable confidence. I am thinking once more of the fighters of that day twenty-one years ago who also set an example to us for the future of our people and the greater German Reich.

GENERAL EISENHOWER'S ARMY HOUR BROADCAST FROM PARIS ON THE NEED FOR AMMUNITION

November 19, 1944 [1]

Allied fighting men have achieved in Europe since June sixth one of the remarkable military victories of all time. They have eliminated more than a million German soldiers. In the great breakthrough in Normandy in late July, and in the sweeping exploitation that carried them all the way to the German frontier, the tactical pattern was always the same: sudden and devastating air attack, followed by intensive artillery bombardment, and then the forward surge of infantry and tanks to break defenses, capture towns, and hurry forward once again. In their relentless advance, they liberated France, Belgium and Luxembourg. This achievement of your sons, brothers and husbands and their gallant Allies was possible only through great expenditure of bombs and ammunition. The huge stocks that we had accumulated in England before the beginning of the invasion were rushed, by day and by night, to the front so that our fighting men would not be handicapped.

[1] War Department.

All the way from the North Sea to the Mediterranean, tactical victories followed swiftly upon earlier ones, each worthy of its own chapter in our military history, but each adding to the inevitable drain upon the stocks of ammunition that you produced. Your toil and skill share with the courage and stamina of the front line soldiers the credit for the stunning successes of the summer and fall. But today we are firing ammunition that we would not have used until next February or March if we had been content with slower advance, with less crushing victories, or if we had been ready to sacrifice soldiers to save materials. Now we are hammering at the massive crust of armor surrounding the German Fortress. Appalling conditions of rain, fog, snow and mud make difficult the employment of our Air Forces and the maneuver of our tanks, even of our foot soldiers. But wretched weather cannot stop artillery shells. More than ever before we need ammunition. In the capture of Aachen the First Army used three-hundred-thousand rounds of 105 mm ammunition in a two-weeks' period, and, even so, the reduction of that place was delayed because of shortage of ammunition.

In spite of all we continue to attack. Five-thousand pounds of ammunition are being poured every minute against the German defenses. Each month our guns are hurling six-million rounds against the hostile trenches, forts and pill boxes, while our mortars add two-million additional rounds to this figure. Expenditures have raced ahead of our receipts from home but I know that you do not want us to give the enemy one second's rest. You do not want the leaders of American soldiers to substitute additional cost in lives for the ammunition that could so surely save those lives. I owe it to every G. I. American soldier in this greatest fighting force that America has ever put into the field, to urge upon you increased production of ammunition, signal equipment, winter clothing, engineering materials, vital medical instruments —and again, *ammunition,* always *ammunition.* We are well aware that this calls for superhuman effort on your part. But you have already accomplished miracles in war production. We know that when you understand that your increased work will shorten the war and save thousands of lives, you will perform this new and even greater miracle.

RESIGNATION OF CORDELL HULL
AS SECRETARY OF STATE

November 21, 1944 [1]

The text of Mr. Hull's letter of resignation to the President follows:

November 21, 1944

MY DEAR MR. PRESIDENT:

It is with inexpressible disappointment that I find it necessary, for considerations of health, to retire from public service. I, therefore, with utmost regret, tender herewith my resignation as Secretary of State.

It is a matter of special satisfaction to me that throughout my almost twelve years at the Department of State, our personal relations have been uniformly and invariably agreeable and that, by our joint efforts, many difficult tasks growing out of the foreign relations of this country before and during this war have been brought to partial or full completion; many great questions have been faced successfully; and many forward movements of

[1] State Department Bulletin.

surpassing importance to friendly relations among nations have been instituted.

As the war draws to a close there remains a vast area of complex and difficult conditions and problems which must be dealt with in the months and years immediately ahead. It is a supreme tragedy to me personally that I am unable to continue making my full contribution to such great international undertakings as the creation of the post-war peace organization, the solution of the many other problems involved in the promotion of international cooperation, and the final development of a full and complete structure of a world order under law.

When I recover my strength, I shall individually be always at your service in every possible way.

Sincerely yours,

CORDELL HULL

The President's reply to Mr. Hull follows:

November 21, 1944

MY DEAR CORDELL:

Your letter of this afternoon has hit me between wind and water. It has been very sad for me even to contemplate the ending of our close relationship during all these twelve years. It is not merely that our personal relations have been so uniformly and invariably agreeable, or that our joint work has borne true success in so many fields, as it is the personal feeling of not being able to lean on you for aid and intimate interchange of thought.

This is especially true because we have come so far along the road of friendly relations among nations that I have counted so much on your help in carrying this work through the final stage of complex and difficult conditions which still face us.

Your health is honestly my first thought, and I am really confident that you will be on your feet again in a relatively short time, even though you are limited to special tasks and avoid the daily routine of Department work. As of today, therefore, you must devote all your thought to getting back on your feet and on this all your friends will join in helping.

I will, of course, accept your resignation as Secretary of State if you want me to do so. But I wish you would, as an alternative, allow me to accept it as of January twentieth, which is the end of our Third Term. Perhaps sentiment enters into this suggestion a little bit, but it would give me great satisfaction if we should round out the three terms. That means two months more, and during that time I could see you from time to time and get your advice on some of the things that will come before us.

Incidentally, when the organization of the United Nations is set up, I shall continue to pray that you as the Father of the United Nations may preside over its first session. That has nothing to do with whether you are Secretary of State or not at the time, but should go to you as the one person in all the world who has done the most to make this great plan for peace an effective fact. In so many different ways you have contributed to friendly relations among nations that even though you may not remain in a position of executive administration, you will continue to help the world with your moral guidance.

With my affectionate regards,

As ever yours,

FRANKLIN D. ROOSEVELT

PRESIDENT ROOSEVELT'S LETTER TO CONGRESS ON LEND-LEASE AND REVERSE LEND-LEASE

November 24, 1944 [1]

I am submitting herewith my seventeenth report to Congress on lend-lease operations.

In fifteen of these reports I have reported on lend-lease aid extended by the United States. One year ago the twelfth lend-lease report to Congress set forth the reverse lend-lease aid received by the United States from the British Commonwealth of Nations under the lend-lease act. That report covered the period up to June 30, 1943.

I now report on reverse lend-lease aid received by the United States from the British Commonwealth of Nations up to June 30, 1944.

One year ago the Governments of the British Commonwealth reported their expenditure for reverse lend-lease aid to the United States, on the basis of estimates carefully prepared from their records, as totaling $1,175,000,000. They now report that by June 30, 1944—one year later—these expenditures had risen to $3,348,000,000—almost three times the previous total.

The first six months of 1944 showed a significant increase in reverse lend-lease aid from the British Commonwealth. These were the months when the final preparations were being made in the United Kingdom for the liberation of western Europe and for the offensive aimed at Germany.

In these six months United States forces in the British Isles received the equivalent of almost 3,851,000 ships' tons of supplies from the United Kingdom under reverse lend-lease exclusive of construction materials and gasoline, compared with 2,950,000 tons in the entire preceding eighteen months. In monetary value, the supplies and services we received in these six months were greater than for the entire preceding year.

By "D" Day, United States armed forces had reached the United Kingdom in vast numbers. From the day our first soldiers arrived in 1942, one-third of all the supplies and equipment currently required by United States troops in the British Isles has been provided under reverse lend-lease. The percentages of total United States Army requirements in the European theatre provided by the United Kingdom have ranged as high as sixty-three per cent in the case of quartermaster supplies and fifty-eight per cent for engineers' supplies.

Reverse lend-lease has played an essential part in the stupendous job of preparing for and supplying the great Allied offensives in Europe.

It would have required a thousand ships to send across the Atlantic what we received for our men through reverse lend-lease from the United Kingdom.

We were able to use these thousand ships instead for carrying supplies and equipment that had to come from the United States.

Without the reverse lend-lease aid that we received from the United Kingdom, we would surely have been forced to delay the invasion of France for many months. Now that this campaign has been successfully launched and is on the road to ultimate success, it is possible to include in this report facts about specific and vitally important reverse lend-lease projects that could not previously be safely disclosed in a public report.

For the war against Japan, United States forces have also received in-

[1] *New York Times.*

creased quantities of supplies and services in the past six months as reverse lend-lease from Australia and New Zealand, and in India. These were the months in which the forces under General MacArthur were completing the New Guinea campaign and were preparing to launch the campaign for the liberation of the Philippines.

Our forces in the Pacific have already received 1,850,000,000 pounds of food alone from Australia and New Zealand, including more than 400,000,000 pounds of beef and other meats.

Another important reverse lend-lease program in this theatre has been the production for our forces of landing craft, small ships and boats, for the campaign we are waging in the Pacific. Tremendous numbers of these boats are needed for landing and supply operations on hundreds of islands scattered across thousands of miles of water. More than 9,500 of these craft had been produced and delivered by Australia alone in time for the Philippines campaign and over 12,000 more are on the way.

In addition, Australia and New Zealand have turned over to our forces many hundreds of coastal steamers, barges, tugs, lighters, yachts and launches.

In India the increased rate of reverse lend-lease aid we have received in the first six months of 1944 has kept pace with the rising tempo of air, land and sea operations in the Burma-India and China theatres.

A significant proportion of the supplies we have received in India has consisted of aviation gasoline and other petroleum products drawn from British oil resources in the Middle East and refined at the British refinery at Abadan. This gasoline provided to us as reverse lend-lease, without payment by us, is helping to power our B-29 Superfortresses in their raids from both China and India on the Japanese homeland and on such enemy occupied strong points as Singapore. It is also being used by the fighter and bomber planes of the Tenth and Fourteenth United States Army Air Forces.

I take the occasion of this report again to point out that the reverse lend-lease aid rendered by nations of the British Commonwealth to the United States is only a part of the aid which we have received from the British in fighting this war. The United States has benefited greatly from reverse lend-lease aid, as the facts set forth in this report indicate. But we have benefited far more, and in a far larger sense, from the total fighting effort of our Allies.

As I have stated in previous lend-lease reports and as the Congress has expressed itself in reports by its appropriate committees at the time of the virtually unanimous renewals of the Lend-Lease Act in 1943 and 1944, lend-lease and reverse lend-lease are not two sides of a financial transaction. We are not loaning money under lend-lease. We are not receiving payments on account under reverse lend-lease. The lend-lease system is, instead, a system of combined war supply, whose sole purpose is to make the most effective use against the enemy of the combined resources of the United Nations, regardless of the origin of the supplies or which of us uses them against the enemy.

Neither the monetary totals of the lend-lease aid we supply, nor the totals of the reverse lend-lease aid we receive are measures of the aid we have given or received in this war. That could be measured only in terms of the total contributions toward winning victory of each of the United Nations. There are no statistical or monetary measurements for the value of courage, skill and sacrifice in the face of death and destruction wrought by our common enemies.

We in the United States can be justly proud of our contributions in men and materials and of the courage and skill and sacrifice of the men and women in our armed forces and of all those others who have devoted themselves selflessly to the war effort at home. We can also be rightly proud of and grateful for the contributions in men and materials of our Allies and the courage and skill and sacrifice of their soldiers, airmen, seamen and peoples.

In this war the United Nations have all drawn strength from each other —our Allies from us and we from them. We can now begin to see the full significance of the overwhelming power that this steadily closer partnership has created. We already know how much it did to save us all from disaster. We know that it has brought and will bring final victory months closer than would otherwise have been possible.

Lend-lease and reverse lend-lease are a system of combined war supply. They should end with the war. But the United Nations' partnership must go on and must grow stronger.

For the tasks of building a workable peace that will endure we shall need all the strength that a permanent and stronger United Nations can provide in winning security from aggression, in building the economic foundations for a more prosperous world, and in developing wider opportunities for civilized advancement for the American people and for all the other peace-loving peoples of the world.

KING GEORGE VI'S SPEECH FROM THE THRONE TO BOTH HOUSES OF PARLIAMENT

November 29, 1944 [1]

My Lords and Members of the House of Commons:

The United Nations look back on a year of resounding achievement. They now look forward with greater confidence than ever to those final victories which will give to the peoples of the world the just peace which is our chief desire. In Western Europe My Forces from the United Kingdom and Canada and their comrades from the United States, with the valuable aid of the Armed Forces of My European Allies and of the peoples who have risen to meet them, have routed the enemy in a series of decisive battles and are now pressing him on the borders of his own country. In Italy the Forces of the United Nations have advanced to the northern plains and in Greece and Yugoslavia the Germans are being driven from the countries which they have oppressed for three bitter years. In the East the massive achievements of My Russian Ally have deprived the Germans of vast stretches of territory which they hoped would feed their armies and provide an impassable barrier to prevent the soil of Germany from becoming a battle-ground. Both in the East and in the West, Germany is invaded. The plight in which her armies now find themselves is a measure of the success which by God's grace has crowned our arms.

In the war against Japan the enemy has been thrown back from India and My American Ally continues to reduce the shriking area still under Japanese control in the Pacific. We intend to reinforce as rapidly and powerfully as possible the United Kingdom Forces who are now sharing with their comrades from all parts of the British Commonwealth and Empire and from the United States, China, the Netherlands and France the burden of the struggle against Japan.

[1] Parliamentary Debates.

My Navies everywhere have maintained their mastery over the enemy and have achieved great successes, in which My Air Forces have fully shared, in driving his surface and submarine forces from the seas. My Air Forces, in concert with the Air Forces of the United States, have delivered increasingly heavy blows against Germany and have maintained their support of military and naval operations in all theatres.

The successes of My Armed Forces would not have been achieved but for the devoted labours of those throughout the Commonwealth and Empire who have striven ceaselessly to arm and equip them. It is over five years now since My peoples first took up the struggle to free the world from aggression and the contribution of the civil population is beyond all praise.

The United Nations await with sober confidence the unrolling of future events. Joined in an unbreakable alliance and fortified by constant collaboration between the Governments concerned and by frequent personal meetings between their leaders, they look forward to that day on which the aggressor is finally defeated and the whole world can turn to the rebuilding of prosperity and the maintenance of an unassailable peace.

Members of the House of Commons:

You will be asked to make further financial provision for the conduct of the war and for the other necessary services.

My Lords and Members of the House of Commons:

Victory remains our supreme aim and to this end you will be invited to pass such further legislation as may be required for the effective prosecution of the war.

Once, however, the war in Europe is over, the transition from war to peace will begin; and My Ministers are actively preparing plans to ensure that, without in any way prejudicing the active prosecution of the war against Japan, an increasing part of our resources is made available for civilian production. They will try to create conditions favourable to the expansion of our export trade and the re-equipment of our industry and to maintain a high level of food production at home. They are considering the methods by which the policy for the maintenance of a high level of employment can be implemented, especially with regard to the distribution of industry in the Development Areas. Progress will be made in fulfilling the urgent tasks of providing additional housing accommodation and of increasing supplies of civilian goods. My Ministers will continue their policy of ensuring a fair distribution of the necessaries of life so long as there is any scarcity.

My Government intend that, as opportunity serves, progress should be made with legislation arising out of the proposals already made public for a comprehensive health service, an enlarged and unified scheme of national insurance, a new scheme of industrial injury insurance and a system of family allowances. They will also invite you to approve measures embodying proposals for a national water policy which have already been presented to you.

A Bill will be laid before you dealing with electoral reform based on the recommendations of Mr. Speaker's Conference, and a Bill providing for the resumption of local elections at the appropriate time. You will be invited to pass measures relating to the provision of finance for the capital expenditure which local authorities will incur after the end of hostilities in Europe and proposals for the adjustment of local government areas in England and Wales will also be laid before you.

You will be asked to approve legislation designed to extend export credit facilities and to conserve, subject to appropriate safeguards, the use or value of assets created at the public expense on requisitioned and other land.

Measures will also be laid before you making further provision for the regulation of wages and conditions of employment and for the development of the public educational system in Scotland.

There will be presented to you legislation making further provision for assistance towards the development of the Colonial Empire both by prolonging the period covered by the Colonial Development and Welfare Act of 1940 and by substantially increasing the provision of funds authorised to be made under that Act.

I pray that the Almighty may give His blessing to your counsels.

PRIME MINISTER WINSTON CHURCHILL'S SPEECH FOLLOWING THE KING'S SPEECH FROM THE THRONE

November 29, 1944 [1]

Everyone will agree with my right hon. Friend who has just sat down that this has been a long Parliament. We need not embark on historical controversy as to the claims to continuous life which would be put forward on behalf of a Parliament much longer than this, but I am very glad that the closing Session of this long ten years' Parliament should show all the respect for the traditional and ceremonial occasions which ignorant, unthinking people who have not meditated upon matters or studied the true movement of events and of forces in the human breast might easily regard as meaningless performance. Here in the Speech from the Throne and in the Debates on the Address may be seen all the workings of the British Constitution or all the principal workings. The Sovereign, advised by His Ministers, delivers the Gracious Speech. The House then proceed to express their thanks, but have a perfect right to move Amendments saying that they regret that this or that has been put in or left out of the Gracious Speech, and if they carry such an Amendment, the Government of the day is defeated on a major point of confidence, and it is not easy to conceive a situation in which they could continue to retain their office. I have on another occasion reminded the House that this Debate on the Address is the beginning of what is called "the grand inquest of the nation." A new Session begins, and at this moment and in this progress of the Address, there is nothing that can be held back from discussion. Amendments can be moved on any matter and considerable periods are left by Mr. Speaker, either at the beginning or during the course of the Debate, when the Debate is general and open. There is no time similar to the period of the Debate on the Address where real trials of strength can be brought about in days of party conflict between the Government and the Opposition.

I have always been of opinion that the wishes of the House in respect to the Debate on the Address should be met by the administration. If the House wish for a few more days to discuss the special Amendments and so forth, the Government should put no obstacle in the way within reason. Of course, we are governed by the end of the year as well as by 31st March, in regard to certain legislation. I have always felt that the Debate on the general aspects

[1] Parliamentary Debates.

of the Address should be a considerable feature. Perhaps I am trespassing beyond my duty, but I have always rejoiced that the Debate on the general aspects of the Address was a considerable feature, because then is the time when a Member who has got no friends and has got no group can get up and speak about anything in the world which he thinks will advance his fellow creatures.

Mr. Quibell (Brigg): If he catches Mr. Speaker's eye.

The Prime Minister: If he should catch Mr. Speaker's eye. This is customary in a Parliamentary sense, a democratic feature in our annual procedure. Of course, I must admit, as an aged Member of this House, and as one who has done some forty-two years of service here—unhappily for me there was a break of two years, two Parliaments which lasted for a year apiece—that after all this long experience and service in the House, I find it very unpleasant to have the Debate on the Adjournment one day, and the Debate on the new Session the next. In the high and far-off times when I first entered this building, there was usually a six months' or five months' Recess, between the grouse on the 12th August and the latter part of January or the beginning of February, when the House reassembled. I do not consider those days were without their wisdom. Do not—and this has a bearing on some of the remarks which have recently been made—ever suppose that you can strengthen Parliament by wearying it, and by keeping it in almost continuous session. If you want to reduce the power of Parliament, let it sit every day in the year, one-fifth part filled, and then you will find it will be the laughing-stock of the nation, instead of being, as it continues to be, in spite of all the strains of modern life, the citadel as well as the cradle of Parliamentary institutions throughout the world; almost the only successful instance of a legislative body with plenary powers, elected on universal suffrage, which is capable of discharging, with restraint and with resolution, all the functions of peace and of war.

This digression on general topics will, perhaps, be excused by another digression which I find it my duty to make, and this is a more sober and more sombre digression. All our affairs, down to the smallest detail, continue to be dominated by the war. Parliamentary business is no exception. I must warn the House and the country against any indulgence in the feeling that the war will soon be over. It may be, but do not indulge that feeling, and think that we should now all be turning our thoughts to the new phase in world history which will open at the close of this war. The truth is that no one knows when the German war will be finished, and still less how long the interval will be between the defeat of the Germans and the defeat of the Japanese. I took occasion some months ago, to damp down premature hopes by speaking of the German war running into January and February. I could see disappointment in several quarters as I looked around the House, and I followed this up quickly by indicating the late Spring or the early Summer as periods which we must take into account as possibilities. My present inclination is not at all to mitigate these forecasts, or guesses, as my hon. Friend the Seconder of the Address said, "guesses" is the right word, for they can be little more. Indeed, if I were to make any change in the duration of the unfolding of events it would be to leave out the word "early" before the word "summer."

The vast battle which is in progress in the West has yielded to us important gains. The enemy has everywhere been thrust back. The capture of Metz and Strasbourg are glorious and massive achievements. The brilliant fighting and manœuvring of the French Army near the Swiss Frontier and their piercing of the Belfort Gap and their advance on a broad front to the Rhine is not only a military episode of high importance, but it shows, what many of us have never doubted, that the French Army will rise again and be a great factor in the life of France and of Europe, and that the French soldier, properly equipped and well led, is unsurpassed among the nations. I had the opportunity of visiting this Army, and one had hoped to be there at the moment when its attack was delivered upon the Belfort Gap, but in the night twelve inches of snow fell and everything had to be put off for three days. Nevertheless, I had the opportunity of seeing a very large number of the troops who were going to be engaged, if not in the first stage, in the second stage of this battle. For an hour or more they marched past in a swirling snow-storm and as the light faded I had a good look, at close quarters, at their faces. These are all young men from eighteen to twenty-two, average twenty. What a fine thing to be a Frenchman, twenty years of age, well-armed, well-equipped, and with your native land to avenge and save. The light in these men's eyes and their alert bearing gives one the greatest confidence that in our nearest neighbour and long friend in war and in these great struggles of our life time will rise in power and force from the ruins, the miseries and the disgraces of the past and will present us once more with a France to be numbered among the Great Powers of the world.

I have spoken of the fighting in the Belfort Gap and I have mentioned Strasbourg, and, further to the North, the very great battles which the Americans have gained around Metz. Opposite Cologne and north of it the fighting has been most severe and it is here that the gains of ground will be most important and consequently are most disputed. The weather, which it is always customary and excusable, even legitimate, to abuse at this season of the year, in these regions has made the tasks of the American troops and those of the British on their left flank extremely difficult. What is called the fourth element in war—mud—has played a formidable part. We have not yet succeeded in driving the enemy back to the Rhine, let alone have we established a strong bridgehead across it. The battle there is continuing still with the greatest vigour. Immense losses have been inflicted upon the enemy. The wearing down process here, burdensome as it has been to the United States and British Forces has been far greater upon the enemy, and, of course, any large and effective break in the German front in these regions— Cologne and northwards—would have the highest strategic consequences.

I may mention that in the interval between the liberation of France and that of the greater part of Belgium Field-Marshal Montgomery's group of armies, with substantial United States assistance, drove the enemy back to the line of the Maas, or lower Meuse and established a sure flank guard, a flank barrier, in Holland protecting the whole line of the main armies operating eastwards. It also opened the great port of Antwerp, which was captured intact, to the reception of large convoys of ocean-going ships, thus making an incomparable sea-base available for the nourishment of the northern group of British Armies and the various groups of American Armies also deployed. In these operations, including the storming of the islands, which contained episodes of marvellous gallantry, grand feats of arms, the British and Canadian forces suffered about 40,000 casualties—that is, in the interval between the two great battles. In the new battle which runs from General Montgomery's Army, broadly speaking opposite Venloo, down to the Vosges Mountains, where the French take up the long line, the whole front is held by the Americans, who are bearing the brunt with their customary distinction and courage.

I am not giving a review of the war situation, I have no intention of doing so; later on, perhaps when we meet after Christmas, it will be right to review it, and it may be very much more easy than it is now. There may be hard facts and cheering facts to put before the House. The House knows that I have never hesitated to put hard facts before it. I know the British people and I know this House, and there is one thing they will not stand, and that is not being told how bad things are. If it is humanly possible to do it without endangering affairs one is always well advised to tell people how bad things are. I remember occasions when I have greatly revived the energy and ardour of the House by giving them an account of the shocking position we occupied in various quarters, and how very likely things were to get worse before they would get better.

MR. BELLENGER (Bassetlaw): So did some of us.

THE PRIME MINISTER: We share the glory, but my motive in doing so was to strengthen the position of the Government. I say that I am not giving a review of the war situation to-day, but I mention these outstanding, these commanding, facts in order to dissipate lightly-founded sensations that we can avert our eyes from the war and turn to the tasks of transition and of reconstruction, or still more that we can turn to the political controversies and other diversions of peace, which are dear to all our hearts, and rightly dear to the democracies in action, because without controversy democracies cannot achieve their health-giving process. But I do not think we can look on any of these matters with a sense of detachment from the war issue, which is right over us, which weighs intensely and preponderantly upon us and upon every form of our national life. All else must be still subordinated to this supreme task. It is on the foe that our eyes must be fixed and to break down his resistance demands and will receive the most intense exertions of Great Britain, of the United States and of all the United Nations and converted satellites—all forces that can be brought to bear.

This is just the moment not to slacken. All the races which the calendar holds, or nearly all of them, are won in the last lap, and it is there, when it is most hard, when one is most tired, when the sense of boredom seems to weigh upon one, when even the most glittering events, exciting, thrilling events, are, as it were, covered by satiation, when headlines in the newspaper, though perfectly true, succeed one another in their growing emphasis and yet the end seems to recede before us, like climbing a hill when there is another peak beyond—it is at that very moment that we in this island have to give that extra sense of exertion, of boundless, inexhaustible, dynamic energy that we have shown, as the records now made public have emphasised in detail. Tirelessness is what we have to show now. Here I must observe that it is one thing to feel these tremendous drives of energy at the beginning of war, when your country is likely to be invaded and you do not know whether you will not all have to die honourably but soon; it is one thing to exhibit these qualities, which certainly the House has never been estranged from, at such a moment, and quite another thing to show them in the sixth year of a war. On the other hand we must remember that the enemy whose country is invaded has also these supreme stimuli which we ourselves responded to in the very dark days of 1940 and 1941.

I have said enough to emphasise the preponderance of the war, weighing down upon us all—the German war—and after the German war we must not forget there is the war with Japan. It is on this footing and in this mood that we must address ourselves to the Gracious Speech and to the loyal Address which it is now our duty to present to His Majesty. My right hon.

Friend who spoke from the bench opposite and my right hon. Friend who spoke for the Liberal Party have both paid their compliments to the Mover and the Seconder of the Address. It has become almost a hackneyed phrase to say that their performances have never been surpassed. In the forty-two King's Speeches—or something like it—which I have heard I think that that phrase must have been used twenty times at least and it certainly can be used on this occasion. But what is the note that is struck by those two young Members of the House of Commons? It is Youth, Youth, Youth; efficient youth marching forward from service in the field or at the coal face, marching forward to take their part in Parliament; and I am of opinion that those who have toiled and sweated, and those who have dared and conquered, should receive, whatever party they belong to, a full share of representation in any new House of Commons that may be called into being. I must say I thought they were extremely good speeches, and I cannot doubt that those two young Members will be real additions for a long period of time, as I trust and pray, to the membership of this House.

Remember, Sir, we have a missing generation, we must never forget that— the flower of the past lost in the great battles of the last war. There ought to be another generation in between these young men and we older figures who are soon, haply, to pass from the scene. There ought to be another genera- tion of men, with their flashing lights and leading figures. We must do all we can to try to fill the gap, and, as I say, there is no safer thing to do than to run risks with youth. It is very difficult to live your life in this world and not to get set in old ways, rather looking back with pleasure to the days of your youth. That is quite right, and tradition is quite right. A love of tradition has never weakened a nation, indeed it has strengthened nations in their hour of peril, but the new view must come, the world must roll forward.

"Let the great world spin for ever down the ringing grooves of change." as Tennyson said many years ago. Let us have no fear of the future. We are a decent lot, all of us, the whole nation. Wherever you go you need have no fear. I was brought up never to fear the English democracy, to trust the people. We need have no fear in these matters, and those speeches made by those two young Members give one the feeling that there must be rich reserves in the Army, in the industries and in the workshops of men of assured quality and capacity who, whatever their differing views on political affairs, are none the less absolutely united in maintaining the historic greatness of Britain and of the British Commonwealth of Nations throughout the world.

I must now refer to several matters which concern the business of the Session and the business of the House before I come to topics of a more engaging character. We intend to allow reasonable time for the Debate on the Address, and under your guidance, Mr. Speaker, we shall endeavour to meet the wishes of the House in regard both to the general Debate and De- bates on specific subjects, as may be desired. The course of the Debate on the Address is a matter for consultation, and the proposed arrangements will be announced in the usual business statement. Before the end of the year it will be necessary for us to ask the House to pass the Expiring Laws Con- tinuance Bill through all its stages, as well as a short Bill to continue in operation the Local Elections and Register of Electors Act until 31st March next. The existing Act expires on 31st December, according to my right hon. Friend who has assisted me in this portion of my speech, and it will be neces- sary to pass that Measure before that date.

As regards the future, a Bill providing for the resumption of local elec- tions and dealing with the assimilation of the Parliamentary and local gov-

ernment franchise—an important step on which both parties have agreed—
is being prepared with a view to its introduction, if possible, before Christmas, and its passage into law early in the New Year. Certain Supplementary
Estimates will also be required, including one to provide a grant-in-aid to
Jamaica for the relief and repair of damage following the hurricane, and a
special Consolidated Fund Bill must be passed for the issue of money. Any
other business will be brought forward as and when required.

I have also to inform the House that it is the Government's intention to
propose a Motion to-morrow to give precedence to Government business, to
provide for the presentation of Government Bills only, and to stop the ballot
for private Member's Bills—all following the precedents of the last five
years, as well as of the last war. I regret to have to ask Members again to
forgo their rights and privileges. They have been induced to make this
sacrifice readily, if not cheerfully, in the past when our whole energies have
been concentrated upon the war. The moment has not yet arrived for us
to resume our normal arrangements, and I fear I must ask for the whole
time of the house to be put at the disposal of the Government in view of the
heavy programmes and the many months of hard work which lie before us,
into which a contingent of my hon. Friends on this side are so eager to plunge.

On a previous occasion I gave my reasons for believing that we are entering
upon the last Session of the present Parliament. The Gracious Speech contains
references to a number of important Measures which we hope to bring forward
this Session, in continuance of the progress of the reform programme and social
advancement upon which the Coalition Government embarked two years ago.
If events take the course I have previously indicated, if we are to attempt
to complete our legislative programme, if we are to attempt to make any
marked progress in our legislative programme, we shall require all the available time of the House. In recent Sessions Members have had many opportunities of raising matters of general interest, and we hope most sincerely
that such occasions will be available from time to time. The Debate on
the Address is supposed to clear a lot of things out of the way, but in Parliamentary usage we have never been reluctant to give to any large number
of Members who may request a Debate on a particular topic the opportunity
they deserve and desire. Of course, anyone who chooses to learn Parliamentary procedure will see that in the course of a Session there are very few
topics that he cannot find occasion to vent, but careful study of the rules
of procedure is recommended to those who wish to find these opportunities.

There is one further matter which concerns our proceedings to-day. It
will be necessary to renew the Motion relating to the hours of sittings of the
House. We must obtain this Motion to-day to regulate our future proceedings,
and I hope it will be possible to adjourn the Debate on the Address at a
reasonable hour in order that my right hon. Friend the Leader of the House
will be able to explain and carry it.

All this may be considered to be preliminary to the very few words I have
yet to say. No one can complain that the King's Speech is not heavily loaded
with legislation—a more elaborate and substantial King's Speech in regard
to legislation has rarely been produced. I have here a paper which sets out
all the Bills—of which I think there are twelve, it might easily have been
thirteen—which figure in the programme: the great health and national insurance group—the National Health Service Bill, the National Insurance Bill,
the Industrial Injury Insurance Bill; Family Allowances holds a high place;
the Water Bill, the River Board Bill, Reform of Parliamentary Franchise
Bill, Local Elections Bill, Public Authorities Loans Bill, Adjustment of Local

Government Areas Bill—a topic which offers itself to expansive conversation —Export Credit Bill, Requisitioned Land and War Works Bill, Wages Council Bill, Education (Scotland) Bill—which has already been given a special emphasis by the seconder of the Address and Colonial Development and Welfare Bill. All these are mentioned, and that is the order in which they are mentioned in the King's Speech, but not necessarily the order in which they will be taken in our Business procedure.

I myself should like to put in word for a decision on the Report of the Select Committee on the Rebuilding of the House of Commons, because I think a Resolution from the House on that subject would liberate certain energies, not on a large scale, which might be detached from the war—some very aged lapidaries exist who can be getting on with the work. We really will need a House to sit in, I can assure hon. Members, after this war is over, when so many great matters will have to be decided on which agreement will not be so perfect and so unanimous as it has been found to be in respect to the general structure of the new Chamber.

We shall proceed with this programme which has been unfolded in the King's Speech. We shall proceed with it as opportunity serves—one cannot do more than that—and we shall proceed with it also in accordance with the time which is left to this Parliament. Our tenure now depends upon the official end of the German war. It is a great inconvenience not to be able to forecast that date. I can only say that we shall press forward perseveringly with the great programme of legislation which this remarkable Coalition has framed, and we shall press steadily forward until the hour of our separation arrives. Hurried legislation is not usually successful; prolonged sittings do not necessarily mean rapid progress. The Dissolution undoubtedly hangs over us, and there is no question of postponing the Dissolution in order to carry a programme of legislation which, with the best will in the world, could not be carried this Session. If, most unhappily, the end of the war in Europe should be unexpectedly deferred, we shall make more progress in the social field, but if it should come to pass at dates which it is reasonable to hope, the summer, the early summer, or earlier if good fortune crowns our arms, then we cannot expect to accomplish more than a small part of what is set down in the Gracious Speech. Much will turn on the result of an appeal to the nation conducted under extraordinary circumstances out of our reverence for democracy, with many difficulties not present in peace time, with an electorate which has not voted for ten years, and with scarcely any voter under thirty years who has had the chance to vote before. I shall not attempt to pierce the veils of the unknown. I see there are already some prophets in the field who know exactly how all these complex forces and circumstances will in the end express themselves.

MR. ELLIS SMITH (Stoke): One a close friend of yours.

THE PRIME MINISTER: I should like further and better particulars.

MR. SMITH: The right hon. Member for Rushcliffe (Mr. Assheton).

THE PRIME MINISTER: I have not had the pleasure of reading in detail his statement, but I was not aware that he had predicted results—results are, of course, often predicted by people who wish to encourage their followers— and as to the time when it would take place. It is only natural that one who is responsible for the actual marshalling of the armies should set the time and date a little in front of what may actually prove to be zero hour.

However, whatever may be the doubts as to when the election will come, and how it will finish up, and where we shall all find ourselves sitting at the end of it, and what our relations with each other will be—all these are uncertain—there is one thing which is quite certain, all the leading men in both the principal parties—and in the Liberal Party as well—are pledged and committed to this great mass of social legislation, and I cannot conceive that whatever may be the complexion of the new House, they will personally fail to make good their promises and commitments to the people. There may, therefore, be an interruption in our work, but it is only an interruption and one which must not be allowed in any circumstance to turn us from our purposes on which our resolves have been taken. This is a matter on which anyone has a right to speak for himself, irrespective of what may be the consequences of the General Election. No one can bind any future Parliament, but some of us, I suppose, will get back, and I cannot believe that any of those who have set their hands to this great social programme—insurance, health, compensation and the other matters that are in it—I cannot believe that any of us, whether in office or in Opposition, who have been sponsors of this programme will fail to march forward along the broad lines that have been set forth.

As I have said, I could not at this stage lay out the exact order of priority of the various legislative Measures which have been set down. The Debate on the Address and the necessary legislation which must be passed before the end of the year will take up our time until we return. There is then a great deal of necessary financial business to be discharged, in getting you, Mr. Speaker, out of the Chair—sometimes arduous—on the Army, Navy and Air Force Votes and the Civil Service Votes. This will all take time. The Consolidated Fund Bill must be disposed of: here is another opportunity for a great many topics to be raised for which Members come along asking for special days to be given. They should just study the precedents of the past and see all the things that have been worked in on that Bill. Easter falls early this year. It falls on April Fool's Day. I hope that is not an irreverent thing to say, but in case anybody thinks it is perhaps I may be allowed to say April 1st. We must have a Budget of a more or less uncontroversial character to tide us over the election period, and as much legislation as possible will be fitted in with these obligatory features of our Parliamentary work. More than that it is premature to define.

There is one matter which was referred to by my right hon. Friend the Member for South-West Bethnal Green (Sir P. Harris). Housing is the most threatened sector in the home front. I have for some time been disquieted by the situation. During the last four or five months I have been continually referring to it by minute and by personal discussion. The objective is painfully plain, namely, to provide in the shortest time the largest number of weather-proofed dwellings in which our people can live through this winter in reasonable comfort. The subject is divided, like ancient Gaul, into three parts—repair, prefabricated and permanent; or, using the code names which have become so common in military matters, "repair," "prefab.," and "perm." At the summit of this problem sits Lord Woolton and what I will venture to call somewhat disrespectfully "the housing squad," including not only War Cabinet Ministers—it is not usual to give details of Cabinet Committees—but also some who are not ministerial at all. These collect, co-ordinate, and in a great many cases, decide, subject to the War Cabinet in the last resort, what is to be done. I have reserved to myself the right to take the chair when and if at any time I think it is necessary or desirable.

That is the function, the relationship, of Lord Woolton to this general scheme. I may say that Lord Woolton has shown a very great deal of energy and grip in trying to meet the difficulties of the past, difficulties which are being continually added to by the fire of the enemy. He has taken a number of steps, but I did not consider that the situation, borne in upon me by questions and answers which I have had to give in this House, was such that we did not require to smooth out and make more precise the arrangements for gripping this problem. Naturally, with the war going on, one's mind is drawn to the focusing of the executive forces of an emergency character upon the really serious parts of the problem. On a lower level, but of equally practical importance, an importance which outweighs the superior level, is the great field of emergency executive action.

I can say a word—and it is only a word—on this matter of the relations between the Minister of Works and the Minister of Health in this field of London repair. The Ministry of Health is the great ambassador Department which deals with local authorities, and nothing must be done to hamper that long usage. Therefore, the Ministry of Health is the ambassador for the Ministry of Works in respect of the taking over of areas, streets and so forth that really require more power than any local authority can bring to bear. For the rest, executive power will increasingly rest with the Ministry of Works which will have to discharge all the tasks of repair which cannot be undertaken, or are not being effectively undertaken, by the local authorities; which will have to produce the prefabricated houses which I spoke of at the beginning of the year but which cannot be produced in the numbers I then mentioned but, still, can be produced in very great number and of varying types. Further, they have to make, with the assistance of the Board of Trade in the closest liaison, as the military would say, the fittings and parts of all kinds which must be made not only for the repairs and for the "prefabs.," but also for the "perms.," which must get forward as fast as they possibly can under the driving power of the Minister of Health and, of course, the Secretary of State for Scotland. I do not want to go more into this now, because we shall very likely have a special Debate on the subject, either on an Amendment to the Address or on the resumption, if desired, and if Mr. Speaker would permit, of the general Debate on the Address. People sometimes do not like to have an Amendment to the Address, because it must take the form of a Vote of Censure, but we are in the hands of the House and under the orders of the Chair.

I do not think it is any use for me at this time to enter upon the subject of foreign policy. I have a list of twenty-five countries on which I am prepared to give information about their tangled politics and their relations to ourselves, but the House may rest assured that I have no intention of doing so, as no sufficient provocation has been offered to His Majesty's Government to induce me to embark upon this lengthy excursion. After all, a Foreign Affairs Debate can be brought on as part of the Debate on the Address. All I have tried to do at this time is to give a general survey of the tasks which lie before us, of the limitations which may be assigned to our powers to discharge these tasks, of our duty to persevere in all we are pledged and committed to, and of the sense of the overlying obligations which we have to carry the war through in its closing stages with all energy and unity, not only at home among ourselves but among the great united Powers of the Grand Alliance, whom, I am happy to say, were never more closely and intimately and comprehendingly united than they are at this time.

PRIME MINISTER WINSTON CHURCHILL'S STATEMENT IN COMMONS ON LEND-LEASE

November 30, 1944 [1]

I think it proper to take this opportunity to tell the House the outcome of the discussions which have been taking place the last few weeks in Washington between the British mission headed by Lord Keynes and the American Administration.

The mission has been occupied in examining the manner in which the continuation of the war after the defeat of Germany is likely to affect the best use of our joint resources, and, in particular, changes in the program of supplies which the American Administration feels it is proper and right for us to have in accordance with the terms of the Lend-Lease Act, an act which we must remember was for the defense of the United States and strictly limited to what was necessary for the effective prosecution of the war by the United States and its Allies.

The end of the war with Germany will make possible large reductions in some of our requirements. We expect our needs will be met by the program at a rate not much more than half of what we have been receiving in 1944. All of these supplies and services will be exclusively for the joint war effort against the common enemy.

The prolongation of the war into what will be for us the sixth and seventh year means that certain improvements are essential if our national economy is to be as fully effective as possible for the prosecution of the war. Fatigue and abstinence carried too far, endured too long, can impede the effectiveness of a people at war at least as much as a more sensational form of privation.

After the defeat of Germany some release in manpower to increase the supply available for essential civilian consumption must follow in due course, and some improvements in the standards and variety of the national diet and devotion of resources to the provision of emergency housing and serious efforts to rebuild the export trade which we deliberately gave up in the extremity of our emergency, but without which we cannot live in the future.

These are forms of sacrifice which it is both possible and right to make over a limited period, but they become self-defeating if they are continued too long.

All these matters, both military and economic, have been jointly examined, supported with a wealth of detail, by our representatives in Washington with the heads of the American departments concerned. We have put at their disposal every particular and every relevant fact in our possession. Relevant material has been made available to the public both here and in the United States in the White Paper published a few days ago.

During the recent brief recess (of Parliament) our representatives in Washington have been in position to make a full report.

I take this opportunity to express our very great appreciation of the practical sympathy with which the realities of the situation have been examined and of the results which have been achieved.

I may remind the House that it is no part of the Lend-Lease Act to provide general relief or to provide for post-war reconstruction or to aid our export

[1] *New York Times.*

trade. That great act has stood us and our Allies in good stead, and we have neither asked nor expected any assistance which is not strictly within its terms and provisions.

Nevertheless, as the war proceeds, the nature of the aid which forwards its prosecution most effectively, though unchanged in major matters, gradually will change in detail. Accordingly, so that we can play our full part in continuing the struggle, the program of lend-lease aid against Japan after the defeat of Germany has now been planned with the American Administration to maintain our fighting power against Japan. Without any reduction in our proportionate efforts, we shall be able, along with the United States, to release some of our manpower to produce some more civilian goods.

Some improvement in the variety of civilian diet will be made possible. We shall be able to do more to build temporary and emergency houses. We must necessarily, for the most part, depend on our own efforts in this field. But in addition to those efforts resulting from the planned and proportional program, we anticipate aid from American sources, not only in materials but also in complete houses to meet some of our needs for temporary emergency houses for war workers in war areas. These items are being closely examined with the help of experts sent by the Ministry of Works during the tenure of Lord Portal.

It is too soon to say on what scale the possibilities of physical production and shipping will allow this most generous assistance to be realized in practice. It is not too soon to say that the principle is recognized that provision of emergency shelters for bombed-out war workers is an essential part of fully effective contribution to final victory.

Finally, we have been able to reduce the lend-lease program so that there will be no obstacles to the efforts we must ourselves begin at once and intensify to defeat Germany and to increase the export trade, which will be absolutely vital to us when, at the termination of the war, the present system of lend-lease necessarily and properly comes to an end. This is a matter on which I am well aware the members are anxious to hear in some detail what our position will now be.

The defeat of Germany will make possible reductions in the lend-lease program, and in certain fields we have been able to anticipate these changes and to work out the basis of a new program from the beginning of 1945. Thus, from that date we shall no longer get shipments to this country under lend-lease of any manufactured articles for civilian use which enter into the export trade, nor of many raw materials and semi-fabricated materials such as iron, steel and some nonferrous metals. We shall then be free to export a wide range of goods made from those materials.

Naturally, we have not used in export, and do not propose to use, any critically scarce material except where export is essential to the effective prosecution of the war.

Until the German war is at an end, however, there can, of course, be no significant release of resources. Prosecution of the war (against Japan) must still continue to have first call on our resources after that, but after the defeat of Germany it will be both possible and necessary to turn over an increasing part of our resources to civilian production, including the export trade. As as result of recent discussions with the United States, exports will then only be subject to those inevitable limitations dictated by the needs of the war against Japan.

There is not and never has been any question of re-exporting in commerce any articles we received under lend-lease, nor in general shall we receive in this country under lend-lease finished articles identical with those we export.

All such articles will be paid for by us. Where we continue to receive any raw materials, the quantities supplied under lend-lease are limited to our domestic consumption for the manufacture of munitions and the maintenance of our essential wartime economy. We shall pay cash for any additional supplies we wish to take from the United States for export purposes. This one uncertainty about our future conditions has now been removed.

It should be possible for exporters henceforward to make plans with the assurance that they will be able to give effect to those plans with the least possible time lag when the defeat of Germany releases manpower capacity and materials.

I should like to add one word. The White Paper on reciprocal aid lately published and the President's lend-lease report provide vivid evidence of the extent to which community and interdependence of effort between the two great Atlantic communities proceeded.

Never has there been a more thorough understanding of the facts of the economic position and the problems of Great Britain and the United States than we have now been able to reach. If men of good-will start out from the same premises and agreed facts, they do not necessarily find it impossible to reach the same conclusions.

(Laborite Emmanuel Shinwell interrupted to ask: "Are we to pay for the goods and raw materials imported from the United States out of our foreign assets still available, or would the United States take in return goods exported from this country?")

Everything is as I said. This statement was agreed upon almost sentence by sentence by our American colleagues, and I would be grateful if Mr. Shinwell would put the question, which is a perfectly valid question, to me after reading the paper either tomorrow or the next day.

I would not like to give the answer offhand, which may not correspond with exactly what was decided upon. I must add that I consider the statement I have made one of a highly satisfactory nature, and it gives real hope for the future and for the smooth development of economic affairs between the two countries in the future.

DECEMBER

December 1, 1944

Propaganda Minister Joseph Goebbels decreed: "No doubts must be expressed as to the final outcome of the war—that is the paramount ruling."

2

Premier Stalin and General de Gaulle conferred in Moscow.

American troops entered Saarlautern, Saar basin industrial town and Juelich, a key point to the Cologne Plain.

Spanish Foreign Minister José Felix Lequerica repeated Dictator Franco's demand that Spain should be given an important place at the peace table. He said: "Spain's history, services to civilization and peaceful attitude give her more than enough rights to intervene in the future organization of the world."

Six Greek Cabinet Ministers belonging to the National Liberation Front (EAM) resigned in protest against the "unilateral decisions" of Lieut. Gen. Ronald M. Scobie, British commander of Allied troops in Greece, in ordering the disbanding of the Greek guerrillas.

3

At least twenty-one persons were killed and 140 wounded when members of the National Liberation Front (EAM) defied a Government ban and paraded through the streets of Athens. Government police fired into the crowd.

Japanese Premier Kuniaki Koiso warned that the military "situation is critical." He declared: "This war has a long way to go."

General Charles de Gaulle defined the purpose of his Moscow mission as tightening and clarifying Russian-French friendship, not only for victory in the war but for lasting peace.

4

George Papandreou's British-supported Greek Government issued an ultimatum to the EAM (National Liberation Front) to quit the Athens area, after the latter had refused to disarm and disband its military arm, the ELAS. Royalist troops sent to disarm the ELAS were met with determined opposition near the Acropolis.

Generalissimo Chiang Kai-shek appointed his brother-in-law, Foreign Minister T. V. Soong, as Premier of China.

President Roosevelt nominated Joseph C. Grew, former Ambassador to Japan, to be Under-Secretary of State. He also accepted the resignations of Assistant Secretaries Adolf Berle, Jr., Breckinridge Long and G. Howland Smith, nominating as their successors, William L. Clayton, retiring Surplus War Property Administrator; Nelson Rockefeller, Co-ordinator of Inter-American Affairs, and Archibald MacLeish, Librarian of Congress.

5

British tanks and Rightist Greek Mountain Brigade troops attacked units of the ELAS, the fighting arm of EAM (National Liberation Front).

Scale: 0 5 10 20 30 MILES

LINE OF FARTHEST GERMAN PENETRATION

LINE AT START OF GERMAN ATTACK DEC. 16, 1944

American counter-thrusts in progress

American counter-thrusts in prospect

Area regained by Allies

Area won in Nazi thrust and still held

Courtesy New York Times

The German Breakthrough in Belgium
December, 1944

588

6

The Japanese drove rapidly toward Kunming, threatening to cut the India-China supply route and cripple the U. S. 14th Air Force.

7

Premier Ivanoe Bonomi reconstructed the Italian Cabinet with representatives from four anti-fascist parties: Liberal, Communist, Christian Democrat and Democracy of Labor.

8

By a vote of 279 to 30 Prime Minister Churchill was upheld in the House of Commons in his policy of intervention in liberated countries, but most of the Labor body, anxious for war unity, abstained from voting as an expression of protest.

9

An ELAS (National Liberation Front) spokesman made a blanket denial of Prime Minister Churchill's charges that the Greek patriot resistance organization was seeking to seize power in Greece. He declared: "If the ELAS desired to take over the reins of authority by force it could have done so immediately after the liberation of Athens when there were no Allied troops or sufficient police or Quisling forces in the capital."

In response to a request by War Mobilization Director James F. Byrnes, Selective Service ordered the resumption of induction of men in the age group twenty-six through thirty-seven.

11

Japanese Foreign Minister Mamoru Shigemitsu, in a speech on the third anniversary of the signing of the Axis military alliance, said: "There is no doubt that the war is definitely in our favor. There is not a shred of doubt in my mind that Hitler and Mussolini will save Europe."

12

Civilians were reported evacuating Tokyo as Superfortresses appeared over the Japanese capital.

14

The opposition in the House of Commons launched a furious attack on Prime Minister Churchill's policy in Greece.

15

The American Seventh Army entered Germany at three points.

American troops landed on Mindoro Island, 155 miles south of Manila.

17

Royal Air Force Spitfires and rocket-firing Beaufighters attacked ELAS forces in Athens.

Large-scale demonstrations in London, Manchester and other English cities, protested British policy in Greece as "protection for Greek fascism."

Going on the offensive for the first time since Normandy, the German Army launched a powerful counter-blow against the southern flank of the United States First Army on a seventy-mile front into Belgium and across the Luxembourg border.

18

On its third day of counter-offensive the German Army advanced twenty miles on its northern flank into Belgium.

19

The U. S. Supreme Court ruled unanimously that Japanese-Americans of unquestioned loyalty could not be detained in war relocation centers.

The British War Office charged that 25,000 out of 60,000 white prisoners of war died while being forced by the Japanese to work under worse-than-slavery conditions to speed through the Thailand-Burma railway and road.

20

Thirteen German divisions drove through a forty-five mile gap in the U. S. First Army defenses in Belgium and Luxembourg.

21

RAF rocket planes and British tanks attacked ELAS concentrations in Athens.

22

Secretary of War Stimson said the German counter-offensive was a gamble of desperation and if it failed would "definitely shorten the war."

The unchecked German offensive moved westward through Belgium for its seventh consecutive day, making a total gain of thirty-five miles.

23

Five thousand Allied planes slowed the German counter-offensive in Belgium and Luxembourg.

24

A Provisional Hungarian Government with Col. Gen. Bela Miklos, former commander of the Hungarian First Army, was formed by the Hungarian National Assembly in Debrecen.

The Rightist EDES Army of Gen. Napoleon Zervas in Epirus was practically destroyed by the ELAS, two-thirds of its soldiers deserting to the latter en masse.

Dr. Joseph Goebbels, German Propaganda Minister, broadcast an appeal to Germany to celebrate the sixth war Christmas with "yet more unbounded faith in our Fuehrer," whose health, spirit and morale, he said, "had never been better."

25

Prime Minister Churchill and Foreign Secretary Anthony Eden arrived in Athens and immediately called leaders of the ELAS forces to a conference.

26

Premier Gen. Kuniaki Koiso warned the Japanese people that the "spirit of the special attack (suicide units), which should be manifested also on the home front in response to the fighting front, is not yet fully expressed."

Greek leaders of all political parties and factions met with Prime Minister Churchill to find a way out of the "fratricidal strife."

Red Army troops, closing the escape corridor for many thousands of Germans in Budapest, completed the encirclement of the Hungarian capital.

27

A Third Army relief column smashed through to Bastogne and freed the encircled American troops who had been defending the town since December 18th.

30

King George II of Greece issued a royal proclamation in London appointing Archbishop Damaskinos as his Regent in Greece.

In his New Year's proclamation Reichsmarshal Hermann Goering said: "Our glorious Wehrmacht has repulsed the enemy on all frontiers of the Reich and the year end again finds it bravely attacking on the Western Front.

Propaganda Minister Joseph Goebbels taunted the Allies: "The enemy completely underestimated the war potential of the Reich and he must now recognize that the time factor has again become an element in his calculations."

The Hungarian Provisional Government at Debrecan declared war on Germany and asked the Allies for the conclusion of an armistice.

31

Gen. Patton's Third Army launched a new and initially successful drive into the southern flank of the German positions between St. Hubert and Bastogne.

The Polish National Council, representing the underground and Resistance Movement in liberated Poland, held a special meeting and established the Polish Provisional Government with Boleslaw Bierut as President and Edward B. Ossubka-Morawski as Prime Minister and Minister of Foreign Affairs.

In a New Year's message to the Chinese people Generalissimo Chiang Kai-shek promised that as soon as the military situation permitted he would "convene a People's Congress to adopt a constitution which would enable the Kuomintang to transfer the power of government to the people."

Field Marshal Baron Carl Gustav Mannerheim resigned the command of Finland's armed forces but continued as President.

STATEMENTS BY THE U. S. NAVY AND ARMY ON PEARL HARBOR

December 1, 1944 [1]

Navy

Public Law No. 339, 78th Congress, approved June 13, 1944, directed the Secretary of War and the Secretary of the Navy, severally, to proceed forthwith with an investigation into the fact surrounding the Pearl Harbor catastrophe, and to commence such proceedings against such persons as the facts might justify.

A Court of Inquiry, consisting of Admiral Orin G. Murfin, USN, retired; Admiral Edward C. Kalbfus, USN, retired, and Vice Admiral Adolphus Andrews, USN, retired, with Commander Harold Biesemeier, USN, as judge advocate, was appointed on July 13, 1944.

The court was directed to convene on July 17, 1944, or as soon thereafter as practicable, for the purpose of inquiring into all circumstances connected with the attack made by Japanese forces on Pearl Harbor, Territory of Hawaii, on Dec. 7, 1941; to inquire thoroughly into the matter, and to include in its findings a full statement of the facts it might deem to be established.

The court was further directed to state its opinion as to whether any offenses were committed or serious blame incurred on the part of any person or persons in the naval service, and, in case its opinion was that offenses had

[1] New York Times.

been committed or serious blame incurred, to recommend specifically what further proceedings should be had.

The Court of Inquiry commenced its proceedings on July 31, 1944, and submitted the record of its proceedings on Oct. 20, 1944. During its investigation, the court took the testimony of thirty-nine witnesses and received seventy-seven exhibits. Certain portions of the record of proceedings before the court, including the findings and opinion of the court, have been classified "top secret" and the balance "secret."

By letter dated Oct. 21, 1944, the Secretary of the Navy requested the Commander in Chief, United States Fleet, and Chief of Naval Operations to advise as to how much of the records of the Pearl Harbor Court of Inquiry bear such a relation to present military operations as to require high security classification.

The Commander in Chief, United States Fleet, and Chief of Naval Operations advised, in a letter dated Nov. 3, 1944, that a substantial part of the records of Pearl Harbor Court of Inquiry bears such a relation to the national security and to current military operations as to make it essential that that information not be revealed publicly.

After thorough review of the record of proceedings of the Pearl Harbor Court of Inquiry, the Secretary concurs with the view of the Commander in Chief, United States Fleet, and Chief of Naval Operations, as expressed in his letter of Nov. 3, 1944, and accordingly has directed that in the best interests of the present and future military operations of the United States, the existing "top secret" and "secret" classifications of the record must be continued. The record of the court will not be made public while the war is in progress.

The net result of the findings of fact and opinion of the Pearl Harbor Court of Inquiry, as reviewed by the Judge Advocate General of the Navy, and the Commander in Chief, U. S. Fleet, and Chief of Naval Operations, and by the Secretary of the Navy, is that the evidence now available does not warrant and will not support the trial by general court martial of any person or persons in the naval service.

The Secretary, in his findings upon the evidence before the Court of Inquiry and all the other proceedings in the matter to date, has found that there were errors of judgment on the part of certain officers in the naval service, both at Pearl Harbor and at Washington.

The Secretary is not satified that the investigation has gone to the point of exhaustion of all possible evidence. Accordingly, he has decided that his own investigation should be further continued until the testimony of every witness in possession of material facts can be obtained and all possible evidence exhausted.

Some of the testimony will be much delayed because certain witnesses who are actively engaged in combat against the enemy are not available and will not be available within the predictable future. The present decision of the Secretary will be reviewed when the investigation has been finally completed in the light of evidence then at hand.

The Secretary makes this personal statement:

"In reaching the above conclusions and decisions I am fully mindful of the wide and legitimate public interest in the Pearl Harbor attack. However, there is one consideration which is paramount to all others, and that is: What will best serve the continued successful prosecution of the war? The actions I have taken, in my judgment, are taken in the light of that consideration, and I accept full and complete responsibility for them."

Army *(by Mr. Stimson)*

By joint resolution of the Congress, approved June 13, 1944, the Secretary of War and the Secretary of the Navy were severally directed to proceed with an investigation into the facts surrounding the Pearl Harbor catastrophe of Dec. 7, 1941, and to commence such proceedings against such persons as the facts might justify. In order to meet the wishes of Congress as expressed in this resolution, I have conducted such an investigation.

In order to assist me to this end, there was appointed by order dated July 8, 1944, a board of three general officers which was directed "to ascertain and report the facts relating to the attack made by Japanese armed forces upon the Territory of Hawaii on 7 December, 1941, and to make such recommendations as it might deem proper."

This Army Pearl Harbor Board has conducted an extensive and painstaking investigation. It has held hearings in Hawaii, San Francisco and Washington. It has examined a total of 151 witnesses and received many exhibits. I have read its report and reviewed the recorded evidence. The Judge Advocate General of the Army, at my direction, has also examined the report and the record and has given me fully the benefit of his views.

I recognize the importance to any individual concerned of having a decision taken as to what, if any, action is to be instituted against him and, after weighing all the considerations, I am clear that the public interest as well as justice and fairness will best be served by a statement of my present conclusions.

So far as they now may be made public, consonant with the public interest, my conclusions are as follows:

"The Army Pearl Harbor Board, although it recommended no disciplinary or other action, concluded that there were several officers in the field and in the War Department who did not perform their duties with the necessary skill or exercise the judgment which was required under the circumstances. On the recorded evidence, I agree with some but not all of the board's conclusions.

"So far as the commanding general of the Hawaiian Department is concerned, I am of the opinion that his errors of judgment were of such a nature as to demand his relief from a command status. This was done on Jan. 11, 1942, and in itself is a serious result for any officer with a long record of excellent service, and conscientious as I believe General Short to be. In my judgment on the evidence now recorded, it is sufficient action.

"Furthermore, I am satisfied that proper steps were taken to correct such inadequacies of either personnel or organization as were shown to exist either in the War Department or in the field at the time of the Pearl Harbor disaster. My conclusion is that under all the circumstances the evidence now recorded does not warrant the institution of any further proceedings against any officer in the Army.

"In accordance with the opinion of the Judge Advocate General, I have decided that my own investigation should be further continued until all the facts are made as clear as possible and until the testimony of every witness in possession of material facts can be obtained, and I have given the necessary directions to accomplish this result.

"Some of the testimony may be much delayed where witnesses are engaged in combat in active theaters of operation. My present decision will be reviewed when the investigation has been finally completed.

"Finally, I am absolutely clear that it would be highly prejudicial to the successful prosecution of the war and the safety of American lives to make public during the war the report of the Army Pearl Harbor Board or the record on which it is based.

"Statement as to Col. Theodore Wyman, Jr. and certain others:

"I have today made a separate statement of my conclusion on the basis of the evidence now recorded not to institute further proceedings against any officer of the Army in respect to the Pearl Harbor disaster.

"The Military Affairs Committee of the House of Representatives, by a report of June 14, 1944, called attention to certain relationships of Hans Wilhelm Rohl to military construction in Hawaii under the direction of Col. Theodore Wyman, Jr., district engineer, and indicated that this may have contributed to the Pearl Harbor catastrophe. Accordingly, the phases of the committee report bearing thereon were referred to the Army Pearl Harbor Board for further investigation.

"I have reviewed the results of this investigation. I do not find from this review that the Pearl Harbor disaster was in any way contributed to or caused by any alleged misconduct, neglect or disloyalty on the part of Rohl, the Hawaiian constructors, the organization with which he was connected, Colonel Wyman, or others directing construction activities in Hawaii, and I do not find that there is any evidence that Rohl or anyone else directing such construction gave any information to the enemy.

"As to certain other alleged misconduct and neglect of Colonel Wyman and others in construction matters, I have referred the question of the commencing of any proceedings to the Under-Secretary of War and the Judge Advocate General."

MAIN POINTS OF PREMIER KUNIAKI KOISO'S SPEECH ASKING MORE GREATER EAST ASIA COLLABORATION

December 4, 1944 [1]

There should be no distinction made between the front line and the home front under the present situation. Each and every one of the 100,000,000 people should maintain and increase fighting power as combatants in response to the loyalty of (word missing).

This does not apply to Japan alone. Each and every one of the G.E.A. races not only should prepare against the enemy counterattacks with the object of the consummation of the G.E.A. War in view, but also should exert their utmost in the increasing and strengthening of fighting power by pursuing their respective mission, thereby (words missing) and fighting to the last for the peace of East Asia. Today the Asia Promotion Movement does not limit itself simply to a people's movement but is itself the G.E.A. War. (One sentence missing.)

In other words, I want you to understand that the present stage of the Asia Promotion Movement is (a portion) of the G.E.A. War. To secure stability of East Asia should be the underlying spirit of the Asia Promotion Movement. The Joint Declaration of Greater East Asiatic nations too, clearly indicates the design to establish a Co-Prosperity order based on righteousness to contribute to the (advancement) of the world.

[1] Office of War Information.

The purpose of the movement should be to further consolidate cooperation among the various races of the G.E.A. in accordance with the great ideal, and to promote the strengthening of the determination of the 1,000,000 peoples of the G.E.A. to willingly (advance) to the frontmost line of the G.E.A. War together with the Imperial Army.

STATEMENT BY SECRETARY OF STATE EDWARD R. STETTINIUS, JR., ON BRITISH POLICY IN ITALY

December 5, 1944 [1]

The position of this Government has been consistently that the composition of the Italian Government is purely an Italian affair except in the case of appointments where important military factors are concerned. This Government has not in any way intimated to the Italian Government that there would be any opposition on its part to Count Sforza. Since Italy is an area of combined responsibility, we have reaffirmed to both the British and Italian Governments that we expect the Italians to work out their problems of government along democratic lines without influence from outside.

This policy would apply to an even more pronounced degree with regard to Governments of the United Nations in their liberated territories.

PRIME MINISTER WINSTON CHURCHILL'S STATEMENT IN COMMONS ON THE SITUATION IN GREECE

December 5, 1944 [2]

So far as has been ascertained, the facts are as follows: The Greek organization EAM had announced their intention of holding a demonstration on Dec. 3. The Greek Government at first authorized this, but withdrew their permission when EAM called for a general strike to begin on Dec. 2. The strike, in fact, came into force early on Dec. 3.

Later in the morning the EAM demonstration formed up and moved to the principal square of Athens in spite of the Government's ban.

On the evidence so far available I am not prepared to say who started the firing which then took place.

The police suffered one fatal casualty and had three men wounded. The latest authentic reports give the demonstrators' casualties as eleven killed and sixty wounded.

The demonstration continued during the afternoon, but there was no further shooting, and by 4:30 the crowd had dispersed and tranquillity was restored.

It is deplorable that an event like this should take place in Athens scarcely a month after the city's liberation and feeding.

Greece is faced with the most desperate economic and financial problems

[1] *New York Times.*
[2] *Ibid.*

apart from civil war, which we are trying to stop. We and our American Allies are doing our utmost to give assistance and our troops are acting to prevent bloodshed.

But sometimes it is necessary to use force to prevent greater bloodshed. The main burden falls on us. The responsibility is within our Allied military sphere—that is, our military sphere agreed upon with our principal Allies.

Our plans will not succeed unless the Greek Government and the whole of the Greek people exert themselves on their own behalf. If the damage of four years of war and enemy occupation is to be repaired and if Greek life and economy are to be rebuilt, their internal stability must be maintained and, pending a general election under fair conditions, the authority of the constitutional Greek Government must be accepted and enforced throughout the country.

The armed force must be dependent on the Greek Government. No Government can have a sure foundation so long as there are private armies owing allegiance to a group, party or ideology instead of to the state and the nation.

Although these facts should be clear to all, the left wing and Communist Ministers have resigned from the Greek Government at this dangerous crisis rather than implement measures to which they had already agreed for the replacement of the EAM police and guerrillas by regular national services.

(William Gallacher, Communist: Why have they resigned?)

I say they have resigned. I am stating the facts. I thought the House would like a full answer.

In addition, the EAM leaders have called a general strike which is, for the time being, preventing the food we and America are providing from reaching the mouths of the population we are trying to feed.

Our own position, as I have said, is extremely clear. Whether the Greek people form themselves into a monarchy or republic is for their decision. Whether they form a government of the right or left is for their decision. These are entirely matters for them. Until they are in a position to decide we shall not hesitate to use the considerable British army now in Greece, and being reinforced, to see that law and order are maintained.

It is our belief that in this course His Majesty's Government has the support of an overwhelming majority of the Greek people. The gaping need is to receive relief for the immediate requirements and conditions which give them a chance of earning a livelihood. In both of these ways we wish to help them, and we are working continually with experts, financial and otherwise, to assist in every possible way, but we cannot do this if the tommy guns which were provided for use against the Germans are now used in an attempt to impose by violence a Communist dictatorship without the people being able to express their wishes.

(F. E. Pethic Lawrence, Laborite, asked whether the Prime Minister was "aware of the very grave anxiety which is felt in all sections of this country with regard to what is taking place, and will he undertake to keep this House informed from time to time in the immediate future so that we can know what the situation is from day to day?" Mr. Lawrence also asked whether Mr. Churchill would take care that the Government action in suppressing disorder "shall not take the form of support to any one faction in Greece."

(Mr. Lawrence continued: "We all recognize that law and order must be maintained, but there is evidence, I think, that mistakes have been committed on both sides and this terrible shooting affair on Sunday is one which suggests, at any rate, that a mistake was made by the Greek Government. Can he [Mr. Churchill] assure the House that if the armed forces of Britain and the Allies are to be used in support of the Greek Government that the British Government will impress on the Greek Government the need for a conciliatory policy and not to assume that because they have the support of the British forces that they can take such action as they like?")

The answer to the first part of the question is that the newspapers give most full and continuous reports from Athens and Greece and that in the event of anything important occurring which is not public property I shall be ready to answer any question.

I have no other wish but to keep the House informed. I quite agree that we take a great responsibility in intervening to preserve law and order in this capital city so lately delivered by our troops from the power of the enemy.

It would be very much easier for us to allow everything to degenerate, as it would, into anarchy or a Communist dictatorship.

But we do not feel, having taken the position we have—having entered Athens and brought food and made great efforts to restore its currency and doing our utmost to give those conditions of peace and tranquillity which will enable the Greek people as a whole to vote on their future—having gone so far as that, that we should look back or take our hand from the plow.

It is the Greek Government we are supporting, or perhaps acting in conjunction with would be a better expression, because General Scobie is for the moment in charge of order. We shall certainly take care that that Government is not used to fasten any rule of a faction upon the Greek people. They will have the fullest opportunity of a free election. The Government of Mr. Papandreou three days ago represented all parties, including the Communist and EAM representatives. They left suddenly on the eve of a quite evident attempt to overthrow a settled Government which was on foot.

(Dr. Haden Guest, Laborite, interrupted to ask if it were not a fact that the demonstration which was fired upon on Sunday consisted of 200 unarmed children and youth with a sprinkling of adults. He quoted the correspondent of *The Times* of London as saying the firing went on for an hour—savagely and wildly. Dr. Guest asked whether it was "not a further fact that there was a good deal of feeling in Greece that collaborationists had not been dealt with, and that the security battalions appointed by the Germans to fight against the Greek movement are now being maintained by the present Government and by us."

(Dr. Guest continued: "Is it not time that the whole of the Athens police force was disarmed, as they have shown themselves thoroughly untrustworthy as people to keep the peace?")

So far as the incident is concerned, I told the House that the British Government reserve judgment upon that. It was a shocking thing that firing should be made by the police force on unarmed children; that is a matter we should all reprobate. We should also reprobate the massing or leading of large numbers of unarmed children to a demonstration center which had been banned by the Government in a city full of armed men liable at any moment to an explosion.

The question of the Security Battalions is not to be dismissed as easily as you have done. According to information that I have most carefully sifted, the Security Battalions came into existence gradually in a large measure to protect Greek villages from the depredations of some of those who, under the guise of being the saviors of their country, were living upon the inhabitants and doing very little fighting against the Germans.

(Mr. Lawrence again broke in: "I quite appreciate that the British Government are holding the ring for a future election in Greece. Will you assure us that, so far as the British Government are concerned, any support that we give to the Government of Greece is accompanied by recommendations that the Greek Government should use a conciliatory attitude toward all sections in Greece?")

Oh yes, certainly a conciliatory policy, but that should not include the running away from or the lying down under a threat of armed revolution and violence.

(Sir Percy Harris, Laborite, asked whether, in addition to military authorities, Britain had a political representative in Greece to advise on political problems.)

We have an Ambassador in Greece with whom the Government is in hourly consultation and whose telegrams arrive with the greatest frequency, wiring having not been cut so far. Mr. Harold MacMillan [Minister Resident in the Middle East] is advising General Wilson, the Supreme Commander in the Mediterranean [who is continuing until Field Marshal Alexander assumes command] on the political aspects of the military measures which he takes.

SUMMARY OF AGREEMENTS ADOPTED BY THE INTERNATIONAL CIVIL AVIATION CONFERENCE IN CHICAGO

December 5, 1944 [1]

The preamble sets out that whereas the future development of international civil aviation can greatly help to maintain world understanding and friendship because abuse of flying can threaten the general security, the Governments signing the convention have agreed on certain principles and arrangements.

The articles in brief follow:

1. The complete and exclusive sovereignty of each nation over its air space is recognized.

2. Territory is defined as the land and adjacent waters under the sovereignty, suzerainty, protection or mandate of a state.

3. Applies only to civil aircraft.

4. Agrees "not to use civil aviation for any purpose inconsistent with the aims of the convention."

5. Foreign aircraft not engaged in scheduled international air services may fly into or across its territory and make stops for non-commercial purposes without obtaining prior permission.

6. Prohibits scheduled air services over the territory of a state except with specific authorization.

7. Each nation reserves the privileges of offering air services between points within its territory and agrees not to yield this privilege on an exclusive basis to any one or to seek such an exclusive right for itself.

8. Bans aircraft capable of being flown without a pilot except with specific authority.

9. Permits uniform restriction of foreign aircraft for military or public safety reasons.

10. A nation may require foreign aircraft crossing its territory to land for customs and other examination.

[1] New York Times.

11-12-13. Provide for uniform application of national air regulations for foreign planes; for air navigation rules; for customs, immigration and quarantine laws.

14. Requires each state to try to prevent the spread of communicable diseases.

15. Requires that airports open to public use shall be opened uniformly to foreign aircraft and forbids discrimination as to services and charges.

16. Confers rights to search for aircraft and inspect certificates.

17-18-19. Gives aircraft nationality of state in which they are registered. Limits registration of aircraft to one state but provides for transfer of registration; provides that registration or transfer comply with national laws.

20. Every aircraft flying internationally must be properly marked.

21. Calls for registration of such aircraft with International Civil Aviation Organization (ICAO).

22. Agrees to facilitate the navigation of aircraft and prevent unnecessary delays.

23. Calls for an effort to establish customs and immigration procedures.

24. Establishes freedom from duty for aircraft fuel and equipment on board.

25. Nation agrees to assist aircraft in distress over its territory and to help search for lost planes.

26. Provides for inquiry into accidents.

27. Prevents seizure of foreign aircraft on grounds of patent infringements.

28. Calls upon each state to provide airports, radio and meteorological services and other air navigation facilities.

29-30-31. Requires international aircraft to carry documents such as certificates of registration.

30-31. To carry radio transmitters and a certificate of airworthiness.

32. Requires licenses for personnel operating the planes.

33. Requires recognition of other's certificates equaling international minimums.

34. Requires aircraft to carry log books.

35. Forbids carrying munitions of war except by special permission.

36. Permits regulation of use of photographic apparatus in aircraft over its territory.

37. Calls for collaboration in securing the highest practicable degree of uniformity in regulations, standards and procedures.

38. State unable to meet accepted standards must notify the ICAO council.

39-40. Calls for endorsement of aircraft to show in what respects it may not comply; provides such aircraft may not fly over foreign territory without permission.

41-42. Limits applicability requirements to aircraft which do not make their first flight until three years after the adoption of world airworthiness standards; of personnel licenses to those granted more than a year after adoption of international standards.

43-44-45. Establishes international civil aviation organization to be composed of an assembly, a council and such other bodies as may be necessary; outlines its aims; fixed permanent seats of ICAO.

46. Interim council to call first meeting of ICAO.

47. Gives ICAO "legal capacity" necessary.

48-49-50. Fixes rules for meetings; outlines powers and duties; fixes membership of council at twenty-one; forbids membership to anyone personally interested in an international airline.

51-52. Fixes term of council president at three years; provides that he may not vote, that council decisions be made by majority.

53. Permits any contracting state to participate in council consideration of matters affecting its interests, but does not permit party to dispute to vote.

54-54. Lists mandatory functions of the council; its permissive functions such as establishing subordinate commissions, conducting research.

56. Provides for air navigation commission of twelve members appointed by council.

57. Lists as duties of the commission consideration of changes in annexes to convention, establishment of technical groups, and advising the council of information it may collect.

58-59-60. Empowers the council to fix the qualifications and hire the personnel of the ICAO; makes the personnel responsible to secretary general; grants them immunities, privileges accorded corresponding personnel of other international organizations.

61-62. Provides for financial arrangements; suspension of voting power of country which fails to pay assessments.

63. Provides that each country pay expenses of its delegation to the assembly.

64-65. Authorizes ICAO to enter into arrangements with whatever world security organization may be established; also with other international bodies for maintenance of common services.

66. Authorizes ICAO to carry out functions placed upon it by documents known as "two freedoms" and "five freedoms," which are separate from the main agreement.

67. Requires each country to file with the council traffic reports, cost statistics and financial statements for its international airlines.

68. Authorizes each country to designate route to be followed across its territory.

69. Authorizes council to recommend means by which State may bring inadequate facilities up to agreement level, but provides no penalty if recommendations are ignored.

70. Permits State to arrange with council execution of latter's recommendations; permits council to bear cost.

71. Permits council, if a country requests, to provide, man, maintain and administer facilities required for airline operations across the country.

72-73-74. Provides for acquisition of land, spending of money, authority to pay cost of operating facilities on request.

75-76. Provides that a State may buy back facilities purchased by the council; latter may return funds to the States which advanced money when such facilities are repurchased.

77. Permits two or more countries to establish joint airline operation.

78-79. Authorizes council to suggest joint operation. Permits private companies to participate.

80. Requires signatory States to denounce the 1919 Paris Convention and the 1928 Havana Pact. (Superseded by new convention.)

81-82. Calls for registration with council of all aeronautical agreements in force between the contracting States; abrogation of all existing obligations which conflict with terms of convention.

83. Permits member State to negotiate with non-member.

84-85. Provides for settlement of disputes and appointment of an umpire.

86. Covers effectiveness of council decisions in disputes pending appeal to permanent court of international justice.

87. Requires member to forbid operation of foreign airline above its territory if airline is not conforming to council decisions.

88-89. Authorizes assembly to suspend voting power; suspends convention participation of member States affected by war.

90-91-92. Provides for adoption of technical annexes; for ratification of convention; for admission by four-fifths of assembly of States not described as "United Nations" or "neutrals" in World War II.

93-94. Provides for amendment of the convention by two-thirds vote; for denunciation of convention after one year's notice.

95. Defines certain convention terms.

International Air Services Transit Agreement

The states which sign and accept this international air services transit agreement, being members of the International Civil Aviation organization, declare as follows:

ARTICLE I

Section 1. Each contracting state grants to the other contracting states the following freedoms of the air in respect of scheduled international air services:

(1) The privilege to fly across its territory without landing;

(2) The privilege to land for non-traffic purposes.

The privileges of this section will not be applicable with respect to airports utilized for military purposes to the exclusion of any international air services. In areas of active hostilities or of military occupation, and in time of war along the supply routes leading to such areas, the exercise of such privileges shall be subject to the approval of the competent military authorities.

Section 2. The exercise of the foregoing privileges shall be in accordance with the provisions of the interim agreement on international civil aviation and, when it comes into force, with the provisions of the convention on international civil aviation, both drawn up at Chicago on Dec. 7, 1944.

Section 3. A contracting state granting to the airlines of another contracting state the privilege to stop for non-traffic purposes may require such airlines to offer reasonable commercial services at the points at which such stops are made.

Such requirement shall not involve any discrimination between airlines operating on the same route, shall take into account the capacity of the aircraft, and shall be exercised in such a manner as not to prejudice the normal operations of the international air services concerned or the rights and obligations of a contracting state.

Section 4. Each contracting state may, subject to the provision of this agreement,

(1) Designate the route to be followed within its territory by any international air service and the airports which any such service may use;

(2) Impose or permit to be imposed on any such service just and reasonable charges for the use of such airports and other facilities; these charges shall not be higher than would be paid for the use of such airports and facilities by its national aircraft engaged in similar international services: provided that, upon representation by an interested contracting state, the charges imposed for the use of airports and other facilities shall be subject to review by the council of the ICAO established under the above-mentioned convention which shall report and make recommendations thereon for the consideration of the state or states concerned.

Section 5. Each contracting state reserves the right to withhold or revoke a certificate or permit to an air transport enterprise of another state in any case where it is not satisfied that substantial ownership and effective control are vested in nationals of a contracting state, or in case of failure of such air transport enterprise to comply with the laws of the state over which it operates, or to perform its obligations under this agreement.

ARTICLE III

This agreement shall remain in force as long as the above-mentioned convention; provided, however, that any contracting state, a party to the present agreement, may denounce it on one year's notice given by it to the Government of the United States of America, which shall at once inform all other contracting states of such notice and withdrawal.

ARTICLE IV

Pending the coming into force of the above-mentioned convention, all references to it herein, other than those contained in Article II, Section 2, and Article V, shall be deemed to be references to the interim agreement on international civil aviation drawn up at Chicago on Dec. 7, 1944; and references to the International Civil Aviation Organization, the assembly, and the council shall be deemed to be references to the provisional international civil Aviation Organization, the interim assembly, and interim council, respectively.

ARTICLE V

For the purposes of this agreement, "territory" shall be defined as in Article 2 of the above-mentioned convention.

PRIME MINISTER WINSTON CHURCHILL'S SPEECH IN COMMONS ON BRITISH POLICY IN LIBERATED COUNTRIES

December 8, 1944 [1]

The value of Sir Richard Acland's speech (Sir Richard rose just before Mr. Churchill) was that it showed how extremely complex these Greek politics are. He made a very large number of assertions, some of which were accurate and some of which, according to my information, are the reverse. . . .

I address myself to the amendment as a whole.

I must point out that it does not only deal with Greece, but with other parts of Europe and with the suppression of these popular movements which have valorously assisted the defeat of the enemy in other countries besides Greece.

The House will therefore, I am sure, permit me to deal with the whole of this question of our intervention in Europe—the tone, the character, the temper, the object of our intervention where we have to intervene by dealing with other countries besides this one. . . .

Before I come to particular countries and cases, let me present to the House the charge which is made against us.

[1] *New York Times.*

It is that we are using His Majesty's forces to disarm the friends of democracy in Greece and in other parts of Europe and to suppress these popular movements which have valorously assisted in the defeat of the enemy. Here is a pretty direct issue and one on which the House will have to pronounce before we separate this evening.

Certainly the British Government would be unworthy of confidence if His Majesty's forces were being used by them to disarm the friends of democracy in Greece and other parts of Europe.

The question, however, arises and one may be permitted to dwell on it for a moment: Who are the friends of democracy and also how is the word democracy to be interpreted?

My idea of it is that the plain, humble common man—just the ordinary man who keeps a wife and family, who goes off to fight for his country when it is in trouble and goes to the poll at the appropriate time and puts his cross on the ballot paper showing the candidate he wishes to be elected to Parliament—that is the foundation of democracy.

[Emmanuel Shinwell, Laborite, interjejcted a reference to Spain.].

I am not at all afraid to go into that discussion, but I have a great deal of ground to cover. It is one of those great misinterpretations that I have said pleasant words about Franco. All I said was that Spanish politics did not really consist in drawing rude cartoons about it.

It is really no use for my honorable friend to screw his face up as if he were taking a nasty dose of medicine.

[Shinwell: That is precisely what I and many people in the country are doing.]

Everyone can have their opinion about that, but so far as the honorable gentleman is concerned, I expect there are some other nasty gulps to follow. . . .

We stand upon the foundation of fair, free elections based on universal service and suffrage. That is what we consider the foundation of democracy. I feel quite different about a swindle-democracy—a democracy which calls itself a democracy because it is Left Wing. It takes all sorts to make democracy, not all Left Wing or even Communists. . . .

The last thing that resembles democracy is mob law with bands of gangsters armed with deadly weapons forcing their way into Greek cities, seizing police stations and key points of Government, and endeavoring to introduce a totalitarian regime.

The last thing that represents democracy is mob law that attempts to introduce a totalitarian regime and clamors to shoot every one who is politically inconvenient as part of a purge of those who are very often said to be—but often have not been—collaborators with the Germans during the occupation.

Do not let us rate democracy so low as if it were merely grabbing power and shooting those who do not agree with us. That is not democracy. That is the antithesis of democracy. . . .

[William Gallacher, Communist: That is what happened.]

Mr. Gallacher must not get so excited, because he is going to have much the worse of the argument and much the worse of the division. . . .

Democracy is not based on violence or terrorism but on reason, on fair play, on freedom, on respecting other people's rights as well as your own ambition. Democracy is not a harlot to be picked up in the street by a man with a tommy gun.

We have trusted the mass of the people in almost every country, but we would like to make sure that it was the people and not a gang of bandits from the mountains or countryside who thought that by violence they could overturn state authority.

That is a general description of the foundation upon which we should approach the various incidents on which I am going to dwell.

During the war, of course, we have had to arm anyone who could shoot a Hun. We accepted them as friends and tried to enable them to fulfill their healthy instincts. We are paying for it in having this debate today, which personally I have found rather enjoyable so far. We are paying for it also with our treasure and our blood. We are not paying for it with our honor or by defeat.

But when countries are liberated, it does not follow that those who have received our weapons should use them in order to engross themselves by violence and murder and bloodshed in all those powers and traditions the continuity of which many countries have highly developed. . . .

If what is called in this amendment the action of the friends of democracy is to be interpreted as a carefully planned coup d'état by murder gangs and by the iron rule of ruffians seeking to climb into the seats of power without a vote ever having been cast in their favor—if that is to masquerade as democracy, I think the House will be united in condemning it as a mockery.

. . . War criminals, the betrayers of their countrymen, the men who sincerely wish Germany might win—these may be the object of popular disgust, of boycott and maybe in extreme cases should be brought before the courts of law and punished with death.

But I hope they will be courts of law with fair trials, not mere expressions of mob juries or political rivals. But let me try to establish this point: That these men who went up into the hills with rifles and machine guns given them by the British Government have by fee simple claimed the right to govern vast complex communities such as Belgium, Greece, or Holland—it may be next. I say I repulse that claim. They have done good service and it is for the state and not for them to judge the rewards they should receive. It is not for them to claim ownership of the state. It cannot be admitted. That is what is being fought out now.

I say we march along our onerous and painful path. Poor old England, perhaps I should say poor old Britain, we have to assume the burden and the most thankless tasks and be shot at, criticized, and abused from every quarter. But at least we know what is our aim, our object. It is that these countries shall be freed from the German armed power and that, under conditions of normal tranquillity, they shall have a free universal vote to decide the Government of their country, except the fascist regime, and whether that Government shall be to the left or to the right.

That is our aim, and we are told we seek to disarm the friends of democracy. Because we do not allow gangs of heavily armed guerrillas to descend from the mountains and install themselves in the great capitals and in power and in office we are told we are traitors to democracy. I repulse that claim, too. I shall call upon the House as a matter of confidence in His Majesty's Government and confidence in the spirit with which we have marched from one peril to another until victory is in sight. I shall call upon them to reject this with the scorn that they deserve.

The amendment on the paper has particular reference to Greece, but it is a general attack on the whole policy of His Majesty's Government as supporting reactionary forces everywhere, trying to install by force dictatorial Governments contrary to the wishes of the people.

I deal therefore not only with Greece, I pin myself at this moment in the first instance to other parts of Europe, because this theme is also to some extent opened up in the last sentence of an American press release with which we were confronted a few days ago.

It is not only in Greece that we appear to some eyes to be disarming the friends of democracy and those popular movements which have assisted the defeat of the enemy. There is Italy; there is Belgium. Let me come to Belgium.

Belgium is another case of what the amendment calls the friends of democracy being disarmed in favor of the organized constitutional administration. If so, that is grave and it deserves scrutiny.

At the end of November there was to be what the Germans called a putsch organized in Belgium to throw out the Government of M. Pierlot, which Government was the only constitutional link with the past and the only link we have recognized during the war. This Government has received a vote of confidence of 132 members to only twelve, with six abstentions, from the Belgian Parliament.

However, the friends of democracy, the valorous assisters in the defeat of the enemy, took a different view. They organized an attack upon the Belgian state. A demonstration largely attended by women and children marched up to the Belgian Parliament House and lorry loads of friends of democracy came along from Mons and other places heavily armed.

Here you see the hard-worked Briton whom we are asked to censure. What did this reactionary undemocratic Government do? Its orders were sent to stop the lorries on the way and to disarm their loads. Moreover, we British placed light tanks and armored cars in the streets near the front of the Parliament House, which the Belgian gendarmerie were defending in the name of the Belgian Constitutional Government.

Now here was intereference in a marked form. Here was an attempt to stand between the friends of democracy and the valorous anarchic overthrow of the Belgian state. And we British stood in the way of that. I have to admit these things to you.

But on whose orders and under whose authority did we take this action? General Erskine, the British officer, made various proclamations like those General Scobie [commander in Greece] has made under the press of the situation. These proclamations had a highly salutory effect, and those concerned in the movement of the Allied force acted accordingly.

Who is General Erskine? He represents, he is directly responsible to, and derives his authority from General Eisenhower, that remarkable American supreme commander, whose wisdom and good fellowship we admire and whose orders we have promised to obey.

I have no hesitation in saying not only did we obey General Eisenhower's orders, but we thought those orders were wise and sensible.

After all, we British who are now said to be poor friends of democracy lost 35,000 to 40,000 men in opening up the great port of Antwerp. And our Navy has cleared the Schelde River. The sacrifice of these men has also to be considered as well as the friends of democracy advancing in lorries from Mons to start up a bloody revolution.

[Aneurin Bevan, Laborite, asked whether the Belgian Premier had not been unwarranted in asking for the intervention of British troops, since there was "no such threat as the Prime Minister pretends."]

I should have thought it was hardly possible to state the opposite of the truth with more precision.

I back up all those who seek to establish democracy and civilization on a basis of law and also popular untrammeled, unintimidated, free universal suffrage voting. It would be pretty hard on Europe if, after four or five years of German tyranny, she liquefied and degenerated and plunged into a series of brutal civil and social wars. If there is a democracy and its various defenders believe they express the wishes of the majority, why can't they wait until the general election—a free vote of the people which is our sole policy in every country into which British and American armies are marching?

That, they say, is one of their fundamental rights and it belongs naturally to any country which has unconditionally surrendered even if it has done most grievous injuries to the Allied cause. We have not attempted to put a veto on the appointment of Count Sforza. If tomorrow the Italians were to make him Prime Minister or Foreign Secretary, we have no power to stop it except with the agreement of the Allies. All that we should have to say about it is that we do not trust the man and we do not think he is a true and trustworthy man, nor would we put the slightest confidence in any Government in which he is a dominating member.

The story of Belgium, which I submit with the utmost respect and affection to the American people as well as to the House of Commons, carries many lessons which are applicable to other parts of the world.

Now I come to the case of Italy, which, as I gather oddly enough, embodies in it the case of Count Sforza.

It is a great mistake, as the Foreign Secretary has said, and not only a mistake but quite untrue to say that we have vetoed Count Sforza's appointment to be the Prime Minister or the Foreign Secretary of the Italian Government. The Italians alone could do that. The Italians, having unconditionally surrendered, have a perfect right to choose anyone they please for any office of the State.

I think we shall have to put a great deal of responsibility of what might happen on those who called him to power.

[Mr. Shinwell, interrupting, asked whether the Prime Minister had not previously made a statement reflecting upon Gen. Charles de Gaulle.]

How little helpful it is to our debate to have such interruptions. I am not speaking about France today. I certainly never felt about de Gaulle the sentiments which experience has engendered in me about Count Sforza.

De Gaulle is a man of honor and has never broken his word, and that is what I am coming to because these things have to come out. I say we should have to put a great deal of responsibility on those who called Sforza to power. We are not avid of becoming deeply involved in the politics of the liberated countries. All we require from them is a government which will guarantee us the necessary protection and facilities for the lines of communication from Naples to Ravenna, lately taken, and to the north.

Our interest in Italy is the front where we have armies engaged under General Alexander and Gen. Mark Clark, that daring and skillful American general under whom we have confidently placed an army which is at least three-quarters British or British-controlled.

We have a joint arrangement with America about Italy, and we should be very sorry if it were proved that we have broken away from this joint arrangement. We have not done so in any way.

When in the shifting tangles and contortions of Italian politics, with six parties ruling over one another, with all their personal and political interests, none of them being hampered by having been elected by anyone, in this confused scene we were suddenly told that Count Sforza was to become Foreign

Secretary. The British Minister did undoubtedly say to the Italian inquiry that we did not think Count Sforza a particularly good choice, or words to that effect.

We had a perfect right to say this. We could not stop his being chosen, but we had a right to say our say.

I must go back to the time of the Italian collapse and surrender in 1943. Count Sforza had been living for twenty years in America. He was very anxious to get back to Italy. We did not think this would be a good thing in the disordered and tumultuous state in which Italy was left on the morrow of her revolt against Germany. On Sept. 23 Count Sforza sent the following message to Marshal Badoglio and repeated it in a letter to Mr. Berle, then an American Assistant Secretary of State, from which I have the President's permission to quote.

(Mr. Churchill quoted Count Sforza as writing that he would support Marshal Badoglio fully and that "the only way to destroy the last criminal remnants of fascism" was to adjourn the matter of internal Italian politics for the period of the struggle. He added: "I pledge my honor to do this myself and urge this course upon my many friends and associates.")

When Count Sforza passed through London I was anxious to ascertain whether this was his sincere resolve. . . . I went through this letter with Count Sforza almost line by line, and he assured me that it was his most profound conviction.

But no sooner, however, had Count Sforza got back to Italy than he began a long series of intrigues which ended in the expulsion of Marshal Badoglio from office.

Now I come to Greece, which forms the mainspring of the vote of censure we have to meet today. I have taken great responsibilities for our foreign policy toward Greece and also in respect of what has taken place in Athens, and the Foreign Secretary and I have worked in the closest agreement. . . .

We have a right to express this point of view on the Greek question because in an attempt to redeem our pledged word we had sustained 30,000 casualties in what might perhaps be called the chivalrous resolve to share the miseries of Greece when she was invaded by Germany and Italy in 1941. At that time we were all alone. . . .

My honored friend, the President, was of the opinion we should certainly have plans made, and accordingly at the Quebec conference it was proposed by the combined chiefs of staff that the British should prepare the forces to occupy the Athens area and pave the way for the commencement of relief and for the establishment of law and order and for the installment of the Greek Government which we and the great bulk of the United Nations had formally recognized.

The Americans and ourselves began to accumulate large masses of food and shipping, and the UNRRA began to grow up in Alexandria and other arrangements for food distribution were actively made at the cost of the food of this country. A large part of this and supplies for medical relief were provided by America out of her riches. The rest of the burden fell upon us.

The proposal of the combined chiefs of staff was initialled by the President and me, and on Sept. 14 a directive was issued. . . .

When he (Premier Papandreou) came out, he restored order to the Greek Government, which is the Constitutional Government of Greece and can only be displaced by the free vote of the people. At the same time we prepared in deep secrecy our British expedition. We did not think it necessary to tell anyone about it, not even the Greek Government. . . .

Meanwhile the forces of Elas were planning to descend upon Athens as a military political operation and the seizure of power by armed force.

Elas is a mixed body, and it is unfair to stigmatize them all as being self-seeking in their aim and action. Nevertheless, during the years of Greek captivity Elas devoted more attention to beating up and destroying representatives of Edes, commanded by Colonel Zervas, a man of the left by our standards but less extreme than the Eam.

For the last two years Elas have devoted themselves principally to preparations for seizing power. . . .

As to Elas, they did not hesitate on occasions to help the German catch and kill supporters of Edes.

From the depradations and ravages of Elas there developed, as we can now well see, a well organized plot by which Elas should march down to Athens and seize it by armed force and establish a reign of terror under the plea that they were purging collaborationists.

How much the Germans knew about this beforehand I cannot tell, but a number had been left behind and are acting in Elas ranks.

. . . We came, therefore, to Greece with American and Russian consent at the invitation of the Government of all parties, bearing with us such good gifts as liberty, order, food and the assurance of an absolute right to determine their own future as soon as conditions of normal tranquillity were regained.

I told the House I would be frank with them. I have stated our action in detail. I must admit that not everyone agrees with the course we have taken, for which I accept the fullest responsibility. But the Government . . . agreed that we should see what we could do to give this unfortunate people a fair chance of extricating themselves from their misery and starting on a clear road again.

I repudiate the idea that democracy can stand upon the violent seizure of power by unrepresentative men or by terrorism and the killing of political opponents. No doubt there are others who take a different view. . . .

Moreover, I do not feel it compatible with our honor or with the obligations into which we have entered with many people in Greece in the course of our presence there to wash our hands of the whole business, make our way to the sea as we easily could, and leave Athens to anarchy, misery and tyranny. We have always been ready to risk our blood in defense of our honor.

In the small hours of Tuesday morning . . . I directed General Scobie to assume complete control of Athens and the districts around and to use what force was necessary to drive out and if necessary to extricate Elas bands. . . .

I also directed our Ambassador to do his utmost to prevail on Papandreou, who seemed to wish to resign, to remain in power. . . .

If I am blamed for this action, I will gladly accept dismissal of the House. But if I am not dismissed, make no mistake, we shall persist in this policy of clearing Athens and the Athens regions of all rebels to the Constitutional Government of Greece.

They are mutineers to the order of the Supreme Commander in the Mediterranean, under whom all guerrillas have undertaken to serve.

I hope I have made the position clear, both generally as it affects the world and the war, and Government.

I have no fear at all that the most searching inquiries into the policy we have pursued in Europe, in Belgium, in Holland, in Italy and in Greece, will entitle any man in whose breast fair play enters to accuse us of a reactionary policy, of hampering the free expression of the national will or endeavoring to enable countries which have suffered the curse of German occupation to resume again the normal free democratic life which they desire and which, as far as this House can act, we shall endeavor to secure for them.

TREATY OF ALLIANCE AND MUTUAL ASSISTANCE BETWEEN THE PROVISIONAL GOVERNMENT OF THE FRENCH REPUBLIC AND THE SOVIET UNION

December 10, 1944 [1]

The Provisional Government of the French Republic and the Praesidium of the Supreme Council of the Union of Soviet Socialist Republics.

Resolved to pursue together, and until the end, the war against Germany;

Convinced that, once victory has been achieved, the re-establishment of peace on a stable basis and its maintenance for a lasting future require the existence of close collaboration between them and with all the United Nations;

Resolved to collaborate with a view to creating an international system of security, making possible an effective maintenance of general peace and guaranteeing the harmonious development of relations between nations;

Desirous of confirming reciprocal commitments resulting from an exchange of letters on Sept. 20, 1941, relating to joint action in the war against Germany;

Certain of meeting, through the conclusion of an alliance between France and the U.S.S.R., the feelings as well as the interests of the two nations, the demands of war as well as the requirements of peace and of economic reconstruction in full conformity with the aims adopted by the United Nations,

Have resolved to conclude a treaty and to this effect have appointed as their plenipotentiaries:

The Provisional Government of the French Republic, M. Georges Bidault, Minister of Foreign Affairs; the Praesidium of the Supreme Council of the Union of Soviet Socialist Republics, M. Vyacheslaff Mikhailovitch Molotoff, People's Commissar for Foreign Affairs. Their appointments having been recognized as being fully valid, they have agreed on the following provisions:

ARTICLE I

Each of the high contracting parties will continue to fight by the side of the other and of the United Nations until final victory over Germany. Each of the high contracting parties undertakes to afford to the other help and assistance in this struggle by all the means at its disposal.

ARTICLE II

The high contracting parties undertake not to enter into separate negotiations with Germany or to conclude, without mutual consent, an armistice or a treaty of peace with either the Hitlerite Government or any government or authority set up in Germany with the aim of prolonging or maintaining the German policy of aggression.

[1] *New York Times.*

ARTICLE III

The high contracting parties undertake to adopt in complete agreement, at the end of the present conflict with Germany, all measures necessary to eliminate any new threat on the part of Germany and to oppose any initiative of a nature capable of making possible a new attempt at aggression on her part.

ARTICLE IV

If one of the high contracting parties should find itself involved in hostilities with Germany either as the result of an aggression committed by Germany or as the result of the provisions of the above Article III, the other high contracting power will immediately give the contracting power so involved all the help and assistance in its power.

ARTICLE V

The high contracting parties undertake not to conclude alliances and not to participate in any coalition directed against one of them.

ARTICLE VI

The high contracting parties agree to give each other all possible economic assistance after the war in order to facilitate and hasten the reconstruction of the two countries and in order to contribute to the prosperity of the world.

ARTICLE VII

The present treaty in no way affects the commitments previously undertaken by the high contracting parties toward third parties by virtue of published treaties.

ARTICLE VIII

The present treaty, of which the French and Russian texts are equally valid, will be ratified and instruments of ratification thereof will be exchanged in Paris as soon as possible. It will take effect immediately on the exchange of instruments of ratification and will remain in force for twenty years. If this treaty is not denounced by one of the high contracting parties at least one year before the expiration of this period, it will remain in force without limitation as to its duration, each one of the high contracting parties being then able to terminate it by means of declaration to this effect subject to one year's notice.

The plenipotentiaries above named have hereunto set their hands and seals. Made in Moscow in duplicate on Dec. 10, 1944.

BIDAULT,
Minister of Foreign Affairs.
MOLOTOFF,
Commissar for Foreign Affairs.

PRIME MINISTER CHURCHILL'S SPEECH IN COMMONS ON THE SOVIET-POLISH FRONTIER

December 15, 1944 [1]

In opening this debate I find myself in a position to read to the House again some extracts from the carefully considered statement that I made to them in February after I returned from Teheran and also in October of the present year.

When I read them over again last night in preparation for this debate, I found it very difficult to improve upon them or to alter them in any way. This may accuse me of infertility of mind, but it also gives me some confidence that I have not misled the House or felt myself stultified, in all respects at any rate, by the harsh, unforeseeable movement of events.

It is not often that one wishes to repeat what one has said two months ago, still less ten months ago. But I propose to do so because in no other way and in no other words can I remind the House and bring home to them the grim, bare bones of the Polish problem.

On Feb. 22 I said that at Teheran I took occasion to raise personally with Marshal Stalin the question of the future of Poland. I pointed out that it was in fulfillment of our guarantee to Poland that Great Britain declared war on Nazi Germany and that we had never weakened in our resolve, even in the period when we were all alone, and the fate of the Polish nation held a prime place in the thoughts and policies of the British Government and the British Parliament.

It was with great pleasure that I heard from Marshal Stalin that he, too, was resolved upon the creation and maintenance of a strong, integral, independent Poland as one of the leading Powers in Europe. He several times repeated this declaration in public. I am convinced that that represents the settled policy of the Soviet Union.

Here I may remind the House that we ourselves have never in the past guaranteed on behalf of the British Government any particular frontier line to Poland. We did not approve the Polish occupation of Vilna in 1920, and the British view in 1919 stands expressed in the so-called Curzon Line, which attempted to deal, at any rate partially, with the problem.

I have always held the veiw that all questions of territorial settlement and adjustment should stand until the end of the war and that the victorious Powers should then arrive at a formal and final agreement governing the articulation of Europe as a whole.

However, the advance of Russian armies in the Polish regions in which the Polish underground army is active makes it indispensable that some kind of friendly working agreement should be arrived at to govern wartime conditions and to enable all anti-Hitlerite forces to work together against the common foe.

During the last few weeks the Foreign Secretary and I have consulted with the Polish Government in London, with the object of establishing a working agreement upon which the fighting forces can act and upon which I trust a loyal comradeship may be built between Russians and Poles.

I have intense sympathy with the policies of that heroic race, whose national

[1] New York Times.

spirit centuries of misfortune cannot quench, and I also have sympathy with the Russians. Twice in our lifetime Russia has been violently assaulted by Germany, many millions of Russians have been slain, and vast tracts of Russian soil have been devastated as a result of repeated German aggression. Russia has the right of reassurance against future attacks from the west and we are going all the way with her to see that she gets it, not only by the might of her arms, but with the approval and assent of the United Nations.

The liberation of Poland may presently be achieved by Russian armies after those armies have suffered millions of casualties in breaking the German military machine. I cannot feel that Russian demands for reassurance about her western frontiers go beyond the limit of what is reasonable or just. Marshal Stalin and I also spoke of, and agreed upon, the need for Poland to obtain compensation at the expense of Germany, both in the north and west. I said that nearly a year ago. I have nothing to alter in it from the point of view of His Majesty's Government.

On Oct. 27, more recently, I reported upon my last visit to Moscow and said the most urgent and burning question was, of course, that of Poland. Here again I speak words of hope, of hope reinforced by confidence—but I am afraid this does not hold in the same degree at the present time. To abandon hope in this matter would indeed be to surrender to despair.

In this sphere there are two crucial issues. The first is the question of the western frontier of Poland and new territory to be added to Poland in the north and west. The second is the relation of the Polish Government with the Lublin National Liberation Committee. On these two points, apart from many subsidiary and ancillary topics, we held a series of conferences with both parties.

I could tell the House we reached a solution of these problems. It is certainly not for want of trying. I am quite certain we have got a great deal nearer—this is subject to some review in the light of events. I hope Mr. Mikolajczyk will soon return to Moscow and it will be a great disappointment to the sincere friends of Poland if an agreed arrangement cannot be made which will enable him to form a Polish Government on Polish soil, a Government recognized by the Great Powers and indeed by all these Governments of the United Nations which now recognize the Polish Government in London.

Though I do not underrate the difficulties which remain, it is a comfort to feel that Britain and Russia and, I do not doubt, the United States are all firmly agreed on the re-creation of a free, independent, sovereign Poland, loyal to the Allies and friendly to her great neighbor and liberator Russia.

Speaking more particularly for His Majesty's Government, it is our persevering and constant aim that the Polish people, after their suffering and vicissitudes, should find in Europe an abiding home and resting place which, though it may not entirely coincide or correspond with the pre-war frontier of Poland, will nevertheless be adequate for the needs of the Polish nation and not inferior in character and quality, taking the picture as a whole, with that they previously possessed.

These are critical days and it would be a great pity if the time were wasted in indecision or protracted negotiations. If the Polish Government had taken the advice we tendered at the beginning of this year, the additional complications produced by the formation of the Polish National Committee of Liberation at Lublin would not have arisen; and anything like prolonged delay in settlement can only have the effect of hampering common action which the Poles and Russians and the rest of the Allies are taking against Germany. I hope no time will be lost in pressing these discussions to a successful conclusion.

The hopes I thought it necessary to express in October have failed. When Mr. Mikolajczyk left Moscow, my hope was that he would return within a week or so with the authority of the Polish Government in London to agree about the Polish frontier on the basis of the Curzon Line and its prolongation to the southward called the Curzon Line "A," which passed on the Russian side of Lwow.

I have several times drawn Mikolajczyk's attention to the dangers of delay. Had he been able to return after the very friendly conversations which passed between him and Mr. Stalin and also the conversations which he had with the members of the Lublin National Committee—had he been able to return with the assent of his colleagues, I believe that the difficulties inherent in the formation of a Polish Government in harmony with the Lublin Committee might well have been overcome.

In that case he would be at this moment at the head of a Polish Government on Polish soil recognized by all the United Nations and awaiting the advance of Russian armies moving farther into Poland as the country is delivered from the Germans. He was also assured in this task the friendship and friendly help of Marshal Stalin.

Thus he could, at every stage, have established good relations between the Polish underground movement and the advancing Russians, and a Polish administration would have been set up by him in newly delivered regions as they expanded. I have the greatest respect for Mr. Mikolajczyk and his able colleagues whom we met, Mr. Romer and Mr. Grabski. I am sure that they are more qualified to fill the place of the late General Sikorski than any other of the Polish leaders.

After endless discussions, into some of which we were drawn on Mr. Mikolajczyk's return from Moscow, the Poles utterly failed to obtain agreement. In consequence, on Nov. 21 Mr. Mikolajczyk and Mr. Romer and other Ministers resigned from the Polish Government, which has been almost entirely reconstituted in a form which, in some respects, I am certainly not able to applaud.

Mr. Mikolajczyk and his friends remain, in the view of His Majesty's Government, the only light that burns for Poland in the immediate future. Just as I said that if the Polish Government had agreed in the early part of this year upon a frontier, there never would have been any Lublin Committee to which Soviet Russia has committed herself, so now I say that if Mr. Mikolajczyk could swiftly have returned to Moscow early in November, as he hoped and expected to do, with the power to conclude an agreement of frontier line, Poland might now take her full place in the ranks of nations contending against Germany and would have the full support and friendship of Marshal Stalin and the Soviet Government.

That opportunity, too, is for the time being suspended. This prospect vanished like the last and it remained one of the stories of the Sibylline Books in which, on every occasion, the price remained the same and the number of volumes decreased until at the last they had to be bought on the most unfavorable of terms.

Mr. Mikolajczyk's ordeal has been a most severe and painful one. Torn between love of his country and an intense desire to reach a settlement with her mighty neighbor, which was most abhorrent to many of his fellow-countrymen, and confronted with the obstinate, inflexible resistance of his London colleagues and their veto, like the veto which played so great a part in the former ruin of Poland, in these circumstances Mr. Mikolajczyk decided to resign.

Almost a month has passed since then and, I imagine, the prospects of reconciliation between the Polish Government and the Lublin Committee with the Soviet Government behind them. They have definitely receded, though they might perhaps advance again were Mr. Mikolajczyk able to speak with authority for the Polish nation. The consequence of this recession of hopes of this working agreement between Russia and the Poles has been masked to British eyes by the fact that the Russian armies on the long Vistula front have been motionless and if and when they move forward, as move forward they surely will, and the Germans are expelled from large new tracts of Poland, the authority of the Lublin Committee and the area it administers will grow in its contacts with the Soviets more intimate and strong.

I do not know what misfortunes will attend such developments. The absence of agreement may well be grievous for Poland and the relationship and misunderstanding between the advancing Russian armies and the Polish Underground movement may take forms which will be most painful to all who have the permanent well-being of Poland and the relationship between Poland and Russia at heart.

The fact that a Prime Minister resigns from a Government and that a new Government is born does not, of course, affect the form of diplomatic relationships between States. We still recognize the Polish Government as the Government of Poland, as we have done since they reached our shores in the early part of this war. This, of course, has been continued up to the present by all the rest of the United Nations, except Russia only, which is most concerned and is the power whose armies will be the first to enter the heart of Poland.

It is a source of grief to me that these forces have not been joined together more closely against the common foe. I cannot accept the view that the arrangements proposed about the frontier are not solid and satisfactory or that they would not give to Poland that abiding home I spoke about in February.

If Poland gives Lwow and the surrounding area on the south known as the Curzon Line A, if Poland makes this concession and these lands are joined to the Ukraine, Poland will gain in the north all of East Prussia south and west of Koenigsberg, including Danzig, one of the most magnificent cities in the world, famous for centuries and the great gathering place for the trade of the Baltic and indeed of the world. Instead of the threatened and artificial corridor built up so laboriously after the last war, Poland would stretch broadly along the Baltic on a front of 200 miles. The Poles are free, so far as Russia and Great Britain are concerned, to extend their territories at the expense of Germany to the west.

I do not propose to go into the exact details, but an extension in which they will be supported by Britain and Russia, bound together as they are by a twenty-year alliance—this extension will mean in the west and north territories more important and more highly developed than those they lose in the east.

We hear of one-third of Poland to be ceded, but that includes vast tracts of the Pripet Marshes, a most desolate region which, though it swells acreage, does not add to the wealth of those who own it.

Thus I have set before the House what, in outline, is the offer which the Russians, on whom the main burden of liberation still falls, make to the

Polish people. I cannot believe that such an offer should be rejected by Poland. It has, of course, to be accompanied by the disentanglement of peoples in the west and north and transference of several millions of people would have to be effected from east to west, or to north, and because that is what is proposed, the total expulsion of Germans from the areas to be acquired by Poland in the west and north, for expulsion is the method which, so far as we have been able to see, will be most satisfactory and lasting.

There will be no mixture of population to cause endless struggle, as in Alsace-Lorraine. A clean sweep will be made. I am not alarmed at the prospect of the disentanglement of population, nor even am I alarmed by these large transferences which are more possible than they ever were before, through modern conditions.

The disentanglement of populations which took place between Greece and Turkey after the last war was in many ways successful and has produced friendly relations between Greece and Turkey ever since. That disentanglement which at first seemed impossible to achieve and about which it was said that it would strip Turkish life in Anatolia of so many extra services, and about which it was said that the extra population could never be assimilated and sustained by Greece, that disentanglement solved problems which before had been the cause of immense friction, of wars and of rumors of wars.

Nor do I see that there should not be room in Germany for the German population of East Prussia and of other territories I have mentioned. After all, six million or seven million Germans have been killed already in this dreadful war into which they did not hesitate for a second time in this generation to plunge all Europe and the world.

At present we are told that there are ten million or twelve million prisoners, or foreigners, used as slaves in Germany, who will, we hope, be restored to their own homes and lands when victory is gained. Moreover, we may expect that many more Germans will be killed in fighting which will occupy spring and summer and which will involve the fiercest and largest battles fought in this war.

When these matters which arose were first foreshadowed by me to the House, British and American armies had not landed on the Continent. France had not been liberated. She was powerless, not like now when she is rising with great rapidity to a strong and fine position among the nations of the world. The armies of General Eisenhower were still gathering on this island and not along the Rhine where they are now growing in strength as great waves of American manhood cross the Atlantic and take their place in the crusade and in the line of battle.

Nor had the Russians advanced to the Vistula. Vast distances separated them even from the frontiers of Poland. Nor was one large German Army cut off in the peninsula which has Memel and Libau as its bases. There was not that great position which Russian armies hold in the extreme north, nor was their left hand reaching out beyond Budapest in the south, threatening to advance into the very heart of Austria. Nor had Rome been occupied, nor the Apennines pierced.

In those days the Poles might well have had some show of reason in asking whether the Great Allies would have power, even if they were so minded, to deliver new territory to Poland which was to compensate her for what she was giving up in the east.

But the situation has changed vastly in favor of the Allies and it seems also extremely unlikely that after the spring and summer campaigns have been fought, if it be necessary to go so far in the business, and we shall go whatever distance is necessary to complete our object, it seems extremely unlikely that the evil, hateful forces in Germany who conceived and planned and began this war will have power to restrict the decision of the peace conference or armistice-peace conference at which the principal victorious powers will be assembled.

The prospects of final victory have in the time that has passed since these matters were first discussed at Teheran become for the Allies solid and spacious. Therefore I say what has always been said by the Poles when I have been discussing with them: "Here we know what we have to give up; what certainty have we of recovering compensation in other quarters?"

They have much more certainty of it now than they had at this time last year. I cannot see any doubt whatever that the Great Powers, if they agree, can effect this transference of population.

I find great difficulty in discussing these matters because the attitude of the United States has not been defined with the precision which the British Government have thought it wise to use. The friendship of the United States Government for Poland, no less than our own, the large mass of Poles who have made their homes in the United States and who are, or are becoming, American citizens, constitutional difficulties of the United States in making treaties—all these have not enabled the Government of that great nation to speak in terms which I have thought it my duty, with the assent of my colleagues, to use in this House.

We know, however, that the Government and the people of the United States have set their hearts upon world organization to prevent outbreak of future wars and this world organization will be fatally ruptured by a quarrel between any of the three most powerful empires which compose the Grand Alliance of the United Nations.

The President is aware of everything that has passed and of what is in the minds of the Russians and British. He had at Moscow in Mr. Averell Harriman a most accomplished representative in the capacity of observer and he was present at all, or nearly all, our Polish talks on the occasion of our last visit. The President, therefore, has been kept fully informed, not only by the British Government but also by his own highly competent and distinguished representative and by all the many sources and channels that are open to the unceasing vigilance of the State Department.

I am particularly careful not ever to pretend to speak in the name of any other Power unless so directed beforehand and I hope the House will make allowance for the care with which I pick my words upon this point. All I can say is that I have received no formal disagreement during all these long months upon the way in which the future of Poland seems to be shaping itself, or is being shaped.

There is no doubt that when the time comes the United States will make their own pronouncement upon these matters, bearing in mind, as they will, the practical aspects which these matters assume and also how much failure on the part of the three greatest Powers to work together would damage all our hopes for the future structure of a world government which, whatever else it might fail to do, will at any rate be equipped with all powers necessary to prevent outbreak of further war.

It is asked why cannot all questions of territorial changes be left over to the end of the war. I think that a most pertinent question and it is one, in fact, which I and the Foreign Secretary gave in almost every case that has been presented to us. They must wait until the end of war. Armies, it is said, move here or there as they advance or recede. They may be in occupation of this ground or the other, but it is at the peace table alone that the permanent destiny of any land or people will be decided. Why cannot that be said in this case? It may be said in every case, or almost every case except in that of Poland. So why should Poland be excepted from this general rule?

It is only for the Polish advantage and to avoid the great evils which might occur. Russian armies—I know nothing of their intentions, but speaking only of what is obvious to anyone who studies war maps—Russian armies will probably during the early part of next year traverse large areas of Poland, driving Germans before them. If during those marches fierce quarrels and fighting break out between large sections of the Polish population and Russian troops, very great suffering, which can still be avoided, will infallibly occur and new poisoned wounds will be inflicted upon those who must dwell side by side in peace and in confidence and in good neighborliness.

They must dwell side by side in peace and friendship if the tranquillity of Europe is to be assured or a smooth working world organization for the maintenance of peace is to be created and maintained. All these matters are among the most serious which can possibly be imagined so far as our present lights allow.

Our British principle has been enunciated in what I have said, that all territorial changes must await the conference at the peace table after victory has been won, but there is exception in principle and that exception is "changes mutually agreed." It must not be forgotten that words are inserted in the Atlantic Charter, "No changes before the peace table, except changes mutually agreed."

I am absolutely convinced that it is in the profound future interest of the Polish nation that they should reach an agreement with the Soviet Government about their disputed frontier in the east before the march of Russian armies through the main part of Poland takes place. That is the great gift that they have to give Russia, a settlement now at this time which gives firm title of mutual agreement to what might otherwise be disputed at the peace conference.

I must, however, say, because I am most anxious that the House should understand the whole position, speaking on behalf of His Majesty's Government, and in a way which I believe will probably be held binding by our successors, that at that conference we shall adhere to the line which I am now unfolding to the House and shall not hesitate to proclaim that the Russians are justly and rightly treated in being granted the claim they make to the eastern frontiers along the Curzon Line as described.

The Foreign Secretary and I have labored many months. We have spared no labor or travel, no risk of political rebuffs and consequent censure in our efforts to bring about that good understanding between the Poles, whom we still recognize, and the mighty ally which has so heavily smitten German military power.

We have never weakened in any way in our resolve that Poland shall be restored and stand erect as a sovereign independent nation, free to model her social institutions, or any institution, in any way her people choose. Provided, I must say, that these are not on Fascist lines and provided that Poland stands loyally as a barrier and friend of Russia against German aggression from the west.

In this task Poland will be aided to the full by Russian and British guarantee and assistance and will also, I cannot doubt though I cannot declare, be aided by the United States, acting at least through world organizations which we are determined to erect, which she and the whole of the United Nations are determined to erect for the salvation of mankind toiling here below from the horrors of repeated wars.

Another great war, especially an ideological war, fought as it would be not only on frontiers but in the heart of every land with weapons far more destructive than men have yet wielded, will spell doom perhaps for many centuries of such civilization as we have been able to erect since history began to be written. It is that peril which, according to the best judgment of this National Government of all parties, has so lately renewed its troth to stand together for the duration of the war against Germany, that we have labored and are striving sincerely and faithfully to ward off.

Other powerful States are with us on every side, some more powerful, perhaps, than the British Empire and Commonwealth of Nations. We can only trust and can only try our best, and if we cannot solve the problems, we can at least make sure that this problem is faced in all its somber magnitude while time remains. I have spoken of fading hopes and of disappointment at failure to reach a Russo-Polish agreement.

But there has been another disappointment. It has been found impossible to arrange any meeting of the Three Great Powers. We had good grounds for believing we might have met before Christmas. Indeed, I confidently expected that we should. So far, however, although the prospect is earnestly desired and looked forward to, nothing definite has been settled. Therefore, strong, authoritative, if provisional decisions which are now required, not only on the Russo-Polish question, but on a host of vital matters, political, international, military, economic—apart from such progress as can be made by correspondence and individual visits, so far these decisions stand at bar and wait. There ought to be a meeting at least of the Three Great Powers at the earliest possible moment.

So far as I and the Foreign Secretary are concerned, we can only repeat what we have so often said, that we will proceed to any place at any time, under any conditions where we can meet the heads of our two chief Allies and that we should welcome above all a meeting in this island, in Great Britain, which has waged war from the very outset and risked, without flinching, annihilation in the cause of freedom.

STATEMENT BY SECRETARY OF STATE
EDWARD R. STETTINIUS, JR.,
ON POLAND

December 18, 1944 [1]

The United States Government's position as regards Poland has been steadfastly guided by full understanding and sympathy for the interests of the Polish people. This position has been communicated on previous occasions to the interested Governments, including the Government of Poland. It may be summarized as follows:

1. The United States Government stands unequivocally for a strong, free and independent Polish state with the untrammeled right of the Polish people to order their internal existence as they see fit.

[1] *New York Times.*

2. It has been the consistently held policy of the United States Government that questions relating to boundaries should be left in abeyance until the termination of hostilities. As Secretary Hull stated in his address of April 9, 1944, "this does not mean that certain questions may not and should not in the meantime be settled by friendly conference and agreement." In the case of the future frontiers of Poland, if a mutual agreement is reached by the United Nations directly concerned, this Government would have no objection to such an agreement which could make an essential contribution to the prosecution of the war against the common enemy.

If, as a result of such an agreement, the Government and people of Poland decide that it would be in the interests of the Polish state to transfer national groups, the United States Government, in cooperation with other Governments, will assist Poland, in so far as practicable, in such transfers. The United States Government continues to adhere to its traditional policy of declining to give guarantees for any specific frontiers. The United States Government is working for the establishment of a world security organization through which the United States, together with other member states, would assume responsibility for the preservation of general security.

3. It is the announced aim of the United States Government, subject to legislative authority, to assist the countries liberated from the enemy in repairing the devastation of war and thus to bring to their people the opportunity to join as full partners in the task of building a more prosperous and secure life for all men and women. This applies to Poland as well as the other United Nations.

The policy of the United States Government regarding Poland outlined above has as its objective the attainment of the announced basic principles of United States foreign policy.

STATEMENT ON BRITISH POLICY IN GREECE BY FOREIGN SECRETARY ANTHONY EDEN IN COMMONS

December 20, 1944 [1]

We could perhaps have been censured for not having interfered in Athens on behalf of law and order at an earlier date, but I refute the suggestion made by Mr. [William] Gallacher [Communist] that someone "whispered in the ear" of Papandreou [Greek Premier] to ban a demonstration. He gave the impression the British Minister had whispered, and that is quite untrue.

The European Advisory Commission was set up to agree on plans for the surrender terms of Germany and plans for the occupation of Germany and other enemy states. It was set up on our initiative.

Regarding the general machinery of international collaboration, there is nothing we should welcome more than closer machinery of collaboration than there is now.

We would welcome quarterly meetings between the Foreign Secretaries of the great powers, such as we used to have before, to deal with some of these matters. The Prime Minister and I have said over and over again that we would go anywhere.

[1] *New York Times.*

As to the decision to go into Greece, I do not know what other decision we could have taken in the circumstances. We knew there were risks, but I still think that the decision was right. Before we took that decision we did consult our United States Ally. We did go there with their agreement. We did tell our decision also to our Soviet Ally and they also approved that decision. There was no question of our having done this without having consulted our Allies, or by a movement of our own.

The only criticism that could have been made is that we ought to have brought contingents of the others with us as well. The Government, I say quite frankly, did not foresee matters would turn out as they have done, and in a fashion all of us deeply deplore.

For reasons of operational security we did not, before we went to Greece, describe in detail all our plans and intentions, even to our Greek Allies. We could not give them a clear answer to many appeals they were making to us to go into Greece. They saw developments and wanted us to drive elements of Germans out. We were unable to describe our plans because we did not want to reveal our military plans.

But as we drew near the date on which we did enter Greece, we did tell them of our plans to some extent and invited their collaboration in respect of the guerrilla bands in Greece.

Two leaders, General Saraphis of the Elas and General Zervas of the Edes, were invited to come to Caserta and meet the Supreme Commander and there was drawn up an agreed formula between them, known as the Caserta Agreement. Items in this agreement do show the immense trouble taken to try to get an agreement between all parties, the Greek Government and guerrilla leaders, before we went into Greece at all.

It was agreed to by Mr. Papandreou, as Prime Minister of the Government of all parties, in the presence of Eam leaders, and signed by General Saraphis and General Zervas at a conference presided over by the Supreme Commander, Mediterranean Theatre, and by Greek guerrilla leaders.

The following decisions were recorded as having been accepted unanimously:

1. All guerrilla forces operating in Greece place themselves under orders of the Greek Government of National Unity. The Greek Government places these forces under the orders of General Scobie, who has been nominated by the Supreme Allied Command as the general officer commanding in Greece.

2. In accordance with a proclamation issued by the Greek Government, the guerrilla leaders declare they will forbid any attempt by any units under their command to take the law into their own hands. Such action will be treated as a crime and punished accordingly.

3. In Athens no action is to be taken except under orders of General Scobie. Security battalions are considered instruments of the enemy unless they surrender.

4. All Greek guerrilla forces, in order to put an end to past rivalries, declare they will form a national union to coordinate their activities in the best interests of the common struggle.

In accordance with the powers conferred on him by the Supreme Allied Command, General Scobie issued operational orders concerning the spheres of various guerrilla forces. [One member asked for the date of this document and Mr. Eden replied Sept. 25.]

At the time the Greek Government was a Government of all parties. There was complete agreement between guerrilla leaders, and in so far as any document expressed agreement, that document did.

Before the actual entry into Greece there was no issue that divided the Greek Ministers among themselves and no issue that divided us from any part of our Greek friends. What was our purpose in going to Greece? We seek nothing for ourselves in Greece. Neither strategic advantage nor economic advantage nor any other advantage of that kind at all. In this action we are taking we have no ulterior motive whatever. I don't know why some members should be always so eager to think that we have some sinister purpose.

Of course, it is true that we have an interest in the Mediterranean. That has never been denied by anyone.

But in respect of this action we took in Greece, we took it only in order to bring food and supplies to Greece because we know the position Greece would find herself in. If Greece was largely a self-supporting country and could provide her people with food, we certainly should not have gone in for this vast organization to try to provide food and supplies for the people of Greece.

If we could not get food in, there was no chance of the Greek people's escaping starvation or of their industries being restarted. Those are the reasons we went into Greece. No one can complain of that. We knew the risks because of disturbed conditions. If we had not done this, there would have been certain mass starvation all over Greece and we would have been asked why we did not do something to help our Allies. UNRRA was coming in, but now unfortunately has had to pull out.

[Mr. Eden then gave the figures on one week's supply, ending Nov. 24, as an indication what the British had done in Greece in providing food and other supplies. He said that in Piraeus alone more than 20,000 tons of food were landed and at other places the total was nearly another 20,000 tons.]

Concerning the matter of terms for an armistice, what is the position? Elas forces undertook to obey General Scobie's orders as agreed.

He has asked that Elas supporters in Athens and Piraeus must cease resistance and hand in their arms. It is limited to that area. He has not asked that Elas supporters outside who have withdrawn shall hand in their arms. I fear that is the minimum which must be there, because if arms are left in the hands of members of the public, many in civilian clothes in Athens, over a long period, even when this immediate emergency is over and political division arises, you will have this same thing happening again. I think these terms are the minimum. They apply only in that area.

We have not asked that dissolving of guerrilla bands outside Athens should be done otherwise than by agreement subsequent to the cessation of hostilities. There is no question of leaving security battalions in possession of their arms nor of any right-wing organization in Athens.

I ought to tell the House in fairness that General Scobie some little time ago refused assistance offered to him by a right-wing organization against Elas. General Scobie said these men offered to join with our forces against Elas and he refused and disarmed them. We desire that all should lay down their arms. We are not trying to impose right-wing or left-wing government.

All we wish is that the ship should be on an even keel. We wish that arms should be laid down and we are against reprisals by one side or the other after this event is over, and we shall do everything we can to stop them.

Aircraft today dropped leaflets containing a warning by General Scobie to civilians in and around Athens and in Piraeus that rebel guns still firing after 9 A.M. tomorrow will be attacked with all arms at his disposal. Guns have for some time been firing at the center of Athens and General Scobie now says he will attack them and he warns the civilian population to get out of the way of the guns.

I do not think that is at all the picture which Mr. Bevan [Laborite Aneurin Bevan] gave. I must say in justice to our commanders that I am absolutely convinced that they used every possible means they could to avoid unnecessary loss of life in this operation.

We were told again today that we were trying to impose a King on the Greek people. It is really not so. We all know the King is still in this country. It is on the advice of the Prime Minister and myself that the King is still here. Very likely he would have taken that decision on his own account. We were perfectly conscious that his arrival might be the cause of political controversy, which he wants to avoid.

That is not imposing a King with British bayonets on the Greek people. We are not against a regency and we were not throwing our weight against a regency.

I had not intended to reveal this but many hard things have been said about our Ambassador in Athens. The first suggestion for a regency was made by our Ambassador in Athens himself. When Mr. Macmillan [Harold Macmillan, British Minister of State in the Middle East] got out there he confirmed the judgment of the Ambassador.

As I understand his position, the King feels that before he can make a decision on a matter of this kind he must get recommendations from leaders of the parties in Greece. The King naturally will be guided by the advice of his Ministers. If this is the desire in Athens, then an expression of the desire can come back to the King.

We are not opposed to a regency. I think the Greeks themselves and the leaders of the political parties have a right to express their own opinion, and should express it to the King. Then the King will make his decision on their advice.

I have said we have not the slightest objection to a regency if it is going to provide a solution; on that we must get advice from the Greeks themselves.

[Tom Driberg, Independent: "If the Government can give advice to the King, about remaining in this country, cannot they advise him against sending messages to Greece in a form which is hardly likely to promote reconciliation?"]

I do not think that is a reasonable request.

[Dr. Haden Guest, Laborite: "Surely it is not worth spending the life or the wounding of one British soldier to defend the King's prerogative."]

Dr. Guest is most unfair. The King is behaving with concrete constitutional propriety. He has not gone to Greece at our request and his present decision is that he awaits the advice of his ministers and, so far as I am aware, he will take that advice. I have tried to avoid bringing controversy into this. We want to bring this present conflict to an end as speedily as possible by whatever means can be devised.

Apart from the tragic loss of life, we must bring it to an end because otherwise we cannot get supplies in, and there will be tragedy of starvation. With the help of the Red Cross, some supplies have been sent, but they are pitifully small. The population of 1,500,000 to 2,000,000 in Athens are faced with serious threat of starvation and disease. Most of the Greeks are in great need of supplies, which cannot reach them because of the disturbed conditions.

We shall use all means at our disposal to try to bring this conflict to an end and to insure that this conflict is not made the excuse for a lasting vendetta either of right against left or left against right when the conflict is over.

Our aim is to maintain law and order to establish a Greek Government broadly representative of all the opinion in Greece, including the Eam, and to enable the Government to establish its authority in all Greece. The first task of the Government will be to get relief going and food for their people. The second task will be to organize free and fair elections, and if our help is needed our help here will be available. And if our Allies will come and help, their help will be welcomed.

We wish to bring our troops away as soon as practicably possible. We only ask that order shall be established so that the people shall be fed with supplies, the greater part of which we collected with great pains.

This is an unhappy phase in Anglo-Greek relations. For more than 100 years our nations have been friends, though there have been incidents from time to time. I hope this chapter will soon be closed and that there will be once again that friendship in which we have taken pride and that the Greek people—all Greek people—and all our own will be united and friends together.

GENERAL EISENHOWER'S ORDER OF THE DAY ON THE GERMAN COUNTEROFFENSIVE IN BELGIUM AND LUXEMBOURG

December 22, 1944 [1]

To every member of the Allied Expeditionary Force:

The enemy is making his supreme effort to break out of the desperate plight into which you forced him by your brilliant victories of the summer and fall.

He is fighting savagely to take back all that you have won and is using every treacherous trick to deceive and kill you. He is gambling everything, but already in this battle your gallantry has done much to foil his plans. In the face of your proven bravery and fortitude, he will completely fail.

But we cannot be content with his mere repulse.

By rushing out from his fixed defenses the enemy may give us the chance to turn his great gamble into his worst defeat.

So I call upon every man of all the Allies to rise now to new heights of courage, of resolution and of effort. Let everyone hold before him a single thought—to destroy the enemy on the ground, in the air, everywhere— destroy him!

United in this determination and with unshakable faith in the cause for which we fight, we will, with God's help, go forward to our greatest victory.

Dwight D. Eisenhower

[1] *New York Times.*

PRESIDENT ROOSEVELT'S CHRISTMAS MESSAGE TO THE AMERICAN PEOPLE

December 24, 1944 [1]

It is not easy to say "Merry Christmas" to you, my fellow Americans, in this time of destructive war. Nor can I say "Merry Christmas" lightly tonight to our armed forces at their battle stations all over the world—or to our Allies who fight by their side.

Here, at home, we will celebrate this Christmas Day in our traditional American way—because of its deep spiritual meaning to us; because the teachings of Christ are fundamental in our lives and because we want our youngest generation to grow up knowing the significance of this tradition and the story of the coming of the immortal Prince of Peace and Good-Will.

But, in perhaps every home in the United States, sad and anxious thoughts will be continually with the millions of our loved ones who are suffering hardships and misery, who are risking their very lives to preserve for us and for all mankind the fruits of His teachings and the foundations of civilization itself.

The Christmas spirit lives tonight in the bitter cold of the front lines in Europe and in the heat of the jungles and swamps of Burma and the Pacific islands. Even the roar of our bombers and fighters in the air and the guns of our ships at sea will not drown out the messages of Christmas which come to the hearts of our fighting men.

The thoughts of these men tonight will turn to us here at home around our Christmas trees, surrounded by our children and grandchildren and their Christmas stockings and gifts—just as our own thoughts go out to them, tonight and every night, in their distant places.

We all know how anxious they are to be home with us and they know how anxious we are to have them—and how determined every one of us is to make their day of home-coming as early as possible. And—above all—they know the determination of all right-thinking people and nations that Christmases such as those that we have known in these years of world tragedy shall not come back again to beset the souls of the children of God.

This generation has passed through many recent years of deep darkness, watching the spread of the poison of Hitlerism and fascism in Europe and the growth of imperialism and militarism in Japan—and the final clash of war all over the world. Then came the dark days of the fall of France and the ruthless bombing of England and the desperate battles of the Atlantic and of Pearl Harbor and Corregidor and Singapore.

Since then the prayers of good men and women and children the world over have been answered. The tide of battle has turned, slowly but inexorably, against those who sought to destroy civilization.

And so, on this Christmas Day, we cannot yet say when our victory will come. Our enemies still fight fanatically. They still have reserves of men and military power. But they themselves know that they and their evil works are doomed. We may hasten the day of that doom if we here at home continue to do our full share.

And we pray that that day may come soon. We pray that until then God will protect our gallant men and women in the uniforms of the United Nations

—that He will receive into His infinite grace those who make their supreme sacrifice in the cause of righteousness and the cause of love of Him and His teachings.

We pray that with victory will come a new day of peace on earth in which all the nations of the earth will join together for all time. That is the spirit of Christmas, the holy day. May that spirit live and grow throughout the world in all the years to come.

CHRISTMAS BROADCAST BY POPE PIUS XII

December 24, 1944 [1]

The goodness and kindness of God our Saviour appeared. [Epistle to Titus, iii, 4.]

For the sixth time since the opening of the dreadful war, the Christmas liturgy again hails with these words, redolent of peaceful serenity, the coming into our midst of God our Saviour.

The humble, mean cradle of Bethlehem, by its wonderful charm, focuses the attention of all believers. Deep into the hearts of those in darkness, affliction and depression there sinks and pervades a great flood of light and joy.

Heads that were bowed lift again serenely, for Christmas is the feast of human dignity, "the wonderful exchange by which the Creator of the human race, taking a living body, deigned to be born of a Virgin, and by His coming bestowed on us His divinity." [First Antiphon of First Vespers for the Feast of the Circumcision.]

But our gaze turns quickly from the babe of the crib to the world around us, and the sorrowful sigh of John the Evangelist comes to our lips: "and the light shineth in darkness, and the darkness did not comprehend it" [John, i, 5].

For alas! for the sixth time the Christmas dawn breaks again on battlefields spreading ever wider, on graveyards where are gathered the remains of victims in ever increasing numbers, on desert lands where a few tottering towers tell with silent pathos the story of cities once flourishing and prosperous, and where bells fallen or carried off no longer awaken the inhabitants with their jubilant Christmas chimes.

They are so many silent witnesses to denounce this blot on the story of mankind which, deliberately blind to the brilliance of Him who is the splendor and light of the Father, deliberately straying from Christ, has descended and fallen into chaos and into the denial of its own dignity.

Even the little lamp is out in many majestic temples, in many modest chapels, where before the tabernacle it had shared the watches of the Divine Guest over a world asleep. What desolation! What contrast! Can there then be still hope for mankind?

Blessed be the Lord! Out from the mournful groans of sorrow, from the very depths of the heart-rending anguish of oppressed individuals and countries there arises an aura of hope. To an ever increasing number of noble souls there comes the thought, the will ever clearer and stronger, to make of this world, this universal upheaval, a starting point for a new era of far-reaching renovation, the complete reorganization of the world.

[1] *New York Times.*

Thus, while the armed forces continue to engage in murderous battles with weapons ever more deadly, the statesmen, responsible leaders of nations, meet for talks, for conferences to determine the fundamental rights and duties on which should be built a community of states, and to blaze the trail toward a better future, more secure and more worthy of mankind.

A strange paradox this, of a war whose bitterness bids to reach the limits of paroxysm, and of the notable progress made in aspirations and proposals for a solid and lasting peace! Undoubtedly one may well discuss the worth, the feasibility, the efficacy of this or that proposal; judgment may well be suspended in their regard, but it remains none the less true that the process has begun.

Moreover—and this is perhaps the most important point—beneath the sinister lightning of the war that encompasses them, in the blazing heat of the furnace that imprisons them, the peoples have, as it were, awakened from a long torpor. They have assumed, in relation to the state and those who govern, a new attitude—one that questions, criticizes, distrusts.

Taught by bitter experience, they are more aggressive in opposing the concentration of dictatorial power that cannot be censured or touched, and call for a system of government more in keeping with the dignity and liberty of the citizens. These multitudes, uneasy, stirred by the war to their innermost depths, are today firmly convinced—at first perhaps in a vague and confused way but already unyieldingly—that had there been the possibility of censuring and correcting the actions of public authority, the world would not have been dragged into the vortex of a disastrous war, and that to avoid for the future the repetition of such a catastrophe we must vest efficient guarantees in the people itself.

In such a psychological atmosphere, is it to be wondered at if the tendency toward democracy is capturing the peoples and winning a large measure of consent and support from those who hope to play a more efficient part in the destinies of individuals and of society?

It is scarcely necessary to recall that, according to the teaching of the Church, "it is not forbidden to prefer temperate, popular forms of government, without prejudice, however, to Catholic teaching on the origin and use of authority," and that "the Church does not disapprove of any of the various forms of government, provided they be per se capable of securing the good of the citizens." [Leo XIII, Encyclical "Libertas," June 20, 1888.]

If, then, on this feast day which commemorates both the benignity of the Incarnate Word and the dignity of man (both in its personal and social aspects) we direct our attention to the problem of democracy, examining the forms by which it should be directed if it is to be a true, healthy democracy answering the needs of the moment, our action shows clearly that the interest and solicitude of the Church looks not so much to its external structure and organization—which depend on the special aspirations of each people—as to the individual himself, who, so far from being the object and, as it were, a merely passive element in the social order, is, in fact, and must be and continue to be, its subject, its foundation and its end.

Given that democracy, taken in the broad sense, admits of various forms, and can be realized in monarchies as well as in republics, two questions come up for our consideration: First, what characteristics should distinguish the men who live under democracy and a democratic regime? Second, what characterization should distinguish the men who hold the reins of government in a democracy?

I. *Characteristics Proper to Citizens in a Democratic Regime*

To express his own views of the duties and sacrifices that are imposed on him; not compelled to obey without being heard; these are two rights of the citizen which find in democracy, as its name implies, their expression.

From the solidity, harmony and good results produced by this between the citizens and the Government one may decide which democracy is really healthy and well balanced, and what is its life energy and power of expansion.

If, then, we consider the extent and nature of the sacrifices demanded of all the citizens, especially in our day when the activity of the State is so vast and decisive, the democratic form of government appears to many as a postulate of nature imposed by reason itself.

When, however, people call for "democracy and better democracy," such a demand cannot have any other meaning than to place the citizen ever more in the position to hold his own personal opinion, to express it and to make it prevail in a fashion conducive to common good.

Hence follows a first conclusion with its practical consequence. The state does not contain in itself and does not mechanically bring together in a given territory a shapeless mass of individuals.

It is and should in practice be the organic and organizing unity of a real people. The people and a shapeless multitude (or as it is called "the masses") are two distinct concepts.

The people lives and moves by its own life energy; the masses are inert of themselves and can only be moved from outside. The people lives by the fullness of life in the men that compose it, each of whom—at his proper place and in his own way—is a person conscious of his own responsibility and of his own views.

The masses, on the contrary, wait for the impulse from outside, an easy plaything in the hands of anyone who exploits their instincts and impressions; ready to follow, in turn, today this flag, tomorrow another.

From the exuberant life of a true people, an abundant rich life is diffused in the state and all its organs, instilling into them, with a vigor that is always renewing itself, the consciousness of their own responsibility, the true instinct for the common good.

The elementary power of the masses, deftly managed and employed, the state also can utilize. In the ambitious hands of one or of several who have been artificially brought together for selfish aims, the state itself, with the support of the masses, reduced to the minimum status of a mere machine, can impose its whims on the better part of the real people, the common interest remains seriously and for a long time injured by this process, and the injury is very often hard to heal.

Hence follows clearly another conclusion: the masses as we have just defined them—are the capital enemy of true democracy and of its ideal of liberty and equality.

In a people worthy of the name the citizen feels within him the consciousness of his personality, of his duties and rights, of his own freedom joined to respect for the freedom and dignity of others.

In a people worthy of the name all inequalities based not on whim but on the nature of things, inequalities of culture, possessions, social standing—without of course prejudice to justice and mutual charity—do not constitute any obstacle to the existence and the prevalence of a true spirit of union and brotherhood.

On the contrary, so far from impairing civil equality in any way, they give it its true meaning, namely, that, before the State, everyone has the right to live honorably his own personal life in the place and under the conditions in which the designs and dispositions of Providence have placed him.

As against this picture of the democratic ideal of liberty and equality in a people's government by honest and farseeing men, what a spectacle is that of a democratic State left to the whims of the masses:

Liberty, from being a moral duty of the individual becomes a tyrannous claim to give free rein to a man's impulses and appetites to the detriment of others.

Equality degenerates to a mechanical level, a colorless uniformity, the sense of true honor, of personal activity, or respect for tradition, of dignity— in a word all that gives life its worth—gradually fades away and disappears.

And the only survivors are, on the one hand, the victims deluded by the specious mirage of democracy, naively taken for the genuine spirit of democracy with its liberty and equality; and on the other the more or less numerous exploiters who have known how to use the power of money and of organization in order to secure a privileged position above the others, and have gained power.

II. *Characteristics of Men Holding Power in a Democratic State*

The democratic state, whether it be monarchical or republican, should like any other form of government be entrusted with the power to command with real and effective authority.

The absolute order itself of beings and purposes, which shows that man is an independent person, namely the subject of inviolable duties and rights, who is the source and end of his own social life, comprises the state also as a necessary society endowed with authority, without which it could neither exist nor live.

And if men, using their personal liberty, were to deny all dependence on a superior authority possessing coercive power, they could by this very fact cut the ground from under their own dignity and liberty, by violating, that is, the absolute order of beings and purposes.

As they are established on this same foundation the person, the State, the Government, with their respective rights, are so bound together that they stand or fall together. And since that absolute order, in the light of right, reason, and in particular of the Christian faith, cannot have any other origin than in a personal God, our Creator, it follows that the dignity of man is the dignity of the moral community willed by God; the dignity of political authority is the dignity deriving from its sharing in the authority of God.

No form of State can avoid taking cognizance of this intimate and indissoluble connection—least of all a democracy. Accordingly, if those in power do not see it, or more or less discount it, their own authority is shaken and social morality and that specious appearance of a purely formal democracy may often serve as a mark for all that is in reality least democratic.

Only a clear appreciation of the purposes assigned by God to every human society, joined to a deep sense of the exalted duties of social activity, can put those in power in a position to fulfill their own obligations in the legislative, judicial and executive order with that objectivity, impartiality, loyalty, generosity and integrity without which a democratic government would find it hard to command the respect and the support of the better section of the people.

The deep sense of the principles underlying a political and social order that is sound and conforms to the norms of right and justice is of special importance in those who in any kind of democratic régime have, as the people's delegates, in whole or part, the power to legislate.

And since the center of gravity of a democracy normally set up resides in this popular assembly from which political currents radiate into every field of public life—for good or ill—the question of the high moral standards, practical ability and intellectual capacity of parliamentary deputies is for every people living under a democratic régime a question of life and death, of prosperity and decadence, of soundness or perpetual unrest.

To secure effective action, to win esteem and trust, every legislative body should—as experience shows beyond doubt—gather within it a group of select men, spiritually eminent and of strong character, who shall look upon themselves as the representatives of the entire people and not the mandatories of a mob, whose interests are often unfortunately made to prevail over the true needs of the common good—a select group of men not restricted to any profession or social standing but reflecting every phase of the people's life; men chosen for their solid Christian convictions, straight and steady judgment, with a sense of the practical and equitable, true to themselves in all circumstances; men of clear and sound principles, with sound and clear cut proposals to make; men, above all, capable, in virtue of the authority that emanates from their untarnished consciences and radiates widely from them, to be leaders and heads especially in times when the pressing needs of the moment excite the people's impressionability unduly and render it more liable to be led astray and get lost; men who in periods of transition, generally stormy and disturbed by passion, by divergent opinions and opposing programs, feel themselves doubly under the obligation to send circulating through the veins of the people and of the State, burning with a thousand fevers, the spiritual antidote of clear views, kindly interest, a justice equally sympathetic to all and a bias toward national unity and concord in a sincere spirit of brotherhood.

Peoples whose spiritual and moral temperament is sufficiently sound and fecund find it themselves and can produce the heralds and implements of democracy who live in such dispositions and know how effectively to put them into practice.

But where such men are lacking, others come to take their places in order to make politics serve their ambition, and be a quick road to profit for themselves, their caste and their class, while the race after private interests makes them lose sight of completely and jeopardize the true common good.

A sound democracy, based on the immutable principles of the natural law and revealed truth, will resolutely turn its back on such corruption as gives to the State Legislature an unchecked and unlimited power and moreover, makes of the democratic régime, notwithstanding an outward show to the contrary, purely and simply a form of absolutism.

State absolutism (not to be confused, as such, with absolute monarchy, of which we are not treating here) consists in fact in the false principle that the authority of the State is unlimited and that in face of it—even when it gives free rein to its despotic aims, going beyond the confines between good and evil—to appeal to a higher law obliging in conscience is not admitted.

A man penetrated with right ideas about the State and authority and the power that he wields as guardian of social order will never think of derogating the majesty of the positive law within the ambit of its natural competence. But this majesty of positive law is only inviolable when it conforms—or at least is not opposed—to the absolute order set up by the Creator and placed in a new light by the revelation of the gospel.

It cannot subsist except in so far as it respects the foundations on which human personality rests, no less, than the State and the Government. This is the fundamental criterion of every healthy form of government, including democracy. It is the criterion by which the moral value of every particular law should be judged.

III. *Nature and Conditions of an Effective Peace Settlement, Unity of Mankind and Society of Peoples*

We were anxious, beloved sons and daughters, to take the occasion of Christmastide to point out along what lines a democracy befitting human dignity can, in harmony with the law of nature and the designs of God as manifested in Revelation, secure happy results. Indeed we are deeply convinced of the supreme importance of this problem for the peaceful progress of mankind.

But we also realize the exalted claims that this form of government makes on the moral maturity of the individual citizen; a moral maturity to which he could never hope to attain fully and securely if the light from the cave of Bethlehem did not illumine the dark path along which the peoples are going forward through the stormy present toward a future which they hope will be more serene.

But how far will the representatives and pioneers of democracy be inspired in their deliberations by the conviction that the absolute order of beings and purposes, of which we have repeatedly spoken, comprises also, as a moral necessity and the crowning of social development, the unity of mankind and of the family of peoples?

On the recognition of this principle hangs the future of the peace. No world reform, no peace guarantee can abstract from it without being weakened and without being untrue to itself.

If, on the other hand, this same moral necessity were to find its realization in a society of peoples which succeeded in eliminating the structural defects and shortcomings of former systems, then the majesty of that order would regulate and inspire equally the deliberations of that society and the use of its instruments of sanction.

For this reason, too, one understands why the authority of such a society must be real and effective over the member states, in such wise, however, that each of them retains an equal right to its own sovereignty. Only thus will the spirit of sane democracy be able to pervade the vast and thorny ground of foreign relations.

There is a duty, besides, imposed on all, a duty which brooks no delay, no procrastination, no hesitation, no subterfuge: it is the duty to do everything to ban once and for all wars of aggression as legitimate solution of international disputes and as a means toward realizing national aspirations.

Many attempts in this direction have been seen in the past. They all failed. And they will all fail always, until the saner section of mankind has the firm determination, the holy obstinacy, like an obligation in conscience, to fulfill the mission which past ages have not undertaken with sufficient gravity and resolution.

If ever a generation has had to appreciate in the depths of its conscience the call, "War on war," it is certainly the present generation.

Having passed, as it has, through an ocean of blood and tears in a form perhaps never experienced in past ages, it has lived through the indescribable atrocities with an intensity such that the recollection of so many horrors must remain stamped in its memory, and even in the deepest recesses of its soul, like a picture of a hell against which anyone who cherishes a sense of humanity desires more than anything else to close the door forever.

The decisions already published by international commissions permit one to conclude that an essential point in any future international arrangement would be the formation of an organ for the maintenance of peace, of an organ invested by common consent with supreme power to whose office it would also pertain to smother in its germinal state any threat of isolated or collective aggression.

No one could hail this development with greater joy than he who has long upheld the principle that the idea of war as an apt and proportionate means of solving international conflicts is now out of date.

No one could wish success to this common effort, to be undertaken with a seriousness of purpose never before known, with greater enthusiasm than he who has conscientiously striven to make the Christian and religious mentality reject modern war, with its monstrous means of conducting hostilities.

Unquestionably the progress of man's inventions, which should have heralded the realization of greater well being for all mankind, has instead been employed to destroy all that had been built up through the ages.

But by that very fact the immorality of the war of aggression has been made ever more evident. And if now, to the recognition of this immorality there is to be added the threat of a judicial intervention by the nations and of chastisement inflicted on the aggressor by the society of states, so that war will always be subject to the stigma of proscription, always under surveillance and liable to preventive measures, then mankind, as it emerges from the dark night in which it has been so long submerged, will be able to hail the dawn of a new and better era of its history.

But only on one condition: Namely that the peace settlement which should be strengthened and made more stable by mutual guarantees and, where necessary, economic sanctions and even armed intervention, should not give definite countenance to any injustice, does not imply any derogation of any right to the detriment of any nation (whether it be on the side of the victors, the vanquished or the neutrals) and does not impose any perpetual burden, which can only be allowed for a time as reparation for war damage.

That any people, to whose government—or perhaps even partially to themselves—the responsibility for the war is attributed, should have for a time to undergo the rigors of security measures until the bonds of mutual trust, violently broken, should be gradually welded together again, is quite understandable from a human point of view, and in practice will in all probability be inevitable.

Nevertheless even these peoples must have a well-founded hope—commensurate to their effective collaboration in the work of reconstruction—of being able, together with the other States with equal consideration and with the same rights, to be associated with the great community of nations.

To deny them that hope would be the reverse of far-seeing wisdom, it would be to assume the grave responsibility of barring the way to a general liberation from all the disastrous consequences, material, moral and political, of the gigantic cataclysm which has shaken the poor human family to its very foundations, but which, at the same time, has shown it the road to new goals.

We will not renounce our confidence that the peoples, who have all passed through the school of suffering, will be able to retain the stern lessons learned.

And in this hope we are strengthened by the words of men who have had a greater share in the sufferings of the war and who have found generous words to express, together with the insistence on their own need of security against any future aggression, their respect for the vital rights of other peoples and their aversion to any usurping of those rights.

It would be vain to expect that this sage judgment, dictated by the experience of history and a high political sense should be—while men's spirits are still burning white-hot—generally accepted by public opinion, or even by the majority.

Hatred and the impossiblity of mutual understanding have given rise in peoples that have fought against each other to a mist too dense to hope that the hour has already come when a ray of light may shine out to clear the tragic panorama on either side of its dark wall.

But one think we know: That the moment will come, perhaps sooner than the people think, when both sides realize that, all things considered, there is only one way of getting out of the meshes in which war and hate have wrapped the world, namely a return to the solidarity, too long forgotten, a solidarity not restricted to these or those peoples, but universal, founded on the intimate connection of their destiny and rights which belong equally to both.

No one certainly thinks of disarming justice in its relations to those who have exploited the war situation in order to commit real and proved crimes against the common law, and for whom supposed military necessity could at most have offered a pretext, but never a justification.

But if justice presumed to judge and punish not merely individuals but even whole communities together, who could not see in such a procedure a violation of the norms which guide every human trial?

IV. *The Church as Guardian of Man's True Dignity and Liberty*

At a time when the peoples find themselves with duties such as perhaps they have never met before in the course of their history, they feel deeply in their tortured hearts the desire, impatient and almost instinctive, to take the reins of their destiny in their own hands with more independence than heretofore, hoping that thus they will find it easier to defend themselves from the periodic invasions of violence which, like a boiling lava torrent, spares nothing of all that they hold sacred and dear.

Thank God, one may believe the time has passed when the call to moral and gospel principles to guide the life of States and peoples was disdainfully thrust aside as unreal.

The events of these war years have given ample evidence to confute, in a harder way than one could ever have imagined, those who spread such doctrines.

The disdain that they affected toward this supposed unreality has been changed into stark reality: brutality, iniquity, destruction, annihilation.

If the future is to belong to democracy, an essential part in its achievement will have to belong to the religion of Christ and to the church, the messenger of our Redeemer's word which is to continue His mission of saving men. For she teaches and defends supernatural truths and communicates the supernatural helps of grace in order to actuate the divinely established order of beings and ends which is the ultimate foundation and directive norm of every democracy.

By her very existence the church rises before the world as a shining beacon to remind it constantly of that divine order. Her history reflects clearly her providential mission. The struggles, which, coerced by the abuse of power, she has had to sustain in defense of the liberty given her by God, were at the same time struggles for man's true liberty.

The church has the mission to announce to the world, which is looking for better and more perfect forms of democracy, the highest and most needed message that there can be: the dignity of man, the call to be sons of God. It is the powerful cry, which from the manger of Bethlehem to the furthest confines of the earth resounds in the ears of men at a time when that dignity is tragically low.

The holy story of Christmas proclaims this inviolable dignity of man with a vigor and authority that cannot be gainsaid—an authority and vigor that infinitely transcends that which all possible declarations of the rights of man could achieve.

Christmas, the great feast of the Son of God who appeared in human flesh, the feast in which Heaven stoops down to earth with ineffable grace and benevolence, is also the day on which Christianity and mankind, before the crib, contemplating the "goodness and kindness of God our Saviour" become more deeply conscious of the intimate unity that God has established between them.

The birth of the Saviour of the world, of the restorer of human dignity in all its fullness, is the moment characterized by the alliance of all men of good will. There to the poor world, torn by discord, divided by selfishness, poisoned by hate, love will be restored, and it will be allowed to march forward in cordial harmony, toward the common goal, to find at last the cure for its wounds in the peace of Christ.

V. *Crusade for Charity*

We do not want to close this Christmas message without addressing a word of heartfelt gratitude to all those—states, governments, bishops and peoples—who at this time of untold misfortunes have lent us valiant aid as we hearken to the cry of suffering which reaches us from so many parts of the world and give a helping hand to so many of our beloved sons and daughters whom the misfortunes of war have reduced to extreme poverty and misery.

And in the first place it is but just to record the immense work of assistance achieved in spite of the extraordinary difficulties of transport, by the United States of America and, with regard to Italy in particular, by his excellency the personal representative of the President of the Union.

It is a pleasure for us to express equal praise and gratitude for the generosity of the head of the State, the Government and people of Spain, and the Governments of Ireland, Argentina, Australia, Bolivia, Brazil, Canada, Chile, Italy, Lithuania, Peru, Poland, Rumania, Slovakia, Hungary and Uruguay who have vied with one another in noble rivalry of brotherly love and charity, of which the echo will not resound in vain through the world.

While men of good-will are endeavoring to bridge the gulf and bring the peoples together, this purely disinterested act of charity assumes an aspect and a value of unique importance.

When—as we all wish—the dissonance of hate and discord that dominates the present moment will be but a tragic memory, the good effects of this victory of active and magnanimous charity over the poison of selfishness and enmity will ripen into even a larger harvest of good.

May all who have had a share in this crusade of charity receive as an incentive and a token of gratitude our apostolic benediction and the thought that on the feast of love from numberless hearts in anguish, but not forgetful in their anguish, there rises to Heaven the grateful prayer for them: Deign to reward, O Lord, all those who do good to us for Your name's sake with eternal life!

PRESIDENT ROOSEVELT'S STATEMENT ON SEIZURE OF MONTGOMERY WARD FACILITIES BY THE SECRETARY OF WAR

December 27, 1944 [1]

We are today at a crucial point in the war. Great battles which will determine the fate of the world are raging in Europe and in the Pacific. The tempo and the fury of the conflict are mounting.

Our commanders in the field are demanding weapons in increasing quantities so that they may hit the enemy harder and harder. The supreme effort of all of us here at home is imperative if we are to give them what they need. Nothing less will suffice.

The Government of the United States cannot and will not tolerate any interference with war production in this critical hour.

Nearly three years ago we set up wartime labor relations machinery to insure that our troops and our Allies would get essential supplies without interruptions caused by industrial disputes. This machinery, embodied in the National War Labor Board, has had the support of all responsible elements in American management and American labor. It has been a vital element in the attainment of our unparalleled record of war production.

Now the confidence which employers and workers rightly place in this structure for the impartial adjudication of disputes is being threatened by consistent and willful defiance of its decisions by the head of one of the great corporations of this country—Sewell Avery, chairman of the board of Montgomery Ward & Co.

This company, under Mr. Avery's leadership, has waged a bitter fight against the bona fide unions of its employes throughout the war, in reckless disregard of the Government's efforts to maintain harmony between management and labor. Its record of labor relations has been a record of continuous trouble.

Twice the Government has had to seize properties of Montgomery Ward as a result of Mr. Avery's defiant attitude, once in Chicago and once in Springfield, Illinois where the Hummer Manufacturing Company, a Montgomery Ward division, has been operated by the War Department since last May.

For more than a year the company has refused to accept decisions involving workers in ten of its retail stores. Four of these stores are in the Detroit area, the very heart of war production from the viewpoint of urgency. A strike is in progress in these four stores, and strikes are threatened in other cities where the company's stores are located. There is a distinct threat that workers in some of our most critical war plants may join the strike in support of the Montgomery Ward employes if the Government fails to act. We are not going to let this happen.

[1] *New York Times.*

Strikes in wartime cannot be condoned, whether they are strikes by workers against their employers or strikes by employers against their Government. All of our energies are engrossed in fighting a war on the military battlefronts. We have none to spare for a war on the industrial battlefronts.

It is up to us to uphold and strengthen our machinery for settling disputes without interruptions of production. We cannot do this in a total war if we permit defiance to go unchallenged.

The findings submitted to me by the War Labor Board were unanimously adopted by the board including the representatives of industry.

We cannot allow Montgomery Ward & Co. to set aside the war-time policies of the United States Government just because Mr. Sewell Avery does not approve of the Government's procedure for handling labor disputes. Montgomery Ward & Co., like every other corporation and every labor union in this country, has a responsibility to our fighting men. That responsibility is to see that nothing interferes with the continuity of our war production.

It is because Montgomery Ward & Co. has failed to assume this obligation that I have been forced to sign an executive order directing the Secretary of War to take over and operate certain properties of Montgomery Ward & Co.

The Executive Order

Whereas the National War Labor Board has found and reported to me that labor disturbances involving nearly 12,000 workers now exist in the plants and facilities of Montgomery Ward & Co., Inc., in Jamaica, New York; Detroit, Michigan; Chicago, Illinois; St. Paul, Minnesota; Denver, Colorado; San Rafael, California, and Portland, Oregon; that in the exercise of the authority conferred upon it by the War Labor Disputes Act, the National War Labor Board has issued directive orders deciding the labor disputes that gave rise to the said disturbances; that the said directive orders provide terms and conditions, of a kind customarily included in collective bargaining agreements, to govern the relations between the parties to such disputes; that the terms and conditions provided for by the said directive orders are fair and equitable to employer and employe under all the circumstances of the cases; that Montgomery Ward & Co., Inc., has refused to put into effect the terms and conditions contained in these directive orders; that as a result of the refusal of Montgomery Ward & Co., Inc., to put into effect the terms and conditions contained in the directive orders issued by the National War Labor Board in the dispute in the plants and facilities of Montgomery Ward & Co., Inc., in Detroit, Michigan, a serious strike involving approximately 1,800 employees is now in progress in that city; that there is a present danger that the strike now existing in the plants and facilities of Montgomery Ward & Co., Inc., in Detroit, Michigan, will spread to plants and facilities of Montgomery Ward & Co., Inc., located in other cities and will adversely affect the operation of other plants and facilities, located in the Detroit area and elsewhere, that are engaged in the production of materials used in the prosecution of the war; and

Whereas the National War Labor Board has also found and reported to me that Montgomery Ward & Co., Inc., employs approximately 70,000 workers and serves approximately 30,000,000 customers; that an interruption of the company's activities would unduly delay and impede the war effort; that the preservation of the wartime structure of labor relations and the prevention of interruptions of war production depend upon the peaceful settlement of labor disputes by the National War Labor Board in the manner provided for by the Congress; that the preservation of the national stabilization program requires peaceful settlement of wage disputes during the war by the procedure provided for by the Congress; that the persistent refusal of Montgomery Ward & Co., Inc., to put into effect the terms and conditions contained in directive orders issued by the National War Labor Board, pursuant to the War Labor Disputes Act, threatens to destroy both the wartime structure of labor relations and the procedure established by the Congress for the peaceful settlement of wage disputes during the war, and unduly impedes and delays the war effort; and

Whereas after investigation I find and proclaim that the plants and facilities of Montgomery Ward & Co., Inc., located in Jamaica, N. Y.; Detroit, Dearborn and Royal Oak, Mich.; Chicago, Ill.; St. Paul, Minn.; Denver, Col.; San Rafael, Calif.; and Portland, Ore., are plants and facilities that are equipped for the production of articles or materials which may be required for the war effort or which may be useful in connection therewith, within the meaning of the War Labor Disputes Act; that Montgomery Ward & Co., Inc., is engaged in the distribution of articles and materials that are essential to the maintenance of the war economy; that as a result of labor disturbances there are existing and threatened interruptions of the operation of the said plants and facilities of Montgomery Ward & Co., Inc.; that the war effort will be unduly impeded or delayed by these interruptions; that the operation of other plants and facilities essential to the war effort is threatened by the labor disturbances at the plants and facilities of Montgomery Ward & Co., Inc., and that the exercise as hereinafter specified of the powers and authority vested in me is necessary to insure, in the interest of the war effort, the operation of these plants and facilities, and of other plants and facilities that are threatened to be affected by the said labor disturbances; and

Whereas, after investigation I also find and proclaim that these existing and threatened interruptions result from the failure of Montgomery Ward & Co., Inc., to adjust labor disputes of long standing with respect to the terms and conditions of employment at the company's plants and facilities; that the National War Labor Board has considered these disputes and issued directive orders determining and providing methods for their adjustment; that the labor unions involved have expressed their willingness to adjust the disputes involved in accordance with the directive orders of the National War Labor Board, but Montgomery Ward & Co., Inc., has persistently refused to accept the provisions of the directive orders as a basis for the adjustment of such disputes; and that this refusal unduly impedes and delays the successful prosecution of the war;

Now, therefore, by virtue of the power and authority vested in me by the Constitution and laws of the United States, including the War Labor Disputes Act (57 Stat. 163) and Section 9 of the Selective Training and Service Act of 1940 (54 Stat. 892) as amended by the War Labor Disputes Act, as President of the United States and Commander in Chief of the Army and Navy of the United States, it is hereby ordered as follows:

1. The Secretary of War is hereby authorized and directed, through and with the aid of any persons or instrumentalities that he may designate, to take possession of the plants and facilities of Montgomery Ward & Co., Inc., that are located in Jamaica, New York; Detroit, Dearborn and Royal Oak, Michigan; Chicago, Illinois; St. Paul, Minnesota; Denver, Colorado; San Rafael, California, and Portland, Oregon, and any real or personal property or other assets used or useful in connection with the operation of such plants and facilities, and to operate or to arrange for the operation of such plants and

facilities in any manner that he deems essential for the successful prosecution of the war. The Secretary of War is also authorized to exercise any contractual or other rights of Montgomery Ward & Co., Inc., to continue the employment of, or to employ, any persons; to do any other thing that he may deem necessary for the operation of the said plants and facilities, including the production, sale and distribution of the articles and materials customarily produced in or sold or distributed from the said plants and facilities; and to take any other steps that he deems necessary to carry out the provisions and purposes of this order.

2. The Secretary of War shall operate the said plants and facilities under the terms and conditions of employment that are in effect at the time possession of the said plants and facilities is taken, and during his operation of the plants and facilities shall observe the terms and conditions of the directive orders of the National War Labor Board, including those dated June 6 and 16, 1944, and Dec. 14 and 15, 1944, provided that the Secretary of War is authorized to pay the wage increases specified in said directive orders, from the effective dates specified in said directive orders to the date possession of said plants and facilities is taken under this order, only out of the net operating income of said plants and facilities during the period of their operation by the Secretary of War; that in the event that it appears to the Secretary of War that the net operating income of said plants and facilities will be insufficient to pay the aforesaid accrued wage increases, the Secretary shall make a report to the President with respect thereto.

3. All Federal agencies, including, but not limited to, the War Manpower Commission, the National Selective Service, the Department of Justice and the Reconstruction Finance Corporation, are directed to cooperate with the Secretary of War to the fullest extent possible in carrying out the purposes of this order. The Secretary of War may request other Federal agencies, including those mentioned above, to assign personnel to assist him in the performance of his duties hereunder.

4. Possession, control and operation of any plant or facility taken under this order shall be terminated by the Secretary of War within sixty days after he determines that the productive efficiency of the plant or facility prevailing prior to the existing and threatened interruptions of operations, referred to in the recitals of this order, has been restored.

5. The words "plants and facilities of Montgomery Ward & Co., Inc.," whenever used in this order, shall be deemed to include, without limitation, any mail order house, warehouse, office, retail store, factory, or production or assembly unit, owned or operated by Montgomery Ward & Co., Inc., in the areas specified in this order.

FRANKLIN D. ROOSEVELT

THE WHITE HOUSE,
   Dec. 27, 1944.

CHANCELLOR ADOLF HITLER'S NEW YEAR'S BROADCAST TO THE GERMAN PEOPLE

December 31, 1944 [1]

German people, National Socialist men and women, my Volksgenossen: Only the turn of the year causes me to speak to you today, my German

[1] *New York Times.*

men and women. The present time has demanded more than speeches from me. Events of the past twelve months and the happenings of July 20 in particular have forced me to devote my whole attention and working capacity to the only task I have lived for for many years past—the faithful struggle of my people.

Although our enemies have predicted our collapse during every one of the past years, they set special hopes on the year 1944. Never before did victory appear as near to them as during the August days of the past year, when one disaster appeared to tread closely on the other's heels.

But we have been once again, as so often before, successful in turning fate away. Some credit is due—apart from the struggle and work of all my countrymen at home and at the fronts—to my own work and my own devotion.

I have acted in accordance with the conviction I gave expression to during the memorable Reichstag session on Sept. 1, when I said that in this struggle Germany would be forced to her knees neither by armed blows nor by time and that a Nov. 9, 1918, would never be repeated in the German Reich.

Anyone who only knew Germany in the days of her weakness might have thought this country would be granted neither reassertion nor strength to maintain itself against the whole world of enemies. Thus the Jewish-international world conspiracy has lived on hopes from the very first day. Every time the people threatened to become suspicious, prophecies were fashioned from hopes and, with a certain propagandistic impudence, represented to the eyes of the masses as being absolutely certain and matters of course.

This propaganda used two methods although, like all lies, they will prove in the end shortlived. On one side, in order to allay the impatience of the masses in Allied countries, dates are fixed by which German collapse is to be expected with certainty; on the other side problems are being tackled, the solution of which will be necessary for the Allies after such collapse.

Before the war had even begun, the first English utterance was already at hand to the effect that the joint Anglo-French declaration of war would, after seven to eight days at the latest, lead to internal revolution in Germany and thus to the collapse of the German Reich.

With almost astronomical regularity, this was followed in the spring and autumn, and sometimes also in between, by ever renewed assurances of the unconditional collapse of Germany and thus the surrender—both these things would be, of course, identical—was now just around the corner. As early as autumn, 1939, one such assurance came on the heels of another. Once it was General Mud, then General Hunger, and then again General Winter, that were to defeat us.

The year 1940 particularly was abundantly blessed at its beginning with such Allied proclamations. New prophecies were propounded after the French campaign—namely, that if Germany did not now succeed in ending the war within two months, by September at the latest, the German collapse would irrevocably occur in the spring of 1941.

That spring hardly passed when new dates in the summer and finally in the winter of 1941 were once again given as the time of our certain destruction.

Since then this game has repeated itself year by year. Once it was said the war would be over before the leaves would fall. Then again it was said Germany would be confronted with capitulation before the new winter would have set in.

With the certainty of a sleepwalker, one called August, 1944, the month of unconditional surrender and prophesied shortly afterward a joint meeting of the leading statesmen in Berlin before Christmas. A short while ago the new date was January. Then March, 1945.

Now it is declared more carefully, as these two months are rapidly coming nearer, that it was to be August.

In June, they will surely again talk about the winter of 1946, except that the war will in fact end in the meantime and not by German capitulation— this will never come—but by German victory.

Parallel to these prophecies, however, takes place the theoretical setting-up of ever new commissions—in order to reinforce psychologically the correctness of the assumptions—to deal with European problems after the war, the foundation of companies for the regulation of food supplies after a German collapse, in other words re-establishment of those racketeer institutions which we know from the World War proclamation of economic agreement, the setting-up of transport regulations and air bases, and the drafting and announcement of laws for the treatment of German people, which are truly idiotic in parts.

All this is done in a manner as if the war had already been won and as if it was even now possible to think over at leisure all the measures necessary for the Government of Europe by States which, however, themselves afford sorry examples of how people should not be governed.

This propaganda maneuver can be rehearsed before unintelligent masses in democratic states for an astonishingly long time. Yet one day it will even there become apparent that this is nothing else but one of those frauds which are the regular custom in these countries. If, nevertheless, one or another of the leading men in the Western democracies really should believe what is dished up to the nations, this could only be explained by three causes:

First, that they do not know the German people at all, and particularly that they do not know that the last 300 years of German history were not a true picture of the character of the German people and its ensuing disunity, but that this German people has, since it entered history, been not only one of the most decisive, but the most decisive factor in European history, and thus in the history of the world, and that it is this today, and that it will be this all the more in the future.

Secondly, that they have not the faintest idea about the meaning of the National Socialist State, and that they completely fail to grasp the essence of this national idea. The achievements the National Socialist regime has accomplished under the most difficult conditions have remained unknown to most of the people in countries surrounding us and have remained hidden because information for the public, and hence the formation of public opinion, was there completely in the hands of the Jews and had been carried out in completely distorted and mendacious manner.

Thus it seems as if even now it would be unknown to them that the National Socialist State can neither be replaced by Bolshevism nor by democratic-plutocratic ideology—as far as it is at all possible to speak of such a thing. Both of them have shown themselves by their actions in Germany itself to be completely incapable and, in addition as regards their achievements in their own countries under their rule, merely to represent a deterrent example.

Thirdly, that on the other hand in these countries something else has existed, something which, it is true the overwhelming mass of sound German people does not know, namely, a small clique of drawing-room politicians and armchair generals who, in complete ignorance of their intellectual, political and military insignificance, have tried to convince the world that some day they would come to power by a coup d'état, and would then be easily able to offer capitulation on the lines of those of Italy, Finland, Hungary, Rumania and Bulgaria.

Just as little knowledge as our enemies therefore had concerning Germany, and smaller their knowledge was concerning the essence of the National Socialist State, all the more gladly did they count upon assurances of these people, completely lacking in any character, believing their fantastic thoughts and fulminations to be the truth, and rewarded them not only with firm belief, but also with payments in cash.

I should like to state once more, in contrast to all this, now at the termination of a year which has given us ample opportunity of furnishing proof that this nation, this state and its leading men are unshakable in their will and unswerving in their fanatical determination to fight this war to a successful conclusion in all circumstances—if it means taking in our stride all reverses which fickle fate may impose upon us—I wish once more to state the conclusions which can be drawn from the past and the present and which must be known by all for the future.

Firstly, we know from the past and the present the aims of our enemies. What the British-American statesmen intend to do with the German Reich, what measures the Bolshevist rulers and finally the international Jews, who are behind everything, intend to apply against the German people is fully known to us.

Their successful application would not only entail the complete tearing asunder of the German Reich, deportation of 15,000,000 to 20,000,000 Germans abroad, the enslavement of the remnants of our German people and the corruption of our German youth, but would particularly result in the complete starvation of millions of people of our nation.

But apart from all this, one can only live either in freedom or die in servitude. If in the past these realizations were decried as mere National Socialist propaganda phrases or were dismissed as such, today they are the openly admitted aims of the leading statesmen and the press and the Jews of these countries and thus represent an official statement of the enemy Governments.

In the second place, in contrast to this we are resolved to go to the extreme. The world must know that this State will, therefore, never capitulate, that the German Reich of today—like all great states of the past—may on its road be exposed to reverses, but that it will never be deflected from this road. The world must know that the present leaders of the State share the sorrow and suffering with its people but will never capitulate on account of suffering and sorrow; that, on the contrary, it is resolved to meet every crisis with still greater effort, to make up by increased working zeal for what has been lost by tardiness.

The world must know these leaders not only express their highest appreciation to every German who does his duty, but also give him assurance that in times to come his individual contribution to the shaping of our nation will not be forgotten, but that, on the other hand, they will annihilate everyone who intends to evade this contribution, thus degrading himself to be the tool of foreigners.

Because we know the aims of our enemies, because they themselves offer us all the necessary enlightenment, thanks to the propagandistic talkativeness of their statesmen and journalists, the entire German nation perceives what fate would be destined for it should it ever lose this war; therefore it will not lose it. It must and will win it.

What our enemies are fighting for—the Jews excepted—they do not know themselves; what we fight for, however, is clear to us all. It is the preservation of the German man and woman. It is our Fatherland. It is our 2,000-year-old civilization. It is the children and the children's children of our people. It is, in fact, all which makes our lives worth living. That is the reason why this people displays that spirit and that bearing which entitle it to believe in its own future and in its reward by Providence.

That this fight itself is an incredibly hard one is due to the enemy's aims I have mentioned before. For, as they intend to exterminate our people, they are already trying this out during the war by means hitherto unknown to civilized mankind. When destroying our towns, they do not only hope to kill German women and children but also to eliminate manifestations of our 1,000-year-old civilization which they cannot in any way rival. This also was the meaning of the war of annihilation against Italy's cultural monuments and their intention in continuation of the struggle in France, Belgium and in the Netherlands.

However, like the phoenix from the ashes, so first of all from the ruins of our towns German determination has risen in spite of all. It has taken possession not only of millions of soldiers but also of millions of workers, female workers, of women and even of children. The suffering inflicted on these millions individually is immeasurable, but equally immeasurable is the greatness of their bearing.

When one day this time of trial has come to an end every German will be boundlessly proud to declare himself a member of such a nation. One day the time will come in which the violation of culture practiced by our enemies will continue to burn in our memory and will be felt as a disgrace by themselves.

I know, my Volksgenossen, what this war is demanding of you. There is hardly a man in any great country of this world who knows his people and their homes better than I know Germany. To all those German towns, localities and landscapes which are being destroyed today, I have come so infinitely close, speaking from both the historical and the personal viewpoint. For decades I was bound to them not only in historical and cultural-historical and personal (menschlicher) love but I also participated to the utmost in the fate of their future development.

But it is just this which makes it rather easier for me to bear all this sorrow, because I more than anybody else know that the German people with such determination have time and again risen from abject misery and I also know that, once at the end of this period, German towns will again rise from the ruins as new proof of the magnificence of the German towns.

The National Socialist State, with its energy and initiative, will newly erect in a few years all that which is liable to destruction today. Outwardly our towns will be more impressive and more beautiful than ever before. The place of destroyed tenements will be taken by healthier homes for the German people and our social and cultural requirements will find more careful consideration than has been possible before.

Nevertheless, we shall no longer possess many irreplaceable documents of art and culture and no longer be in a position to build them anew. Above all we can never replace the sacrifices of numerous people dear to us and we shall not be able to replace the loss of their accumulated memories which had grown dear to them in the course of long life. All these great treasures and small memories will in the end find, if not replacement, then at least compensation in the common memories of our people of a time of the hardest battle of destiny that any people has ever had to endure and which they have borne with such heroism common to them all.

The year of 1944 was a year of the heaviest strain in this gigantic struggle. It was also a year in which it was proved once and for all that the bourgeois social order was no longer in a position to defy the storms of the present or the gales of tomorrow's situation.

State after State, which does not find the way to truly social reorientation, will take the road to chaos. The liberal age is a thing of the past. To hold the opinion that this upsurging of people can be met by proletarian-democratic compromises is childish; just as childish as Metternich's when confronted with tendencies toward national unity of the nineteenth century.

The consequences of the absence of any truly new social reorientation of life are lack of moral will to resist not only of the people, but also lack of moral strength of their leaders to resist. We have seen in all countries that the attempt at the renaissance of democracy was a complete failure. The tangled knot of these political amateurs and military politicians of a bygone bourgeois epoch, with their petty feuds, is preparing with a fatal certainty to plunge into chaos and—in Europe at any rate—economic catastrophe on a nationwide scale.

Indeed, here is one factor which has already shown itself to be true: This most densely populated continent on earth either lives under an order which guarantees the greatest consideration for individual abilities and which, with the strongest suppression of all egoistic tendencies, prevents their excesses; or in States such as we see in central and western Europe which are incapable of living, that is to say nations which are doomed to destruction.

Following the example of royal Italy, Finland, Rumania, Bulgaria and Hungary collapsed during this year. This collapse was, in the first place, due to cowardice and lack of determination of their leaders. They themselves and their actions can be understood only in relation to the corrupt and socially immoral atmosphere of the bourgeois world. The hatred expressed by many statesmen, particularly of these countries, toward the Germany of today is nothing but the voice of an uneasy conscience; the expression of an inferiority complex vis-a-vis our organization of a human community which frightens them because it successfully represents aims which do not correspond to their economically confined egotism and the political short-sightedness that goes with it.

For us, however, my German Volksgenossen, it merely means a fresh obligation to realize with increasing clarity that the existence or non-existence of the German future depends on the consistent development of our people's State and also that all the immeasurable sacrifices which our people have made are thinkable only if an order of society is presupposed which does away with all privileges and thus makes the whole people not only the bearer of equal duties but also of equal vital rights—a society, moreover, that makes war without mercy on social illusions of a time that has outlived itself, and which sets in their place the most valuable reality there is—namely, a nation in which the mass of human beings is joined together by the same blood, the same character and experience of long history, whose origin as substance we do not owe to the arbitrariness of mortals but to the unfathomable will of the Almighty.

The knowledge of the moral value of this, our conviction, and the resulting aims of our struggle for existence, give to us, and above all to me, strength to continue the struggle in the gravest hours with the strongest faith and an unshakable confidence. The people, also and in particular, are bound to their leaders by this conviction in such hours. It has secured that unprecedented response to the appeal which I had to address to the German people this year with particular emphasis.

Millions of Germans of all callings and all classes, men, women, boys and girls, even to children, took up spade and shovel. Thousands of Volkssturm battalions sprang up and are still coming into existence; division after division has been newly raised. The people's artillery corps, anti-aircraft and assault gun brigades, as well as armored formations, were brought into being overnight; fighter formations were replenished and equipped with new machines.

Above all, German factories, through German workers, men and women, have reached unprecedented achievements. They are more and more being joined—I may say this today—by those thinking people of other nationalities who, as workers in Germany, perceive the essence of our social community.

Thus, whatever our enemies smashed was rebuilt with superhuman industry and unparalleled heroism and this will continue until one day our enemy's undertaking comes to an end. The German spirit and German determination will enforce this. This, my Volksgenossen, will one day go down in history as the miracle of the twentieth century.

The nation that reaches such immeasurable achievements on the front and at home, that submits to and bears such terror, can therefore never be destroyed. On the contrary it will emerge from the fiery furnace of trial stronger and firmer than ever before in its history. The power, however, to which we owe all this, the Jewish-international enemy of the world, will not only be foiled in its attempt to destroy Europe and exterminate its peoples but will bring about its own destruction.

At the end of this year, I wish to thank from my heart, filled to overflowing, uncounted millions of my Volksgenossen, as spokesmen of the nation and at this moment also as leader of their fate, for all they have suffered, submitted to, done and achieved. I wish to thank them all, men and women, right down to our children in the Hitler Youth, in cities and townships, in villages and in country.

I want to ask them not to falter in the future either, but to have faith in the leaders of the movement and to fight to the end with extreme fanaticism in this difficult struggle for the future of our people.

What I personally can do to aid our success will be done in the future as it was in the past. I am at present speaking less frequently, not because I do not want to speak or because I cannot speak, but because my work leaves little time for speeches and because I believe it is my duty today to think and toil every hour in order to increase the strength of resistance of our armies, introduce better weapons, set up new formations and form out of my nation all the forces which can be mobilized. My enemies may already have gathered that I have not been sleeping all this time.

For the rest, I want today to assure you again, my Volksgenossen, just as during the long years of our struggle for power, that my faith in the future of our people is unshakable. He who has been given such a difficult test by Providence is called to achieve the greatest results. It is therefore my only care to lead my people through this time of peril and thus to open to the people the gates to that future in which we all believe and for which we fight and work.

I cannot conclude this address without thanking the Almighty for the support which he has given time and again to the leaders and the nation and for the strength which he gave us and which made us stronger than peril and danger. If at the same time I thank Him for my own escape, I am doing it only because I am happy to be able to continue to serve my people with my life. I want, therefore, in this hour, as spokesman of Greater Germany to promise solemnly to the Almighty that we shall fulfill our duty faithfully and unshakably in the new year too, in the firm belief that the hour will strike when victory will ultimately come to him who is most worthy of it, the Greater German Reich.

INDEX

All direct references to speeches and documents are set in **bold face type** to facilitate location.

All other references are in light face type.

645